Advance Pr:
*Undergraduate Research at* ~~~~~~ *~~~~~~~~.*
*Equity, Discovery, and Innovation*

"The transformative power of an undergraduate research experience has been well documented, and colleges and universities continue to explore opportunities to scale the experience in order to broaden participation for their students. The capacity to achieve greater participation has grown in recent years as a result of the expanding role of community colleges. With her decades of experience in higher education, Hensel provides her thoughtful and comprehensive perspectives on the state of undergraduate research at our nation's community colleges. This is a must-read for community college faculty and administrators committed to adopting this high impact practice on their campuses."—*James A. Hewlett, Executive Director, Community College Undergraduate Research Initiative*

"The Council on Undergraduate Research and Community College Undergraduate Research Initiative collaborated with community colleges to expand opportunities for students to participate in undergraduate research as part of their 2-year college experience. This important book provides a wealth of excellent examples of transformative undergraduate research practices and describes their impact on the wide diversity of students who attend community colleges before they transfer to four-year institutions, enter the workplace, or both. I highly recommend it as it will inspire readers to develop creative course-based, community-based, basic and other research programs of their own."—*Elizabeth J. Teles, Retired ATE/NSF Colead and Community College Mathematics Faculty*

"This is an invaluable resource for faculty, college leaders, and even policymakers who want to see community college students gain opportunities for a richer education and better career outcomes. Nancy Hensel has made a compelling case for community colleges to embrace undergraduate research, and this book is full of inspiring examples of authentic opportunities for students to research topics ranging from the needs of student veterans to the behaviors of birds, rattlesnakes, and other fauna found on campuses across the country."—*Marcella Bombardieri, Senior Fellow, Center for American Progress*

"This book is loaded with invitations to use and develop new strategies and tactics for teaching with research in all settings, but especially community colleges. It offers examples from multiple disciplines, embracing core concepts in student development, student learning, and course-based undergraduate research. At a time when community colleges are poised to become even more important in higher education this book adeptly addresses innovation and equity in education."—*Julio C. Rivera, William B. Yersin Professor of Applied Business Analytics, Carroll University*

UNDERGRADUATE RESEARCH AT
COMMUNITY COLLEGES

# UNDERGRADUATE RESEARCH AT COMMUNITY COLLEGES

*Equity, Discovery, and Innovation*

*Nancy H. Hensel*

COUNCIL ON UNDERGRADUATE RESEARCH

1996-2021 25TH ANNIVERSARY

Stylus
PUBLISHING, LLC.

STERLING, VIRGINIA

COPYRIGHT © 2021 BY STYLUS PUBLISHING, LLC.

Published by Stylus Publishing, LLC.
22883 Quicksilver Drive
Sterling, Virginia 20166-2019

Library of Congress Cataloging-in-Publication Data
The CIP data for this title has been applied for

13-digit ISBN: 9-781-62036-994-4 (cloth)
13-digit ISBN: 9-781-62036-995-1 (paperback)
13-digit ISBN: 9-781-62036-996-8 (library networkable e-edition)
13-digit ISBN: 9-781-62036-997-5 (consumer e-edition)

Printed in the United States of America

All first editions printed on acid-free paper
that meets the American National Standards Institute
Z39-48 Standard.

Bulk Purchases

Quantity discounts are available for use in workshops and for staff development.
Call 1-800-232-0223

First Edition, 2021

# CONTENTS

FOREWORD                                                      vii
*Gail O. Mellow*

PREFACE                                                        xi

ACKNOWLEDGMENTS                                              xiii

## PART ONE: BACKGROUND

1   ACCESS AND EQUITY                                          3

2   UNDERGRADUATE RESEARCH AT COMMUNITY COLLEGES              17

3   OVERVIEW OF FIVE SYSTEMS                                  31

4   ENSURING STUDENT OPPORTUNITIES AND SUCCESS               46

## PART TWO: EXAMPLES OF UNDERGRADUATE RESEARCH

5   BASIC AND APPLIED RESEARCH                                61

6   COURSE-BASED RESEARCH AND EDUCATIONAL EQUITY             76

7   COMMUNITY-BASED RESEARCH                                  91

8   INTERDISCIPLINARY RESEARCH                               107

9   COMMUNITY COLLEGE PARTNERSHIPS                           122

## PART THREE: NEXT STEPS

10  INCLUSIVE PEDAGOGY                                    141

11  ASSESSING UNDERGRADUATE RESEARCH                      157

12  ADVANCING UNDERGRADUATE RESEARCH                      175

    REFERENCES                                            189

    ABOUT THE AUTHOR                                      213

    INDEX                                                 215

# FOREWORD

*Give the pupils something to do, not something to learn; and if the doing is of such a nature as to demand thinking, learning naturally results.*

John Dewey, 1916

Nancy Hensel's book, *Undergraduate Research at Community Colleges: Equity, Discovery, and Innovation*, is a counterbalance to the lack of attention to what faculty do in their classrooms, and why it matters. Her experience comes from her tenure as the President of the University of Maine at Presque Isle, and her leadership in the Council on Undergraduate Research. If you ask a college faculty member about their teaching, invariably the conversation is centered around "What do you teach?" The much more interesting question is "*How* do you teach that?" This book highlights undergraduate research as an important tool in faculty's pedagogical practice. Meeting the faculty in community colleges across the country, entering their classrooms, and watching research in action distinguishes this book. Despite their heavy teaching load within underresourced colleges, these faculty and their institutions insist on high-quality experiences that challenge and support students to take on the unscripted inquiry of research, and to reap its benefits.

The author acknowledges her own initial lack of understanding of the role community colleges play in the U.S. higher-education systems. She notes that her peers at 4-year colleges often view community colleges as a lesser form of college and question (without evidence) their intellectual rigor. The disenfranchising elitism of too many 4-year college administrators and faculty is a stealth guarantee of structural inequality in higher education. Perhaps Hensel's book, by highlighting the against-the-odds commitment of faculty who provide the rich experiences of undergraduate research at community colleges, will expose the bias against community colleges for what it is—a thinly veiled and deeply rooted exclusionary policy cloaked as merit-based analysis. The inequity of funding is inextricably braided to the demographics of who community colleges serve. Compared to every other sector in higher education, community college students are more likely to be low-income, female, working more hours to support themselves, parents, first generation, and Black or Latinx. Hensel brings to life the state systems, faculty, and administrators who push to offer undergraduate research as a part of the curriculum. It should not escape notice that these faculty and administrators are also more likely to be to be female, paid less, and probably teach more courses and more students in one semester than their 4-year counterparts do in a year.

Detractors of community colleges often point to their lower graduation rates as evidence of their tarnished reputation without regard for either the radically unequal funding or the realities of how poverty affects their students. It is plausible that the radically unequal funding is evidence that these results are exactly what the tiered system of colleges are intended to produce. It is by peeling back the veil of the unconscious bias that this book reveals the truer nature of what is happening at community colleges across the United States, where faculty commitment to providing experience in doing scientific research for their diverse student body forms part of the solution to addressing inequity.

Undergraduate research over the years has been especially prominent in science, technology, engineering and mathematic (STEM) curriculum at 4-year colleges, where faculty presume that students will enter the fields of medicine and science. Hensel's incisive interviews show that the same assumptions about students' career aspirations must be held for community college students if America is to diversify STEM fields.

The book's wide-ranging look at how different colleges, and different community college systems, have made undergraduate research a part of their curriculum is both instructive and inspirational. Through its engaging case studies and interviews, undergraduate research is shown to engage community college students in unscripted and creative problem solving that not only advance their scientific understanding but also to develop the transferable intellectual skills that make a difference in students success in college and careers.

There is a growing development of apprenticeship-based education that is linked to the emphasis on undergraduate research. Educational practices that intentionally marry thinking, application of knowledge, and reflection is certainly not a new idea, as the John Dewey quote that began this foreword affirms. Pedagogical strategies that engage students deeply in their academic work are a partial answer to the critique of students who have degrees but no ability to function effectively in the world of work.

Undergraduate research can produce outsized learning. Its practice is further buttressed by brain-based science, which stresses the importance of application and reflection that is coupled with regular feedback as key elements of deep learning. Like any effective apprenticeship, where learning is occurring within a lab or other real-world setting, students emerge understanding the theory and the practice, and their ability to learn in the future is enhanced. Nancy Hensel's *Undergraduate Research at Community Colleges: Equity, Discovery, and Innovation* opens the doors to classrooms and lets the reader encounter the faculty who deploy undergraduate research and the students who benefit from their work.

Gail O. Mellow
Executive Director, New York Jobs CEO Council
President Emeritus, LaGuardia Community College,
City University of New York

American higher education frequently underrates community colleges. Many people think that only less capable students attend 2-year colleges. However, in my work with community colleges, while I was the executive officer for the Council on Undergraduate Research (CUR), I met faculty who were passionate about teaching, enjoyed doing research, and understood the benefits to students of participation in undergraduate research. I hope this book encourages others to appreciate, as I do, the quality of education at community colleges.

My original plan for the book was interviewing faculty and administrators about undergraduate research projects on their campuses. I chose to focus on five systems that I got to know through two National Science Foundation grants CUR received to support community colleges' efforts to establish undergraduate research programs. However, COVID-19, with the forced closing of all campuses, disrupted my plans for extensive visits. While I was able to visit several colleges in the five systems, I had hoped to make a second and possibly third visit, but instead completed the remaining interviews by telephone and Zoom. I appreciated the graciousness of the interviewees when many were overwhelmed by suddenly moving all of their classes online. Fortunately, before campuses closed, I attended several undergraduate research conferences and saw firsthand the work of many talented students.

Through the interviews, I became even more positive about the commitment of community college faculty to students' success. The professors I met are serious scholars, often with many publications in professional journals. They are also innovative teachers who develop supportive relationships with their students. Many told me how their students kept in touch after graduation and sometimes came back to assist with ongoing research efforts. The professors proudly shared information about where their students transferred, and in some cases, where they went for graduate work. When meeting with one professor, I asked him if he took his students to visit nearby California Institute of Technology. He said yes, they visited Cal Tech, and Cal Tech accepted one of his students. However, the student decided not to attend Cal Tech because Massachusetts Institute of Technology also admitted him. Many community college graduates transfer to research institutions and other prestigious universities or colleges. Others have successful experiences at 4-year colleges and may continue for a master's or doctoral degree. Others directly enter the workforce and find a satisfying career and employment.

As we talked about undergraduate research, several professors commented that they had been encouraged to apply for positions at 4-year colleges. However, they loved teaching at their community college because they felt their work was making a significant difference in their students' lives. The community college mission of student success resonated with their values and aspirations. I hope that in this book I have conveyed the deep commitment and enthusiasm that the faculty I interviewed have about their work.

Chapters 1, 2, and 3 provide background information about community colleges, undergraduate research, and the systems I worked with: California, City University of New York, Maricopa Community College District–Arizona, Oklahoma, and Tennessee. Chapter 4 examines success strategies.

In the next five chapters, we look at five approaches to undergraduate research: basic/applied, course-based, community-based, interdisciplinary, and partnership research. When community college professors engage students in research, it may be predominantly one approach, or it may overlap with one or more approaches. Some may question how 1st- or 2nd-year students can do basic research, but they can.

Occasionally, they make original discoveries. Frequently a project starts as basic research and then questions lead to applied research. The reverse may also happen. A course may include a basic research project, but it can also be community-based. Sometimes the questions a community asks lead to basic research. In organizing each of the research chapters, I wanted to highlight the advantages and challenges of the particular approach. I think what is different about student research at community colleges from 4-year colleges may be that community college faculty are flexible as they choose their research topics. Sometimes a request comes from the community, and it may be a project to incorporate into the curriculum. In other cases, it may be a question from a student that determines the research approach. A significant strength of community colleges is their ability to adapt and engage in different kinds of research. Their commitment to finding ways to engage students in research is another strength.

Chapters 10, 11, and 12 discuss ways to assess and evaluate undergraduate research experiences, inclusive pedagogy, and ways to advance undergraduate research.

I have tried to capture the passion, enthusiasm, and commitment of the faculty I interviewed in the descriptions of their work. It is my hope that you will enjoy reading about the fascinating and exciting student research as much as I enjoyed talking with the faculty mentors.

# ACKNOWLEDGMENTS

In some ways this book is a collaborative effort. It could not have been written without the involvement and expertise of the many professors who spoke with me in person, on the telephone, and Zoom about their inspiring work with students. You will meet them in this book. They were generous with their time and shared student posters, videos, coauthored articles, and other artifacts with me. Each person I interviewed read the section about their work and sometimes the whole chapter. Their suggestions were always valuable and welcome. The final product, of course, is my responsibility and I hope that each interviewee will feel the time committed to this project was worthwhile.

There were also many other people who were helpful in writing this book. I would like to thank Avrom Caplan, Effie MacLauchan, and Ron Neiro for suggesting CUNY faculty to be interviewed. They also shared their assessment of undergraduate research at CUNY's 2-year colleges with me. Their help gave me a better understanding of the history and culture of CUNY and was invaluable. They are largely responsible for the expansion of student research across the seven 2-year CUNY campuses. Robin Cotter, Phoenix College; Thomas Ekman, Volunteer State Community College; Joan Peterson, Queensborough Community College; JoAnn Russell, Kingsborough Community College; Allyson Sheffield, LaGuardia Community College; and Shiang-Kwei Wang at Queensborough Community College were all helpful in arranging meetings for me with several faculty involved in research in many disciplines. Heidi Leming at the Tennessee Board of Regents generously shared with me Tennessee's work with assessing undergraduate research. John Barthell, Lori Gwen, and Greg Wilson arranged my attendance at Oklahoma Research Day, which was a meaningful experience.

Mary Crowe, James Hewlett, Jill Singer, Dan Weiler, Jane Weis, Pam Wilson, and Greg Young read chapters and provided insightful comments. I also benefited from talking with Andy Baldwin, Emily Berg, Bill Billingsley, David Brown, Nicole Cerveny, Patricia Cross, Francesca Di Martini, Hugo Fernandez, Janice Hammer, Shirley Hess, Richard Jarman, Dionne Miller, Pushpa Ramakrishna, Mark Swanson, Bronwen Steele, Rebecca Tally, and Richard Van Niel.

I am grateful for the opportunity to publish this book with Stylus Publishing. This is my second book with Stylus and the support the staff provides to authors is exceptional. I would especially like to thank editor David Brightman. From the email I received while in Uganda that the book proposal was accepted to the final work on this project, David has been helpful and supportive. It has been my pleasure to work with him.

# PART ONE

## BACKGROUND

# I

# ACCESS AND EQUITY

When I began working on this project, a friend asked me why I was writing a book about community colleges. It was a good question, as I had never attended a community college, nor had I ever taught at one. My first involvement with community colleges came when I was president of the University of Maine at Presque Isle (UMPI). Houlton, Maine, a nearby town, had asked the chancellor of the University of Maine System, the chancellor of the Maine Community College System, and me to come to a town meeting. They were interested in bringing a "community" college to their town. They did not necessarily mean a 2-year college but rather any college as long as it was in their community. Maine already had seven public universities and seven community/technical colleges and an interactive television system that brought college classes to towns all across the state. However, this was not sufficient for Houlton residents, who saw having a brick-and-mortar college in their community as encouraging economic development and increasing access to higher education.

Developing a new college in Houlton was not possible. However, we were able to create an outreach center with a donated vacant building from a grocery store chain and a $1.2 million allocation from the state legislature. The Houlton Higher Education Center, opened in 2001, included courses offered by UMPI, the Northern Maine Community/Technical College, a GED program, and in-person and interactive television courses. As president of UMPI, I enjoyed attending the Houlton Center graduation ceremonies to celebrate our students' achievements. I was inspired by the women and men from recent high school graduates to senior citizens studying together and striving to achieve their sometimes-delayed lifelong goals. Through the partnership, I began to learn more about community colleges. Students attended the Houlton Center for many reasons. Some wanted to transfer to a 4-year college. Others wanted vocational training, and others just wanted an opportunity to learn. And this is what I find exciting about community colleges, as they are committed to giving all students a chance to achieve their dreams. So, to my friend, I said, "Community colleges are places where every student is welcome, where faculty, staff, and administrators are committed to students successfully meeting their personal goals." These were the goals of the Houlton Center as well. The opening of the Houlton Center was an occasion for celebration. Nearly one third of the Houlton population visited during the all-day open house, an indication of how important access to higher education is to the people of this small, rural community. And they clearly saw the Houlton Center as a "community" college.

While community colleges provide geographical and affordable access to millions of students, the general population is not always aware of the depth and quality of the education they provide. When President Obama (2009) announced his American Graduation Initiative, he called community colleges the stepchildren of higher education. He suggested that "they're an afterthought if thought of at all (para. 26)." Many of my 4-year college peers may have also viewed community colleges as stepchildren and perhaps had some doubt about their intellectual rigor. I admit that at the beginning of my career, I was not particularly interested in community colleges. As I had an opportunity to work with community college faculty, however, I understood the role 2-year colleges play in providing access to higher education. I also came to appreciate the commitment of faculty and their institutions to educational justice and second chances. I became a believer. This book aims to highlight the exciting work of 2-year colleges to prepare students for their future careers through engagement in undergraduate research. I hope I can convey to the reader the enthusiasm and passion of the community college faculty I met and their excitement about the research they are doing with students. Community colleges provide educational opportunities for students to earn prebaccalaureate certificates or degrees, transfer to 4-year institutions, or complete workforce and skill development programs. Students pursuing these programs are more prepared for the next step in their education or careers after participating in quality undergraduate research experiences.

Today there are 936 public community colleges in the United States (AACC, 2021). In 2019, they provided affordable access to 6.8 million students who enrolled for credit in one of the public 2-year institutions in the United States. These students earned 878,900 associate's degrees and 619,711 certificates in 2019, and 20,700 baccalaureate degrees (AACC, 2021). The range of degrees offered by community colleges to provide career-ready training and liberal arts courses for possible transfer to a 4-year college has expanded since the beginning of the community college movement. William Rainey Harper developed the concept of a community college at the beginning of the 20th century. Harper was president of the University of Chicago, and he wanted to both enhance the role of the research university and find a way to encourage practical studies. What he called a *junior college* was his answer. Institutions like the University of Chicago, in his view, would become leaders in research and discovery while junior colleges would prepare students for the world of work. Joliet Junior College, the first public junior college in the United States, was the result of conversations between President Harper and Joliet Superintendent of Schools J. Stanley Brown (Joliet Junior College, n.d.).

The term *junior college* was dropped sometime in the 1970s. Community colleges still prepare students to enter the world of work after 2 years of training, but they also serve as a starting point for many students for a 4-year degree. In suggesting that community colleges are the stepchildren of higher education, President Obama recognized that many people believe community colleges are inferior to 4-year colleges. However, President Obama (2009) was wrong when he said community colleges are "an afterthought if thought of at all (para. 26)." Community colleges have been on the minds of U.S. presidents, governors, legislators, and business leaders for many decades. Several United States presidents have proposed initiatives to expand and improve community colleges. President Truman, who did not have a college degree, appointed a President's Commission on Higher Education. The Commission's report called for the expansion of community colleges and broadened the services they provide to increase educational opportunity and diversification. We are still dealing with these issues today (President's Commission on Higher Education, 1948). President Clinton wanted a community college education to be an entitlement, and he proposed a tax deduction for tuition (Postrel, 1997). President George W. Bush sought to provide more flexibility in job training programs and proposed community colleges to achieve his goal (Brush, 2005). While President Obama believed strongly in community colleges' value, he was not successful in implementing the American Graduation Initiative, which would have invested $12 billion in community colleges and increased the number of college graduates by five million. He proposed another initiative in 2015, the American College Promise, that would provide free tuition for the first 2 years of postsecondary education at a community college. The $60 billion community college initiative would assist nine million students a year. The bill did not pass and although it was introduced in subsequent years, it has still not passed. Despite the bill's failure, President Obama challenged states to implement the goals of the Promise program. Today College Promise reports that 360 Promise programs in 47 states offer free community college tuition across the country (College Promise, 2020).

America's College Promise program set the following goals in 2015 (White House Office of the Press Secretary):

- Enhance student responsibility and cut college cost for all Americans
- Build high-quality community colleges
- Ensure shared responsibility with states
- Expand technical training for middle-class jobs
- Build on state and local programs
- Increase access and educational equity

The conversation about the vital role that community colleges play in higher education and workforce development continues. Many governors and state legislators see community colleges as a way to address the increasing cost of higher education, expand access for more students, and meet the regions' job training needs. Business leaders see community colleges as playing a pivotal role in workforce development and narrowing the skills gap. The Business Roundtable (BRT) issued a report in January 2019 that called on Congress to expand community college/private sector partnerships to facilitate pathways between high school, higher education, job training, and entry-level positions. President Biden, in his April 28, 2021 address to the Joint Session of Congress, called for free college tuition. Free tuition will support low-income students and efforts to address racial and class equity through education (Carnevale et al., 2020).

Four-year colleges are increasingly interested in the transfer aspects of community colleges as demographic changes show a decline in recent high school graduates. In 2016, the Western Interstate Commission for Higher Education (WICHE) predicted a significant drop in the number of U.S. high school graduates over the next 10 years (Seltzer, 2016). WICHE also suggested that there will be more diversity in high school graduating classes. Demographic changes suggest that colleges will need to find new ways of recruiting students and more effective ways of retaining students. Rising costs of 4-year colleges and universities lead some students to choose community colleges for the first 2 years. Almost half of all college graduates earned some credit at a community college. Also, nearly 40% of elementary and secondary teachers begin their college education at a community college, and 44% of recent science and engineering graduates have attended a community college (National Student Clearinghouse Research Center, 2019). To sustain current enrollment levels, many 4-year colleges and universities, including those in the private sector, have eased transfer policies and developed articulation agreements with local community colleges (Marcus, 2015).

Community colleges play an increasingly important role in the delivery of higher education to students of all ages and are likely to receive more attention during President Biden's administration. First Lady Jill Biden is a professor at Northern Virginia Community College and a passionate advocate for 2-year colleges. In addition, Miguel Cardona, newly appointed U.S. Secretary of Education also strongly supports community colleges.

## Why Community Colleges Are Important

As open access institutions, community colleges play an important role in making a college education available to everyone. They also offer a wide range of programs for either transfer to a 4-year college or career preparation. Meeting workforce needs of their region is another significant role for community colleges.

### Equity, Access, and Workforce Development

By providing access and equitable opportunities to develop employment skills, community colleges play a critical role in fulfilling democracy's aspirations. As open-access institutions, community colleges have a diverse student body. Public community colleges in the United States enroll students from a wide range of ethnic, economic, and social backgrounds. Slightly over one quarter of community college students are Hispanic, exceeding 18.1% of Hispanics in the U.S. population. Community college enrollment for African Americans, Native Americans, and Asians/Pacific Islanders is very close to the percentages in the U.S. population. White enrollment in community colleges is 45%, while whites make up 76.6% of the U.S. population (U. S. Census, 2019). These statistics suggest that public community colleges are attractive and accessible to a diverse range of students.

Several characteristics differentiate the community college student body from that of 4-year colleges. First-generation students make up 29% of the community college student body, 15% are single parents, and the average age of students is 28, with a median age of 24 (American Association of Community Colleges, 2021). The large number of part-time students enrolled in community colleges suggests that many students work part- or full-time while also attending college. Some part-time students are attending community colleges to retool for changes in their employment or a new career. Community college students may live with their parents or may have families and homes of their own. Few community colleges have residence halls.

Equal access and workforce preparation are essential for individuals and our society for several reasons. Educational opportunity is key to economic mobility and community vitality. We expect that our children will grow into self-sufficient adults. We hope they will be productive and engaged citizens. Obtaining a good job that pays a livable wage and provides a degree of job satisfaction is central to personal fulfillment. The job market is changing from an industrial economy to a knowledge-based economy. Postsecondary education with either an associate degree or job-specific training is critical. Carnevale et al. (2013) predicted that by 2020, 65% of all jobs would require postsecondary education and training beyond high school; 35% of job openings would need at least a bachelor's degree, and 30% would require an associate's degree. Nicole Smith, one of the authors of the Center on Education and Workforce (CEW) 2013 report, said in an interview with the *Chronicle of Higher Education* that they were surprised by the changes in the number of people getting an education. However, she also said CEW predicts that by 2027, 70% of all jobs will require some postsecondary education (Blumenstyk, 2020).

Community colleges are the entry point for postsecondary education and entry-level jobs for a large segment of the U.S. population. For example, many 2-year degrees, such as chemical laboratory technicians, air traffic controllers, and dental hygienists, lead directly into the workforce and provide excellent pay (LaPonsie, 2018). Certificates in areas like information technology, electronics, and business and office management can also lead to good-paying jobs (Carnevale et al., 2017). In other cases, students begin their education at a community college and then transfer to a 4-year institution. The National Student Clearinghouse Research Center (2019) found that 46% of 4-year graduates began their college education at a community college.

Community colleges play a major role in societal development by providing accessibility to underserved ethnic and low-income groups, credentialing, and immediate entry into the workforce (Brint and Karabel, 1989; Dougherty et al., 2017; Franco, 2006). While the paths students follow to their eventual careers may be different, there are skills that most employers value for all types of work. For several years the Association of American Colleges & Universities (AAC&U), with Hart Research Associates, conducted surveys to determine what skills employers see as essential. In the 2018 survey, Hart Research found that employers highly value the following skills (Hart Research Associates, 2018):

- Effective oral and written communication
- Critical thinking, analytical reasoning

- Ethical judgment and decision-making
- Effective work in teams
- Ability to work independently
- Self-motivation, initiative, proactive: ideas/solutions
- Applying knowledge/skills to real-world settings

They also identified a secondary list of desirable skills:

- Find, organize, evaluate information from many sources
- Analyze/solve complex problems
- Analyze/solve problems with people from different backgrounds and cultures
- Able to innovate and be creative
- Stay current on changing technology/applications to the workplace
- Able to work with numbers and statistics
- Proficiency with a language other than English

The primary desirable job skills have remained nearly the same over the many years that AAC&U has commissioned the surveys. However, secondary job skills are responses to changes in the type of work employees are doing now. The second list reflects changes as the workforce transitions into a knowledge economy. The prevalence of technology in all kinds of jobs, the need for continuing education and training, and the ability to work within a multicultural society are skills needed in a global knowledge economy. Comprehensive research training is also considered critical to private sector employment.

Approximately 95% of businesses and organizations that employ individuals who attended a community college recommend a community college education. A 2008 report by the Government Accountability Office (GAO) concluded that community colleges play a crucial role in a knowledge-based economy. Participating in undergraduate research can develop many of these skills and better prepare students to work in the new knowledge-based economy regardless of the type of work they do.

There are several employment areas where community colleges play an especially significant role, such as science, technology, engineering, and mathematics (STEM). *Rising Above the Gathering Storm*, a National Academies of Science, Engineering, and Medicine (2007) report, warned that the STEM pipeline's weakness was becoming a major crisis that has been mounting gradually over several decades. Many in Congress and the scientific community believed that the United States was in danger of losing its preeminent global position for innovation and scientific discovery. The future of the economy and job creation is dependent on our ability to be innovative, primarily in science and engineering, with 96% of the jobs created in the United States dependent upon the efforts of scientists and engineers, according to the authors of *The Gathering Storm.*

Business leaders also warned that the critical shortage of skilled American workers hinders their ability to compete globally. In 2005 the BRT called for doubling the number of STEM bachelor's degrees by 2015. Progress has been minimal despite significant national attention to the narrowing of the STEM pipeline. Five years after the initial *Gathering Storm* report, the National Academy, in an updated document, called the storm a category five (National Academies of Sciences, Engineering, and Medicine, 2010).

Carnevale et al. (2013) reported that the growth of STEM jobs in the past decade was three times greater than the growth of non-STEM jobs. According to the Bureau of Labor Statistics, the two fastest-growing STEM jobs are web developers and computer support specialists at 12.8% growth (Fayer et al., 2017). Universities will be able to provide only about 30% of the demand for trained specialists for the estimated 1.4 million job openings for computer specialists in 2020 (Rosenbaum, 2015). One way to address this shortage is by recruiting a more diverse student body. The participation of women and minorities in the workforce and higher education at the community college level is significant and may be a potentially critical source for STEM recruitment. Congressional commissions have investigated the status of women and minorities in science, engineering, and technology (Congressional Commission on the Advancement of Women and Minorities in Science, Engineering, and Technology Development, 2000; U.S. Congress Joint Economic Committee, 2012). They found that while women and minorities represent two-thirds of the American workforce, they are significantly underrepresented in STEM areas. Community colleges can be involved in fulfilling workforce needs. Community colleges enroll 41% of all undergraduates; 38% of all first-time freshmen, 43% of Black, 53% of Hispanic, 38% of Asian/Pacific Islander, and 56% of Native American undergraduate students (AACC, 2021). Females who completed bachelor's or master's degrees in science or engineering fields were more likely than their male counterparts to have attended community college (Tsapogas, 2004). If women and minorities were to enter into STEM fields in the same proportion as their representation in society, the report suggested, the shortage could be significantly decreased. Unfortunately, women and minorities are less likely to enroll in STEM programs during college, and they are more likely to drop out of such programs when they enroll. Biology is the exception, with nearly 60% of biology students being female and master's degrees and PhDs being slightly above 50% (Catalyst, 2019). Community colleges' commitment to access and student success can address shortages in the STEM workforce and contribute significantly to increasing workforce diversity. However, increasing access will not address the totality of the issue. The educational environment must become more welcoming and inclusive.

In addition to access and offering programs that lead to good jobs, attention to equity-minded teaching strategies and services is highly desirable. For example, many 2-year colleges house financial aid, business, and counseling offices in the same area and keep them open in the evening to accommodate working students. Offering evening, weekend, or online courses accommodate students' work and family demands. Some campuses offer childcare for students with children. Carnevale and Smith (2017) found that 42% of students worked for low wages that put them at or below 200% of the federal poverty line. There is growing recognition that many low-income college students do not have a place to stay or enough to eat. The Wisconsin Hope Lab, in a survey of 43,000 students at 66 institutions in 20 states, estimates that 42% of community college students experienced food insecurity, 46% experienced housing insecurity, and 9% were homeless (Goldrick-Rabb et al., 2018). To address these issues, many colleges participate in Single Stop USA. The Single Stop initiative coordinates access to food pantry programs, legal assistance for eviction, clothing, childcare options, and other kinds of support that students need. Often the Single Stop programs are housed near the registrar's office and are promoted by the college. Estela Mara Bensimon developed a list of indicators campuses can use to assess their progress in developing equity-minded campus practices (Bensimon and Malcolm, 2012). Among the items included are undergraduate research and other high-impact practices. Later chapters will discuss the pedagogical aspects of equity.

## Retention and Completion

Retention and completion rates for college students are a concern of every college in the United States. Rates are documented and publicly available in the Integrated Postsecondary Education Data System (IPEDS) reports. Students, parents, donors, and legislators can check IPEDS information online. High retention and completion rates are considered an indication of quality. Low retention and completion rates suggest a lack of quality but are also of economic concern. Low retention and completion rates have plagued community colleges for a long time. The National Student

Clearinghouse Research Center (2019) reported a 48.9% retention rate for students who started in the fall of 2017 and returned to the same institution in the fall of 2018. There are several complicating factors in retaining community college students. A high proportion of community college students are low-income, first-generation, or nontraditional age and struggle with various issues while attending college. Many students work full- or part-time and may have families to support. Also, students may intentionally attend a community college for a semester or year and then transfer to a 4-year college. Community colleges believe that transfer can be a positive decision by students and should not be counted as a negative when calculating retention rates. Students who take a few classes to enhance their career skills count as dropouts in completion rates. However, community college administrators also see these students as successes rather than dropouts. Tracking students' movement is complicated for all institutions, but it is especially difficult for community colleges because their mission includes such a wide range of enrollment possibilities.

The ability of community college students to transfer to 4-year colleges is vital for students, and it has been a frequent topic for state legislatures and Congress. The National Center for Education Statistics (2021) reports that about 37% of first-year students in 2019 began their education at community colleges. Because slightly more than one-third of first-time students start their education at a community college, 4-year colleges have proactively involved community colleges in their recruitment efforts. For students intending to transfer to a 4-year college, their first 2 years must be rigorous and include experiences that prepare them for the transition. Undergraduate research is one way in which campuses can ensure students have the necessary skills for success at a 4-year college.

An excellent place to begin to analyze the completion issue is to start with students. There are many reasons why students do not complete their degrees at community colleges. A survey of 6,000 community college students from nine states asked students their reasons for dropping out of school (Porter & Umbach, 2019). The need to work and paying for college were the top two issues for noncompletion, as reported by 34% of the students surveyed. Meeting the needs of family and friends was the third reason for noncompletion. Childcare, family health issues, or lack of family support for college attendance were additional reasons given. Other causes include problems with online classes, parking on campus, developmental courses, faculty, health and disability, difficult college-level work, and registering for classes. Many business leaders and legislators see online instruction as a way to provide courses at times that are convenient for students. However, students reported finding it challenging to use the course technology, learn independently, or stay motivated without interaction with faculty and other students. Some of the reasons for dropping out of college were surprising. Parking, for instance, was sometimes expensive, and it often took a long time to find a place to park. When students have very tight work and class schedules, finding a parking place was frustrating and frequently made them late. Students wanted more weekend hours for tutoring and library usage. Textbooks were costly, and students couldn't afford to buy them. The need to take developmental courses was discouraging because it took time, delaying degree completion. Some students found that faculty were not available after class, were not responsive to email, or took too long to grade assignments. Sometimes registration presented problems when courses weren't available at convenient times, were filled, or were not available at all.

The survey also found that students were attending a 2-year college for two reasons. Of the students surveyed, 53% attended because they wanted to increase job and career opportunities. Of these students, 85% felt that their college was preparing them either very well or reasonably well for their chosen career. Another 38% of students expected to transfer to a 4-year college and 85% also felt the college was doing a good job preparing them to transfer. Of all students surveyed, 95% indicated they would recommend their college to a friend. Despite the many challenges students face, they are generally satisfied with their experiences as a community college student.

Degree completion is a concern for campus administrators, legislators, boards of trustees, and the general public. An American Enterprise Institute report found that "Cutting the dropout rate by half would generate substantial gains: the 160,000 'new' graduates would earn $30 billion more in lifetime income—and create an additional $5.3 billion in total taxpayer revenue" (Schneider & Yin, 2012, p. 1). The authors of the report suggest that using online courses and a competency-based education model could boost graduation rates. In Arizona, Rio Salado College increased its graduation rate by 42% by offering 500 online courses with flexible schedules and 50 start times each year. In Florida, Valencia College increased its graduation rate by 40% using competency-based education (CBE). CBE is an approach that allows students to advance at their own pace and has a focus on learning outcomes rather than seat time. However, these approaches may not be as feasible as the authors believe for the majority of community college students. Carnevale and Smith (2018) suggest that this approach may be challenging for many community college students. For students who find the interaction with faculty and students valuable, online instruction may not be the right solution. Other students may experience time management and motivation problems with competency-based programs. Mature highly motivated students are more likely to be successful in online and competency-based programs than traditional-age students.

## Guided Pathways

There have been many community college reform efforts in the past several years that have had varying success. A promising new initiative is a model developed by the Community College Research Center, Completion by Design, with support from the Bill and Melinda Gates Foundation (Bailey et al. 2015). The Completion by Design model led to what Bailey et al. are calling Guided Pathways. Guided Pathways' premise is that students need significant guidance and direction as they progress through the components of seeking a 2-year degree. The typical community college student experience is like a kid in a candy store with too many choices. With no clear direction, students can be overwhelmed by the options and may not fully understand the consequences of the decisions they make. Guided Pathways attempt to address this issue and has the following components:

- Mapping pathways to student end goals
- Helping students choose and enter a program pathway
- Keeping students on the path
- Ensuring that all students are learning

*Mapping Pathways to Student End Goals*
Pathway maps lay out a direction for students for the courses needed to graduate and meet career goals. Faculty and advisers need to develop the pathways, and students need to see how the sequence of courses and experiences will get them to their end goal. Campus websites post the Pathways maps. Pathways encourage student choice but offer direction and one that will lead to where the student wants to go.

*Helping Students Choose and Enter a Program Pathway*
Advising and mentoring are essential parts of the pathway program. The advising process starts before the student begins a program. Students need to understand the requirements for the career they wish to enter. A Guided Pathways model works with local high schools to ensure that high school graduates have the courses they need to begin college. The community college needs to know the requirements for transferring into a particular major at a 4-year college or for career entry after the 2-year program. While students

are in charge of the direction they choose, advisers and mentors help them to make choices appropriate for their goals.

*Keeping Students on the Path*
Students need to make timely progress toward their goals. Achieving this Pathways goal may mean changes in the scheduling of courses and possibly a redesign of the curriculum. Classes need to be scheduled and available in the sequence of the Pathway. Some students need developmental courses, and campuses find ways of incorporating developmental needs into courses in the curricular sequence.

*Ensuring Students Are Learning*
The campus needs a system to track student progress and provide alerts to various campus offices when students may be veering off the path. Program-specific learning outcomes assessment results need to be communicated to the student. Including applied learning experiences; project-based, collaborative learning; and other high-impact practices such as undergraduate research support student engagement on the Pathway.

Guided Pathways have been adopted by many community colleges with modifications to fit their student body, faculty, resources, and campus culture. The American Association for Community Colleges (AACC) offers Pathways institutes, customized technical assistance, and workshops at the AACC annual meeting. Other organizations involved in Guided Pathways are Achieving the Dream, the Aspen Institute, Center for Community College Student Engagement, Complete College America, the Charles A. Dana Center, Jobs for the Future, National Center for Inquiry and Improvement, and Public Agenda. Such widespread support for Guided Pathways suggests that this reform movement has a strong possibility of successfully meeting the goal of significantly increasing retention and degree completion.

The success of the program, of course, depends on what students think about Guided Pathways. The Community College Research Center conducted one-on-one interviews with 149 students enrolled in four of the seven City Colleges of Chicago (CCC) that launched a Guided Pathways program in 2010 (Fink, 2017). Of the 149 students interviewed, 48 expressed definite opinions about some aspects of CCC's Guided Pathways program. The majority of the students (37) commented positively, and 19 students were frustrated or had concerns about the Pathway program. Students thought that the program maps, educational plans, and the tracking process were helpful and encouraged them to continue their studies. A few students worried that program maps and curricular sequences could limit their choices, and some were overwhelmed by the multiple steps in their plans.

The Center for Community College Student Engagement identified 13 high-impact practices specific to Guided Pathways and investigated the relationship between high-impact practices and degree completion. High-impact practices included logistical practices such as orientation, academic goal setting and planning, registration, alert and intervention, assessment and placement, and class attendance. It also included instructional strategies such as accelerated developmental education, student success courses, tutoring, supplemental instruction, experiential learning beyond the classroom, and structured group learning experiences. The data analysis suggests that participation in one or more Guided Pathways high-impact practice can impact degree completion (Jenkins, 2014).

There is some overlap between the Guided Pathways high-impact practices and the educational high-impact practices identified by George Kuh and promoted by the Association of American Colleges & Universities (Kuh, 2008). Undergraduate research is a high-impact practice on Kuh's list, and it could be part of the Guided Pathways experiential learning strategies. The engagement of community colleges in undergraduate research and its impact on student learning is the focus of the remainder of this book. We will look in-depth at five community college systems or districts: California, CUNY, Oklahoma, Tennessee, and the Maricopa district of Arizona.

# UNDERGRADUATE RESEARCH AT COMMUNITY COLLEGES

Engaging undergraduate science students in research has been common practice for many years in the majority of American 4-year colleges and universities. Its capacity for developing students' critical thinking, problem-solving skills, deeper understanding of the discipline, oral and written communication skills, and self-confidence have been well documented (Hunter et al., 2007; Lopatto, 2003, 2010; Nagda et al., 1998; Russell et al., 2007; Seymour et al., 2004). Undergraduate research has also proven to be a particularly effective method for developing student work habits, improving student retention in STEM majors, connecting classroom experiences to the world of work, and motivating students to continue their studies (Hunter et al., 2007; Kuh, 2008; Lopatto, 2010; Nagda et al., 1998; Russell et al., 2007). Positive economic growth depends on attitudes and skills for innovation and entrepreneurship, often developed through undergraduate research (Lazear & Marron, 2009). Recognizing the value of undergraduate research to student learning and degree completion, the humanities, social sciences, the arts, and some professional programs such as business and teacher education are also beginning to embrace student engagement in research.

## Basis of a Successful Research Experience

Undergraduate research at colleges and universities began in the sciences, and the scientific method formed the basis for developing undergraduate research programs. In 2003 David Lopatto, professor of psychology at Grinnell College, identified the essential features of undergraduate research projects in science (Lopatto, 2003). While Lopatto's list of essential features addressed scientific research, several features can apply to students in any field. Lopatto suggests that students should participate in the design and conduct of the research project, feel ownership of the project, have an opportunity for oral and written communication, attend professional meetings, and receive either pay or credit. Students need to have a meaningful and focused research question that can have a significant finding. Students also need the guidance of a faculty member and research tools appropriate for the discipline. Ten years after Lopatto's article, several undergraduate students from the University of Central Florida identified five critical skills needed to help students move from acquiring knowledge to creating knowledge (Showman et al., 2013). The skills the students identified—creativity, judgment, communication, organization, and persistence—are skills that cut across all disciplines.

The CUR definition of *undergraduate research* emphasizes originality, contribution to the discipline, and communicating results. While many find the focus on originality problematic, most definitions reference original or creative thinking. Creativity leads to innovation, and innovation takes many forms of originality.

The Florida students discussed judgment in the context of research ethics. Being responsible and using good judgment in research are essential and necessary behaviors outside of the classroom and research project. Considering ethical dilemmas in research, of which there are many, is excellent preparation for dealing with ethical decisions in the context of work and community activities. The point of developing new knowledge is to share it so that others might benefit from it. Acquiring effective oral and written communication skills is a part of successful undergraduate research programs and are skills that also carry over to the workforce.

Additionally, organizational skills developed through engaging in a research project can carry over to other classes and the workforce. The Florida students saw that persistence is necessary for any project, but they also saw that failure is frequently an outcome of research. Most of us are fearful of failure and fear can prevent us from taking risks that might lead to new skills and new knowledge. Understanding that failure is a part of the research process helps to build persistence and appropriate risk-taking. Students who recognize the role of failure in developing new knowledge are more likely to excel in the long run.

## Student Characteristics

Russell et al. conducted possibly the most extensive study of undergraduate research. The study's purpose was to conduct a "broad-based, nationwide evaluative study of NSF's support for undergraduate research" (Russell et al.,

2005, p. 1). Russell et al. surveyed over 4,500 STEM undergraduates and 3,400 STEM, social, behavioral, and economic science (SBES) graduates. They wanted to develop a better understanding of the demographic characteristics of undergraduates who participate in student research experiences, why they chose to participate, and the effects of the experience on their academic and career decisions. In addition to the surveys, the study also included site visits to 20 universities. The site visits included both summer and academic-year programs. The principal investigators of campus NSF grants, individual faculty, and groups of undergraduate and graduate students were interviewed. The key findings of the study were that about half of STEM graduates had participated in an undergraduate research experience ranging from academic-year research, junior/senior thesis, intern/co-op program, or full-time summer research. About seven in 10 respondents said their undergraduate research experience shaped their career decisions; and six in 10 said their research experience increased their interest in a STEM career. Most students seem to have been interested in STEM since childhood. They chose to participate in research because they wanted hands-on experiences to reinforce what they learned in class, thought it would be fun, or thought it would help them get into graduate or medical school. Students were generally positive about their research experiences and believed they increased their understanding of the discipline and developed more self-confidence and awareness. The benefits were more significant for longer research experiences.

The study also looked at students who had started at 2-year colleges and found that one in six STEM graduates began their education at a 2-year college. Among students of color, Hispanics/Latinx were more likely to have started their education at a 2-year college than Blacks, Asians, or whites.

While the Russell et al. study provides needed documentation about the characteristics of 4-year students who engage in undergraduate research, the findings may not be applicable to 2-year college students. Many students surveyed by Russell and colleagues indicated that they had been interested in science since childhood. Also, they seemed to understand the value of undergraduate research in their future career. It is less likely that the same proportion of community college students thought about science as a career when they were children. First-generation students, a large proportion of community college enrollment, may not have considered science as a career when they were young. They also may not have thought about the importance of undergraduate research for their future careers before their college research experiences.

While 4-year colleges are making significant strides in expanding research across the curriculum, many community colleges are still developing robust undergraduate research programs. For many reasons, implementing undergraduate research may be more complicated for community colleges than it is for 4-year colleges. However, community colleges play an important role in the smorgasbord of college choices available to students, and it is, therefore, crucial for community colleges to engage students in research to provide them the same benefits their 4-year counterparts receive.

As a professor and university administrator at several 4-year colleges, I recognized the value of student research and encouraged the development of undergraduate research programs at the campuses I served. My interest in undergraduate research at community colleges, however, didn't begin until shortly after I became the executive officer for the Council on Undergraduate Research (CUR) in 2004. My interest was awakened when I attended a session at a science conference where the presenters discussed their partnership between a research university and a community college. The impetus for the partnership was to facilitate student opportunities for transfer from the community college to the research university. The presenters found that science students who did not have undergraduate research experience before transferring to a 4-year college needed an additional year to complete their baccalaureate degree and they wanted to address this issue. Transferability struck me as an issue that CUR, as the only national association with a singular focus on undergraduate research, might want to address. Founded in 1978 by ten chemists from private liberal arts colleges, CUR's focus had always been on 4-year colleges. In 2005 the CUR Board of Directors realized that its focus needed to expand to include community colleges. At the time we had no knowledge about what was happening at community colleges in regard to undergraduate research. Since we needed to learn about the extent of student research at 2-year colleges, we looked to the National Science Foundation Advanced Technological Education (ATE) program for support.

In 2006 CUR and the National Council of Instructional Administrators (NCIA), an organization focused on 2-year colleges, received a 2-year ATE planning grant to host a series of regional conversations about undergraduate research at community colleges (NSF Award #0603119). We held six conversations primarily with community college faculty and administrators between October 2006 and October 2007 in California, Georgia, Illinois, Massachusetts, Oklahoma, and Washington State. The facilitated conversations addressed three broad questions (Cejda & Hensel, 2009):

- What is currently happening regarding undergraduate research at community colleges?
- In what kind of research activities would community colleges like to involve undergraduates?
- How could CUR and NCIA assist community colleges to realize their goals for students' participation in undergraduate research?

As we engaged in these discussions around the country, we discovered that undergraduate research was an emerging pedagogy at community colleges. Although we recognized that community college professors would likely define *student research* differently from 4-year professors, we shared the CUR definition of *undergraduate research* as part of the premeeting materials sent to discussion participants: "An inquiry or investigation conducted by an undergraduate student that makes an original intellectual or creative contribution to the discipline" (Wenzel, 1997).

As we discussed how to define undergraduate research, it became clear that some faculty felt helping students develop research skills was very important while other faculty were more interested in providing opportunities for students to engage in independent research projects similar to those at 4-year colleges. Others discussed how undergraduate research can support community colleges' workforce development mission. Many of the participants felt that undergraduate research added value to the curriculum and wanted to expand the use of research as a teaching strategy. While the issues discussed were similar to the challenges that 4-year colleges face as they implement student research programs, community colleges face additional challenges.

The differences between 2-year and 4-year colleges impact the ways in which undergraduate research is implemented. Two-year colleges work with beginning college students and some question the feasibility of engaging beginning students in research.

Because most community colleges have open admissions, students may need academic support through developmental courses. Faculty at 2-year colleges typically teach five classes per semester and, as a result, 2-year faculty have limited time to continue their own research and to supervise student research. The 2-year student turnover rate is another challenge for faculty and can discourage some faculty from investing in preparing students to do research. This is especially true for scientists who benefit from investing in 1st-year students with the expectation that they will eventually have juniors and seniors who will become true research collaborators. Criteria for promotion and tenure may not include research and publications. Some community colleges reported that their campus did not have a grants office or policies, such as Institutional Review Boards, to support research. We also heard that that some administrators and trustees saw the community college mission as teaching, did not understand the relationship between teaching and research, and thought community colleges should focus solely on teaching and not engage in research. As faculty persisted in engaging students in research, they found ways to meet these challenges and administrators began to see the value of research for student learning. Later chapters will demonstrate the many successes of community college faculty and their campuses.

Because of the emphasis on originality, the CUR definition of *undergraduate research* is challenging, particularly for 2-year colleges. Many campuses have modified the definition to better reflect their campus culture and resources. In an effort to clarify the choices campuses face, Beckman and Hensel (2009) suggested a continuum of the various aspects of undergraduate research in Figure 2.1.

Campuses can choose to emphasize some practices from both sides of the continuum. For example, community colleges may choose to emphasize the student learning process of research while focusing on faculty-initiated projects. Research projects are more likely to be original to the student rather than making an original contribution to the discipline. It is also likely that honors students have more opportunities for research than other students whether it is in the academic year or a summer fellowship. Community college students typically present their research at a campus event but may also present at professional conferences that offer venues for student presentations and at the National Conference on Undergraduate Research.

As a result of our initial foray into undergraduate research at community colleges, we felt that CUR and NCIA could provide support to further the expansion of undergraduate research at community colleges. There are many reasons why it is important to support the development of engaged learning at community colleges and particularly the inclusion of undergraduate research in the curriculum. Access and educational equity, societal development, and workforce development are among the most important and potentially impactful reasons for including undergraduate research in the community college curriculum.

**Figure 2.1.** Continuum of undergraduate research activities.

| Student process-centered | Outcome product-centered |
| --- | --- |
| Student initiated | Faculty initiated |
| All students | Honors students |
| Curriculum-based | Cocurricular |
| Collaborative | Individual |
| Original to the student | Original to the discipline |
| Multi-or interdisciplinary | Discipline-based |
| Campus audience | Professional audience |

*Source:* Beckman and Hensel, 2009.

In addition, this is an especially important time to explore further development of undergraduate research programs at community colleges and partnerships between the major stakeholders. The literature clearly supports the benefits for science students at 4-year colleges. Undergraduate research experiences encourage students to pursue degrees in science fields; encourage them to continue learning, either in advanced degree programs or in the workplace; and develop essential career skills. As a result, interest in expanding the scope of undergraduate research is growing. The growth in transfers to 4-year institutions has spurred significant increases in 2-year college STEM programs. Political and business leaders who are looking for ways to ensure that the United States has a highly educated workforce in STEM areas reinforce these developments. With legislative pressures for better retention and degree completion, 2-year institutions might consider that undergraduate research programs have increased retention rates (Nagda et al., 1998), helped recruit students with higher educational expectations, improved academic reputations (Perez, 2003), and increased the level of grants and other academic support at 4-year colleges. Undergraduate research at 2-year colleges can also increase retention, degree completion, and transfer rates when implemented in the sciences but also across all disciplines.

While many faculty at 2-year institutions recognize the benefits of providing research opportunities for students, structural realities such as high teaching loads, lack of institutional expectations, and a culture to support and reward faculty mentoring hinder their efforts. Science faculty may be further hindered by limited laboratory space for undergraduates to set up and leave experiments and lack of research-grade equipment. Despite these challenges, 2-year colleges are finding ways to provide research opportunities for their students. Through our NSF ATE grant we found that the community colleges we met with were using primarily three approaches to undergraduate research: (a) incorporating research into the curriculum; (b) conducting applied research on campus; and (c) conducting basic research on campus (Cejda and Hensel, 2009).

## *Incorporating Research Into the Curriculum*

Science faculty who taught lecture/laboratory classes were looking for ways to reduce or eliminate "cookbook experiments" where the experimental results were known and instead engage students in more research-oriented experiments where the results were unknown. Other faculty were breaking down the research process into its component parts and then introducing students to elements such as a literature review, developing a research hypothesis, or learning how to use certain software programs, such as SPSS or SAS.

At Bellevue College, a 2-year college in Bellevue, Washington, *undergraduate research* is defined as

> purposefully structured activity that results in the generation of noteworthy data that did not exist before, the analysis of that data leading to specific inferences/conclusions and making these results available to a community of scientists able to take advantage of those data. (Bangera et al., 2018. p. 14)

Gita Bangera, dean of undergraduate research at Bellevue, incorporates this definition into work with her students in the biology course she teaches. In Biology 275, students conduct original research that includes developing a literature review, framing a hypothesis, keeping a research journal, and communicating the results of the research at a campus forum. Bangera, a prolific researcher herself, is the leading force behind undergraduate research at Bellevue College and has been successful in converting "cookbook" research into authentic research appropriate for the developmental level of beginning science students. She is also a national leader in how to integrate undergraduate research into the curriculum at community colleges.

## *Conducting Applied Research*

Communities have many resources available for applied research. Rattlesnakes, for example, presented a problem for Mesa Community College (MCC). The snakes could often be found outside the classroom or office building doors. Rather than dispose of the snakes, MCC decided to have students study the rattlers. The snakes were banded, and a study was begun to see what they ate, where they lived, and when and where they mated. The snakes became a low-cost research project (Makin, 2011).

Finger Lakes Community College (FLCC) had a similar natural resource problem. In the mid-1990s the local bear population experienced a significant increase. Bears were starting to wander into residential areas and could be potentially dangerous to humans or cause property damage (Van Niel, 2014). The New York State Department of Environmental Conservation (DOEC) was responsible for wildlife management; however, their resources were not sufficient to manage educating the public about how to behave in bear country and to gather baseline data to better understand the population increases and where they were occurring. FLCC had a DOEC and Horticulture that was one of the largest in the United States. The College's service area overlapped with the bear range. Initially, faculty developed an educational presentation to meet the need for more community knowledge about bears. Students became involved in the project when FLCC began collecting data. Professionals from the State DOEC attached collars to the bears, but FLCC students monitored the data collected from the collars. As the project progressed and the bear population receded to its more normal level, the DOEC had two additional questions they wanted to study, "When were the cubs were born, and what is a typical bear den like?" (Van Niel, 2014, p. 81). John J. Van Niel and his students began to study these questions. After several years Professor Van Niel introduced two courses in black bear management that continue to this day.

## Conducting Basic Research

The integration of community colleges with the local community also provides opportunities for students to engage in basic research that might address a community issue or support community agencies or businesses. A College of DuPage research project is an excellent example of basic research conducted by 2-year students and also of the benefits and challenges of research partnerships. The Green Fuels Depot was a collaborative research project to determine the feasibility of transforming yard waste into energy. The partners in the collaboration with the College of DuPage were the City of Naperville, Argonne National Laboratory, and Packer Engineering (Jarman, 2014). The College of DuPage portion of the project, led by Richard Jarman, professor of chemistry, had the following goals:

- develop training and educational materials for future operators of the project;
- train and mentor students in the operation of the depot's equipment; and
- perform basic research on the gasification process.

This is an especially interesting project because it engaged a city government, a national research laboratory, a campus, and a local business to find ways to address renewable energy for the benefit of the local community. The City of Naperville, a participant in the U.S. Department of Energy Smart Grid Initiative, is a leader in energy conservation and has a long history of commitment to finding renewable energy solutions to reduce cost and support environmental sustainability. Naperville's goal for the project was to eventually fuel all 300 city vehicles through converting yard waste into useable fuel. Argonne National Laboratory is a multidisciplinary science and research center that has extensive experience in collaborations involving diverse partners. A major focus area for Argonne is energy innovations through science. Packer Engineering developed the technology that was used in the project and considered itself a solution-oriented engineering firm. Combining engagement in basic research with learning how to operate sophisticated equipment added to the value of the project as did the development of training materials for future equipment operators.

Two students were selected for the 10-week project. During the course of their work, they encountered several problems relating to the science that needed to be addressed. For example, they had to analyze the woody biomass for discarded metal because some materials in the biomass could damage the gasifier. In addition, they had to become familiar with Environmental Protection Agency standards for testing liquids. The project led to another research question to study different types of switch grass as a possible alternative for replacing the biomass fuel. A campus outcome for the project was the development of a new course, Scientific Concepts in Sustainable Energy, to examine a range of sustainable energy sources. The campus also developed the curriculum for a Biomass Energy Technology Certificate to train operators of the type of equipment used in the Green Fuel Depot project. The challenge of the collaboration came from two of the partners. According to Jarman,

> Packer Engineering, which was the lead entity in the collaborative, declared bankruptcy shortly after the opening of the Green Fuels Depot. Some of the personnel formed an enterprise called TGER Technologies that explored the application of the Green Fuels Depot technology to the conversion of garbage into energy in the military arena. Currently a company called Green Fortress Engineering owns the intellectual property related to the Green Fuels Depot and is actively pursuing commercialization. All-in-all, the project ultimately didn't fulfill the objective of truly demonstrating a sustainable local source of power from yard and agricultural waste. That said, I do believe that it was conceptually sound, and I think something of the sort could still serve as a model for other communities to create sustainable energy sources. (R. Jarman, personal communication, April 23, 2019)

Even though the project did not meet its goals, the students learned not only about the science and federal regulations involved in the project, they also learned about how collaborations can be created and the uncontrollable issues that can derail a project. These are important learnings about work outside the classroom.

## Challenges to Undergraduate Research at Community Colleges

At the completion of the six regional discussions we found that there were several significant challenges if undergraduate research was to be adopted by community colleges with any degree of scale. The teaching mission of community colleges is the overarching challenge. In order to implement undergraduate research, campuses need to discuss how student research can be integrated into the current mission. Will teaching loads need to be adjusted to accommodate mentoring students in research? Will extensive curricular changes be needed to include research skills into existing courses? What other resources might need to be added such as equipment, proposal writing and grant support, and faculty professional development? After the regional discussions we felt that the following systemic changes would be needed (Cejda & Hensel, 2009):

- Trustees need to understand the value of undergraduate research as a powerful teaching tool and they need to affirm faculty efforts to engage students in research.
- State legislatures need to understand the potential economic development value of undergraduate research and provide support for infrastructure needs for up-to-date buildings, libraries, and laboratory equipment.
- Community college administrators need to support and encourage faculty members' involvement in their disciplinary or professional organizations so that professors can remain current in their fields and be aware of future directions.
- Community college administrators also need to find ways of supporting faculty members for outside-the-classroom mentoring of students engaged in collaborative research.
- Faculty members need to consider ways in which the development of research skills can be incorporated into the curriculum.
- Student affairs personnel at community colleges need to recognize the importance of undergraduate research for students' transfer and career opportunities and encourage students to participate in research activities.
- Local employers need to provide research opportunities for community college students as well as students from 4-year institutions.
- Community college administrators need to provide support for faculty members to write proposals for external funding.

- Community colleges should expand their partnerships with nearby 4-year colleges, local industries, and local government and nonprofit agencies to provide additional research opportunities for students.

## Expanding Opportunities for Undergraduate Research

Building on what we learned from the regional conversations, our next step was to obtain a Course, Curriculum, and Laboratory Improvement (CCLI) grant from National Science Foundation (NSF Award #0920083). The main objectives of the project were to: (a) develop a workshop curriculum tailored to the needs of community colleges considering the planning or implementation of undergraduate research; (b) train a cadre of workshop presenters to deliver the CUR workshop curriculum to community college faculty and administrators; and (c) provide workshops for colleges considering or just beginning undergraduate research programs, employing expert community college presenters to help participants plan changes at their institutions and address implementation issues.

Participation in the workshops was by an application that included a self-study of the status of undergraduate research at the institution. A letter of administrative support was also required with the application as we had found that administrative support was essential if the undergraduate program was to expand across the campus. The selected campuses were expected to send a team to the workshop that consisted of three faculty members and an administrator who had authority to designate funds to support undergraduate research. Community colleges from large and small, rural and urban campuses submitted applications for the workshops and we deliberately sought a mix of campus types.

While we were reviewing workshop applications, we also identified 12 facilitators from community college faculty we had met during the ATE regional conversations. The facilitators attended a 2-day training workshop and observed a traditional CUR workshop prior to serving as community college workshop leaders. Part of their charge was to adapt the workshop curriculum and format to fit the needs of community college faculty. Three facilitators led each workshop and typically facilitated four workshops. As one of the principal investigators, I attended six of the workshops and Brent Cejda attended the other six workshops.

By the completion of the project, we had worked with 380 educators from 95 institutions, about 10% of public community colleges. We held workshops in 12 states: Alabama, Arizona, California, Illinois, Kansas, Maine, Minnesota, New York, Oklahoma, Texas, Virginia, and Washington, and 28 states were represented among the participating campuses. None of the participating campuses had an institutionalized undergraduate research program though some had pockets of undergraduate research in one or two departments, often by one or two professors. A major expectation for the workshop teams was the development of an action plan to take back to their campus for further discussion and to begin the implementation process for an undergraduate research program. The highlight of the workshop was sharing the plans and discussing each plan among all participants. The plans reflected campus cultures and generally included practical implementation strategies. Sharing of the plans created the possibility of a supportive community for faculty about to embark on a major and challenging curricular change. Some of the plans included seeking partnerships with 4-year colleges while other plans wanted to take advantage of nearby national research laboratories. Other plans included developing a course that would include a research component. All of the plans included strategies for developing interest and support for undergraduate research on campus. While the workshop participants needed to come from disciplines supported by NSF, our hope was that robust undergraduate research programs in science would eventually lead to undergraduate research in other non-NSF disciplines.

The 2-year follow-up of the workshops found that nine out of ten campus teams were using what they at learned in the workshops as they sought to implement an undergraduate research program (Weiler, 2013). The majority of teams also found the action plan they developed was a useful guide for their implementation efforts. A number of continuing challenges were also identified in the follow up report. Resource limitations and difficulties in adjusting faculty workload are challenges that 4-year colleges also face. Workshop participants identified additional challenges to address such as constraints on student time, lack of student awareness, and difficulty in obtaining faculty buy-in for student research. In the regional conversations that were part of the ATE grant we heard that administrative and trustee support was a significant issue. The fact that this issue was not mentioned as a significant challenge suggests that administrative involvement in the workshop and the development of the action plan helped to gain presidential and possibly trustee interest if not actual support. In the next chapters we will look at some of the campuses where teams were able to achieve a level of success, by providing more opportunities for student learning and preparation for transfer to a 4-year college or entry into the workforce.

While access is central to the community college mission, community college faculty, administrators, and staff are also committed to the full spectrum of human development for low-income, first-generation, immigrant, and minoritized students. Undergraduate research contributes particularly to the public good because of its emphasis on stimulating curiosity, problem-solving, and discovery—necessary skills for the innovations needed to maintain a healthy economy. As our economy becomes increasingly knowledge-and idea-based, we become more dependent on innovative ideas, research, and development to maintain our standard of living and to remain competitive in the global marketplace. Future employees at all levels will need more skills and more education in order to obtain jobs in a knowledge-based economy. The role of community colleges in economic development, workforce preparation, and social justice is critical to the well-being of our nation.

# 3

# OVERVIEW OF FIVE SYSTEMS

The five community college systems or districts described in this chapter are institutions that I came to know through CUR National Science Foundation grants. Each system/district is different and distinctive in specific characteristics.

These five community college systems/districts combined have 2,537,307 students, which is approximately 37% of the U.S. community college student population. They represent four regions; east coast, west coast, south, and southwest, and five states—Arizona, California, New York, Oklahoma, and Tennessee. Some are closely aligned systems, and one is loosely aligned. The California system is the most extensive community college system in the United States, with a range from large urban campuses to suburban and rural campuses. The City University of New York (CUNY) enrolls more students than any other urban system in the country. The remaining smaller systems/districts include both urban and rural colleges.

## California Community College System

With 116 colleges, 73 districts, and 2.1 million students enrolled, the California Community College System (CCCS) has the distinction of being the largest system of higher education in the United States (California Community Colleges, 2019). Located up and down the state, the CCCS serves both urban and rural areas. A chancellor leads each district with an elected board, and a president leads each individual campus. Districts have significant autonomy from the state system office.

As the state with the largest population and third largest geographic size, it is not surprising that California has the most extensive community college system. Perhaps because of its size, California has played an essential role in the recent history of higher education. In 1907 California became the first state to pass a law establishing public junior colleges (Galizio, 2019). California's Master Plan for Higher Education became a model for other states and in some cases, other countries. A committee appointed by the University of California Regents and the State Board of Education developed the Master Plan in 1960. Governor Edmund "Pat" Brown signed it into law in April 1960. Designed to address cost containment for higher education in California, the Master Plan provided access to higher education for California residents. The plan "delineated responsibilities and defined the missions of the public segments of California Higher Education" (Governor's Office of Planning and Research, 2018, p. 8). It also more clearly defined missions of the three higher education sectors and stated eligibility expectations for each segment:

- The University of California would focus on academic research and award bachelor's, master's and doctoral degrees. It would admit the top 12.5% of high school graduates.
- The California State Colleges (now the California State Universities or CSU) would offer bachelor's and master's degrees with a focus on liberal arts and sciences and admit the top 33.3% of high school graduates.
- The community colleges would provide open access to the remaining students and focus on 2-year preparation for transfer to 4-year colleges or developmental and vocational training.

A significant part of the Master Plan was free tuition for each segment, which is no longer available. Challenging the Master Plan is its capacity to meet current state educational needs for a growing population. The population has more than doubled since the Master Plan was approved in 1960. California's colleges and universities remain among the most diverse and highest quality institutions in the United States. Several UC campuses, such as Berkeley and UCLA, are internationally acclaimed (Keller, 2009). Open access has led to California community colleges having the highest rate of public attendance, with one in five community college students in the United States attending a California community college. Three out of every 10 college students in California attend one of the 116 community colleges (Foundation of California Community Colleges, 2017).

As with other community colleges, completion rates for California community colleges are low. Only 13% of community college students graduate with an associate degree in 2 years, and only 31% graduate within 3 years. The 6-year completion rate is approximately 48% (Public Policy Institute of California, October 2019). The completion rate varies by racial and ethnic identity, with white and Asian students more likely to graduate than African American and Latinx students. Over 40% of the students attending California community colleges are 25 years old or older and are working full-time. Work and adult responsibilities may partially account for the low completion rate.

The Master Plan addressed the issue of transfer from a community college to either the UC or the CSU system. Transfer rates are low, with approximately 80,000 students transferring to one of the 4-year institutions each year (California Community Colleges, 2019). There are many obstacles to transfer with articulation agreements often being specific to a particular campus. To address concerns about transfer, the Chancellor's Office is supporting the Guided Pathways Initiative with a one-time state investment of $150 million over 5 years (Foundation for California Community Colleges, 2017). Through a competitive process, 20 community colleges were selected to participate in the full implementation of the Guided Pathways Initiative. The Community College Research Center (Bailey et al., 2015) developed expectations. The CCCS Chancellor's office encourages all campuses, whether or not they were selected, to fully participate in the Guided Pathways project to:

- Strive to meet the Board of Governor's goal of having 100% of students complete an education plan.
- Augment and enhance student services to monitor student progress more closely and intervene more assertively.
- Take steps to foster deeper, more personal relationships between faculty and students.
- Strive to carve out more time for faculty to work together to define clear, relevant learning outcomes and prioritize professional development. (Foundation for California Community Colleges, 2017, p. 22)

Improving the completion rate and, therefore, the number of college-educated California residents is of great importance to the state economy. California is the fifth largest economy in the world, but the pipeline for future workers is aging, and the state is not educating enough young people to replace retiring workers (The Campaign for College Opportunity, 2018). Estimates suggest that California will be short by 1.1 million bachelor's degrees to meet economic demand by 2030 (Public Policy Institute of California, April 2016). The Campaign for College Opportunity projects that California needs 60% of adults in the state to have a college credential if it is to maintain California's economic place in the world. The state will need 1.65 million more people to reach the goal. Meeting workforce demand and closing racial/ethnic gaps are also crucial if California is to retain its role as one of the leaders in the technology industry and other areas of innovation.

Affordability and access are critical challenges to meeting the demand for more educated citizens. California Promise Legislation (AB19) passed in 2018 to increase access and affordability (Rauner et al., 2018). Renamed the California Promise Grant, the new legislation builds on previous programs. There are currently more than 50 California Promise programs. California community colleges are also aggressively participating in the College Completion Agenda.

While the various national initiatives for retention and completion do not include undergraduate research as a strategy, it is, nevertheless, a strategy that has proven successful (Lopatto, 2010; Nagda et al. 1998; Russell et al., 2007; Seymour et al., 2004). Participating in undergraduate research develops innovative and entrepreneurial predispositions. Nine California community colleges participated in CUR's NSF funded workshops on developing undergraduate research, and 15 campuses are participating in the CCURI professional development programs for undergraduate research. California hosts several events for students to share the results of their research. The University of California Irvine hosts the Honors Transfer Council of California annual student research conference in April each year. The Bay Area Consortium hosts a similar conference each May. The Southern California Council for Undergraduate Research hosts a student conference that is open to students from all universities and colleges in California. Some community colleges collaborate to host regional undergraduate research conferences. These meetings recognize the importance of undergraduate research and support efforts to expand research opportunities for students.

## City University of New York

The City University of New York system is a high-enrollment urban system, with 270,00 undergraduate students and 18 colleges, including 2-year and 4-year colleges. What makes this system distinctive, in addition to the population it serves, is its emphasis on quality of teaching and research for all faculty. Promotion and tenure guidelines are similar for community colleges and 4-year universities. Faculty and student research receive support at both 2-year and 4-year institutions. Because of the diversity of its student body, the early commitment of the first city colleges and current CUNY system to access and social mobility has remained a consistent goal deeply embedded in the mission.

The roots of the City University of New York as a democratic institution go back to the founding of the Free Academy of the City of New York in 1847. Providing free education for immigrants and the poor was its purpose. The first president of the Free Academy, Horace Webster, said:

> The experiment is to be tried whether the children of the people, the children of the whole people, can be educated and whether an institution of the highest grade, can be successfully controlled by the popular will, not by the privileged few. (Landa, 2011)

It was a grand experiment, and the present CUNY system still holds dear the idea of diversity and equal access to higher education. The experiment has made available quality education for many who might not otherwise have access to higher education. Like many experiments, however, the city colleges in New York have had many ups and downs during their 172-year history. There were debates about the education of women, free tuition, open access, remedial education, and power struggles over who would control the city colleges. Community colleges were a late addition to the network of New York City colleges. Bronx Community College, the first community college, was founded in 1957, followed by Queensborough in 1959, Borough of Manhattan and Kingsborough in 1963, Hostos in 1968, LaGuardia in 1971, and most recently, Gutmann in 2008. It wasn't until 1961 that New York created the CUNY system. On April 11, 1961, Governor Nelson A. Rockefeller signed into law the creation of a centralized system of higher education for New York City colleges and universities. The State Board of Higher Education previously approved the legislation. The new system consisted of five senior colleges and two community colleges (CUNY, 2011). There are now seven CUNY community colleges, which enrolled 95,592 students in 2018.

Though the CUNY community colleges are relatively young, they have developed several programs that are models for other community colleges. The goal of the Accelerated Study in Associate Programs (ASAP) is to increase the number of students who graduate in 3 years (Gupta, 2017). The program provides tuition waivers, free use of textbooks, and unlimited MetroCard usage, so students have transportation to classes, advising appointments, use of the library, and computer centers. To further support the program, advisers received reduced caseloads. Students can access individual career and employment counseling and tutoring for 3 years. The MDRC evaluation found that the project has been highly successful, with 40% improvement in the 3-year graduation rate (Gupta, 2017). CUNY helped Ohio develop an ASAP demonstration program. CUNY also provides technical assistance to

Skyline College in California and Westminster Community College in New York to implement the ASAP framework (Smith, 2019).

In 2011 the CUNY system, including 2-year and 4-year institutions, began developing a Guided Pathways program to facilitate retention and completion rates as well as a more effective transfer process. Initially, the plan was quite controversial, particularly with the faculty union. A significant part of the opposition was the top-down approach to exert control over the curriculum (Vitale, 2011). Alexandra Logue, who led the Pathways effort, describes the process in her 2017 book, *Pathways to Reform: Credits and Conflict at The City University of New York*. Despite the controversies and conflicts, CUNY implemented the Pathways project in 2013. Essentially, Pathways established general education requirements and transfer guidelines across the system. There is a 30-unit general education Common Core that, when completed, will transfer to any CUNY institution.

The relationship between Guided Pathways and the ASAP generated many questions (MDRC, 2016). While there are differences, the two programs are compatible. ASAP is a targeted intervention program that addresses inadequate support and academic preparedness by intrusive advising, acceleration, financial and educational support, and using data for improvement. Guided Pathways, an integrated, institution-wide reform effort, includes changes such as program streamlining through curricular mapping and creating faster approaches to remediation. The overlap between ASAP and Guided Pathways occurs in making transfer easier and emphasizing tracking and feedback support. Two CUNY community colleges, LaGuardia and Kingsborough, also participate in the Achieving the Dream project.

The CUNY Research Scholars Program (CRSP) is an example of how the system is supporting undergraduate research. Students at every CUNY community college have the opportunity to participate in a yearlong faculty-mentored research experience. The emphasis of the program is engagement in authentic research to increase persistence in STEM disciplines; CRSP is restricted to STEM. Some of the participating colleges, however, incorporate social science students in the program if they are participating in experimental research. One college incorporates English students because they are studying audiology and they conduct research in an audiology laboratory. Each year the CRSP program hosts a symposium at one of the CUNY campuses where students from all disciplines present their work. The CUNY Office of Research recently completed a comprehensive study of the CRSP program's impact and continues to assess the program (Neiro et al., 2019). A later chapter discusses the study in more detail. There are plans to expand CRSP into the humanities and social sciences pending funding. Humanities students are able to participate in undergraduate research through the grant-based program Research in the Classroom. Nearly every community college campus hosts an annual research day for students to present their work. In addition to system initiatives, Queensborough hosted one of the NSF workshops and the Borough of Manhattan, Bronx, Hostos, Gutmann, and Kingsborough Community Colleges participated in the CUR workshop. Three community colleges, LaGuardia, Queensborough, and Bronx, also belong to the CCURI project.

## Maricopa Community College District, Arizona

Maricopa Community College District (MCCD) in Arizona has ten community colleges, serving more than 220,000 students in Phoenix and the surrounding area. Maricopa Community College District employs 10,000 professors who teach a diverse population that includes 2.4% Native American and 32.6% Latinx students.

Arizona's first community college began in 1920 as Phoenix Junior College (now Phoenix College). The formation of the system in 1962 led to the development of eight new colleges over the next 30 years. Mesa and Glendale Colleges opened in 1965, GateWay College followed in 1968, and Scottsdale in 1969. South Mountain opened in 1978 and Paradise Valley in 1985. The 1990s saw the development of two new colleges in 1992, Chandler/Gilbert and Estrella Mountain. Maricopa is a Hispanic Serving System, and seven of its ten colleges have designations as Hispanic serving (MCCD, n.d.).

In 2017 the Maricopa Governing Board approved the Chancellor's vision for the transformation of the district and allocated $26 million to fund the institutional changes. The Transformation Project's overarching goal was for Maricopa community colleges to become a leading force in higher education and drive economic development in Arizona. Aligning the college system with "current community needs and expectations" and transforming the student experience were significant changes to be implemented. The project will eventually involve all employees of the district in a review of district policies, practices, structures, procedures, and culture to further a student-centered and student-focused mission. Three areas for implementing the transformation vision are Guided Pathways and Integrated Student Support, Industry Partnerships, and Enterprise Performance (MCCD, 2017).

### *Guided Pathways and Integrated Student Support*

As with other Guided Pathways projects, Maricopa will develop a comprehensive curriculum map that aligns with student career goals and provides proactive student support to stay on the pathway. The district has a particular focus on ensuring equity in the comprehensive design of its programs. In 1918 MCCD received a $325,000 grant from The Teagle Foundation for implementation of Guided Pathways (MCCD, 2018). Maricopa worked with the National Center for Inquiry and Improvement (NCII) for 2 years to support the implementation of Guided Pathways in all 10 colleges. NCII provided professional development for cross-functional teams and also made site visits to each college and the district office. Success of the project will be measured by:

- Length of time and number of credits a student earns in meeting their educational goal.
- Persistence and completion rates.
- Develop a curriculum map for degrees, certificates, and transfer options.
- Align programs with industry goals.
- Close the equity gap in student success.
- Foster natural cohorts of students pursuing similar goals.
- Scale-up high impact practices.

## *Industry Partnerships*

The newly established Workforce and Economic Development Office responds to community business partner needs for solutions to workforces concerns. The new office also supports students hands-on work experience. In the future, these industry partnerships can support student research projects as well as provide work experience (MCCD, 2020a). Shortly after the creation of the new Workforce and Development Office the Covid-19 pandemic caused U.S. colleges and universities to close their campuses. Many American industries and businesses also closed normal operations. In response to the Covid-19 closures, MCCD began working with the National Governor's Association (NGA) and the American Association of Community Colleges (AACC) to train workers in new skills for a workforce altered by the pandemic (MCCD, 2020b). The goal of a network of community colleges formed by the NGA and AACC is to prepare workers to successfully enter an economy transformed by the pandemic. The goals of the network are:

- Engage with a collaborative network of like-minded state leaders to strategize economic and workforce recovery efforts;

- Receive access to innovative tools designed by peers in the field and be paired with experts engaged by the NGA Center and AACC; and
- Access technical assistance, including webinars, facilitated peer-to-peer learning, virtual state site visits, and more community (MCCD, 2020b).

## *Enterprise Performance*

Efficiency, collaboration, and talent identification are necessary processes for improving the management of MCCD. Underlying the improvement process is ensuring support for a culture of accountability and employee development. The goals for enterprise performance fall into two areas: Organization and employees, and budget and finance. The organization and employee goals include developing a salary competitiveness ratio to evaluate the competitiveness of compensation options and making sure that all employees receive a regular performance review.

## Undergraduate Research Possibilities

Maricopa's Transformation project is an ambitious endeavor. Students and the Phoenix community will benefit from the full implementation of the plan.

Each of the transformational goals presents possibilities for undergraduate research projects that could lead to future jobs as well as support the local economy. Colleges in the Maricopa district actively engage their students in undergraduate research projects. The projects often focus on local interest topics. Estrella Mountain Community College hosts a conference each year for students from all Maricopa colleges. Mesa Community College was an early adopter of undergraduate research and hosted one of CUR's NSF workshops. Several Maricopa colleges participate in the CCURI network.

## Oklahoma State System of Higher Education

Established on March 11, 1941, by constitutional amendment, the Oklahoma State System of Higher Education includes two research universities, ten regional universities, one public liberal arts college, and 12 community colleges. The first Oklahoma Territorial Legislature passed legislation in 1890 to create three higher education institutions. This legislation was necessary to fulfill a Congressional requirement to become a territory. Three types of public higher education were mandated to provide: liberal arts and professional education; agricultural and mechanical arts education; and teacher training. Oklahoma became a state in 1907. Initially, Oklahoma wanted the Oklahoma Territory and the Indian Territory to be two separate states. However, the U.S. government insisted on unification. Equalizing educational opportunities of the Indian Territory to that of the Oklahoma Territory was a provision of the unification. Statehood was granted after reaching an agreement that new institutions would be developed to provide geographical access across the state (Oklahoma State Regents for Higher Education, n.d.).

Beginning in the 1920s local school boards began creating public junior colleges. While there were 20 such colleges by 1939, the total enrollment was only about 1,600 students. On the establishment of the state system, these junior colleges began to disappear. Over the years some of the junior colleges became part of the Oklahoma State System of Higher Education, and by 1987 all remaining public junior colleges were merged into the system. The state is mostly rural, with ten of the 12 community colleges located in rural areas. The colleges range in size from 24,500 students at Oklahoma City Community College to Western Community College, with 2,076 students. Despite having higher education available in the rural areas of the state, Oklahoma is falling behind the nation in the number of adults with postsecondary education degrees. Oklahoma needs to increase the number of associates degrees in the state from 67,574 in 2019 to 274,664 in 2025 to close the workforce skills gap (Oklahoma Works, 2017).

Oklahoma has taken several steps to increase participation in postsecondary education and college completion. Oklahoma's Promise, created by the legislature in 1992, is one of its most successful programs. It pays tuition at 2-year or 4-year colleges or universities for students who have met academic and student conduct requirements and with family incomes below $55,000. In 2018, 73.6% of the graduating class completed the requirements for Oklahoma's Promise, the highest level in the history of the program (Oklahoma's Promise, 2018).

In addition to state initiatives, Oklahoma has also joined national initiatives such as the Complete College Agenda (CCA). Through CCA, the Oklahoma State Regents for Higher Education (OSRHE) developed Guided Pathways to assist students in planning their college progression. The OSRHE Task Force for the Future of Higher Education set a goal of increasing the number of degrees and certificates earned to 67% by 2023 (OSRHE, 2018). Oklahoma initiatives include a focus on college readiness, transforming remediation, strengthening pathways to certificates and degrees, increasing adult degree completion, and performance-based funding for campuses. GEAR UP, through partnerships with public schools in the state, engages minoritized students in math courses through concurrent enrollment and aligning high school and college-level math classes. Math is considered a gateway course, and such courses often prevent students from entering the major or career that has the most interest for them. This issue was studied in depth by a committee as part of the Future of Higher Education task force. The committee recommended a New Math Pathways program and OSRHE approved it in 2017. The Math Task Force Recommendations report (Math Pathways, 2017) included the following five recommendations:

1. Establish statewide college metamajors and corresponding math pathways, ensuring transferability across institutions.
2. Increase student engagement and teaching of applications in gateway math classes.
3. Increase support for academic success in gateway math classes.
4. Provide professional development and resources for faculty and advisers.
5. Improve student preparation, including efforts in K–12 education and remediation reform.

Competence in mathematics is essential to the state's efforts in research and economic development. Success in math courses is critical for a student's advancement in STEM areas and participation in STEM undergraduate research. Oklahoma has been falling behind in the production of research at its major universities. For example, between 2000 and 2005, public university research in Oklahoma grew by only 15% while in the nation, the growth rate was 52%. Increasing research productivity has been an essential goal for the state, and Oklahoma has had considerable success. Between 2006 and 2010, federal funding for research in Oklahoma grew by $34 million. Public universities developed several areas of excellence, including environmental sciences, engineering, mathematics, and computer sciences, and earth sciences to support Oklahoma's agricultural industries (Battelle Technology Partnership Practice, 2013).

OSRHE sees research and undergraduate research as a path toward economic development and have put considerable resources into supporting faculty and student research. When the state began its efforts to increase university research, Linda Mason, coordinator for grant-writing and external funding assistance (now retired), thought that tying undergraduate research with the attempt to expand university research would move the effort forward. Campuses were enthusiastic about the idea and began engaging students in research (L. Mason, personal communication, June 26, 2019). One of my first invitations, when I came to CUR, was from Central Oklahoma University asking me to speak at the statewide student research conference Oklahoma Research Day. It was an impressive gathering of students from across the state and posters of their research. Later Oklahoma participated in a CUR NSF grant, and then Oklahoma invited CUR to offer another workshop. OSRHE supports a statewide faculty conference each year. Each campus selects one student to present research at a State Capitol conference and compete for a prize presented by a legislator. Community colleges have been active in the undergraduate research initiative.

## Tennessee Board of Regents for Higher Education

The Tennessee Board of Regents (TBR), with 13 public community colleges, enrolling 87,220 students in 2017, became the first state in recent years to offer free tuition to high school graduates. The Tennessee Promise program launched free education in 2015 for students graduating in that year. It is open to all students regardless of socioeconomic status (Tennessee Board of Regents, 2019). Between fall 2015 and fall 2017 Tennessee Promise has given scholarships to over 41,000 students. The program is an extension of Drive to 55, an initiative of former governor Bill Haslam. Drive to 55's goal was to increase the number of Tennesseans with a college degree or certificate to 55% by 2025. In 2014, 32% of Tennessee citizens had some level of postsecondary education or a credential, and in 2018, it was 42.7% (Lumina Foundation, 2019). Haslam, a Republican, believed free community college tuition would do more for left-behind Tennesseans than typical Republican tax incentive programs (Wermund, 2019). While he saw education as a way out of poverty, he also believed that postsecondary education plays a significant role in state-level economic development. Tennessee Reconnect, established in 2018, expands the free tuition program to adults who do not have an associate degree or higher to obtain an associate degree or credential. In 2016 Governor Haslam proposed and the state legislature passed a bill to separate the six 4-year colleges from the TBR. While the move was somewhat controversial, the Governor thought it would strengthen community colleges and assist them in fully implementing Drive to 55 (Sher, 2016).

Free tuition is not the only way in which Tennessee is a national leader in community college education. The Community College Research Center said that the TBR "is probably the furthest along in implementing Guided Pathways reforms" (Jenkins et al., 2018. p. 1) All 13 colleges are engaged in the reform process. Tennessee's focus on completion practices incorporated the goals of the Community College Research Center (Bailey et al., 2015):

- mapping pathways to student end goals
- helping students choose and enter a program pathway
- keeping students on the path
- ensuring that all students are learning

There are several unique features about the Tennessee degree completion approach, some of which are supportive of undergraduate research. Corequisite courses in math and English, for example, align developmental courses with students' academic focus areas. Program learning outcomes are aligned to reflect the skills needed for success in further education or future employment for student interest areas. And the emphasis on high-impact practices suggests that undergraduate research might be made more available to many Tennessee students. Another feature of the Tennessee approach to degree completion is the level of support and mentoring that students receive. With mentoring and support, students develop the academic skills they need as well as planning and goal-setting skills. These skills are necessary for nearly every career and are essential for undergraduate research projects.

Tennessee community colleges define undergraduate research as (adapted from CUR)

> an inquiry or investigation conducted by an undergraduate student in collaboration with a faculty member that makes a unique intellectual, scholarly, or creative contribution to the discipline, and for which the student receives academic credit either through a course or independent study. The student's contribution may be part of a new or ongoing faculty research project. (TBR website, 2019)

Tennessee community colleges differ in the level of development of undergraduate research programs, and the adapted definition leaves room for varying approaches to student research. The TBR has made a significant effort to codify undergraduate research and creative activities. Ten program elements have been identified and categorized as minimal, moderate, or intensive levels of engagement in undergraduate research. The ten levels are:

- Institutional Commitment
- Faculty Commitment
- Infrastructure
- Curriculum Integration

- Duration/Time
- Scope of Activities
- Scale
- Integration with Other High-Impact Practices
- Equity in Access
- Campus Assessment Plan

The identified elements of undergraduate research reflect the standards developed by CUR in *Characteristics of Excellence in Undergraduate Research* (COEUR; Hensel, 2012). Efforts are underway to aggregate data on student research activities in courses and outside of classes through the system's student information program. The scale of the project and the possibility for multiple interpretations of definitions in the taxonomy are challenges. The Tennessee elements of undergraduate research are likely common to most programs. However, three areas stand out: (a) integration with other high-impact practices; (b) equity in access; and (c) the campus assessment plan. Faculty can become overwhelmed with expectations for engaging students in high-impact practices, but integration can be efficient while also encouraging creativity. Access to undergraduate research in all disciplines is an important goal that few campuses have achieved. Providing access to low-income and minoritized students is a further challenge and suggests that multiple entry points to participate in undergraduate research are needed. Colleges across the country are only beginning to look at the structural and curricular changes necessary to provide equal access for all students to engage in research. Finally, many campuses struggle with how to know whether or not their student research programs are successful. Tennessee's taxonomy is a beginning step to document engagement in undergraduate research. While more specificity in the criteria for each level would be desirable, the taxonomy is an excellent first step.

Some community college campuses have taken advantage of national professional development opportunities offered by CUR and the Community College Undergraduate Research Initiative (CCURI). TNSCORE, in collaboration with Vanderbilt University, the University of Tennessee, and the TBR, invited CUR to provide a workshop for 4-year and 2-year colleges in Tennessee. The purpose of the TNSCORE project was to engage more faculty in undergraduate research from colleges that focused on teaching rather than research. Volunteer State College participates in the CCURI program.

In 2017 The National Association of System Heads (NASH) selected TBR to participate in a national project to identify and implement high-impact practices that would improve student opportunities for success

(Tennessee Board of Regents, 2017). Undergraduate research is one of the high-impact practices that are part of this initiative. NASH recognized TBR for its proactive work on learning and work-based learning.

## Concluding Comments

The five systems/districts highlighted in this chapter are all committed to student success and working toward higher retention and completion rates. They also play a significant role in workforce development and creating a vibrant state economy. The challenges the five systems face differ somewhat because of geography, size of the state population, state economic challenges and opportunities, and state history and culture. While these five systems cannot be said to be representative of all community colleges, it is likely that the missions, goals, and challenges are similar to community colleges across the country.

# 4

# ENSURING STUDENT
# OPPORTUNITIES
# AND SUCCESS

Community colleges provide access to higher education for millions of people each year. But access is not sufficient to ensure that community college students have a genuine opportunity to learn. Many community college students come from low-income homes and are the first in their family to attend college. Students also may have jobs and families of their own to support. The conditions needed for their success can be very different from what middle-class students need. Addressing the learning needs of first-generation and minoritized community college students requires attention to the logistical and structural issues of their daily lives and their emotional and psychological needs to ensure a learning environment for optimum success. Logistical and structural challenges can include food and housing insecurity, lack of transportation, time constraints, and childcare needs.

First-generation and minoritized students may experience doubts about their ability to learn and feelings that they don't belong. And they may lack knowledge about the culture, rules, and expectations of the academic world. Sometimes they need extra assistance in improving their math, reading, or writing skills. In this chapter, we will look at these challenges and how community colleges are addressing them.

## Logistical and Structural Challenges

The needs of students who enroll in 2-year colleges are often quite different from the needs of students enrolling in 4-year colleges. Many community college students are low-income, first-generation students, and may be immigrants. They may also work full- or part-time jobs while attending college and may have families to support. Community colleges address these issues in various ways.

## Food and Housing Insecurity

In 1962 Michael Harrington wrote a ground-breaking book, *The Other America: Poverty in the United States,* that galvanized national attention to hunger. Harrington found that about 10% of the U.S. population were starving and living below the poverty line. His book was instrumental in moving forward President Johnson's antipoverty program. While Johnson did much to address poverty, it is still with us today. Public elementary and secondary schools have free lunch programs because we know that students cannot learn if they are hungry. But what about hungry college students? In the last 10 years or so, many scholars and social activists have brought national attention to the degree of hunger and lack of housing for college students. Sara Goldrick-Rab et al. (2019) found that of 86,000 students surveyed, 45% of respondents were hungry in the prior 30 days, 56% were housing insecure in the previous year, and 17% were homeless in the last year. Like public K–12 students, college students need adequate nutrition and shelter if they are to learn. Goldrick-Rab, while a professor at the University of Wisconsin, founded the Wisconsin HOPE Lab to conduct research that would lead to more equitable outcomes in post-secondary education. Now a professor at Temple University, Goldrick-Rab continues her work on this issue and speaks forcefully about student hunger. A recent GAO report took a comprehensive look at the status of food insecurity in U.S. colleges. The GAO (2018) found only 31 studies that looked at food insecurity rates for college students.

An Urban Institute report (Blagg et al., 2017) found that between 2011 and 2015, nearly one in five families with a community college student family member experienced food insecurity. Families with students at 2-year colleges persistently experienced higher rates of food insecurity than families with students at 4-year colleges. The level of food-insecure 2-year college students peaked in 2012 at 23.8%. It fell to 13.3% in 2015. However, Goldrick-Rab et al. (2019) found food insecurity significantly increased in 2019 to 39%. In a February 2020 expanded survey, it was found that food insecurity for community college students was 44% (Baker-Smith et al., 2020). The GAO estimates that in 2018, nearly two million students who are potentially eligible for nutritional support through the Supplemental Nutrition Assistance Program (SNAP), were not receiving aid. Federal government discussions in 2019 about the SNAP program attempted to make it more difficult for students to access SNAP (Capps, 2019). On January 22, 2021, President Biden issued an executive order to increase SNAP benefits (Brown, 2021).

CUNY serves a high percentage of low-income students. A survey of food and housing insecurity in 2011 found that 39.2% or nearly two in five students experienced food insecurity in the 12 months before the study. The CUNY study defined food insecurity by four questions:

- How often did you worry that you would not have enough money for food?
- How often did you cut or skip a meal because you didn't have enough money to buy food?
- How often were you unable to eat balanced or nutritious meals because of a lack of money?
- How often did you go hungry because of a lack of money? (Freudenberg et al., 2011, p. 3)

The study led to a guide for faculty and staff on how to address food insecurity at CUNY (Clarke et al., 2018). One approach the guide suggested is to integrate food security issues into the curriculum and classroom discussions. Such steps could include developing a course on food security, adding readings on the topic to current classes, encouraging visits to public programs related to food security, and sponsoring independent studies. This area, food security, is one in which student research can have a direct impact on communities and institutions. It is also a field in which public presentations and publications are possible. Courses in political science, psychology, sociology, public health, and other areas could address food insecurity. Students could learn how to conduct interviews and surveys and complete a literature review through such undergraduate research projects. A course might also include analysis of government data, thereby introducing students to a comprehensive and readily available resource. The guide suggests that mapping food assistance resources could be a useful study. Food insecurity is personal to many students. It would be a compelling undergraduate research topic, and their perspectives as possible students experiencing food insecurity could be an informative addition to the existing literature.

Goldrick-Rab et al. (2019) also investigated housing insecurity and homelessness. Of the 167 students from 101 community colleges and 68 4-year colleges and universities, they found that 46% of respondents were housing insecure in the previous year and 17% experienced homelessness. In a more recent report, the Hope Center found that 50% of community colleges reported some kind of housing insecurity (Baker-Smith et al., 2020). Housing insecurity included difficulty in paying rent or mortgage, paying full utilities, moving in with people due to financial problems, and moving several times.

CUNY also investigated housing insecurity among its students and found that 41.7% of CUNY students, or two in five students, reported housing instability. The most common issue was the lack of enough money to pay the rent (Tsui et al., 2011). They also found that women, students over 25, and students raising children were more likely to experience housing problems. Community college students who don't live with their parents must find rental housing. Finding suitable accommodations is challenging because many students don't have a rental history and lack funds for a security deposit or money for first and last month's rent. Also, they may not have someone to act as a guarantor for rent (Office of Policy Development and Research, n.d.). Lack of housing, eviction, and housing discrimination may also be topics for undergraduate research. Including food and housing insecurity in the curriculum can make students more comfortable discussing their issues in this area because they will realize that they are not alone.

## Childcare

In addition to food and housing insecurity, childcare is another challenge for community college students with children. Nearly one third of the 5.8 million community college students are raising children while attending college. The Institute for Women's Policy Research (IWPR) (2014) found that approximately 2.1 million community college students are parents, and many of them are single mothers. Childcare is a pressing need for these parents, and their attendance at college is often dependent on the availability of affordable childcare. IWPR found that four in ten women at 2-year colleges said they might need to drop out of college because of their childcare obligations (Kruvelis et al., 2017).

Many campuses have early childhood laboratory schools that may be part of the teacher training program, and students can place their children in these centers. Even when fees are typically adjusted depending on the parent's status as college staff, student, or member of the community, childcare costs are prohibitive. These programs are frequently considered preschool rather than daycare programs. This distinction is noteworthy because the emphasis at laboratory schools is on the education of the child and teacher training provided for education students rather than serving the childcare needs of parents. Daycare centers focus primarily on the needs of parents for affordable and convenient childcare without sacrificing quality early childhood education. For example, some parents attend school in late afternoon or evening, and campus childcare centers are frequently not open after six o'clock. A state-by-state assessment of campus childcare found that 81% of California community colleges have campus childcare centers (Eckerson et al., 2016). After reading this study, I looked at a small sample of California campus childcare websites, and I called two campus centers. I found that community college students' costs could range from $500 per month (Saddleback Community College) to approximately $1,300–1,400 for preschool children (Glendale Community College), depending on the age of the child. Subsidies are available for low-income students through various state programs and can help to reduce costs. When campus childcare centers are open to the community, spaces for college staff and students are more limited. Whether offered on a college campus or in the private sector, childcare is expensive. Also, there is frequently a shortage of space, regardless of cost.

Unpredictable work hours can add to childcare challenges. Many community college students work part-time or sometimes full-time while at places with extended hours and peak and low times. Employers like to develop work schedules based on peak/low times, holiday, and seasonal needs, and other schedule variations. Sometimes employees won't have regular schedules and won't know their work hours far enough in advance to arrange for childcare. Employers who find ways to post schedules well in advance and consider childcare needs are likely to have happier and more loyal employees.

## Transportation

Community college students live off-campus, whether they live with their parents or in their own homes, and transportation can be a considerable challenge. The cost of buying a car, insurance, gasoline, and maintenance can be out of reach for low-income students. Public transportation, when available, is an alternative but can also be costly. When I was an undergraduate student, perhaps like students today, I bought my bus tokens on payday to ensure that I had bus fare for the whole month. CUNY provides free monthly Metro passes for eligible students to attend classes, meet with their advisers, and use the library (C. Kim, personal communication during campus visit, October 2019). Other urban campuses, such as Peralta Community College District in California, negotiate a reduced fare for their students (Orozco & Mayo, 2011). The Peralta contract reduced the bus fare from $116 to $31 per semester in 2011 and the contract continues bus fare reductions today.

Rural campuses face a different challenge because public transportation is often not an option. Some colleges can afford to offer van services, but this is too costly and probably inefficient for most campuses. A better alternative is to facilitate ride-sharing and encourage carpooling by providing parking spaces for carpoolers.

## Campus Support Services

Community college students are more likely to be successful in completing their degree if campus administrators and faculty consider all aspects of the students' day. Making registration, financial aid, and student support services available in one place can immensely help students who are juggling classes and off-campus jobs. Single Stop USA helps students to access information and benefits for food, housing, childcare, taxes, legal services, and other resources that a student may need. Students who took advantage of Single Stop were 6–11% more likely to persist than students who did not use it (Daugherty et al., 2020). All seven CUNY community colleges participate in Single Stop USA. The RAND Corporation suggested that Single Stop programs, based on their findings, play a vital role in supporting student success as they pursue their degrees (Daugherty et al., 2020). Recognizing that food and housing insecurity, transportation, childcare, and other life issues impact student success, colleges are developing programs that make essential services more transparent.

## Emotional and Psychological Needs

Just as campuses strive to make their support services more transparent to students, it is also essential to make the learning process more transparent. Many students come to college, not understanding the culture, rules, and expectations of the academic world. Even though they may have been successful students in high school, they still may not think of themselves as scholars who are capable of success in college. Community colleges are noted for the many ways they support students and the commitment of faculty and staff to student attainment. The Guided Pathways initiative is just one example of how community colleges strive to increase the possibility of degree completion and future career achievement. In addition to advising and curricular changes included in Guided Pathways, there are also classroom practices that can support students' learning process by incorporating mentoring into class meetings. Faculty are frequently the best mentors for students and play a vital role in the campus support system. We typically think of mentoring as a one-on-one experience, and while that is perhaps the best kind of mentoring, it is impossible to provide individual mentoring for every student. We can extend mentoring to more students if we think about mentoring a class rather than a single student. Class mentoring to introduce students to academic culture, rules, and expectations is especially important for students in their first year. Mentoring a class can take many forms. Key aspects are developing a sense of belonging for students by uncovering the hidden curriculum, recognizing the assets they bring to the classroom, and further developing students' capacities.

Developing a sense of belonging is critical for success in college (Packard, 2016). Creating an open and welcoming classroom is essential for fostering a feeling of belonging and begins by learning students' names. Extending that openness to more personal engagement with students plays a part in further building a sense of belonging. Overcoming a feeling of marginalization can be addressed by specific attention to uncovering the hidden curriculum of higher education.

## Uncovering the Hidden Curriculum

Head Start supplements the learning of low-income preschool children by making the hidden curriculum of the middle class transparent. The middle-class hidden curriculum includes reading to young children at night, going to museums, taking dance or music lessons, and family travel vacations in the summer, activities that may be out of reach for less affluent families. There is also a higher-education hidden curriculum, which involves the values, expectations, and norms of the academy that are not made explicit to students (Smith, 2013). First-generation students might not have had dinner table conversations about the college experiences of their parents or siblings. As a result, knowledge about higher education practices is not as implicitly understood as they are for young people whose parents graduated from college. College is very different from high school, and it can be intimidating. Recent immigrants may also be unfamiliar with the practices of higher education in the United States. College professors can uncover the hidden curriculum for their students by explicating American higher education values as they teach their courses and encouraging students to ask questions about hidden curriculum areas.

Anthony Abraham Jack, the author of *The Privileged Poor: How Elite Colleges Are Failing Disadvantaged Students* (2019), investigated students' experiences in attending elite high schools and entering Ivy League colleges. Even though Jack was a scholarship student at a private high school, he did not fully understand academic culture when he entered Amherst College. The *privileged poor* (PP) he described in his book are students like him who had the opportunity to have a glimpse of the hidden curriculum when given a chance to attend an elite preparatory school. Students who graduated from public high schools that were frequently underresourced came to college lacking knowledge about academic culture, practices, and unspoken rules. Jack called these students the *doubly disadvantaged* (DD). In *The Privileged Poor*, Jack compared the 1st-year experiences of the two groups. DD students lacked the language of higher education, awareness of the meaning of office hours, and many other aspects of higher education that are second nature to other students. When the college environment is unfamiliar, it can be intimidating and make DD students feel they don't belong. DD students in Jack's study were attending an elite institution where only exceptional students were accepted. Even so, they often doubted whether they were smart enough. Community college students can also feel they don't belong in college. Attending an open-admission institution doesn't necessarily translate into a feeling of belonging.

In the United States, we expect every child to attend high school, so the feeling of belonging develops somewhat naturally for most high school students. Middle-income families typically assume that their children will continue their education at a college or university. Lower-income families may have the same aspirations for higher education but are less likely to have the same certainty of achieving their aspirations.

First-generation, minoritized, and low-income students often feel marginalized. They lack a sense of belonging when they enter college because they do not understand institutional norms, expectations, and values. Simple issues such as whether to call your professor, "Professor X," "Doctor X," or "Mr., Mrs., or Ms. X" can intimidate new college students. More serious issues, such as not knowing how to ask for help or not knowing how to study, are likely to negatively impact student progress. Campuses have begun to recognize that marginalized students need a more comprehensive orientation to college (Rosenberg, 2017). For example, Georgetown University (2018) offers a 5-week, one-credit summer course that includes research and theory about first-generation college students. It also introduces students to academic and cultural capital and develops students' writing, analytical, and public speaking skills. Students viewed as disadvantaged and the PP are invited to attend the summer program. However, few community colleges or their students have the resources to spend five weeks in a summer orientation course. Another approach is needed. There are many ways that faculty, while mentoring students in their class, can begin to uncover the hidden curriculum for students.

*Introducing Academic Language*
Each profession has its distinct language, and higher education is no exception. Not knowing the language of the academy puts students at a disadvantage. First-year students may not know what a syllabus is or may not understand what is meant by *discipline, interdisciplinary*, or *canon. Liberal arts* may also be a confusing term. Professors can make the meaning for these terms explicit through class discussions. The introduction of the syllabus includes explaining the word and its purpose. Lacking an understanding of some words can be harmful. Students need to understand what is meant by *plagiarism*, how to avoid it, and why it is essential to understand it. Students also need to understand concepts like *intellectual property* and *critical perspectives* toward publications and other source materials. They also need to

understand what is meant by *primary* and *secondary sources, peer-reviewed,* or the differences between magazines and journals. Finding ways to regularly introduce students to the academic language in an integrated approach can be immensely helpful.

## Anticipating Questions

When explaining assignments, professors might anticipate questions that students may be afraid to ask and raise the question and answer it herself for all students to hear. Students might be asked to write down their questions on a 3x5 card, and the professor can answer them in class. This technique lets students know that other students may have the same questions; thereby assuring them that they are not the only one who does not understand. It is also a way to encourage questions without putting any particular student on the spot.

## Office Hours

*Office hours* is an example of a term that students may not understand. Students may not know that office hours are times when their professor is available to talk with them. Even if they know the purpose of office hours, they may not feel confident enough to make an appointment to meet with a professor. Faculty can be proactive by inviting students to meet with them at a specific time to break the ice for a first one-on-one conversation. Explaining the process of making an appointment and posting an appointment on a class website invites students to visit the professor's office. Office hours can be useful for learning more about each student and how to engage them in the class more effectively.

## Becoming Scholars

Students may also believe that they don't belong because they do not see themselves as scholars. Assisting students to see themselves as scholars can play a part in retention and degree completion. Undergraduate research is one way to help students become comfortable with their role as scholars. Because research is the essence of scholarship, providing students with an early research experience engages them in authentic scholarship and strengthens their identity as a scholar. Research methodology in nearly every discipline relies on four primary skills: observing, asking questions, making connections, and using evidence. These are important skills for students to acquire and need to be developed through hands-on or experiential activities.

Scientists know that observation skills are critical to developing new knowledge, but observation skills are also crucial for other professions such as writers, sociologists, psychologists, and artists. First-year students can learn to be good observers. Becoming a good observer can assist students in being more focused and engaged in the learning process.

Observations can lead to asking questions, and the heart of the research process is the ability to frame a researchable question. However, many students have been taught at home, and possibly in their elementary and secondary schools, not to ask question (Ross, 2016). In some cultures, asking questions may be considered disrespectful of one's elders or intrusive, so students need to learn that asking questions is an integral part of the learning process (Alrubail, 2016).

Developing answers to questions can entail making connections between one observation and another. Many discoveries, such as the microwave oven, came from connecting two observations and asking a question (Tweedie, 2015). Students need the ability to see relationships between ideas, theories, and events. Students who make connections are more likely to discover the interrelationships between what they are learning in their various classes. The ability to find connections may lead the student to a discovery or new interpretation of existing knowledge.

The development of new knowledge is also dependent on the use of evidence. Students must learn how to separate bogus research and sham ideas from legitimate research and accurate information. It is possible to build the development of these four skills into the curriculum of nearly every 1st-year course. In addition to embedding observing, questioning, connecting, and using evidence into the course's content, pedagogical changes are also crucial to address the needs of first-generation and minoritized students. Chapter 10 discusses in more detail these four fundamentals of research and other pedagogical issues.

### Student Assets

For students who may feel that they don't belong in college, it is essential to understand that while they may lack knowledge about the academy, they bring assets to the classroom. A significant asset for many students is their drive and perseverance. Overcoming innumerable obstacles to arrive at college is a collective experience for a substantial number of first-generation, immigrant, and low-income students. Drive and determination got them to college and are significant attributes that should be recognized and fostered. Supreme Court Justice Sonia Sotomayor (2013), a first-generation student, said, "There are uses to adversity, and they don't reveal themselves until tested" (p. 11). She credits her success in life to her "native optimism and stubborn perseverance," (p. 11) but she also says that the support from her family and others made a decisive difference. Professors can use these attributes to help students when they feel overwhelmed by the challenges of college. Asking students to reflect on how they met problems in the past can help them see that they can successfully address their current challenges. By sharing personal challenges, professors can strengthen students' beliefs in their power to overcome. Supporting the aspirations of students also encourages their ability to overcome their challenges. Ryan Speedo Green (Pelley, 2019), now an international opera singer, provides an excellent example of how teachers can support students' aspirations. Green had a troubled childhood that led him to juvenile detention. He was fortunate to have teachers at critical points in his life who believed in his abilities. On a high school field trip to the Metropolitan Opera, Green saw Denyce Graves perform in *Carmen.* He came away thinking that a Black man could become an opera singer and told his music teacher of his dream. Green's teacher could have said how few students ever achieve success in the opera world and suggest that Green consider a different path. Instead, his teacher told him he would need to graduate from high school, learn several languages, go to college for music, and then he would be ready to audition at the Metropolitan Opera. Green's teacher set out a path for him, and Green's drive and perseverance led to accomplishing his goals.

Knowledge and skills gained from work experiences are additional assets for many community college students. Students' jobs, whether part- or full-time, are often viewed as low-skill jobs that only serve the purpose of paying the bills while in school; however, students learn valuable lessons from their work. They learn responsibility, to show up and be on time, they may learn customer relations and how to deal with difficult people, how to work as a member of a team, how to take the initiative in addressing work tasks, and how to manage their finances. They may also learn skills specific to the job, such as computer skills, how to accept constructive criticism, and in some instances, how to evaluate another employee.

Students' cultural and economic experiences are also an asset. Different cultures and economic status bring different ideas and perspectives to the table, and these can be valuable commodities in the classroom, undergraduate research projects, and future professional employment. Appreciating the students' perspectives and bringing diversity into class discussions helps students value their own experiences and respect such differences as an asset. Diversity can also expand the cultural and socioeconomic understanding of all students in the class.

## *Building Capacity*

In addition to recognizing assets, building capacity creates additional assets. Mentoring, of course, is a typical way to develop student capacity. Mentoring is also an essential part of undergraduate research, and mentorship has proven to be a useful tool for retention and degree completion. Typically mentoring in undergraduate research occurs in a one-on-one relationship as students and professors work together on a project. Few community colleges have the resources to provide one-on-one mentoring for every student—nor do other higher education institutions, for that matter. While faculty may find one-on-one mentoring the most gratifying, it is possible to mentor a whole class collectively if professors look at the class members as a team working toward a common goal. And large classes can be divided into smaller research teams. Many industries and professions value people who can work well together as a team. Businesses also know that utilizing the different skills of team members can contribute to a successful product. Teams work best when the contributions of each member are valued. The concept of democratic leadership can create an inclusive and productive classroom team. Democratic leadership places a high value on inclusiveness, equality, and shared decision-making. An open classroom where student ideas and opinions are encouraged and valued can model democratic leadership (Hensel, 2018). An open classroom can also include several additional teaching/learning strategies to foster the notion that all team members, including the professor, are learners. The basis of scholarship is the idea that we are all trying to find out more than what is already known and then share our discoveries.

### Sharing Challenges

Students often think that they are the only ones who feel challenged by the course content. When a professor shares problems he or she experienced in college, it tells students that even successful people did not succeed all of the time. Letting students know that failure is part of the path to success is reassuring. I often share with students that it took me 7 years to complete my baccalaureate degree and I failed a genetics class.

### Transparent Teaching

Inviting students to provide feedback as the professor experiments with new teaching strategies conveys to students that the teacher is also a learner and that the teaching/learning process can be a topic for discussion. Soliciting students' comments regarding the effectiveness of a particular teaching strategy provides insight into how students are learning and where the stumbling blocks are.

### Modeling

For students who may not know how to learn or understand their learning process, the instructor can model his or her thinking process. When a topic is difficult to understand, the professor may tell students that he also found the topic difficult, share the questions he had about the topic, and describe how he came to his conclusions. Asking students to share their thinking process can be insightful for students and instructors. Professors may also share their techniques for learning and mastering a topic.

## Concluding Comments

Initiatives like Guided Pathways require campus-wide commitment and a great deal of energy from several sectors to achieve the desired goals. It is also a long-range initiative, and results will not be known for several years. Changing the pedagogy is a process that the instructor can control, and the results will be readily apparent as students become more comfortable and engaged in the class. We will look more closely at new pedagogies in chapter 10.

Sonia Sotomayor comments on her first experiences at Princeton:

> I came to accept during my freshman year that many of the gaps in my knowledge and understanding were simply limits of class and cultural background, not lack of aptitude or application as I'd feared. That accept-ance, though, didn't make me feel less self-conscious and unschooled in the company of classmates who'd had the benefit of much more worldly experience. Until I arrived at Princeton, I had no idea how circumscribed my life had been, confined to a community that was essentially a village in the shadow of a great metropolis. . . . I was enough of a realist not to fret about having missed summer camp, or travel abroad, or a casual familiar-ity with the language of wealth with so much to offer, of which I'd tasted almost nothing. . . . The agenda for self-cultivation that had been set for my classmates by their teachers and parents was something I'd have to develop for myself. (Sotomayor, 2013, p. 135)

We know a great deal more now about supporting first-generation, low-income or minoritized students than we did in 1972 when Sotomayor entered Princeton. While we have progressed, we still have a long way to go before students no longer feel alone addressing the gaps in their knowledge and understanding of college culture.

# PART TWO

# EXAMPLES OF
# UNDERGRADUATE RESEARCH

# 5

# BASIC AND APPLIED RESEARCH

Traditionally, scientific research has been categorized as basic or applied research. Vannevar Bush, President Roosevelt's science advisor, published a report in 1945 where he described basic research as "pure research" that does not have practical applications but may sometimes develop useful outcomes (Shneiderman, 2016, p. 21). Bush also believed in a linear approach to research with applied research following basic research. Basic research is said to be "curiosity- driven" while applied research is "mission- or solution-driven" (Shneiderman, 2016).

In *Science, the Endless Frontier*, Bush (1945) contrasts basic and applied research:

> Basic research is performed without thought of practical ends. It results in general knowledge and understanding of nature and its laws. The general knowledge provides the means of answering a large number of important practical problems, though it may not give a complete specific answer to any one of them. The function of applied research is to provide such complete answers. The scientist doing basic research may not be at all interested in the practical applications of his work, yet the further progress of industrial development would eventually stagnate if basic research were long neglected. (Chapter 3)

The National Research Council (2005) provided the following updated definition:

> Research is systematic study directed toward fuller scientific knowledge or understanding of the subject studied. Research is classified as either basic or applied according to the objectives of the sponsoring agency.

> Basic research is defined as systematic study directed toward fuller knowledge or understanding of the fundamental aspects of phenomena and of observable facts without specific applications toward processes or products in mind (Appendix D, p. 46).
>
> Applied research is defined as systematic study to gain knowledge or understanding necessary to determine the means by which a recognized and specific need may be met. (Appendix D, p. 47)

The distinction between basic and applied research is becoming less clear. Peter Medawar, in his book *Advice to a Young Scientist* (1979), described basic research as "snobbish" because the science community looked down on applied science. Medawar won a Nobel Prize in 1960 for work that began with an applied question. At the beginning of World War II, Medawar was asked by the Medical Research Council of England to investigate skin grafting and why skin taken from one person would not form a permanent graft on another person (Nobel Media, 2019). He received the Nobel Prize for his discovery of acquired immunological tolerance. Medawar was able to demonstrate that it is possible to experimentally induce tolerance when he successfully transplanted tissue from one mouse embryo to another. The adult mouse would accept tissue only from the original donor. Another example of a practical problem that led to a basic science breakthrough is Louis Pasteur's work on milk spoilage and the lack of fermentation in wine. Pasteur discovered that heating milk reduces the presence of bacteria (Stokes, 1997). Most milk on the market today undergoes a pasteurization process making the milk safer for everyone to drink. Many other examples of the interrelationship between applied and basic research can be found in scientific and historical literature.

Ben Shneiderman argues in his recent book, *The New ABCs of Research: Achieving Breakthrough Collaborations* (2016), that "combining applied and basic research produces higher-impact research, compared to doing them separately" (p. 1). Shneiderman says academic researchers should work in teams that are diverse and address significant societal problems. He provides an example of integrating basic and applied research when Thomas Jefferson directed Lewis and Clark to explore the West and make detailed notes about the geology, geography, water, astronomy, and meteorology as they forged a trail across the country. Jefferson also asked for documentation about the language, traditions, laws, and customs of the Native Americans that they met on their journey. The research on bears by John Van Niel at Monroe Community College, referred to in chapter 2, is an example of applied research that led to basic research. Initially, students collected data from the monitors attached to bears, which is applied research. The data then led to basic research questions when students began studying other aspects of the bear population. Undergraduate research at community colleges is often research that combines applied and basic research, as suggested by Shneiderman.

Industry and government are interested in research conducted at universities because the interplay of basic and applied research opens lines of inquiry that are less likely at laboratories, whose function is limited to developing or testing a product. In 2007, a bipartisan committee of the United States Congress published their report, *Rising Above the Gathering Storm: Energizing and Employing America for a Brighter Economic Future*, examining the status of science productivity and innovation in the United States (National Academies of Science, Engineering, and Medicine, 2010). Concern about America's competitiveness compared to other countries, particularly India and China, was the impetus for the study (American Academy of Arts and Sciences, 2014). Following the report's publication, the National Science Board (NSB), overseer of the National Science Foundation (NSF), created a Task Force on Transformative Research. The NSB issued its report in 2007 and recommended that the NSF adopt the following definition of *transformative research*:

> Transformative research is defined as research driven by ideas that have the potential to radically change our understanding of an important existing scientific or engineering concept or leading to the creation of a new paradigm or field of science or engineering. Such research also is characterized by its challenge to current understanding or its pathway to new frontiers. (National Science Board, 2007, para. 1)

Proposals to the NSF must address the intellectual merit and broader impact of the proposed project. In response to the NSB report, the NSF revised one element of the criteria for proposals. The phrase *potentially transformative* concepts was added to the intellectual merit criterion: "To what extent does the proposed activity suggest and explore creative, original, *or potentially transformative concepts?*" (NSF news release, August 9, 2007).

When the NSB report was released, members of CUR were concerned about whether the NSF emphasis on potentially transformative research would limit the amount of funding available to colleges focused on teaching undergraduates. CUR applied for an NSF grant to host a summit on transformative research at predominantly undergraduate institutions (PUIs). A report of the summit (Karukstis and Hensel, 2010) suggested that transformative research is possible when faculty, departments, and institutions create an environment that expects and supports high-quality research. Incorporating research into the curriculum is one way to support high-quality research. Collaborations between colleges, universities, and industry can support the generation of transformative ideas and provide a process and structure for implementing those ideas. Potentially, transformative research is more likely to occur when there is collaboration between various sectors such as research universities, liberal arts colleges, community colleges, national laboratories, and industry.

It is maybe harder for community colleges to engage students in transformative research than 4-year colleges and universities, where students have possibly had more opportunities to compete in prestigious high school science contests. Transformative research may require more time than the 2 to 3 years students spend at a community college. Despite the challenges, some community college students are conducting transformative research. In fact, community colleges have several advantages when engaging students in research. First, they typically have strong ties to the local community and can provide needed research, basic and applied, to local agencies and industries. Second, young students often come to research with interesting and unusual questions because they do not yet know what they don't know. When given encouragement and opportunity, students may ask questions that would not occur to a trained scientist. And finally, because research and publication are not usually part of the promotion and tenure process at community colleges, professors may feel freer to take risks with the questions they investigate. Partnering with 4-year institutions, industry, and research laboratories may provide community college students with additional opportunities to participate in basic, applied and also transformative research. Chapter 9 will describe research partnerships at community colleges.

Strong basic research programs at community colleges will continue to be important in the future. The NSB released an update of Bush's *The Endless Frontier* in May 2020, *Vision 2030*. The report calls for increasing science, technology, engineering, and math skills for all Americans to retain America's leadership role in fundamental research. With the report's emphasis on partnerships and inclusion, community colleges should play a role in the implementation of the 2030 vision.

## Basic Research at Community Colleges

Students at 2-year colleges are doing basic research in several areas. They present their research at conferences and sometimes are able to copublish research with their faculty mentor. I attended several undergraduate research conferences to view student posters. I also interviewed faculty and they frequently shared student posters with me.

### Posters at the Southern California Conferences on Undergraduate Research

The Southern California Conferences on Undergraduate Research (SCCUR), an annual event, is an example of how 4-year and community colleges can collaboratively support research. In November 2019, I attended the SCCUR held at California State University, San Marcos. Community colleges actively participate in SCCUR, and two posters stood out to me as examples of basic and applied research and possibly transformative research. One poster was in cryptography, and the other was in music.

## Pasadena City College

### Cryptography

I met Juan Leon, professor of computer science and applied mathematics, at SCCUR and later at his Pasadena City College office. He is a professor who encourages students to step out of their comfort zone to take advantage of possible new experiences. One of Leon's students, Adam Ismail, was interested in encryption and had some ideas he wanted to pursue. Leon told Ismail he didn't know much about cryptography but agreed to support his study and said they would learn together. Seeking new knowledge with a faculty member is an empowering experience for a student and rewarding for a professor. Ismail began developing his ideas under his professor's guidance. Professor Leon suggested Ismail submit a proposal to the SCCUR conference. His poster, *Replacing Public Cryptographic Key Exchanges with Quantum Resistant Implementations* (Ismail, 2019), was accepted, and that is where I met him.

Pasadena City College participates in the Cisco Advanced Network Engineer program. Students can earn an Occupational Skills Certificate that leads to entry and midlevel jobs in information technology, one of the significant growth areas for employment. Industry partnerships in this field are crucial because of the fast-changing nature of technology and work. In 2002, the National Science Foundation and American Association of Community Colleges held a summit on community colleges' role in cybersecurity. The summit brought together educators and corporate leaders from cybersecurity firms to strengthen college and industry partnerships. Community colleges are uniquely suited to deliver undergraduate cybersecurity programs because they can quickly develop new programs and respond to industry changes.

Through their workforce development programs, community colleges have close relationships with business and industry professionals who serve as program advisers (NSF & AACC, 2002). Advisers assist computer technology programs to incorporate topics such as the role of security in new technologies, understanding of vulnerability, threats, acceptable risks, risk mitigation, and knowledge of the Information Technology Security Evaluation Criteria into the curriculum.

Encryption is necessary for cybersecurity and is a fertile area for research and development. For many years the Diffie-Hellman key exchange was used to protect electronic communications and financial transactions. While the development of the Diffie-Helman key exchange was groundbreaking, as electronic communications and transactions expanded, businesses needed a more efficient cybersecurity method. Researchers explored the use of elliptic curves, a branch of mathematics, as a better solution for secure encryption (Ismail, 2019). Elliptic curve key exchanges could provide even more security if a quantum-resistant algorithm is used. This is the problem that intrigued Ismail.

Ismail investigated whether the use of the supersingular isogeny elliptic curve Diffie-Hellman would be a quantum-resistant algorithm. He was using reverse engineering on Cisco's Linux architecture to develop a more effective debugger relationship. Ismail states in his poster, "If this can all be accomplished, interesting benchmarks can be performed to gauge the relative performance of the most prominent contenders for quantum-resistant encryptions." According to Ismail, many researchers are currently working on this issue (Ismail, 2019). Professor Leon told me that quantum encryption is a significant area of research because it can potentially render current encryption techniques obsolete. According to Leon, the possibility that quantum computing can encrypt in seconds piqued Ismail's interest and led to the research described in his poster. If Ismail is successful with his efforts, it would place his research in the forefront of "what the future of computing holds for information security" (J. Leon, personal communication, January 30, 2020).

## Mira Costa Community College

### Music

Music is perhaps an unusual area for basic or applied research. Humanities and arts scholars are more likely to engage in theoretical research that builds on existing knowledge but may offer fresh interpretations or create new concepts. Greg Young, professor of music at Montana State University, suggests that music majors should have opportunities to engage in "innovative techniques, analyses, and practices" (Young & Shanahan, 2018, p. 3). Music technology is one of those innovative areas. It is an emerging field that is of particular interest to undergraduate researchers. Jonathan Cline's (2019) SCCUR poster, *Metal vs. Make-up: The Musical Composition Formulas Within the 2019 Albums of Tool and Taylor Swift*, is an example of computational music analysis. Cline, a student at Mira Costa Community College, analyzed the music of two performers on several criteria: artistic complexity, lyrical content, instrumentation, song structure, and variation. Computational music analysis (CMA) is an emerging field of study and presents significant challenges to the researcher. The researcher must balance the objectivity and scientific rigor of computer analysis with the interpretive nature of musical analysis (Anagnostopoulou & Buteu, 2010). Scholars have developed various approaches to CMA, but all depend on the explicitness of the analytical criteria (Meredith, 2016). Cline (2019) developed a new tool for harmonic analysis and form. He created circular, color-coded graphs to represent the areas of analysis he defined. This work could be considered basic research because it is both creative and potentially adds new interpretation to the discipline. Indeed, in Cline's oral presentation at the SCCUR, an audience member commented, "You've provided new tools that are inventive, interesting, and perhaps groundbreaking" (Oral presentation, personal communication from audience member, SCCUR, November 23, 2019). Cline's research may potentially provide a better understanding of how the elements of music appeal to various listeners. The length of the piece, for example, the number of instrument entrances and exits, and repetition in the lyrics and composition can be measured and considered when composing music or writing lyrics. In the future, musicians might consider CMA as they develop new songs and compositions and think about how their ideas might make their work more attractive to a commercial market. While Cline did not discuss musical plagiarism, this is another possible application of CMA. The precise and rigorous analysis of a musical piece could help the courts determine the originality of a given piece.

## CUNY Kingsborough Community College

### Linguistics

The CUNY system promotion and tenure policy is atypical because the criteria is nearly the same for 2-year and 4-year faculty. CUNY expects community colleges professors to engage in research and publish the results. While the imperative to pursue publishable research might seem to be in conflict with the undergraduate teaching mission of community colleges, faculty scholarship can encourage and complement student research in much the same manner as at research universities. An advantage for 2-year CUNY college students is that 1st- and 2nd-year students are more likely to have a scholar engaged in research as their teacher than their counterparts at research universities where senior faculty often don't teach introductory courses. The CUNY Office of Research created the CUNY Research Scholars Program (CRSP) in 2014 to fund laboratory experiences for associate degree students. Their program's goal is to encourage participation in authentic research and increase persistence in STEM disciplines, and it requires faculty mentoring of student research. To date, approximately 1,300 students have received funding to participate in CRSP (R. Nerio, personal communication, February 14, 2020).

Laura Spinu, assistant professor of linguistics at Kingsborough Community College, is an active researcher, and her CRSP students are engaging in original research. Spinu and I spent several hours talking about her work at the New York Public Library café on January 21, 2020. Spinu grew up in Romania and came to the United States to pursue a master's degree at SUNY Stony Brook and eventually a doctorate at the University of Delaware. She has taught at several universities in Canada but says that CUNY Kingsborough is the best place for her because her first passion is teaching. She and her students conduct research on bilingual cognition. They are collecting data to create a linguistic map of Kingsborough Community College's diverse students. Spinu has 35 publications listed on Google Scholar. She exudes enthusiasm for teaching, research, and mentoring students. In addition to teaching and research, she advises the speech and debate clubs. One wonders how she can successfully juggle so many professional activities at a very active pace. Her classes sound like great fun. For example, in her fall voice and articulation class she has a competition for spooky voices at Halloween. Whoever designs the spookiest voice on the software program receives ten points for extra credit.

Spinu's students are working on a wide range of research projects. One student is developing an application that will eventually help children with autism improve their tonal skills. Three of her students presented posters at the Acoustical Society of America December 2019 annual meeting in San Diego. Each of the students learned how to use the scientific method, although they used different procedures. They learned to conduct a literature review, develop a hypothesis, analyze the results of the experiment, draw conclusions, and suggest questions for further study. Vali Valizade's project investigated the relationship between native language, degree of bilingualism, and voice onset time. Often, people who learn a second language have an accent. Valizade and Spinu wondered whether the degree of bilingualism positively correlates with native-like voice onset time (VOT). The hypothesis also asked how different language groups affect English VOT in different ways. Native Chinese speakers, for example, produce values similar to those of English speakers while Russian and Spanish speakers do not (Valizade & Spinu, 2019). The study concluded that native language effects were strong in speakers of languages with different VOT patterns regardless of the degree of bilingualism. In this study, Valizade developed a questionnaire about participants' linguistic backgrounds, designed a research study, and selected participants.

Beckie Dugaillard investigated articulatory control in speakers of diverse linguistic backgrounds. Dugaillard and Spinu (2019a) hypothesized that bilingual articulatory skill is superior to monolinguals. The study did not find any differences overall between bilinguals and monolinguals. However, they did find support for a bilingual advantage in terms of articulatory skill depending on the specific type of multilingual (early, mid, late, bilingual and trilingual) with mid and late bilinguals. The researchers concluded that their study "stands out in having found an advantage with mid/late young adult bilinguals" and suggested that follow up studies are needed. This work was presented at the 2019 International Symposium on Monolingual and Bilingual Speech in Chania, Greece, and published in the conference proceedings (Dugaillard & Spinu, 2019b).

Sholom Gutleizer studied monolingual and bilingual reading fluency. Earlier research suggests that speaking more than one language fluently produces a cognitive advantage called the *bilingual advantage* (Gutleizer & Spinu, 2019). Gutleizer and Spinu hypothesized that bilingual reading fluency would be reduced compared to monolingual and that trilingual reading fluency will be reduced compared to bilinguals. They also found that females were more fluent than males in all groups, especially in the monolingual group. The study was not conclusive in terms of bilingual advantages or disadvantages and the findings are in line with previous published work. Through this study, Gutleizer learned the meaning of independent and dependent variables and how to do a multivariate ANOVA. The work of these three students is original research, and they are contributing to their discipline. Spinu and her students are producing valuable basic research.

Two other of Spinu's mentees distinguished themselves through their tireless work just before and during the COVID-19 crisis. Rawan Hanini, who has always been interested in speech disorders and language phonology, worked on a project involving the attrition of Arabic geminate consonants. Arabic consonants come in both short and long forms, whereas English only possesses the former. When native speakers of Arabic immigrate to an English-speaking environment, their Arabic consonants gradually come to resemble those of English, such that the length distinction becomes less robust and may eventually disappear—a process known as *attrition* in linguistics. Mariana Vasilita, another of Spinu's research students, explored monolinguals and bilinguals' ability to learn a number of new speech patterns in an artificially constructed accent of English, establishing that bilinguals possess an advantage on this task across the board. Hanini and Vasilita presented their posters at the 178th Meeting of the Acoustical Society of America in San Diego in December 2019, and later at the 2020 CUNY CRSP Virtual Symposium (where Hanini won the best poster award). One of Hanini's latest accomplishments was an invitation to speak at Columbia University, where she shared insights of her research experience with 21 bilingual education seminar students. Both Vasilita and Hanini made presentations in December 2020 at the International Seminar on Speech Production, jointly organized by Yale University and Haskins Laboratories.

After distinguishing themselves through CRSP, Vasilita and Hanini were hired as research assistants for K-CORE (Kingsborough Collaborative Research Bootcamp), a new initiative Spinu created to train students to do collaborative research. Participants work in groups and receive guidance from faculty and experienced students (L. Spinu, personal communication, May 15, 2021). Vasilita and Hanini coached undergraduate students from several community and senior CUNY colleges and assisted them with performing literature reviews, data entry, data analysis using acoustic analysis software, and poster design. Hanini also presented and published her original and follow-up studies, which were conducted jointly with a group of undergraduates (Ciccone et al., 2020) in the proceedings of the 36th Northwest Linguistics Conference (University of Seattle) and the 2020 Web Summer School for Logic, Language, and Information (Brandeis University), while Vasilita coauthored a paper with Spinu and other collaborators (Spinu et al., 2020), which was accepted for presentation at Interspeech 2020, an annual conference with a 47% acceptance rate attended by over 1,000 participants from all over the world. The conference content is enriched by a number of satellite workshops and a Scientific and Industrial Exhibition, making it a particularly valuable experience for undergraduate researchers (L. Spinu, personal communication, October 6, 2020).

Spinu's work never stops; she is currently mentoring four CRSP students, but also students outside the CRSP program, and students who have already transferred to senior institutions (some already accepted to graduate school). The more experienced students are taking on leadership roles and doing their part in helping to mentor the newcomers in the context of group work. Spinu feels very fortunate to receive financial support from her institution.

It allows her and her students to use specialized equipment and software and present their work at international conferences. Their work is primarily basic research although there are applications related to speech-language pathology, accent coaching, speech synthesis and recognition (especially as far as accented speech is concerned), public speaking, and even forensic phonetics. The work also has implications for theories of language learning and teaching (L. Spinu, personal communication, October 4, 2020). While the COVID-19 crisis has impacted Spinu's work by decreases in funding, she continues to work with four students with reduced CRSP funding.

One benefit from COVID-19 is that Spinu's students had the opportunity to present virtually at a higher number of conferences than in-person meetings would have allowed (a total of 14 conference presentations delivered in 2020), and publish their work in conference proceedings. She has also been able to use previously awarded CRSP funds to purchase an ultrasound system for speech research that will significantly expand research possibilities for her and her students.

## CUNY Queensborough Community College

### Biology

Andrew Anh Van Nguyen is a professor of biology at Queensborough Community College (QCC). As a graduate of Albert Einstein College of Medicine and Ruth Kirschstein postdoctoral fellow in the Howard Hughes Medical Institute laboratory, Nguyen could have obtained a tenured track position at a flagship university but chose to stay at QCC. His more than 34 publications have over 3,156 citations. He has conducted research on the biology of tumors, their growth, and metastasis. More recently, he has worked on inflammatory diseases and the role of inflammation in bone development. Nguyen's work demonstrates that not only basic research but applied research is possible at community colleges.

Since his tenure at QCC, Nguyen has mentored over 20 students; nine are CRSP students. In his basic research, Nguyen and his students published a paper on how inflammation stimulates tumor formation and its role in tumorigenesis (Nguyen et al., 2013). Currently, he and his students are examining how bone cells, osteoblasts, and how osteoclasts interact to maintain healthy bone development (A. Nguyen, personal communication, January 16, 2020). As part of his applied research, Nguyen and his students are examining microbes in environmental water and samples (Nguyen et al., 2020).

Nguyen, with a team of investigators at QCC, have been able to expand their research with QCC students by creating a new biotech core facility with state-of-the-art instrumentation like Cytoflex flow cytometry, confocal laser scanning microscope, and recently, a Quanstudio6 real-time PCR obtained through an NSF grant in which Nguyen is the principal investigator. QCC is very fortunate to have a modern laboratory with the equipment that students need for their work. The relatively new laboratory means that students can do all of their lab work at QCC rather than travel to another lab at 4-year colleges or universities.

While Nguyen's students come to QCC without a background in science, they have achieved extraordinary success. Nguyen attributes the students' success to the time and effort that QCC faculty put into mentoring and encouraging student development (A. Nguyen, personal communication, October 16, 2020). Nguyen also commented that straight-A students are not necessarily the best in the laboratory. C students, he said, might listen more carefully to the professor and are more likely to ask, "am I doing this right?" Because C students have experienced failure, they have learned that failure means you need to try again, and in the lab, that means persistence. Regardless of students' past performance, Nguyen and his colleagues have high expectations for all of their students. C, B, and A students strive to meet those expectations.

Several of Nguyen's students are doing original basic research. For example, Oscar Bermudes was one of 400 students who was accepted into a NSF Research Experiences for Undergraduates program at Northeastern University (QCC, 2018). An immigrant from Ecuador, Bermudes spent 3 years serving in the United States Army before beginning his studies at Queensborough. He worked with a team of students under Professor Nguyen's supervision to develop a less expensive method for detecting methicillin resistant staphylococcus aureus (MRSA), a common bacteria found in hospitals and the environment (Gaozhen et al., 2018). MRSA can cause severe complications for hospital patients. The team used loop-mediated amplification (LAMP) that does not require expensive equipment to amplify a specific target. The reaction is relatively easy to perform and is quicker than other methods of amplification. The LAMP method is especially useful for 1st- and 2nd- year students. Bermudes and his teammates' poster was a winner at the 2018 CUNY Research Scholar Program Symposium. Bermudes's research poster also took first place at the 26th annual statewide CSTEP student conference in April 2019 (Bermudes, 2019). He is continuing his education in a joint Bachelor's/Master's degree in science program at St. John's University.

Kaylynn Pubill is also doing original basic research. She didn't know what she wanted to do after graduating from high school, so she worked as a waitress for a few years (QCC, August 6, 2019). Eventually, she found her way to QCC and graduated with a science degree in 2019. At QCC, she found several colleagues who provided support and encouragement that led her to study science. She also found a research mentor, Andrew Van Nguyen, who encouraged her to become involved in research. Pubill's research focuses on the prevalence of *Salmonella* bacteria around the QCC campus. Salmonellosis is an infectious disease caused by ingesting contaminated food or water with *Salmonella*. Pubill hypothesized that because of birds and geese, common carriers of *Salmonella*, this microorganism can be detected in the environment. To prove the hypothesis, she examined standing water on the Queensborough campus (Pubill & Nguyen, 2019). Like Bermudes, Pubill used the loop-mediated isothermal amplification to identify *Salmonella* bacteria. Her poster took first place at the Metropolitan Association of College and University Biologists 2019 annual meeting. Pubill was not a CRSP recipient but was a part of the NSF-funded program Bridges to Baccalaureate at QCC. Pubill will be attending Hunter College to study biology after completing her associate's degree at QCC. She has won a $5,000 scholarship from the Finch College Alumni Foundation.

Nguyen also supervises students who are doing applied research. Another student uses the LAMP molecular beacon method to monitor the level of Enterococci in the East River in New York City. Enterococci are indicators of the presence of fecal matter in water, which can indicate the presence of disease-causing bacteria and viruses. The pathogens can sicken swimmers and also fish. New York City has many water-treatment centers that sometimes overflow when there are heavy rains. Nguyen and his student hypothesized that runoff from heavy rain in New York City will increase the level of Enterococci in the East River (Fox & Nguyen 2019). The student modified the novel LAMP technique by adding the molecular beacon component to the testing procedure. This new procedure is less expensive and easier to use than the process currently used by the Environmental Protection Agency (EPA). This student's research is an excellent example of how basic and applied research are combined. Adding a molecular beacon to the LAMP method was original research. The findings may eventually be used by the EPA to reduce the cost of monitoring Enterococci and more effectively determine the presence of harmful bacteria. The student's poster took first place in Microbiology and Immunology at the 52nd MACUB conference at Monmouth University, New Jersey.

Disseminating the results of research is an important part of undergraduate research. Presenting posters allows students to discuss their work with others and to receive feedback. Students also improve their writing skills when they have the opportunity to publish their work in professional journals. Nguyen encourages his students to publish and has coauthored many articles with them.

Nguyen, like many of his colleagues I interviewed at QCC, can succeed in both teaching and research at a community college because of programs like CRSP, Bridges to Baccalaureate, and the Minority Science and Engineering Improvement Program (MSEIP), which provide some financial assistance to the students. At the same time, mentors can capitalize on CUNY's internal competitive grant mechanisms. CUNY offers several types of internal funding, like the Community College Research Grant Program, Research in the Classroom grant, and Interdisciplinary Climate Crisis Research Grant to help start the research project. These grants foster collaboration between faculty members within university networks. Nguyen is grateful for these internal grants and can keep his lab running because of these grants and NSF funding he receives.

## Tulsa Community College

### *Sign Language*

Rhoda Smietanski is an assistant professor of American Sign Language Education at Tulsa Community College (TCC). She is also a practicing ASL/English interpreter. She developed her interest in languages when, as a teenager, she moved with her family to Belgium. It was a formative experience for her. She experienced culture shock when she could not communicate with her classmates. Eventually she learned French. When she came back to the United States, she enrolled at TCC. Remembering how she felt when she could not communicate with anyone when she first moved to Belgium, she enrolled in TCC's American Sign Language (ASL) program. After practicing as an interpreter for a decade, she began teaching at TCC as an adjunct professor. She discovered that she loved teaching, so she went back to school and earned a graduate degree in Interpretive Studies from Western Oregon University (R. Smietanski, personal communication, September 11, 2020).

When she began teaching full-time, Smietanski introduced high-impact practices to her students. During the first semester of the ASL Interpreter Education program, students participate in a service-learning translation project for a specific audience so students can experience an authentic context in the translation process. In the second and third semesters students engage in an embedded research project. Every student in the course records two interpretations. The first interpretation is a basic sample and the second has very specific instructions to focus on one particular skill, such as spatial mapping or nonmanual markers. Then all of the students do the coding and interpretation of the skills. One of the skills students practiced is spatial mapping, which doesn't exist in English.

In March 2020 I attended Oklahoma Undergraduate Research Day and came across a poster on American Sign Language/English interpreting, *The Impact of Deliberate Practice on Spatial Mapping in American Sign Language/English Interpretation*. Felicia Dunlap, Smietanski's student, wanted to learn more about focused practice. Dunlap and Smietanski's (2020) unpublished study investigated the effectiveness of focused practice on students' application of spatial mapping techniques. Focused practice involves goals, extended time, cognitive challenges, repetition, self-analysis, and feedback. There are two contradicting beliefs in the role of practice in learning interpretation. One belief is that innate talent and individual practice can lead to excellence. The other belief is that a structured and focused approach to practice is more effective. This study was the first to test the effectiveness of focused practice using spatial mapping in ASL/English interpretation. Learning sign language is not the same as learning interpretation and interpretation is not easy to learn. Continuing professional development is an ethical expectation of the interpretating profession. This expectation was the foundation of Dunlap's study. She found that deliberate practice had greater gains than general practice. The study is likely to impact educational practices of ASL/English interpreting. It is an excellent example of the kind of basic research undergraduate students can do and the possible impact of their research.

These examples of basic and applied research exemplify the kinds of scholarly work that community college faculty and students are doing together. Basic and applied research are most common in the sciences but, as we have seen, students in other disciplines are also doing this type of research. In the next several chapters we will find that basic research at community colleges overlaps with other approaches to research.

# 6

# COURSE-BASED RESEARCH
# AND EDUCATIONAL EQUITY

Course-based research, the integration of research into the curriculum, is an emerging pedagogy and research strategy. Biologists began implementing course-based research, known as CUREs, as a response to the American Association for the Advancement of Science (AAAS) 2011 report, *Vision and Change in Undergraduate Education: A Call to Action*. The report called for an early introduction to the scientific process and its integration into undergraduate biology courses. While there have been many changes in the undergraduate biology curriculum as a result of the AAAS report, introducing research into the curriculum is perhaps the most innovative change. Embedding research into the curriculum is a way of stimulating student curiosity and interest in science. Biology is a national leader in the development of course-based research. CUREnet, an online community of scholars who share how they are integrating research into the curriculum, is a force in promoting course-based research. Erin Dolan, University of Georgia, was one of the founders of CUREnet while she was a professor at the University of Texas. According to Dolan (2016), CUREs provide students the opportunity to "collect and analyze data, to interpret and communicate results, and even determine what questions to pursue" (p. 3). Generally, STEM CUREs include five components: (a) use of scientific practices; (b) discovery; (c) broadly relevant or important work; (d) collaboration; and (e) iteration (Auchincloss et al., 2014). Biologists are now exploring developing CUREs for nonmajors, and other STEM disciplines are also developing CUREs (Ballen et al., 2017). As faculty became involved in course-based research, they realized that it was an especially effective pedagogy for minoritized and first-generation students (Auchincloss et al., 2014). CUREs, because they involve the whole class in the research project, are more inclusive than the apprentice model of undergraduate research (Bangera &

Brownell, 2014; Hensel, 2018). Engaging students in course-based research in the first 2 years has a positive impact on the retention of STEM students. The National Academies of Sciences, Engineering, and Medicine in a 2015 report on integrating research into the curriculum found that:

- "Course-based research can provide many benefits for students from first year to senior year and also to underrepresented students.
- Many faculty members are not familiar with course-based research or are not aware of local and national models that already exist.
- Well-designed course-based research projects use many of the 'best practices' identified by pedagogical research." (pp. 7–8)

As faculty in non-STEM disciplines became aware of the benefits of course-based research, they began experimenting with ways to develop CUREs in areas such as English literature, history, sociology, and theater. As more disciplines have become involved in course-based research in the first 2 years, the criteria could be adapted to be more inclusive. Hensel (2018) suggested the following:

- Research is embedded into the course curriculum.
- All students engage in the research or scholarship project.
- Students work collaboratively on the project.
- Research projects introduce students to the research or scholarship methodology of the discipline.
- Outcomes of the project are unknown.
- Student outcomes of the research or scholarship are communicated in some manner.

As community colleges become more involved in undergraduate research, they are also developing CUREs. Because community colleges serve a diverse population, course-based research is an especially appropriate pedagogy. Many minoritized and first-generation students can be intimidated by research. However, students begin to see themselves as scholars when they are part of a classroom research project. Pyles and Levy (2009) suggested that the early introduction of students to research can "demystify" research for students. Course-based research can also facilitate a closer working relationship between professor and student and foster collaboration among students.

While there are many advantages to course-based research, there are also challenges. Finding developmentally appropriate research topics that can be implemented and managed with an entire class is not easy. Finding research topics that can be completed within a semester and do not require sophisticated and costly equipment is a significant challenge. Networks such as the Science Education Alliance-Phage Hunters Advancing Genomics and Evolutionary Science (SEA-PHAGES) project through the Howard Hughes Medical Institute have provided exciting projects that lead to discoveries with minimal cost. Online archival materials have been helpful to humanities and social science faculty. Many faculty, whether in STEM, humanities, the arts, or social sciences, have found topics and access to materials through citizen research projects. Citizen science engages amateurs in the research process by involving them in collecting data through crowdsourcing and providing volunteer support to researchers in science, history, social sciences, and other disciplines. There are thousands of citizen research projects that are appropriate for developing course-based research (Citizen Science, n.d.).

## CUNY Kingsborough Community College

### Biology

Mary Ortiz is a professor of biology at Kingsborough Community College (KBCC). She attended the 2012 CUR NSF workshop at QCC. In a telephone interview, Ortiz told me she left the workshop thinking, "I need to do something with undergraduate research, but we have no money" (M. Ortiz, personal communication, March 14, 2021). After thinking about how she could engage her students in research, she realized that she had a readily available and cost-free resource—birds. KBCC is surrounded on three sides by water, and the water attracts a large and diverse population of birds. After the workshop, in the fall of 2013, Ortiz introduced her Comparative Anatomy students to a research project to identify and catalog birds at several locations near the water. Previously, Comparative Anatomy included 3 hours of lecture and 3 hours of lab. It evolved into a writing-intensive hybrid course with 1 hour of lecture and 3 hours of lab. After Ortiz participated in the CUR NSF workshop, she introduced the additional innovation of course-based research that would fulfill her goal of engaging students in authentic research.

Including a longitudinal ornithology research project in Comparative Anatomy transformed the course and lab (Ortiz & Taras, 2014). Students have been collecting data for over 7 years. Spending 15 minutes each week in the field making observations, recording the location, time, date, weather conditions, tide, numbers of species of birds, and their characteristics, students have made significant contributions to knowledge about the local bird population.

Regardless of the weather, students go out each week to record their observations. Some students take photos of the birds while other students make drawings. When students have difficulty identifying the species, especially the juvenile birds, they use the *National Geographic Field Guide to the Birds of North America*. Sometimes the identification is not clear, and students need to make a decision as they assign species. As Ortiz continued the project, she asked one of her students to design a data collection template that all students now use. Eventually, it can be shared with conservation organizations or professors of ornithology to use in their research. Students are learning observation and questioning skills and the ups and downs of fieldwork. Some students are hesitant to ask questions. Ortiz tells them, "You are paying me, I don't pay you, so ask questions." When students come in from the field, they discuss what they found out that day, what happened, and why something is happening. As students begin to see trends, they talk about the implications of those trends. One semester, for example, they saw more cormorants than the previous semester. Another time they saw more herring gulls on the beach during a particular week. After Hurricane Sandy in 2012, they noticed that many gulls were nesting on the roof of campus buildings, providing students with the opportunity to study nesting behaviors, how many eggs the gulls laid, and how many survived.

For fieldwork, students divide into groups of four, and they collaborate on recording data and species identification. Each group submits a comprehensive lab report at the end of the semester that is part of the college Writing Across the Curriculum requirement. They also make PowerPoint presentations to the entire class as part of their final project. Ortiz's students are learning the basics of how to do scientific research. Groups often have questions about what they observe and develop hypotheses that they can test in the field. For example, they might ask if there will be fewer birds as the weather gets colder toward the end of the fall semester. During the first 3 years of the bird study, Ortiz worked with CRSP students on individual projects, and students presented their work at the summer CUNY CRSP conference. Some students also presented their work at the Metropolitan Association of College and University Biologists. And one student had his work accepted for publication in the honors program journal. The project has given students an appreciation of birds, and several have continued their interest as they have transferred to a 4-year college. One of Ortiz's students has entered a PhD program in marine biology in Florida. Even after students have graduated from KBCC, they come back periodically to see the results of current students' research and talk with Ortiz about their ongoing work.

It was clear from my conversation with Ortiz that she loves teaching. She commented that engaging students in undergraduate research is more work, but she says it makes her teaching more fun and she also learns from her students. Ortiz's father, who was a professor, told her, "if every decision you make in academia is best for the students, you will never go wrong." She lives by that, and her students understand and appreciate her commitment to them.

Christina Colon is also a professor of biology at KBCC, where she teaches ecology. She, too, found a way to engage students in authentic research with minimal cost. Colon's students study horseshoe crabs. When we met at the New York Public Library, Colon said all she needs for her research is a ruler, paper, and a pencil (C. Colon, personal communication, 2020). Her students find the crabs at Plumb Beach, the mouth of Jamaica Bay, and regularly monitor six sites. Plumb Beach is part of the Gateway National Park, a large, protected wetland in Brooklyn near JFK airport. The conditions of the sites vary. One site is near the parking lot and is quite polluted, and another site, where they find the most crabs, is at a relatively clean beach. Horseshoe crabs are a unique species to study. The blood of the crabs detects bacterial contamination in surgical equipment. It can identify MRSA, Gram-positive bacteria, making it a significant product for hospitals. The horseshoe crab's blue blood is a $112 million dollar per year industry in the United States (Lander, 2018).

An ancient species, horseshoe crabs have survived for over 480 million years (Van Roy et al., 2015). However, the crabs are declining worldwide due to increased pollution levels, habitat loss, beach erosion, shoreline hardening, and sea-level rise. While adult horseshoe crabs are resilient, juvenile crabs are vulnerable and subject to high rates of predation. Harvesting horseshoe crabs at Gateway National Park is illegal and subject to arrest (Somma, 2017). KBCC students study the juvenile crabs that they find on the beach. As the juvenile crabs grow over several seasons, they move offshore into deeper waters where students cannot study them. There have been few studies of the juveniles. Colon's students are doing basic research and making original contributions to knowledge about horseshoe crabs. In the fieldwork, students look for baby crabs and eggs and compare the sites where they found them. Students develop hypotheses. For example, one student asked about crab behavior and discovered that they swim in a clockwise manner. Another student was interested in egg survival and looked at the ratio of live eggs between beach sites. According to Colon, the students are excited about the research, participating in citizen science, and contributing to conservation. When Colon first started the project, a timid student was doing a presentation to the KBCC faculty. At the question and answer time, Colon was going to answer the question, and the student was so excited that she took the microphone and responded herself.

Colon said that the students become so enthusiastic about the horseshoe crab project that they want to rescue every crab. Several have won awards at regional and national conferences, others were featured on TV shows and a documentary, and one is a coauthor on an upcoming book chapter. Their enthusiasm and passion carry them through to graduation, and some continue their work when they transfer to a 4-year university. CUNY's NSF CSTEP program supports the research. CUNY also funded two students through CRSP. The majority of the students are interested in continuing their education in biomedical research.

Colon has conducted research in Belize and Singapore. She also had a Fulbright Fellowship to do her doctoral research in Borneo. She is part of the International Union for the Conservation of Nature and collaborates with many leading scientists on the topics she studies. Colon's academic journey is not dissimilar from the path of her students. She said that in high school, she was a mediocre student in science. Near the completion of high school, she learned about Lamarckian theories, the precursor of the theory of evolution. Through Lamarck's reference to giraffes, she realized her biology classes ignored animals. A high school physics teacher encouraged her to study the physics of bird flight while she had a part-time job at the Philadelphia Academy of Natural Sciences. After high school graduation, she enrolled at Drew University because they had a hands-on nature-based program in biology. While at Drew, she studied raptors and marine biology and realized she wanted to work in conservation. She completed an MA in conservation education at NYU and then pursued her PhD at Fordham University in ecology. For Colon, it was one teacher who recognized her interests and encouraged her to pursue them. She hopes she is that kind of teacher for her students. By engaging students in research, she communicates her respect for their potential and encourages them to think for themselves and pursue their interests.

## *Economics*

Dorina Tila is an assistant professor of Business at KBCC. She engages microeconomics and macroeconomics students in course-based research. She has also assessed the impact on learning through engagement in research. Microeconomics students participate in basic economic experiments, incorporating the ideas of Vernon Smith. In 2002 Smith won a Nobel Prize in Economics for his research to test economic theories by using economic experiments. Tila wondered whether the experiments she devised, even though they are not run in a lab and students are not paid real money, would work in a classroom and would improve students' learning and their attitudes toward economics (D. Tila, Personal communication, October 2, 2019).

The experiments involved setting up an economic environment that required students to make decisions and see how those decisions and "their interactions create the market forces predicted by the economic theory (D. Tila, personal communication October 2, 2019). To understand the concept of equilibrium and market demand and supply, students participated in a mock double auction by making bids to buy and offers to sell a product. By recording the process on a whiteboard, students saw how the transaction prices would eventually reach equilibrium. The second experiment demonstrated the concept of elasticity. As consumers, students received a fixed income and the cost of four products. They had to spend all of their income and choose what they wanted to buy. The next phase of the experiment involved different prices or a different salary for the same products. Students learned how to determine market demand by calculating elasticity of demand, cross elasticity, and income elasticity. After completion of the experiments, students responded to a questionnaire developed by Tila. The results suggest the experiments improved student learning and their interest in the subject. Students perceived the experiments as helpful in understanding economic concepts.

Students in Tila's macroeconomics course engage in a process that is similar to the research of professional economists. Tila developed a scaffolded process that begins with students selecting a country for analyzing its economic performance and ends with a formal paper that includes recommendations. In addition to learning about how economists conduct research, students improve their writing skills through the Writing Across the Curriculum pedagogy. The opportunity to choose the country they wish to study also addresses culturally responsive teaching and the college's global competence requirement.

The first step of the research process is developing an economic investigation map. The economic map is a tool that directs students to the appropriate sequence of the research process by starting with data collection, data analysis, and interpretation using economic theory. Students work individually on research about the country they have chosen and discuss findings and ideas with the whole class throughout the semester. Tila's approach to teaching this class is an example of both course-based research and applied research. In addition to a textbook, Tila introduces students to the World Bank, International Monetary Fund, and their chosen country's data bank. Students need to look at the impact of the country's labor laws, unemployment rates, and economic theories that inform the country's economic policies. Students learn how to interpret data, ask questions, read graphs, and apply economic theory. Class discussions provide a forum for sharing economic indicators, fiscal policy, and any economic events, such as a recession, during the semester. The capstone project is a paper and presentation that describes the current status of the economy in the chosen country and specific recommendations based on their findings. The student research has elements of originality as they develop economic recommendations.

## English

Jane Weiss is the literature program director in the English Department at KBCC. She is an active researcher and has contributed chapters to several books about life in 17th-century New England. She teaches Themes in American Literature and English Composition. When we met at the New York Public Library on January 21, 2020, Weiss had recently returned from a trip to France to study women who worked in textile factories during the 17th century.

As a literary scholar, Weiss is interested in having her students engage in a similar process appropriate for beginning students. Her students start doing literary research almost at the beginning of their studies. In the first semester of the writing class, students develop an essay that requires analysis and interpretation. Weiss does not expect her students to be particularly skilled in this type of work, but she believes it is essential to introduce them to the methodology of literary scholarship. The ability to analyze and interpret, of course, are skills that extend beyond literary research. As she introduces students to scholarly research, she also introduces students to the vocabulary of the field such as *point of view* and *voice*, terms describing the genre, such as *realist* and *gothic*, and concepts like *linear narrative* versus *nonlinear narrative*. Students learn to use research methodology by doing a literature review, using primary sources, and identifying possible gaps in the literature about a given text. After completing a literature review, students begin developing an original analysis, formulate an interpretation by close reading, and finally support their interpretation. She does not give her students a template or detailed instructions for the assignment, as she wants them to develop their approach and structure and learn how to flesh out their ideas. She uses Project Gutenberg, which gives students free access to texts used in her course. Students can download digitized texts on books whose U.S. copyright has expired. Students continue to develop their skills as Weiss responds to multiple versions of their papers. The second semester of the writing course includes a more substantial look at literary works, and students produce their own more complex interpretations. In this course, Weiss thinks about some students who might be ready to develop a presentation or begin writing a paper for possible publication. For example, a recent student looked at descriptions of places of refuge in books by Louisa May Alcott, Mark Twain, and Theodore Dreiser in her final examination. Weiss is hoping the student will develop the essay into an article as she compares past places of refuge to staying at home during the COVID-19 pandemic.

American literature courses offered online engage students in discussions through Blackboard. The conversations bring forward different perspectives for argument and disagreement about what the text means. For example, students had read some of Washington Irving's writings about Native Americans and the concept of the noble savage. They then read an 1827 memoir of an indigenous American writer about a tribal nation in New England. The students contrasted the views and perspectives of the two authors. Sometimes they relate the ideas from historical readings to contemporary issues. Some students have written about different voices, how it is meaningful to current discussions, and they have related historical voices to current debates.

They also asked, "who has the authority to speak?" as they read Irving and the Indigenous author and other authors with different points of view. In one of the American literature courses, students read poetry and other writings by Francis Ellen Watkins Harper, an African American abolitionist and suffragist. Weiss said that one student had an original interpretation of Harper's work, which changed how Weiss thought about the text.

CUNY provides some funding for faculty and student work in the humanities. Some of the projects are cofunded by the faculty union. There are also presidential awards that fund student projects and faculty pedagogy related to undergraduate research or other high-impact practices. KBCC's Honors Program's student scholarly journal, *Distinctions*, is funded by the provost's office and the support is beneficial to undergraduate research efforts. The possibility of publication is a strong motivator for literature students to produce original scholarly work. The journal considers articles authored by all students, not only those in the Honors Program.

Students from KBCC participated in CUNY's first community college literary studies conference at LaGuardia Community College. (The second conference was canceled because of COVID-19.) Weiss hopes for a second conference on campus or virtually in 2021.

Undergraduate research in the humanities and particularly in literary studies is not well developed at community colleges or 4-year institutions. It is an emerging field as faculty find ways to engage students in authentic disciplinary scholarship. Jane Weiss is a pioneer in the emerging area of student research.

## CUNY LaGuardia Community College

### *Biology*

Olga Calderon is an associate professor of biology at LaGuardia Community College (LGCC). She is also a graduate of the college. During her time as a student at LGCC, she was given an internship in a biology lab and eventually offered a lab technician position. During our interview in her office on January 15, 2020, she said she always wanted to be a scientist. After completing her studies at LaGuardia, she went on to earn a baccalaureate degree from Queens College, City University of New York, CUNY, and then a PhD from the CUNY Graduate Center in Urban Education. She shares some personal experiences with her LGCC students: she is an immigrant; Spanish was her first language; she worked full-time while a student, and also had children while getting her degree. Calderon said it took a long time to achieve her goals, becoming a full-time professor in 2014. She tells her students that achieving their goals is what is important, not how long it takes. Focusing intently on how she teaches and what she teaches, Calderon encourages her students to persist in achieving their goals.

Calderon teaches microbiology, and her course meets the Writing Across the Curriculum and global learning competency requirements at LGCC. Amid the COVID-19 pandemic, her class is especially timely and engaging. Students investigate microorganisms found in nature, industry, and diseases. Virology, bacteriology, immunology, epidemiology, and pathology are the main areas introduced to students. The class considers topics from a global perspective, such as preventing disease spreading and how health departments and governments manage and prevent disease spreading. Students also look at the social issues that arise from conditions such as spread in factories, social stigmatism, and needed changes in health care laws.

In Calderon's microbiology course, students make connections between the bacteria they identify in their laboratory experiments and the bacteria they find on their shoes, kitchen sink, or other places. In 2014, Calderon began giving students a swab at the start of the semester, and they collect specimens, isolate them, and then do the DNA analysis. While they wait for the analysis, students analyze other specimens. At the end of the course, they compare the laboratory specimens to their home specimens. Students write up their results in the format of a scientific manuscript. Calderon gives them an example of one of her publications and asks students to follow the same format. She introduces them to the kind of writing that 4-year universities expect and the foundations of the scientific method. Calderon encourages students to ask questions and develop an inquiry mindset. She says that "as professors, we don't think about what students don't know, we take many things for granted." For example, she has learned that her students need to know that it is okay to ask questions. They often come from cultures where questions are not allowed or encouraged. To encourage question-asking, she provides her students with articles, links to TED talks, etc. Then she follows up with questions allowing students to share their thoughts about what they have read or heard. While Calderon loves science and discovering the unknown, she recognizes that not all students share her enthusiasm for science. She does hope, however, that they will develop a passion for whatever they want to do. To encourage her students' career aspirations, she focuses on developing generalizable skills.

At the beginning of each class, realizing that many of her students have significant challenges in their lives, Calderon introduces 3 minutes of silent meditation, or just silence for those who don't want to meditate. She tells them that research suggests that meditation and quiet time can increase their attentiveness and focus. She sees the period of silence as a time of transition. Students can set aside the crowded train ride, minimum wage job, or demanding family responsibilities while in their biology class. Calderon says, "I want them to improve their writing, communication skills, express their ideas, and be reflective. I teach holistically, not just about science, but to see connections."

She has also introduced the concept of *radical listening*, a strategy that encourages students to express themselves completely and to listen to others, without interruption or judgment (Gilligan & Eddy, 2017). Gilligan and Eddy suggest asking questions of the speaker with curiosity and an open mind. They suggest, "coming from a place of genuine curiosity or not knowing, the researcher becomes open not only to surprise or discovery but also to having one's view of the world shaken" (p. 76). Students in Calderon's course practice radical listening as they discuss the global and cultural perspectives of the topics they are studying. In addition to the skills of radical listening, students are encouraged to listen with respect, empathy, and compassion (Calderon, 2017). Coteaching is part of the course activities, and students practice radical listening when their peers are making presentations. They practice nonjudgment, respect, and empathy as they critique a peer's presentation. After one talk, a student commented,

> Lucy, I admire the fact that even though your English is not the best, you didn't shy away from the role of actually taking a firm part and a major role in this discussion and there was no fear, so I encourage you to keep practicing and it will get better! (Calderon, 2017, p. 62)

Cogenerative dialogue is another teaching strategy that Calderon incorporates into her classes to give students a stronger sense of agency and empowerment. Rachel Smith (2016) suggests that cogenerative discussion calls for shared responsibility between instructors and students in an active learning environment giving students a voice in their education. In addition to learning the basics of scientific research methodology, improving writing skills, and understanding the globalization of science, students are also gaining significant abilities in working together, asking researchable questions, and being more curious by practicing radical listening. These are all skills that will transfer to other courses and future career success.

## CUNY Queensborough Community College

### *Biology*

Nidhi Gadura, chair of biological sciences and geology at Queensborough Community College (QCC) was an early adopter of undergraduate course-based research. She attended the CUR NSF workshop that was hosted by QCC. She realized that her students had work and family responsibilities and would not be able to participate in one-on-one student research. Yet she firmly believed that every student should have hands-on research experiences (Gadura, 2018). She developed a partnership with Cold Spring Harbor DNA Barcoding Lab (CSHL). The Urban Barcode Research Program developed an "integrated biochemical and bioinformatics workflow for DNA barcode analysis" (N. Gadura, personal communication, January 16, 2020). It is a safe, relatively easy, and inexpensive way to engage students in open-ended research that can result in an original discovery. Gadura began the project as a pilot program with teams of three honors students. The pilot project's success led her to integrate the barcoding research into her courses to provide more students with authentic research experiences. Since her pilot project, Gadura tried three approaches to engaging students in DNA barcoding research: a traditional mentor-mentee experience, a course-based authentic research experience, and a peer-led authentic research experience. In the traditional approach, students registered for a two-credit research internship. A nearby body of water was a source for collecting water samples. A local nonprofit group, Coalition to Save Hempstead Harbor, wanted to see if the growth of plankton species impacted water quality. Students analyzed the water samples collected by the Coalition to Save Hempstead Harbor and extracted the DNA. The analysis was followed by "polymerase chain reaction (PCR) using plant-specific primers to look for phytoplankton species in the water samples" (Gadura, 2018, p. 155).

Students in the course-based approach worked in groups of three and developed a hypothesis-driven project on biodiversity on campus and in the surrounding area. They collected samples from plants and animals and used the Cold Spring Harbor protocol to log in the data. Students conducted the following experiments (Gadura, 2018):

- Genomic DNA extraction
- gel electrophoresis
- PCR amplification specific to mitochondrial or chloroplast gene sections
- DNA sequencing
- aligning sequences using National Center for Biotechnology Information Basic Local Alignment tool
- analyzing gene sequences and making phylogenetic trees using DNA Subway software developed by CSHL DNA Learning Center (p. 157)

The Peer-Led Authentic Research Experience was part of a National Science Foundation STEM grant from Brooklyn College. Two graduates of the biotechnology class, chosen based on their grades in the course and their interpersonal skills, were hired as peer mentors. After a training course, the peer mentors prepped the lab, assisted students during the experiment, and analysis of the results. They also reviewed the student presentations.

In comparing the results of the approaches, Gadura found strengths and weaknesses in all three approaches. She concluded, however, that the course-based plan worked best for community college students. While an excellent experience for the participating students, the traditional method took a great deal of out-of-class time that limited participation for many students. Also, the traditional method could only accommodate a few students. More students can be reached through the course-based approach, although it also necessitated out-of-class time. The peer-led approach was the least effective because students volunteered for the experience, and there were frequent absences. Students need structure during the semester and the guidance of the professor, Gadura concluded. Careful planning before beginning the course is also essential. Gadura's work is interesting because she tried three versions of implementing a high-impact practice and was able to see that course-based research provides many of the benefits of traditional research experiences. Her conclusions are similar to those of the National Academies of Science, Engineering, and Medicine (2015).

## Estrella Mountain Community College

### Psychology

I met with Erica Wager in her office at Estrella Mountain Community College on November 7, 2019. As an instructor of psychology, Wager actively engages with her students in experimental research. In addition to teaching her courses, she supervises independent student research projects, advises the college's psychology club, and works with the college's chapters of Phi Theta Kappa and Psi Beta. Phi Theta Kappa is the honor society of community college students, similar to Phi Beta Kappa for baccalaureate students. Psi Beta is the honor society for 2-year students who are interested in psychology. While Wager embeds research in her courses, she also engages her cocurricular students in collaborative research similar to what one might do in a course-based research class.

Wager is a friendly and approachable professor. Many students come to talk with her about personal issues, perhaps because she is a psychology professor or maybe because she is friendly and very open to meeting informally with students. She tells them that she is not a therapist and will refer students to the campus counseling service when they come to her to discuss personal problems. However, she is happy to be an ear and wants her office to be a safe place for students. She has flyers about all kinds of resources in her office that she can give to students. She also includes information about food pantries, counseling services, and legal aid on her course syllabus. She mentioned one student who was being evicted from his apartment because a roommate had gotten into trouble. She referred him to legal aid services. On the day I visited Wager, several students stopped by her office to check in about their research projects and upcoming research events. Wager has taken students to national and regional conferences. "Some students," she said, "had never been out of Arizona." When students present their work, whether on campus or at a professional conference, Wager believes it increases their self-confidence and sense of self as a scholar.

Psi Beta students initiated a research project on the stigma of mental illness. They are looking at differences in the views toward mental illness of different racial groups. The qualitative part of the study asked students what myths or facts they had heard about mental illness. In the next step, club members collaborated on developing a survey in Google Forms. They also learned how to submit a proposal to the Institutional Review Board for project approval. The Google Forms were made available to participants in the study by using a QR (Quick Response) code printed on flyers distributed around the campus. Survey respondents could scan the QR and respond through Snapchat. The response was confidential and easy to do. Unfortunately, the study was interrupted when the campus closed down because of COVID-19.

Phi Theta Kappa students designed a research project to determine what veterans on campus need for success and identify possible barriers. Wager calls this project an "Honors in Action Project" because the students first do the research and then act on what they have learned. On the day I visited Wager, the project coordinator stopped by to discuss plans for a spring event to distribute a survey to the veterans. There were concerns about whether veterans would attend the event. Often veterans do not want to be identified on campus as veterans. To get to know veterans and encourage their participation in the research project, Phi Theta Kappa students assist the veterans' group in their annual run by taking care of their children during the event. Past action research projects have investigated food and housing insecurities that led to setting up a food pantry on campus.

At the time of my visit, Estrella Mountain Community College had just received a $15,000 grant for student research travel. This grant is an indication of the significant support provided for undergraduate research at Estrella and in the Maricopa district. Estrella Mountain Community College hosts the Maricopa Community College district Undergraduate Research Conference each year. The conference was founded by the late Brian Tippett who, as vice president for academic affairs, was a strong advocate for undergraduate research at community colleges.

Course-based research is an effective way for community colleges to provide all students with undergraduate research experiences. If every required course included a CURE students would leave the community college with the basic benefits of research. It is possible to include CUREs in most classes because research projects can be implemented using local or readily available resources that are cost effective. While course-based research often takes more time than traditional teaching, it can sustain faculty interest in the project and create enthusiasm and excitement in students.

# 7

# COMMUNITY-BASED RESEARCH

C ommunity-based research (CBR) is collaborative research between a university or college and the local community to address a community need. It is not a new strategy, but it has become increasingly prominent as higher education has been encouraged to be more responsive to community needs. Faculty have also encouraged community-based research to relate service-learning projects directly with student learning outcomes. Strand et al. (2003) identified three central features of CBR:

- "A collaborative enterprise between academic researchers (professors and students) and community members.
- Seeks to democratize knowledge by validating multiple sources of knowledge and promoting the use of multiple methods of discovery and dissemination.
- A goal of social action for the purpose of achieving social change and social justice." (p. 6)

The collaboration process includes identifying the problem, developing the research question, and designing a research process that might consist of survey instruments, collecting, analyzing, and interpreting the results. Finally, it communicates the results back to the community. Recommendations suggested by the research project should be jointly agreed upon by the researchers and the community group. It is essential for the project's success that the participants are equal partners. The community benefits from an increased understanding of the issue and possible choices for a solution. Students benefit primarily by gaining experience in doing research. Students have an opportunity to develop skills for civic engagement that may be helpful to them later in life. They also learn the importance of confidentiality and privacy, negotiation skills, and how to respond to unexpected circumstances.

While there are benefits for researchers and communities from community-based research, there are also challenges. Time is a major factor for both researchers and community participants. It takes time to develop trust and time to plan the research project. Students may find that CBR involves significant time demands outside of class instruction. Supervision of student work also requires time from the professor and the community project leader.

Community colleges are unique in engaging in CBR because of their close ties to the community and their workforce development programs. Community college students are typically from the same city as the college. So, they understand the local area, may have contacts with community agencies, and know about community issues that CBR could address. These students may have a deeply held commitment to their home community. For example, Sentz and Stout (2018) found that 61% of community college students stay within 50 miles of the college they attended.

Sometimes students identify a problem they want to study. This was the case at Mercer University, as I discovered when I visited the campus. On the drive from the Atlanta airport to Macon, Georgia, I noticed several billboards advertising various spas, such as Asian spas. I wondered what they were. Mercer students wondered as well. In 2008, 1st-year students, enrolled in the course Engaging the World, began asking questions about the Macon spas. They discovered that the spas were brothels holding sex-trafficked girls and women. The students formed an organization, Sex Trafficking Opposition Project (S.T.O.P.), to raise awareness about the problem. They hosted a national conference that brought several experts on the topic to the Mercer campus and 900 conference participants. They were able to rescue some victims, and the police made several arrests of spa clients. The project directed statewide attention to sex trafficking (Sex Trafficking Opposition Project, n.d.). I was so impressed with the students' work that I invited two student leaders to be keynote speakers at the CUR biennial conference in 2010. It is not unusual for a particular community issue to stimulate faculty and student research. The Mercer University project is an example of how impactful student community-based research can be in the local area and sometimes beyond.

## CUNY LaGuardia Community College

### Environmental Science

Faculty at LaGuardia Community College (LGCC) connect to their community through research in many different ways. LGCC is near Newtown

Creek, which was declared a Superfund site by the Environmental Protection Agency in 2010. It is one of the most polluted superfund sites in the United States. Newtown Creek is a 3.8 mile long part of the Hudson River Estuary that empties into the East River. It has long been a polluted area, with more than 40 industrial facilities along its banks in the mid-1800s. More recently, in 1978, there was a significant oil spill in the creek (New York DOEC, n.d.). A water treatment plant near the college overflows when it rains, because the plant runs out of capacity. Raw sewage from the overflow goes into the creek, then into the East River, and eventually into the Hudson River (I. Veras, personal communication, January 15, 2020). The Newtown Creek Alliance and LGCC developed a plan to clean up the creek.

Professor of Biology and Director of the Environmental Science Program Holly Porter-Morgan is the "go-to" person at LGCC for community-based research and community partnerships. I met her briefly when I visited the LGCC campus in January 2020. She was extremely busy meeting with students and on the telephone with the various community agency research partners. On February17, 2020, we had a lengthy follow-up telephone interview. Porter-Morgan teaches a capstone course that prepares students for transfer to a 4-year college. The students have a full semester of individual laboratory research that is part of the larger water quality projects. While students don't design their projects, they are engaged in authentic research by collecting and analyzing data. Porter-Morgan provides students with citizen science site maps so they can collect samples from a safe site. Students bring in water samples every week, develop a hypothesis, and compare their sample to class samples' through analysis. They also compare still pond water to moving river water. Students test for nine to ten trace metals such as aluminum, lead, copper, zinc, chlorine, nitrate, phosphate, and bacteria. Students work in teams to test for one of the elements. They learn responsibility because the team depends on them each week for the testing.

Porter-Morgan also connects with many citizen science organizations in New York City. NSF funds some of the citizen science programs. One organization has a boat, and during boating season, students collect samples of fecal indicator bacteria that reveal sewage in the water. Queensborough Community College is the only testing site in the area, so many citizen science programs bring their samples to Queensborough, and then students do the analysis. Students are doing original, basic research. The New York City Water Trail Association (n.d.) posts the students results. Citizens Water Quality Testing Program posts the students' results on their website. Students also present their work at the Newtown Creek Alliance (n.d.) monthly meetings and regional conferences. Because of the experience students gain in this work, Porter-Morgan encourages them to seek external internships. Porter-Morgan has three to five students work in her lab doing 15–20 samples per week for students who cannot find an external internship.

According to Porter-Morgan, when students test their samples and citizen science groups' samples and then report the results to a longitudinal database, they say it makes them feel like real scientists. Working on a longitudinal project, students understand that scientific research can be tedious, but they also know they are doing original research that might lead to a discovery. They are learning the logistics of research, to request permission to collect samples in certain areas, and to practice ethical research behavior. Students in the capstone course write their final paper following the format of a scientific journal. Porter-Morgan tells her students that the class is a safe place to learn, making mistakes are part of the research process, and asking questions is okay. She is preparing students for transfer to a 4-year college and possibly for graduate school. The relationship students have with Porter-Morgan, and their positive feelings about their research stay with them after graduation. Students often come back to campus to volunteer, and they follow the continuing work of the project online.

Ingrid Veras, associate professor of biology, is another LGCC science professor who involves her students in studying the problems of water pollution in the local community. She engages her students in community-based and course-based research when they enroll in her introductory biology course. Veras also works with the Newtown Creek Alliance on remediation efforts for the polluted water. Students collect water samples and look for dissolved oxygen, fecal matter nitrates, chlorine, and sulfates. They also check water temperature and turbidity. Students report their results to the Newtown Creek Alliance. Veras wants her students to gain knowledge that they take with them after they complete their studies. She wants them to learn how to use the scientific method and understand the importance of evidence. In another class, students walk around their home and college neighborhoods to test air quality. In these projects, students write up their results and give an oral presentation.

Veras has a special connection with her students because her life experiences are similar to many LGCC students. She is an immigrant from the Dominican Republic. She did not understand English when she arrived in the United States nor the U.S. system of education. She didn't know what the SAT is or about the New York Regents diploma. Despite not understanding the system, Veras graduated from high school and briefly attended a private liberal arts college but found it was too expensive. She transferred to a community college but did poorly and dropped out. She finally became a serious student at another community college. After completing her AA degree, she transferred to another liberal arts college and discovered biology and research. During her graduate studies, she fell in love with teaching. Her passion for teaching is apparent. Her small office is bright, colorful, and crowded with a small refrigerator, an extra table and chairs. Students come by to keep their lunch in the refrigerator. Sometimes they eat their lunch in her office or use her office as study space. During the November meeting, she spent more than an hour telling me about the problems of the Newtown Creek overflow, the difficulty of remediation, and how her students were benefitting from their engagement in the project. Veras and her students participate in two community events, Newtown Creek Field Day and the Riverkeeper Sweep, as volunteers clean up the sites. In all of the activities related to Newtown Creek, students document their experiences through photographs. Students added photos, poster presentations, and reflections on their experiences and work to their ePortfolios (see chapter 11). A series of ePortfolio prompts ask students to comment on their most significant piece of learning and how they would apply their learning process to a higher-level course (Radhakrishman et al., 2018).

Veras also engages her students in other kinds of research. With six CRSP students, she studies sea stars, commonly called starfish. Sea stars are dying out. Students studying sea star wasting disease (SSWD) are doing basic research. Sea stars are keystone organisms because they are critical to the environment. Veras and Porter-Morgan are two of several faculty at LGCC who provide various research opportunities for their students. The group presents several community events each year to keep the community informed about student research findings. Presentations have included topics of noise pollution and data collection, air pollution, taking care of street trees, and stenciling storm drains to discourage further water pollution. The group has also published articles about their research with their community partners in scientific journals (Calderon et al., 2017).

## Estrella Mountain Community College

### *Biology*

Rachel Smith, biology professor at Estrella Mountain Community College, part of the Maricopa Community College District, works with a local conservation organization to protect and study burrowing owls. I met with Smith in October 2020 to talk with her about her introductory biology course and the burrowing owls research. The burrowing owls research project could be considered basic and applied research and community-based research. While Smith is very interested in basic research, she says students should ask only questions that they have the capacity to answer. Smith began her work with burrowing owls when the biology faculty were invited by Wild at the Heart, a nonprofit conservation organization, to answer an applied question; Wild at the Heart needed to know how to determine the sex of the owls in order to release rescued owls in pairs. Smith began to involve students in analyzing owl DNA to determine sex. Students learned how to extract the DNA and use the equipment. Smith teaches the scientific method, guides the assignment for students to learn by doing, and when something fails, they stop and ask questions about what went wrong. Smith feels that through troubleshooting, students understand the scientific method. Because she has only limited time with students, they cannot develop a hypothesis from scratch. They generally follow the professor's questions. However, once students understand more about doing research, they can develop their ideas and questions about burrowing owls. While they previously relied on a trial-and-error approach, in fall 2020, Estrella Mountain offered a research methods course to delineate the steps from observation, questioning, developing a hypothesis to conducting the study.

Burrowing owls are an excellent subject for an undergraduate research project. They are adorable, charismatic, don't fly away, and are the only owls out in the daytime. These characteristics make them especially attractive to students as well as the campus development office and local media. Once students determined how to identify the sex of burrowing owls, Smith and her students became interested in other questions. The Wild at the Heart agency wanted to know if there was an ideal height for the perches. They also began to look at how the owls' diet changes during the year, determined by DNA analysis. Arizona owls migrate south from Phoenix in the winter, although some do stay. The females migrate to Mexico. The males who remain over the winter cohabit in the burrows. In the spring, when the females return, the males fight over who will retain the burrow. These discoveries have further increased interest in burrowing owls. The engineering department at Estrella Mountain, for example, is looking for a way to place cameras in the burrows.

There is a strong commitment at Estrella Mountain Community College to protect the burrowing owls. When the campus was expanding parking lot space, they realized that the new parking lot would infringe on the owls' burrows. The campus purchased plastic storage containers from Home Depot and buried them in the ground. Smith said the owls began occupying the boxes on completion of the work.

Students become attached to the borrowing owls during the year-long biology course. Studying the owls prepares them for the next phase of their education. Most of the students in the introductory biology class are science majors, and they are career-focused. As first-generation students, the undergraduate research project prepares them for transfer to a 4-year college, typically Arizona State University (ASU). Before the course, many of the students had never been in a laboratory and often had little understanding of college. She compares the research process to cooking, where the cook makes mistakes while learning but tries again. She makes the process seem less intimidating. Smith encourages her students to use the ASU library because she wants to show them primary literature and help them be comfortable in a research library and at a research university.

## CUNY Guttman Community College

### *Anthropology*

As an urban institution, Guttman Community College commits to social justice, equity, and community engagement. The City of New York offers diverse opportunities for field studies. Pressing Public Issues, a collaboration between CUNY community colleges, the James Gallery at the CUNY Graduate Center, the Teaching and Learning Center, and the CUNY Humanities Alliance, is an example of a system-wide exploration of community issues. Each year Pressing Public Issues brings together a small group of liberal arts faculty and teaching artists to develop creative teaching practices and pedagogies to incorporate into projects that address a current pressing issue in New York City. Associate Professor of Anthropology Kristina Baines participated in a recent Pressing Public Issues project. Her topic was environmental ethics. Students studied environmental issues in their communities while concurrently learning about environmental activism's theoretical roots. Topics included gentrification, air pollution, and lack of adequate health care. Coleader and artist Vaimoana Niumeitolu, along with a field trip to the Interference Archive in Brooklyn, guided students in learning about protest art. Students displayed posters and distributed a student-produced zine at a James Gallery reception in spring 2019 (Guttman News, 2019b).

In addition to her teaching and research, Baines with Victoria Costa cofounded Cool Anthropology, an organization whose purpose is to tell transmedia stories and solve problems. Cool Anthropology is a collective of academics, artists, technologists, and filmmakers committed to public scholarship. An example of student involvement in Cool Anthropology is the multimedia *Shifting Stereotypes*, an ongoing interactive project that addresses stereotypes through brief videos discussing contemporary stereotypes. The short videos eventually are combined into a documentary. Students research the backgrounds of the stereotypes, conduct the interviews, and do the videotaping. A team of students presented their *Shifting Stereotypes* work at the 2015 and 2016 American Anthropological Association conference in Denver and Minneapolis. The University of Massachusetts–Amherst invited them to also share their work at the anthropology department's student and faculty colloquium. The Guttman students, along with Baines and Costa, provided a professional development opportunity for UMass faculty. Students are often the best advocates for new and innovative pedagogies (K. Baines, personal communication, August 20, 2020).

Baines was named as a Course Hero Fellow in 2019 by what was then the Woodrow Wilson Foundation. The Foundation chooses eight fellows each year; four are tenure-track faculty, and four are nontenure track. The only community college recipient, Baines is the first Fellow from CUNY (Guttman News, 2019a). The award has been compared to the MacArthur "genius award" for outstanding college teachers (Hannan 2019). It emphasizes the balance between teaching and research. The $30,000 grant stipulates that $20,000 goes toward hiring a research or teaching assistant. Hannia Delgado, a Guttman graduate who transferred to Baruch College and graduated with a marketing specialization, was hired as Baines's research assistant. Delgado worked with the Cool Anthropology project to introduce ethnographic methods to the public through a social media campaign, Ethnography Matters. Delgado designed a website where people can post their thoughts and experiences about ethnography. In September 2020, Cool Anthropology gave a virtual workshop as part of the New York Academy of Sciences–Anthropology Division's Distinguished Lecture series. Baines is exploring ways to engage students and the public in integrating learning and hands-on research through ethnography.

As an anthropologist, Baines sees developing an "ethnographic mindset" as an essential part of her teaching approach (K. Baines, personal communication, August 15, 2019). She summarizes the ethnographic mindset thus:

- Thinking like an ethnographer requires training yourself to observe the details of a culture or community without passing judgment.
- The concept of cultural relativism, first developed by Franz Boas, means that each culture should be evaluated only by its own standards and not by the standards of the observer's own culture, and this guides ethnographic thinking.
- Empathy, humility, openness, curiosity, and the ability to separate yourself from your own cultural norms are all qualities that good ethnographic thinkers develop.

Baines is also a proponent of open pedagogies. This pedagogical approach centers on active learning experiences that engage students in producing knowledge rather than merely consuming knowledge (Baines and Costa, 2020). An open pedagogy uses nondisposable assignments (NDA). These assignments develop new knowledge about a real problem instead of the typical research paper that students must write and throw away after receiving a grade (Seraphin et al., 2019). Undergraduate research projects are nondisposable because they produce knowledge rather than simply communicate existing knowledge. Baines and Costa (2017) discussed how faculty design courses for students to produce knowledge. Baines's course, Sexuality and Gender in Urban Life, provides an example of how students produce knowledge. Ethnography was the basis for a three-part assignment. Students went into the community to observe and take field notes and applied gender norm theories to their observations. To complete the project, they made videos and shared them with a community audience. The structure of the course linked knowledge from readings and class discussions with gathering data through fieldwork. Baines suggests students are fulfilling their civic responsibility to share what they learned by communicating the results of their work. Sharing the videos meets the expectations of undergraduate research and provides feedback to students about their work.

Educational equity is a central focus of Guttman Community College, and undergraduate research experiences are part of the emphasis on equity. Creating international opportunities through Global Guttman, students can develop a deeper understanding of themselves in a global context; understand their personal and social responsibility; consider the complexity of global interdependence, and develop intercultural skills (Baines and Wilson, 2017). In 2017 students traveled to Belize with Professor Baines as part of an environmental ethics program. Ethical environmental decision-making was studied through an individual, community, national, or international lens and multidisciplinary perspectives. Students met with environmental community organizations, local and international activists, and indigenous communities. Within the context of environmental ethics, issues of habitat loss, indigenous livelihoods, resource extraction, and climate change were examined. Students documented their observations, perceptions, and reflections through their field journals. They also added photographs and drawings to the journals. Sharing their reflections with other students deepened the transformative travel experience. When the students returned home, they adapted their field notes to an ePortfolio, a guided process for students to reflect on their learning process (Eynon and Gambino, 2017). The ePortfolio makes the learning process visible to the professor, and it can be a mechanism for sharing the project with a broader community.

During the summer of 2020, Guttman students, like students across the country, were studying virtually because of COVID-19. Baines asked her students to digitally map the health resources in their community. Defining what *health* means to a community was another part of the project. Students made lists of words that were related to *health* and used a "pile sort" of related terms to see how various communities think differently about health. Students then became involved in the University of Connecticut's pandemic journaling project. The project's goal is to record the experiences and voices of ordinary people with COVID-19 through an open website (University of Connecticut, n.d.). A sample assignment, designed by Baines, is posted on the website. Students can participate by reading the public posts on the Featured Entries page, reflecting on a post of their choice, and sharing their reflections by text, audio recording, or photos on the class discussion forum. Students have the option of commenting on the class discussion privately or publicly. Participation in the project is available in English and Spanish. Guttman students also analyzed the entries regarding how they reflect community views of health and healthy lives. This project used a readily available resource, and students had the experience of contributing to a real-world project (Baines, 2020).

Guttman Community College is fortunate to have a rich source of possible community-based research projects in New York City. Located in the heart of Manhattan, the community is at the center of Guttman's mission. Through its academic and undergraduate research programs, Guttman students engage in the nation's largest city's challenging issues. Rural and small-town communities present different but equally interesting issues for community college students to study.

## Multidisciplinary

Deep and rigorous experiential learning is the core of Guttman Community College's program. Campus-based courses and short-term, faculty-led study abroad courses integrate global issues. Students can study in Germany, Ecuador, Nicaragua, Jamaica, Chile, Belize, China, and several other countries. Students who participate in Global Guttman programs may participate in undergraduate research, interdisciplinary studies, and engage with local communities. To provide additional opportunities for students, Guttman established a partnership with the Pulitzer Center's Campus Consortium for Education and Hunter University's journalism department in 2017 (Global Guttman, 2018). Students can propose international reporting projects to the consortium. Journalists and Center staff mentor selected students, and the Center's website publishes students' articles. Two Global Guttman participants joined the Pulitzer Center Student Fellows. The first student, in 2018, went to China and wrote about why Chinese women are delaying starting a family. In 2019, the second student traveled to Ecuador to report on conservation efforts in the Chocóan Rainforest. She traveled with Derek Tesser, who has led four trips to the Ecuadorian rain forest.

Derek Tesser's students study endemic species, biodiversity indicators, and deforestation from Ecuador's changing ecosystem (D. Tesser, personal communication, September 16, 2020). They participate in authentic research experiences involving identifying species not yet cataloged, installing microclimate research sensors, and validating ecosystem science satellite remote sensing products. The Itapoa Reserve, where students conduct their research, is located within the Chocó Hotspot of Biodiversity, a narrow ecoregion west of the Andes Mountains that is more threatened and diverse than the Amazon rainforest. The students spend 7 days in the rainforest. Tesser wants his students to experience what it is like to work in the field. He says that some students believe that doing research is too high a level for them. However, when students can shadow field scientists trained in fundamental data collection techniques, students realize that they are capable of conducting research and see pathways of access into geoscience fields. Before leaving for Ecuador, students meet with Tesser for lectures, films, and readings about ecosystem science, tropical deforestation, socioeconomic pressures, and biology conservation. Students develop research questions they would like to explore while in Ecuador. They conduct interviews and collect data while in Ecuador and complete the research project when they return home.

Arriving in Ecuador, students spend a few days exploring Ecuador's history and culture and learning about whale migration, coastal habitats, and marine ecotourism (D. Tesser, personal communication, September 16, 2020). Once they reach the Itapoa Reserve in the lowland Chocó rainforest, where they camp for the week, students assist in data collection by installing microclimate stations, supporting drone surveys, and photographic cataloging endemic species. Many of these species are collected during night hikes, where students often walk with biologists for hours to observe the unique nocturnal diversity of the Chocó rainforest. Global Guttman affiliates with the Itapoa Project, and the director, Raul Nieto, talks with students about deforestation and conservation policy in the Ecuador–Columbian Chocó ecoregion. Students also hear lectures by renowned neotropical biologists and learn about the critical ecological roles of endangered reptiles and amphibians endemic to the region.

Tesser is currently working on his dissertation in earth and environmental science at the CUNY Graduate Center. His research utilizes remote sensing measurements of the environment from satellites to map

ecosystem dynamics. Ground-based data collections are important vali-
dation of satellite information. To support this research, Tesser mentored
two research students to build a drone quadcopter for data collection in
Ecuador. The quadcopter would allow students to see forest fragmentation
in the rainforest and support the development of vegetation structural char-
acterizations to support the assessment of recent land-use change activity
in the region. Since little aerial imagery of these areas exists in the cloudy
tropics, the project provides critical data to local conservation projects. The
research students designed the quadcopter in collaboration with students at
the City College of New York, a senior college in the CUNY system, and
based on designs from collaborating scientists at NASA's Jet Propulsion
Laboratory. The quadcopter design "required programming, building,
testing, and a variety of design modifications to achieve a balanced flight
capable of delivering high-definition video from the mounted camcorder"
(Global Guttman, 2016). For the information technology majors, building the quadcopter was a unique learning experience in programming and
research. They saw their project's practical application in a trial run at City
College in New York.

In the fall after the Ecuador trip, students share the findings from their
research at an evening campus event, Global Guttman Presents A Night in
the Chocó. Students who participated in the 2017 trip described what they
learned about endangered monkey species, Ecuadorian fronted capuchins,
Ecuadorian mantled howler monkeys, and brown-headed spider monkeys.
Two students studied glass frog indicator species, concluding that there are
ten species of glass frogs in the rainforest, more than any other location in
the world, that face survival challenges. The changing climate in the region
and agricultural expansion of oil palm plantations impacts the population
of endemic amphibians and reptiles. A significant problem in the rainforest is deforestation, and the quadcopter helped in observation and data collection. One student studied this issue and found the problem results from
the mass production of cheap palm oil. There is a belief that palm oil is
sustainable. The fact that it is not, is one of the challenging socioeconomic
issues that students learned about. Students need to understand the breadth
of conservation issues and the connections that extend beyond the immediate problem. The last student to speak at the event discussed how farmers
working with the Itapoa Project cultivate sustainable cacao plantations. As
an alternative to harmful palm oil, cacao also provides more economic benefits and decreases farmers' dependence on the palm oil industry. Students
described the Ecuador trip as transformational and that it opened their minds
and made them more aware of the world beyond New York. The Guttman
Foundation pays the fees for the Ecuador experience.

The Ecuador project exemplifies many of the principles of community-based research. The Ecuadorian community is involved in the project. Tesser said that all the project experts are Ecuadorian or Latin American. Students studied issues of concern to Ecuadorian conservationists. The project introduced students to research, and they began to see themselves as scholars. They further developed their observation and question-asking skills, and they started to see connections that extended beyond the immediate topics of study.

## Tulsa Community College

### Child Development

Participatory action research (PAR) is not community-based research. However, the two approaches do have some things in common. PAR involves working with a community; the community is the students and teacher. It is also group-centered, and there is an element of collaboration as the teacher's interactions with students are studied. And PAR includes the possibility of change. Debbie Deibert at Tulsa Community College (TCC) is a practitioner of PAR. She began a study with students who were working toward a Child Development Associate (CDA) certificate (D. Deibert, personal communication, September 10, 2020). The research project also included Tulsa Educare, the preschool program where students interned. The study's purpose was to explore the impact of child development internships on student attitudes toward persistence in their program and their trajectory into professional teaching positions. Deibert's role in the project was as an observer-participant in collaboration with four students. As in more traditional research types, she made observations, took field notes, and facilitated interviews with a focus group. The project collected data primarily from photos. She and the students used a technique called Photovoice. By photographically documenting community activities and events through Photovoice, the community is represented and enhanced (Wang and Burris, 1997). It is a process that produces new knowledge with three goals: (a) to record and reflect on a community's strengths and concerns; (b) to promote dialogue and knowledge through discussion of the photos; and (c) to provide information to policy-makers.

Students took hundreds of photos in the preschool classroom where they were interning, particularly photos of interactions with children. Students learned about consent forms, institutional review board requirements, and subject privacy in doing the study. They were also introduced to PAR methodology and tools for analyzing the data. The photos were uploaded and then printed. Deibert and the interns met to look at the pictures and respond to five questions for each photo:

- What do you see here?
- What is happening?
- How does this effect our lives?
- Why does this strength or weakness exist?
- What do we do about it? (D. Deibert, personal communication, September 10, 2020)

After answering the questions, students and Deibert sorted the photos by recurring objects/activities, common trends, and unique experiences. Deibert and the students used the zoom method to analyze the data, a method that encourages looking at documents from different perspectives as the interns told the stories from the photographs (Pamphilon, 1999). The researchers looked at the interns' connections to the teaching profession, their feelings about their experiences as students, and their interactions with the preschool children they observed (Deibert, 2019). In addition to the photovoice data, classroom observations provided additional data through semistructured observations of interactions among interns, mentor teachers, and children. Biweekly reflections with mentor teachers and interns with responses to the previous five questions contributed to the data collection.

The findings suggest that relationships with the mentor teacher provided significant support for the interns; interactions with the children were valuable experiences for interns, and persistence was encouraged when interns were recognized as part of the teaching profession. TCC has also successfully converted interns to employed teachers after the program. Perhaps what was most valuable about this project was that students learned how to observe their students, ask questions about what they observed, and problem-solve when the observations and questions identified a concern. These are essential skills for providing a quality educational experience for children and improving teacher professional skills. Participatory action research is a methodology that the interns can use when they fully enter the teaching profession.

## Additional Options for Community-Based Research

Colleges and universities are also communities, and they present many opportunities for undergraduate research. I always looked at the institution where I worked as a community with resources that could address a given university problem. We did not have a robust undergraduate research program when I was president of UMPI; however, some students engaged in research. One example was in the planning for the new health and physical education building. We wanted to make the new building as environmentally friendly as possible. We invited students in an honors course to investigate the possibilities for environmentally friendly construction and develop a set of recommendations for the administration. Although we could not include all of the students' ideas, the architects used many of them. In contemporary times, it might be interesting to invite students in the business program, for example, to investigate how the campus might reduce costs by collaborating with other campuses. It would be an excellent learning opportunity for students, and they might come up with new ideas because they are not operating within the constraints of past practice.

The 2020 pandemic offered students other opportunities to document oral histories of how local people managed the quarantine. Many years ago, students at Ball State University conducted a study of Muncie, Indiana, to update the 1929 sociology classic *Middletown: A Study on a Modern American Culture*, a book I read in my 1962 sociology class. *Middletown* only studied Muncie's white community, and students in 2003 wanted to replicate the study with Muncie's Black community. They eventually compiled all of their oral interviews into a published book, *The Other Side of Middletown: Exploring Muncie's African American Community* (Lassiter et al., 2004). Communities are rich with opportunities for oral histories to add to the local historical society. As cities change, students at community colleges could document those changes through interviews and, in the process, learn how to do sociological research.

When I was a dean of education, the Maine State Board of Education invited our campus to make recommendations for changes to the state's teacher certification requirements. We established a student committee to develop our campus recommendations. One might ask, "How do teacher education students know enough to make recommendations about credential requirements?" They didn't. However, with the faculty's guidance, students explored the issues, thought about their training, what they wanted and needed to know, and eventually came up with recommendations. The new requirements adopted by the State Board of Education reflected the students' work. It was a wonderful affirmation for our students, and they also developed a better understanding of why they were studying certain things.

Political science also offers significant opportunities for community-based research. Members of city councils and state legislatures, particularly in small towns and states, have to address many issues in their roles for which they don't have a great deal of knowledge. A state legislative representative, for example, must make decisions about judicial matters, education, health, noise and air pollution, and taxes. They often don't have the staff to research these issues. Students could do some of the research so legislators could have more understanding of the issue's background. Students might also survey the community on changes under consideration by the legislative body. Students could also make recommendations based on their research.

Community-based research can reinforce students' connections to their communities. Through community-based research, they can learn valuable collaboration skills, listening, interviewing, documenting, and sometimes problem-solving. These skills may contribute to their continued community engagement and also may be useful in their future work. Communities, of course, also benefit from the attention to their issues and support.

# 8

# INTERDISCIPLINARY RESEARCH

Nearly every college and university includes critical thinking in their student learning outcomes and vision statements. Employers list critical thinking as one of the skills they seek in employees. Interdisciplinary research offers students multiple ways of thinking. For example, historians think differently from sociologists, artists, or scientists, and when students do research that includes more than one discipline, they can develop a broader range of thinking skills. Thinking from the perspective of several disciplines provides more options for addressing research questions and solving problems.

Scientists recognize that the questions and problems they investigate often require knowledge from other disciplines. New disciplines have emerged in recent years, such as bioengineering, behavioral economics, chemical physics, biomedicine, and biotechnology. Funding agencies addressed the trend toward interdisciplinary research in several reports over the last 20 years. The National Academies, in a 2004 release, said, "Interdisciplinary research (IDR) can be one of the most productive and inspiring of human pursuits—one that provides a format for conversations and connections that lead to new knowledge" (p. 16).

Undergraduate students are often interested in problem-driven questions that address social issues. They see interdisciplinary research as a way to explore the topics of most concern to them. Several organizations, such as the National Academy of Engineering and the United Nations, have identified society's grand challenges. These challenges frequently require an interdisciplinary approach. The grand challenges of the National Academy of Engineering, for example, include the provision of clean water for everyone or making solar energy economical. The United Nations has 17 sustainable development goals that address many young students' topics of interest, such as zero hunger and no poverty.

The National Academies, Committee on Facilitating Interdisciplinary Research (2004) defines IDR broadly as:

> a mode of research by teams or individuals that integrates information, data, techniques, tools, perspectives, concepts, and/or theories from two or more disciplines or bodies of specialized knowledge to advance fundamental understanding or to solve problems whose solutions are beyond the scope of a single discipline or area of research practice. (p. 26)

Ten years after the National Academies published this definition, the National Research Council (NRC) (2014) published a report describing the concept of convergence. The idea of convergence is an expansion of interdisciplinarity. According to the NRC report, convergence merges ideas, approaches, and technologies from a broad spectrum of disciplines. High-level integration is a critical approach to solving complex problems. In part, it is a response to the emergence of new fields in the sciences and new technologies.

The goals of convergence, however, can extend beyond STEM disciplines. The report suggests the following curricular goals for undergraduate education that are appropriate across all disciplines:

- to develop in students the intellectual capacity to deal with real, complex problems;
- to build student confidence and willingness to approach problems from multiple perspectives;
- to build student ability to communicate with scientists from other disciplines;
- to develop student ability to make decisions in the face of uncertainty (reflective judgment); and
- to help students understand strengths and limitations of different disciplinary perspectives. (NRC, 2014, p. 81)

In addition to STEM, these goals are compatible with social science and humanities disciplines. They are also skills that students will need in their future careers. The ability to think across disciplines is an essential strategy for problem-solving as it gives students many more approaches to the issue they are investigating. The goals of convergence can inform the university's general education programs. The integration of knowledge from fundamental disciplines seeks a balance between depth of study in an area and breadth of study.

Increasingly, employers see skills in teamwork as a highly desirable competency (AAC&U, 2018). Atlassian, a global technology company, said, "Teamwork has never been more important than it is today," with 90% of companies reporting that their work is so complex that it requires teams to work on projects (Atlassian, n.d.). Interdisciplinary research for undergraduates can build the teamwork skills they need for their future careers.

Interdisciplinarity education is not without its challenges. If team-taught, interdisciplinary projects take more time than teaching a course on their own, and community college faculty have heavy teaching loads and other demands on their time. In some community college systems or districts, there is a process for making curricular changes. Interdisciplinary courses may meet objections from faculty who do not see the value of interdisciplinary studies. Community college students who want to transfer to a 4-year college may encounter difficulty when they try to transfer interdisciplinary courses. Despite these challenges, some colleges and faculty are introducing interdisciplinary research to their students.

Community colleges may have advantages when it comes to interdisciplinary courses. Close ties with the local community might suggest interdisciplinary studies to address community needs. The concerted efforts of community colleges to engage students in hands-on learning may also encourage interdisciplinary courses.

## Saddleback Community College

### *Dance and Science*

Deidre Cavazzi is a choreographer and science communicator. She combines these two areas in her work at Saddleback Community College. I learned about Deidre's work when I attended an undergraduate research conference hosted by Saddleback Community College and Irvine Valley Community College on November 2, 2019. Cavazzi, the founder, choreographer, and artistic director for ArchiTexture Dance Company (2017a) was one of the keynote presenters. She spoke about her 2017 experience in the Arctic. The Arctic Circle, an international residency program, selected 30 artists and scientists to participate in the residency. Participants spend approximately two and a half weeks on a ship off the coast of Svalbard with the goal of creating a project that incorporates both disciplines.

Having been to Svalbard several years ago, I wanted to learn more about her project. We met over coffee at a Starbucks near her campus. Cavazzi's passion for dance and the environment is compelling, as is her enthusiasm for engaging students in dance and environmental science.

She is passionate about involving students in collaborative projects and sharing the results with the broader community. She always chooses cross-disciplinary projects and frequently ones that explore the relationship between art and science. She often selects topics from the United Nations' (n.d.) sustainable development goals. She is a strong advocate for creative investigation, discovery, and experimentation and believes that creative activities should be available to all students regardless of their major. It is undoubtedly this philosophy that led to her participation in the Arctic Circle program.

On returning home from Svalbard, Cavazzi and her students developed a dance theatre production focusing on climate change and Arctic ecosystems. I watched the multimedia production, *Ice Memory: Arctic Musings and Movement Inspired by the Journey North* on video (Architexture Dance Company, 2017b). Even on a small computer screen, watching the performance was a powerful experience. It began with five dancers, holding a paper mâché polar bear head and legs. The backdrop was a beautiful photographic mural of arctic ice. In the next scene, the sounds of ocean waves and a creaking boat created a feeling of being on the ocean while the dancers moved in wave-like motions. A later segment focused on pollution with plastic bottles scattered around the stage and evolving from quiet, meditative music to sharp and jarring sounds. The scenery changed gradually from the ice to polluted waters to busy, noisy, and smoggy cities. The dance ended on a hopeful note, suggesting that we can address climate change and environmental degradation. Cavazzi included a geologist, an architect, a light designer, and visual artist in the Arctic ballet's production.

I attended Cavazzi's 2020 dance theatre production *Bloom! Exploring California Ecology Through Dance Theatre.* Two brief talks with a PowerPoint presentation, by Morgan Barrows, environmental science department Chair, about Monarch butterflies' migratory routes and a talk by Robert Farnsworth, professor of horticulture and landscape design, about seed dispersal patterns and dandelions preceded the performance. Cavazzi and her students also developed a dance theater piece combining dance and physics, *Entangled States: Exploring the Intersection of Dance and Physics.* Todd Brei, professor of physics at the college, met with Cavazzi regularly as she was choreographing the production. After the project, a student commented that she previously had difficulty understanding the physics lectures. When students put the physics concepts into motion through dance, she felt she had a better understanding of physics (D. Cavazzi, personal communication, December 12, 2019).

Physics and dance are perhaps not such an unusual combination for interdisciplinary study. Richard Feynman (1988), a Nobel physicist, often talked about atoms and their dance patterns. The students also studied the properties of light, particle waves, and color spectrum and frequency. After the Arctic Circle program, Cavazzi was invited to the National University of Ireland at Galway to work with students and the community on a similar dance theater production as part of the 2018 National Science Ireland week and the Galway Science and Technology Festival. She has been invited to return to collaborate on a new project in Ireland centered on nanophysics, neurobiology, and medical technology. Cavazzi welcomes all students to participate in her interdisciplinary projects regardless of their major. In her courses, she stresses the skills of observation, asking questions, and using evidence. She wants students to fall in love with research, and I am sure many do after participating in her program.

## CUNY–Queensborough Community College

### Theater and Communication

When I visited Queensborough Community College (QCC), several faculty I met said, "You have to talk with Heather Huggins." When I got home, I connected with Huggins by Zoom and was very glad I did. Huggins is an assistant professor of speech communication and theatre arts. She is an interdisciplinary artist and supports student-centered work and engagement in collaborative research. She is involved in Social Presencing Theater (SPT), an international program that is part of the Presencing Institute. SPT are a series of practices founded by a collaboration between Arawana Hayashi; Otto Scharmer, a senior lecturer at MIT; and colleagues. Arawana Hayashi is a choreographer, performer, and educator who has been engaged in collaborative improvisation for many years. She is also a practitioner of meditation and a social justice advocate (Hayashi, 2021a). In her recent book published about SPT, *Social Presencing Theater: The Art of Making a True Move*, Hayashi (2021b) writes:

> (The practices) invite deep reflection and brave action. They engage the whole person—body, mind, and heart. They work quickly—they get to the point. They engage people's natural creativity and deep care for one another. Social Presencing Theater appeals to our true human nature to work together to bring something beneficial in the world. It is for people looking for insights into both how change happens and how they can best shepherd new approaches and initiatives (p. 21).

Social Presencing Theater brings together art and contemplative traditions to develop a clearer understanding of relationships, human dynamics, and the possibilities for change and the future. Theater in this context speaks to "making visible" rather than a traditional theatrical performance; SPT has been used for over 10 years in business, government, and civil society settings (Hayashi 2021a). Huggins first introduced her students to SPT to investigate how it might support authentic communication at a campus where 87 languages are spoken. These students have a range of interests and plans for their future careers, and Huggins works with a small group outside of her normal teaching responsibilities. Working mostly with first- and second-generation students from several countries, Huggins found that students were interested in exploring equity and inclusiveness issues.

The students asked to continue practicing SPT and suggested using SPT to devise theater. Huggins modeled a devising process that centered SPT as a research tool. An initial process of *seeding* brings key issues to the surface. The next step is *co-initiating*, to reach consensus on ideas worthy of further investigation. After reaching consensus on the issue, participants engage fully in exploring the issue through *presencing* (a blend of presence and sensing, according to Scharmer, quoted in Hayashi, 2021b, p. 6). Participants make connections to sources of deeper knowledge. Then they engage in a process called *co-creating*, in order to imagine new possibilities for the future through active engagement.

Student participation in SPT eventually led to their first performance at QCC's Shadowbox Theater, entitled *Borders and Migration* in December 2018. In the activities leading up to the production and in the performance, they examined implicit and explicit borders. Three members of the community—Joseph Distl, Geovanny Guzman, and Yineng Ye—extended their research on borders to present a poster, *Social Presencing: Practices for Diversity*, at CUNY's Faculty Diversity and Inclusion Conference. They concluded that "Diversity is not only creating a diverse space; it is allowing those diverse people to change the space they inhabit . . . by reclaiming their bodies, participants can also reclaim their minds, and become a part of the change they want to see," (Distl et al., 2019, slide 22).

Each year in December, QCC hosts an Undergraduate Research Day. While the majority of the students present posters, some students have the opportunity to make oral presentations. Three of Huggins' students gave oral presentations about their work with SPT. Geovanny Guzman (2019) discussed how SPT provides a framework for "suspending habitual patterns, awakening the senses, letting go." The letting-go process can then lead to "letting come" new ideas and experiences. Kristopher Harris looked at the role of self-discovery as a path to cocreative art. Harris was one of three undergraduate researchers who responded to a Kennedy Center American College Theater Festival (KCAACTF) national devised theater prompt that led to a public performance and juried response with industry professionals at the KCACTF Region II Festival on January 18, 2019 at Montclair

State University (Harris, 2019). Isabel Vazquez explored the SPT practice of "stuck." Stuck is a body-based exercise that moves from the current reality to the emerging future (Presencing Institute, 2007–2021). She used it to gain fresh insights about her relationships with the Dominican Republic and the United States. Stuck informed her devising process, and a variation of the exercise was included in the *Borders and Migration* performance; she extended this research for UR Day (Vasquez, 2019).

Guzman and Vasquez also collaborated with Mayan youth at an international social art studio residency in Yucatan, Mexico, hosted by La Vaca Independiente (2020). The theme of the residency was Youth and Nature and the program explored new ways of thinking, doing, and feeling about the disruptive challenges of contemporary life. The goal was to both make visible the challenges and then to consider possible solutions through SPT, including a performance in the town square of Izamal that blended SPT practices with applied theatre (H. Huggins, personal communication, March 31, 2020).

SPT is a highly interactive and personal activity, yet Huggins and her students have managed to continue and even expand their work during COVID-19. In addition to sharing their work internationally through various SPT meetings and conferences, they presented "Cultivating Communities of Care Through Action Research" at the 2021 CUNY Faculty Diversity and Inclusion Conference. At the first session of recent two-part workshop series, presented via Zoom in partnership with the Harriet and Kenneth Kupferberg Holocaust Center (KHC) on the QCC campus, Huggins's research team developed and shared a program on peacebuilding through awareness and improvisation. Reflecting on the event, Laura Cohen, KHC executive director, remarked that:

> So much of the work we do at the Kupferberg Holocaust Center is about the past. This work today reminds me . . . that our programming is about life, making these connections between the past even more resonant in the future, and talking about what it means to not only live with these memories, but to put them into conversation and to really harness the power of peacebuilding and relationships.

Arawana Hayashi herself, who presented as part of the workshop, observed that this:

> art form (that Heather and the group are creating) links the deeply personal with the systemic, with the bigger view of the global and the spiritual world that we all live in. These moments, the gestures, the words of these poems . . . they open from the most minute moment of the heart, of the individual person up into a real sense of global humanity, and beyond that.

Huggins has found that practice-based research at community colleges is very rare. She hopes it will find traction through interdisciplinary course offerings and funding for students, because the action research makes visible many of the social issues that confront community college students. She suggested that SPT is "decolonizing the space" for students, many of whom feel that their intersectionality has been tokenized. Once students are introduced to the concept of Social Presencing they take on leadership roles in developing workshops and presentations. The students are learning that they have agency to make changes in their community as they already do at work, at home, and in their off-campus communities. Developing the student-led performances has led to collaborative writing. In addition to developing an individual sense of agency, students are also learning how to be a contributing member of a team. I asked Huggins if her students continue their education in theatre. Some do, she said, but others become engaged in social change organizations, and some see the potential of Social Presencing Theater for leadership training.

## CUNY Guttman Community College

### *Sociology and Anthropology*

Guttman Community College, opened in September 2012, views college as a place and an idea. The place is midtown Manhattan. The idea is using the city as an environment to explore through experiential learning, considering different perspectives and cultures, and collaborating to foster inclusivity. A hallmark of the student experience is a year-long social science course, Ethnographies of Work (EOW), where students study the workplace as social science researchers. Associate Professor of Sociology Mary Gatta, along with colleagues, developed the course and teaches it each year. Gatta is the author of several books and articles about work-related issues ranging from women's employment and unemployment, flexible workforce development, low wage work, and retirement. She used an ethnographic methodology in her research and applied her research background to the development of EOW. She believes that students need to look critically at the world of work as they consider career decisions (M. Gatta, personal communication, August 13, 2020).

While it has a career focus, EOW is not the typical career preparation course. In EOW, students don't develop a resume, write letters of application, participate in skills assessment, practice job interviews, or enter the work environment as an intern. Students enter the work environment as researchers. The first semester of the EOW course introduces students to the sociological and anthropological perspectives on work. "The course approaches work as a cultural system invested with meanings, norms, values, customs, behavioral expectations, and social hierarchies" (Guttman Community College, n.d.). Students learn about discriminatory practices in work environments, workplace dynamics, and how work matters to people in all employment hierarchies. Students study literature about work and research design. They learn how to observe in the workplace. To prepare for the second semester, students choose an occupation they are interested in and do an ethnographic investigation of that occupation in a real-work environment. They also develop skills in workplace mapping, interviewing, and gathering quantitative data and employment trends. As a final project, students compose and present ethnographic accounts of workplace relations and vocational pathways as they think about their future careers.

Second-semester students apply what they have learned about sociological and anthropological perspectives of work through fieldwork. The research requires students to use observation, interviewing, and analytical skills learned in the first semester as they study work's cultural, social, and economic aspects. They apply their research skills to the specific occupation selected in the first semester. After the year-long course, students have a deeper understanding of the meaning of work and the labor market. They have more knowledge about navigating the work environment and exercising their agency within that environment. Initially, EOW students enrolled in a course about how to be a successful student. The linkage between the student success course and EOW provided an intellectual basis for the study of work and practical work skills. After the fall of 2020, the two courses are no longer aligned by coenrollment, but the student success course will still be offered in the first year. The EOW course is an excellent example of introducing 1st-year students to research methodology within a discipline. When I was CUR's executive officer, I often heard faculty say that 1st- and 2nd-year students did not know enough about the discipline to engage in research. Guttman students enrolled in EOW learned the basics of ethnographic research and something about the sociology and anthropology of work, group dynamics, and employment hierarchies. Gatta and colleagues designed a course that is scaffolded for 1st-year students' developmental level.

The course is having a positive impact on students. Students in the 2012 inaugural course began to think about work differently. According to a *New York Times* article on the program, at the end of the course, one student wrote, "Work is the foundation of purpose" (Giridharadas, 2012). Another student realized that there is more to work than earning a living; some decided to follow their interests rather than following a more typical path. Giriharadas interviewed nine students, and six said that the class made them see that passion and work are compatible. Mary Gatta and Nancy Hoffman (2018) also interviewed students about their experiences with EOW. They found that students began to identify themselves as researchers and ethnographers and that the research process increased their self-confidence. Students learned how to introduce themselves to the professionals they interviewed, and the experience gave them a feeling of self-worth. Learning ethnographic methodology taught students to see in new ways. One student commented that after the class she "kind of saw ethnographies everywhere" (Gatta & Hoffman, 2018, p. 9). Students also reported having a better understanding of workplace and societal structures and constraints. The authors said that when students see work in a theoretical and evidence-based context, they are more informed about the range of career possibilities. By visiting professional workplaces, students gained a sense of the profession and what it means to be a professional. EOW introduced students to people they were unlikely to meet in their everyday lives. In the 2012 inaugural class, one student commented that he got to go to the 52nd floor of a building, something he had never done even though he grew up in New York City and had always wanted to do (Giriharadas, 2012). Perhaps the most significant impact of the course is students' expanding view of what they might do with their lives; this is also part of the campus ethos.

Other institutions have noticed the success of Guttman and the EOW. Colleges in New Hampshire, New Jersey, Massachusetts, and other New York institutions are studying how Guttman has embedded career development into the curriculum by engaging students in an ethnographic study of the workplace.

## Reedley Community College

### Art History

The mostly agricultural San Joaquin Valley of California is the home of Reedley Community College, which serves approximately 8,000 mostly Hispanic students. Reedley College is making a significant effort to engage its students in undergraduate research that is frequently interdisciplinary. Recent posters by Reedley College honors students described research projects that looked at group relations in Chaucer's *Canterbury Tales* or developed a novel intermediate-parcel delivery system design. Another study asked if legal cannabis would impact California's food prices or if community activity could reconstitute Dhegiha tribal culture.

Jamie Buettner is a part-time instructor of art history at Reedley College, and her career is an excellent example of interdisciplinarity. She is a licensed physical therapist and owned a private practice for many years. Buettner is also an art historian and costume designer; teaches art history and costume design; and publishes and presents papers on these topics. Her art history course incorporates a multidisciplinary perspective. She encourages students to consider personal interests as they select paintings to study (J. Buettner, personal communication, August 25, 2020).

For example, one student wanted to become a physical therapist, and Buettner directed her to a 1642 painting by Jusepe de Ribera, *The Clubfoot*. The painting is of a young boy who appears happy and confident. A closer look at the boy shows that he may have a clubfoot and possibly other problems. Buettner's student diagnosed the young boy's condition and provided textual support for her position. Medical doctors who have looked at the painting speculated that the child might have had polio, which was unknown then, or cerebral palsy (Abdul et al., 2018; Ramachandran & Aronson, 2006). The student did not believe the boy had a clubfoot but rather a neurological issue.

Another student was interested in color theory and studied Picasso's color periods (Duarte-Diaz, n.d.). When Picasso's close friend died, he experienced sadness and possibly depression. His paintings reflected his feelings in the blue and gray colors he used. Later, as his personal life improved, he began painting in happier colors in red, peach, and pink. Duarte-Diaz compared two paintings, one in blue and the other in shades of rose, with Picasso's mood when he did the paintings. He interviewed community members to view the two paintings and asked if the paintings changed their mood. A follow-up question asked why their mood changed. Duarte-Diaz concluded that color impacts mood. Another student asked, "What was the impact of suppressed homosexuality on the symbolism and design within art created during the Italian Renaissance period?" To answer this question, the student looked at the symbolism of wingless angels in Michelangelo's paintings, the sociopolitical context of Renaissance Italy, and several Saint Sebastian paintings as a symbol of homosexuality.

Leonardo Da Vinci's *The Last Supper* inspired another student's research to investigate Leonardo's painting of hands and the relationship with sign language. The student was interested in Audism, the hearing community's oppressive attitudes toward the deaf community, and how the deaf community painted hands (Ensz, n.d.). Author Ross King (2012) says Leonardo was fascinated by the expressive possibilities of human hands. He painted a wide range of emotions in the disciples' hands. During Leonardo's time, the Dominican friars practiced silence for several hours a day in the refectory. During periods of silence, the friars communicated with hand gestures and facial expressions. At other times the friars spoke publicly and many were excellent orators who used hand gestures and facial expressions in their speeches. Leonardo often told his students to watch the friars' sermons. Ensz concluded that Leonardo was inspirational for deaf artists because of the way he painted hands.

In each of these projects, the student studied in depth one or more paintings, investigated the artist's life and times, and drew conclusions using textual support. As these projects demonstrate, Buettner encourages her students to look at art through different lenses: gender, politics, society, and so on. She sometimes uses a strategy she calls *slow art*, asking students to look carefully at all of the objects in a painting and decode them. Other times students are asked to look for evidence of their views using a forensic approach when looking at a painting.

In our telephone interview, Buettner commented that her students often see things as right or wrong, and she wants them to develop trust in their observations. By making in-depth observations of specific paintings, she also teaches her students to ask questions and think critically about possible answers. They are learning how to use evidence or textual support when they investigate the artist's life, the social and political situation at the time, and the artist's intent in doing the painting. She often asks students to think about how audiences might respond to a given painting in different periods.

Reedley students present their posters at the Central Valley Honors Symposium and other regional conferences. Usually, Buettner takes her students on a field trip to art museums in either Los Angeles or San Francisco. Students in the fall of 2020 had a unique opportunity to have a virtual behind-the-scenes tour of the Vatican, because they could not visit museums closed by COVID-19.

While I enjoyed my college art history course many years ago, I think how much more exciting and meaningful art history must be for Jamie Buettner's students. Not only are they learning about art and its history, but students are also learning skills of observing, questioning, critical thinking, and using evidence that will serve them well in their future careers and community activities.

## Tulsa Community College

### Music History and Music Theory

In 2015 the George Kaiser Family Foundation created an endowed chair for undergraduate research at Tulsa Community College (TCC). The gift provided the cornerstone for the development of a robust and creative undergraduate research learning community at TCC. Diana Spencer, associate professor of biotechnology, was selected to hold the first endowed chair. Spencer created the SEArCHH and ASPIRE program (Sustainability, Energy, ACcessibility, Happiness, Health, and [or] Social Policy Interdisciplinary Research Explorations). As she began her role as endowed chair for undergraduate research, she organized faculty conversations to explore how faculty could further engage students in research. She encouraged the group to think about how they could work across disciplines to create innovative and exciting student research opportunities. She credits faculty who participated in the discussions for the clear emphasis on interdisciplinarity that is a significant part of TCC's undergraduate research program. In 2019 Spencer developed a professional development course for faculty to expand undergraduate research across the four Tulsa campuses. Faculty who complete the course receive an Undergraduate Research Certificate (D. Spencer, personal communication, September 1, 2020). Spencer recently retired but left an inspiring legacy of student research and faculty commitment to interdisciplinary undergraduate research.

Robert Katz, associate professor of music, now holds the endowed undergraduate research chair. Katz and music professor Heidi Rigert work collaboratively with a cohort of students taking concurrent classes. The collaboration between music history and music theory developed over 5 years and is an excellent example of collaborative interdisciplinary research. Katz and Rigert wanted to create a project that would work for both courses. Their goal was to build a meaningful project that would lead to a new stage in students' pedagogical development. The result is a course that combines analytical skills from the music theory course with research and writing skills from the music history class.

Each class has a syllabus and project guidelines, but they are closely aligned. Students choose a composition that they would like to study in depth. In the music history course, they learn the history, background, and musical genre of the composition. They listen to two performances from different time periods and compare the versions on tempo, dynamics, articulation, phrasing, tonal quality, and expression. The music theory class builds on the music history class by having students complete a project to identify a clear goal, question, or focus; define main points, and explain the history class investigation results with specific examples. Students have options in how they present their results. Many students plan to be teachers, so they might choose to develop a lesson plan. Other students might design a website, a Prezi or PowerPoint, or a traditional research paper. Whichever presentation approach students choose, they need to examine the project through three lenses: historical, analytical, and technical. Students are evaluated on the projects' creativity, the content, style and organization, and overall quality. Katz and Rigert grade the assignments separately, but they have worked together long enough that they seldom have differences in their grading. Katz and Rigert teach their courses from their disciplinary perspectives, but students have an interdisciplinary experience because the professors collaborate on their two courses (R. Katz and H. Rigert, personal communication, August 25, 2020). Other professors might replicate Katz and Rigert's interdisciplinary collaboration in other areas such as literature and history, philosophy and business, and many other possibilities.

## CUNY LaGuardia Community College

### Biology and Ecology

Several professors at LaGuardia Community College (LGCC) designed and implemented an undergraduate research module to study the relationship between water pollution and leukemia. The U.S. Department of Education provided funding for the project through its Continuous Intensive Learning Environment in STEM (CILES) program. Enhancing recruitment into STEM programs by introducing students to authentic research was the goal of the program. Two community colleges and one 4-year college participated in the program. As several faculty at LGCC were conducting cancer research as part of their research program, it made sense to include students. A causal relationship between water pollution and cancer is currently not clear, making it an ideal topic for original student research. LGCC is near the highly polluted Newtown Creek, where other LGCC faculty have taken students to do fieldwork. The creek is an accessible and logical location for the study. The undergraduate research module integrates several high-impact practices. First, it connects basic biological concepts with environmental issues that are of particular importance to students because of their proximity to Newtown Creek. Newtown Creek's pollution personalizes the global aspect of ecological challenges for students. Incorporating a global perspective into the project is the second high-impact practice. The third aspect was peer mentorship. A student who had been involved in faculty research served as a peer mentor for the project (Xu et al., 2016).

The researchers studied the impact of polluted water on fruit flies. Fruit flies are an excellent species for research for several reasons. They are inexpensive, easily obtainable, and require minimal care, space, and equipment. They have transparent bodies making it easy to see the tumors that the flies developed from polluted water. The students were very excited the first time they saw a tumor in the fruit fly's body. The tumors, floating in the blood, are readily visible to the naked eye (N. Xu, personal communication,

September 21, 2020). The students also were curious about the fruit flies and enjoyed taking care of them. By careful observations, students learned to identify male and female flies, body structures, and the cycle of life from newborn flies to death. The anesthetized flies allowed students to see the flies through a dissection microscope. Discovering the link between polluted water and fruit fly tumors engaged the students' interest. Studying the fruit flies stimulated students' curiosity and led to other questions. Students wondered whether temperature or long periods in darkness or light made a difference in tumor development.

Some of these questions became part of summer research with CRSP students. Each student did a literature review, wrote lab reports, and added personal reflections to their portfolio. The project's success as a learning experience was assessed by a student survey and an analysis of students' reflections in their lab reports regarding integrative learning. LGCC uses a rubric for integrative learning across the curriculum to assess students' experiences with connections between and among academic disciplines. The rubric also assesses students' experiences, the ability to apply learning across diverse contexts, and student reflections and self-assessment. As part of the reflection process students were asked to take digital photographs to demonstrate the relationship between the project and their lives. Faculty found that students made connections between pollution and cancer and their personal lives. The emphasis on questioning and making connections is a strength of this project for student learning.

This project is an example of how the various research models overlap at community colleges. The fruit fly project included the whole class in course-based research. It is also basic research because the researchers documented the relationship between water pollution and leukemia. Learning more about what causes leukemia might lead to preventative measures. Identifying preventative measures is applied research. Finally, it is interdisciplinary research because it involved biology and environmental studies. The project demonstrates that 1st-year students can do authentic, original research in the classroom with minimal cost. The faculty involved in the original project continue the fruit fly research each year with different research questions.

# 9

# COMMUNITY COLLEGE PARTNERSHIPS

From their earliest beginnings, community colleges have engaged in partnerships. They partner with 4-year colleges and universities to enhance the possibilities for transfer after completing a 2-year degree. Industry partnerships provide internships for community college students and help sustain currency in the college curriculum, particularly in technology areas. Government agencies and national laboratories are also excellent sources for internships and research partnerships.

## University–Community College Partnerships

University–community college partnerships can be formal or informal. Arizona State University (ASU), for example, has a program called Motivated Engineering Transfer Students program (METS). It was initiated by ASU engineering professors to support community college students who wanted to transfer to ASU's engineering program (VanIngen-Dunn, 2016). The NSF partially funds the program. Students receive support while completing their 2-year degree and encouragement to take as many engineering courses as possible at the community college. Students admitted to the program, about 100 students each year, have access to daily contact with other transfer students, study and networking space, and advising support. The METS 2017 graduation rate exceeded 95%, and of those, 50% continued directly to graduate school (Southwest Institute for Engineering Transfer Excellence, n.d.). Designed to encourage first-generation students to consider an engineering career, the expansion of community college engineering programs and recruiting efforts was a secondary result. METS is part of the Southwest Institute for Engineering Transfer Excellence (SWIETE). It bases its practices on the goals and research-based methods of the Academic Success & Professional Development Academy (ASAP). One of the ASAP goals is creating "tomorrow's leaders, researchers, and innovators" (ASAP, 2018, para. 1). Community colleges play an essential role in this goal as they bring diversity, new questions, and different ways of thinking to the discovery process (SWIETE, n.d.).

The NSF provides funding for universities to support community college students through its Research Experience for Undergraduates (REU) program. The University of California, Berkeley (2015) and Rice University (2018) received funding for NSF REU programs to serve community colleges in their state. The Berkeley REU addressed engineering research that engaged community college students in nanotechnology research on novel nanomaterials, biotechnology research on advanced biofuels and bio-based chemicals production, and robotics research. The Rice University project also focused on nanotechnology with the goals to:

- facilitate the development of engineering students from minoritized groups;
- educate community college students about STEM careers;
- provide experiences in research laboratories;
- build and sustain mentoring relationships with REU participants; and
- promote effective interinstitutional partnerships between Rice University and community colleges in the Texas Gulf Coast Region.

Many of the faculty I interviewed talked about informal partnerships with nearby universities or with the university where they received their doctorate. They often kept in touch with their doctoral adviser or dissertation committee members and might spend the summer doing collaborative research. Sometimes students would come with them for the summer research, or they might visit the university during the academic year to allow students to see research at a major university. At Estrella Mountain Community College, for example, Erica Wager brought her students to Arizona State so they could become familiar with a big university where they might wish to transfer (E. Wager, personal communication, November 7, 2019). Sometimes community college faculty will connect with a university expert in the field they are studying and develop a partnership. Christina Colon, KBCC, developed such a relationship with Mark Botton, professor of biology at Fordham University (C. Colon, personal communication, January 14, 2020). He is considered one of most prominent researchers on horseshoe crabs in the world. Recognized for his many years of horseshoe crab research, when a new species was discovered, Albalimulus bottony, it was named after him (Stoelker, 2020). Christina Colon and her students have done fieldwork with Botton.

## Industry Partnerships

There is widespread support for community college–industry partnerships (CCIPs) from industry, community colleges, and state and federal legislators. Industry sees the benefits of CCIPs as developing employee skills the industry needs and community colleges benefit by adding programs that meet community needs and keeping up with advancements in their workforce programs (Soares, 2010). Student research is not usually a part of these partnerships. However, there are partnerships based on students doing research that can be helpful to an employer. David Brown, now an emeritus professor of chemistry from Southwestern Community College in Chula Vista, California, received an NSF Small Business Innovation Research Program and Small Business Technology Transfer Program grant to work with Ondax, Inc., a California company. Ondax manufactures high-performance holographic optical filters and wave-length stabilized sources for industrial, scientific, defense, and consumer applications. Southwestern students worked with Ondax to develop new material used with the latest laser technology that Ondax would eventually market (Radelat, 2011). Southwestern students won several awards for their discoveries and were among the first community college research teams to present at CUR's Posters on the Hill.

The Green Fuels Depot project at College of DuPage, described in chapter 2, is an example of an industry, government agency, national laboratory, and community college partnership. A four-way partnership is exceedingly difficult to develop and manage. However, it can have genuinely innovative and far-reaching results. This project's goals were to investigate the gasification process, with the hope that waste from the city of Naperville, Illinois, could be converted to gas to fuel city vehicles. When the engineering company went bankrupt, the partnership, unfortunately, did not survive either (Jarman, 2014).

## National Laboratories Partnerships

As community colleges offer more student research opportunities, colleges can partner with national laboratories, government agencies, and nonprofit organizations. National laboratories like Brookhaven National Laboratory (n.d.) offer Department of Energy Community College Internships (CCI) and Science Undergraduate Laboratory Internships (SULI), open to 2-year and 4-year students. Its purpose is to encourage students to pursue careers in STEM by providing authentic research experiences. Through the Community College Internship, Argonne Laboratory (n.d.) encourages community college students to enter technical careers. During the internship, students work on technologies or instrumentation projects that support the Department of Energy's mission. Other National Laboratories also partner with community colleges and universities.

## Queensborough Community College and Brookhaven National Laboratory

Sharon Lall-Ramnarine is a professor of chemistry at Queensborough Community College (QCC). A prolific scholar and researcher with 28 research grants from the Department of Energy, Con Edison, CUNY, and other agencies and 23 publications in major scientific journals, she also actively engages students in research. She understands the importance of collaboration, partnerships, and mentoring as she reaches out to other universities and organizations to advance her research efforts and those of her students.

Lall-Ramnarine began her work with Brookhaven National Laboratory (BNL) while a doctoral student at Queens College. She and her adviser Robert Engel, wrote a paper about ionic liquids that caught the attention of James Wishart, a chemist at BNL. Lall-Ramnarine and Wishart began a research collaboration that continues today. Soon after becoming an assistant professor of chemistry at QCC in 2004, she began involving her students in her research on campus and at BNL. Lall-Ramnarine is a strong advocate for engaging her students in authentic research projects on campus and at BNL during the summer. She recruits students to work with her on research through her chemistry courses. She reads their lab reports, observes how they perform in class, and then asks students if they are interested in doing research. The students selected for research internships at BNL receive $500 stipends and live and work at BNL for 10 weeks. Lall-Ramnarine conducts cutting-edge research in liquid salts or ionic liquids. The design and development of ionic liquids could lead to the creation of efficient nonflammable batteries needed in cell phones, laptops, solar cells, and other energy storage devices. Lall-Ramnarine collaborates with scientists who also study ionic liquids at Yale, Rutgers, and the University of Iowa (S. Lall-Ramnarine, personal communication, January 16, 2020).

Through her collaborations with BNL and other universities, she and her students continuously learn about new techniques and discoveries. She encourages her students to present their work at national and regional conferences, and she and her students have coauthored many published articles. Students published two peer-reviewed articles in 2019 in the *Journal of Physical Chemistry A* and *The Journal of Chemical Physics* (Doyle, 2019). Many of her students have gone on to earn doctorate degrees and continue the research they began in Lall-Ramnarine's and BNL's labs.

For many years, QCC students participated in the BNL Faculty and Student Teams (FaST) program, now called Visiting Faculty Program (VFP). The VFP is a collaborative program between BNL, the Department of Energy, and the NSF that supports teams for a BNL researcher, a faculty member with two or three undergraduate students. In addition to the opportunity to be part of a team doing high-level research, VFP also builds long-term and sustainable relations that benefit students throughout their STEM careers. Faculty participants also benefit from the program. Lall-Ramnarine, like other faculty members, recognizes that she would not be able to do her research without the support of the Brookhaven National Laboratory and her research university partners. In a BNL report (Blackburn et al., n.d.) Lall-Ramnarine commented:

> Being involved in the BNL FaST program has allowed me to stay current in my research field and to be involved in the most exciting and current research. I am able to bring this new knowledge to my classroom discussions and my research students. I am also able to take my research with my students to a level that I could not duplicate on my home campus. After the FaST experience many of my students decided to pursue science degrees and now consider graduate school as a career option. My BNL FaST mentor is a very valued collaborator who looks out for opportunities for me on a continuous basis. (p. 29)

### Walters State College and Oak Ridge National Laboratory

Eugene de Silva is a professor of physics and chemistry at Walters State Community College in Morristown, Tennessee. De Silva's broad educational interests include science literacy for K–12 students and multidisciplinary research in science for undergraduate students. A passionate advocate for science education, he has developed a network of international scholars who participate in virtual conferences hosted by Walters State. Students have an opportunity to hear scholars from England, the Philippines, Israel, Cyprus, Australia, Singapore, and other colleges in Tennessee and the United States. The scholars are available so students can contact the researchers and possibly participate remotely in their research projects. Conference themes have included science's role in intelligence, security, terrorism, and nanotechnology. De Silva is continuing to hold symposiums for students to present their research virtually and virtual conferences. The June 2021 conference was titled *Intelligence and Law Enforcement in the 21st Century*. As president of the Tennessee Association of Science Department Chairs, de Silva also created a statewide conference for science students to present their research (E. de Silva, personal communication, July 10, 2020).

At Walters State Community College, students take multidisciplinary research modules developed by de Silva based on his published educational model, START, a syllabi-tracking system. START also includes assessment methods, research components, and testing (de Silva & de Silva, 2016). Following these research modules, students build their final research projects and present them at research conferences. A recent example of multidisciplinary research is an investigation into land acquisition by the Tennessee Valley Authority (TVA). The study involved an analysis of the method TVA used to acquire land and the free market value of acquired lands (Gerard et al., 2020). It was supervised by de Silva, a history professor, and a psychology professor. Students collected and compared property deeds with court records to determine how many landowners fought to keep their land. Census records identified descendants of the original landowners and students surveyed their opinions about TVA's land acquisition practices.

In 2011 de Silva contacted the Oak Ridge National Laboratory (ORNL) regarding a potential partnership. The partnership, approved in 2012, assists Walters State in addressing training needs for the community's workforce. ORNL provides advice to the college regarding the needs of employers based on newly developed technologies. The partnership also includes training and hands-on research experience for Walters's students. When the partnership was announced, de Silva said, "Research is the application of knowledge." Research is so crucial to the learning process that de Silva often calls research the fourth R (Walters State, n.d.).

Oak Ridge participates in the Department of Energy Community College Internships program (CCI), sponsored by the Department's Office of Science Workforce Development for Teachers and Scientists. The program provides a 10-week summer internship that includes a weekly stipend. Sharon Smith, a civil engineering major, was the first intern in the summer of 2013. Over the summer, she worked with scientists entering data on weather patterns' effects on biomass productivity. The project studied the economics of growing crops for use in energy creation. Smith felt that she was part of a project that could ultimately impact the nation's energy efficiency. Working with world-class scientists on critical societal issues has to be an inspiring experience for a young student (Walters State, 2013). Three more students have gone through Oak Ridge internships after completing their studies at Walters State Community College.

## National Aeronautics and Space Administration (NASA)

### *Queensborough Community College and Goddard Space Flight Center*

A professor at Queensborough Community College (QCC), CUNY, M. Chantale Damas said she was, "Captivated by stars from an early age." She came to the United States from Haiti when she was 11. Learning about Albert Einstein in school, she commented, "It was love at first sight. Maybe it was the hair, but I was totally mesmerized by what he did. I wanted to be just like that" (Damas, n.d., para. 1). The little girl who grew up to become a space scientist and an international scholar developed a particular interest in space weather. NASA, NSF, and CUNY fund her research. Damas is the recipient of several teaching and research awards.

The partnership Damas developed with the Community Coordinated Modeling Center (CMMC) based at the NASA Goddard Space Flight Center opened many opportunities for her students. NASA defines *space weather* as weather created by the sun's surface (NASA Science, n.d.). Space weather is not something that 1st-year students are likely to know about. However, Damas et al. (2019) say that space weather impacts our technological society, and once students learn about space weather, they can relate to the topic. Space weather provides three areas for student research: (a) using archival and real-time data; (b) understanding the causes and drivers of storms; and (c) forecasting.

In 2015, Damas received at $750,000 3-year grant from NASA (Momberg, 2015). QCC is one of only four community colleges to receive this grant to train students in space science. The NASA funded project, CUNY-NASA Solar and Atmospheric Research Program and Education Partnership (SOLAR PREP), expands QCC's Space Weather Research and Education Program (QCC SWREP). The focus of the project is training and retaining women and minoritized students in space science. The goals of the grant are to provide community college students:

- "long-term integration of space weather into the undergraduate curricula;
- experience in analyzing large geospacer data sets, which increases students' computational, critical thinking, and analytical skills, useful in any career; and
- increase students' interest in and motivation to study STEM, as well as preparing them for choosing a career path in space science and related fields" (Damas et al., 2019).

The grant provides funds for community college students to engage in a year-long study of space weather. QCC students enroll in a course-based undergraduate research (CURE) class to conduct research about real-world space weather problems. After the course, they can participate in a summer internship at NASA, City College of New York, or other partner institutions. The summer program also funds community college students and 4-year college students nationally.

The study of space weather is interdisciplinary and includes applied research in solar, geospace, and atmospheric physics. Damas's students presented a poster, *Investigation of Long Duration Positive Ionospheric Storms and ICME Interplanetary Structures*, at the December 2019 American Geophysical Union conference in San Francisco (Damas et al., 2019). The research focused on how space weather impacts the ionosphere. The ionosphere is a layer of electrically charged particles that play a role in satellite-based communication and navigation. Geomagnetic storms can damage satellites and high-frequency transmission and impact the electric power grid. Students identified long-duration storms between 1996–2018 and then used GPS data to determine total electron content changes. Another group of students looked at storm-generated disturbances that could potentially modify the planet's upper atmosphere. Space weather scientists debate the impact of events like long-lasting storm enhanced density (LLSED). Damas's students are doing cutting edge, original research. They could not do this exciting research without the partnership Damas developed with NASA and her commitment to engaging students in significant research.

## California Space Grant Consortium, NASA, and NSF

NASA initiated the National Space Grant College and Fellowship Project in 1989. The program's purpose was to enhance science and engineering education, research, and public outreach efforts (NASA, 2020). Now there is a Space Grant program in all 50 states, the District of Columbia, and the Commonwealth of Puerto Rico. In 2017 the California Space Grant Consortium expanded to include community colleges. The Consortium issued a call for proposals to fund ten 2-year colleges. The new program's goal was to enhance STEM preparation and increase graduation rates for community college students. Improving bridge opportunities to 4-year colleges was an additional goal (California Space Grant Consortium, 2017).

Before the 2017 call for proposals, however, several community colleges were already involved in space studies. Under the leadership of Timothy Usher, professor of physics at California State University, San Bernardino

(CSUSB), the NASA Curriculum Improvement Award for the Integration of Research (CIPAIR) awarded a 3-year grant to CSUSB and College of the Desert. An outcome of the CIPAIR grant was the development of the College of the Desert's (COD) winternship program. Math, Science, Technology Center (MESA) Director Carl Farmer established winter internships that last for 2 weeks and provide an enhanced learning opportunity to prepare students for transfer to a 4-year college and apply for summer internships. During the winternship, working as a team, students complete a literature review, design a poster describing their project, and give an oral presentation to faculty and other students. Completing three applications for summer internships is an expectation for winternship students. The 2-week program introduces students to the research process and offers a mentored introduction to research and other available opportunities. When mentors know the student participants, they can write more informed recommendations for a summer internship (C. Farmer, personal communication, July 21, 2020).

Following the CPAIR grant, CSUSB requested NSF funding through its Center for Research Excellence in Science and Technology (CREST) program. Three community colleges were involved in the CREST grant: College of the Desert, Irvine Valley Community College, and Victor Valley Community College. The project provided community college students with a wide range of training on research-grade instruments. Students also gained experience with specific computational packages, gained hands-on experience in synthetic organic chemistry, and general laboratory techniques and procedures (NSF CREST #1345163). The collaborations also provided professional development opportunities for faculty.

The College of the Desert winternship students investigated several important topics:

- *"An investigation of the particulate matter emissions from the Sentinel Power Plant.* The study of atmospheric chemistry and its correlation with Coachella Valley's diminished air quality has shown its origin from outside sources and the desert environment. The impact of a recently opened natural gas turbine power plant on the valley air quality was also investigated.
- *Investigative analysis on the air quality in the Coachella Valley.* Using emissions and back trajectories via computational methods to calculate the traversal of incoming air, students concluded that most of the emissions must occur elsewhere, namely the Los Angeles basin.
- *NXT Robotics: Solving Daedalus' Labyrinth.* The program involved students working collaboratively to develop Lego Mindstorm NXT robotic systems utilizing the LabView programming

language to navigate a maze and create decision-making Artificial Intelligence systems.
- *Selenium content of the Salton Sea.* Values for the concentration of selenium in water, sediment, and biota from literature and previous studies and compared to samples of the biota, sediments, and air in the Salton Sea environment" (Usher, 2016).

Victor Valley Community College, under the leadership of Michael Butros, professor of physics and mathematics, developed a 4-week winternship program (M. Butros, personal communication, August 25, 2020).

Butros felt that students needed structure in their first research experiences, so he designed projects in five areas:

- *Predator–Prey Model*: A biological-based model that looks at how the interaction between a predator and its prey changes when the predator or prey is taken out or a third species is introduced. This model can be adapted to explain other dynamic systems in physics. As the students worked with this model, they discover that it is more complicated than they initially thought because additional environmental variables such as mating season and migration needed to be considered.
- *Double Pendulum Analysis*: This is a research model that looks at the dynamic behavior of two pendulums. Students were introduced to equations of motion and various ordinary differential equations.
- *The Wave Equation and Solitons*: Students investigated the nature of the wave equation and solitons to produce models using mathematical software and differential equations to describe linear and nonlinear waves.
- *The Heat Equation:* Students used mathematical models to produce three-dimensional graphs to show how heat will eventually reach thermal equilibrium over a region if enough time elapses.
- *N-Body Problem*: The n-body problem involves the interaction of celestial objects due to gravity. Students analyzed the mutual gravitational forces that make the bodies move and then analyzed the problem mathematically to find the equations of motion."

Irvine Valley College engages students in research during a semester course:

- "*Primary research on aerodynamic design to land on Mars (PRANDLT-M).* Thirty students from seven institutions developed a Mars glider. The program is multidisciplinary covering flight design aspects, flight control systems, communication systems, environmental sensing, and flight body prototyping.

- *Solar tracking systems.* Students designed and built a series of smart solar tracking systems that implemented simple and cost-effective Arduino microcomputer platforms. Students developed multiple axis and simple axis solar systems to compare efficiency curves and development data.
- *Quad-copter control systems.* Students built a fully autonomous flight control system for an F450-style quad-copter. They implemented strategies to identify targets and act on available information to achieve a specific goal or outcome using sonic, LIDAR, or infrared sensors. Flight control systems are developed using the Arduino platform allowing for a cost-effective, expandable dynamic, microcontroller platform" (Usher, 2016).

The National Science Foundation awarded a CREST 2 grant to CSUSB (Award #1914777). CSUSB added San Bernardino Community College to the new CREST grant and the College of the Desert and Victor Valley Community Colleges continue as partners. Also, the grant allows CSUSB and the community colleges to continue their partnership with the NASA Armstrong Flight Center. CSUSB's Center for Advanced Functional Materials manages the project, and its focus is supporting the development of new functional materials and promoting understanding of structure/function relationships. The Center continues its emphasis on undergraduate research and addressing the STEM pipeline from high school to 4-year degrees and graduate work (P. Cousins, personal communication, August 26, 2020).

The 2017 California Space Grant partnership supported the transfer of 2-year students to a 4-year college. It also provided professional development opportunities for community college faculty. For example, Irvine Valley physics professor Alec Sim spends summers at the NASA Armstrong Flight Research while his and other partnership students are at Armstrong. Sim continues his professional research through his collaboration with NASA Armstrong. He also mentors summer student interns and serves as a bridge between students and world class-scientists (A. Sim, personal communication, August 4, 2020). Michael Butros also sends students to NASA Armstrong. He encourages students from various science disciplines to apply for NASA internships because he believes that students benefit when they broaden their perspectives. For example, he encouraged a chemical engineering student to apply for the NASA internship, and the student was amazed by how useful his background was at NASA. When the Space Grant funding ends, Butros plans to develop a one-credit winternship honors course that will focus on computational projects. This course can be offered virtually, does not require expensive equipment, or classroom space, and it will prepare students to enter a growing field (M. Butros, personal communication, August 25, 2020).

The collaboration continues with CSUSB's 2018 grant from NASA's Minority University Research and Education Project (MUREP). The grant supports COD's continued efforts to engage minoritized students in space science and technology. Students will specifically study the field of entry, descent, and landing (EDL) phases of space projects through laboratory work (Pennamon, 2018). Six students continue their work by participating in a summer internship at Jet Propulsion Laboratory (JPL) after participating in an undergraduate experience in EDL. Studying EDL is helpful to students as they transition to a 4-year college and has the possibility of leading to a career at NASA or other space organizations. The College of the Desert's involvement in space studies has engaged over 120 minoritized STEM research and summer internship students. Many of these students have completed 4-year degrees, and some have earned graduate degrees.

Los Angeles City College (LACC) had 21 students, led by engineering professor Jayesh Bhakta, participate in the California Space Grant Consortium. Bhakta worked with students during the academic year and the summer. The program's goals included recruiting minoritized students to STEM, offering them authentic research projects, introducing them to research methodology, and serving as a bridge for transitioning to a 4-year college. Students visited nearby JPL and the California Institute of Technology to meet with professional research scientists. The visits also encouraged students to apply for summer internships at NASA Armstrong, JPL, and other sites. Bhakta introduces students to a microcontroller, designed by the Italian firm Arduino, to design and build a broad range of projects (J. Bhakta, personal communication, July 16, 2020). For example, Arduino supported a project to develop a sensor vest to measure heart rate, skin conductivity, and acceleration along six axes for amusement park riders. The vest's eventual applications may be useful for monitoring space stress.

Students work in small groups to brainstorm possible research topics. They need to select topics to complete within the semester. Once students have settled on a collaborative project, they break it down into manageable steps. Sometimes the project doesn't work out the way students anticipated, but that is also part of the learning process.

Students worked on a wide range of projects such as:

- Four students studied LIDAR (light detection and ranging) to create a 2D map of the environment by collecting data from a rotating LIDAR-lite V3 sensor. The students were successful in developing a working prototype that has potential applications for robotic autonomous navigation.

- Five students' project goal was to measure each finger's electrical activity and then use it to control the corresponding finger on a prosthetic hand. They found that the system they developed works but only at a rudimentary level. They identified the challenges for future work and possible next steps.
- Three students looked at ways to address water contamination that occurs after natural disasters. The students proposed using solar energy to conduct water filtration. They developed a low voltage DC water pump that required only moderate pressure to feed the Reverse Osmosis (RO) membrane. The system design would save energy and prevent overflows.

LACC developed a six-wheeled rover, Earth Rover, for use in student projects. Three students designed, built, and installed a system to control all six wheels. In the design process, they discovered that the Arduino UNO could not provide enough power for the project necessitating a design to expand the control board's capacity. The team was successful in designing a six-wheeled steering system using their custom-made components.

Another team created an autonomous rover that used LIDAR to detect obstacles and calculate the rover's appropriate degree to move forward. While the team faced several challenges, their rover successfully navigated through openings and obstacles. They had hoped to increase the speed of the rover while still controlling the navigation. However, they were not able to complete that part of the project within the available timeframe. All of these projects are examples of original basic research with the possibility of applications to current issues. The last two projects highlight the continuous nature of research and how projects build on past results. Students also learned how to analyze their results and identify steps for future research.

The Consortium for Undergraduate Research Experiences is an NSF Research Experience of Undergraduates program that offers paid internships at JPL to work with scientists in astronomy, astrophysics, planetary science, and space exploration. LACC and other Southern California community colleges participate in the program. Student work relates to ongoing or future JPL projects that engage students in observations, data analysis, instrumentation development, and space missions engineering (Los Angeles City College, n.d.).

## *Tulsa Community College and Oklahoma Space Grant Consortium*

Tulsa Community College (TCC) began its partnership with NASA's Space Grant Consortium several ago. As often happens in new ventures, the circumstance that led to their involvement was serendipitous. Mary Wells

Phillips, associate professor of biology, attended an Oklahoma Association of Community Colleges' conference presentation by a NASA JPL scientist. After inquires with JPL, JPL invited Phillips to work with researchers in the microfluidics lab in Pasadena, California, for a summer. She discovered that community college students were interning at JPL. Phillips decided that it would be a life-changing experience for TCC students and sought to make that opportunity available to them. She created a research challenge course focusing on NASA's mission research. The college received funding from the TCC Foundation and community supporters to send students to JPL. Phillips successfully submitted a proposal to NASA (Project UR NASA) that supported undergraduate research and student internships at JPL. In 2017, the Oklahoma NASA Space Grant Consortium invited TCC to become a partner. The Oklahoma Space Grant Consortium program and TCC Foundation continue to support JPL student internships. Students also participated in the NASA Community College Aerospace Scholars program and a summer internship program at Arizona State University—L'Space (M. W. Phillips, personal communication, August 26, 2020).

While at TCC, students participated in several undergraduate research projects related to space. One student investigated the effects of alcohol, caffeine, and valium on heart rates of daphnia to G-Forces (Stevens and Phillips, n.d.). Another team of students addressed the issue of nonrenewable food and crew waste on a spaceship. They investigated producing a complete nutritional diet using waste management (Corbit et al., n.d.).

TCC has been very successful in providing students opportunities for future success. For example, a student who participated in TCC's space program achieved a BA degree in chemical engineering and obtained work for a big data and technology company. Another student received a $120,000 Jack Kent Cooke scholarship to study engineering. Several TCC students have returned to JPL for a second internship, and JPL invited one student to remain and continue his work at the lab. Several students made presentations at Oklahoma Research Day, NCUR, and other conferences. Students who studied renewable foods and crew waste published an article in *Electrophoresis* (Noell et al., 2018).

## Partnerships With Nonprofit Organizations

### Howard Hughes Medical Institute

The Howard Hughes Medical Institute (HHMI) supports a program called Science Education Alliance (SEA) to engage thousands of beginning undergraduate students in course-based research. The Science Education Alliance-Phage Hunters Advancing Genomics and Evolutionary Science program

(SEA-PHAGES) program is a two-semester laboratory research course for students with little or no research experience. SEA-PHAGES can take the place of introductory biology courses or become part of the curriculum. Students have an authentic discovery-based research experience when they isolate and characterize novel bacteriophages from their local environment. They annotate the genomes they discover, and then send the annotated sequences to the National Center for Biotechnology Information GenBank database. HHMI invites students and faculty representatives to a SEA symposium each year where students share their discoveries with peers. In the 2018–2019 academic year, more that 5,500 1st- and 2nd-year students from 126 colleges and universities took part in the program, including 12 community colleges. SEA-PHAGES is an excellent program for community college students because it involves them in original research, is designed for beginning students, allows them to make their first discovery, and their work becomes part of a national research project. It is a relatively inexpensive program, and HHMI provides support for faculty who incorporate the program into their classes. Each year HHMI invites program participants to use the SEA-PHAGES assessment instrument, Persistence in Science, that assesses the program's impact on student development and persistence.

Elvira Eivazova at Columbia State Community College in Tennessee and Urszula Golebiewska at QCC in New York, are part of the HHMI SEA-PHAGES project. Eivazova and Golebiewska are active scholars with many publications in scientific journals. They are also committed to engaging students in research and have done so before their involvement in SEA-PHAGES.

QCC joined the SEA-PHAGES project in 2010. It was the first community college to become part of the project, and 225 students have participated in SEA-PHAGES to date. Columbia State College joined in 2018 and more than 100 students have participated to date (www.seaphages.org).

Urszula Golebiewska is one of the coauthors of an article about phage discovery in genomics published by the American Society for Microbiology (Jordan et al., 2014). The authors state that the genomics project increases students' interest in science, positively influences academic achievement, and enhances student persistence in STEM. It is also making substantial advances in phage genomics.

Golebiewska and 38 of her students contributed to a 2015 publication in *elife*, "Whole genome comparison of a large collection of mycobacteriophages reveals a continuum of phage genetic diversity" (Pope et al. 2015). Being listed as coauthors on the publication was thrilling for students. When students have an opportunity to present or publish their work, it affirms Golebiewska's goal for students to learn to think like a scientist. Each year QCC students present their research results at the HHMI annual symposium. They also present posters at the CUNY Annual Honors Conference. A video of Bridgett Carvajal's SEA-PHAGES presentation at the HHMI annual symposium documents the success of Golebiewska in mentoring young scientists. Carvajal was confident, articulate, and spoke without notes. She also comfortably answered questions from the audience (Carvajal, 2016). Golebiewska's students have won awards and scholarships to continue their education. Biling Chen is the most recent QCC student to earn the prestigious Jack Kent Cook Scholarship. The $40,000 scholarship will support Chen's transfer to a 4-year university (Queensborough News, April 28, 2020). The National American Chemical Society accepted the student's project with Golebiewska and included her abstract in the society's archives.

Golebiewska is an active and highly successful researcher. She began her career as a high energy physicist and worked with the Super Kamiokande, the world's largest neutrino detector. The Super Kamikande collaboration discovered neutrino-oscillations that led to a Nobel Prize in Physics in 2015. Golebiewska was a member of the collaborative, and it was awarded the Breakthrough Prize in Fundamental Physics in 2016. She continues to have wide-ranging interests such as evolution, paleontology, astrobiology and poetry. She has also written several articles and given public talks on these topics. She currently serves as vice president of the New York Paleontological Society.

Eivazova began her research career as a microbiologist and immunologist at the University of London before moving to Vanderbilt University. While at Columbia State Community College, she established its undergraduate biology research program and developed research-based courses. For her efforts, Eivazova received the League of Innovation's Excellence Award in teaching in 2019.

Eivazova mentored biology students in Columbia State's Honors program before her involvement with SEA-PHAGES. Three of her honors students engaged in a research project about whitetail deer in middle Tennessee. They presented their work at the 2017 Undergraduate Research Conference in Austin, Texas, and the conference included the project's results in the proceedings. One of the students spent the summer of 2017 at the Harvard Undergraduate Research program, where he researched the effects of long-term soil warming on soil respiration and carbon release. He also presented a poster at the Austin conference. Columbia State students have the opportunity to participate in Vanderbilt University's summer internship program, Aspirnaut, where they work in a variety of research laboratories. Aspirnaut is a science boot camp that provides "hands-on and mentored laboratory experience for undergraduate students interested in a career in biomedical science" (Aspirnaut, 2020, para. 1).

Eivazova believes it is vital for Columbia State students to expand their horizons by participating in undergraduate research programs at 4-year universities. She wants to familiarize her students with research opportunities and the culture of research universities to encourage them to continue their education and ease their transition to a 4-year institution. A long-term advocate for collaborative undergraduate research, Eivazova encouraged Columbia State to join the SEA-PHAGES program in 2018. When I visited Columbia State and met with Eivazova I saw her passion for collaborative student research firsthand. As several students stopped by her office, I also saw how much students appreciated her commitment to them and her advocacy for student research. Her office door is always open for students, as she feels it is imperative to make a personal connection with her students. She has high expectations for her students, but because she is approachable and knows her students, her courses' attrition rate is very low. She encourages students to develop questions, as she believes that being able to frame researchable questions is an important skill not only for STEM, but also in other professions. Participation in HHMI's SEA-PHAGES programs has given more visibility to undergraduate research at Columbia State College and opened up research opportunities to many more students (E. Eivazova, personal communication, March 20, 2019).

Partnerships provide significant benefits to students when they have an opportunity to engage in authentic research under the supervision of professional scientists. Working with partners introduces students to various issues scientists face when experiments don't work, potential ethical dilemmas, and requirements of funding agencies.

# PART THREE

---

# NEXT STEPS

# IO

# INCLUSIVE PEDAGOGY

Several years ago, I attended a planning meeting for a conference on inclusive education. The discussion centered on how to make the curriculum more all-encompassing of diverse cultures and perspectives. Higher education has paid substantive attention to diverse curricular content. Colleges and universities have made significant strides to broaden the curriculum to reflect various cultures and schools of thought, even though there is still more to do. As I listened to the speakers around the table, I thought the discussion was missing how pedagogy also needs to change to make the instruction and student/professor interaction more inclusive. Others have had similar observations (Gannon, 2018; Quaye and Harper, 2007). One area where we have made pedagogical changes is in addressing concerns regarding career preparation. Though controversial, we have made a noteworthy effort to weave work-related skills into the curriculum. Skills such as communication, critical thinking, and ability to work as part of a team are skills that employers value and recent pedagogical changes reflect. Undergraduate research is a pedagogy that addresses work-related skills, encourages collaborative interaction between students and faculty, and builds inclusiveness.

## Pedagogical Changes

The prevalence of undergraduate research across the curriculum has led to additional pedagogical changes. As students and their professors work together to construct new knowledge, their relationship profoundly changes. The professor retains a position of authority; however, the balance of power shifts to a more level partnership.

In *Teaching to Transgress: Education and the Practice of Freedom*, bell hooks (1994) sees the classroom as a "communal place that enhances the possibility of a collective effort in creating and sustaining a learning community" (p. 8). She describes a classroom where all students contribute to the learning process, and the collective effort generates excitement and commitment. A classroom or laboratory engaged in research becomes the classroom hooks envisions.

Angela Brew takes hook's "collective effort" concept even further. Brew (2006) suggests countries such as Australia, the United States, and other Western countries are governed by participatory democracy. Such democracies, she says, value "respect for human life, liberty, equality, and justice," yet university culture doesn't necessarily reflect these values in the institutional hierarchy (p. 117). Students, student affairs personnel, faculty, academic administrators, and other campus areas each have their lane. Yet, all of the institutional departments are necessary for the university's success and ability to educate. For example, as a university president, I remember when the physical facilities staff was upset about the changes proposed by the facilities director to rotate responsibilities across all buildings. When I met with the staff over breakfast, I heard comments such as, "we take pride in our building, and we want it to be well-taken care of so students can learn." I was surprised by the intensity of the custodial staff's commitment to the direct connection between their role and student learning. Given the facilities staff's strong feelings, we did not make the suggested change. In other cases, it may be the departmental administrative assistant who knows when a student needs help with an assignment, is having family problems, or whose car broke down and can direct the student to the appropriate resource. Participatory democracy suggests that all campus constituents are part of the learning community. Brew suggests that the separation of the university's various parts reflect the separation that many see between research and teaching. She advocates for viewing students as scholars and creating research partnerships that engage students and faculty equally in experiencing the excitement of discovery.

A shared vision, team learning, and systems thinking are three of Peter Senge's (2006) five disciplines that are particularly pertinent to higher education. The facilities staff in Maine felt that the campus had a shared vision, and they were part of the team. Many campuses identify a common reading for 1st-year students to cultivate shared learning. At Presque Isle, to facilitate collective learning, we offered all employees a book relating to the learning theme for the year. Embedding undergraduate research into campus culture fosters a shared vision across campus and nurtures teamwork. The CUNY 2-year colleges share a vision of the campus' role in student learning. The system office provides opportunities for team learning through programs like the Pressing Issues Project. Senge's fifth discipline, systems thinking, suggests that we are all part of the larger organization and the organization's problems and solutions are within our control.

The Association of American Colleges and Universities (AAC&U) believes that all students benefit from an inclusive pedagogy, and inclusivity must also embrace excellence. AAC&U calls this concept *inclusive excellence* (McNair et al., 2020). The goal of inclusive excellence is to create equitable opportunities for minoritized students to achieve equal outcomes. AAC&U advocates incorporating essential learning outcomes and high-impact practices into all programs. Recognizing and valuing the achievements of all students moves a campus toward inclusive excellence. Increased undergraduate research participation, as one of the high-impact practices, plays a critical role in realizing inclusive excellence.

## Inclusive Pedagogy

Inclusive pedagogy includes four basic concepts: a sense of belonging, consideration of capacity, attention to student interest, and the process of becoming a scholar (Packard, 2016). Faculty interviewed in previous chapters conveyed the belief to students that they belong on campus. Students feel welcome when their professors express genuine interest in students' learning success. Professors are interested in students' ideas and goals. Community college professors take many steps to get to know each student. Holly Porter-Morgan believes that the classroom needs to be a safe place to learn, a place where students can make mistakes and receive the assistance they need. A safe place to learn is an environment that respects students' abilities, interests, and goals. It is a place that minimizes the barriers to students' work. One of those barriers is the emotional labor that is often part of the lives of minoritized students.

### Emotional Labor and Belonging

Understanding the demands of emotional labor can help professors make students feel that they belong and have a place on campus. Arlie Russell Hochschild, in her 1983 book, *The Managed Heart: Commercialization of Human Feeling,* coined the term *emotional labor,* which she defines as "the management of feelings to create a publicly observable facial and bodily display"(p. 7). It is the feeling that emotional responses to certain topics must be suppressed. Students may have to deal with emotional labor in the classroom. Classroom discussions about poverty, racial issues, sexuality, and abuse are all topics that can create the need for students to quash their feelings. The sense that they need to hide feelings of anger, frustration, sadness, or embarrassment generates tension for the student and makes learning more difficult. By recognizing the concept of emotional labor, professors can thoughtfully encourage discussions about sensitive issues and provide relief and also foster a sense of belonging.

Erica Wager addresses emotional labor in several ways. She recognizes that some of her students struggle financially so she includes resources to address food insecurity and other issues on her syllabus. She is letting students know that they are not alone and that others may be facing similar problems. She also discusses racism in her classes. She opens the discussion by asking students to reflect on personal experiences when they faced discrimination, either as the recipient or the perpetrator. Students are introduced to Black researchers whose work has been pivotal in the creation of legislation designed to reduce segregation and prejudice in general. White privilege is examined in intelligence tests, health care, and children's textbooks. Wager's students become aware of bias, stereotypes, discrimination, prejudice, and racism that infiltrates many aspects of our everyday lives (E. Wager, personal communication, October 23, 2020). These are difficult conversations; however, they are guided by a supportive facilitator who creates a safe environment for such conversations.

Heather Huggins recognizes her students' emotional labor and uses social presencing to ease their burden. Her students discuss uncomfortable issues and, by confronting the issues within a safe and supportive environment, they find positive ways to address personal and community problems. Olga Calderon begins her classes with a few minutes of quiet time or meditation. She knows that her students face many obstacles in their daily lives, and she wants them to set aside those obstacles for the hour or so that they are in her classroom. She tells her students that research supports the idea that meditation can help people to focus.

## Student Assets

While community college professors recognize that some students arrive on campus with deficits in math and reading and some are still learning English, they also acknowledge their students' capacity and the personal assets students bring to class. Professors respect students' abilities and see them as capable of learning complex subjects. Several of the professors I interviewed have backgrounds similar to the students they teach. Many grew up in low-income homes, and their parents may have been immigrants. Sometimes the professors were not successful when they first started college. When they share these experiences with students, it creates a common bond, and students can see the possibility for their success. Olga

Calderon had children while she was working on her bachelor's degree. It took her many years to complete two master's degrees and her doctorate and begin teaching full-time at LGCC. She tells her students that it is not important how long it takes to meet your goals, but only that you keep working toward them. Several faculty shared with me that it was not until they experienced research that they became genuinely enthusiastic about their education. Ingrid Veras shares her academic history with her students. When students see Veras as a successful teacher and researcher who did poorly in her first attempt at college, it encourages persistence. When professors share their academic challenges with students, it also helps to build a sense of belonging and community.

## *Valuing Student Interests*

When students feel they belong in college and that their capacities are recognized, they have more confidence to raise questions of personal interest. Students are encouraged to express those interests when faculty help them pursue their learning interests. Jamie Buettner incorporates student interest into her art history course when she asks students to select a painting related to their interests for more in-depth study. Juan Leon agreed to oversee a student project when he was not an expert on the topic; he and the student would learn together. Professors who practice course-based research encourage their students to develop individual projects after completing the course project. Christina Colon encourages students to follow up on their questions by developing a hypothesis and pursuing answers. Sharon Lall-Ramnarine observes her students and asks those who are interested in the course if they would like to participate in research with her at a national laboratory. The professors I interviewed understand the importance of recognizing students' interests. They know that valuing student interest supports persistence and can lead to students seeing themselves as scholars.

## *Becoming a Scholar*

Undergraduate research contributes to students' sense of belonging and feeling that they can achieve as a scholar. Professors take many steps to help students become scholars. Dorina Tila scaffolds her course-based research project to gradually teach students the methodology of economic research. Tila's students pursue their interests in economics when they choose the country they wish to study. Rachel Smith teaches her students the scientific method by encouraging her students to troubleshoot. She asks them to think about what went wrong, why it went wrong, and how it can be corrected. By engaging students in research, professors encourage student curiosity and to see themselves as scholars. Becoming a scholar means developing skills in four major areas: observing, asking questions, making connections, and using evidence. These four areas are aspects of research or scholarly methodology in nearly every discipline and can be taught in the first year.

## Developing Research Skills

Research practices differ across academic disciplines. While biology, chemistry, physics, and geology follow the scientific method and the humanities, social sciences, and creative arts have different research methodologies, there are four skill areas that cut across all disciplinary research. Observation, framing a research question, making connections, and using evidence are research skills for every discipline and can be incorporated into the curriculum.

### *Observation*

Observation skills are critical to developing new knowledge. Every academic discipline depends on the ability to pay careful attention. Employees who are good observers have a better chance of success in their chosen careers. Observation skills can be taught to first-year students. Mary Gatta, in the EOW course at Guttman College, demonstrates that first-year students can learn observation skills. The development of observation skills permeates the curriculum at Guttman Community College. In another example, Kristina Baines focuses on developing an ethnographic mindset in her students. Her students learn to objectively pay attention to details. Mary Gatta, Christina Colon, and Mary Ortiz encourage their students to become good observers when doing fieldwork. John Stilgoe, Harvard Professor of Landscape History, engages his students in what he calls acute observation (Gibson, 2016). Rather than look specifically at places of work, birds, or horseshoe crabs, Stilgoe's students go for a walk and notice the details of their everyday surroundings and things they had never paid attention to before (Stilgoe, 1998). Author Annie Lamott (1994) believes that writers should become people-watchers. Writers' and actors' acute observation skills help them to develop strong and interesting characters.

Many might say that observation is a part of every course as students learn research methodology. However, it may not be taught explicitly, and specific teaching encourages students to be careful observers by letting them know how and why the skill is important. It also gives them strategies to continue their development of observation skills. Rob Walker has written a book, *The Art of Noticing* (2019), about ways to encourage paying attention.

For example, he suggests going on a color walk and looking for colors not usually noticed or making a sensory map of how things feel, or scents encountered during a walk. James Benning, an independent filmmaker, commented, "I always believe that any learning comes through concentration and patience, and that you have to train yourself to have that patience and to perceive" (Bradshaw, 2013). Amy Herman (2016), a visual perception consultant, brings her clients to the Metropolitan Museum of Art to acutely observe details in paintings. She sees this as a way to improve policemen's observation skills when they look at a crime scene, or doctors when they interview patients, and businesspeople when they study customer behavior. Jamie Buettner teaches her students to be good observers by asking them questions about what they see in a painting. She tells them there are no right or wrong answers because she wants them to trust their observations. When she asks students to look at paintings through a different lens, she is also encouraging students to understand that people can see things differently. Becoming a good observer can assist students in becoming more focused and engaged in the learning process. It is also a skill that will be immensely helpful in their future careers.

Jennifer Landin, a North Carolina State University biology professor and a scientific illustrator, has her students draw what they are studying in their biology class. Drawing, Landin believes, improves observational skills, and also develops a more positive attitude toward biology. She says, "Observational skills are crucial. The abilities to see without bias and focus on detail and pattern require training, not talent" (Landin, 2015, p. 5).

"A pencil is one of the best eyes," a phrase familiar to many scientists and artists, is from a story that Samuel Scudder, a Harvard entomologist, told. Scudder studied with Louis Agassiz, a preeminent Harvard Professor of Natural History. Scudder was studying specimens of fish in the laboratory, and Agassiz told him to look carefully at the fish and record what he saw. Scudder acutely observed the fish for 3 days, and Agassiz kept telling him to look further, that Scudder had missed vital parts of the fish. Finally, Scudder drew the fish and realized what he had missed. He was always grateful to Agassiz for teaching him how to observe (Scudder, 1997).

Laura Hills, professor of English literature at George Mason University, having heard Scudder's fish story, wondered if drawing could enhance students' ability to notice and record details in the literature they were reading. She suggests reading a poem and then asking students to draw what they read or heard when the poem was read aloud. Students could also draw portraits of a character in a novel. She goes a step further and suggests students use color to represent a verb. Hills (2008) believes that drawing can lead to new discoveries about the text.

Urszula Golebiewska (2018) loves poetry and wondered how she could incorporate poetry into her biology course. She sees similarities in poetry and science's descriptive techniques and how those techniques can foster creative, critical, and metaphoric thinking. She read poems associated with ecology to her students during class time. Students read a poem on a quiz and then are asked to figure out what components of a cell were described in the poem. After exploring several ways to use poetry in her biology course, Golebiewska felt that poetry in the classroom could encourage new ways of seeing science in everyday life. Golebiewska 's work is part of a pilot study at QCC to look at poetry across the curriculum (Traver et al., 2018).

Paying attention to what we hear might be considered another form of acute observation. As we saw in chapter 6, Olga Calderon uses radical listening in her classes. *Radical listening* is hearing both what is spoken and unspoken with genuine curiosity and without judgment (Gilligan and Eddy, 2017). When someone listens intently and tries to understand what another is saying, it can be a transformative process that leads to questions, making connections, and deeper learning. Setting aside opinion or judgment in radical listening can lead to probing questions that explore ideas and concepts and identify evidence. There are many creative ways to explicitly teach observation skills in any discipline.

## Asking Questions

Asking questions based on observations is the heart of the research process. The ability to frame a researchable question is not inherent; it must be learned. Many students have not been encouraged to ask questions. In some families, asking questions may be considered disrespectful of one's elders or intrusive. Kathleen Ross (2016), president emerita and professor of cross-cultural communication at Heritage University, found that she had to explain to students that asking questions is necessary for learning. Other students may be too intimidated in the classroom to ask questions. Mary Ortiz addressed intimidation when she told students they were paying her, so they should ask all the questions they wanted. Like observation skills, questioning can be explicitly taught. Learning how to ask good questions is not easy, however. Ken Bain, author of *What the Best College Teachers Do* (2004), found that the professors he interviewed saw questioning as crucial to learning. One professor commented, "When we can successfully stimulate our students to ask their own questions, we are laying the foundation for learning" (p. 31). How do we stimulate students to ask good questions? Some professors begin the course by asking "what do you think are the big questions in this field?" or "what do you hope to learn in this course?" For example, Robert Full, Chancellor's and Goldman Professor of Integrative Biology at the University of California, asks his 1st-year biology students what they want to know, what they are curious about. Full's (2012) pedagogy is based on *curiosity-driven research*. The process of curiosity-driven research is involvement, imagination, invention, and innovation. Matthew H. Bowker (2010) practices what he calls a *question-centered pedagogy*. He suggests that it encourages independent thinking when students ask questions as they engage with the course content. Probing questions to discover relationships and new possibilities are the kind of questions he wants students to ask. Bowker tells his students that they will begin the class with answers and end with questions. Such an approach suggests that students can question assumed knowledge. When a student feels free to ask questions of the professor or about the course readings, the academic playing field is leveled, and students are engaging in authentic scholarship. Bowker says encouraging *what if* and *why* questions rather than *what* questions or questions where the answer cannot be easily found on Google lead to better question-asking skills. Warren Berger, author of a *More Beautiful Question: The Power of Inquiry to Spark Breakthrough Ideas* (2014), says a good question is one that "is an ambitious yet actionable question that can begin to shift the way we perceive or think about something—and that might serve as a catalyst to change" (p. 8). Research involves actionable questions that add to our knowledge about or understanding of the course content. The last of the five questions that Debbie Deibert and her students ask of their observations is an actionable question—"what can we do about this?" There are several strategies professors can use to help students learn how to ask probing, actionable questions. Tasking students with developing questions for class discussions, where the answers are not found in the text, emphasizes critical thinking questions. Questions can be asked about questions. For example, is there a bias or viewpoint in the question? Does the question suggest a particular action? Can you look at a question from a different perspective? Would men see this question differently from women? Or would a historian have a different question than a philosopher? Some professors ask students to write down as many questions as they can think of on a particular topic. It is a form of brainstorming that can lead to more comfort with asking questions. A colleague, Andrew Velkey of Christopher Newport University, once said to me, "Research is about the audacity of the question" (A. Velkey, personal communication, October 14, 2010). It is audacious or actionable questions that lead to more learning and new ideas. Students should be encouraged to ask audacious questions. Often students ask questions that would not occur to an expert in the field because students don't yet know what they don't know. These questions might lead to a new path of inquiry.

## Making Connections

Developing answers to questions involves making connections between one observation and another. Many discoveries, such as Velcro, came from connecting observations and asking a question. A Swiss engineer, George de Mestral, liked to hike in the Alps. In 1941, he came home and found several burdock burrs stuck to his clothing. Pulling them off was hard and he noticed the burrs had small hooks that easily attached to the fabric. He began to think about how the burrs worked and realized he could adapt the burrs' stickiness to fasteners. We now use Velcro on shoes, containers, belts and in many other ways when we need to fasten or attach something (Loria, 2018). Students need the ability to see relationships between ideas, theories, and events. Students who can make connections are more likely to see the interrelationships among what they are learning in their various classes. The ability to see connections may lead the student to a discovery or interpretation of existing knowledge. Jane Weiss was thrilled when one of her students connected the refuge sought by characters in the novels the class was reading to the COVID-19 stay-at-home order.

We hope that our students make connections between what they learn in one class to what they learn in another class. Making connections doesn't necessarily happen automatically and may need some encouragement. James Lang, author of *Small Teaching: Everyday Lessons From the Science of Learning* (2016), suggests questions that encourage students to think about connections:

- Write down the most important thing you learned today, and why it matters to you or to society.
- List one way in which the day's course content manifests itself on campus or in your home life.
- Identify a television show, film, or book that somehow illustrates a course concept from class.
- Describe how today's course material connects to last week's material.

The *New York Times* Learning Network is a resource for teachers, students, and parents for making connections between daily events and topics in a course, and students' lives. Katherine Schulten (2018) says that the Learning Network asks two questions every day: (a) What is happening in the world that students need to know about and grapple with?, and (b) how does what's happening in the world connect with the literature, history, civics, science, and math we know our teachers are teaching? The Learning Network questions are adaptable to the college classroom even though designed for middle and high school students. Almost every day, there is something in the news that relates to a course students are taking. Asking them to think about connections not only helps them to see relationships but it also encourages questions. Professors can make their thoughts about connections visible to students. When discussing the text or readings, a professor can mention to the class a connection he saw and ask students for additional connections.

## Using Evidence

The development of new knowledge is also dependent on the use of evidence. With the proliferation of misinformation on the internet, students must learn how to separate bogus research and sham ideas from legitimate research and accurate information. The development of these skills can be built into the pedagogy of every 1st-year course. Students should be encouraged to ask, "what is the evidence to support this idea, statement of conclusion?" For example, when Jamie Buettner's students drew conclusions about the painting they were studying, they had to provide textual support for their conclusions. There are several questions that students can ask when determining the legitimacy of information. First, what is the authority of the person providing the information? It can be expert or personal authority. If expert authority, does the speaker or author have credibility as an expert? Do other experts in the field recognize that authority, whether or not they agree with the statements? Sometimes information may have a bias, and it is essential to understand the bias when determining the value of the information. It is also useful to understand the purpose of the information. Is it intended to inform or persuade? These are questions that can be incorporated into class discussions about reading assignments and the development of a literature review. Sometimes professors ask the class to read an article and discuss it in terms of authority and bias. Positive and negative examples of evidence help students to become more discerning. When students are doing research, they learn about how knowledge is produced. Understanding knowledge production helps students to separate ideas and opinions based on evidence from misinformation.

## Mentoring a Class

Mentoring students is a vital part of an inclusive pedagogy and undergraduate research. Community colleges are exceptionally good at mentoring; however, it is nevertheless challenging. In addition to academics, community colleges pay attention to life skills, preparing students to transfer to a 4-year college or enter the workforce. Support services on campuses help students develop career-related skills and address some of the barriers students face in completing their degrees. However, faculty may be the most crucial source for mentoring. Faculty see students regularly in the classroom and meet with students during office hours. Typically, we think of mentoring as a relationship between a professor and one to three students. If we use this mentoring model, a campus cannot reach very many students. Another, more equitable model is whole class mentoring.

There are several ways to integrate mentoring into regular course instruction. The syllabus may be the beginning of the mentoring process. Can the syllabus be written as an invitation rather than as a set of rules and deadlines? Ken Bain (2004) suggests the syllabus might be an invitation to a feast or a promising syllabus. He found that the "best college teachers" he interviewed included three parts in a promising syllabus. First, professors talked about the opportunities in the course, perhaps field work to study horseshoe crabs or learn about the world of work. Bain suggests that by starting with opportunities students have a sense of control when they see possibilities for learning that matters to them.

Second, Bain found that the best faculty explained what students would be doing in the course. The syllabus might serve as a map for completing the course (Paxton, 2016). Sometimes faculty use graphics or illustrations related to the course content to serve as a visual journey. The syllabus might also anticipate some of the questions students are likely to have about the course and provide answers. It can also consider some of the hidden curriculum barriers and, for example, provide definitions for words that might be unfamiliar to students. An invitation to office hours and a description of the visit's purpose is welcoming to students who are unsure about whether they belong.

The third characteristic Bain identified was that the syllabus described how students and the professor address the learning process. The syllabus is an opportunity for faculty to talk about the learning process, encourage students to ask questions, think about connections, and see learning as a collaborative process between students and professor. The discussion might also be the time to let students know how they should address the professor as this can establish the formality or informality of the student-teacher relationship. Of course, there are mandatory elements included in the syllabus, such as attendance policies, grading, safety procedures in some classes, and plagiarism. Colleges may also have additional mandatory items to be included in the syllabus.

Inviting students to participate in creating the syllabus is an approach some faculty have used to encourage collaboration. Suzanne Hudd (2003) wanted to make her class more collaborative by cocreating the syllabus with her students. She began her sociology course at Quinnipiac University by giving students the topics to be studied and asking them to develop a list of possible graded assignments. She found that students responded positively to participating in designing the syllabus. Hudd concluded, "As a result of this exercise, students learn at the outset that their opinions matter and they are more immediately immersed in the learning process "(Lang, 2006). Professors might look at their courses and see if there are aspects of the syllabus that could engage students to cocreate it.

Once the syllabus is designed, how it is introduced to students can also set the course's tone. Before introducing the syllabus, other activities can help to create an inclusive classroom. Students will be wondering, "Who is this teacher?" "What is she like?" "How will I relate to him?" Professors can briefly introduce themselves by telling students why they love the discipline they teach, perhaps some activities they like outside of the university, and maybe a story about their own educational experience. Students also want to know something about their classmates. Will I feel comfortable talking in class? Is there someone in this class that I might share notes with, or who might be a good study partner for me? Giving students a chance to talk in pairs or small groups can introduce them to each other without putting them on the spot to talk about themselves in front of the whole class. Students might be given a question to get the conversation started, such as what interests you about this course? After students know a little about the professor and each other, it's time to distribute the syllabus. Students might be asked to read the syllabus and then in small groups generate questions they have about the course. Early in the course, it is important to stimulate students' curiosity; thinking about the first day as a preview or similar to a movie trailer might suggest ways that will work for a particular class. A professor of art history might show slides of paintings and ask students in small groups to create a story about the painting. Photographs of historical events could be used in the same way. Introducing a mystery or an unanswered question scholars in the field are discussing, might stimulate students' curiosity. If possible, relating the course to the students in some personal way also inspires interest. For example, students in Ingrid Veras's class might be especially interested in the course because they live near the polluted creek that will be studied in the course.

There are several other strategies professors can incorporate into their teaching to make it more inclusive and collaborative:

- *Making content relevant.* It is helpful for students to know why they need to learn a particular concept. If professors say, "this important because . . ." or "learning this will help you . . ." the context will help motivate students to learn. Learning how to write a persuasive essay, for example, may be helpful in writing a job application letter. Working in teams is an expectation for many jobs; collaborative learning groups help to develop team skills. Some students don't like collaborative learning but if they understand that teamwork is an important skill for their career they might participate with more enthusiasm.

- *Taking risks.* A research project can feel risky because we don't always know if it will be successful. Students can benefit by knowing about risks that did not work out for the professor as well as experts in their field. Knowing that others initially failed can inspire courage to continue. Students need to know that a perceived failure in a research project may also tell us something we did not know. When a project fails, it is also an important learning experience because learning how to fail and then move on is critical for future success. Failure leads to success and students shouldn't be discouraged by a failed research project.

- *Coteaching.* Assigning one or two students to lead discussions on a course topic encourages them to see themselves as capable scholars.

- *Student contributions.* Students bring many experiences to the classroom and these experiences can stimulate questions, offer connections, and sometimes provide personal evidence. When professors encourage students to share how their personal experiences relate to the research topic, students feel a connection to the research, and it kindles continued involvement in the project.

- *Using local resources.* The use of local resources is another way to spark student interest and create a sense of belonging. Studying one's community suggests that the community's resources and activities are worthy of attention. Research based on local resources is cost effective and it also may make it easier for students to find time to access the subject of study.

- *Encourage perspective-taking.* Asking questions such as what perspective is missing from an assigned article or text allows students to bring their ideas and experiences to the discussion. Students can also try taking the perspective of someone else. Would people in various parts of the country, different income levels, or diverse cultural backgrounds look at the text or discussion topic differently? Recognizing that there are many views on a topic tells students that their views are also valuable.

## *Introducing Research*

Sometimes students are intimidated by the idea of research. Students may think research is something only professionals do, not an undergraduate student. Professors can address the intimidation factor in several ways. First, a professor may ask students what they have wondered about, did they ever have questions about what they observed in their neighborhood, for example, or how they could get better at sports, writing songs, or making friends. How could students find out answers to their questions? Most might reply, "I Googled it' and maybe they found the answer to their question. But some questions are more complex, and they might not be satisfied with the Google answer. Students might then suggest going to the library. They are beginning the process of research: looking for an answer. What then is research? The Office of Research Integrity (U.S. Department of Health and Human Services, n.d.) says "Research is the process to discover new knowledge" and this is what students did when they Googled their question or went to the library. Of course, academic research is more complicated, but faculty can make it seem easier when they explain the process.

Academic research is a systematic process to gather, analyze, and interpret information. In a course-based research class, all students will initially be working on the same question. Explaining the question, why is it important, and how we find the answer begins the research process. Students may not know the word *hypothesis* so this is an opportunity to introduce an academic word—that it is an explanation or prediction that leads to a question—is the hypothesis true or not. Students may have hypothesized various ideas without realizing that it is what they were doing. The hypothesis for the course must be something that will stimulate students' curiosity and also involve a question that can be addressed within a semester and using available resources. This is why community resources like birds, horseshoe crabs, or the behavior of people in Starbucks are good subjects for beginning students. Scaffolding the research process by introducing and explaining each step and why it is important develops confidence in students that they can become researchers or scholars. The steps in scientific research are somewhat different from research in literature, economics, or art history, but introducing the system used by professionals in the field is important. Students who are fortunate enough to have a research opportunity in different disciplines will develop a wider range of thinking processes that can be invaluable as they approach their chosen career.

As I talked with faculty during the process of writing this book, they often shared their pride in their students' successes; sometimes, it was completing a course despite many obstacles, admission to a 4-year college, landing a good job, or earning a doctoral degree. Believing in the potential and capacity of all students is inclusive pedagogy. Making students aware of opportunities, such as a poster presentation or a national laboratory internship, is inclusive pedagogy. Ensuring that all students feel respected and part of the class is essential for inclusive learning and teaching. Creating an inclusive pedagogy that honors students' assets, experiences, and hopes for the future, is what community college professors do.

# II

# ASSESSING UNDERGRADUATE RESEARCH

D etermining the impact of undergraduate research is a challenging endeavor. When I was teaching, I wanted to know what my students were learning, and as an administrator, I wanted to know how effective our programs were for students. Finding manageable ways to gather such information is a daunting task. The purpose of this chapter is threefold:

1. It presents a brief overview of research on the benefits of undergraduate research.
2. It gives a review of currently available assessment tools.
3. It describes informal ways for professors to gather information about the research experiences of their students.

Undergraduate research at community colleges is still in the relatively early stages of development, so there are only a few studies addressing assessment in 2-year institutions. Extensive assessment programs are costly and may require external funding. Adapting existing assessment tools for community colleges is a possible solution. Less complicated, informal assessment is likely to be helpful to community college faculty and administrators. However, understanding past studies is useful as community colleges consider the impact and benefits of their undergraduate research programs.

## Benefits of Undergraduate Research

We now have over 20 years of research that documents the benefits of undergraduate research for students. One of the earliest studies (Nagda et al., 1998) found that 1st-year minoritized students were more likely to continue their education when they had an opportunity to participate in undergraduate research. An alumni survey conducted by Bauer and Bennett (2003) found that alumni who had participated in undergraduate research were more likely to pursue graduate degrees and were more satisfied with their undergraduate experiences than alumni who did not have a research experience. Alumni also reported more personal skills and cognitive development than their fellow alums. Hathaway et al. (2002) similarly found that students who participated undergraduate research were more likely to attend graduate school. An often-cited 2004 study (Seymour et al.,) found that students at four liberal arts colleges were "overwhelmingly positive" about their research experience. Students reported that they understood what it is like to be a scientist, were more interested in learning, clarified what they wanted to study, and wanted to attend graduate school. Early reports on the SURE survey support the benefits of undergraduate research (Lopatto, 2004). The study asked three questions:

1. Is the educational experience of undergraduates being enhanced?
2. Are undergraduate research programs attracting and supporting talented students interested in a career involving scientific research?
3. Are undergraduate research programs retaining minority students in the "pathway" to a scientific career? (p. 270).

The survey results found students felt undergraduate research enhanced their educational experience. They learned more about the research process, lab techniques, and scientific problems. Students also thought they gained in tolerance for obstacles and were more able to work independently. The institutions in the study were attracting students who had already expressed an interest in science. The research experience supported their continued interest in science. Finally, the survey found similarity across gender and minoritized students to continue their education at the graduate level. In a later study, Lopatto (2007) also reported that undergraduate research positively influenced students' desire to earn a graduate degree. Russell et al. (2007) summarized the results of an NSF survey of nearly 8,000 STEM and social science students in an article in *Science*. Student respondents reported they experienced an increase in understanding of science and research, an increase in confidence in their research skills, and more awareness of what graduate school is like. They also reported increased interest in a STEM career and continuing their education toward a PhD.

What is interesting about these studies is that they all involved either research universities (Nagda et al., 1998), prestigious liberal arts colleges (Seymour et al., 2004), or a range of 4-year institutions (Russell et al.,

2007). None of the studies included community colleges and probably did not include open access institutions. The community college faculty I interviewed, however, have anecdotally reported similar benefits for their students.

## Essential Elements of Undergraduate Research

David Lopatto, in 2003, also surveyed faculty who had participated in Seymour's project. Faculty were asked what they saw as necessary for an undergraduate research experience. Lopatto compiled a list of what he called *essential features.* The majority of American professors would probably agree with the list. However, there have been significant changes in undergraduate research since 2003. For example, the discussion of research focused primarily on the scientific method. With the expansion of student research to more curricular areas, we need to recognize that methodology and scholarship in other disciplines may differ from the scientific method. Scholarship in the humanities is quite distinct from research in science. Where disciplines agree is that student ownership of the of the process is crucial, students should have opportunities to communicate the results of their work, and they need to learn about research and scholarly ethics. Faculty mentoring is also seen as an essential aspect of undergraduate research.

The five elements identified by students at the University of Central Florida are significant additions to the list of essential elements described by Lopatto. Showman et al. (2013) were interested in aspects of research that would move their educational experience from knowledge acquiring to knowledge producing. The five elements—creativity, judgement, communication, organization, and persistence—are skills that cut across all disciplines and are essential for many future careers. As we think about developing UREs and assessing student research, we should also keep in mind the elements students think are important.

## Impact of Undergraduate Research

The Undergraduate Research Opportunity Program (UROP) at the University of Michigan conducted an early study about undergraduate research. In the late 1980s and early 1990s, Michigan developed a comprehensive plan to expand ethnic and racial diversity throughout the campus called the Michigan Mandate. The project was quite successful in the diversification of the university, and Michigan became a national leader in the implementation of affirmative action. As the campus accepted more historically minoritized students, they noticed a 25 point difference in retention of White students and students of color. The White retention rate was 90%, while the retention rate for students of color was only 65% (Locks and Gregerman, 2008).

Like most U.S. campuses, Michigan developed remediation, tutoring, and social support programs such as mentoring, living/learning residence halls, and social groups for minoritized students. The retention problem, however, remained. As the UROP staff studied the work of retention scholars such as Astin (1993), Pascarella and Terenzini (1991), Kuh et al. (2005), and others, they found several factors that contributed to retention. The factors were:

- the nature of a student's peer group;
- the quality and quantity of student interactions with faculty outside the classroom setting;
- the balancing of students' academic and social lives;
- experiences that make coursework more relevant, especially gateway courses in STEM fields; and
- the invitation from faculty to participate in research, one of the core academic missions of the campus (Locks & Gregerman, 2008, p. 13).

With support from the U.S. Department of Education's Fund for the Improvement of Postsecondary Education (FIPSE), the State of Michigan's Office of Equity, and a NSF Recognition Award for the Integration of Research and Education grant, UROP designed a quasiexperimental study to compare a group of 1st- or 2nd-year UROP students with a control group of nonparticipants (Gregerman, 2008). Two carefully matched groups of approximately 600 students each were assigned to a group by lottery. The UROP students had peer advisers and were assigned to peer research interest groups. They were also able to select a professor and research topic based on their interest. If work-study eligible, students received payment and, if not, they received academic credit. Finally, students had the opportunity to publicly present their research results (Nagda et al., 1998). The study found that African American students who participated in UROP increased their retention rate from 65% to 81%. A follow-up study found that UROP students were also more likely to complete their degree and go on to graduate school.

Perhaps the most exciting finding from this study was the impact of engaging 1st- and 2nd-year students in research. Most UROP programs at the time did not engage students in research until their junior year. While students in this study were attending a highly selective major research university, the results suggest that engaging community college students in research may also be beneficial for retention.

In 2008 the Association of American Colleges and Universities (AAC&U) published *High-Impact Educational Practices: What They Are, Who Has Access to Them, and Why They Matter* by George Kuh, a study that identified undergraduate research as a high-impact practice. The National Survey of Student Engagement (NSSE), administered by hundreds of 4-year colleges and universities, identified 10 high-impact practices that promote deep student learning. Undergraduate research is one of the high-impact practices identified by NSSE. While only students at 4-year colleges take the NSSE, the findings of high-impact practices are also likely to apply to students at community colleges.

## Tools for Assessment

Institutions can use either formal or informal methods to assess undergraduate research. Early assessment efforts used student surveys to measure student attitudes regarding their research experiences. More recent assessment programs have developed additional ways of assessing students' research experiences that include interviews and portfolios. In addition to formal assessment tools, many campuses informally collect information about the success of their programs by looking at campus research activities.

### *EvaluateUR*

EvaluateUR is a proven method for assessing the skills and competencies of undergraduate research students while also contributing directly to student learning. Work on this evaluation method was pioneered at SUNY-Buffalo State, which has had a coordinated campus-wide undergraduate research program for over 20 years.

In 2003 Buffalo State created an Office of Undergraduate Research with Jill Singer, a SUNY Distinguished Teaching Professor, as its first director. The program has promoted and expanded research opportunities for students in all disciplines in order to institutionalize undergraduate research. The Office of Undergraduate research conducted regular evaluations of its programs, mainly relying on surveys of student and faculty reactions to the program. In 2006, Singer joined with Daniel Weiler Associates, an independent consulting firm specializing in education evaluation, to modify Buffalo

State's evaluation process by developing measures beyond surveys of participant reactions to the program. The objectives of their new evaluation design were to:

- Obtain reliable assessments of the impact of participating in student research;
- Provide information to student researchers about their strengths and weaknesses;
- Create a longitudinal database on student outcomes for research, and;
- Serve as a model that could be adapted by other institutions (Singer & Weiler, 2009).

After considerable input from faculty from the physical and social sciences, the arts, and humanities, Singer and Weiler identified 11 outcome areas for gathering data. In a pilot program, students first completed a survey designed to determine their level of motivation and their knowledge about their academic strengths and weaknesses. Faculty mentors then met with students and together they discussed the student survey responses. These conversations were designed to help mentors learn enough about their students' strengths and weaknesses to support a preliminary assessment of student knowledge and skills. Students also completed a preliminary self-assessment, using the same assessment instrument completed by their mentors. Over the course of the research projects both students and faculty mentors were asked to keep journals in which they could record their thoughts, questions, and concerns. Students and faculty collaborative activities included mentor-student meetings to compare and discuss initial assessments as well as comparisons and discussions of mid-project and final assessments that were again completed by both the students and their mentors (J. Singer, personal communication, February 5, 2021).

With support from the National Science Foundation's WIDER program (Widening Implementation and Demonstration of Evidence-Based Research) Singer and Weiler, with the collaboration of CUR and technical support from the Science Education Resource Center at Carleton College, refined this evaluation method, now named EvaluateUR, and made it available to institutions across the country. Details about the development of the method are provided in Singer and Weiler (2009), Singer and Zimmerman (2012), and Singer and Mogk (2020).

EvaluateUR consists of 11 outcome categories, each defined by several descriptive behavioral components that are scored using a 5-point rubric based on the frequency of the observed behavior (1=never to 5=always). The 11 outcome categories are:

- communication
- creativity
- autonomy
- ability to deal with obstacles
- intellectual development
- critical thinking and problem-solving
- practice and process of inquiry
- nature of disciplinary knowledge
- content knowledge and methods
- understanding ethical conduct
- career goals

These outcomes are aligned with the Office of Career, Technical, and Adult Education, U.S. Department of Education, and the National Association of Colleges and Employers thereby supporting the concept that undergraduate research develops work-related skills (Perkins Collaborative Resource Network, n.d.). The integration of workforce skills into assessments of undergraduate research experiences provides a significant rationale for further development of student research at community colleges. Campuses that implement EvaluateUR receive significant technical support, access to instructional videos, guides for using EvaluateUR, and its built-in statistical package called EZStats. EvaluateUR is divided into four phases of the research experience, beginning with an initial student reflection on their thoughts about research. Student self-assessments and mentor assessments (using the same assessment components) are completed at the beginning, midpoint, and completion of student research projects. In this design evaluation is part of the research and mentoring process, because student–mentor conversations about their respective assessments are a means to help students reflect on their academic strengths and weaknesses and strengthen their metacognitive skills. Following the completion of each assessment, the student and mentor receive a score report that shows how each scored each item. This report is particularly useful when the student–mentor pairs meet to talk about how the research is progressing. A web-based dashboard provides administrators with up-to-date information on the progress of each student–mentor pair. Students and mentors have their own version of the dashboard showing their progress (e.g., completed steps and steps remaining to be completed). For each student–mentor pair, EZStats generates summary measures that enable undergraduate research directors to easily import outcome data into reports for administrators, faculty, and governing boards or grant proposals.

What sets EvaluateUR from other evaluations of undergraduate research is that students play an active role in the assessment and discussion of the results. In 2019, during the last year of the NSF WIDER award, 37 institutions with 799 student–mentor research pairs implemented EvaluateUR. Summary findings (EvaluateUR, 2020) concluded that:

- The EvaluateUR method introduced students to skills they would need in graduate work or the workplace;
- Students made positive gains on the outcome measures;
- The assessment sequence contributed to the development of students' metacognitive skills;
- Mentors more easily identified student strengths and weaknesses and could see areas where students over- or underestimated their competencies; and
- EvaluateUR provided undergraduate research directors with clear, reliable evidence of the potential benefits of their research programs.

One of the novel features of this approach to evaluation is that it is embedded into the research and mentoring processes, while at the same time generating reliable data that can be used by directors of undergraduate research programs to document their programs' impacts. The method has several strengths for assessment of undergraduate research. It provides students and their mentors with valuable information, can be implemented for all academic disciplines, and a subscription is now available for a modest cost. EvaluateUR (2021) provides extensive resources including instructional videos and guidebooks.

A second version of EvaluateUR supports shorter duration research programs. An adaptation of EvaluateUR for use in classroom-based undergraduate research (CUREs)—known as EvaluateUR-CURE—has been developed and supports one semester and yearlong CUREs. The structure of EvaluateUR-CURE is similar to EvaluateUR and also includes score reports for the students and faculty member teaching the CURE. Resources for EvaluateUR-CURE include instructional videos on its implementation and a series of short activities focusing on metacognition that can be used as assignments or in-class activities. Another adaptation of the method, called Evaluate-Compete, is being developed in collaboration with the Marine Advanced Technology Education (MATE) Center in Monterey, California, for high school and college students participating in its long running Remotely Operated Vehicle (ROV) competitions. EvaluateUR, EvaluateUR-CURE, and Evaluate-Compete are appropriate for undergraduates at all levels (J. Singer, personal communication, March 10, 2021).

## Research Skills Development Framework (RSD)

John Willison and his colleagues at the University of Adelaide developed a program to measure the acquisition of research skills for all disciplines. The Research Skills Development framework (RSD) measures six areas of skill development (Willison, 2018):

- Embark on inquiry and thus determine a need for knowledge/ understanding;
- Find/generate needed information/data using appropriate methodology;
- Critically evaluate this information or data and the process to find or generate it;
- Organize information collected or generated;
- Analyze and synthesize; and
- Communicate knowledge and understanding and the processes used to generate the advances, with an awareness of ethical, social, and cultural issues (p. 7).

The framework has five levels of attainment in each of the six categories that can assess where students begin the process of research skill development and their improvement based on skills in their specific discipline. Willison (2009) suggests that the "framework, used as a conceptual model to inform the explicit and incremental development of student research skills in the curriculum, has proved to be highly flexible, allowing faculty members to adapt it to their disciplinary contexts . . ." (p. 14). The adaptability of the RSD suggests that it can be a useful assessment tool for community colleges. It also has the advantage of making the sequence of skill development explicit when shared with students. When students understand expectations, they tend to perform better and find the learning process more meaningful.

## Survey of Undergraduate Research Experiences and CURE

David Lopatto developed the Survey of Undergraduate Research Experiences (SURE). The survey has 44 items that ask about demographic variables, learning gains, and evaluation of aspects of undergraduate research programs (Lopatto, 2004). While initially designed to measure students' research experiences over the summer, the survey now measures academic-year research. It also offers a preflection or presurvey, a survey administered immediately after the experience, and a follow-up survey administered six to nine months after the experience. The SURE asks questions about the impact of the research experience on future plans and the value of mentoring and its benefits.

Additionally, Lopatto developed a survey for research embedded in a course, CURE. The CURE survey also includes a pre- and postsurvey. The presurvey asks why students are taking the course, student goals, whether they can visualize being a scientist, and life choices after graduation. In 2018, 3400 students took the SURE (Lopatto, 2018). The surveys are available on the Grinnell College website and are free. Designed for science students, approximately 100 community colleges have used either the CURE or SURE survey (D. Lopatto, personal communication, July 30, 2020).

### Undergraduate Research Student Self-Assessment (URSSA)

The Undergraduate Research Student Self-Assessment (URSSA) is a web-based survey to determine what students gain or don't gain from participating in undergraduate research experiences in STEM (Hunter et al., 2009). It also asks what activities contribute to those gains. This survey addresses questions about increases in personal and professional growth, thinking and working like a scientist, demonstrating norms of professional practice in science, career clarification, and career preparation. It has both multiple-choice and open-ended questions. The survey was developed as part of an 8-year study of undergraduate research at four liberal arts colleges. The results of the study are similar to the results of David Lopatto's work. The developers of URSSA suggest that its flexibility allows it to be used in various program types and institutions, though only in STEM. The URSSA is found on the web platform, designed by Elaine Seymour, for the Student Assessment of Learning Gains (n.d.), where directions and additional information about URSSA can be found.

## Program Assessment

Assessment of undergraduate research can include more than evaluating students' experiences in undergraduate research. While I was the executive officer for the CUR, many members asked questions about what are considered the elements of a quality program. CUR decided to take on the task of providing guidance to campuses about the nature of quality undergraduate research programs.

### Characteristics of Excellence in Undergraduate Research

CUR is the leading voice in the United States that advocates for, encourages, and supports the inclusion of student research in the undergraduate experience. With over 30 years of experience providing professional development support for faculty and institutional development support for colleges and universities, it was not until 2011 that CUR began to develop a best practices guide for undergraduate research. *Characteristics of Excellence in Undergraduate Research* (COEUR), compiled by Roger Rowlett, Linda Blockus, and Susan Larson, and based on CUR's 7000 members' best thinking is the result (Hensel, 2012). The characteristics of excellence emerged from CUR's experience with successful and mature programs. While not an assessment instrument, COEUR is a roadmap for institutions that are just beginning to design their programs and a guide for campuses that want to expand and improve their programs. The framework outlines important programmatic areas in:

- Campus Mission and Culture
- Administrative Support
- Research Infrastructure
- Professional Development Opportunities
- Recognition
- External Funding; Dissemination
- Student-centered Issues; Curriculum
- Summer Research Program
- Assessment Activities
- Strategic Planning

The document does not offer qualitative or quantitative measures. It is designed to allow small colleges and large research universities to use it. The item for scholarly activity, for example, suggests that a thriving undergraduate research environment needs an institutional commitment to scholarly activity but does not specify number of publications or presentations. The document is available to be downloaded from the CUR website (Hensel, 2012). The COEUR has also led to an annual award given to institutions for excellence in undergraduate research, AURA (Award for Undergraduate Research Accomplishments).

### Community College Undergraduate Research Assessment: City University of New York (CUNY)

For several years, the CUNY system has been a leading force in promoting undergraduate research at 2-year colleges. In 2014 CUNY initiated the CUNY Scholars Research Program, known as CRSP. The program involves between 220 and 240 students per year. Although CRSP is a decentralized program, the 2-year campuses follow a standard set of guidelines requiring each CRSP student to receive 400 hours of mentored research support in STEM over the academic year. Also, students receive a $5,000 stipend for program participation. The CUNY Office of Research initiated a longitudinal study of the first 3 years (2014–2017) of the CRSP program to determine whether the impact of a 1-year research experience yielded results similar to the effect on 4-year students' success (Nerio et al., 2019). The study involved a quantitative longitudinal analysis of student outcomes that included the SURE survey adapted for community college students and a survey developed for program students, focus groups with faculty mentors, and outcome measures. The study compared students enrolled in CRSP with a propensity-score matched group of students who did not participate in CRSP.

The treatment group and the comparison group were composed of students from all of the CRSP campuses. The analytic data included demographic characteristics (gender, race/ethnicity, age), enrollment features (class standing, full-time/part-time status), and academic background and standing (high school grade point average, cumulative credits earned, initial remedial status). The results indicate a generally positive impact for retention and graduation rate, with CRSP students significantly more likely to graduate than their counterparts in the comparison group. Disaggregation of data shows that male and female CRSP students had similar graduation rates, and both males and females in the comparison group had slightly lower graduation rates. When disaggregated for ethnicity, the data show little difference between CRSP students and control group students for Asian, Black, or Latinx students. Still, White students in the comparison group were less likely to graduate than CRSP students. The study also found that when students transferred to a 4-year college, more than half the CRSP students, compared to 31% in the nontreatment group, transferred to research universities within the CUNY system. Of the students who transferred externally, a significantly high percentage of CRSP students (70%) entered major research universities relative to members of the comparison group (39%).

Nearly two-thirds of CRSP students reported feeling "comfortable" or "at home" after participating in the CRSP program while only 27% reported feeling so before they entered the program. It may be that faculty mentorship contributed significantly to the feeling of belonging. Faculty mentors commented that the CRSP program helped students to see themselves as scholars and scientists. Mentors reported that the yearlong duration of the program was also a major factor in supporting student success.

This study has made a significant contribution to the literature on undergraduate research at community colleges. It is one of the largest and most comprehensive investigations of the effect of undergraduate research on community college students to date.

## Developing a Plan

There are various considerations when developing a campus plan to assess undergraduate research, but time and cost are primary. Many campuses do not have the funds to do assessments similar to what the CUNY system conducted or the time and personnel to use the SURE/CURE/URSSA, RSD, or EvaluateUR programs. So, what can they do? The spring 2012 *CUR Quarterly* includes several articles on "how to count students in a way that provides both accountability and value to those using the derived number" (Blockus, 2012). In developing an accountability response, every campus needs to have a standard definition for undergraduate research that is broad enough to apply to all disciplines but also specific enough to give guidance to faculty about how to apply the definition.

Administrators, funders, and faculty want to know how many students and faculty on campus are engaged in mentored student research. They also want to know about the quality of student experiences. The numbers can't directly tell you about quality, but quality indicators can be extrapolated from the figures. As a first step, it is useful to have information about the number of students participating in undergraduate research activities; however, gathering this information is complicated.

Some community college systems and individual campuses have tried to gather this information by identifying undergraduate research courses. A clear definition of undergraduate research is the starting point. The TBR developed a taxonomy of undergraduate research. The TBR adapted the CUR definition of *undergraduate research* to fit the needs of its campuses:

> Undergraduate research is an inquiry or investigation conducted by an undergraduate student in collaboration with a faculty member that makes a unique intellectual, scholarly, or creative contribution to the discipline, and for which the student receives academic credit either through a course of independent study. The student's contribution may be part of a new or ongoing faculty research project. (TBR, n.d., para. 1)

Tennessee uses the taxonomy to determine how many courses include undergraduate research in the curriculum and the depth of undergraduate research experiences at system campuses. The taxonomy looks at nine areas:

- faculty commitment
- infrastructure
- curriculum integration
- scope and scale of activities

- scale
- duration/time
- integration with other high-impact practices
- equity in access
- campus assessment plan (Tennessee Board of Regents, n.d.)

There are three levels or milestones for each area. A campus may want to develop its framework, taxonomy, and definition to maintain consistency in what counts.

A campus assessment plan might include using either the free Lopatto SURE/CURE surveys or the URSSA survey available on their respective websites. A campus might also consider the EvaluateUR that is relatively inexpensive and includes all disciplines. Additionally, colleges may want to use more informal accountability measures.

## Informal Assessment

Campus undergraduate research activities can be reviewed to provide indicators of the extent and effectiveness of the student research program. Collecting data on these activities and noting changes can evolve into an informal evaluation of the campus's undergraduate research program.

### Celebration Days

Looking at trends in the number and breadth of presentations at undergraduate research celebration days can suggest an increase in student research activity and the inclusion of more disciplines. Many campuses have found that celebration days create more desire for faculty and students to engage in undergraduate research. Increasing the number of faculty listed as student mentors and more posters from the humanities, social sciences, and natural sciences indicate that undergraduate research is spreading across campus and becoming more deeply embedded in the culture.

### Participation in Conferences

Several conferences are either specifically designed for student presentations or are professional associations that make space in the program for student presentations. The National Conferences on Undergraduate Research (NCUR), hosted by (CUR) is an annual gathering of more than 4,000 attendees each spring. The event welcomes presenters from all institutions of higher learning and from all disciplines. Students from across the globe present their research and creative activity through posters, oral presentations, visual arts, and artistic performances. It is an ideal conference for students' first presentations. Responding to questions from peers and faculty from different universities is an affirming experience for novice student researchers. Each year CUR hosts Posters on the Hill, which is CUR's annual advocacy event. Students present their research and share their experiences with members of Congress to support the message of the importance of undergraduate research funding at the federal level. As a highly competitive event, acceptance for presenting at Posters on the Hill makes it an indicator of quality. Oklahoma and a few other states have state capitol poster events, and also have a competitive process for poster presentations.

Professional associations in STEM, political science, and psychology designate conference program space for undergraduate research. Other organizations are considering adding undergraduate space for posters or presentations. Regional disciplinary conferences are another venue for student posters and oral presentations and are closer to the campus, reducing travel expenses. Some states or districts, such as California, CUNY, Maricopa, Oklahoma, and Tennessee, host conferences for all students in the district, system or state. Often conferences that include student research give awards for best posters, a further indication of a quality program. Several conferences were offered virtually in 2020 and early 2021 in response to COVID-19 restrictions. Some of those conferences may continue the virtual format as it allows for greater participation and eliminates travel costs.

## Publications

Many campuses publish honors journals that are peer-reviewed. The number of accepted articles about undergraduate research projects provides evidence of the prevalence and quality of campus student research efforts. CUR has a list of approximately 245 journals that accept student work from all campuses and a variety of disciplines. *STAR Journal* (n.d.)—Social Science Texts and Academic Research—is an example of a publication designed specifically for community college students in the social sciences. Anoka-Ramsay Community College, the publisher, opens the journal to students from all community colleges. Articles coauthored by students and faculty are additional evidence of the robustness of undergraduate research on campus. Many professional journals now accept coauthored manuscripts, and acceptance indicates the quality of the research and communication of the results. Coauthorship is especially encouraged when faculty promotion and tenure guidelines recognize the value of student/faculty publications.

## *Grant Success*

External funding is another indicator of strong undergraduate research programs. Writing a proposal encourages the campus to take stock of progress in developing a robust undergraduate research program. Grant writing also provides an opportunity to strategically plan for next steps. Success in proposal writing often indicates program quality.

Funding opportunities for undergraduate research at community colleges are expanding. CUR-E News includes information about funding opportunities for undergraduate research for members (see www.cur.org).

The NSF offers the following programs available to 2-year colleges:

- Advanced Technological Education (ATE). This program supports partnerships between academic institutions and employers to improve STEM education. It also supports curriculum development.
- Scholarships-in-Science, Technology, Engineering, and Mathematics (S-STEM). This program supports scholarships for needy students who are academically talented and want to enter the STEM workforce.
- Improving Undergraduate STEM Education (IUSE). The focus of this program is to improve the quality of STEM education. It was formerly the TUES program.
- Tribal Colleges and Universities Program (TCUP). The focus of this program is to strengthen teaching and learning in STEM at tribal colleges.
- Centers of Research Excellence in Science and Technology (CREST). This program provides support to enhance minority-serving institutions' research capabilities through the establishment of centers that effectively integrate education and research.
- Research in Undergraduate Institutions (RUI) and Research Opportunity Awards (ROA). These programs provide funding opportunities to support research by faculty members at predominantly undergraduate institutions.

In addition to these programs, NSF recently introduced the ATE-URE program. This new program resulted from the Undergraduate Research Summit that NSF, American Association of Community Colleges, and CUR hosted in November 2019. The new funding program is available to grantees with an active ATE award, and it supports undergraduate research experiences as part of ATE projects. In addition to supporting research experiences, ATE-URE projects must also promote workforce preparation for students at 2-year institutions.

Other federal agencies, such as the National Institutes of Health (NIH), the Department of Education, and the Department of Energy (DOE), offer grant programs that are available to community colleges.

## Electronic Portfolios

Portfolios can provide insight into how students are understanding and perceiving curriculum, pedagogy, and mentoring. Such insights contribute to other assessment information. LGCC received a Fund for Improving Post-Secondary Education (FIPSE) grant to develop the use of ePortfolios on its campus and to link their efforts with 24 other institutions, including several in the CUNY system. The project asked, "What difference can ePortfolio make?" and "What does it take for an ePortfolio to make a difference?" (Eynon et al. 2014). In answer to the first question, Eynon et al. found that incorporating ePortfolios into the student experience has a positive impact on student success when measured by GPA, pass rates, and retention rates. ePortfolios contribute to student success in several ways. Eynon et al. view ePortfolios as a high-impact practice (HIP). They suggest that the use of ePortfolios be combined with other HIPs such as 1st-year seminars and undergraduate research. Some of the campuses involved in the FIPSE project felt that their success rate resulted from using ePortfolios and other HIPs.

The design of the ePortfolio is a critical factor for enhancing student learning. LGCC and other CUNY community colleges view the ePortfolio as a guided process for students to reflect on their goals and learning in and out of the classroom. Students reflect on several questions such as "Who Am I?," "Who Am I Becoming?," and "Who Do I Dare to Be?" (Eynon & Gambino, 2017, p. 11). The particular advantage of ePortfolios for community college students is that portfolios make the learning process visible to students and professors. Students can see their progress in academic skills through the sequential entry of documents to the portfolio. Faculty can see, from the reflective entries, areas where students may be having difficulty and also areas of particular interest that are leading to success. Portfolios can guide students to see connections across courses and disciplines and connect with their future work. They can also foster further inquiry about course content and applications and the integration of concepts across disciplines. There are many approaches to student portfolios, but with careful design and mentoring, portfolios can be part of the campuses' informal assessment plan.

## Faculty Evaluation

Undergraduate research involves active, engaged learning. It is a collaborative process between students and professors. When the curriculum includes project-based, inquiry-based, and research-based learning, the professor's role is no longer that of lecturer and presenter of content. In this approach, students need to take more responsibility for their learning process. The evaluation of faculty by students must reflect this change in the student/professor relationship. Student evaluations of faculty teaching provide information about how students are learning and what teaching strategies are effective when the questions on evaluation surveys reflect the pedagogical change in the student/professor relationship. Students can be asked to reflect on their learning process, their contributions to the class, their own learning, and their classmates learning. An evaluation process that reflects the new dynamics of student learning might address topics such as questions about how students fulfilled their responsibilities as part of a learning community, whether they talked about the subject matter outside of class with their peers, and if they sought reading materials beyond what was assigned. Faculty also might want to ask students what contributed to their understanding of the course's key concepts and if they changed their assumptions about the material as a result of class discussions (Hensel et al., 2015). An evaluation that encourages students to be responsible for their learning and reflect on the learning process can provide valuable information to the course instructor about how students are receiving the course and how they are learning. A more holistic evaluation process can also encourage students to be more thoughtful about how they learn.

Ultimately, the purpose of assessment is to understand and enrich student learning, enhance teaching, and advance the undergraduate research program. Finding a way to assess these areas that is compatible with institutional resources and campus culture is critical for continuous improvement. When faculty, students and administrators perceive value from the assessment process, the process can be met with interest and enthusiasm.

## Additional Resources

Mary Crowe and David Brakke periodically do a review of the literature and annotated bibliography on assessing undergraduate research. For additional resources see Crowe and Brakke, 2008, 2019.

Another excellent source of assessment information is Roman Taraban & Richard L. Blanton (2008). *Creating Effective Undergraduate Research Program in Science: The Transformation from Student to Scientist.*

# 12

# ADVANCING
# UNDERGRADUATE RESEARCH

When CUR and the National Council on Instructional Administrators began our six regional conversations with community colleges in 2006 we did not know how widespread undergraduate research was at 2-year colleges. At the completion of the conversations in 2007 we felt that undergraduate research was an emerging pedagogy at some community colleges. Since then there has been a confluence of events that suggest undergraduate research is now far more prevalent across community colleges. CUR's 2009 NSF grant engaged 380 professors from 95 colleges around the country in workshops to develop undergraduate research programs. In previous chapters, faculty who participated in the workshops described how they were inspired to engage their students in research and continue to do so.

With a small NSF grant in 2005, James Hewlett began a pilot project to integrate undergraduate research into the FLCC curriculum (Patton, 2019). Hewlett received two additional NSF grants that significantly moved forward undergraduate research at 2-year colleges. A Course, Curriculum, Laboratory Improvement grant (#0816515) provided funds to develop a model for integrating undergraduate research into the curriculum. It included five community colleges, one 4-year college, four environmental research organizations, and a state government agency. The grant led to establishing the CCURI. A 2011 Transforming Undergraduate Education in STEM (#1118679) grant for $3.64 million was the only biology and community college initiative to receive funding from the highly competitive TUES Type III program (Patton, 2019). The NSF funding supported the expansion of CCURI to 27 colleges. The grant also signaled NSF's recognition of the significance of undergraduate research at community colleges. Through grant activities,

CCCURI identified barriers to undergraduate research, investigated the impact of research experiences on students, and the effect of the CCURI program on STEM teaching. Since the TUES grant, CCURI has received additional funding from NSF and other agencies. (Patton, 2019). CCURI now has a national network of over 120 community colleges in 39 states (J. Hewlett, personal communication, October 21, 2020). CCURI is currently leveraging its large network of institutions to better understand the critical forces involved in the development of an undergraduate research culture at a community college.

In 2010 the Association of American Colleges and Universities (AAC&U) expanded its Liberal Education and America's Promise (LEAP) program to include a community college roadmap for student success and degree completion. The Roadmap project initially invited 12 community colleges to participate and added nine campuses in 2013. The project focused on inclusive excellence and engagement in undergraduate research and other high-impact practices. Student success was defined as achievement of essential learning outcomes and degree or certificate completion. The program emphasizes collaboration between academics and student affairs, a clear and comprehensive pathway for student success, use of high-impact practices including undergraduate research, and assessment to measure the quality of learning and student outcomes (AAC&U, 2014). With support from the Bill & Melinda Gates Foundation and Acsendium Education Group, AAC&U has expanded its work with community colleges. In collaboration with the Center for Community College Student Engagement, AAC&U has involved 20 community colleges in a project to strengthen student learning through Guided Pathways.

The NSF and the American Association of Community Colleges (AACC) hosted a Summit on Community Colleges and Undergraduate Research in November 2019. V. Celeste Carter, lead NSF ATE program director, in her Summit remarks, said NSF made the "first ATE award to explore the use of undergraduate research experiences (UREs) at community colleges to the Council on Undergraduate Research" (Patton & Hause, 2020, p. 4). When CUR applied for the 2005 ATE grant, the proposal did not fit the ATE guidelines, so we were surprised and pleased when we received funding. Undergraduate research has become a vital part of the student experience at colleges across the country. The NSF and the AACC acknowledged the significant role of undergraduate research when they convened the Community College Undergraduate Research Experience Summit. The summit's purpose was to accelerate the value and impact of community colleges in STEM workforce development and to raise awareness about the effectiveness of undergraduate research. One result of the summit was the issuing of a March 6, 2020, Dear Colleague Letter inviting current ATE grantees to request supplemental funding to support UREs that promote workforce preparation for community college students (Patton & Hause, 2020). The letter from Karen Marrongelle, assistant director of the NSF Education and Human Resources Directorate, invited requests for supplemental funding that supports UREs for up to 20% of the original ATE grant. The requests need to address the "development and implementation of undergraduate science, technology, engineering and mathematics (STEM) research experiences in the context of ATE projects" (Marrongelle, 2020). Including undergraduate research in the ATE program, a program focused on technician training, is an indication that undergraduate research is viewed as a significant learning strategy for community college students in technical programs as well as transfer programs.

## Challenges to Expanding Undergraduate Research

Even with support from organizations like CUR, AACC, and CCURI and funders like NSF, there remain many challenges to provide undergraduate experiences for all students. Funding is a significant challenge and since most of the available funding is in STEM, other disciplines face an even greater challenge. When CUR offered regional workshops to reach 380 professors, participants had to be in areas funded by NSF. We hoped that if science departments developed robust undergraduate research programs, humanities and social science departments would also begin to offer their students research experiences. This is happening. The interviews in earlier chapters confirm that humanities and social science faculty are involving their students in research.

Despite the visible success of spreading undergraduate research to all community colleges, many barriers remain. Among the obstacles identified at the summit are time, financial, space/college infrastructure, and institutional administration. Specifically, community college faculty have high teaching loads, lack of reassigned time for curricular revision, limited travel funds for faculty and students for undergraduate research conferences, and sometimes lack of funds for equipment, materials, and supplies. STEM laboratories may lack equipment and dedicated laboratory space for student research may not be available. The faculty I interviewed frequently commented that undergraduate research takes more time but it is also very rewarding. Many also commented that travel funds were sparse for faculty and students. When I visited QCC and Estrella Mountain Community College, I saw their new science laboratories with up-to-date equipment and space for students to do research. Other campuses are also finding ways to enhance laboratory space for undergraduate research as they increase their understanding of the impact of undergraduate research on student achievement.

There are also challenges in working with the community college student population that are different from challenges at four-year institutions. Community college students are often unaware of the availability and benefits of undergraduate research. Many students have limited time for research outside of class because they have jobs and families. In addition, financial aid restrictions and credit limit regulations are barriers when the research experience appears outside of course work required for a specific degree program (J. Hewlett, personal communication, October 21, 2020). Commuting time to campus is sometimes a hurdle for students. Spending 2 years as opposed to 4 years on a campus means undergraduate research needs to start in the freshman year. Since many students transfer after degree completion, faculty do not reap the benefits of trained research students who can engage in more sophisticated research in their senior year.

Another challenge that I heard from many professors is that the public perceives community colleges as teaching institutions and the students who attend community colleges as less able than students who begin their college education at 4-year institutions. Several faculty also told me that they were often asked, "why aren't you teaching at a 4-year college?" Their response was that they loved the work they were doing and were enthusiastic about teaching and student research at a community college.

Despite these challenges, community colleges are increasing both the number of students and the disciplines involved in research. Providing student research opportunities is a substantial commitment toward educational equity. As institutions and faculty work to overcome the barriers to involving students in research, they are motivated by how research inspires student achievement. They are also disproving a commonly held view that community colleges are second-class institutions.

## Promising Practices for Advancing Undergraduate Research

There are several promising practices for expanding undergraduate research opportunities. Certainly, the CCURI approach and the support provided by the organization to faculty is a significant factor in the growth of undergraduate research. In my interviews with faculty and administrators, I encountered additional promising practices; some were system-wide and others were single campus initiatives.

## *Financial Support*

The CUNY system has perhaps the most robust financial support for undergraduate research of any system in the country. CUNY's CRSP program provides $5,000 per year to students who participate in mentored research with a professor. While a small program and only for science research, it has given visibility to undergraduate research and its benefits for students. CUNY provides other smaller grants for faculty who work with students in research. These efforts help to expand undergraduate research to additional disciplines and make research available for more students.

Not every system or campus can afford the kind of financial support that the CUNY system provides. However, other systems and campuses also provide small grants to support research. For example, Maricopa Community College District recently provided $15,000 for undergraduate research to Estrella Mountain Community College. Including funds, even if small, into the annual budget for equipment, materials, and travel communicates strong administrative support for UREs.

External funding to support undergraduate research can be found from various sources. Community colleges are becoming more active in seeking federal funding to support student research. The NSF, National Institutes of Health, and Department of Energy are examples of federal agencies that offer grants to community colleges for student research. Funding can also come from a charitable organization. TCC benefited by support from a local organization, the George Kaiser Family Foundation, for an endowed chair. The endowed chair provided Diana Spencer time to work with faculty to further expand TCC's growing undergraduate research initiative (personal communication, D. Spencer, October 23, 2020).

Charitable donations to community colleges are on the rise and the size of gifts has grown substantially. Donors are giving more million-dollar gifts to community colleges and are attracted to the work-force education mission (Di Mento & Theis, 2019). A survey of 104 community colleges by the Council for Advancement and Support for Education (CASE) reported an eight percent increase in private gifts in 2018 (Piper, 2019). Kristin Bennett, vice president for institutional advancement and executive director of the foundation at Trinity Valley Community College, is quoted by Piper, saying that every dollar gift to a community college is similar in campus value to $100 for a 4-year college. The Jay Pritzker Foundation recently gave $100 million to the California Community College Foundation (Los Angeles Times, October 20, 2020). McKenzie Scott recently gave $4.2 billion to colleges and universities, including 12 community colleges. The Borough of Manhattan Community College received $30 million (Redden, 2020).

CASE now offers an annual advancement conference for community colleges. Fund raising is typically used for scholarships and infrastructure, however, donors may also be interested in supporting undergraduate research. Many donors like to see directly where their money is going, and they enjoy meeting student researchers. Supporting laboratory equipment, a research project, or student travel gives donors the opportunity to see the power of their donation. Soliciting support for undergraduate research is a way to engage new donors or smaller donations that might eventually lead to larger donations. Though small, such donations can have a huge impact on the undergraduate research program.

## *Communities of Practice*

Colleague support is a critical factor for broadly implementing pedagogical changes. Knowing that other professors may be struggling with a similar problem opens up discussions that can lead to solutions and decrease barriers to successful change and innovation (Lopatto et al. 2012). The CCURI is a national community of practice for member campuses. Diana Spencer said that the national network "constantly worked together to solve problems of research in the classroom." CCURI's recent biennial meeting expanded the community of learning to include students.

In addition to participation in CCURI, TCC's successful undergraduate research program can be attributed to the campus's community of practice. When Spencer was selected for the undergraduate research chair, she brought together faculty from all departments to talk about how they could engage students in research. She encouraged them to "think outside the box" and how they might work together to develop cross-disciplinary research projects. Faculty enjoyed the gatherings and developed several interdisciplinary undergraduate research projects. Relationships established through the community of practice provided support for faculty who were trying new approaches to teaching. In addition to the benefits undergraduate research affords students, faculty also benefit. Spencer commented that,

> UR allowed me as faculty to participate in current, novel research—often developing techniques that I had not completed in my doctoral program. It stretched me, and my brain and capabilities which kept me engaged and excited about the classroom. And the sweetest spot is when I would find myself WITH my students analyzing data that did not present as expected. At that moment, the faculty member and students became instant colleagues in deciphering the meaning of the data. I was inspired and energized by the work. (D. Spencer, personal communication, October 23, 2020)

Spencer captures the feelings that many faculty have when working with students on a research project.

Colleague support can be built into campus culture. Gita Bangera is the founding dean of Bellevue College's Research, Innovation, Service and Experiential Learning Institute (RISE). Initially RISE's goal was to encourage and support the implementation of student research. It now includes Bellevue's Center for Career Connections and service learning. RISE developed from an NSF funded research program, the Community College Genomics Research Initiative (ComGen). ComGen was an effort to embed authentic research into a biology course. ComGen led to establishing learning communities across campus to support undergraduate research, project-based learning, and service learning that are now coordinated by RISE and Bellevue Undergraduate Research. RISE has a goal of involving 1,000 students in course-based research. In 2018–2019, 800 students and 11 faculty representing four disciplines participated in undergraduate research (G. Bangera, C. Vermilyea, M. Reese, & I. Shaver, personal communication, n.d.). Bangera and her colleagues analyzed the RISE Institute's efforts and identified what they called the "squiggle" or the failures that ultimately led to successfully institutionalizing undergraduate research. Some of the levers of positive change were:

- Funding allows for the freedom to pilot and increases the speed and scale of innovation.
- Shared purpose and narrating the benefits of change is important to innovation.
- Working within current structures is the means for outreach and allows for faculty-driven change.
- The Faculty Learning Committee reduced barriers to change and also facilitated the use of previously successful approaches, lessons learned, and assessment across projects.
- Strategic administrative support was important for providing standing for the change.

RISE is now in the process of spreading lessons learned and the concept of course embedded research to other community colleges in the Washington state system.

## Course-Based Research

As faculty and administrators recognize how students benefit from undergraduate research experiences, they also realize that the traditional model of undergraduate research experiences (URE) limit student participation in research. The traditional apprentice model assumes that students have time to participate in research projects outside of class or in the summer. This is not possible for many community college students because of work and family responsibilities. Course-based research addresses this issue. Embedding research in the course curriculum allows every student in the class to participate in research. Ensuring that all students have an opportunity to participate in a URE is an equity issue. Carnevale and Strohl's (2013) report, *Separate and Unequal: How Higher Education Reinforces the Intergeneration Reproduction of White Privilege*, suggests that access is not sufficient to address higher education's inequities. They believe that the pedagogy must also change to become more inclusive for first-generation and minoritized students. The professors highlighted in the course-based research chapter and other chapters are making the curriculum and pedagogy more inclusive. Involving a whole class of beginning students in research requires an inventive approach about how to scaffold research skills, find projects that can engage simultaneously 20 to 30 students, how to manage preparation and class time, and identify affordable resources.

When CUR began talking about undergraduate research at community colleges, we heard comments that 1st- and 2nd-year students don't know enough to do research. Community college professors have proven the naysayers wrong and are leading the way for 4-year institutions to begin undergraduate research in the first year. Professors are progressively introducing students to the research methodology of the discipline. Students learn how to do a literature review, the difference between primary and secondary documents, and how to cite references and avoid plagiarism. They also learn how to observe and how to frame a researchable question. They may also begin to see connections and develop an understanding of what counts as evidence. We also heard that community colleges lack the resources for student research, especially in STEM. Again, community college professors addressed the problem. Mary Ortiz involves her students in research on birds, a readily available resource. When COVID-19 prevented students from doing their fieldwork, she modified the course to have students observe vertebrates from their home or another safe location. Ortiz said that students were fully engaged in the research and several requested letters of recommendation for summer research internships (M. Ortiz, March 14, 2021). Dorina Tila uses national data banks to engage her students in economic research, thereby introducing students to a wealth of available information. Jane Weiss uses Project Gutenberg for free literary resources. And Mary Gatta and Kristina Baines use New York City for their student research projects. Often local resources become the basis of research embedded in the curriculum. Sometimes local or national citizen science projects become valuable research sources. These professors and others I interviewed are extraordinarily resourceful in finding ways to engage students in research.

Course-based research can also include basic/applied, interdisciplinary, community-based, and partner research. The traditional apprentice model for undergraduate research is a respected model and it can be especially beneficial for students who are interested in pursuing continued work in the discipline. However, embedding research into the curriculum for a whole class is the only way to make research available to all students. It is a particularly constructive teaching and learning strategy for beginning students as it inspires students to think of themselves as scholars and it may encourage students to continue their education. For all students, the skills developed through research will be useful in future employment and civic engagement.

## *Celebrations*

Celebrations or conferences presenting the results of student research have been part of undergraduate research for many years. Community colleges are not an exception. Undergraduate research conferences are important for several reasons. They give students an opportunity to share their work and receive feedback. They also give visibility to undergraduate research and student work. Some conferences are specifically for community college students and other conferences are open to all students. The Honors Transfer Council in California hosts two conferences each year for community college students who wish to transfer to a 4-year university. The southern conference is hosted by the University of California, Irvine. The northern conference is hosted by the University of California, Berkeley. Another conference in California, Southern California Conference on Undergraduate Research (SCCUR), is offered annually on a California campus. SCCUR is open to all students in all disciplines and community colleges are typically well represented. When students have an opportunity to attend a conference at a 4-year college or research university, they see possibilities for transfer. Estrella Mountain Community College in Arizona hosts a conference each year that is open to all students in the Maricopa Community College District. Oklahoma Research Day is an annual event cohosted by Oklahoma EPSCoR and the Oklahoma State Regents for Higher Education. It is open to all students. The administrative support for Oklahoma Research Day is noteworthy and central administration personnel attend the conference. Oklahoma also hosts a research day at the state legislature and a legislator gives out awards for outstanding student research.

CRSP students at CUNY have an opportunity to present their research at the system's summer conference. The CUNY Research Scholars Program was entirely virtual in 2020 because of COVID-19 restrictions. There were several advantages to this format because all students were able to present publicly by recording their presentations, which are available on YouTube. The judges also had more time to provide individual feedback to each presenter. The virtual conference suggested other possibilities for program expansion to conduct cross-college workshops throughout the year.

Individual campuses also have celebration days. They may invite the community or state legislators to attend. Walters State Community College in Tennessee hosts a virtual conference that connects students to other student researchers and professional researchers all over the world.

The National Conference on Undergraduate Research is an excellent opportunity for students to present their work and see what students at other colleges and universities are doing. For community college students the NCUR conference may suggest possibilities for transfer after completing their 2-year degree.

Undergraduate conferences and celebration days are a way for students to gain public speaking experience, receive feedback on their research, and possibly make contacts for transfer or graduate school. The increasing number of undergraduate research conferences, especially those specifically for community colleges students, is an indication of the growing recognition that undergraduate research at community colleges is a significant part of the student experience.


## Promotion and Tenure

Recognizing undergraduate research in the retention, tenure, and promotion process has met with resistance at some 4-year colleges and universities. There is the challenge about how to categorize undergraduate research. Is it teaching or maybe service? Can it be considered scholarship? Are articles coauthored with students as worthy of consideration in promotion decisions as articles coauthored with peers? Because supervising student research is often outside of the traditional faculty workload of teaching, campus service, and research, it is crucial that it is recognized in the faculty evaluation process. Community colleges are looking for ways to support research through various workload adjustments. For example, FLCC initially allowed 5 hours of teaching time for faculty who are doing research until student research became integrated into the curriculum. Once introductory science courses or other courses engaged students in research, the buying out of 5 hours of teaching time was no longer necessary (J. Hewlett, personal communication, February 26, 2021).

Four-year institutions with robust undergraduate research programs have successfully advocated for various ways to recognize student research in the faculty review process (Flaherty, 2014). Expectations for retention, promotion, and tenure for community colleges are not typically the same as expectations for 4-year faculty. The CUNY system, which includes 4-year universities, has essentially the same promotion and tenure expectations for 2-year and 4-year faculty. It is likely that CUNY's expectations for faculty research and publication have encouraged undergraduate research in the 2-year institutions. While the CUNY system guidelines reflect traditional 4-year promotion and tenure criteria, this is not necessary for community colleges and may not be appropriate for other campuses. However, not requiring research and publications does not mean that such work shouldn't be recognized in faculty evaluation.

Community colleges may be moving to recognize supervision of student research. For example, TCC recently created full professorships and a process for becoming a full professor. When TCC created the full professor position, they had to develop criteria for promotion to full professor. The process they created is unique and it is also reflective of campus values. Professors requesting promotion to full professor need to demonstrate active engagement in consistent service to the college, professional development, and collaboration with others (D. Deibert, personal communication, October 22, 2020). In addition, and perhaps most interesting and innovative, they also need to participate in an *action research* project that is described in the TCC (2020) Faculty Handbook as:

> Action Research is an essential component of professional development for faculty who wish to be promoted. It is a scholarly and project-based approach to improve teaching and learning within the context of individual faculty practices inside and outside the classroom. Candidates for the rank of professor should conduct two cycles of action research and complete a scholarly, academic paper as the final product of the research process. (p. 55)

Debbie Deibert was instrumental in developing the criteria for promotion to full-professor and the action research requirement is based on her research with students. She indicated that several faculty have gone through the promotion process. Some successfully completed the action research part of the process while others found it challenging (D. Deibert, personal communication, September 20, 2020). The faculty evaluation process not only values undergraduate research but it also encourages research and reflective teaching.

## Administrative Support

Support of the system office is a critical factor in the success of undergraduate research at the campus level. In addition to the funding that some systems have made available to campuses, supporting programs and conferences is another example of strong support. Oklahoma Research Day involves all 2-year and 4-year campuses in the state and it brings together students, faculty, and administrators. CUNY's Pressing Public Issues forum identifies current issues of concern to New York City and recognizes and promotes the importance of public scholarship. The TBR and system office sponsor annual professional development faculty workshops on high-impact practices. Several community colleges I visited are institutional members of CUR and are able to take advantage of CUR's workshops on curriculum, pedagogy, and grant-writing. Institutional membership provides an electronic subscription to CUR's journal for all campus faculty. CUR offers systems a special rate for a system membership, and this would help expand involvement in undergraduate research.

The results of the 2020 presidential election are promising for undergraduate research and recognition of the value of community colleges. We now have a First Lady of the United States who is an energetic and strong advocate for community colleges and free tuition and is continuing her career as a professor of English at Northern Virginia Community College. The new secretary of education, Miguel Cardona, has also expressed support for free community college tuition, and said, "Our community colleges are gems that are not looked at as the gems they are" (Murakami, 2021).

## Final Thoughts

When Brent Cejda and I edited the monograph about the 2005 NSF ATE project (2009), we wrote that there were several issues community colleges needed to consider regarding their teaching mission and student research. We suggested institutions needed to think about how undergraduate research could become part of the student experience without resulting in unsustainable added costs and burdens. Initially, some workshop participants saw research as a distraction, but others were convinced that authentic, hands-on research is teaching. Community college perceptions about student research have evolved since 2005 into greater acceptance of students' capacity for research and its' value in the learning process.

The faculty I interviewed and their institutions see student research as teaching and they recognize its importance for students who wish to earn a 4-year or graduate degree and also for those entering a career. While challenges remain for faculty and institutions regarding full implementation of undergraduate research, the commitment to undergraduate research experiences is growing and the challenges are becoming less daunting. Based on the faculty I met as I wrote this book and the campuses I visited, I think that undergraduate research has reached the tipping point and in the future will be widespread across the majority of community colleges. If this is the case, students will be better prepared to think critically and creatively about contemporary issues such as climate change, health care, racial and economic equity, and an evolving knowledge economy. They will understand that there are no easy answers to society's challenges but they will know that objective observations, asking audacious questions, thinking about connections, and considering evidence is the process for finding solutions. Our communities can thrive when we have young people prepared to be the change agents we need.

# REFERENCES

Abul, K., Misir, A., & Buyuk, A. (2018). Art in science: Jusepe de Ribera's puzzle in the clubfoot. *Clinical Orthopaedics and Related Research, 476*, 942–945. https://www.semanticscholar.org/paper/Art-in-Science%3A-Jusepe-de-Ribera%27s-Puzzle-in-The-Abul-Misir/256dedd64cf60d545362770711b91cfe73c96590

Academic Success & Professional Development. *Home page.* http://aar.faculty.asu.edu/asap/index.html

Agrawal, N. (2020, October 20). Historic $100 million gift will help California community college students most in need. *Los Angeles Times.* https://www.latimes.com/california/story/2020-10-20/california-community-colleges-announce-100-million-gift-largest-ever-in-nation

Alrubail, R. (2016, January 16). Being mindful of cultural differences. *Student Voices.* https://mystudentvoices.com/being-mindful-of-cultural-differences-48c59e4d6ff5

American Academy of Arts and Sciences. (2014, September). *The vital role of research in preserving the American dream.* https://www.amacad.org/publication/restoring-foundation-vital-role-research-preserving-american-dream

American Association for the Advancement of Science. (2011). *Vision and change in undergraduate biology education: A call to action.* https://live-visionandchange.pantheonsite.io/wp-content/uploads/2013/11/aaas-VISchange-web1113.pdf

American Association of Community Colleges, (2021). *Fact sheet.* https://www.aacu.nche.edu/research-trends/fast-facts/

Anagnostopoulou, C., & Buteau, C. (2010). Can computational music analysis be both musical and computational? *Journal of Mathematics and Music, 4*(2), 75–83. https://www.tandfonline.com/doi/pdf/10.1080/17459737.2010.520455?needAccess=true.reve

Architexture Dance Company. (2017a). *About.* www.architexturedance.org/about.html

Architexture Dance Company. (2017b). *Ice memory.* www.architexturedance.org/ice-memory.html

Argonne National Laboratory. (n.d.). *Educational programs and outreach.* www.anl.gov/education

Aspirnaut. (2020). *Undergraduate summer research internships.* https://aspirnaut.org/undergraduateinternships/

Association of American Colleges & Universities. (2014). *Developing a community college road map.* https://www.aacu.org/sites/default/files/files/Roadmap/RoadmapFall2014Newsletter.pdf

Association of American Colleges & Universities. (2018). *Fulfilling the dream: Liberal education and the future of work.* https://www.aacu.org/sites/default/files/files/LEAP/2018EmployerResearchReport.pdf

Astin, A. (1993). *What matters in college? Four critical years revisited* (2nd ed.). Jossey-Bass.

Atlassian Teamwork. (n.d.) *Teamwork.* https://www.atlassian.com/teamwork.

Auchincloss, L. C., Laursen, S. L., Branchaw, J. L., Eagan, K., Graham, M., Haauer, D. I., Lawrie, G., Pelaez, N., Rowland, S., Towns, M., Trautma, N. M., Varma-Nelson, P., Weston, T. J., & Dolan, E. L. (2014). Assessment of course-based undergraduate research experiences: a meeting report. *CBE Life Science Education, 13*(1), 29–40. https://pubmed.ncbi.nlm.nih.gov/24591501/

Bailey, T. R., Jaggars, S. S., & Jenkins, D. (2015). *Redesigning America's community colleges: A clearer path to student success.* Harvard University Press.

Bain, K. (2004). *What the best college teachers do.* Harvard University Press.

Baines, K. (2019, August 15). Thinking like an ethnographer. In A. R. Tyner-Mullings, M. Gatta, & R. Coughlan (Eds.), *Ethnographies of work* (1–5). Guttman Community College: Open Educational Research. https://academicworks.cuny.edu/nc_pubs/106/

Baines, K. (2020). *The pandemic journaling project.* University of Connecticut. https://pandemic-journaling-project.chip.uconn.edu/

Baines, K., Buttet, S., Fisher, F., Naidoo, V., & Naish, P. D. (2017). *Students as producers in hybrid courses: Case studies from an interdisciplinary learning circle.* Semantic Scholar. https://www.semanticscholar.org/paper/Students-as-Producers-in-Hybrid-Courses%3A-Case-from-Baines-Buttet/c5f239116454c7b0e69496a964476c008142ab55?p2df

Baines, K., & Costa, V. (2020, September 14). *Course materials that last: Collaborative workshop in creating versatile assignments* [Paper presentation]. Course Hero Education Summit. https://www.coursehero.com/faculty-club/education-summit-2020/course-materials-that-last/

Baines, K., & Wilson, K. (2017). From Berlin to Belize: Deepening the global learning experience with ePortfolio pedagogy. In B. Eynon & L. M. Gambino (Eds.), *Catalyst in action: Case studies of high-impact ePortfolio practice* (pp. 141–153). Stylus.

Baker-Smith, C., Coca, V., Goldrick-Rab, S., Looker, E., Richardson, B., & Williams, T. (2020, February). *#Real college 2020: Five years of evidence on campus basic needs insecurity.* The Hope Center. https://hope4college.com/wp-content/uploads/2020/02/2019_RealCollege_Survey_Report.pdf

Ballen, C. J., Blum, J. E., Brownell, S., Hebert, S., Hewlett, J., Klein, J. R., Mcdonald, E. A., Monti, D. L., Nold, S. C., Slemmons, K. E., Soneral, P. A. G. & Cotner, S. (2017). A call to develop course-based undergraduate research experiences (CUREs) for nonmajors courses. *CBE Life Sciences Education, 16*(2), 1–7. https://www.lifescied.org/doi/full/10.1187/cbe.16-12-0352

Bangera, G., & Brownell, S. E. (2014). Course-based undergraduate research experiences can make scientific research more inclusive. *CBE Life Sciences Education, 13*(4), 602–606. https://www.ncbi.nlm.nih.gov/pmc/articles/PMC4255347/

Bangera, M. G., Harrington, K., & Fuller, J. (2018). Developing the pedagogy for classroom-based undergraduate research experience courses. In N. Hensel (Ed.), *Course-based undergraduate research: Educational equity and high-impact practice* (pp. 13–24). Stylus.

Battelle Technology Partnership Practice. (2013, March). *Oklahoma public higher education: Economic and social impacts.* https://www.okhighered.org/studies-reports/misc/battelle-study-2013.pdf

Bauer, K. W., & Bennett, J. S. (2003). Alumni perceptions used to assess undergraduate research experience. *Journal of Higher Education, 74*(2), 210–230. https://www.tandfonline.com/doi/abs/10.1080/00221546.2003.11777197

Beckman, M., & Hensel, N. (2009). Making explicit the implicit: Defining undergraduate research. *CUR Quarterly, 4*(29), 40–44. https://www.mcgill.ca/senate/files/senate/beckman__hensel_making_explicit.pdf

Bensimon, E. M., & Malcom, L. (Eds.). (2012). *Confronting equity issues on campus: Implementing the equity scorecard in theory and practice.* Stylus.

Berger, W. (2014). *A more beautiful question: The power of inquiry to spark breakthrough ideas.* Bloomsbury USA.

Bermudes, O. (2019, April 13–15). *Examining environmental isolates of Staphylococcus aureus using loop mediated (LAMP) amplification* [Poster presentation]. 26th Annual Statewide CSTEP Student Conference, New York, NY.

Biden, J. (April 28, 2020). *Address to the Joint Session of Congress.* https://www.whitehouse.gov/briefing-room/speeches-remarks/2021/04/29/remarks-by-president-biden-in-address-to-a-joint-session-of-congress/

Blackburn, N., Stegman, M. O., & Jansson, L. (n.d.). *Faculty and student teams and national laboratories: Expanding the reach of research opportunities and workforce development.* Department of Energy, Brookhaven National Laboratory. https://www.bnl.gov/isd/documents/45499.pdf

Blagg, K., Gunderson, C., Schanzenbach, D. W., & Ziliak, J. (2017, August). *Assessing food insecurity on campus: A national look at food insecurity among America's college students.* The Urban Institute. https://www.urban.org/sites/default/files/publication/92331/assessing_food_insecurity_on_campus_2.pdf

Blockus, L. (2012). The challenge of "the count." *CUR Quarterly, 32*(3), 4–8.

Blumenstyk, G. (2020, January 22). By 2020, they said, 2 out of 3 jobs would need more than a high-school diploma. Were they right? *Chronicle of Higher Education.* https://www.chronicle.com/newsletter/the-edge/2020-01-22

Bowker, M. H. (2010). *Teaching students to ask questions instead of answering them.* Semantic Scholar. https://www.semanticscholar.org/paper/Teaching-Students-to-Ask-Questions-Instead-of-Them

Bradshaw, N. (2013, October). The *Sight and Sound* interview: James Benning. *The International Film Magazine Sight and Sound.* https://www2.bfi.org.uk/news-opinion/sight-sound-magazine/interviews/sight-sound-interview-james-benning

Brew, A. (2006). *Research and teaching: Beyond the divide.* Palgrave Macmillan.

Brint, S. G., & Karabel, J. B. (1989) *The diverted dream.* Oxford University Press.

Brookhaven National Laboratory. (n.d.) *Workforce development and science education: College students.* www.bnl.gov/education/college-students.php

Brown, H. C. (2021, January 22). *Biden issues an executive order to boost SNAP benefits*. The Counter. https://thecounter.org/biden-issues-executive-order-boost-snap-benefits-covid-19-hunger/

Brush, S. (2005, May 20). Bush's job-training proposals aim to help nontraditional students and community colleges, department official says. *Chronicle of Higher Education*. https://www.chronicle.com/article/bushs-job-training-proposals-aim-to-help-nontraditional-students-and-community-colleges-department-official-says/

Bush, V. (July 1945). *Science, the endless frontier: A report to the president by Vannevar Bush, director of the Office of Scientific Research and Development*. https://www.nsf.gov/about/history/nsf50/vbush1945.jsp

Business Roundtable. (2005). *Tapping America's potential—Governor's workforce development board*. www.gwdb.maryland.gov/pub/pdf/tappingamericaspotential.pdf

Business Roundtable. (2019, January 24). *Innovation nation: An American innovation agenda for 2020*. https://www.businessroundtable.org/business-roundtable-releases-innovation-nation-an-american-innovation-agenda-for-2020

Calderon, O. (2017). Awakening mindfulness in science education. In M. Powietzynska & K. Tobin (Eds.), *Weaving complementary knowledge systems and mindfulness to educate a literate citizenry for sustainable and healthy lives* (pp. 57–78). Sense Publishers.

Calderon, O., Porter-Morgan, H., Jacob, J., & Elkins, W. (2017). Bacterial diversity impacts as a result of combined sewer overflow in a polluted waterway. *Global Journal of Environmental Science Management*, *3*(4), 437–446. https://www.gjesm.net/article_27147.html

California Community Colleges. (2019). *State of the system report*. Chancellor's Office. https://www.cccco.edu/-/media/CCCCO-Website/About-Us/State-of-the-System/Files/2019-sos-final-web.ashx?la=en&hash=E3997F2DC0573E12C28F0877701E91DECF2EC947

California Space Grant Consortium. (2017). *NASA seeks community college STEM students*. https://casgc.ucsd.edu/?p=7211#more-7211

Campaign for College Opportunity. (2018, August). *Our California: A call to action and blueprint to increase college graduates and keep our economy strong*. https://collegecampaign.org/portfolio/california-higher-ed-blueprint/

Capps, K. (2019, December 4). *What the USDA's new food stamp rule will do*. https://www.bloomberg.com/news/articles/2019-12-04/who-will-the-usda-s-food-stamp-cuts-hurt-most

Carvajal, B. (2016, April 6). *7th annual SEA-PHAGES symposium at HHMI Janelia research campus* [Video]. https://seaphages.org/video/28/

Carnevale, A. P., Saban, J. R., Gulish, A., Quinn, M. C., & Cinquegrani, G. (2020). *The dollars and sense of free college*. Center on Education and the Workforce. Georgetown University. https://1gyhoq479ufd3yna29x7ubjn-wpengine.netdna-ssl.com/wp-content/uploads/CEW-The-Cost-of-Free-College-FR.pdf

Carnevale, A. P., & Smith, N. (2017). *Learning while earning: How low income working learners differ from all other American college students.* Association of Community College Trustees. https://www.acct.org/product/learning-while-earning-how-low-income-working-learners-differ-all-other-american-college

Carnevale, A. P., & Smith, N. (2018*). Balancing work and learning: Implications for low-income students.* Center in Education and the Workforce. Georgetown University. https://cew.georgetown.edu/cew-reports/learnandearn/

Carnevale, A. P., Smith, N., & Strohl, J. (2013). *Recovery: Job growth and education requirements through 2020.* Georgetown Center on Education and the Workforce. https://cew.georgetown.edu/cew-reports/recovery-job-growth-and-education-requirements-through-2020/

Carnevale, A. P., & Strohl, J. (2013). *Separate and unequal: How higher education reinforces the intergenerational reproduction of white racial privilege.* Center on Education and the Workforce, Georgetown University. https://cew.georgetown.edu/cew-reports/separate-unequal/

Catalyst. (2019, June 14). *Women in science, technology, engineering, and mathematics (STEM): Quick take.* https://www.catalyst.org/research/women-in-science-technology-engineering-and-mathematics-stem/

Cejda, B. D., & Hensel, N. (2009). *Undergraduate research at community colleges.* Council on Undergraduate Research.

Center for Community College Student Engagement. (2014). *A matter of degrees: Practices to pathways (High-impact practices for community college student success).* The University of Texas at Austin, Program in Higher Education Leadership. https://cccse.org/sites/default/files/Matter_of_Degrees_3.pdf

Ciccone, M., Hanini, R., & Sciannantena, M., (2020). A cross-linguistic examination of geminate consonant attrition. In A. Pavlova (Ed.), *Proceedings of the ESSLLI & WeSSLLI Student Session, 2020* (Vol. 1, pp. 173–184). https://www.brandeis.edu/nasslli2020/pdfs/student-session-proceedings-compressed.pdf

CitizenScience. (n.d.) *Helping federal agencies accelerate innovation through public participation.* citizenscience.gov.

City University of New York. (n.d.). *Pathways: General education requirements.* http://www2.cuny.edu/about/administration/offices/undergraduate-studies/pathways/gened/

Clarke, M., Delgado, K., Dickinson, M., Galvez, A., Garot, R., Mercado, I., Poppendieck, J., & Freudenberg, N. (2018). *Ending food insecurity at CUNY: A guide for faculty and staff.* CUNY Urban Food Policy Institute and Healthy CUNY. http://www.cunyurbanfoodpolicy.org/publications/

Cline, J. (2019, November 23). *Metal vs. make-up: The musical composition formulas with the 2019 albums of Too and Taylor Swift* [Poster presentation]. SCCUR conference, California State University, San Marcos.

College Promise. (2020). *Celebrating 5 years.* https://static1.squarespace.com/static/5e44327a52b88927aaaecabd/t/5fc5037acb3e0f5771ed50f9/1606747007079/2020+Annual+Report+-+College+Promise.pdf

Congressional Commission on the Advancement of Women and Minorities in Science, Engineering, and Technology Development. (2000, September). *Land of plenty: Diversity as America's competitive edge in science, engineering and technology.* https://ascelibrary.org/doi/pdf/10.1061/%28ASCE%291532-6748%282001%291%3A4%2827%29

Corbit, B., Fors-Francis, K., & Francis, W. (2020, March 6) *Producing a complete nutritional diet using waste management* [Poster presentation]. Oklahoma Research Day, Tulsa Community College.

Crowe, M., & Brakke, D. (2008). Assessing the impact of undergraduate research experiences on students: An overview of the current literature. *CUR Quarterly, 28*(1): 43–50.

Crowe, M., & Brakke, D. (2019). Assessing undergraduate research experiences: An annotated bibliography. *SPUR: Scholarship and Practice of Undergraduate Research, 3*(2), 21–30.

CUREnet. (2012). *Course-based undergraduate research experience.* Carleton College, Science Education Research Center. https://serc.carleton.edu/curenet/about.html

Damas, M. C. (n.d.). *Astronomers of the African diaspora.* http://math.buffalo.edu/mad/physics/damas_chantale.html

Damas, M. C., Maghsoudi, A., Asan, J., Martinio, A., Durand, S., & Ngwia, C. M. (2019, December 9–13). *Investigation of long duration positive ionospheric storms and ICME interplanetary structures* [Paper presentation]. American Geographical Union Conference, San Francisco. https://agu.confex.com/agu/fm19/meetingapp.cgi/Paper/538524

Damas, M. C., Ngwire, T. D., Cheung, T. D., Marchese, P., Kuznetsóva, M., Zheng, Y., Chulaki, A., & Mohamed, A. (2019). A model of an integrated research and education program in space weather at a community college. *Space Weather, 18*(1). https://doi.org/10.1029/2019SW002307

Dana Center Mathematics Pathways. (2017, February). *Task force report: Oklahoma—Math pathways task force recommendations.* https://dcmathpathways.org/resources/task-force-report-oklahoma-math-pathways-task-force-recommendations

Daugherty, L., Johnston, W. R., & Berglund, T. (2020) *Connecting college students to alternative sources of support: The single stop community college initiative and post-secondary outcomes.* RAND Corporation. https://www.rand.org/pubs/research_reports/RR1740-1.html

Deibert, D. (May 2019). *Early childhood education/Educare career express ECE2: A program for retention and completion of community college students in the area of child development* [Unpublished doctoral dissertation]. Arizona State University.

de Silva, E., & de Silva, E. (2016). START model in science teaching. In E. A. Railean, G. Walker, A. Elçi, & L. Jackson (Eds.), *Handbook of research on applied learning theory and design in modern education* (pp. 187–200). IGI Global. http://doi:10.4018/978-1-4666-9634-1.ch009

Di Mento, M., & Theis, M. (2019, July 18). As the cost of a 4-year degree soars, community colleges reap more big gifts. *The Chronicle of Philanthropy.* https://www.philanthropy.com/article/as-the-cost-of-a-4-year-degree-soars-community-colleges-reap-more-big-gifts/

Distl, J., Guzman, G., & Ye, Y. (2019, March). *Social presencing: Practices for diversity* [PowerPoint slides]. CUNY's Faculty Diversity and Inclusion Conference. https://docs.google.com/presentation/d/15N6LO2kvfAhHwh8fRbcihHL27i0CUp46y oWPrAtH7v8/edit?usp=sharing

Dolan, E. (2016). *Course-based undergraduate research experiences: Current knowledge and future directions.* https://sites.nationalacademies.org/cs/groups/dbassesite/documents/webpage/dbasse_177288.pdf

Dougherty, K. J., Lahr, H., & Morest, V. S. (2017, November). *Reforming the American community college: Promising changes and their challenges.* Community College Research Center, Teachers College, Columbia University.

Doyle, A. (2019, November 8). *A Sumner to remember: Long hours in the lab yields excellent results for junior researchers.* https://www.qcc.cuny.edu/news/2019/11/Sumner.html

Duarte Diaz, H. (November 22, 2019). *The life and artwork of Pablo Picasso and the significance of how color theory pertaining to the mood of this Blue and Rose period* [Poster presentation]. Fresno City College for Central Valley Honors Symposium.

Dugaillard, B., & Spinu, L. (2019a). An investigation of articulatory skill in monolingual and bilingual speakers. In E. Babatsouli (Ed.), *Proceedings of the International Symposium on Monolingual and Bilingual Speech* (pp. 31–37). Institute of Monolingual and Bilingual Speech. http://ismbs.eu/data/documents/ISMBS-2019-PROCEEDINGS-cmprd.pdf

Dugaillard, B., & Spinu, L. (2019b, December 2–6). *An investigation of articulatory control in speakers of diverse linguistic backgrounds: Do bilingual show enhanced skill?* [Poster presentation]. Acoustical Society of America annual meeting, San Diego, California.

Dunlap, F., & Smietanski, R. (2020, March 6). *The impact of deliberate practice on spatial mapping in American Sign Language/English interpretation* [Poster presentation]. Oklahoma Research Day, University of Central Oklahoma.

Eckerson, E., Talbourdet, L., Reichlin, L., Sykes, M., Noll, E., & Gault, B. (2016, September). *Child care for parents in college: A state-by-state assessment.* Institute for Women's Policy Research. https://www.chronicle.com/blogs/ticker/files/2016/09/Child-Care.pdf

Ensz, C. (November 22, 2019). *Sign language & the oppression of the deaf had a large impact on the art world of De'VIA and Leonardo da Vinci* [Poster presentation]. Fresno City College for Central Valley Honors Symposium, Fresno, CA.

EvaluateUR. (2020). *EvaluateUR: Findings from the NSF report.* serc.carleton.edu/evaluateur/about/findings.html

EvaluateUR. (2021). *EvaluateUR: Supporting undergraduate research experiences with and online evaluation process.* https://serc.carleton.edu/evaluateur

Eynon, B., & Gambino, L. M. (2017). *High-impact ePortfolio practice: A catalyst for student, faculty, and institutional learning.* Stylus.

Eynon, B., Gambino, L. M., & Török, J. (2014). What difference can ePortfolio Make? A field report from the Connect to Learning Project. *International Journal of ePortfolio, 4*(1), 95–114. https://www.theijep.com/pdf/IJEP127.pdf

Farmer, J. C., Sim, A., & Usher, T. (2014, December 15–19). *Intensive training academy during winter breaks (winterships) at a two-year Hispanic serving institution to prepare STEM students for summer internships* [Poster presentation]. American Geophysical Union Fall Meeting, San Francisco, CA.

Fayer, S., Lacey, A., & Watson, A. (2017, January). *STEM occupations: Past, present, and future.* U.S. Bureau of Labor Statistics. https://www.bls.gov/spotlight/2017/science-technology-engineering-and-mathematics-stem-occupations-past-present-and-future/pdf/science-technology-engineering-and-mathematics-stem-occupations-past-present-and-future.pdf

Feynman, R. (1988). *What do you care what people think?: Further adventures of a curious character.* W. W. Norton & Company.

Fink, J. (2017, January). *What do students think of guided pathways?* Community College Research Center. https://ccrc.tc.columbia.edu/media/k2/attachments/what-do-students-think-guided-pathways.pdf

Flaherty, C. (2014, October 16). Faculty work, student success: How the College of New Jersey reimagined what professors do. *Inside Higher Education.* https://www.insidehighered.com/news/2014/10/16/how-college-new-jersey-rethought-faculty-work-student-success-mind

Foundation for California Community Colleges. (2017, July). *Vision for success: Strengthening the California community colleges to meet California's needs.* https://www.cccco.edu/-/media/CCCCO-Website/Files/Workforce-and-Economic-Development/RFAs/19-300-001/appendix-d-vision-for-success-a11y.pdf

Foundation of California Community Colleges. (2017, August). *Facts and figures.* https://foundationccc.org/About-Us/About-the-Colleges/Facts-and-Figures

Fox, M., & Nguyen, A. (2019, October). *Developing a LAMP molecular beacon method to monitor the level of Enterococci in East River water of NYC* [Poster presentation]. MACUB Conference, Monmouth University, Monmouth, NJ.

Franco, R. W. (2006, November 17). *The civic role of community colleges: Preparing students for the work of democracy.* Campus Compact. https://compact.org/resource-posts/the-civic-role-of-community-colleges-preparing-students-for-the-work-of-democracy/

Freudenberg, N., Manzo, L., Jones, H., Kwan, A., Tsui, E., & Gagnon, M. (2011). *Food insecurity at CUNY: Results from a survey of CUNY undergraduate students.* Campaign for a Healthy CUNY.

Full, R. J. (2012, December 20). *Curiosity, discovery, and gecko feet* [Video]. TEDEd. https://ed.ted.com/lessons/curiosity-discovery-and-gecko-feet-robert-full

Gadura, N. (2018). Barcoding undergraduate research tool can be scaled from traditional to course-based research project with ease. In N. Hensel (Ed.), *Course-based undergraduate research: Educational equity and high-impact practice* (pp. 153–165). Stylus.

Galizio, L. (2019, April 18). *The origin of California's community colleges.* Community College League of California. https://www.ccleague.org/blog/origin-californias-community-colleges

Gannon, K. (2018, February 27). The case for inclusive teaching. *Chronicle of Higher Education.* https://www.chronicle.com/article/the-case-for-inclusive-teaching/?cid=gen_sign_in

Gaozhen, L., Mata, D., Bermudes, O., Fernandes, M., & Van Nguyen, A. (2018, July). *Examining environmental isolates of Staphylococeus aureus using loop mediated (LAMP) amplification* [Poster presentation]. CUNY Research Scholar Program Symposium, New York, NY.

Gatta, M., & Hoffman, N. (2018, October 18). *Putting vocation at the center of the curriculum: The student experience in CUNY's ethnographies of work course.* https://guttman.cuny.edu/faculty-staff/center-on-ethnographies-of-work/ethnographies-of-work/

Georgetown University. (2018). *Mastering the hidden curriculum, MHC fall 2018 syllabus (public).* https://futures.georgetown.edu/mastering-the-hidden-curriculum

Gerard, Z., de Silva, E., Webb, S. T., & Jarnagin, W. (2020, April 24). *An investigation into TVA's land acquisition in the Cherokee Lake area* [Poster presentation]. 2020 Research Symposium for Community College Students. Tennessee Association of Science Department Chairs.

Gibson, L. (2016, August 15). John Stilgoe on "acute observation." *Harvard Magazine.* https://www.harvardmagazine.com/2016/08/john-stilgoe-harvard-summer-course-on-acute-observation-of-the-landscape

Gilligan, C., & Eddy, J. (2017). Listening as a path to psychological discovery: An introduction to the listening guide. *Perspectives on Medical Education, 6*(2), 76–81. https://link.springer.com/article/10.1007/s40037-017-0335-3

Giridharadas, A. (2012, December 14). School takes new tack on work study. *New York Times.* https://www.nytimes.com/2012/12/15/us/15iht-currents15.html?smid=tw-share

Global Guttman. (2016, July 14). *Two Guttman students build drone to support scientific research.* https://guttman.cuny.edu/2016/07/14/two-guttman-students-build-drone-to-support-scientific-research/

Global Guttman. (2018, May 21). *Guttman's first Pulitzer fellow writes about China travel experience.* https://guttman.cuny.edu/2018/05/21/guttmans-first-pulitzer-fellow-writes-about-china-travel-experience/

Goldrick-Rab, S., Richardson, J., Schneider, J., Hernandez, A., & Cady, C. (2018). *Still hungry and homeless in college.* Wisconsin HOPE Lab. https://hope4college.com/wp.../Wisconsin-HOPE-Lab-Still-Hungry-and-Homeless.pdf

Goldrick-Rab, S., Baker-Smith, C., Coca, V., Looker, E., & Williams, T. (2019, April). *College and university basic needs insecurity: A national #realcollege survey report.* https://hope4college.com/wpcontent/uploads/2019/04/HOPE_realcollege_National_report_digital.pdf

Golebiewska, U. (2018). Poetry in the biology curriculum. In A. E. Traver, S. Kincaid, & F. Jacob (Eds.), *Poetry across the curriculum: New methods for writing intensive pedagogy for U.S. community college and undergraduate education* (pp. 43–52). Brill.

Government Accountability Office. (2008, May). *Workforce development: Community colleges and one-stop centers collaborate to meet 21st century workforce needs.* https://files.eric.ed.gov/fulltext/ED501277.pdf

Government Accountability Office. (2018, December). *Food insecurity: Better information could help eligible college students access federal food assistance benefits.* https://www.gao.gov/assets/700/696254.pdf

Governor's Office of Planning and Research. (2018, December 19). *The master plan for higher education in California and state workforce needs: A review*. https://opr .ca.gov/docs/20181226-Master_Plan_Report.pdf

Gregerman, S. (2008, October 13–14). *The role of undergraduate research in student retention, academic engagement, and the pursuit of graduation education* [Commissioned paper presentation]. Evidence on Promising Practices in Undergraduate Science, Technology, Engineering, and Mathematics (STEM) Education Workshop, the National Academies of Science, Engineering, and Medicine.

Gupta, H. (2017, October). *The power of fully supporting community college students*. MDRC. https://www.mdrc.org/publication/power-fully-supporting-community-college-students

Gutleizer, S., & Spinu, L. (2019, December 4–6). *Monolingual and multilingual reading fluency* [Poster presentation]. Acoustical Society of America annual meeting, San Diego, California.

Guttman Community College. (n.d.). *Ethnographies of work*. https://guttman.cuny.edu/faculty/staff center-on-ethnographies-of-work/ethnographies-of-work/

Guttman News. (2019a, May 6). *Professor Kristina Baines receives Course Hero-Woodrow Wilson Fellowship for Excellence in Teaching*. https://guttman.cuny.edu/2019/05/06/professor-kristina-baines-receives-course-hero-woodrow-wilson-fellowship-for-excellence-in-teaching/

Guttman News. (2019b, June 5). *Guttman collaborates on CUNY's Pressing Public Issues Project*. https://guttman.cuny.edu/2019/06/05/guttman-collaborates-on-cunys-pressing-public-issues-project/

Guttman News. (2020, April 11). *Guttman professor and alumna join forces to share why ethnography matters with the public*. https://guttman.cuny.edu/2020/04/11/guttman-professor-and-alumna-join-forces-to-share-why-ethnography-matters-with-the-public/

Guzman, G. (2019, December 6). *Growth: Letting go/letting come* [Panel presentation]. Queensborough Community College, Undergraduate Research Day.

Hannan, F. (May 6, 2019). *Course Hero, Woodrow Wilson Foundation celebrate innovative professors with the excellence in teaching fellowship*. https://woodrow.org/news/course-hero-fellows-2019

Harrington, M. (1962). *The other America: Poverty in the United States*. Simon & Schuster.

Harris, K. (December 6, 2019). *Self-journey: Creativity unbound* [Panel presentation]. Queensborough Community College, Undergraduate Research Day.

Hart Research Associates. (2018, July). *Fulfilling the American dream: Liberal education and the future of work: Selected findings from online surveys of business executives and hiring managers*. https://www.aacu.org/sites/default/files/files/LEAP/2018EmployerResearchReport.pdf

Hathaway, R. S., Nagda, B. A., & Gregerman, S. R. (2002). The relationship of undergraduate research participation to graduate and professional education pursuit: An empirical study. *Journal of College Student Development, 43*(5), 614–631. https://eric.ed.gov/?id=EJ653327

Hayashi, A. (2021a). *Arawana Hayashi*. www.arawanahayashi.com/

Hayashi, A. (2021b). *Social presencing theater: The art of making a true move.* PI Press.

Hensel, N. (Ed.). (2012). *Characteristics of excellence in undergraduate research (COEUR).* Council on Undergraduate Research. https://www.cur.org/assets/1/23/COEUR_final.pdf

Hensel, N. (2009). Context, implications, and recommendations. In B. D. Cejda & H. Hensel, *Undergraduate research at community colleges* (pp. 65–69). Council on Undergraduate Research.

Hensel, N. (Ed.). (2018). *Course-based undergraduate research: Educational equity and high-impact practice.* Stylus.

Hensel, N. H., & Cejda, B. D. (2006). *Two-year technician education and transfer programs: Tapping the potential of undergraduate research.* National Science Foundation Award # 0603119.

Hensel, N., Hunnicutt, L., & Salomon, D. A. (2015). *Redefining the paradigm: Faculty models in support of student learning.* The New American Colleges and Universities.

Herman, A. E. (2016). *Visual intelligence: Sharpen your perception, change your life.* Houghton Mifflin.

Hills, L. (2008, March 2). *Teaching the reading of literature: A pencil is one of the best eyes.* http://www.samplereality.com/gmu/spring2008/610/03/02/a-pencil-is-one-of-the-best-eyes/

Hochschild. A. R. (1983). *The managed heart: Commercialization of human feeling.* University of California Press.

hooks, b. (1994). *Teaching to transgress: Education as the practice of freedom.* Routledge.

Hudd, S. (2003, April). Syllabus under construction: Involving students in the creation of class assignments. *Teaching Sociology, 31*(2), 95–202. https://blogs.baruch.cuny.edu/ctlworkshop2016/files/2016/05/Suzanne-Hudd-Syllabus-Under-Construction.pdf

Hunter, A. B., Laursen, S., & Seymour, E. (2007). Becoming a scientist: The role of undergraduate research in students' cognitive, personal, and professional development. *Science Education, 91*, 36–74. https://doi.org/10.1002/sce.20173

Hunter, A. B., Weston, T. J., Laursen, S. L., & Thiry, H. (2009). URSSA: Evaluating student gains from undergraduate research in the sciences. *CUR Quarterly, 29*(3), 15–19.

Institute for Women's Policy Research. (2014, November). *4.8 million college students are raising children.*https://iwpr.org/category/iwpr-publications/fact-sheet/

Ismail, A. (2019. November 23). *Replacing public cryptographic key exchanges with quantum resistant implementations.* [Poster presentation]. SCCUR. California State University San Marcos.

Jack, A. A. (2019). *The privileged poor: How elite colleges are failing disadvantaged students.* Harvard University Press.

Jarman, R.H. (2014). The green fuels depot: Demonstrating local sustainable energy conversion. In N. H. Hensel & B. D. Cejda (Eds.), *Tapping the potential of all: Undergraduate research at community colleges* (pp. 66–72). Council on Undergraduate Research.

Jenkins, D. (2014, October). *Redesigning community colleges for student success: Overview of the guided pathways approach.* Community College Research Center Teachers College, Columbia University. https://www.ccsse.org/docs/CCRC_Guided_Pathways_Overview.pdf

Jenkins, D., Brown, A., Fink, J., Lahr, H., & Yanagiura, T. (2018). *Building guided pathways to community college student success: Promising practices and early evidence from Tennessee.* Community College Research Center, Teachers College, Columbia University.

Joliet Junior College. (n.d.). *First community college.* https://www.jjc.edu/about-jjc/history

Jordan, T. C., Burnett, S. H., Carson, S., Caruso, S. M., Clase, J., DeJong,, R. J., Dennehy, R. J., Denver, D. R., Dunbar, D., Elgin, S. C. R., Findley, A. M., Gissendanner, C. R., Golebiewska, U. P., Guild, N., Hartzog, G. A., Grillo, W. H., Hollowell, G. P., Hughes, L. E., Johnson, A., . . . & Hatfull, G. F. (2014, February 4). A broadly implementable research course in phage discovery and genomics for first-year undergraduate students. *mBio, 5*(1), e01051–13. https://mbio.asm.org/content/5/1/e01051-13

Karukstis, K. K., & Hensel, N. (Eds.). (2010). *Transformative research at predominately undergraduate institutions.* Council on Undergraduate Research.

Keller, J. (2009, June 11). California's "gold standard" for higher education falls upon hard times. *Chronicle of Higher Education.* https://www.chronicle.com/article/Californias-Gold-Standard/44468

King, R. (2012). *Leonardo and the Last Supper.* Bloomsbury.

Kruvelis, M., Cruse, L. R., & Gault, B. (2017, September 20). *Single mothers in college: Growing enrollment, financial challenges, and the benefits of attainment. institute for women's policy research.* https://iwpr.org/iwpr-issues/student-parent-success-initiative/single-mothers-in-college-growing-enrollment-financial-challenges-and-the-benefits-of-attainment/

Kuh, G. D. (2008). *High-impact educational practices: What they are, who has access to them, and why they matter.* Association of American Colleges & Universities.

Kuh, G. D., Kinzie, J., Schuh, J. H., & Whitt. E. J. (2005). *Student success in college: Creating conditions that matter.* Jossey-Bass.

La Vaca Independiente. (2020). *La Vaca Independiente, culture in evolution.* https://lavaca.edu.mx/

Lamott, A. (1994) *Bird by bird: Some instructions on writing and life.* Anchor.

Landa, R. (2011, September 16). *The birth of a modern university.* https://eport-folios.macaulay.cuny.edu/hainline2014/files/2014/02/Landa-The-Birth-Of-a-Modern-University---CUNY-Newswire.pdf

Lander, M. (2018, January 19). People pay $112 million a year for horseshoe crab blood. A company wants Georgia's coast in on it. *Savannah Morning News.*

Landin, J. (2015, September 4). Rediscovering the forgotten benefits of drawing. *Scientific American.* https://blogs.scientificamerican.com/symbiartic/rediscovering-the-forgotton-benefits-of-drawing/

Lang, J. (2006, August 28). The promising syllabus. *The Chronicle of Higher Education.* https://www.chronicle.com/article/the-promising-syllabus/

Lang, J. (2016, February 8). Small changes in teaching: Making connections. *Chronicle of Higher Education.* https://www.chronicle.com/article/small-changes-in-teaching-making-connections/

LaPonsie, M. (2018, February 27). *20 high-paying jobs you can get with a 2-year degree.* Money Talks News. https://www.moneytalksnews.com/20-high-paying-jobs-2-year-degree/

Lassiter, L. E., Goodall, H., Campbell, E., & Johnson, M. N. (2004). *The other side of Middletown: Exploring Muncie's African American community.* Altamira Press.

Lazear, E. P., & Marron, D. B. (2009). *Economic report to the president.* https://www.govinfo.gov/content/pkg/ERP-2009/html/ERP-2009-appendixA.htm

Locks, A. M., & Gregerman, S. R. (2008). Undergraduate research as an institutional retention strategy: The University of Michigan model. In R. Taraban & R. L. Blanton (Eds.), *Creating effective undergraduate research programs in science: The transformation for student to scientist* (pp. 11–32). Teachers College Press.

Logue, A. W. (2017). *Pathways to reform: Credits and conflict at the City University of New York.* Princeton University Press.

Lopatto, D. (2003). The essential features of undergraduate research. *CUR Quarterly, 24*, 139–142.

Lopatto, D. (2004). Survey of undergraduate research experiences (SURE): First findings. *Cell Biology Education, 3*(4), 270–277. https://www.doi.org/10.1187/cbe.04-07-0045

Lopatto, D. (2007). Undergraduate research experiences support science career decisions and active learning. *CBE Life Science Education, 6*(4), 297–306. https://www.lifescied.org/doi/full/10.1187/cbe.07-06-0039

Lopatto, D. (2010) *Science in solution: The impact of undergraduate research on student learning.* Council on Undergraduate Research and Research Corporation for Science Advancement.

Lopatto, D. (2018, July 2). *Assessment of undergraduate research.* Paper presented at Council on Undergraduate Research (CUR) Biennial Conference, AGU Blogoshere. https://blogs.agu.org/geoedtrek/2018/07/02/lopatto/

Lopatto, D., Hauser, C., Jones, C. J., Paetkau, D., Chandrasekaran, V., Dunbar, D., MacKinnon, C., Stamm, J., Alvarez, C., Barnard, D., Bedard, J. E. J., Bednarski, A. E., Bhalla, S., Braverman, J. M., Burg, M., Chung, H-M., DeJong, R. J., DiAngelo, J. R., Du, C., Eckdahl, T. T., Emerson, J., Frary, A., Frohlich, D., Goodman, A. L., Gosser, Y., . . . & Elgin, S. C. R. (2012). A central support system can facilitate implementation and sustainability of a classroom-based undergraduate experience (CURE) in genomics. *CBE-Life Science Education, 13*(4), 711–723. https://www.ncbi.nlm.nih.gov/pmc/articles/PMC4255357/

Loria, K. (2018, April 4). These 18 accidental and unintended scientific discoveries changed the world. *Business Insider.* https://www.sciencealert.com/these-eighteen-accidental-scientific-discoveries-changed-the-world_

Los Angeles City College. (n.d.). *Physics/engineering: Consortium for undergraduate research experiences* (CURE). https://www.lacitycollege.edu/Departments/Physics-Engineering/Cure.

Lumina Foundation. (2019). *Stronger nation report, TN.* https://strongernation.luminafoundation.org/report/2019#state/TN

Lynd, R. S., & Lynd, H. M. (1957). *Middletown: A study in modern American culture.* Harcourt Brace and Company.

Makin, A. E. (2011, March 6). *Rattlesnakes under the radar at Mesa Community College. upcloseaz.com/rattlesnakes-under-the-radar-at-mesa-community-college/*

Marcus, J. (2015). *Private colleges target community college grads they once shunned.* The Hechinger Report. https://hechingerreport.org/private-colleges-target-community-college-grads-they-once-shunned/

Maricopa Community College District. (n.d.). *Home page.* http://www.maricopa.edu

Maricopa Community College District. (2017, August 22). *MCCD governing board minutes.* https://district.maricopa.edu/sites/default/files/minutes/7.1%2008.22.17%20RBM%20Minutes.pdf

Maricopa Community College District. (2018, February 16). *Guided pathways benefit college students, transforms institutions.* https://news.maricopa.edu/press-releases/guided-pathways-benefit-college-students-transforms-institutions

Maricopa Community College District. (2020a, January 28). *MCCCD to launch a workforce and economic development office to better meet workforce and industry needs.* https://news.maricopa.edu/news-articles/mcccd-launch-workforce-and-economic-development-office-better-meet-workforce-and

Maricopa Community College District. (2020b, August 4). *MCCCD partner's with national governor's association to reskill workers during the pandemic.* https://news.maricopa.edu/news-releases/mcccd-partners-national-governors-association-reskill-workers-during-pandemic

Marrongelle, K. (2020, March 6). *Dear colleague letter.* National Science Foundation.

McNair, T. B., Bensimon, E. M., & Malcolm-Piqueux, L. (2020). *From equity talk to equity walk: Expanding practitioner knowledge for racial justice in higher education.* Jossey-Bass.

MDRC. (2016, December). *How does the ASAP model align with guided pathways implementation in community colleges?* https://www.mdrc.org/publication/how-does-asap-model-align-guided-pathways-implementation-community-colleges

Medawar, P. B. (1979). Advice to a young scientist. Harper & Row.

Meredith, D. (Ed.). (2016). *Computational music analysis.* Springer International.

Momberg, T. (2019, October 3). *Queensborough selected for NASA grant program.* https://qns.com/story/2015/10/03/queensborough-selected-for-nasa-grant-program/.

Motivated Engineering Transfer Students (METS). (n.d.). *Mission, vision, and goals.* http://aar.faculty.asu.edu/mets/about-mets

Murakami, K. (January 14, 2021). Biden's choice for education secretary. *Inside Higher Education.* https://www.insidehighered.com/news/2021/01/04/biden-selects-miguel-cardona-education-secretary

Nagda, B. A., Gregerman, S. R., Jonides, J., von Hipple, W., & Lerner, W. J. S. (1998). Undergraduate student-faculty research partnerships affect student retention. *Review of Higher Education, 22*(1), 55–72. https://sites.lsa.umich.edu/wp-content/uploads/sites/439/2016/10/1998_6.pdf

NASA. (2020, November 17). *About the space grant project.* https://www.nasa.gov/stem/spacegrant/about/index.html

NASA Science. (2021, June 2). *Space place: What is space weather?* https://spaceplace.nasa.gov/spaceweather/en/

National Academies, Committee on Facilitating Interdisciplinary Research, Committee on Science, Engineering, and Public Policy. (2004). *Facilitating interdisciplinary research.* National Academy Press.

National Academies of Sciences, Engineering, and Medicine. (2007). *Rising above the gathering storm: Energizing and employing America for a brighter economic future.* The National Academies Press. https://www.nap.edu/catalog/11463/rising-above-the-gathering-storm-energizing-and-employing-america-for

National Academies of Sciences, Engineering, and Medicine. (2010). *Rising above the gathering storm, revisited: Rapidly approaching category 5.* The National Academies Press. https://www.nap.edu/catalog/12999/rising-above-the-gathering-storm-revisited-rapidly-approaching-category-5

National Academies of Sciences, Engineering, and Medicine. (2015). *Integrating discovery-based research into the undergraduate curriculum: Report of a convocation.* The National Academies Press. https://www.nap.edu/catalog/13362/discipline-based-education-research-understanding-and-improving-learning-in-undergraduate

National Association of Colleges and Employers. (2021). *What is career readiness?* www.naceweb.org/career-readiness/competencies/career-readiness-defined

National Center for Education Statistics. (2021, February). D*igest of Education Statistics, 2019* (55th ed.). www.https://nces.ed/pubs2021/2021009.pdf

National Research Council. (2005). *Assessment of Department of Defense basic research (Appendix D).* The National Academies Press. https://www.nap.edu/read/11177/chapter/8

National Research Council. (2014). *Convergence: Facilitating transdisciplinary integration of life sciences, physical sciences, engineering and beyond.* National Academies Press. https://www.nap.edu/catalog/18722/convergence-facilitating-transdisciplinary-integration-of-life-sciences-physical-sciences-engineering

National Science Board. (2007, May 7). *Enhancing support for transformative research at the National Science Foundation.* https://www.nsf.gov/nsb/documents/2007/tr_report.pdf

National Science Board. (2020, May). *Vision 2030.* https://www.nsf.gov/nsb/NSBActivities/vision-2030.jsp

National Science Foundation. (2007, August 9). *News release.* https://www.nsf.gov/news/news_summ.jsp?cntn_id=109853

National Science Foundation. (n.d.) *Changes to NSF merit review criteria.* https://www.nsf.gov/about/transformative_research/merit_review_criteria.jsp

National Science Foundation. (2004). *Federal funds for research and development: Fiscal years 2002, 2003, and 2004, technical notes.* https://wayback.archive-it.org/5902/20150628155948/http://www.nsf.gov/statistics/nsf05307/htmstart.htm

National Science Foundation and American Association of Community Colleges. (2002). *The role of community colleges in cybersecurity education: A report from a workshop.* Community College Press.

National Student Clearinghouse Research Center. (2019, July 10). *Persistence & retention—2019.* https://nscresearchcenter.org/snapshotreport35-first-year-persistence-and-retention/

Nerio, R., Webber, A., MacLachlan, E., Lopatto, D., & Caplan, A. J. (2019). One-year research experience for associate's degree students impacts graduation, STEM retention, and transfer. *CBE-Life Sciences Education, 18*(2). https://www.lifescied.org/doi/10.1187/cbe.19-02-0042

New York City Water Trail Association. (n.d.). *2020 citizens water quality testing program.* nycwatertrail.org/water_quality.html

New York Department of Environmental Conservation. (n.d.). *Green Point remediation project.* http://www.nysdecgreenpoint.com/projecthistory.aspx

Newtown Creek Alliance. (n.d.) *Water quality sampling.* www.newtowncreekalliance.org/water-quality-sampling/

Nguyen, A. V., Orlofsky, A., Pubill, K., Tawde, M., Li, G., Mata, D., Bermudes, O., Fernandez, M., Santana, J., Kim, W., Chimbay, E., Kim, Y., Nguyen, T., Fox, M., Eralte, J., Metz, M., Smyth, D. S., Panzeca, C., & Khan, M. I. (2020, December 9). Loop-mediated isothermal amplification (LAMP) as a rapid, affordable and effective tool to involve students in undergraduate research. *Frontiers in Microbiology, 11,* 1–10. https://www.frontiersin.org/articles/10.3389/fmicb.2020.603381/full

Nguyen, A., Wu, Y., Liu Q., Wang, D., Nguyen, S., Loh, R., Pang, J., Friedman, K., Orlofsku, A., Augenlicht, L., Pollard. J. W., & Lin, E. Y. (2013, September). Stat3 in epithelial cells regulates inflammation and tumor progression to malignant state in colon. *Neoplasia, 15*(9), 998–1008. https://doi.org/10.1593/neo.13952

Nobel Prize. (2019). *Peter Medawar–Facts.* https://www.nobelprize.org/prizes/medicine/1960/medawar/facts/

Noell, A. C., Fisher, A. M., Fors-Francis, K., & Sherrit, S. (2018, January 18). Subcritical water extraction acids from Mars analog soils. *Electrophoresis, 0,* 1–10. https://onlinelibrary.wiley.com/doi/abs/10.1002/elps.201700459

Office of Policy Development and Research. (n.d.). *Barriers to success: Housing insecurity for U.S. college students.* U.S. Department of Housing and Urban Development. https://www.huduser.gov/portal/periodicals/insight/insight_2.pdf

Oklahoma's Promise. (2018). *What is Oklahoma's promise?* https://www.okhighered.org/okpromise/about.shtml

Oklahoma State Regents for Higher Education. (n.d.) *A guide to the history, organization, and operation of the State System.* https://ww.okhighered.org./state-system/overview/part2.shhtml

Oklahoma State Regents for Higher Education. (2018, February 1). *Report on the future of higher education.* https://www.okhighered.org/future/docs/final-report.pdf

Oklahoma Works. (2017, November). *Launch Oklahoma strategic plan.* https://oklahomaworks.gov/wp-content/uploads/2017/04/Launch-OK-Strategic-Recommendations-2017.pdf

Orozco, V., & Mayo, L. (2011, January). *Keeping students enrolled: How community colleges are boosting financial resources for their students.* Demos. https://www.demos.org/sites/default/files/publications/KeepingStudentsEnrolled_Demos.pdf

Ortiz, M., & Taras, L. B. (2014). Undergraduate research in an urban community college's comparative anatomy class. In N. Hensel & B. D. Cejda (Eds.), *Tapping the potential of all: Undergraduate research at community colleges* (pp. 41–43). Council on Undergraduate Research.

Packard, B. W.-L. (2016). *Successful STEM mentoring initiatives for underrepresented students: A Research-based guide for faculty and administrators.* Stylus.

Pamphilon, B. (1999, September 1). The zoom model: A dynamic framework for the analysis of life histories. *Qualitative Inquiry, 5*(3), 393–410. https://www.mendeley.com/catalogue/32926c5a-ce26-3418-9394-32a20617aaa4/

Pascarella, E. T., & Terenzini, P. T. (1991). *How college affects students.* Jossey-Bass.

Patton, M. (2019). *Redefine, reinvent, reinvigorate: Recommendations from the meeting on the sustainability and growth of the Community College Undergraduate Research Initiative (CCURI).* https://38ee22dd-6114-4625-898b-718021ffc55d.filesusr.com/ugd/e84dcd_4065c35c83474d24bc300eb78a76ab9e.pdf

Patton, M., & Hause. E. (2020). *Community college undergraduate research experience summit proceedings report.* American Association of Community Colleges. https://www.aacc.nche.edu/wp-content/uploads/2020/04/AACC_URE_REPORT-FINAL.pdf

Paxton, K. (2016, March 10). *Tempering the syllabus: From contract to invitation, map, and guide.* The Scholarly Teacher. https://www.scholarlyteacher.com/post/tempering-the-`syllabus

Pelley, S. (Reporter). (2019, June 16). Ryan Speedo Green: From juvenile delinquency to opera stardom. *60 Minutes.* CBS News.https://www.cbsnews.com/video/ryan-speedo-green-from-juvenile-delinquency-to-opera-stardom-60-minutes-2019-06-16/

Pennamon, T. (2018, August 1). *Diverse issues in higher education.* https://diverseeducation.com/article/author/tpennamon

Perez, J. A. (2003). Undergraduate research at two-year colleges. In J. Kinkead (Ed.), Valuing and supporting undergraduate research (New Directions for Teaching and Learning, no. 93, pp. 69–78). Wiley. https://doi.org/10.1002/tl.89

Perkins Collaborative Resource Network. (n.d.). *Employability skills.* https://cte.ed.gov/initiatives/employability-skills-framework

Piper, J. (2019, March 10). The job in which every single dollar matters. *The Chronicle of Higher Education.* https://www.chronicle.com/article/the-job-in-which-every-single-dollar-matters/

Pope, W. H., Bowman, C. A., Russel, D. A., Jacobs-Sera, D., Asai, D. J., Cresawm, S. G., Jacobs, Jr., W. R., Hendrix, R. W., Lawrence, J. G., & Hatfull, G. F. (2015). Whole genome comparison of a large collection of mycobacteriophages reveals a continuum of phage genetic diversity. *eLife 2015*(4), e06416. https://elifesciences.org/articles/06416

Porter, S. R., & Umbach. P. D. (2019). *What challenges to success do community college students face?* Perconter. https://www.acct.org/files/Financial%20Wellness%20 and%20Student%20Success.pdf

Postrel, V. I. (1997, March 30). Clinton's college plan: Educational inflation. *Washington Post.* https://www.washingtonpost.com/archive/opinions/1997/03/30/ clintons-college-plan-educational-inflation/af4e8303-63d0-4967-be40-f18 c494b11c9/

Presencing Institute. (2007–2021). *Stuck exercise.* https://www.presencing.org/ resource/tools/stuck-exercise-desc

President's Commission on Higher Education. (1948). *Higher education for American democracy: A report.* Harper & Bros.

Pubill, K., & Nguyen, A. (2019, October). *Examining the prevalence of Salmonella bacteria in standing water using loop mediated isothermal amplification method, an alternative to polymerase reaction* [Poster presentation]. The 52nd Metropolitan Association of College and University Biologists, Monmouth University, Monmouth, NJ.

Public Policy Institute of California. (2016, April). *Californians for education.* https:// www.ppic.org/content/pubs/survey/S_416MBS.pdf

Public Policy Institute of California. (2019, October). *Improving college completion.* https://www.ppic.org/wp-content/uploads/higher-education-in-california- improving-college-completion-october-2019.pdf

Pyles, R. A., & Levy, F. (2009). Opening the door to early student involvement in scholarly activity: Coordinating efforts and providing financial support. In M. K. Boyd & J. Wesemann (Eds.), *Broadening participation in undergraduate research: Fostering excellence and enhancing the impact* (pp. 134–139). Council on Undergraduate Research.

Quaye, S. J., & Harper, S. R. (2007). Faculty accountability for culturally inclusive pedagogy and curricula. *Liberal Education, 93*(3), 32–39.

Queensborough Community College. (2018, June 4). *Veteran & immigrant is only community college student in U.S. accepted into NSF REU at Northeastern University.* Queensborough Community College, Marketing and Communications.

Queensborough Community College. (2019, August 6). *Ability and judgment lead to medical studies.* Queensborough Community College, Marketing and Communications.

Queensborough Community College. (2020, April 28). *Queensborough Community College student awarded prestigious Jack Kent Cooke Foundation Undergraduate Transfer Scholarship.* Queensborough Community College, Marketing and Communications.

Radelat, A. (2011). Taking dreams to market. *Latino Magazine.* http://www. latinomagazine.com/winter11/journal/dreams_market.htm

Radhakrishman, P., Hendrix, T., Mark, K., Taylor, B. J., & Veras, I. (2018). Building STEM identity with a core ePortfolio practice. In B. Eynon & L. M. Gambino (Eds.), *Catalyst in action: Case studies of high-impact ePortfolio practice* (pp. 223–240). Stylus.

Ramachandran, M., & Aronson, J. K. (2006). The diagnosis of art: Arthrogryposis and Ribera's *The Clubfoot. Journal of the Royal Society of Medicine, 99*(6), 321–322. https://journals.sagepub.com/doi/10.1177/014107680609900622#articleCitationDownloadContainer

Rauner, M., Perna, L. W., & Kanter, M. J. (2018, November). *California College Promise: Program characteristics and perceptions for the field.* WestEd. https://californiacollegepromise.wested.org/wp-content/uploads/2018/11/College-Promise-Landscape-Scan-2018.pdf

Redden, E. (2020, December 16). McKenzie Scott gives away $4.2 billion, and colleges rejoice. *Inside Higher Ed.* https://www.insidehighered.com/quick-takes/2020/12/16/mackenzie-scott-gives-away-42-billion-and-colleges-rejoice

Rice University. (2018). *Nanotechnology REU with a focus on community colleges.* Award # 1757967. https://www.nsf.gov/awardsearch/showAward?AWD_ID=1757967&HistoricalAwards=false

Rosenbaum, M. (2015, August 12). *How to fix the tech talent shortage.* CIO. https://www.cio.com/article/2969298/how-to-fix-the-tech-talent-shortage.html

Rosenberg, J. S. (2017, November–December). Mastering the "hidden curriculum." *Harvard Magazine.* https://harvardmagazine.com/2017/11/mastering-the-hidden-curriculum

Ross, K. (2016). *Breakthrough strategies: Classroom-based practices to support new majority college students.* Harvard Education Press.

Russell, S. H., Hancock, M. P., & McCullough, J. (2007). Benefits of undergraduate research experiences. *Science, 316*(5824), 548–559. https://doi.org/10.1126/science.1140384

Russell, S. H., Hancock, M. P., McCullough, J., Rossner, J. D., & Storey, C. (2005, November). *Evaluation of NSF support for undergraduate research opportunities: Survey of STEM graduates.* SRI International.

Scharmer, O. (2019, April 15). Vertical literacy: Reimagining the 21st-century university. *Medium.* https://medium.com/presencing-institute-blog/vertical-literacy-12-principles-for-reinventing-the-21st-century-university-39c2948192ee

Schneider, M., & Yin, L. M. (2102, April). *Completion matters: The high cost of low community college graduation rates, report 2.* American Enterprise Institute.

Schulten, K. (2018, December 7). Making it relevant: Helping students connect their studies to the world today. *New York Times.* https://www.nytimes.com/2017/12/07/learning/lesson-plans/making-it-relevant-helping-students-connect-their-studies-to-the-world-today.html

Scudder, S. (1997) Take this fish and look at it. In M. F. Moriarty (Ed.), *Writing science through critical thinking* (pp. 205–208). Jones and Bartlett. https://digitalcommons.hollins.edu/cgi/viewcontent.cgi?article=1047&context=facbooks

Seltzer, R. (2016, December 6). The high school graduate plateau. *Inside Higher Education.* https://www.insidehighered.com/news/2016/12/06/high-school-graduates-drop-number-and-be-increasingly-diverse

Senge, P. (2006). *The fifth discipline.* Doubleday.

Sentz, R., & Stout, K. (2018, November 13). Community colleges' crucial role in powering local economies. *Governing.* https://www.governing.com/gov-institute/voices/col-community-colleges-vital-role-powering-economies.html

Seraphin, S. B., Grizzzell, J. A., Kerr-German, A., Perkins, M. A., Grzanka. P. R., & Hardin, E. E. (2019). A conceptual framework for non-disposable assignments: Inspiring implementation, innovation, and research. *Psychology, Learning, and Teaching, 18*(1), 84–97. https://journals.sagepub.com/doi/full/10.1177/1475725718811711

Sex Trafficking Opposition Project. (n.d.). *S.T.O.P sex trafficking: The call to end 21st century slavery.* stop.mercer.edu/who_we_are.htm

Seymour, E., Hunter, A. B., Laursen, S., & DeAntonni, T. (2004). Establishing the benefits of research experiences for undergraduates in the sciences: First findings from a three-year study. *Science, 88*(4), 493–534. https://doi.org/10.1002/sce.10131

Sher, A. (2016, April 4). Bill splitting apart Tennessee Board of Regents approved senate, goes to governor. *Chattanooga Times Free Press.* https://www.timesfreepress.com/news/politics/state/story/2016/apr/04/bill-splitting-apart-tennessee-board-regents-approved-senate-goes-governor/358723/

Shneiderman, B. (2016). *The new ABCs of research: Achieving breakthrough collaborations.* Oxford University Press.

Showman, A., Cat, L. A., Cook, J., Holloway, N., & Wittman, T. (2013). Five essential skills for every undergraduate researcher. *CUR Quarterly, 33*(3), 16–20. https://www.cur.org/assets/1/7/333Spring13Showman16-20.pdf

Singer, J., & Mogk, D. (2020). *Assessment of undergraduate research.* https://serc.carleton.edu/NAGTWorkshops/undergraduate_research/assessment_pedagogy.html

Singer, J., & Weiler, D. (2009). A longitudinal student outcomes evaluation of the Buffalo State College Summer Undergraduate Research Program. *CUR Quarterly, 29*(3), 20–25.

Singer, J., & Zimmerman, B., (2012) Evaluating a summer undergraduate research program: Measuring student outcomes and program impact. *CUR Quarterly, 32*(3), 40–47.

Single Stop USA. (n.d.). *Services.* singlestopusa.org/services

Smith, A. (2019, June 26). CUNY expands student success programs and helps export them. *Inside Higher Education.* https://www.insidehighered.com/news/2019/06/26/cuny-expands-student-success-programs-and-helps-export-them

Smith, B. (2013). *Mentoring at-risk students through the hidden curriculum of higher education.* Lexington Books.

Smith, R. (2016). *Co-generative dialogue's communicative effectiveness in higher education entry-level college courses.* [Master's thesis. University of Rhode Island]. https://digitalcommons.uri.edu/theses/852

Soares, L. (2010, October 4). *The power of the education-industry partnership.* Center for American Progress. https://americanprogress.org/issues/economy/reports/2010/10/04/8518/the-powerpfo-the-education-industry-partnership/

Somma. D. (2017, May 2). *Illegal taking of horseshoe crabs.* https://www.nps.gov/ gate/learn/news/illegal-taking-of-horseshoe-crabs.htm

Sotomayor, S. (2013). *My beloved world.* Alfred A. Knopf.

Southern California Conference on Undergraduate Research. (n.d.). *Home page.* www.sccur.org

Southwest Institute for Engineering Transfer Excellence. (n.d.). *Mission statement.* http://aar.faculty.asu.edu/asap/index.html

Spinu, L., Hwang, J., Pincus, N., & Vasilita, M. (2020). Exploring the use of an artificial accent of English to assess phonetic learning in monolingual and bilingual speakers. *Proceedings of Interspeech 2020.* http://www.interspeech2020.org/ uploadfile/pdf/Wed-1-10-4.pdf

STAR Journal. (n.d.). *Home page.* https://star-journal.org/

Stevens, R., & Phillips, M. W. (2019). *Effects of various substances on heart rates of daphnia subjected to g-forces* [Poster presentation]. National Conference on Undergraduate Research, Kenesaw State University.

Stilgoe, J. R. (1998). *Outside lies magic: Regaining history and awareness in everyday places.* Walker and Company.

Stoelker, T. (2020, January 21). *Albalimulus bottoni: Horseshoe crab named for Professor Mark Botton.* Fordham News. https://news.fordham.edu/science/albalimulus- bottoni-horseshoe-crab-named-for-professor-mark-botton/

Stokes, B. E. (1997). *Pasteur's quadrant: Basic science and technological innovation.* Brookings Institution Press.

Strand, K., Marullo, S., Cutforth, N. J., Stoecker, R., & Donohue, P. (2003). Principles of best practice for community-based research. *Michigan Journal of Community Service Learning, 9*, 5–15. https://quod.lib.umich.edu/m/mjcsl/3239 521.0009.301?rgn=main;view=fulltext

Student Assessment of Their Learning Gains. (n.d.). *Welcome to the SALG website.* www.salgsite.org

SWIETE. (n.d.). Southwest Institute for ENG Transfer Excellence. https://aar .faculty.asu.edu

Taraban, R., & Blanton, R. L. (Eds.) (2008). *Creating effective undergraduate research program in science: The transformation from student to scientist.* Teachers College Press.

Tennessee Board of Regents. (n.d.). *HIP taxonomy: Undergraduate research & creative activities.* https://www.tbr.edu/student-success/hip-taxonomy-undergraduate- research-creative-activities

Tennessee Board of Regents. (2017, December 20). *College system selected to work on two high-level student success initiatives.* https://www.tbr.edu/news/college-system- selected-work-two-high-level-national-initiatives-improve-college-student.

Tennessee Board of Regents. (2019, August). *Tennessee promise at community colleges: Student success for the second cohort of promise students*, 1–2. https://www.tbr.edu/ sites/default/files/media/2020/03/TN-Promise-2016_Executive%20Summary_ July2019_0.pdf

Tila, D. (December 1, 2020). Economic experiments improve learning and attitudes towards economics: A case study at a community college of the City University of

New York. *The Journal of Education for Business, 96*(5), 308–316. https://doi.org /10.1080/08832323.2020.1812489

Traver, A. E., Kincaid, S., & Jacob, F. (Eds.). (2018). *Poetry across the curriculum: New methods for writing intensive pedagogy for U.S. community college and undergraduate education.* Brill.

Tsapogas, J. (2004, April). The role of community colleges in the education of recent science and engineering graduates. *InfoBrief, Science Resources Statistics,* National Science Foundation, NSF 04-315. https://wayback.archive-it .org/5902/20150628084151/http://www.nsf.gov/statistics/infbrief/nsf04315/ nsf04315.pdf

Tsui, E., Freudenberg, N., Manzo, L., Jones, H., Kwan, A., & Gagnon, M. (2011, April). *Housing instability at CUNY: Results from a survey of CUNY undergraduate students.* Healthy CUNY Initiative, City University of New York. http://web .gc.cuny.edu/che/cunyhousingstability.pdf

Tulsa Community College. (2015, November 9). *College names George Kaiser Family endowed chairs.* https://www.tulsacc.edu/about-us/news-and-events/publications/ weekgeorge-kaiser-family-foundation-endowed-chairs

Tweedie, S. (2015, July 3). *How the microwave was invented by a radar engineer who accidentally cooked a candy bar in his pocket.* Business Leader. https:// www.businessinsider.com/how-the-microwave-oven-was-invented-by-acci- dent-2015-4.

United Nations. (n.d.). *Sustainable development goals.* www.un.org/sustainabledevel- opment

United States Census Bureau. (2018, July 1). *Census quick facts.* https://www.census .gov/quickfacts/map/INC110213/00

United States Census Bureau. (2019). https://www.census.gov/quickfacts/

United States Department of Health and Human Services, Office of Research Integrity. (n.d.) *Module One.* https://ori.hhs.gov/node/1198/printable/print

U.S. Congress, Joint Economic Committee. (2012, April). *STEM education: Preparing for the jobs of the future.* https://www.jec.senate.gov/public/_cache/ files/6aaa7e1f-9586-47be-82e7-326f47658320/stem-education---preparing-for- the-jobs-of-the-future-.pdf

U.S. Department of Education, Office of the Under Secretary. (2016). *America's college promise playbook.* http://www2.ed.gov/documents/press-releases/college- promise- playbook.pdf

University of California, Berkeley. (2015). *Advancing California community college students through engineering research.* Award # 1461157. https://www.nsf.gov/ awardsearch/showAward?AWD_ID=1461157&HistoricalAwards=false

Usher, T. (2016). *Undergraduate research collaborations between TYCs universities, and industry/government* [PowerPoint presentation].

Valizade, V., & Spinu, L. (2019, December 4–6). *Consonant production in bilinguals: The relationship between native language, degree of bilingualism, and voice onset time* [Poster presentation]. Acoustical Society of America annual meeting, San Diego, CA.

Van Niel, J. J. (2014). Bears in our backyard. In N. H. Hensel & B. D. Cejda (Eds.), *Tapping the potential of all: Undergraduate research at community colleges* (pp. 78–83). Council on Undergraduate Research.

Van Roy, P., Briggs, D. E. G., & Gaines, R. R. (2105). The Fezouata fossils of Morrocco: An extraordinary record of marine life in the Early Ordovician. *Journal of the Geological Society, 172*, 541–549. https://doi.org/10.1144/jgs2015-017

VanIngen-Dunn, C. (2016). *Making a difference: Community colleges are key drivers of rural development*. Science Foundation of Arizona. http://www.sfaz.org/making-difference-community-colleges-key-drivers-rural-development/

Vasquesz, I. (2019, December 6). *Stuck between two worlds* [Panel presentation]. Queensborough Community College, Undergraduate Research Day.

Vitale, A. (2011). *The fight against pathways at CUNY*. AAUP. https://www.aaup.org/article/fight-against-pathways-cuny

Walker, R. (2019). *The art of noticing: 131 ways to spark creativity, find inspiration, and discover joy in the everyday*. Alfred A. Knopf.

Walters State Community College. (n.d.). *Walters State announced partnership with ORNL*. https://www.ws.edu/academics/research/news/

Walters State Community College. (2013, September 12). *One outstanding student spent the summer at ORNL*. Walters State Community College News. https://ws.edu/news/current/article.aspx?story=473

Wang, C., & Burris, M. A. (1997). Photovoice: concept, methodology, and use for participatory needs assessment. *Health Education Behavior, 24*(3), 369–387. doi:10.1177/109019819702400309

Weiler, D. (2013). *Developing undergraduate research at community colleges: Tapping the potential of all students evaluation report*. Daniel Weiler Associates.

Wenzel, T. (1997). What is undergraduate research? *Council on Undergraduate Research Quarterly, 17,* 163.

Wermund, B. (2019, January 16). *The red state that loves free college*. Politico Pro. https://www.politico.com/agenda/story/2019/01/16/tennessee-free-college-000867/

White House, Office of the Press Secretary. (2009, July 14). *Remarks by the president on the American Graduate Initiative in Warren, MI*. https://obamawhitehouse.archives.gov/the-press-office/remarks-president-american-graduation-initiative-warren-mi

White House Office of the Press Secretary. (2015, January 9). *White House unveils America's College Promise proposal: Tuition-free community college for responsible students* [Fact Sheet.] https://obamawhitehouse.archives.gov/the-press-office/2015/01/09/fact-sheet-white-house-unveils-america-s-college-promise-proposal-tuitio

Willison, J. (2009). Multiple contexts, multiple outcomes, one conceptual framework for research skill development in the undergraduate curriculum. *CUR Quarterly, 29*(3), 10–14.

Willison, J. (2018). Research skill development spanning high education: Critiques, curricula and connections. *Journal of University Teaching & Learning Practice, 15*(4), 1–15.

Young, G., & Shanahan, J. O. (2018). *Undergraduate research in music: A guide for students*. Routledge.

Xu, N., Porter-Morgan, H., Doran, N., & Keller, C. (2016, October 12). Water pollution and leukemia: A model for interdisciplinary research in the classroom experiences incorporating effective pedagogical appraoches for community college general biology 1 lab students. *International Journal of Higher Education*, *5*(4), 122–133. https://files.eric.ed.gov/fulltext/EJ1116851.pdf

Zeng, H. J., Johnson, M. A., Ramdihal, J. D., Sumner, R. A., Rodriguez, C., Lall-Ramnarine, S. I., & Wishart, J. F. (2019). Spectroscopic assessment of intra- and intermolecular hydrogen bonding in ether-functionalized imidazolium ionic liquids. *Journal of Physical Chemistry*, *123*(39), 8370–8376. https://www.osti.gov/pages/servlets/purl/1558252

# ABOUT THE AUTHOR

**Nancy Hensel** has been a faculty member, dean, provost, and university president. She served as executive officer of the Council of Undergraduate Research (CUR) for 7 years. In that role she served as co-PI for several National Science Foundation grants to assist colleges in developing undergraduate research programs. She has written or edited a variety of books about undergraduate research, including *Course-Based Undergraduate Research* (Stylus, 2018); *Transformative Research at Predominately Undergraduate Institutions* with Kerry K. Karukstis (CUR, 2007); and *Faculty Support and Undergraduate Research: Innovations in Faculty Role Definition, Workload, and Reward* with Elizabeth L. Paul (CUR, 2012). She coedited two monographs on undergraduate research that specifically address student research at community colleges. She has given many speeches on undergraduate research and is a recognized national and international leader on the topic.

AAAS. *See* American Association for the Advancement of Science

AACC. *See* American Association of Community Colleges

AAC&U. *See* Association of American Colleges & Universities

Academic language, 53–54, 155

Academic Success & Professional Development Academy (ASAP), 123

Accelerated Study in Associate Programs (ASAP), 35–36

Acoustical Society of America, 68, 70

Action plan, for undergraduate research, 29, 169

Action research, 185–86

Administrators, undergraduate research and, 27, 28–29, 167, 169, 186

Advanced Technological Education (ATE), 20, 23, 28, 172, 176–77

Advantage, bilingual, 69

*Advice to a Young Scientist* (Medawar), 62

Advising, of students, 14–15, 36

Agassiz, Louis, 147

"Alumni perceptions used to assess undergraduate research experience" (Bauer & Bennett), 158

American Academy of Arts and Sciences, 63

American Anthropological Association, 98

American Association for the Advancement of Science (AAAS), 76

American Association of Community Colleges (AACC), 15, 176

American College Promise, 5–6

American Enterprise Institute, 13

American Geophysical Union, 129

American Graduation Initiative, 4, 5

American literature, courses on, 84

American Sign Language (ASL), 74–75

American Society for Microbiology, 136

A Night in the Chocó (student event), 102

Anthropology, 97–98, 114–15

Anticipation, of questions, 54

Applied research, 24–25, 61–63, 71–73

ArchiTexture Dance Company, 109

Arctic Circle, 109–11

Argonne National Laboratory, 25–26, 125

Arizona, 13, 37–39, 122

Arizona State University (ASU), 122

Art History, 116

Articles, coauthorship of, 171

Articulation agreements, 6, 33

Articulatory control, 69

*The Art of Noticing* (Walker), 146

ASAP. *See* Academic Success & Professional Development Academy; Accelerated Study in Associate Programs

ASL. *See* American Sign Language

ASL Interpreter Education Program, 74

Aspirnaut program, Vanderbilt University, 137–38

Assets, of students, 55–56, 144–45
Association of American Colleges &
    Universities (AAC&U), 8–9, 16,
    143, 161, 176
ASU. *See* Arizona State University
ATE. *See* Advanced Technological
    Education
Atlassian, 109
Attrition, 70
Audism, 117–18
AURA, 167
Authentic communication, 112
Award for Undergraduate Research
    Accomplishments (AURA), 167

Bacteria experiment, 85
Bain, Ken, 148–49, 152
Baines, Kristina, 97–98
Ball State University, 105
Bangera, Gita, 24, 181
Basic research, 25–27, 61–63,
    64–66
Bauer, K. W., 158
Bears, research on, 24–25, 62–63
Belize, 99
Bellevue College, 24, 181
Benefits, of undergraduate research,
    157–58
"Benefits of undergraduate research
    experiences" (Russell), 18–19
Bennett, J. S., 158
Benning, James, 147
Bensimon, Estela Maria, 11
Berger, Warren, 149
Bermudes, Oscar, 72
Bhakta, Jayesh, 133
Biden, Jill, 7, 186
Biden, Joe, 6, 47, 187
Bilingual advantage, 69
Bilingual cognition, 68
Biology, 71–73, 76, 78–81, 84–88,
    95–96
Birds, research on, 78–79
*Bloom!* (Cavazzi), 110

BNL. *See* Brookhaven National
    Laboratory
Boas, Franz, 98
*Borders and Migration* (SPT students),
    112, 113
Botton, Mark, 123–24
Brew, Angela, 142
Brookhaven National Laboratory
    (BNL), 124–26
Brown, David, 124
Brown, Edmund, 32
Buettner, Jamie, 116–18, 145, 147,
    151
*Building guided pathways to community
    college student success* (Jenkins),
    42–43
Bureau of Labor Statistics, 10
Burrowing owls, 95, 96
Bush, George W., 5
Bush, Vannevar, 61, 64
Business Roundtable, 6
Butros, Michael, 131

Cacao, 102
Calderon, Olga, 84–87, 144–45
California
    California State University San
        Bernardino (CSUSB), 129–30,
        132
    Community College System of
        (CCCS), 31–34
    Space Grant Consortium, 129–30,
        133
    Campaign for College Opportunity,
        33
Campus, parking on, 13
Cardona, Miguel, 7
Career preparation, 141
Carnevale, A. P., 8, 10, 11, 13,
    182
Carter, V. Celeste, 176
Carvajal, Bridgett, 137
CASE, 179–80
Cavazzi, Deidre, 109–11

CBE. *See* competency-based education

CBR. *See* Community-based research

CCA. *See* Complete College Agenda

CCC. *See* City Colleges of Chicago

CCCS. *See* California Community College System

CCCSE. *See* Center for Community College Student Engagement

CCI. *See* Department of Energy Community College Internships

CCIP. *See* Community College Industry Partnerships

CCLI. *See* Course, Curriculum, and Laboratory Improvement

CCURI. *See* Council on Undergraduate Research and the Community College Undergraduate Research Initiative

Cejda, Brent, 20, 23, 28, 186–87

Celebration Days, 170, 183–84

Census, U.S., 127

Center for Community College Student Engagement (CCCSE), 16

Center for Research Excellence in Science and Technology (CREST), 130–31, 172

Center on Education and Workforce (CEW), 8

CEW. *See* Center on Education and Workforce

Changes, Pedagogical, 141–42

Characteristics of Excellence in Undergraduate Research (COEUR), 44

*Characteristics of Excellence in Undergraduate Research* (COEUR), 167

Chen, Biling, 137

Childcare, 12, 49–50

Child Development, 103–4

Chocó Hotspot of Biodiversity, 101

*Chronicle of Higher Education* (newspaper & website), 8

CILES. *See* Continuous Intensive Learning Environment through STEM

CIPAIR. *See* NASA Curriculum Improvement Award for the Integration of Research

Cisco Advanced Network Engineer program, 65

Citizen science, 80, 93

City Colleges of Chicago, 15

City University of New York (CUNY), 31, 34–37, 47–48, 51, 167–68, 185

Civic engagement, 91

Climate change, 110

Cline, Jonathan, 67

Clinton, Bill, 5

*The Clubfoot* (de Ribera), 117

CMA. *See* Computational Music Analysis

Coachella Valley, 130–31

Coalition to Save Hempstead Harbor, 87

Coauthorship, of articles, 171

COD. *See* College of the Desert

COEUR. *See* Characteristics of Excellence in Undergraduate Research

Co-generative dialogue, 86

Cognition, bilingual, 68

Cohen, Laura, 113

Co-initiating, 112

Cold Spring Harbor, 87–88

College of DuPage, 25–26, 124

College of the Desert (COD), 130, 132–33

Colleges, rural, 40

Colon, Christina, 80, 123–24, 145

Columbia State Community College, 137–38

Communication, authentic, 112

Communities of practice, 180–81

Community-based research (CBR), 91, 92–106

Community College Genomics
Research Initiative (ComGen),
181
Community College Industry
Partnerships (CCIPs), 38, 65–66,
124–38
Community College Research Center,
14, 15, 33, 43
Community colleges, 6, 178
number of in U.S., 4
reasons for dropping out, 12–13
Community College Undergraduate
Research Experience Summit,
176–77
Community resources, in research, 155
Comparative Anatomy, 78
Competency-based education (CBE),
13
Complete College Agenda (CCA), 40
Completion, of degree, 11–12
composition project, 119–20
Computational Music Analysis (CMA),
67
Conferences, virtual, 171
Congress Joint Economic Committee,
of United States, 63
connection, of students to community,
92
Connections, in research, 55, 150–51
Conservation, 101
Constraints, time, 178
Continuous Intensive Learning
Environment through STEM
(CILES), 120
Continuum, of undergraduate research
activities, *22*
Contributions, by students, 154
Control, articulatory, 69
Convergence, of ideas, 108
"Cookbook" experiments, 23, 24
Cool Anthropology, 97–98
Costa, Victoria, 97–98
Co-teaching, 86
Coteaching, by students, 154

Council for Advancement and Support
for Education (CASE), 179–80
Council on Undergraduate Research
(CUR), 18, 20–22, 28, 31, 78
biennial conference, 92
COEUR and, 167
regional conversations and, 175
Council on Undergraduate Research
and the Community College
Undergraduate Research Initiative
(CCURI), 44, 175–76, 180
Country project, 82
Course, Curriculum, and Laboratory
Improvement (CCLI), 28, 175
Course-based research (CURE), 76–81,
83–84, 88–90, 164, 181–83
at QCC, 71–72, 78, 87, 129
traditional, 87, 88
Course Hero Fellow, 98
COVID-19, 70–71, 100, 150, 184
CREST. *See* Center for Research
Excellence in Science and
Technology
Critical thinking, 107
CRSP. *See* CUNY Research Scholars
Program
Cryptography, 65–66
CSUSB. *See* California State University
San Bernardino
"Cultivating Communities of Care
Through Action Research"
(Huggins), 113
Cultural capital, 53
CUNY, 31, 34–37, 47–48, 51, 167–68,
185
CUNY Graduate Center, 85, 97, 101
CUNY-NASA Solar and Atmospheric
Research Program and Education
Partnership (SOLAR PREP), 128
CUNY Research Scholars Program
(CRSP), 36, 68, 70–71, 95, 121
financial support and, 179
graduation rates and, 167–68
student satisfaction with, 168

CUR. *See* Council on Undergraduate Research
CURE. *See* Course-based research
CUREnet, 76–77
curiosity-driven research, 149
*CUR Quarterly* (journal), 169
Curriculum, Course, and Laboratory Improvement (CCLI), 28

Damas, M. Chantale, 128–29
Daniel Weiler Associates, 161–62
Da Vinci, Leonardo, 117
Days, Celebration, 170
DD. *See* Doubly disadvantaged
Definition of undergraduate research, 18, 21, 43, 169
degrees granted, number of, 4, 32
Deibert, Debbie, 103–4, 149, 185–86
Delgado, Hannia, 98
Democracy, participatory, 142
Democratic leadership, 57
Department of Education, U.S., 120
Department of Energy, U.S. (DOE), 173
    Community College Internships (CCI), 124–25, 127
    Office of Science Workforce Development for Teachers and Scientists, 127
    Smart Grid Initiative of, 25–26
de Ribera, Jusepe, 117
de Silva, Eugene, 126–27
Different perspectives, of students, 154
Diffie-Hellman key exchange, 66
*Distinctions* (journal), 84
Distl, Joseph, 112
Diversity, in community colleges, 7, 10–11, 32–33, 85, 94
DOE. *See* Department of Energy, U.S.
DOEC. *See* New York State Department of Environmental Conservation
Dolan, Erin, 76–77
Doubly disadvantaged (DD), 52–53

Drive to 55, 42
Drone, 101, 102, 132
Dropping out, reasons for, 12–13
Duarte-Diaz, H., 117
Dugaillard, Beckie, 69
Dunlap, Felicia, 75

Earth Rover, 134
Economic investigation map, 82
Economics
    concern with, 11–12
    development, 3, 8, 10, 17, 27, 30, 33
    at KBCC, 81–82
Economy, knowledge-based, 8, 30
Ecuador, 101, 102, 103
Eddy, J., 86
EDL. *See* Entry, descent and landing
Educational equity
    Guttman Community College, 99
    MCCD and, 38
    TBR and, 44
    undergraduate research and, 22, 182
    workforce development and, 6, 7, 8, 10–11, 45, 187
Educational practices, of U.S., 52
Eivazova, Elvira, 136, 137–38
Elasticity, in economics, 82
Elements of undergraduate research, at Tennessee community colleges, 43–44, 169–70
*elife* (journal), 136–37
Emotional labor, 143–44
Encouragement, of questions, 55, 64, 79, 85–86, 148–49
Encryption, 65–66
English literature research, 83–84
Ensz, C., 118
*Entangled States* (Cavazzi), 110
Enterococci monitoring, 73
Enterprise Performance, 38–39
Entry, descent, and landing (EDL), 133
Environmental ethics, 97, 99
Environmental Protection Agency, U.S., 26, 73, 93

Environmental Science, 92–93, 109–10
EOW. *See* Ethnographies of Work
ePortfolio, 95, 99, 173
Equal access, to education, 8, 10–11,
    30, 33, 35, 38
  Guttman Community College, 99
  undergraduate research and, 22, 182
  workforce development and, 6, 7, 8,
    10–11, 45, 187
Equilibrium, 82
Essential features, of undergraduate
    research, 17–18, 159
"The essential features of undergraduate
    research" (Lopatto), 17–18
"Establishing the benefits of research
    experiences for undergraduates in
    the sciences" (Seymour), 159
Estrella Mountain Community College,
    88–90, 95–96, 179, 183
Ethnographic mindset, 98
Ethnographies of Work (EOW),
    114–16
Ethnography, 98–99, 115
Ethnography Matters, 98
Evaluate-Complete, 164
EvaluateUR, 161–63, 164
EvaluateUR-CURE, 164
Evaluation, of faculty, 173–74
Evidence, use of, 55, 151
Expanding opportunities, for
    undergraduate research, 28–29
Experience, knowledge from, 56
Eynon, B., 173
EZStats, 163

Faculty
  evaluation of, 173–74
  guidance from, 18, 27, 33, 51, 187
  as mentors, 51–52, 57, 72, 87, 88,
    151–52, 168, 174
  office hours of, 54
  research initiated by, 22
  teaching load of, 27
Farmer, Carl, 130

Features of undergraduate research,
    essential, 17–18, 159
Feynman, Richard, 110–11
Fieldwork, 80
Financial goals, of Maricopa
    Community College District, 39
Financial support, for undergraduate
    research, 179–80
Finger Lakes Community College
    (FLCC), 24–25, 175, 184–85
First-generation students, 7, 12, 30,
    46, 58
  course-based research and, 76–77,
    97, 158
  struggles of, 53
FLCC. *See* Finger Lakes Community
    College
Focused practice, 75
Focused research question, 18
Food insecurity, 11, 47
  research into, 48
4-year universities
  community colleges contrasted with,
    20, 21
  transfer rates to, 33, 168
Free Academy of the City of New York,
    35
Free tuition, 5, 6
Fruit flies, 120–21
Full, Robert, 149
Full professor, promotion to,
    185–86
Fund for Improving Secondary
    Education (FIPSE), 173
Funding programs, of NSF, 172
Future of Higher Education Task Force,
    41

Gadura, Nidhi, 87–88
GAO. *See* Government Accountability
    Office
Gap, workforce skills, 40
Gatta, Mary, 114–16, 146
GEAR UP, 41

George Kaiser Family Foundation, 118
Georgetown University, 53
Gilligan, C., 86
Giridharadas, A., 115
Global Guttman, 99, 100–101
Goals, of students, 13, 14
Goddard Space Flight Center, 128–29
Goldrick-Rab, Sara, 47–48
Golebiewska, Urszula, 136–37, 148
Government Accountability Office (GAO), 9, 47
Graduation rates, CRSP and, 168
Grant Success, 172–73
Graves, Denyce, 56
Green, Ryan Speedo, 56
Green Fuels Depot project, 25–27, 124
Guidance, of faculty, 18, 27, 33, 51, 187
Guided Pathways, 14–16, 51
  at California colleges, 33
  at CUNY, 35–36
  at MCCD, 37–38
  at Oklahoma colleges, 40
  at Tennessee colleges, 42–43
Gutleizer, Sholom, 69
Guttman Community College, 97–100, 114–15
Guzman, Geovanny, 112

Hanini, Rawan, 69
Harper, Francis Ellen Watkins, 84
Harper, William Rainey, 4–5
Harrington, Michael, 47
Hart Research Associates, 8
Haslam, Bill, 42
Hayashi, Arawana, 111–14
Head Start, 52
Herman, Amy, 147
HHMI, 135–36, 138
Hidden curriculum, 52
*High-Impact Educational Practices* (Kuh), 160
High Impact practices (HIP), 44, 74, 173

Hills, Laura, 147–48
HIP. *See* High Impact practices
History, Art, 116
Hochschild, Arlie Russell, 143
Hoffman, Nancy, 116
Holton Higher Education Center, 3–4
Honors in Action Project, 89
Honors Transfer Council of California, 183
hooks, bell, 141–42
Horseshoe crabs, research on, 80, 123–24
Housing insecurity, 11, 48–49
Howard Hughes Medical Institute (HHMI), 135–36, 138
Hudd, Suzanne, 153
Huggins, Heather, 111–12, 144
Humanities, research in, 36–37
Hypothesis, development of, 155

Ideas, convergence of, 108
IDR. *See* Interdisciplinary research
Impact, of undergraduate research, 159–60
*The Impact of Deliberate Practice on Spatial Mapping in American Sign Language/English Interpretation* (Dunlap), 75
Implementation strategies, for undergraduate research, 29
Improving Undergraduate STEM Education (IUSE), 172
Inclusiveness, 112, 141–56, 182
Incorporation, of research in curriculum, 23–24, 27
Industrial economy, 8
Informal Assessment, 170–71
Information Technology Evaluation Criteria, 66
*In Memory* (ArchiTexture Dance Company), 110
Insecurity
  food, 47–48
  housing, 48–49
Institutional Review Board, 21, 89, 103

Instruction, online, 13–14
Integrated Postsecondary Education Data System (IPEDS), 11
Integrated Student Support, 37–38
*Intelligence and Law Enforcement in the 21st Century* (conference), 127
Interdisciplinary research (IDR), 107, 108, 109
Interests, of students, 145
International Symposium on Monolingual and Bilingual Speech, 69
International Union for the Conservation of Nature, 81
Interns, in research, 103–4
Invention, of Velcro, 150
Ionic liquids, 125
IPEDS. *See* Integrated Postsecondary Education Data System
Irvine Valley College, 131–32
Irving, Washington, 84
Ismail, Adam, 65
Itapoa Reserve, 101
IUSE. *See* Improving Undergraduate STEM Education

Jack, Anthony Abraham, 52
Jarman, Richard, 25–26
Jenkins, D., 42–43
Jet Propulsion Laboratory (JPL), NASA, 133, 135
Johnson, Lyndon B., 47
Joliet Junior College, 5
*The Journal of Chemical Physics* (journal), 126
*The Journal of Physical Chemistry A* (journal), 126
JPL. *See* Jet Propulsion Laboratory
Junior college, 5
Justice, social, 91

Katz, Robert, 119–20
KBCC, 35, 67–68, 78–84
KCAACTF. *See* Kennedy Center American College Theater Festival

K-CORE. *See* Kingsborough Collaborative Research Bootcamp
Kennedy Center American College Theater Festival (KCAACTF), 112–13
King, Ross, 117–18
Kingsborough Collaborative Research Bootcamp (K-CORE), 70
Kingsborough Community College (KBCC), 35, 67–68, 78–84
Knowledge, from experience, 56
Knowledge-based economy, 8, 30
Kuh, George, 16, 161

Laboratory work, students and, 72
LACC. *See* Los Angeles City College
LaGuardia Community College (LGCC), 36, 84–85, 92–95, 120–21, 173
Lall-Ramnarine, Sharon, 125, 145
Lamott, Annie, 146
LAMP. *See* loop-mediated amplification
Landin, Jennifer, 147
Lang, James, 150
Language, academic, 53–54, 155
Lassiter, L. E., 105
La Vaca Independiente, 113
Leader in innovation, U.S. as, 9, 23, 63
LEAP. *See* Liberal Education and America's Promise
*Learning while earning* (Carnevale & Smith), 11
Leon, Juan, 65, 66, 145
Leukemia, 120–21
Levers of positive change, in undergraduate research, 181
Levy, F., 77–78
LGCC, 36, 84–85, 92–95, 120–21, 173
Liberal Education and America's Promise (LEAP), 176
LIDAR. *See* Light detection and ranging
*The life and artwork of Pablo Picasso and the significance of how color theory*

*pertaining to the mood of this Blue and Rose period* (Duarte-Diaz), 117

Light detection and ranging (LIDAR), 134

Linear narrative, 83

Linguistics, 67–69

Liquids, ionic, 125

"Listening as a path to psychological discovery" (Gilligan & Eddy), 85

Logistical challenges, 46–47, 177–78

Logue, Alexandra, 36

Loop-mediated amplification (LAMP), 72–73

Lopatto, David, 17–18, 158–59, 165–66

Los Angeles City College (LACC), 133–34

Lynd, H. M. and R.S., 105

Macon, Georgia, 92

Maine, 3, 4

*Making it relevant* (Schulten), 150–51

*The Managed Heart* (Hochschild), 143

Map, economic investigation, 82

Mapping, spatial, 74

Maricopa Community College District (MCCD), 37, 38–39, 90

Mars, research on, 131–32

Mason, Linda, 41–42

Math classes, and STEM jobs, 41

Math Task Force, 41

MCC. *See* Mesa Community College

MCCD. *See* Maricopa Community College District

Medawar, Peter, 62

Mental illness, 89

Mentors, faculty as, 51–52, 57, 72, 87, 88
   with classes, 151–52, 174
   CRSP and, 168
   EvaluateUR, 163, 164

Mercer University, 92

Mesa Community College (MCC), 24

*Metal vs. Make-up* (Cline), 67

Methicillin resistant staphylococcus aureus (MRSA), 72, 80

Metropolitan Association of College and University Biologists, 73, 79

METS. *See* Motivated Engineering Transfer Students

Michigan Mandate, 159–60

Microbiology, 85

Microclimate, 101

*Middletown* (Lynd), 105

Minority students, 46, 49, 53, 133

Mira Costa Community College, 66–67

Modeling, of thought process, 57–58

Monroe Community College, 62

*A More Beautiful Question* (Berger), 149

Motivated Engineering Transfer Students (METS), 122–23

MRSA. *See* Methicillin resistant staphylococcus aureus

Multidisciplinary research, 100

"Multiple contexts, multiple outcomes, one conceptual framework for research skill development in the undergraduate curriculum" (Willison), 165

Musical analysis, computational, 67

Music History, 118

Nanotechnology, 123

Naperville, Illinois, 25–26, 124

NASA. *See* National Aeronautic Space Administration

NASH. *See* National Association of System Heads

National Academies of Sciences, Engineering, and Medicine, 9, 77, 107

National Academy of Engineering, 107–8

National Aeronautic Space Administration (NASA), 102, 128–30, 135

National Association of System Heads (NASH), 44–45

National Center for Biology Information GenBank, 136
National Center for Education Statistics, 12
National Center for Inquiry and Improvement (NCII), 38
National Conference on Undergraduate Research (NCUR), 22, 170–71, 184
National Council of Instructional Administrators (NCIA), 20, 22, 175
National Institute of Health (NIH), 173
National Laboratories, 25, 124–25
National Research Council, 61–62, 108
National Science Board (NSB), 63
National Science Foundation (NSF), 19, 20, 23, 28, 29, 63
  CREST and, 131–32
  funding programs of, 172
  SWIETE and, 123
National Student Clearinghouse, 8, 11–12
National Survey of Student Engagement (NSSE), 161
National University of Ireland at Galway, 111
Native Americans, in New England, 84
NCIA. *See* National Council of Instructional Administrators
*The New ABCs of Research* (Shneiderman), 62
New England, Native Americans in, 84
New knowledge and evidence, 55
Newton Creek Field Day, 95
Newtown Creek, as Superfund site, 92, 95, 120
Newtown Creek Alliance, 93–94
New York State Department of Environmental Conservation (DOEC), 24–25
*The New York Times* (newspaper), 115
*New York Times* Learning Network, 150

Nguyen, Andrew Anh Van, 71–72
Nieto, Raul, 101
Nobel Prize, 62, 137
Non-STEM disciplines, CUREs and, 77, 177
Northern Maine Technical Community College, 3
NSB. *See* National Science Board
NSF. *See* National Science Foundation
NSSE. *See* National Survey of Student Engagement
NXT Robotics, 130–31

Oak Ridge National Laboratory, 126–27
Obama, Barack, 4, 5
Observation, poetry and, 148
Observations, from students, 55, 146
Office Hours, of faculty, 54
Office of Research Integrity, 155
Office of Undergraduate Research, 161
Oklahoma, 39–42
Oklahoma Research Day, 42, 75, 183, 186
Oklahoma Space Grant Consortium, 134–35
Oklahoma's Promise, 40
Oklahoma State System of Higher Education (OSRHE), 39–42
Online instruction, 13–14
Open access, 7, 32
Open pedagogies, 58, 99
Original research, 22
Ornithology, 78–80
Ortiz, Mary, 78–80, 148, 182
OSRHE. *See* Oklahoma State System of Higher Education
*The Other America* (Harrington), 47
*The Other Side of Middletown* (Lassiter), 105

Packer Engineering, 26
Palm oil, 102
PAR. *See* Participatory action research

Parking, on campus, 13
Participation in Conferences, 170–71
Participatory action research (PAR), 103
Participatory democracy, 142
Partnerships
    4-year universities, 23, 25, 28, 29, 64, 122–23
    industry, 38, 65–66, 124–38
    private sector, 6
Pasadena City College, 65–66
Pasteur, Louis, 62
*Pathways to Reform* (Logue), 36
Pedagogical Changes, 141–42
Peer-Led Authentic Research, 87, 88, 120
Perception, of community college, 178
Performance, enterprise, 38–39
Phillips, Mary Wells, 134–35
Phi Theta Kappa, 89
Phoenix College, 37
Photovoice, 103
Physics, dance and, 110–11
Picasso, Pablo, 117
Plankton, research on, 87
Poetry, observation and, 148
Point of view, 83
Political Science, 105–6
Porter-Morgan, Holly, 93–94, 143
Posters on the Hill (conference), 171
PP. *See* Privileged poor
Practice, focused, 75
Practices, for advancing undergraduate research, 178–79
Practices, high impact, 44
Preparation, career, 141
Presencing, 112
President's Commission of Higher Education, 5
Pressing Public Issues, 97, 186
"Principles of best practice for community-based research" (Strand), 91

Privilege, White, 144
Privileged poor (PP), 52
*The Privileged Poor* (Jack), 52
Problem-solving, 108
Progress, of students, 15, 33
Project Gutenberg, 83
Promotion, to full professor, 185–86
Prosthetics, research on, 134
Psi Beta, 89
Psychology, research projects on, 88–89
Pubill, Kaylynn, 72–73
Publications, of undergraduate research, 171
Pulitzer Center's Campus Consortium, 100–101
Pyles, R. A., 77–78

QCC. *See* Queensborough Community College
QCC SWREP. *See* Space Weather Research and Education Program
QR. *See* Quick Response code
Quadcopter project, 101, 102, 132
Quantum encryption, 66
Queensborough Community College (QCC), 35, 71–72, 78, 87–88, 111–12
    Brookhaven National Laboratory and, 125–26
    NASA and, 128–29
question-centered pedagogy, 149
Quick Response code (QR), 89

Racism, 144
Radical listening, 86, 148
Rattlesnakes, research on, 24
*Recovery* (Carnevale), 8
Recruiting, of students, 6
Reedley Community College, 116–17
Relevant content, for students, 153–54
*Replacing Public Cryptographic Key Exchanges with Quantum Resistant Implementations* (Ismail), 65

Research, 9, 12, 17–18, 19–20, 100
    applied, 24–25, 61–63, 71–73
    basic, 25–27, 61–62, 64–66
Research, Innovation, Service and
    Experiential Learning Institute
    (RISE), 181
Research Experience for
    Undergraduates (REU), 72, 123,
    134
Research question, focused, 18, 64
"Research skill development spanning
    high education" (Willison), 165
Research Skills Development
    Framework (RSD), 165
Retention, 11–12, 23
Rice University, 123
Rigert, Heidi, 119–20
Rio Salada Community College, 13
RISE. See Research, Innovation, Service
    and Experiential Learning Institute
Rising Above the Gathering Storm
    (National Academies of Science,
    Engineering and Medicine), 9–10,
    63
Risks, in research, 154
Roadmap project, 176
Rockefeller, Nelson A., 35
RSD. See Research Skills Development
    Framework
Rural colleges, 40
Russell, S., 18–19, 158–59

Saddleback Community College,
    109–10
Salton Sea, 131
SBES. See Social, behavioral and
    economic science
SCCUR. See Southern California
    Council for Undergraduate
    Research
Scharmer, Otto, 111
Schedules, work, 50
Scholars, students as, 54–55, 77, 94,
    145–46

Scholarships-in-Science, Technology,
    Engineering and Mathematics
    (S-STEM), 172
"School takes new tack on work study"
    (Giridharadas), 115
Schulten, Katherine, 150–51
Science (journal), 159
Science, Technology, Engineering and
    Mathematics (STEM), 9, 17, 19,
    23, 36
    at CUNY, 68, 120
    CUREs and, 76–77
    interdisciplinary research and, 108
    women in, 10, 93–95, 128–29
Science, the Endless Frontier (Bush, V.),
    61, 65
Science Education Alliance-Phage
    Hunters Advancing Genomics
    and Evolutionary Science (SEA-
    PHAGES), 78, 134–38
Science Undergraduate Laboratory
    Internships (SULI), 124–25
Scudder, Samuel, 147
SEArCHH and ASPIRE. See
    Sustainability, Energy,
    Accessibility, Happiness,
    Health, and (or) Social Policy
    Interdisciplinary Research
    Explorations
Sea stars, research on, 95
Seeding, 112
Senge, Peter, 142
Separate and Unequal (Carnevale &
    Strohl), 182
sex, of owls, 96
Sex Trafficking Opposition Project
    (S.T.O.P), 92
Seymour, Elaine, 159, 166
Sharing, of challenges, 57
Shifting Stereotypes (Cool
    Anthropology), 97–98
Shneiderman, Ben, 62
Sign language & the oppression of the deaf
    had a large impact on the art world

*of De'VIA and Leonardo Da Vinci* (Ensz), 118
Sim, Alec, 132–33
Singer, Jill, 161–62
Single Stop USA, 11, 50–51
Skills, research, 146
Small Business Innovation Research Program and Small Business Technology Transfer Program, 124
"Small Teaching" (Lang), 150
Smietanski, Rhoda, 74–75
Smith, Nicole, 8, 11, 13
Smith, Rachel, 86–87, 95–96
Smith, Sharon, 127
Smith, Vernon, 81–82
Social, behavioral, and economic science (SBES), 19
Social justice, 91, 111, 114
Social Presencing (Distl), 112
*Social Presencing Theater* (Hayashi), 111
Social Presencing Theater (SPT), 111–14
*Social Science Texts and Academic Research (STAR) Journal*, 171
Sociology, research on, 114–15
Solar tracking systems, 132
Sotomayer, Sonia, 55–56, 58
Southern California Council for Undergraduate Research (SCCUR), 65–68, 183
Southwestern Community College, 124
Southwest Institute for Engineering Transfer Excellence (SWIETE), 122–23
Space weather, 128
Space Weather Research and Education Program (QCC SWREP), 128
Spatial mapping, 74
Spencer, Diana, 118–19, 179, 180
Spinu, L., 68–71
SPT. *See* Social Presencing Theater

S-STEM. *See* Scholarships-in-Science, Technology, Engineering and Mathematics
STAR. *See Social Science Texts and Academic Research Journal*
START system, 127
State Board of Higher Education, New York, 35
State legislative representatives, research for, 106
STEM. *See* Science, Technology, Engineering and Mathematics
S.T.O.P. *See* Sex Trafficking Opposition Project
Strand, K., 91
Strohl, J., 182
Struggles, of first-generation students, 53
Stuck exercise, 113
Student-mentor pairs, in EvaluateUR, 163
Students, 13, 14, 18, 55, 146, 154
    minority, 46, 53
    number of, 4, 31, 32, 34, 40
    process-centered research of, *22*
    satisfaction with CRSP and, 168
    as scholars, 54–55, 77, 94, 145
Success, grant, 172–73
Summer School for Logic, Language, and Information, 70
SUNY-Buffalo State, 161
Superfund site, Newtown Creek as, 93
Supplemental Nutrition Assistance Program (SNAP), 47–48
Survey of Undergraduate Research Experiences and CURE, 158, 165–66
Sustainability, Energy, Accessibility, Happiness, Health, and (or) Social Policy Interdisciplinary Research Explorations (SEArCHH and ASPIRE), 119
Svalbard project, 109, 110

SWIETE. *See* Southwest Institute for Engineering Transfer Excellence
Syllabus, 152–53

Task Force on Transformative Research, 63
TBR. *See* Tennessee Board of Regents
TCC. *See* Tulsa Community College
TCUP. *See* Tribal Colleges and Universities Program
Teaching load, of faculty, 27
*Teaching to Transgress* (hooks), 141–42
Teamwork, 109
Tennessee, 42–45
Tennessee Board of Regents (TBR), 42–45, 169
Tennessee community colleges, elements of undergraduate research at, 43–44, 169–70
Tennessee Promise, 42
Tennessee Reconnect, 42
Tennessee Valley Authority (TVA), 127
Tenure, at community colleges, 67–68, 184–85
Tesser, Derek, 101
Theater, Communication and, 111–12
thinking, Critical, 107
Thought process, modeling of, 58
Tila, Dorina, 81–83, 182–83
Time constraints, 178
Tippett, Brian, 90
TNSCORE, 44
Tracking systems, solar, 132
Transfer rates, to 4-year universities, 32, 168
Transformation goals, of Maricopa Community College District, 38–39
Transformative research, 63–64
Transparent teaching, 57
Transportation, 50
Tribal Colleges and Universities Program (TCUP), 172
Truman, Harry, 5

Trustees, research and, 27, 29
Tulsa Community College (TCC), 74, 103, 118–19, 134–35, 179–80
tenure at, 185
Tulsa Educare, 103
TVA. *See* Tennessee Valley Authority

UC. *See* University of California
UMPI. *See* University of Maine at Presque Isle
Undergraduate Research Experiences (URE), 176–77, 181–82
Undergraduate Research Opportunity Program (UROP), 159–60
Undergraduate Research Student Self-Assessment (URSSA), 166
United Nations, 107
United Nations Sustainable Development Goals, 110
University of California (UC), 32, 33, 34, 123
University of Connecticut, 100
University of Maine at Presque Isle (UMPI), 3–4, 105, 142
University of Michigan, 159–60
Urban Barcode Research Program, 87
UROP. *See* Undergraduate Research Opportunity Program
Use, of syllabus to mentor, 152
Usher, Timothy, 129–30

Valizade, Vali, 68
Vanderbilt University, 137–38
Van Niel, John, 25, 62–63
Vasilita, Mariana, 70
Vazquez, Isabel, 113
Velcro, invention of, 150
Velkey, Andrew, 149–50
Veras, Ingrid, 94–95, 145, 153
Veterans, 89–90
VFP. *See* Visiting Faculty Program
Victor Valley Community College, 131
Virtual conferences, 171
*Vision 2030* (Bush, V.), 64

*Vision and Change in Undergraduate Education* (AAAS), 76
Visiting Faculty Program (VFP), 126
Voice-onset time, 69

Wager, Erica, 88–89, 123, 144
Walker, Rob, 146–47
Walters State College, 126–27
Water pollution, 120–21, 134
Water sampling project, 93–94
Webster, Horace, 35
Weiss, Jane, 83–84, 150
Western Interstate Commission for Higher Education (WICHE), 6
"What difference can ePortfolio Make?" (Eynon), 173
*What the Best College Teachers Do* (Bain), 148–49
White privilege, 144
WICHE. *See* Western Interstate Commission for Higher Education
Widening Implementation and Demonstration of Evidence-Based Research (WIDER), 162

WIDER. *See* Widening Implementation and Demonstration of Evidence-Based Research
Wild at the Heart, 96
Wildlife, of Ecuador, 102
Willison, John, 165
Wintership program, 130–31
Wisconsin Hope Lab, 11, 47
Wishart, James, 125
Women, in STEM, 10, 93–95
Workforce development, 7, 9, 21, 33–34, 45, 163
Workforce skills gap, 40
Work schedules, 50
Workshop, on undergraduate research, 28–29
Writing Across the Curriculum, 79, 82, 85

Young, Greg, 67

Zoom conferencing, 111, 113
Zoom method, 104

COURSE-BASED
UNDERGRADUATE
RESEARCH
Educational Equity and
High-Impact Practice

Edited by NANCY H. HENSEL
Foreword by CATHY N. DAVIDSON

# Course-Based Undergraduate Research

*Educational Equity and High-Impact Practice*

Edited by Nancy H. Hensel

Foreword by Cathy N. Davidson

Undergraduate research has long been recognized as a high-impact practice (HIP), but has unfortunately been offered only to juniors and seniors, and to very few of them (often in summer programs). This book shows how to engage students in authentic research experiences, built into the design of courses in the first two years, thus making the experience available to a much greater number of students.

"If you are an educator who believes in the importance of all students engaging in undergraduate research as a way to develop the competencies needed to thrive in an innovation-driven economy, then this book is a must-read. Course-based Research provides practical, equitable, and inclusive strategies for making undergraduate research accessible and engaging for every student."—*Tia Brown McNair, Vice President, Office of Diversity, Equity, and Student Success – Association of American Colleges and Universities*

UNDERGRADUATE
RESEARCH
IN ONLINE,
VIRTUAL, AND
HYBRID COURSES
Proactive Practices
for Distant Students

Edited by Jennifer G. Coleman,
Nancy H. Hensel, and William E. Campbell
Foreword by Lynn Pasquerella

# Undergraduate Research in Online, Virtual, and Hybrid Courses

*Proactive Practices for Distant Students*

Edited by Jennifer C. Coleman, Nancy H. Hensel, and William E. Campbell

Published in association with AAC&U and CUR

With the growing interest in undergraduate research as a high-impact practice, and the recognition that college education is increasingly moving online, this book—the first to do so—provides a framework, guidance from pioneering practitioners, and a range of examples across disciplines on how to engage remote students in research.

While the examples range across the behavioral sciences, business, education, the health professions, the humanities, social sciences, and STEM, readers will find much of value and inspiration from reading the chapters beyond their disciplines.

"If you're committed to socially just educational practices, this book is vitally important. We shortchange students who take online courses (often from historically marginalized and underserved populations) if we exclude research projects in virtual classes. With examples from across the disciplines, you'll find impactful ideas on fostering equitable online student success."
—*Flower Darby*, *Faculty and Lead Author of* Small Teaching Online

"Essential reading for educators focused on equitable student success, the thoughtful chapters provide key insights to increasing affordability and ubiquity of undergraduate research through investment in online models."
—*Elizabeth L. Ambos*, *CUR Executive Officer, 2012–2019*

Edited by George R. Boggs
and Christine Johnson McPhail

Foreword by Eloy Ortiz Oakley

## Team Leadership in Community Colleges

Edited by George R. Boggs and
Christine Johnson McPhail

Foreword by Eloy Ortiz Oakley

This edited collection is the first book to address
the topic of how leaders work with teams to
manage and transform community colleges. There
is a need to develop better leadership teams in
order to administer community colleges effectively and to improve these
organizations, whether it be an individual campus, multicollege system, or
state-wide organization. Edited by two long-time leaders in the field, the
book includes contributions from many other experienced leaders and scholars of community colleges.

"Boggs and McPhail have assembled an all-star troupe of experts from within
and outside our community college sector. The chapters present a thorough
and exhaustive examination of the power and purpose of leadership at all levels.
Leadership is a team sport—Boggs and McPhail have been both practitioners
and champions in the field. They know firsthand the power of leadership
and its role in advancing a culture of success necessary for our students to
achieve their hopes and dreams. This book should serve a guiding narrative
for anyone privileged to play a leadership role in community colleges."
—*J. Noah Brown,* *President and CEO of the Association of Community College
Trustees*

# Transformational Change in Community Colleges

*Becoming an Equity-Centered Institution*

Christine Johnson McPhail and Kimberly Beatty

Foreword by Walter G. Bumphus

The authors had three main goals for this text:

*Relevance:* This book is the result of many years of teaching, leading, researching, and coaching individuals and institutions about equity inside higher education. The authors place a clear emphasis on awareness and teaching skills first, but also ensure that those skills are based on practical application in the field.

*Practical Application:* To describe and explain equity and transformational change concepts, this book provides step-by-step implementation approaches that can be used to integrate equity-centered principles into practices and policies to implement or improve equity work into the organizational culture.

*A Purposeful Approach:* The authors defined the act of becoming an equity-centered institution in terms of a transformational change approach using Kotter's eight-stage process. Kotter's model and AACC's leadership competencies for community college leaders are introduced in chapter 1 and integrated throughout the book. This integrated framework allows practitioners to place the intersectionality of equity, transformational change, and requisite leadership competencies into the larger context of higher education. While using Kotter's 8-step change model, the authors emphasize that operations and situations inside higher educational institutions are not linear as implied in Kotter's model. They show how the stages of change may occur at different times and different situations at different institutions, and demonstrate what leadership competencies are recommended for each stage in the change process.

*Also available from Stylus*

### Community Colleges as Incubators of Innovation

*Unleashing Entrepreneurial Opportunities for Communities and Students*

Edited by Rebecca A. Corbin and Ron Thomas

Foreword by Andy Stoll

Afterword by J. Noah Brown

While community colleges have traditionally focused on providing students with opportunities to gain credentials for employment, the increasingly important question is: Are they preparing students for the looming dynamic, disruptive, and entrepreneurial environments ahead?

This book addresses the urgent need for community colleges to prioritize entrepreneurship education both to remain relevant in a changing economy and to give graduate students the flexible and interdisciplinary mindsets needed for the future of society. It argues that entrepreneurial education should be offered broadly to a wide range of students, and across all disciplines; defines the key constructs for achieving this objective; and describes how to create entrepreneurial learning environments.

"Entrepreneurial thinking has the power to facilitate transformational change within our colleges, and this book captures the essence of not only how it can, but why it should. Whether energizing educators to seek innovative curriculum designs, or creating partnerships to better address complex workforce issues in the 21st century, the contributing authors make it clear that the entrepreneurial college is the new standard of excellence."—*Edwin Massey, President, Indian River State College*

22883 Quicksilver Drive
Sterling, VA 20166-2102      Subscribe to our e-mail alerts: www.Styluspub.com

The mission of the Council on Undergraduate Research (CUR) is to support and promote high-quality mentored undergraduate research, scholarship, and creative inquiry. Among the many activities and networking opportunities that CUR provides, the organization also offers support for the professional growth of faculty and administrators through expert-designed institutes, conferences, and a wide range of volunteer positions. The CUR community continues to provide a platform for discussion and other resources related to mentoring, connecting, and creating relationships centered on undergraduate research. CUR's advocacy efforts are also a large portion of its work as we strive to strengthen support for undergraduate research. Its continued growth in connections with elected representatives, private foundations, government agencies, and campuses worldwide provides value to its members and gives voice to undergraduate research.

CUR is committed to inclusivity and diversity in all of its activities and our community.

We are your resource. We are community. We are mentoring. We are CUR.

# Reconstructed Marriage Records of Owsley County, Kentucky
## 1843-1910
## Part 1 (A-L)

Margaret Millar Hayes

Heritage Books, Inc.

Published 1998 by

HERITAGE BOOKS, INC.
1540E Pointer Ridge Place
Bowie, Maryland 20716

1-800-398-7709
www.heritagebooks.com


ISBN 0-7884-1058-X

# PREFACE

Owsley County, Kentucky was created on 23 January, 1843 from Breathitt, Clay, and Estill Counties. The county was named for William Owsley, Judge of Kentucky Court of Appeals and the sixteenth Governor of the state of Kentucky. The effective date for Owsley's formation was 1 June, 1843. Booneville is the county seat.

Present day Owsley County is surrounded by the counties of BREATHITT (formed in 1839 from Clay, Estill, & Perry), LEE (formed 1870 from Breathitt, Estill, Owsley, & Wolfe), JACKSON (formed 1858 from Clay, Estill, Laurel, Madison, Owsley, & Rockcastle), CLAY (formed 1806 from Floyd, Knox, & Madison), LESLIE (formed 1878 from Clay, Harlan, & Perry), and PERRY (formed 1820 from Clay, & Floyd).

A fire in the court house in 1929 destroyed all records up to that time, which leaves us without access to marriages, deeds, etc., except those filed with the state and the federal government.

This book is an effort to reconstruct the missing marriages from available sources. It is not to be considered a complete list. I am certain there are marriages which took place in Owsley which will never be found.

Most of the marriage dates in this book are estimates, based on the age of the oldest child plus one year.

I have also included some marriage records from surrounding counties for those couples who lived in Owsley County at one time or another during the years 1843-1910. If a marriage took place in a county other than Owsley, the county is listed after the marriage date and underscored, so as to avoid confusion.

iii

The records contained in this book were taken from the following sources:

Main source:
   Microfilmed copies of the records filed with the state of Kentucky during the years 1852-1859, 1874, 1876-1879, and 1903-1910. If no source is cited after a marriage it is taken from the "main source".

NOTE:   If the word "Ows." does not appear after a marriage date, then it is an assumption on my part that this person was married in Owsley County, but I have found no record to confirm it.

Other sources (listed after marriage record in parenthesis)
1830, 1840, 1850, 1860, 1870, 1880, 1900, 1910, & 1920 = Owsley Co., KY census
1830-county abbreviation, 1840-county abbreviation, etc. For example, 1850-B = 1850 Breathitt Co., KY census; 1840-C = 1840 Clay Co., KY census; 1870-L = 1870 Lee Co., KY census.
(see County abbreviations on page 23)
1850-#, 1860-# etc. = oldest child listed as age #. For example, if the oldest child was 8 in the 1850 census, it would be listed as 1850-8; or if in Breathitt, as 1850-B-8.
1850-MWY, 1860-MWY, 1880-MWY = listed as married within the census year.
1850Inx = 1850 Kentucky Index book at Archives
1860 NOTE:   The 1860 Breathitt & Clay census list the County of birth of each person.
1860MS, 1870MS, 1880MS = Owsley Co. Mortality Schedules
1860SS = 1860 Owsley Slave Schedules
   [NOTE:   For the most part, Blacks were not listed in census records prior to the Civil War, except on the slave schedules, which lists the owner and only the age, sex, and color (Black or Mulatto) of the slaves.]
1860SS-B = 1860 Breathitt Slave Schedules

iv

Sources (cont.)

1870 NOTE: The 1870 Owsley & Lee census list
the month of marriage if a couple were
married within the census year.

1870Inx = 1870 Kentucky Index book; researched
by Floyd John Ratz

1870MS-L, 1880MS-L = Lee Co. Mortality
Schedules

1880Sx, 1900Sx, 1910Sx, 1910Sx = Soundex
(see County abbreviations on page 23)

1890 = 1890 Special Census of Civil War
Veterans - Owsley Co.

1900-J annot. = "Jackson County Census, 1900"
(annotated), by Doug Ramsey, sold by
Jackson Co. Public library

1900-OK = 1900 Oklahoma census

1900 NOTE: 1900 census lists the number of
years a couple were married.

1910 NOTE: The 1910 census lists the number
of years a couple were married & whether it
is their 1st, 2nd, 3rd marriage, etc.

3Fks. = "The Three Forks Tradition," date;
Beattyville, Lee Co. newspaper on microfilm
from 1883; plus articles called "A Look at
our Past" & obituaries from recent years
(sent to me by Sam & Faye Stamper and Lucy
Noe Gay)

AB = Records of Arch Bowman (from Pat Ball;
Marge Turner; Ruth Moran)

ABB = Records of A. B. Burns (Re: DEATON)

ACB = Anna Carole Bays, Dayton, OH

AJ = "The Johnsons of Buckhorn, Perry County
Area," compiled from Asbury Johnson's &
Harrison B. Johnson's material, by Bertha
Noble, Lerose, KY    (photocopy sent to me
by Clay Co. Historical Society)

AM = Adelene Mullins of Ft. Thomas, KY

ARS = Annette Russell Shannon of Amelia, OH

B-county abbreviation = Birth records
(microfilmed), covering the 1850's, 1870's
and 1900-10. For example, B-C = Birth Clay
B-L = Birth Lee; B-O = Birth Owsley
(see County abbreviations on page 23)

B&L = "Early Settlers of Lee County, Virginia,
and Adjacent Counties," by Bales &
Lanningham

BBG = Betty Bowman Gabbard of Booneville, KY

Sources (cont.)
BC = birth certificate or delayed birth
certificate of child in Owsley Co.;
original birth certificates ordered from
Frankfort; Kentucky Index researched by
Anna Carole Bays & myself
BC-county abbrevation = birth certificate or
delayed birth certificate of child in
a county other than Owsley.  For example,
BC-B = birth certificate, Breathitt Co.
(see County abbreviations on page 23)
BCN = "Breathitt County News" newspaper, date
(on microfilm)
BE = "Beattyville Enterprise" newspaper,
date   (on microfilm from 1896)
BJE = Betty J. Estep of Alexandria, KY
BJN = Records of Mrs. Granville (Bertha J.)
Noble of Lerose, KY  (Re: NOBLE)
BS = "Booneville Sentinel" newspaper, date
(on microfilm from 1976)
BTF = Betty Thomas Finger of Gold Hill, OR
CB = Carol Barnett (Re: TURNER)
CC = Charles Chamberlain of Hamilton, OH
CED = Carl E. Depew of Fairfield, OH
CH/DM = Carlene Ho of Kailua, HI, info from
Dee McGuire
COJ = "Genealogy, Jett Family," by C. Otis
Jett (researched by Marge Turner)
CRC = book about the Caudill family by
Clayton R. Cox of the East Kentuckian,
abstracts sent to me by Anna Carole Bays
D-county abbreviations below
Death records (microfilmed), covering the
1850's, 1870's and 1900-10.  For example,
D-B = Breathitt = Death Breathitt
D-O = Death Owsley
(see County abbreviations on page 23)
DB = Records of David Brandenburg (from TR)
DC = death certificate
DDN = Dolores Deaton Nader of Jackson, MS
Desc/Snowden = "The Descendants of Joseph
Snowden (1725/30-1799)," by Virginia
Whitman Snowden, Gateway Press, 1981
(Researched by Jeff Akers)
DGS = David G. Moore (see TCS)
DSG = Denise Spencer Greer
DSS = Dorothy Stidham Stein of Roswell, NM

vi

Sources (cont.)
ECP = "Estill County and Its People," Vols. 1
     & 2, by Estill Co. Historical Society
EDS = Elmer D. Scalf (through TCS)
EERS = Charts of Emily Euphemia Rowland Selby
     (sent to me by Pat Ball)
EJ = Elsie Johnson· of Lebanon, OH
EPW = McGuire Genealogy, Descendants of
     James McGuire and wife Elizabeth Black,
     by Eric Passmore White, 1977
ES = Elora Stewart (through TCS)
EVR = Edna V. Rice of Sycamore, IL
FB = family Bible records
FH = funeral home records from Newman's
     Funeral Home, formerly Congleton Bros.
     Funeral Home, researched by Lucy Noe Gay
FJR = Floyd J. Ratz of Del City, OK
GLM = Goldie L. Miller of Odessa, FL
HC = "Harlan Connections," by Frances Y.
     Dunham, copy loaned to me by Pat Horne
HET = Hugh Edwin Tuttle of Winchester, KY
HH = "The Hazard Herald," Perry Co. newspaper,
     date
HJ = Herbert Jewell
HJN = "The Hamilton Journal News," Hamilton,
     OH newspaper, date   (obits sent to me
     by Thelma Robinson & Virginia K. Dutze)
HPH = Helen Pat Horne of Hazard, KY
HTB = Harley Tucker Bowling of Cincinnati,
     OH; Clay Ancestral News 11/96
IBW = Ida B. Wells of Tucson, AZ
JA = Jeff Akers of West Alexandria, OH
JAB = James A. Bowman family chart, printed
     in Estill Co. Newsletter 8/97
JC = Janice Coffey, Tyner, KY
JCH = "The Hursts of Shenandoah," and "The
     Strong Family in Kentucky," by J. C. Hurst
JDW = Jess D. Wilson's article in "Clay
     County Ancestral News," June, 1991
JEM = John E. McIntosh of Jackson, KY
JEW = James E. Welch of Manchester, KY
JFB = microfilmed records of James F. Bowman,
     deceased  (loaned to me by Thelma Robinson)
JGN = Janette G. Nolan (through TCS)
JJDD = John J. Dickey Diary
JL = Jackie Little
JM = Jeannie Maines of Hamilton, OH

Sources (cont.)
JMC = Judy Murray Cunagin
JO = James Owen of San Diego, CA
JS = Jack Stidham of Morristown, TN
JSG = Judy S. Gabbard of Jackson, KY
JT = "The Jackson Times," Breathitt Co.
    newspaper, date  (on microfilm)
JTB = Jackie T. Burton of Hamilton, OH
    (information on Baker Cemetery, Cortland,
    Owsley Co., KY; and correspondence)
JWFW = John William Frederick Williams, who
    wrote several newspaper articles for the
    "Beattyville Enterprise"  (thru Moran)
KAS = Kay A. Spencer of Novi, MI
KCM = Karen Caudill McGraw of Cincinnati, OH
KY-Exp. = "Kentucky Explorer Magazine,"
    date, submitter
KY-H = "Kentucky, a History of the State," by
    W. H. Perrin, J. H. Battle, G. C. Kniffin,
    1888
LBH = Lavonne Bedal Hughey of San Jose, CA
LCent = "Lee County Centennial Book"
LDS = Chart filed with the Library of the
    Latter Day Saints
LG-art. = article by Lucinda Gipson of
    Lexington, KY, researched by Pat Ball
LHS = Lee Historical and Genealogical
    Society
LM = Leon Morris of Union, MI
LNG = Lucy Noe Gay of Beattyville, KY
LNG/TW = information given to Lucy Noe Gay
    by William Thomas
LP = Records of Leland Porter
LS = Records of Lyman States of Hamilton, OH
LSS = Mrs. Lydia Spencer South, Jackson, KY
M-county abbreviations = Marriage records*,
    name of county;
    #:# =  marriage book and page number;
    mf = microfilm records
    (see County abbreviations on page 23)
M-cons. = Marriage consent

Sources (cont.)
NOTE: (Marriage records taken from published and non-published sources), as follows:
M-B = "Reconstructed Marriage Records of Breathitt County, Kentucky, 1839-1873," by author, Revised ed. 1994; "Breathitt County Marriage Records, Books 1A-8, 1869-1900," by Judy Kilburn McGuinn, 1997; "Breathitt County Marriage Records, Books 9-19, 1900-1915," by Judy McGuinn & Jamie Oaks, 1997; "Breathitt County Marriage Records, Books 20-43, 1915-1927," by Brenda Robinson Moore, 1997, published by Breathitt Co. Historical & Genealogical Society; also microfilm records and marriages on file in the Court House
M-C = "Clay County Marriage Index, Book 1, 1807-1859," "Clay County Marriage Index Book II, 1860-1889," and "Clay County Marriage Index Book III, 1890-1909," all by Clay Co. Historical Society; also taken from microfilm records and records on file in the Court House
M-E = Estill Co. marriage records sent to me by ACB & MT; microfilm records; records from Court House
M-Hawk, TN = Hawkins Co., TN marriage records printed in "Distant Crossroads", published by Hawkins Co. Genealogical Society; and "Hawkins County, Tennessee Marriage Records, 1789-1866," by Hawkins Co. Genealogical Society, 1993
M-L = "Lee County, Kentucky Births, Deaths, and Marriages, 1874-1878 and 1900-1910," by author 1992; also marriages researched at the Court House by LNG
M-O = Marriage records of Owsley Co., KY on microfilm. Marriages after 1910 are from Court House (researched by LNG).
M-P = "Perry County, Kentucky Marriages, Books A-F," "Perry County, Kentucky Marriages, Book G, H, I," and "Perry County Marriage Book J," all by the Perry Co. Historical Society.
M-W = "Wolfe County, Kentucky Marriages," by Wilma Johnson, Helen Pat Horne, Mary Walker

Sources (cont.)
MAR = Mary Ann Riddle of Lewisburg, OH
MCA = "William Congleton, Kentucky Pioneer,"
    by Marie Congleton Allega, researched by
    LNG
ME = "Mountain Echo," date; originally a Knox
    Co. newspaper published in Bourbourville;
    from 7/2/1875 on, a Laurel Co. newspaper,
    published in London, KY (on microfilm)
    usually under the heading of Owsley Co.
    news from Booneville, Buck Creek, Island
    City, Travellers Rest, etc.
MGL = Myra G. Lantz of Columbus, IN
MGS = Myrna Gulley Seal of Connersville, IN
MJC = Martha Jo Carr of Corinth, KY
ML = Marriage license
MLJ = Margie L. Jones of Sunman, IN
    (Re: Fox & Pace)
MM = Marilyn Morris
MMH = my personal research
MNC = "Early Pioneers of the Three Forks of
    the Kentucky River," by Miles N. Crawford,
    1984; also correspondence with Miles
MRS = Records of Manuel Spencer of
    Independence, KY
MS = Owsley Co. Mortality Schedules
MS-L = Lee County Mortality Schedules
MT = Marge Turner of Leesburg, FL

Newsletters:
N-abbreviations below, date, submitter:
    N-B = Breathitt "The Record"
    N-C = "Clay Co. Ancestral News"
    N-DCr = "Distant Crossroads" Hawkins Co, TN
    N-E = Estill
    N-E.KY = "Back Home Again in Eastern
        Kentucky" (containing newspaper articles
        from Eastern Kentucky) published by Allen
        Watts, Cincinnati (Historical Indexing)
    N-E.KYN = "The East Kentuckian," article by
        Clayton Cox on the Holbrook family;
        abstract sent to me by Anna Carole Bays
    N-EM = Estill newsletter, marrriage records
        after 1900, submitted by Diana C.
        Frymyer, 1/90 - 6/97
    N-L = Lee
    N-P = Perry

Sources (cont.)

NC = Nevyle Cable of Okmulgee, OK

NSB = "Longs Creek, Breathitt County,
     Kentucky, 1900-1991," by Nancy Stamper
     Begley, deceased   (data from Marge Turner)

NVP = Records of Norma V. Pierson of
     Oklahoma City, OK   (through Moran)

OB = Order Book, Owsley Co., KY Court,
     book #: page #

OCC = "Owsley County Courier," date -
     Booneville newspaper, articles researched
     by Allen Watts (on microfilm, 1934-1943)

OCN = "Owsley County News," date - Booneville
     newspaper   (on microfilm, 1949-1958)

P-CW = Pension, Civil War

P-Mex. = Pension, Mexican War

P-Rev. = Pension, Revolutionary War

P-Sp.Am. = Pension, Spanish American War

Peters = "Peters Family of Scott County,
     Virginia," by J. N. Peters (researched by
     Betty Bowman Gabbard)

PF-C = "Pioneers of Clay County, Kentucky,"
     by Kelly Morgan   (researched by PWB)

PF-Les. = "Pioneer Families of Leslie County,
     Kentucky," by Sadie Stidham

PWB = Pat Wilson Ball of Richmond, IN

PWR = Phyllis Weaver Rogers (through TCS)

RB = Rufus Bruner (through TCS)

REM = Ruth Eager Moran of Oklahoma City, OK

REM/BM = Ruth Eager Moran, information
     from Barbara Mahaffey

Rich.IN - obits from Richmond, IN newspaper
     "The Palladium Item"   (sent to me by PWB)

RM = Roy McDaniel of Franklin, TN

Rom.Lee = "Romance of Lee," by Nevyle
     Shackelford, 1947, 2nd printing 1979

RP = Ruby Prescott of Dallas, TX

RW = Ruby Wilson (through TCS)

SD = "The Eastern Kentucky Davidsons," by
     Seldon Davidson   (copy of this book loaned
     to me by Dorothy S. Stein)

SE = Shirley Evans (thru Lucy Gay)

SES = Samuel E. Sebastian of North
     Wilkesboro, NC

Sources (cont.)
SF = Family Group sheet of Steve Fugate
    (descendant of Moses Spencer & Elizabeth
    Deaton through their son Joseph Charles)
    (sent to me by Marge Turner)
S&FS = Sam & Faye Stamper of Walled Lake, MI
SMO = Sharon Maloney Ogzewalla of West
    Minister, CO
TCS = "The Computer Says," compiled by David
    G. Moore, Knightstown, IN; information
    from AB, BBG, BJN, EDS, ES, JFB, JGN, KCM,
    LP, MGS, MNC, MT, PWR, RB, REM, RW, WJM;
    WOG; also Rev. Dennis Brewer, Georgia Moore
    Burch, Mrs. Sam Cornett, Adalene Moore
    Davis, Josephine Flannery, Ike Gabbard,
    Taylor P. Gabbard, Helen C. Helton, Jimmie
    Herald, Nettie Jackson, Emily Mae Rowland
    Moore, Herman B. Moore, Hobert Moore,
    Granville Noble, Darlene Sizemore, Henry
    Sizemore, Violet Stepp, Vol Taylor, Fred
    Tirey, Maude Moore Tirey, Christine L.
    Wilson, Jess Wilson, Joyce Wilson, et al
TD = Mrs. Terry David
TL = listed on Owsley Co., KY tax lists
    (microfilm records 1844-1858)
TR = Thelma Robinson of Hamilton, OH
TS = Tombstone dates, followed by initials of
    the person who sent data to me.
    (for example: TS-LNG = tombstone dates
    sent to me by Lucy Noe Gay)
TS-WE = Tombstones read by Wallace Edwards of
    Booneville and submitted to "Clay Co.
    Ancestral News," 7/96
TS-Wlf = "Wolfe County Cemeteries," Vols. 1 &
    2, by Anna Carole Bays
TW = Records of Tom Walters
VH = Vandela Howell of Cincinnati, OH
VKD = Virginia K. Dutze of Hamilton, OH
W&PS = Wallace & Phyllis Stamper of Troy, MI
WEB = Records of Dr. Wilgus E. Back, deceased,
    of Breathitt Co., KY
WEJ = William E. Johnstone's article in
    Lee Co. Newsletter, Summer, 1997
    Re: John P. Gum's Civil War Pension
WGO = "Dozens of Cousins," by Wm. G.
    O'Connor and correspondence with William

Sources (cont.)
will #:# = will, Owsley Co., KY, book number,
    page number
    will-F = father's will
    will-H = husband's will
    will-W = wife's will
WJ = Wilma Johnson
WJM = Records of Dr. William J. Moore of
    Richmond, now deceased  (thru Moran)
WN = letter from Wm. "Bill" Newman to Pat Ball
WOG = Wilson O. Gabbard (thru BBG)
WTM = records of Willard Thomas McHone of
    Richmond, KY
Yest. = "This Was Yesterday, A Romantic
    History of Owsley County," by Joyce Wilson,
    1977

* * * * *


Marriage records are set up as follows:
GROOM (residence, age, marital status,
    occupation [only if other than farmer],
    birthplace) birthplaces of father & mother;
    names of parents
    BRIDE (residence, age, marital status,
    birthplace) birthplaces of father & mother
    names of parents
    Date & place of marriage; by whom married;
    witnesses; Remarks

The amount of information may vary with each
entry, depending upon the source it was taken
from.  For example:

ABNER
ENOCH (c27 b.KY)  [s/o Elijah Abner & Nancy
    Loving - 1850]
    MARTHA GILBERT (c19 b.KY)
    c1857      (1860-2; B-O ch.)

The above entry was reconstructed from two
sources:  the 1860 Owsley census, wherein the
first child was age 2; and Owsley Co. birth of
a child, listing the mother's maiden name.

ANDERSON
JACOB M. (R.Ows.; 22 S b.KY) P/VA-KY     [s/o
    Frank Anderson & Jane Anderson - 1870]
    ANNIE GABBARD (R.Ows; 24 S b.KY) P/KY-TN
    [d/o James Gabbard & Eliz. A Frost - MT]
    28 Aug, 1878, Ows.  [R.Ows. 1880-1900-1910]

The above entry was listed on the microfilmed
marriages filed with the state.  Information
in  brackets  tells  where  they  resided  in
following years.

    The counties listed in each entry are in
Kentucky, unless otherwise noted.  The towns
listed are (or were) in Owsley County, unless
otherwise noted.
    Race is only listed (and underscored) if
other than white.
    Anything in brackets [---] has been added
by me for the sake of clarification or as an
annotation.
    Words in quotation marks are spelled as is,
such  as  "Claborn"  Co.,  TN,  instead  of
Claiborne Co., TN.
    Names  are  listed  alphabetically.  When
there is more than one listing for a certain
name, they are listed by date (the earliest
date being first), discounting the use of
middle initials or middle names.
    For example, if we had three Joseph Smiths:
Joseph Walter Smith married 1845; Joseph Smith
married 1855; and Joseph Allen Smith married
1869, they would be listed as follows:

        JOSEPH WALTER        1845
        JOSEPH               1855
        JOSEPH ALLEN         1869

Abbreviations:
#/# ch. = per 1900-1910 census, mother had
    # children, # living
---- = left blank or unknown
----? = unreadable
1st ch-# = first child listed age # or born --
2nd = 2nd marriage
3rd = 3rd marriage (etc.)
1x = one time
2x = two times
3x = three times, etc.
@ = at
A-dau. = adopted daughter
A-d/o = adopted daughter of
A-son = adopted son
A-s/o = adopted son of
abt. = about
abv. = above
admr/o administrator of
aff/o = affidavit(s) of
a/k/a = also known as
a/L = also listed
al. = alive
anniv. = anniversary
appar. = apparently
apptd. = appointed
art. = article
asst. cash. = assistant cashier
B-O ch-# = Owsley  births, child born (date)
b. = born
b/d = born dead; or born & died same day
Bapt. = Baptist
Bapt. Min. = Baptist Minister
Bday = birthday
betw. = between
BiL = brother-in-law
Blk = black
Bo. = Boarder
bro. = brother
bro/o = brother of
B'smth = blacksmith
bur. = buried
c = circa (about)
cab.mkr = cabinet maker
CClk = County Clerk
cem. = cemetery
cen. = census

Abbreviations (cont.):
cert. = certified or certificate
ch. = child(ren)
CH = court house
ch/o = child(ren) of
Chr. Church = Christian Church
Cir.Ct. = Circuit Court
Cir.Ct.Clk = Circuit Court Clerk
C.minr = coal miner
Co. = county
Conf.sold. = Conferate soldier, Civil War
cons/o = consent of
cont. = continued
Cpl. = Corporal in the army
Cr. = Creek
crp = carpenter
Ct. rec. = court records
cuz(s) = cousin(s)
C.W. or CW = Civil War
d. = died
d/o = daughter of
da. = days
dau. = daughter
decd. = deceased
diff. = different
DiL = daughter-in-law
Div. = divorced
div/f = divorced from
DOB = date of birth
DOD = date of death
domst = domestic
Dr. = doctor or physician
d.s. = died single
dur. = during
Eld. = Elder
engr. = engineer or engineering
est/o = estate of
F = father
F/as = father as
fam. = family
fam/o = family of
FiL = father-in-law
fore. st-mill = foreman, stave mill
f/w/o = formerly widow of
G-GD = great-granddaughter
G-GF = great-grandfather
G-GM = great-grandmother

G-GP = great-grandparents
G-GS = great-grandson
G-G-GD = great-great-granddaughter
   (etc.)
Gch. = grandchild(ren)
GD = granddaughter
GD/o = granddaughter of
gdn/o = guardian of
GF = Grandfather
GM = Grandmother
GP or Gpar. = grandparents
Gro.kpr. = grocery keeper; keeping grocery
GS/o = grandson of
H1 = first husband
H2 = second husband (etc.)
H = husband or husband's
   H-# = husband's age
   H-2nd = husband's 2nd marriage
   H/as = husband listed as
   H/o = husband of
   HF = husband's father
   H-GF = husband's grandfather
   H-GM = husband's grandmother
   HM = husband's mother
   H-NL = husband not listed
   HP = husband's parents
   H-remd. = husband remarried
   HS = husband's sibling(s)
   H-sgl. = husband single   (etc.)
H&W = husband & wife
Hkpr. = housekeeper or keeping house
hosp. = hospital
Hot-kpr. = hotel keeper
hs-pntr = house painter
hus. = husband
hus/o = husband of
Hwf = housewife
illegit = illegitimate
inc. = including
Inx = index
jewl. = jeweler
JPC = Judge, Perry Co.
JPJC = Justice of the Peace, Jackson Co.
JPLC = Justice of the Peace, Lee Co.
JPOC = Justice of the Peace, Owsley Co.
JPPC = Justice of the Peace, Perry Co.

<u>Abbreviations (cont.):</u>

k.C.W. = killed during the Civil War
lab. = laborer
last ch-# = last child listed age # or born --
Law. = lawyer
lic. = license
liv. = living or lived
Lum.Insp. = lumber inspector
Lum. = lumberman or lumberer
M = mother
M/as = mother listed as
m-# = married # years (1900-1910 census)
m2-# = married 2nd # years (1910 census)
m3-# = married 3rd # years (1910 census) (etc)
MB = Marriage Book
MC = Marriage Certificate
MC-NFI = Marriage Certificate not filled in
mcht. = merchant
md. = married
ME = Methodist Evangelical Church
mech. = mechanic
Meth. = Methodist
mf = microfilm
mg. = marriage
MG = Minister of the Gospel (sometimes listed
    as GM)
MiL = mother-in-law
mill = miller
Min. = Minister
minr = miner
ML = marriage license
M/M = Mr. & Mrs.
m/o = mother of
mo. or mos. = months
Mul = mulatto
N#L = census does not list the number of years
    couple were married.
Neph/o = nephew of
NFI = not filled in
Ni/o = niece of
NL = not listed
no occ. = no occupation
Nur.H. = Nursing Home

Abbreviations (cont.):
ob. or obit = obituary
   ob-H = obit husband
   ob-H&W = obits husband & wife
   ob-HF = obit husband's father
   ob-HM = obit husband's mother
   ob-HS = obit husband's sibling
   ob-W = obit wife
   ob-WF = obit wife's father
   ob-WM = obit wife's mother
   ob-WS = obit wife's sibling
orph/o = orphan of
P, P/, or par. = parents
P/as = parents listed as
P/o = parents of
Pct. = Precinct
Plft. = Plaintiff
PM = Postmaster
poss. = possibly or possible
Presb. = Presbyterian
prev. = previous or previously
prob. = probably
pub.wks. = public works
Pvt. = Private in the army
R. = Residence or residing
rec. = recorded or record(s)
rel. = related or relative
remd. = remarried
remd-# - remarried # years (1900-1910)
res. = residence or residing
repr/o = reprint of newspaper
Retl. dry gds = retailing, dry goods
Rev. = Reverend
RR = Railroad worker; railroading
S = single
s-b = stepbrother
s-bro. = stepbrother
s-ch = stepchild(ren)
s-d = stepdaughter
s-dau. = stepdaughter
s-F = stepfather
s-GD = step-granddaughter
s-Gch. = step-grandchild(ren)
s-GS = step-grandson
s-M = stepmother
s-mill = Saw mill worker
s-s or s-son = stepson

## Abbreviations (cont.):

s-s/o = stepson of
s-sis = stepsister
Sadl = saddler
Sal.kpr = saloon keeper
s/b = should be
sch.cen. = school census
sch.tchr. = school teacher
SClk = store clerk
sgl. = single
Sgt. = Sergeant in the army
sib = sibling (brother or sister)
SiL = sister-in-law or son-in-law
sis = sister
sis/o = sister of
sm. = small
S-mason = stone mason
smstss = seamstress
s/o = son of
spin. = spinster or spinstress
stats = statistics
step-ch. = step-child(ren)
st-mill = stave mill (worker/laborer)
svt. = servant
sur. = surety
tchr. = teacher
Terr. = Territory
Tmbr = timberman
tmstr = teamster
uk = unknown
w = white
W1 = 1st wife
W2 = 2nd wife (etc.)
w/ = with
W or W/ = wife or wife's
   W-# = wife's age
   W-2nd = wife's 2nd marriage
   W/as = wife listed as
   WF = wife's father
   W-GF = wife's grandfather
   W-GM = wife's grandmother
   WM = wife's mother
   W-NL = wife not listed
   W/o = wife of
   WP = wife's parents
   W-remd. = wife remarried
   WS = wife's sibling
   W-sgl. = wife single  (etc.)

## Abbreviations (cont.):

wf = wife
wf/o = wife of
wid. = widow
widr. = widower
wid/o = widow of
widr/o = widower of
wits. = witnesses
wkr = worker
yrs. = years

## Name abbreviations:

Abr. = Abraham
Alex. = Alexander
Archd. = Archibald
Benj. = Benjamin
Cath. = Catherine
Chas. = Charles
Edw. = Edward
Eliz. = Elizabeth
Geo. = George
Hen. = Henderson
Jeff. = Jefferson
Jer. = Jeremiah
Jno. = Jonathan

Jos. = Joseph
Kath. = Katherine
Margt. = Margaret
Nath. = Nathaniel
Nich. = Nicholas
Richd. = Richard
Robt. = Robert
Saml. = Samuel
Theo. = Theophilus
Thos. = Thomas
Val. = Valentine
Wash. = Washington
Wm. = William
Zach. = Zachariah

## Surname abbreviations:

BBurg. = Brandenburg

## town/area abbreviations & names:

|  |  |  |
|---|---|---|
|  | Ages | (Harlan Co.) |
|  | Anna |  |
|  | Annville | (Jackson Co.) |
|  | Arvel | (Lee Co.) |
|  | Athol | (Lee Co.) |
|  | Avendale | (poss. Clay) |
| Beattyv. = | Beattyville | (Lee Co. seat) |
|  | Belle Point | (Lee) |
|  | Berea | (Madison Co.) |
|  | Bernstadt | (Laurel Co.) |
|  | Benge | (Clay Co.) |
| Blk. Water = | Black Water | (Morgan or Laurel) |
|  | Blake | (Owsley) |

xxi

| | | |
|---|---|---|
| Boonev. = | Booneville | (Ows. Co. seat) |
| | Buck Creek | (Owsley) |
| Buff.Cr. = | Buffalo Creek | (Owsley) |
| | Campton | (Wolfe Co.) |
| | Canyon Falls | (Lee) |
| | Carlisle | (Nicholas Co.) |
| | Carters Chapel | (Lee Co.?) |
| | Clay City | (Powell Co.) |
| | Coal Branch | (Lee Co.) |
| | Congleton | (Lee Co.) |
| | Conkling | (Owsley) |
| | Cortland | (Owsley) |
| Cov. = | Covington | (Kenton Co.) |
| Cow Cr. = | Cow Creek | (Owsley) |
| Crockettsv. = | Crockettsville | (Breathitt Co.) |
| | Delvinta | (Lee) |
| Dev. Cr. = | Devil's Creek | (Owsley) |
| | Doorway | (Owsley) |
| | Drip Rock | (Jackson) |
| Earnestv. = | Earnestville | (Owsley) |
| | Egypt | (Jackson Co.) |
| | Ender | (Owsley) |
| | Esau | (Owsley) |
| | Evelyn | (Lee) |
| | Eversole | (Owsley) |
| | Fixer | (Lee) |
| | Floyd | (Owsley) |
| | Frenchburg | (Menifee) |
| | Gabbard | (Owsley) |
| | Gray Hawk | (Jackson Co.) |
| | Green Hall | (Owsley) |
| | Hazel Green | (Wolfe Co.) |
| Haz. | Hazard | (Perry Co.) |
| Hlbg. | Heidelberg | (Lee Co.) |
| | Idamay | (Lee) |
| Ind. Cr. = | Indian Creek | (Owsley) |
| | Irvine | (Estill Co.) |
| Is. City = | Island City | (Owsley) |
| Is. Cr. = | Island Creek | (Owsley) |
| | Jackson | (Breathitt Co.) |
| | Jetts Creek | (Breathitt Co.) |
| KY Riv. = | Kentucky River | |
| Lanc. | Lancaster | (Garrard Co.) |
| L.F.Rock = | Left Fork, Rock Creek | |
| | Leeco | (Lee Co.) |
| | Leighton | (Lee Co.) |

|              | Lerose          | (Owsley)                |
|--------------|-----------------|-------------------------|
|              | Levi            | (Owsley)                |
| Lex.         | Lexington       | (Fayette Co.)           |
|              | London          | (Laurel Co.)            |
|              | Lost Creek      | (Breahtitt Co.)         |
| Low.Buff. =  | Lower Buffalo   |                         |
|              | Lynch           | (Harlan Co.)            |
|              | Major           | (Owsley)                |
|              | Manchester      | (Clay Co.)              |
|              | Maulden         | (Jackson Co. near Clay Co. line) |
|              | McKee           | (Jackson Co.)           |
| Mid. Fk. =   | Middle Fork     |                         |
|              | Mistletoe       | (Owsley)                |
|              | Monica          | (Lee)                   |
|              | Moore's Creek   | (Jackson Co.)           |
|              | Moore's Station | (Owsley)                |
|              | Mt. Pleasant    | (Clay or Harlan)        |
|              | Mount Sterling  | (Montgomery Co.)        |
|              | Mount Vernon    | (Rockcastle)            |
| No. Fk. =    | North Fork Kentucky River |               |
|              | Oil             | (Lee)                   |
|              | Old Landing     | (Lee Co.)               |
|              | Oneida          | (Clay Co.)              |
|              | Orpho           |                         |
|              | Pattonsville    | (Lee Co.)               |
| Peb.         | Pebworth        | (Owsley)                |
|              | Pleasant Flat   | (Lee)                   |
|              | Posey           | (Owsley)                |
|              | Preuit(?)       |                         |
|              | Prestonsburg    | (Floyd Co.)             |
|              | Primrose        | (Lee Co.)               |
|              | Proctor         | (Lee Co.)               |
|              | Pryse           | (Estill Co.)            |
|              | Puncheon        | (Magoffin Co.)          |
|              | Ricetown        | (Owsley)                |
|              | Risner          | (Floyd Co.)             |
|              | Rogers          | (Wolfe Co.)             |
|              | Sassafras       | (Knott Co.)             |
|              | Scoville        | (Owsley)                |
|              | Sebastian       | (Owsley)                |
|              | Sexton Creek    | (Clay Co.)              |
|              | Somerset        | (Pulaski)               |
| So. Fk. =    | South Fork Kentucky River |               |
|              | St. Helens      | (Lee Co.)               |
|              | Standing Rock   | (Lee)                   |

## town/area abbreviations & names (cont.):

|  |  |  |
|---|---|---|
|  | Stanton | (Powell Co.) |
|  | Station Camp | (Estill) |
|  | Stillwater | (Wolfe Co.) |
|  | Stone Coal | (Lee Co.) |
| Sturg. = | Sturgeon (Cr.) | (Owsley) |
|  | Taft | (Owsley) |
|  | Tallega | (Lee) |
|  | Taylor's Landing |  |
|  | Teges | (Clay Co.) |
|  | Terry | (Breathitt Co.) |
| Trav. Rest = | Travelers Rest | (Owsley) |
|  | Turin | (Owsley) |
|  | Turkey Creek | (Breathitt) |
|  | Tyner | (Jackson Co.) |
|  | Vada | (Lee Co.) |
|  | Vincent | (Owsley) |
|  | Wagersville | (Estill Co.) |
|  | Welchburg | (Jackson Co.) |
|  | Whoopflarea | (Owsley) |
|  | Whynot | (Lee) |
|  | Williba | (Lee) |
|  | Williamsburg | (Whitley Co.) |
|  | Winchester | (Clark Co.) |
|  | Yellow Rock | (Lee) |
|  | Zachariah | (Lee Co.) |
|  | Zoe | (Lee) |

## City abbreviations - state of Ohio:
Cin. = Cincinnati, Hamilton Co., OH
Ham.,OH = Hamilton, Butler Co., OH
Midltwn,OH = Middletown, Butler Co., OH
Rich,IN = Richmond, IN

## Country abbreviations:
Eng. = England
Germ. = Germany
Ire. = Ireland

County abbreviations:

B or Br. = Breathitt          (formed 1839)
Bunc.,NC = Buncombe Co., NC
C = Clay                      (formed 1806)
Claib.,TN = Claiborne Co., TN
Clk = Clark                   (formed 1792)
E or Est. = Estill            (formed 1808)
Fay. = Fayette                (formed 1780)
Fl = Floyd                    (formed 1799)
Frk. = Franklin Co.           (formed 1795)
Gray.,VA = Grayson Co., VA
H or Harl. = Harlan           (formed 1819)
Hanc.,TN = Hancock Co., TN
Hawk,TN = Hawkins Co., TN
J or Jack. = Jackson          (formed 1858)
Jack.,MO = Jackson Co., MO
Jeff. = Jefferson Co.         (formed 1780)
Jess. = Jessamine Co.         (formed 1798)
John. = Johnson               (formed 1843)
John.,Ark. = Johnson Co., Arkansas
John.,MO = Johnson Co., MO
John.,TN = Johnson Co., TN
Knt = Knott Co.               (formed 1884)
Knx = Knox                    (formed 1799)
L = Lee                       (formed 1870)
Lau. = Laurel                 (formed 1825)
Law. = Lawrence               (formed 1821)
Lee,VA = Lee Co., Virginia
Les. = Leslie                 (formed 1878)
Let. = Letcher                (formed 1842)
Linc. = Lincoln               (formed 1780)
M or Mad. = Madison           (formed 1785)
Mad.,Ark. = Madison Co., Arkansas
Mad.,NC = Madison Co., NC
Mag. = Magoffin               (formed 1860)
Menf. = Menifee               (formed 1869)
Merc. = Mercer                (formed 1785)
Montg. = Montgomery           (formed 1796)
Montg.,MO = Montgomery Co., MO
Montg.,NC = Montgomery Co., NC
Morg. = Morgan                (formed 1822)
Nich. = Nicholas              (formed 1799)
Org.,NC = Orange Co., NC
O or Ows. = Owsley
P or Per. = Perry             (formed 1820)
Pitts.,VA = Pittsylvania Co., VA
Pk = Pike                     (formed 1821)

County abbreviations (cont.):
Pow. = Powell            (formed 1852)
Pul. = Pulaski           (formed 1799)
R or Rockc. = Rockcastle (formed 1810)
Russ.,VA = Russell Co., VA
Scott,VA = Scott Co., VA
Taz.,VA = Tazewell Co., VA
W or Wlf = Wolfe         (formed 1860)
Wash. = Washington       (formed 1792)
Wash.,TN = Washington Co., TN
Wash.,VA = Washington Co., VA
Whit. = Whitley          (formed 1818)
Wlk.,NC = Wilkes Co., NC
Woodf. = Woodford        (formed 1788)


* * * * *


| Nicknames (males) | Given Name |
|---|---|
| Ab | Abner, Absolum |
| Abe | Abraham |
| Add | Adoniram |
| Al | Alexander, Allen |
| Alec | Alexander |
| Amie | Ambrose |
| Ance | Anderson, Ansil |
| Andy | Andrew, Andrew Jackson |
| Arch, Archie | Archibald |
| Bart | Barton, Burton |
| Ben | Benjamin, Benjamin Franklin |
| Berry | Asberry, Elsberry, Greenberry |
| Bert | Albert, Burton, Burrell, Burwell |
| Bige | Abijah |
| Bill, Billy | William |
| Bob, Bobby | Robert |
| Bode | Otis |
| Bony | Napoleon Bonaparte |
| Boone | Daniel Boone |
| Brant | Brantley |
| Breck | Breckenridge |
| Buck - Buckhannon, Buckminster, James Buchanan |
| Burt | see Bert |
| Cale | Caleb |
| Cage | McCager, Micajah |
| Cal | Calvin, Caleb, Calloway |
| (cont.) | |

xxvi

| Nicknames (males) | Given Name |
|---|---|
| Calvin | Calloway |
| Cam | Campbell |
| Carr | Hezekiah |
| Charlie, Chuck | Charles |
| Chris | Christopher |
| Clabe | Claiborne |
| Clay | Claiborne, Clayton, Henry Clay |
| Cratie | Socrates |
| Crit | Crittenden |
| Dan, Danny | Daniel, Daniel Boone |
| Dick | Richard |
| Don, Donce | McDonaldson |
| Drew | Andrew, Andrew Jackson |
| Eb | Edmund, Ebenezer |
| Eben | Ebenezer |
| Ed | Edmund, Edward |
| El | Eldridge, Elhannon |
| Eph | Ephraim |
| Fillmore | Millard Fillmore |
| Frank - | Franklin, Frances, Benjamin Franklin |
| Fred | Alfred, Frederick |
| Gabe | Gabriel |
| Gale | Gallin |
| Gran | Granville |
| Grant | Ulysses S. Grant |
| Green | Greenberry, Greenville |
| Hag | Hagerty |
| Harry - | Harrison, Henry, Wm. Henry Harrison |
| Hen, Hence | Henderson |
| Hugh, Huey | Elihue, Houston |
| Ike | Isaac |
| Jack | John, Jackson, Andrew Jackson |
| Jake | Jacob, Jackson, Andrew Jackson |
| Jay | Jasper |
| Jeff | Jefferson, Thomas Jefferson |
| Jerry | Jeremiah |
| Jim, Jimmy | James |
| Joe, Joey | Joseph |
| John | Jonathan |
| Kager | McCager, Micajah |
| Ki, Kier | Hezekiah |
| Kin | McKinley |
| Kit | Christopher |
| Lane, Laney | Delaney |
| Lige | Elias, Elijah |
| (cont.) | |

| Nicknames (males) | Given Name |
|---|---|
| Link | Lincoln, Abraham Lincoln |
| Lish | Elisha |
| Lonnie | Alonzo |
| Lum | Christopher Columbus, Columbus |
| Mack, Mac - | McCager, McCoy, McDonaldson, Micajah, McKinley |
| Matt | James Madison, Matthew |
| Merry | Meriwether Lewis |
| Mertie, Merdie | Meredith |
| Nate | Nathan, Nathaniel |
| Nathan | Nathaniel |
| Neal, Nealy | Cornelius |
| Ned | Edward |
| Newt | Newton; Isaac Newton |
| Nick | Nicholas |
| Nim | Nimrod |
| Niram | Adoniram |
| Ode | Otis |
| Ollie | Oliver |
| Ova | Overton |
| Poley | Napoleon Bonaparte |
| Polk | James K. Polk |
| Randy | Randall, Randolph |
| Rick, Ricky | Richard |
| Robin | Robert |
| Roe | Monroe |
| Rome | Jerome |
| Saul, Sol | Solomon |
| Shade | Shadrack |
| Sim | Simeon, Simpson |
| Squire | Esquire |
| Shelt | Shelton |
| Taylor | Zachary Taylor |
| Ted | Edward |
| Thee, Theo | Theophilus |
| Tice, Tyce | Mathias |
| Tom, Tommy | Thomas |
| Tyler | John Tyler |
| Val | Valentine |
| Van, Van Buren | Martin Van Buren |
| Wash | Washington, George Washington |
| Wes | Wesley, John Wesley |
| Wick | Wilson |
| Will, Willie | William, Wilborn |
| Wils | Wilson, Woodrow Wilson |
| (cont.) | |

| Nicknames (males) | Given Name |
|---|---|
| Woody | Woodrow, Woodrow Wilson |
| Zack | Zachariah, Zachary, Zachary Taylor |
| Zade | Zadock |
| Zeke | Ezekiel |
| Zeph | Zephariah |
| Zera | Isaiah, Izearah |

| Nickname (female) | Given Name |
|---|---|
| Addie or Ada | Adaline |
| Aggy | Agnes |
| Allie | Almira |
| Amy | Amelia |
| Ann | Angeline |
| Anna - | Hannah, Joannah, Orannah, Susannah |
| Army, Armie | Armina |
| Artes, Arty | Artemise |
| Bam | Alabama |
| Bea | Beatrice |
| Becca, Becky | Rebecca |
| Belle | Arabelle, Isabelle |
| Beth, Betsy, Betty - | Elizabeth |
| Bertie, Burtie | Alberta, Roberta |
| Biddy | Bridget, Obedience |
| Bitha | Tabitha |
| Bridie | Bridget |
| Briney | Sabrina |
| Callie | California |
| Carrie | Caroline |
| Cassis | Cassandra, Casseopia |
| Caty, Katy | Catherine, Katherine |
| Chris | Christine, Christina |
| Cinda, Cindy | Lucinda |
| Clara | Clarinda |
| Creaty | Lucretia |
| Darky | Dorcas |
| Debby | Deborah |
| Dellie | Delilah |
| Delphia | Philadelphia |
| Dema, Demmy | Diadema |
| Dicy | Ludicia |
| Dolly | Dorothy |
| Dora | Eldora |
| Dosha | Ludoshia, Theodocia |
| Dot | Dorothy |
| (cont.) | |

| Nickname (female) | Given Name |
|---|---|
| Drew | Druscilla |
| Ebbie | Isabelle |
| Edy | Edith |
| Effie | Effarilla; Ophelia |
| Eliza | Louisa, Elizabeth |
| Ella, Ellie - Ellen, Eleanor, Elender, Helen, Luellen, | |
| Ellen | Eleanor, Elender, Helen, Luellen |
| Em, Emily, Emma, Emmie - Emilia, Emeline | |
| Esther | Hester |
| Etta, Etty - Harriett, Henrietta, Marietta | |
| Fanny | Frances |
| Femie, Feema | Euphemia |
| Flora | Florilla |
| Fran | Frances |
| Franky | Frances |
| Frona | Sophronia |
| Gina | Virginia |
| Greta | Margaret |
| Haley | Mahala |
| Haney | Henrietta, Mahala |
| Hetty | Harriett, Henrietta, Hester |
| Hulda | Mahulda |
| Ibby | Isabelle |
| Icy | Isabelle |
| Jane, Jean | Virginia |
| Jenny, Jennie | Jane, Virginia |
| Jo | Joannah, Josephine |
| Joan | Joannah |
| Josey | Josephine |
| Katy, Caty | Katherine, Catherine |
| Kitty | Katherine, Catherine |
| Kizzy, Kizzie | Keziah |
| Lalie | Eulalah |
| Lear | Euller |
| Lela | Eulalah |
| Lena | Orlena, Salena |
| Letha, Litha | Delitha, Maletha, Taletha |
| Letty | Letitia |
| Liddie, Littie | Lydia |
| Lilla, Lily - Delilah, Drucilla, Pruscilla | |
| Linda | Belinda, Delinda, Malinda |
| Lissa | Malissa |
| Lizzie | Elizabeth |
| Loris | Delores |
| (cont.) | |

| Nickname (female) | Given Name |
|---|---|
| Lotty | Charlotte |
| Lou - Lucinda, Louisa, Luella, Louvisa, Lula | |
| Lucy | Lucinda |
| Lydie | Lydia |
| Maggie | Margaret, Magnolia |
| Mallie | Maletha, Malinda |
| Mancy, Mantha | Samantha |
| Mandy | Amanda, Tymanda |
| Mattie, Matty | Martha, Matilda |
| Melly | Melissa |
| Mecie | Artemise |
| Meldy | Armelda |
| Merca, Merkie | America |
| Milda | Armilda, Almilda |
| Millie | Amelia, Emilia, Permelia |
| Mima | Jemima |
| Mina, Minie, Minnie - Armina | |
| Minta, Mintie | Araminta |
| Mirty, Mirt | Myrtle |
| Missy | Melissa |
| Molly | Mary |
| Myra | Almira |
| Nan, Nannie | Nancy |
| Nealie | Cornelia |
| Nelly, Nellie - Eleanor, Elender, Helen, Luellen | |
| Nettie | Jeanette, Annette |
| Nerva, Nervie - Minerva, Nervesta | |
| Nicy | Eunice |
| Nora | Lenora, Phanorah |
| Ollie | Olive, Viola |
| Omy | Naomi |
| Orpha | Orphelia |
| Patsy | Martha |
| Peggy | Margaret |
| Polly, Pop | Mary |
| Pris | Priscilla |
| Pru, Pruda, Prudy | Prudence |
| Rainey | Lourana |
| Reba | Rebecca |
| Rena | Lurena |
| Retty, Ritty | Henrietta, Loretta |
| Rildy | Serilda, Zerilda |
| Rilla, Rillie | Florilla, Serilda, Zerilda |
| Rinda - Clarinda, Farinda, Lurinda, Marinda | |
| (cont.) | |

| Nickname (female) | Given Name |
|---|---|
| Rody | Rhoda |
| Sally | Sarah |
| Shannie | Nancy |
| Sibby | Sebrina |
| Silla | Drucilla, Priscilla |
| Shugie | Susan, Susannah |
| Sukey | Susan, Susannah |
| Susan | Susannah |
| Tabby | Tabitha |
| Tempy | Temperance |
| Tenny | Tennessee |
| Thena | Barthena |
| Tibbie | Tabitha |
| Tilda, Tildy | Matilda |
| Tina, Teen | Christina, Christine |
| Tish | Letitia, Martisha |
| Vada | Nevada |
| Vaney | Sylvania |
| Vica, Vicey | Levica |
| Vina, Viney | Levina, Malvina |
| Virgie | Virginia |
| Wilda | Alwilda |
| Willie | Wilhelmina |
| Winnie, Winny | Winnifred |
| Zona, Zoney | Arizona |

* * * * *


Corrections or additions welcome.

I want to take this opportunity to express my gratitude to those researchers who have helped me with the annotations for this book. Your assistance has been invaluable. I would especially like to thank my friends of long-standing: Carole, Lucy, Marge, Pat, Ruth, Bertha, Thelma, Kay, Dolores, David, and Floyd.

I also appreciate the assistance of the various court houses in Kentucky whom I have contacted to obtain records; mostly especially Jackson County, for their prompt responses and continuing help.

Also a special thanks to my husband, Marv, for remaining silent when my few minutes at a the court house or library turns into hours, for letting me drag him around to cemeteries way up in the hills, for going with me to meet family he knows nothing about, for being supportive and loving these past twenty-eight years.

# RECONSTRUCTED MARRIAGE RECORDS
## (A - L)

**NO SURNAME**
    _____ (\_\_\_ b.\_\_\_)
  VIRGINIA NEECE (R.Ows. 28 S b.Harl.) P/VA-
  Ows.
  1909, Ows.    [NOTE: There was an error
  in this & several other marriages, wherein
  the bride was listed on the wrong line.  I
  have matched up all the other brides to the
  correct grooms, but it appears that
  Virginia Neeces's husband was omitted.]

**ABNER**
ENOCH (c27 b.KY)  [s/o Elijah Abner & Nancy
  Loving - 1850]
  MARTHA GILBERT (c19 b.KY)
  c1857    (1860-2; B-O ch.; 1870-P;
  NL 1880Sx; NL 1900/B/P)  [H-remd.]
ENOCH (70 2nd b.KY)  [m1 Martha Gilbert above]
  [SARAH] JANE (nee BAKER) BOWLING (65 2nd
  b.Ows.)  [wid/o Wm. Bowling, who d. 1895 -
  TCS]  [1844-1931; d/o John Baker & Lucinda
  Amis - TCS]
  27 Sept., 1910, Cortland, Ows. (HTB; TCS;
  listed M-B as md. 1910, no date, @ Hester
  Riley's, by Andy Eversole; wits. James
  Riley & Joe Johnson)
JOHN (c22 b.Ows.)  [s/o Lacy Abner & Cynthia
  Combs - TCS]
  JOYCE BURNS (c19 b.Ows.)  [d/o Wm. Burns
  & Rachel Asher - TCS]
  1866    (1870-3; 1880; 1900 m-33;
  B-O ch.; wid. Joisy 1910)
(Abner cont.)

1

**ABNER (cont.)**
LEWIS (R.Proctor [27] S b.Clay) [s/o John
   Abner & Milly Noble - TCS; 1850]
   MILLY ANN GUM (R.Ows. 20 S b.Est.)
   [d/o Wm. B. Gum & Lucinda Benton - TR]
   11 July, 1859, Ows. [R.Owsley 1860;
   R.Lee 1870-1880-1900; widr. Lewis 1910 Lee]
LEWIS "KANEY" (c33 S b.KY) [1864-1949; ob-H
   OCN-11/4/49]
   SUSAN HACKER (c21 S b.KY) [1876-1950; d/o
   Hogan Hacker & Nora J. Day - ob-W OCN-
   5/5/50; 1880]
   1897/8      (1900-8/90, m-2; 1910-18, m-14
   = 1895/6, 1st ch. appar. hers, 7/7 ch, all
   7 listed; TCS; 1920)
ROBERT (c21 b.KY)    [s/o Wm. Abner & Jane
   Baker - 1860]
   SARAH A. DEATON (c12 b.KY)    [d/o Isaac
   Deaton & Nancy Smith - DDN]
   c1872        (1880-8; DDN)
SAMUEL (c22 S b.Ows.) [s/o Lacy Abner
   & Cynthia Combs - 1880]
   MARIAH "CHINA/CHANEY" BISHOP (c19 S b.KY)
   1885/6      (1900-11/87, m-14; 1910 m-21 =
   1888/9; DC-ch. 1917; "Chaney" - TCS)
WILEY (c22 S b.Ows.) [s/o John Abner & Joyce
   Burns]
   LETHAN McINTOSH (c17 S b.KY)
   1896        (1900 m-4; 1910 m-13; BC)
WILLIS (c25 b.Clay) [1824-1890; s/o Elisha
   Abner & Nancy Loving - TCS; REM; JTB]
   ELMIRA BAKER (c22 b.Clay) [1828-1890; d/o
   John H. Baker & Lucinda Amis - JTB; TS-TCS]
   c1850        (1860-9; B-O ch.; TCS; NL 1850;
   NL M-C)
**ABSHEAR/ABSHER**
ABRAHAM (c21 b.VA)    [s/o Isaac Abshear & Mary
   Eagle - 1860-70]
   NANCY BOWMAN (c19 b.Ows.) [d/o Levi Bowman
   & Eliz. Turner - TCS]
   c1876           (1880; B-O ch-3/77; M-L ch-
   1908) [NANCY m2 Mr. Brown - TCS]

(Abshear cont.)

## ABSHEAR (cont.)

BEN FRANK (c22 S b.Ows.) [c1882-1968 Clark;
   s/o Jeff Abshear & Sarah Frost - TCS; 1920;
   ob-H BE-7/11/68]
   DELLA FREEMAN (c20 S b.KY) [1883-1910 -TCS]
   1903/4          (DC son Moab; 1910 Frank,
   Della & Moab 3; 1920 Ben w/HM, W-NL, a/L
   1920-Clk as Frank w/W2 & ch.; Moab 13 1920-
   Clk neph/o Henry Frost; M-Clk 1930 Moab b.
   1906 Ows.)     [FRANK m2 c1916, Lillie Bush
   - 1920-Clk, Frank, Lillie & son Ray (listed
   ob-Frank); BC-Clk son Ray; NL M-Clk; Frank
   R.Trapp 1967 - ob-HS BE-12/7/67]
FRANCIS M. (c23 b.VA) [1848-1912; s/o Isaac
   Abshear & Mary Ann Eagle - 1860-70; TS-TCS]
   SALLIE T. MINTER (c30 b.VA)
   1871/2          (1880-J-7, HM w/them; 1900;
   TCS; NL M-J)
FRANK - see BEN FRANK
GEORGE (c31 2nd b.KY) [m1 _____ Palmer - JFB]
   [s/o Isaac Abshear & Mary Ann Eagle - 1880]
   MOLLIE MARSHALL (c16 S b.KY)   [d/o Joseph
   Marshall & Rebecca Thomas]
   24 Nov., 1900, Perry, @ Green Marshall's,
   by Sherman Anderson, MG; wits. Martha Young
   & Logan Marshall   (M-P H:4; 1910 w/WP)
JAMES (c30 b.Lee,VA) [1850-1897 Ows.; s/o
   Isaac Abshear & Mary Eagle - 1850-Lee,VA;
   1860-1870; ME-2/19/97; TS-TCS]
   LUTICIA MARSHALL (c26 b.Ows.)   [1853-1926;
   d/o Joseph Marshall & W1 Caroline Combs
   - TS-TCS]
   1879/80          (1880-MWY; TCS; NL wid.
   1900Sx; wid. Letisha 1910-L; 1920 wid.
   Lutisha w/dau. & SiL Estep; M-L ch-1909;
   ob-ch. BS-3/21/85
JEFFERSON (c28 b.VA) [s/o Isaac Abshear
   & Mary A. Eagle - 1870]
   SARAH ELIZ. FROST (c17 b.KY) [1853-1932;
   d/o Cornelius Frost & Cath. Grindstaff -
   1870; LNG]
   c1879          [DIVORCED 1905-10] (1880-4/80;
   NL 1900Sx H/W; Jeff. widr 1910 w/ch. Martha
   14, Myrtle 10, Roosevelt 5; Sarah div 1910;
   1920 Sarah wid w/ch. Myrtle 20, Ben 35 &
   Roosevelt 15)
(Abshear cont.)

**ABSHEAR (cont.)**

JOHN B. (c29 S b.KY) [1860-1919; s/o Isaac
    Abshear & Mary Ann Engle - 1880; TS-TCS]
    NANNIE BRANDENBURG (c17 b.KY) [1872-1953;
    d/o Kash Brandenburg & Sarah Moore - ob-W&S
    BE-9/17/53, OCN-11/24/50; 1880-L]
    1889/90        (TCS; 1910; wid. Nannie 1920)
JOHN (c18 S b.Ows.) [1883-1966 Boonev.; s/o
    James Abshear & Lutisha Marshall - ob-H BE-
    8/11/66; TS-TCS]
    PARROTT PAYNE (c17 S b.Ows.) [1883-1968
    Boonev.; d/o Thomas Payne & W1 Mary Gibson
    - DC; ob-W&F BE-11/28/68, OCC-9/8/39]
    1900/1        (1910-1920; TCS; BC 1913-1917;
    wid. R.Boonev. 1966-68)
PLEASANT - see WM. PLEASANT
W[M.] S. (R.Ows. 30 S mill b.Ows.) P/VA [1872-
    1906; s/o F(rancis) M. Abshear & Sallie
    Minter - mg.; TS-TCS; ME-10/6/04-12/21/05,
    Wm. S. suffering from hemorrhage of lungs]
    MINNIE P. RAGAN (R.Whitley 22 S b.Pul.) P/
    Pul-Linc. [d/o J. D. Ragan & Nannie Coffey
    - mg.; ME has d/o Rev. J. W. Ragan of
    Williamsburg, formerly of Ows.]
    24 Dec., 1902, Williamsburg, Whitley Co. @
    J. G. Ragan's, by J. G. Ragan, MG; wits. A.
    S. Hill & Flora J. Sullivan (M-Whit.; ME-
    1/9/03; NL 1910Sx)
WILLIAM PLEASANT (c25 S b.Ows.) [1877-1957;
    s/o Abraham Abshear & Nancy Bowman - 1880;
    ob-H OCN-12/26/57]
    ELLA BELLE REYNOLDS (c18 S b.KY) [d/o
    Simeon Reynolds & Eliz. Moore - ob-WS
    OCN-3/28/52, BE-3/25/71]
    1902/3        (1910-1920; ob-ch. BS-1/21/99;
    R.Boonev. 1957-1971)
Z[ARHARIAH] M. (R.Buckhorn, Per; c31 Dr. b.KY)
    [s/o Francis Abshear & Sallie Minter -1900]
    AMANDA GROSS (c16 b.KY) [d/o John Gross
    & Ella        - ME; 1900-P]
    26 Oct., 1904, Perry @ Buckhorn, by Harvey
    S. Murdock, Min. Presbyterian Church; wits.
    Louisa S. Murdock & Emma H. Gordon (M-P
    J:21; ME-11/10/04)

**ABSTON/ABSTANE**
MAR[TIN] W[M.] (R.Lee 22 S Min. b.--) P/--
    MARTHA ROWLAND (R.Ows. 22 S b.Lee) P/Lee
    [c1887-1938; d/o John R. Rowland & Molly
    Connor - EERS; ob-W&S BE-10/6/38-6/6/35]
    2 Oct., 1909, Ows.    [R.Endee 1935; wid.
    R.Hlbg. 1938]
**ACRES**
see AKERS
**ADAMS**
FREDDIE (c23 b.KY) P/KY    [poss. s/o Wm.
    Adams & Louvisa        - 1860-C]
    SARAH J. HORNSBY (c21 b.KY)    [d/o Job
    Hornsby & Catherine Gabbard - TCS; MT]
    c1871        (1880-8; MT; TCS; NL 1900Sx)
    [appar. DIVORCED]    [FRED poss. m2 1/14/87
    Nancy Hornsby - M-C; poss. DIVORCED;
    Nancy Hornsby Adams remd. Green Johnson]
    [a FRED (R.Ows. 76 widr. b.Clay - s/o Wm.
    Adams & Louvisa) md 9/10/1929 Ows., Esther
    Smith (65 wid.) d/o Rural Collins &
    Caroline (Smith) - M-O; Fred NL 1910-20; no
    DC on file]        [SARAH m2 Frank Johnson;
    m3 Irvine Wooton - MT]
JOHN (R.Ows. 21 - b.Clay) P/TN-Clay [1852-
    1917; prob. s/o Wm. Adams & Louvisa
    - 1860-C w/M; TS-TCS; NL DC]
    MARTHA J[ANE] HORNSBY (R.Ows. 19 S b.Clay)
    P/Clay [1857-1918; d/o Job Hornsby & Cath.
    Gabbard - 1860; TS-TCS]
    - Oct., 1876, Ows., @ Catherine Hornsby's
    [R.Owsley 1880; (NL 1900); Jane & ch. 1910]
JOHN (c26 b.KY)
    ANGELINE MOSLEY (c20 b.KY)    [d/o Jim
    Mosley - BBG]
    1879/80            (1910; wid. Angeline 1920;
    NL 1880-1900Sx; BBG; NL M-B]
JOHN (c18 b.KY)
    JANE _____ (c18 b.KY)
    1898/9        (1900)

(Adams cont.)

5

**ADAMS (cont.)**
JOHN (___ b.___)
   ANGELINE McINTOSH (c45 S b.KY) [d/o Wm.
   McIntosh & Mary J. Harris - TCS; 1880]
   18 Jan., 1910, Ows. [rec. Perry], @ John
   Adams', by A. J. Eversole, MG; wits: Andy
   Burns & Isaac Gilbert (M-P J:175; 1900
   "wid" Angeline McIntosh & ch.; TCS & JEM
   say she was not md. 1900, but had ch. by a
   Fox)
SQUIRE (c17 b.KY)
   NANCY SNOWDEN (c16 b.KY)
   c1844     (1850-5; B-O ch.; 1860; 1870-L)
WESLEY (c26 b.KY)
   EMILY ABSHEAR (c25 b.KY) [d/o Isaac
   Abshear & Mary A. Engle - 1880]
   1891     (1900 m-9; TCS)
**ADDISON**
ALBERT (c23 b.Ows.) [1882-1975 Lee; s/o Ben
   Addison & Sally Reese - 1900; AB/JFB PWB]
   BETTY STACY (c18 b.KY) [d/o James Stacy
   & Susan Campell - 1900; ob-WS BE-1/21/60]
   23 Nov., 1905, Ows. (AB/JFB PWB; 1910-L;
   M-L ch-1933; R.Hlbg. 1960)
ALVIN (c23 b.KY)
   ELIZABETH _____ (c15 b.TN)
   1881/2    (1900)
BENJAMIN J. (c21 b.Ows.) [1850-1912 Ows.; s/o
   Isaac Addison & Mary Price - 1860; AB JFB;
   PWB]
   SARAH "SALLY" REESE (c16 b.Ows.) [d/o
   Joseph Reese & Judy Brewer - B-O]
   1871/2    (1880-6; 1900; B-O ch-1/74;
   H-remd. 1910, 2 of their ch. w/son Charlie
   1910-L; M-L ch-1909; ob-ch. BE-12/9/48)
BENJAMIN (c53 2nd b.KY) [m1 Sarah Reese above]
   TEMPA (nee WARD) MARCUM (c35 2nd KY)
   [m1 Henry Marcum - 1900] [1874-c1918 -
   art. BE-9/3/70]
   1909/10    (1910 m2-0 both, Marcum
   s-ch. w/them; BC)


(Addison cont.)

ADDISON (cont.)

CHARLES (R.Lee 23 S b.--[Ows.]) P/-- [s/o
    Benjamin Addison & Wl Sarah Reese - 1880]
    SUSIE REECE (R.Lee 20 S b.--[KY]) P/--
    [c1882-1957; d/o George Reece & Wl Frances
    McQueen - ob-W OCN-2/21/57; P/1880-L]
    28 June, 1902, Lee, @ George Reece's, by
    J. C. Smallwood, Min.; wits. John F. Reece
    & Leslie Jones     (M-L; AB/JFB PWB; 1910-L
    HS w/them; 1920)
CHARLES (c20 S b.KY)    [1887-1976; s/o Elias
    Addison & Eliz. Clemtine Carmack - TS-TCS]
    SARAH SMITH (c22 S b.KY)   [1885-1953 IN;
    d/o James Smith & Lucinda Gumm - TCS ob-W
    OCN-11/20/53]
    1906/7         (1910-1920; ob-W)
ELIAS ERVIN (c25 S b.Ows.)   [1859-1929; s/o
    Isaac Addison & Mary Price - 1880; TS-TCS]
    ELIZABETH CLEMENTINE CARMACK (c17 S b.TN)
    [1865-1955; d/o Jacob Carmack & Elizabeth
    Chadwell - 1880; TS-TCS]
    1882/3          (1900-1910-1920; TCS; PWB)
ELIAS/ELISH (c21 c-minr b.Ows.)   [1881-1931
    Ham., OH; s/o Isaac Addison & Cath. Garrett
    - PWB; 1900; DC]
    SARAH ALLEN (c16 b.Ows.)   [1886-c1908 Lee;
    d/o Joseph Allen & Frances Beard - PWB;
    1900]
    c1902          (PWB, dau. b. 6/1904)
GREELY W. (c20 S b.Ows.)   [s/o Ben Addison
    & Wl Sarah Reese - 1900; AB/JFB PWB]
    MILLIE JANE MATHEWS (c19 S b.KY)   [1886-
    1956; d/o James Madison Mathews & Nancy J.
    Lamb - 1900; ob-W OCN-3/22/56]
    1905/6         (1910-J; AB/JFB PWB; ob-W;
    NL M-J/L; R.Hlbg. 1956)
ISAAC (c24 b.England)
    MARY PRICE (c21 b.KY)   [d/o Adam Price
    & Holly     - PWB AB/JFB]
    c1845          (1850-4; Isaac 1st appears on
    TL 1845; 1844 TL missing for "A"; 1860-
    1870-1880; PWB)

(Addison cont.)

7

**ADDISON (cont.)**

ISAAC, JR. (c21 S b.Ows.) [s/o Isaac Addison
    & Mary Price - 1860-1870]
    CATHERINE GARRETT (c22 S b.Lee,VA) [c1855-
    1898; d/o Geo. W. Garrett & Sarah Thompson
    - PWB; 1870; TS-TCS]
    c1875      (1880; B-O ch-3/76; widr.
    Isaac 1900-1910)
WILLIAM M. (c32 b.KY) [1864-1936; s/o Isaac
    Addison & Mary Price - 1880; TS-AB]
    MARY CATH. ROWLAND (c33 b.KY) [1863-1945;
    d/o John Rowland & Sarah Campbell - 1880;
    TS-AB & TS-TCS]
    1897      (1900 m-3; 1910 m-12, Rowland
    BiL; 1920; EERS; BBG; PWB)

**AGER**

see EAGER

**AIKMAN**

MARTIN (c19 b.KY)
    LUCY SIZEMORE (c20 b.Ows.) [d/o Henderson
    Sizemore & Nancy J. Gabbard]
    early 1900      (1900, m-3 mos., w/WM; MT;
    1910-B; NL M-B)    [LUCY m2 c1914, James
    Crank - MT; TCS; 1920-B; NL M-B]

**AKERS/ACRES**

CLIFTON P. (c28 b.KY) [s/o William Akers
    & Perdelia Pitman - REM]
    ELIZA ANN ASHCRAFT (c20 b.KY) [d/o James
    Ashcraft, Jr. & Eliz. McCollum - REM]
    c1849      (NL 1850; 1860-10; B-O ch.;
    1870)
JOHN J. (R."H.C.", Ows. 21 S b.Ows.) [s/o
    Wm. Akers & Perdelia Pitman - 1850]
    AMANDA SEE (R.Millina; 17 S b.Ows.)
    19 Oct., 1853, Ows., by G. S. Williams
JOHN (R.Ows. 26 S b.Est.) [1829-1875; s/o
    John Akers & Patsy McGuire - 1850; JA]
    ARMINA GRAY (R.Ows. 18 S b.Est.) [d/o
    John Gray & Polly Hatton]
    13 Dec., 1855, Ows. [R.Estill 1860; Lee
    1870; wid. Armina 1880 Lee] [ARMINA m2
    12/11/1901 Lee, John H. Plummer - M-L; JA]

(Akers cont.)

**AKERS/ACRES**
MILTON (c27 S b.KY) [s/o Wm. Akers & Perdelia
    Pitman]
    MARGARET HELTON (___ b.___)
    Nov., 1861        (TCS)
STEPHEN (c20 b.Ows.) [s/o Wm. Acres & Perdelia
    Pitman]
    RHODA JAMESON (c18 b.Est.) [d/o Mordecai
    Jamison & Sarah Winkler - 1860]
    c1864        (1870-L-5; B-L ch.; 1880-L;
    ob-ch. ME-8/2/01)

**ALDER**
WILLIAM (c33 b.Powell Co., VA) P/VA
    SUSAN CORNELIUS (c21 b.Clay) P/KY [d/o Eli
    Cornelius & Mary Paris - 3rd M-L; sgl-1860]
    c1861        (1870-L-8; B-L ch.; 1880-L;
    ob-ch. BE-3/19/36) [SUSAN m2 1/27/92 Lee,
    Joseph Rogers - M-L; 1900-L; SUSAN m3
    10/11/08, Elijah Ross, his 3rd also - M-L]

**ALFORD**
JAMES (c24 b.VA) [s/o Charles Alford & Sarah
    E. Houge - TCS]
    EMILY TREADWAY (c22 b.KY) [d/o Wm.
    Treadway & Margaret Bowman - TCS]
    22 April, 1848, Ows. (TCS; 1850-1; B-O ch.;
    Emily 1870, separated from hus., but they
    later reunited - TCS)

**ALLEN**
ABIJAH (R.Br. 22 S b.Br.) P/KY [s/o Jno.
    Allen & Rhoda Riley]
    ELLA HUTCHISON (R.Br. 18 S b.Br.) P/Br. &
    KY [appar. d/o Sally Hutchison by a
    Sandlin - 1860-B]
    1 Oct., 1874, Ows. (a/L M-B as 25 & 29 Oct,
    Br.; bride ELLA SANDLIN) [R.Breathitt 1880]
ABNER (___ b.TN)
    RHODA SMITH (___ b.Ows.)
    pre-1904        (B-O ch.; NL 1910-1920Sx;
    NL M-B/C)
ADANIRAM (R.Clay 26 S b.Clay) [prob. s/o John
    Allen & Esther Baker - 1850-C; P/M-C]
    EASTER ABNER (R.Ows. 18 S b.Clay) [d/o Wm.
    Abner & Jane Baker - JC; 1850-C; P/M-C]
    15 Sept., 1855 Clay (M-C mf; 1860-1870-C)

(Allen cont.)

**ALLEN (cont.)**
DANIEL G. (R.Clay 24 S b.Clay)
   RHODA JONES (R.Ows. 23 S b.Knox)
   5 March, 1856, Ows.  (R.Clay 1860-1870)
DANIEL (c25 S b.Clay)
   LULIE GROSS (c19 S b.Clay)  [d/o James
   Gross & Cath. Spivey - TCS]
   March/April, 1900        (1900-C m-0 mo.;
   NL M-C; B-O ch. 1904; TCS; 1910-C m-10)
DAVID (___ b.___)
   CLARA GABBARD (c14-29 b.KY)  [d/o Abijah
   Gabbard & Nancy Bishop - 1880; MT]
   1885-1900        (W-sgl. w/P 1880;
   WP 1900-M; NL 1900-1910Sx; NL M-C)
ELI (c21 b.Est.)
   NANCY M. WALLIN (c14 b.VA)
   c1868        (1870-8/69; B-O ch.; 1880-11)
ELIJAH (___ b.KY)
   JENNIE WELLS (c19 S b.KY)
   29 March, 1901, _Clay_  (M-C; MT; 1910 Jennie
   Cope m2-3, Allen s-s, 8)     [JENNIE m2
   Nathan Cope a/k/a Hicks - 1910-1920; TCS]
GEORGE W. (c22 S b.Clay) [1872-1958; s/o Ethan
   Allen - ob-H OCN-8/21/58]
   MARY JANE SAYLOR (c20 S b.Ages, Harl.)
   [1874-1954 - ob-W OCN-2/5/54]
   1894        (1900 m-6; 1910 m-15; B-O ch.;
   1920; ob-ch. BS-12/23/93 & Rich.IN-9/14/94;
   ACB/obit-Wlf; NL M-C)
JOB (c28 b.Clay)
   AMERICA SIZEMORE (c23 b.Clay)  [d/o Smith
   Sizemore & Matilda Hudson - 1860]
   c1872        (W-sgl. w/F 1870; B-O ch-1/74,
   this ch. w/Sizemore GF 1880; NL 1880-1900-
   1910Sx; NL M-C)
JOHN (c21 b.KY)
   LUCINDA "LOU" _____ (c17 b.KY)
   1886/7        (1900 m-13; 1910-R m-30 =
   1879/80; NL M-R)


(Allen cont.)

**ALLEN (cont.)**
JOSEPH "JOE" (c26 S b.Br.)  [1849-1929 Rockc.;
   s/o Jno. Allen & Rhoda Riley - PWB 2nd M-L]
   FRANCES E. BEARD (c22 b.Rockbridge/Lee Co,
   VA) P/VA  [c1850-c1909; d/o Daniel Beard
   & Eliza Jane     - PWB]
   c1872     (1880-7, Frances md., H-NL;
   B-O ch.; 1890; PWB; 1900 m-26 = 1873/4;
   ob-ch. BE-6/4/59; DC ch-1959; also R.Jack.,
   Rockc., & Lee)  [JOE (R.Banford 55 2nd b.
   Br.) m2 1/30/10 Lee, Maggie Deaton (Helton)
   (40 2nd - d/o Wm. Deaton) - M-L; PWB]
JOE (c26 b.Br.)
   MAHALIA "HALLEY" RILEY (c18 b.Cortland,
   Ows.)  [1880-1972; d/o James Hacker Riley
   & Rhoda Riley - 1900; ob-W BE-3/9/72]
   1901/2     (ob-W; 1910-1920-B; ob-ch. BS-
   4/17/86; NL M-B)  [NOTE: B-O ch. lists
   W/as Halley _Thomas_, but ob-W confirms she
   was a Riley]
LEVI (c20 b.Clay)  [s/o Adoniram Allen - MT]
   SALLY STRONG (c18 b.Ows.)  [d/o Alex
   Strong & Anna Wilson - 1850]
   c1857     (JCH; 1860-C-2 & 6 mos.;
   TCS; B-C 1878; NL M-C)
LEWIS (c17 S b.Clay)  [c1885-1972, Is. Cr. -
   ob-H BE-3/2/72]
   LUCY HELEN TAYLOR (c17 S b.Conkling, Ows.)
   [1886-1954 OH; d/o Eli Taylor & Sarah
   Shepherd - 1900; ob-W BE-9/2/54]
   1904/5     (1910-1920; B-O ch.; ob-ch.
   BS-8/20/87; NL M-C)
ROBERT (c28 mcht. b.KY)
   SUSAN ABNER (c18 b.KY)  [d/o Wm. Abner
   & Jane Baker - 1850]
   c1851     (W-sgl. 1850; 1860-C-8;
   1870-13 wid. Susan w/P as ALLEN; 1880 as
   ABNER; 1900 as ALLEN; 1910-L as ALLEN;
   TCS; NL M-C)

(Allen cont.)

**ALLEN (cont.)**
SAMUEL (c23 b.KY)  [s/o Bige Allen & Ella
    Hutchison/Sandlin - TCS]
    RHODA JANE ALLEN (c21 b.Ows.)  [1876-1959;
    d/o Joseph Allen & Frances Beard - ob-W
    BE-6/4/59 & DC as ALLEN]
    1897/8        (1900; PWB TCS; NL M-C)
    [RHODA m2 Thomas Land (c1874-1935); Tom
    killed by W-SiL, who claimed that Rhoda
    paid him to murder Tom - ob-H, W-arrest
    BE-12/19/35; NL M-L/O]
THOMAS (___ b.___)
    EMILY B. STIDHAM (c18 b.KY)  [d/o Thomas
    Stidham & Armilda Morris - JS]
    13 Aug., 1902, Clay  (M-C file 31; ob-ch.
    BS-7/30/92 Alva b. c1903 Ows.; NL 1910Sx
    H/W; R.Newfoundland, KY JS)
WILLIAM (c19 b.KY)
    MARGARET ["PEGGY"] LINCH [LYNCH] (c16 b.KY)
    13 Feb., 1880, Clay  (M-C; 1900 m-20; TCS;
    ob-ch. HJN-9/90)
WILLIAM "WILL" (c27 b.KY)
    MATTIE GILBERT (c24 b.KY)  [1870-1905; d/o
    John Gilbert & Ann Judith Minter - TCS;
    1880; ob-W ME-6/22/05]
    c1894        (1900-9/95, Mattie ALLEN w/P,
    H-NL; R.Winchester; W-d. @ WF's house Ows.;
    widr. Wm. w/WP 1910, 1 ch., 14; NL M-C)
**ALLUMBAUGH/ALUMBAUGH**
JAMES (c25 b.Ows.)  [s/o Wm. Allumbaugh & W1
    Delilah Kelly - 1850]
    MARY D. WARREN (c22 b.Ows.)  [d/o George
    Jordan Warren & Eliza      - 1850-H; 1860]
    1869        (1870-6/70; 1880-1890-1900;
    TCS)
WM. (40's 2nd b.KY)  [widr/o Delilah Kelly -
    1850; M-E 2/28/39]   [s/o Peter Allumbaugh
    & Sarah      - D-O]
    LUCY ANN (nee THOMAS) BOWLES (40's 2nd b.
    VA)  [wid/o Wm. Bowles - REM]
    1850-9        (1860 Wm. w/Lucy Ann, who
    claims mg. rights; REM)    [H-remd.]

(Allumbaugh cont.)

## ALLUMBAUGH (cont.)

WILLIAM (c51 3rd b.KY)   [widr/o Lucy A. Thomas
    above - 1860]
    JULINA [nee PHIPPS] MORRIS (c35 2nd b.VA)
    [wid/o John Morris - M-C 1853]  [d/o Samuel
    Phipps & Mary Hash - TCS; 1850-C]
    21 Sept., 1862, <u>Clay</u>  (M-C; 1870 W/Julia,
    only ch. under 10 was 4; 1880 Julia w/s-ch.
    & dau. Eliz. 14; REM)

## AMBROSE

BARTON P. (c25 b.Ows.)  [1845-c1935 Berea; s/o
    Meredith Ambrose & Anna Clark - 1860-1870]
    ISABELLE "IBBY" CARMACK (c17 b.TN)
    5 May, 1871       (TCS; 1880-8, HM w/them;
    1900 m-29; B-O ch. & D-O ch.; moved to
    Berea - ME-9/14/05; OCN-9/1/50 art. on dau.
    Ruth Wilson; art. BE-7/30/59)
FRANCIS M. (c22 b.KY)  [s/o Meredith Ambrose
    & Anna Clark - REM]
    MARIA L. MINTER (c21 b,VA)
    c1865       (1870-4; TCS; B-J ch-1874;
    went to Ark. TCS)
GEORGE (c23 <u>Mul</u> b.KY)
    LUCY _____ (c19 <u>Blk</u> b.VA)
    c1865       (1870-4)
H. C. (c22 dentist b.KY)
    EMILY _____ (c15 b.KY)
    c1859       (1860, no ch.)
JAMES (c21 b.KY)
    MALINDA ROBERTSON (c21 b.KY)
    21 Jan., 1842, <u>Clay</u>  (M-C; 1850; 1860-C)
JAMES HARVEY (c25 S b.KY)
    LUCY BIGGS (c22 b.KY)  [d/o Wm. Biggs
    & Phoebe Barrett - TCS]
    22 Jan., 1889, <u>Jackson Co.</u>  (M-J; TCS;
    1900-J; 1910-1920)
JOSEPH (c22 b.KY)  [s/o Moses Ambrose & Mary
    Browning - TCS]
    RACHEL BISHOP (c22 b.KY)
    c1845       (1850-9 b.MO, who is prob. a
    rel.; next ch. ages 4 & 3; B-J ch-1859;
    1860-J-14; 1870-1880-J)

(Ambrose cont.)

13

## AMBROSE (cont.)

WILLIAM (20's b.KY)   [1828-1858; s/o Meredith
   Ambrose & Anna Clark - D-O; 1850]
   _____ (___ b.___)
   1850-8        (H-sgl. 1850; D-O 1858, Wm.
   listed as md.)

WILLIAM (c20 b.KY)
   CHARLOTTE M. "LOTTIE" FARMER (c18 S b.KY)
   [d/o Cornelius Nelson Farmer & Letitia
   Tackett - TCS; 1880]
   6 April, 1892, Jackson Co. (TCS; 1900-J
   anot.; B-J ch-1901)   [LOTTIE m2 Mr. Marcum
   - TCS]

## AMIS/AMY/AMEY/AMOS

JEFF (c33 b.KY)
   LYDIA A. SMITH a/k/a OLIVER (c31 b.KY)
   d/o _____ OLIVER & Lucretia (nee SMITH)
   Moore, wid., who later md. Harvey Combs -
   TCS]
   1895/6        [DIV. 1910-20] (1900; 1910
   Lyddia A. m-14, H-NL; 1920 Lydia, div.)

ROBERT (c23 b.Br.) [1866-1948; s/o John Amis
   & Sarah Eversole - 1880; TS-TCS; 2nd M-O]
   ESTHER BAKER (c20 b.KY) [1870-1932; d/o
   James W. Baker & Sarah Davidson - 1880;
   TS-TCS]
   1889/90        (1900-1910; TCS; ob-ch. BS-
   3/7/91; BS-4/5/90 ch-98 Bday) [They are
   s-b & s-sis - TCS]   [ROBERT (R.Ows. 65
   widr. b.Br.) m2 9/15/32 Ows., Martha (nee
   Spivy) Judd (62 wid. b.Ows.) d/o David
   Spivey & Amanda - M-O]

## AMYX

JOHN (R.Jack. 20 S b.TN) P/TN-NC [s/o Sam
   Amyx & Mary      - TCS]
   ALPHA WILSON (R.Ows. 15 S b.Lee,VA) P/VA
   22 Feb., 1877, Ows. @ Lish Walton(?)

W[M.] T. (R.Hindman, Knt c28 Dr. b.Jack.)
   [ELIZABETH] LIZZIE CAMPBELL (R.Boonev. c22
   b.KY)
   13 March, 1895        (ME-3/22/95; 1900-J
   m-5)

14

## ANDERSON

CHARLES M. (c37 S Dr. b.MO)
   FLORENCE ABSHEAR (c26 S b.Jack.) [d/o
   Francis M. Abshear & Sally Minter - 1900]
   Dec, 1902, Ows. @ bride's home, So. Boonev.
   (Tues., 9 a.m.), by Rev. W. W. Baxter of
   Manchester who came to Ows. to officiate
   (ME-1/9/03; 1910 m-6; H-sgl. 1900; B-O ch-
   1904)
ED (c22 b.KY) [s/o Franklin Anderson
   & Jane Combs - TCS; F/P-CW]
   MARY ANN COMBS (c19 b.KY) [d/o Jackson
   Combs & Martha Reynolds - 1880]
   1885/6      (1900-J m-14; TCS; NL M-J)
FRANKLIN (c22 S b.VA) [1827-1898 Ows. - TS-
   TCS; P-CW]
   JANE COMBS (c17 S b.KY) [1832-1920 Jack. -
   P-CW]
   1 April, 1849, Ows. @ Meredith M Ambrose's,
   by Meredith M. Ambrose, JPOC (ML 3/31/49
   Ows.) (P-CW; 1850-5 mos.; B-O ch. W/as
   Anderson; 1860-1870-1880; wid. Jane 1900;
   Jane d. Mildred, Jackson Co.)
FRANKLIN (c25 b. TN)
   NANCY J. _____ (c22 b.KY)
   c1868     (1870-1)
JACOB M. (R.Ows. 22 S b.KY) P/VA-KY [s/o
   Frank Anderson & Jane Combs - 1870; F/P-CW]
   ANNIE GABBARD (R.Ows. 24 S b.KY) P/KY-TN
   [d/o James Gabbard & Eliz. A Frost - MT]
   28 Aug, 1878, Ows. [R.Ows. 1880-1900-1910]
JAMES (c24 S b.MO)
   LOUISA J. McCOLLUM (c19 S b.KY) [d/o Dan
   McCollum & Emily Brewer - 1880]
   1887/8    (1900-1910-1920; TCS)
JESSE (c23 b.TN)
   MARTHA MORRIS (c16 b.KY) [d/o Wm. Morris
   & Margaret Sandlin - TCS]
   c1848/9    (1850-6 mos.; TCS; Jesse
   1st appears on TL 1848; 1860-J-10)
PETER (c18 b.KY) [s/o Franklin Anderson
   & Jane Combs - 1870; F/P-CW]
   _____ (___ b___) [d. pre-1900]
   c1880   (1900-10/81, widr. Peter, HM
   w/him)

(Anderson cont.)

**ANDERSON (cont.)**
SHERIDAN (c24 b.Ows.) [s/o Franklin Anderson
    & Jane Combs - 1880; F/P-CW]
    JOSEPHINE (ANDERSON?) (c25 b.Ows.)
    1895/6          (1900; B-O ch. W/as Anderson)
SHERMAN (c21 S b.Ows.) [s/o Franklin Anderson
    & Jane Combs - 1880; F/P-CW]
    NANCY M. COMBS (c16 S b.Ows.) [d/o
    Granville Combs, Mary Carmack - 1880; TCS]
    1889          (1900 m-11; 1910 m-20; B-O ch.)
THOMAS (c18 S b.Ows.) [s/o Franklin Anderson
    & Jane Combs - B-O; F/P-CW]
    SUSAN JANE THOMAS (c19 S b.Ows.)  [1849-
    1928; d/o Elisha Thomas & Rachel McCollum -
    TCS; 1850-1860)
    c1873          (1880-6; wid. Susan 1900 as
    THOMAS; 1910 as Susan ANDERSON m-35 =
    1874/5; B-O ch.)
WILL C. (R.Ows. 26 S b.Jefferson Co.) [s/o
    Wm. Anderson & Nancy Cheek - 1850]
    SYLVANIA MORRIS (R.Ows. 23 S b.Clay)  [d/o
    George Morris & Eliz. Johnson - 1850]
    21 Aug., 1856, Ows.
WILLIAM (c15 S b.Boonev.) [s/o Frank Anderson
    & Jane Combs - 1880; F/P-CW]
    SARAH CATHERINE MOORE (a/k/a FORD) (c15 S
    b.Boonev.) [1872-1953; d/o Joe LOME
    & Lucinda MOORE, who later md. David Alex.
    FORD - DC; ob-W BE-9/17/53]
    1887/8          (1900-1910-1920; B-O ch.
    W/as Ford; M-L ch. & FH ch. W/as Moore)
**ANDREWS/ANDREW**
CARL (___ b.___)
    LULA BREWER (c14-30 b.KY) [d/o Daniel
    P. Morris Brewer & Lucy Wilson - 1880]
    1894-1910          (TCS; NL 1900-1910Sx)
    [LULA m2 Mr. Roe - TCS]
WILLIAM M. (c27 S b.Wythe Co., VA) [s/o James
    M. Andrews & Hester     - 1870]
    SARAH A. SCHOONOVER (c25 b.Scott Co., VA)
    [prob. d/o Wm. Schoonover & Matilda - 1870]
    1872/3          (1880; B-O ch-5/74; 1900-J)

## ANGEL

ANDREW (c29 b.KY)  [s/o Ephraim Angel & W1
    Eliza       ]
    MALVINA GROSS (c21 b.Br.) [c1845-1878; d/o
    Henry Gross & Louisa Jones - D-L; LNG]
    1866 **Breathitt** (LNG; 1870-L-1; widr.
    Andrew 1880-L)    [H-remd.]
ANDREW (c42 2nd b.KY) [widr/o Malvina Gross -
    D-L 1878; LNG]
    CATHERINE TAYLOR (c34 S b.KY) [d/o Orville
    P. Taylor & Hannah Harvey - LNG; 1860]
    1882, Ows. (LNG; both d. pre-1900; 1900
    dau. Martha Angel w/Robt. Taylor as niece;
    M-L dau. 1919; ob-ch. BE-5/29/41)
BARNIE (R.Ows. 22 S b.Lee) P/Lee
    LINNIE TURNER (R.Ows. 18 S b.Ows) P/Ows-VA
    [d/o Henry Turner & W1    - 1900]
    9 Dec., 1908, Ows.    [R.Owsley 1920]
EDWARD (c22 S b.Lee) [1884-1967 Oneida Mt.
    Hosp.; s/o John Wesley Angel & W1 Mary
    Mays - TS-TCS; 1900-L; ob-H BE-4/6/67]
    ANNIE KELLER (c16 S b.KY)
    1906/7    (1910-1920; TCS; ob-ch. BS-
    4/24/97; wid. R.Lerose 1967)
EPHRAIM (c46 2nd b.Bunc., NC) [widr/o Eliza
    - M-P 1826]    [s/o James Angel, Sr]
    SUSANNAH JANE (nee INGRAM) RICHARDSON (c26
    2nd b.KY)    [wid/o Wm. Richardson - M-E
    3/20/35] [d/o Wm. Ingram & Eliz. Horn - WN]
    c1844    (WN; AB; PWB; 1850, Angel ch-
    12, 9, 5, 3, 1 & 17, Richardson ch-13, 11,
    9; 1860; 1870-1880-L; ob-ch. BE-1/11/45)
HENDERSON (c33 b.KY) [poss. s/o Absolem Angel
    & Themy    - LP]
    REBECCA STEEL (c22 b.Floyd) [d/o Andrew
    Jackson Steel & Nancy King - REM]
    c1863    (1870-L-6; B-L ch.; 1880-L;
    wid. Rebecca 1900-L)
JAMES (c29 b.Ows.) [s/o Ephraim Angel & W1
    Eliza    - PWB; LP]
    REBECCA MAYS (c17 b.Ows.) [d/o Andrew Mays
    & Margaret Barrett - 1850]
    1855/6    (1860-3; 1870-L; AB; B-Lau.
    ch-1875; 1880-Lau; 1900-Lau. m-54, but s/b
    44)

(Angel cont.)

**ANGEL (cont.)**

JOHN W[ESLEY] (20 S b.Br.) [1861-1942; s/o
   Reubin Angel & Cath. Couch - LNG; TS-TCS]
   MARY MAYSE (21 S b.KY) [d/o Andrew Mays
   & Rachel Mays - TCS]
   8 Jan., 1882, <u>Lee</u> (M-L; TCS; LNG; 1900-L)
   [H-remd.]

J[OHN] W[ESLEY] (R.Ows. 47 2nd b.Br.) P/Br.
   [1861-1942; widr/o Mary Mays above]
   [MARY JANE (nee SHOUSE) SPENCER] (R.Ows 28
   "S" b.Ows.) P/Ows. [Div/f Keen Spencer -
   TCS; 1900] [1880-1937; d/o Calvin Shouse
   & Aggie Mullins - DC; MRS; TS-TCS]
   10 June, 1909, Ows. [R.Owsley 1910-1920;
   1910 lists as W-3rd] [NOTE: There was an
   error in this & several others marriages,
   wherein bride listed on wrong line. Wife
   listed as MARY P. WILSON, line above was
   MARY SHOUSE. Wes md. MARY JANE SHOUSE -
   B-O ch.; BC-1912; ob-ch. BS-4/12/90]

[OSCAR] AUSKER (R.Simpson; 31 S b.Lee) [s/o
   John Angel & Jane Thomas - mg.]
   DORA ROBERTS [_____] (R."Sympson"; 24 2nd
   b.Br.) [m1 _____] [d/o John
   Roberts & Bettie Maloney - mg.]
   5 Dec., 1903, <u>Breathitt</u> @ Tom Spencer's
   (M-B 10:455; B-O ch-1908 W/as Dora RHODES;
   1910-B m-8; 1920-B)

ROBERT L (c21 S b.KY) [s/o Andrew Angel
   & Melvina Gross - 1880-L; LNG]
   JEMIMA "MIMA" GABBARD (c18 S b.Ows.) [d/o
   Julius Gabbard & Cath. Thomas - 1880; MT;
   LNG]
   1894, Owsley (LNG's GP; MT; 1900-1910-L;
   M-L ch-1920-1921-1937; ob-ch. 3Fks-8/14/96)

SQUIRE F. (R.Lau. 22 S b.Ows.) [s/o James
   Angel, Jr. & Eliz. Cunningham - 1850]
   MARGARET J[ANE] BRYANT (R.Lau c19 b.Lau.)
   [c1837-1869 Jack. - PWB]
   22 Sept, 1856 <u>Laurel</u> (M-Lau. mf; TCS; PWB;
   B-Lau. ch-1857; B-J ch-1859; 1860-J-7;
   widr. Squire 1870-J) [SQUIRE m2 c1874,
   Mary Johnson - PWB; B-J ch-1875; 1880-J;
   NL M-J]

WESLEY - see J. WESLEY

(Angel cont.)

**ANGEL (cont.)**
WILEY (c19 b.Clay)    [s/o James Angel, Jr.
   & Elizabeth Cunningham - 1850]
   CATHERINE HELTON (c17 b.KY)
   c1851         (1860-J-8; B-Lau. ch-1857; PWB;
   TCS; Wiley on TL 1850; 1870-1880-J; NL M-C)
**ANGLIN**
HARVEY (___ b.KY)  [d. 1864 Andersonville, GA
   while POW C.W.; poss. s/o James Anglin &
   Jane Barrett, listed 1850 as Henry 19]
   JEMIMA PHILLIPS (c20 b.KY)  [c1830-1880;
   d/o Hardy Phillips & Eliz.   - 1850; P-CW]
   19 Sept., 1850, Ows. @ H. Phillips', by Wm.
   Clark, JP    (P-CW; wid. Jemima R.Grant Co.
   1865-1880)
ISAAC (c23 b.KY)
   MARTHA SIMPSON (c24 b.Laurel)
   c1847         (1850-2; B-O ch.; B-Lau. ch-
   1853; Isaac on TL 1845-6 & 1849; TCS;
   NL M-Lau.)
MARTIN (c21 b.KY)
   DEBORAH SIMPSON (c20 b.KY)
   c1848         (1850-1; B-O ch.; Martin 1st
   appears on TL 1849)
**ARNOLD**
JAMES (c20 S b.Lee,VA)  [s/o Lorenzo Arnold
   & Mary         - 1860]
   ARAMINTA STAMPER (c24 S b.Morgan)  [d/o
   John A. Stamper & Lucinda Kash]
   1862         (1870-1880-L; B-L ch.; 1900-L
   m-38; 1910-L m-47)
JAMES L. (R.Ows. 30 S b.Lee) P/Lee & VA  [s/o
   Geo. Arnold & Mary Thomas - 1900-L]
   MARY ["MOLLY"] PORTER (R.Ows. 26 S b.Lee)
   P/-- [c1883-1967 Nur.H. Lex. - ob-W BE-
   3/30/67]
   5 March, 1908, Ows. [Mollie R.Beattyv. at
   death]
NEWTON J. (c18 b.Lee,VA)  [s/o Lorenzo Arnold
   & Mary         - 1860]
   SARAH RILEY (c18 b.Fay.) P/KY
   1863         (1870-1880-L; 1900-L m-37;
   1910-L m-46; B-L ch; ob-ch. BE-11/3/49)

(Arnold cont.)

19

**ARNOLD (cont.)**
WILLIAM D. (c26 b.Lee,VA) [s/o Lorenzo Arnold
    & Mary        - 1860]
    LUCY FAIRCHILDS (c22 b.Hancock Co., TN) P/
    TN-NC
    c1869          (1870-L no ch.; 1880-L-9;
    B-L ch.)
**ASBELL**
HENRY BEATTY (c46 2nd c.minr b.KY) [widr/o
    Eliza Jane Johnson - B-O ch.; M-E 11/8/38
    W1/as Eliza Bennett] [s/o Henry BEATTY
    & Sarah ASBELL, who later md. David Winkler
    - MCA]
    LUCINDA (nee BENNETT) SLONE (c41 2nd b.KY)
    [wid/o Frederick Slone - M-Pk 1829; wid.
    1850-Pk]
    c1858          (B-O ch.-2/53 by W1; 1860 W/as
    Lucinda; D-O Lucinda's ch.)
**ASHCRAFT**
JAMES (c21 miner b.KY)
    NANCY WARNER (c19 b.KY)
    22 July, 1847, Estill (M-E; 1850; TL 1848)
WILBURN (c27 mcht. b.KY) [1880-1934 - ob-H
    OCC-5/18/34; w/Henderson BBurg. 1900-L]
    FIDELIA SPICER (___ b.___) [NL 1900/L]
    23 April, 1908          (ob-H; wid. R.Dayton,
    OH 1961 - ob-ch. BE-3/16/61; NL M-L)
**AVERY/AVEARY**
[BENJAMIN] FRANKLIN ["FRANK"] (c29 Blk S b.NC)
    LUCY GIBBS (___ b.___) [d. 1890-2]
    2 May, 1885, Clay, by Rev. J. W. Colyer;
    wits. Jas. & Letcher Love (M-C file 2;
    H-remd. 1900, 1st ch-10)
[BENJAMIN FRANKLIN] FRANK (c37 Blk 2nd b.NC)
    [m1 Lucy Gibbs above]
    MARIAH [nee CAWOOD] HUDSON (c26 Blk 2nd
    b.KY) [m1 _____ Hudson]
    11 Aug., 1892, Clay Co. @ bride's house, by
    James Gilbert, Min.; wits. James Love &
    Samuel Gibson (M-C; 1900 m-7, wf 9/3 ch--
    Mary 10, Willie 4, Edw. 3; M-L ch-1922; DC
    & ob-ch. OCN-10/6/55, BE-2/22/51; H/as
    Frank & Benjamin Franklin) [H-remd.]


(Avery cont.)

**AVERY (cont.)**
BENJAMIN FRANKLIN "FRANK" (c47 Blk 3rd b.NC)
    [m2 Mariah Cawood above]
    JANE (nee _____) _____ (c27 Blk 2nd b.KY)
    [m1 _____]
    1901/2      (ME-11/3/04 & 11/10/04 Frank
    stabbed Jane in quarrel, but she survived;
    1910 H-m3-8, W-m2-8, ch. Wm. 14, Ed 12,
    Parilee 4; 1920; ob-ch. Frank's son Edward
    lists only one sib, half-sis "Pearlie"
    King; NL M-C)
FRANK - see BENJAMIN FRANKLIN

**BAILEY/BALEY/BALY**
_____ (___ b.___)
    MARY JANE REYNOLDS (c21 S b.Ows.)
    c1872      (W-sgl. 1870; W-2nd M-O & M-B
    9/74 to Fox)   [MARY m2 1874 George Fox]
ALFORD (c32 2nd b.KY)  [m1 _____]
    SURINDA PERKINS (c22 b.KY)
    c1851      (1860; B-O ch-9/52; 1870-80-L;
    1910-L as m-55; REM; TCS; W/as Surinda,
    Surilda, Laurinda)
EARL VANDORIN (c20 b.KY)  [s/o Elhannon Bailey
    & Sarah J.      - 1870-L; 1880]
    ROSA GOODMAN (c19 b.KY)  [d/o _____ Goodman
    & Sarah Taylor, who m3 Wm. Jennings - 1880]
    1881/2      (1900-L; M-B ch-1904, Eugene
    b.1883 Ows.)
ELKANAH (c23 Law. b.VA)
    SARAH J. _____ (c19 b.TN)
    c1861      (1870-L-8; wid. Sarah J. 1880)
EVERETT S. (R.Frankfort 22 stenographer b.Ows)
    P/--
    [CATHARINE] KATE M. FLANERY (R.Ows. 25 S
    b.Ows.) P/--  [1879-1911; d/o Hampton
    Flanery & Nancy Brandenburg - 1880; TS-TCS]
    24 Dec., 1904, Monica, Lee, by Z. Ball, MG
    wits: John & James B. Hieronymus  (M-L; DB;
    TCS)
GEORGE (R.Per. 23 S b.TN) [s/o Catherine
    Bailey - REM]
    MINERVA LANGDON (R.Per. 15 S b.Per.)  [d/o
    Sam Langdon & Mary      - 1850-P]
    13 April, 1858, Perry (M-P B:27, a/L as
    Minerva LACY md. 5/58; 1860-1)
(Bailey cont.)

## BAILEY (cont.)

GEORGE W. (c22 b.KY) [s/o Green Bailey & Eliz.
  Reynolds - 1880]
  ELLEN F. SMITH (c17 b.KY) [d/o Henry
  Smith & Sarah Taylor - P/1880]
  1898/9          (1900, WM w/them; ob-ch. BE-
  1/14/71 son R.Trapp)
GREEN[BERRY] (c18 b.TN) [1842-1887 - TS-TCS]
  ELIZABETH REYNOLDS (c19 b.KY) [1840-1910;
  d/o Wesley Reynolds & Nancy Moore - TS-TCS]
  19 July, 1860, Ows., @ Wesley Reynolds', by
  Joseph C. Reynolds, JPOC; wits. Presley,
  Nickolas & Henderson Moore (P-CW; 1860-MWY;
  TCS; 1870-1880; wid. Eliz. 1890-1900-1910)
GREEN [B.] A. (c26 b.KY) [s/o Hiram Bailey
  & Sarah Parris - 1860; LNG; 2nd M-L]
  LAURA B. EVANS (c18 b.KY)
  1885          (1900-9/86, m-14; LNG; ob-ch.
  3Fks-3/3/96; M-L ch-1911-1919) [H-remd. WS]
G[REEN B.] A. (R.Lee 48 2nd/W1 d; mcht. b.Br)
  [widr/o Laura B. Evans - LNG]
  [DRUSCILLA] ZILLIE [nee EVANS] SIZEMORE (R.
  Lee 28 2nd b.Ows.) [m1 Henry Sizemore -
  LNG; 1900-L] [1871-1948; d/o Hiram Evans &
  Mary Steele - mg.; ACB]
  14 May, 1908, Lee (M-L; ACB; LNG; 1910-L
  m2-2)
HIRAM (c21 b.TN) [appar. s/o wid. Catherine
  Bailey - 1850]
  SARAH PARIS (c17 b.KY) [d/o Joshua Paris
  & Elizabeth Thomas - LNG; P M-E]
  c1849          (1850, no ch., HM&S w/them;
  1860-8; NL 1880/E/L; LNG; M-L ch-1904-1908)
JOHN B. (c21 b.VA) [appar. s/o John Bailey -
  1870-W]
  MARTHA TAYLOR (c19 b.VA)
  c1851          (1860-8; B-O ch.; 1870-W)
JOHN K. (c24 b.Harlan) [s/o Andrew Jackson
  Bailey & Ann Kelly - HC]
  ROSANNAH McKINEY (c23 b.Lee,VA)
  c1851          (1860-8; B-O ch.)
MARION - see WM. MARION
MINTER (c26 b.KY) [s/o Andrew Bailey & Anna
  Kelly]
  LOUISA BAILEY (c18 b.VA)
  c1848          (1860; 1850-H; HC; NL M-H)
(Bailey cont.)

**BAILEY (cont.)**
ROBERT (R.Meadow Cr. 26 S b.VA)
    MARY WILSON (R.Cow Cr. 29 S b.Cow Cr.)
    18 June, 1854, Ows.   [R.Owsley 1860]
SAMUEL (c22 b.Harl.)  [1834-1913 Clay - P-CW;
    1900]
    ELIZABETH COMBS (c17 b.KY)  [c1839-1896;
    d/o Henry Combs & Elizabeth      - P-CW]
    25 March, 1856, Ows., by Joseph Parsons
    (P-CW; 1860; B-O ch-2/57; 1880; widr.
    Samuel 1900)   [H-remd.]
SAMUEL (c72 2nd b.KY)  [widr/o Eliz. Combs
    above]
    LOUISA [nee EVERSOLE] COLE (c46 2nd b.KY)
    [wid/o Robert Cole, who d. 1888 - P-CW H2;
    M-C 9/1/86]
    5 April, 1906, Ows. @ Samuel Bailey's;
    wits. Wm. Deaton & Franklin Cole  (P-CW;
    1910 m2-4 both; wid. R.Burning Springs,
    Clay 1913)
SHELBY (c22 S b.Ows.)  [1879-1955; s/o Green
    Bailey & Eliz. Reynolds - 1880-1900; ob-H&S
    OCN-1/27/55, OCC-5/17/40-7/15/38; will-F]
    LAURA [ELIZABETH] COLE (c21 S b.Ows.)
    [1880-1964 Br.; d/o Lewis Cole & Martha
    Cooper - TCS; TS-LNG; ob-WS BE-9/6/62; DC]
    1901            (1910 m-8, HM w/them; 1920;
    B-O ch.; R.Lerose 1938; ob-H lists W/as
    Eliz.; wid. Laura R.Jackson, Br. Co. 1962;
    ob-ch. BS-4/14/94 b.8/02 Ows.; NL M-B)
WALTER (R.Ows. 20 S b.--) [b.Ows. 1881-1949;
    s/o Green Bailey & Eliz. Reynolds - 1900
    ob-H&S OCN-12/2/49, BE-12/1/49, OCC-
    5/17/40-7/15/38]
    EMMER [EMMA] FOX (R.Lee 19 S b.--)  [b.Lee
    1882-1968; d/o Thomas Fox & Harriett Taylor
    - 1900-L; ob-W BE-1/25/68]
    27 Feb., 1902, Lee @ Thomas Fox's, by J. M.
    Roberts; wits: Keen BBurg. & Jos. Moore
    (M-L; 1910 m-8; TCS; R.St Helens 1938; wid.
    Emma R.Beattyv. 1966 - ob-HS BE-5/5/66;
    Emma R.St. Helens 1968 - ob-W)
WM. MARION (c23 S b.KY) [1868-1948; s/o Sam
    Bailey & Eliz. Combs - 1880; TS-TCS]
    MATTIE THOMAS (c19 S b.KY)  [d/o Elisha
    Thomas & Elizabeth Bowman - 1880]
    1889/90            (1900-1910; TCS)

## BAKER

_____ (___ b.___)
   CHRISTINA _____ (c20 b.KY)
   c1855      (1860-4, wid. Christina)
   [CHRISTINA m2 Sam Barker - TCS; 1870-C]
A. J. (___ b.Boonev.)
   NANCY MILLER (___ b.Boonev.)
   pre-1908     (B-O ch.; NL 1910Sx;
   NL M-B)
ABIJAH "BIGE" (c30 S b.KY)
   AMY SIZEMORE (c30 S b.KY)
   1884      (1900-6/85, m-15 = 1884/5; JTB;
   NL M-C; 1910-C m-27 = 1882/3)
ABIJAH (R.Br. 25 S b.Br) P/Ows-Per.
   NANCY SANDLIN (R.Br. 18 S b.Br.) P/Br.
   15 Dec., 1910, <u>Breathitt</u> [recorded Owsley]
ABNER (c19 S b.Ricetown) [1865-1941; s/o James
   Wilson Baker & Sarah Davidson -1880 TS-TCS]
   NANCY AMIS (c14 S b.Br.) [1870-1943; d/o
   John Amis & Sarah Eversole - 1880; TS-TCS]
   1883      (1900 m-17; 1910 m-26; B-O ch.;
   1920; NL M-B) [They are s-b & s-sis - 1880]
A[BNER] C. (c21 S b.Ricetown) [1880-1958
   Ows.; s/o Andrew J. Baker & Eliz. Amis -
   1880; ob-H OCN-8/14/58]
   ISABELLE MAYES (c19 S b.Br.) [d/o Wm. Mays
   & Eliz. Sebastian - 1900]
   20 March, 1901, Ows., by H. H. Rice, JP;
   wits. James & Lucy Mayes & others   (M-O
   rec. 8/19/33; 1910-1920; B-O ch. 1909 W/as
   <u>Rachel</u> Mays; ob-ch. BS-2/12/87 W/as <u>Eliz.</u>
   Mays & BS-7/25/91 as <u>Isabelle</u> Mays)
   [ABNER m2 1918, Lettie Herald - TCS; ob-H
   d. Boonev.]
ADAM "AD" (c17 S b.KY) [1877-1905; s/o Red
   Bob Baker & Margaret Baker - BBG; JTB]
   NANNIE BELL RICE (c17 S b.KY) [d/o Richard
   Rice & Catherine Brandenburg - BBG]
   1894     (BJE P-CW H2 McIntosh; 1900 m-10
   = 1889/90, W-7/5 ch. b.6/88, 1/90, 12/94,
   5/96, & 2/1900; wid. Nannie 1910 9/7 ch.;
   ob-ch. HJN-4/89 has <u>Robt.</u> Baker & Nancy
   Rice)   [NAN m2 Richard McIntosh - BJE]

(Baker cont.)

**BAKER (cont.)**

ALBERT (c20 S b.Br.)
   SUSIE GABBARD (c19 S b.Br.)  [d/o Michael
   Gabbard & Perlina Baker - 1900]
   1902/3     (1910; B-O ch.; NL M-B)
ALEXANDER (c21 b.TN)  [s/o Benjamin Baker
   & Polly Bradley - REM]
   DEBORAH CAMPBELL (c15 b.KY)  [d/o Stephen
   Campbell & Eliz. Eversole - TCS; REM]
   c1851     (1860; B-O ch-8/52)  [DEBORAH
   m2 c1865, Egbert Moore - N-C-3/96 JEW]
ALFRED (c19 b.KY)  [1875-1948; s/o James Todd
   Baker & Eliza Abner - HTB]
   LIZZIE BOWLING (c18 b.KY)  [1876-1962; d/o
   James Bowling & Mary Ann Baker - HTB]
   9 Nov., 1894, Ows. [rec. Perry], @ James
   Bowling's; wits. L. F. Cole, James Moore &
   Wm. Duff  (M-P G:102; 1900-B m-5, Bowling
   BiL & SiL w/them; their photo N-C 11/96)
ANDREW JACKSON (c23 b.Clay)  [1827-1900; s/o
   John H. "Mucker Jack" Baker & Lucinda Amis
   - TCS; JTB]
   MARGARET RILEY (c20 b.Perry)  [1830-1888;
   d/o John Riley & Jennie Johnson - TCS; JTB]
   1849/50     (1850-MWY, w/HP; B-O ch.;
   1860-1870-1880; widr. Andrew 1900; M-L ch.
   1907; NL M-C)
ANDREW JACKSON (R.Ows. 20 S b.Ows.)  [s/o
   James Baker & W1 Sarah Davidson]
   ELIZABETH ["BETTY"] AMIS (R.Br. 16 S b.Br.)
   P/Per. [d/o John Amis & Sarah Eversole]
   11 Feb., 1875, _Breathitt_ (M-B; 1880-4;
   1900-1910-1920; M-O ch.; ob-ch.BS-10/24/91)
BENJAMIN (___ b.Perry)
   MAUD McINTOSH (___ b.Br.)
   pre-1908     (B-O ch.; NL M-B/C;
   NL 1910Sx)
BIGE - see ABIJAH
BOONE - see DANIEL BOONE
CALLOWAY a/k/a CALVIN (c34 b.KY)  [1873-1936;
   s/o "Black Bob" Baker & Mary Gabbard - 1900
   NSB; JTB]
   SUSAN SMITH (c18 b.KY)
   c1908     (TCS; GGB; NL 1910Sx; 1920-11;
   NL M-C)

(Baker cont.)

**BAKER (cont.)**

DANIEL BOONE (c24 S b.KY)    [1870-1954; s/o
   Black Bob Baker, Mary Gabbard - MT JTB NSB]
   HANNAH FIELDS (c20 S b.KY) [1874-1966 -JTB]
   1894      (1900 m-5; 1910 m-16; 1920; TCS;
   ob-ch. BS-12/30/93)
ELI (c31 b.KY)
   HALLEY _____ (c36 b.KY)
   1894/5      (1900)
ELIHU (c20 b.KY)
   ISABELLE FROST (c16 b.KY)
   1895/6      [poss. DIVORCED because there
   were 2 sm. ch. listed 1900 & they are NL
   w/F 1910]    (1900; TCS)   [H-remd.]
ELIHU (c28 2nd b.KY)  [m1 Isabelle Frost abv.]
   ETTA YEARY (c17 S b.KY) [poss. d/o Morgan
   Yeary & Rhoda       - TCS]
   1904/5      (1910-1920; TCS; ob-ch.
   BS-4/18/85)
ELISHA "BUCK FOX" (c21 S b.Br.)  [1885-1964 -
   TS-TCS; ob-H BE-3/19/64]
   AMERICA DANIEL (c17 S b.Doorway, Ows.)
   [1890-1971 Manchester hosp; d/o George
   Daniel & Lucy Allen - 1900; DC; ob-W BE-
   9/23/71]
   31 Jan., 1907, Ows. [rec. Perry] @ G. W.
   Daniel's, by Rev. M. L. Gayl; wits: G. W.
   Daniel & Irvine Daniel  (M-P J:75; B-O ch.;
   1910; wid. America R.Mistletoe 1964-9; BBG;
   ob-ch. BS-3/11/93-7/1/93; ob-WS BE-4/17/69)
GARRETT - see T. GARRETT
G[EORGE "BALDY"] W (R.Clay 22 S b.Clay) [1837-
   1898; s/o Robt. Baker & Sarah Rogers - BBG]
   RACHEL STRONG (R.Clay 17 S b.Ows.)  [d/o
   Alex Strong & Anna Wilson - JCH; 1850]
   24 Nov, 1859, <u>Clay</u>  (M-C, a/L M-C mf as
   <u>9/10</u>/59 & 11/24/59, H-Geo. & G. W.; JCH;
   TCS; 1860-C, w/them is Emily Hargis, 3)
G[EORGE] M. (c19 b.VA)  [s/o Thomas Baker
   & Joannah Alford - REM]
   JANE GABBARD (c21 b.KY)  [d/o Edw. Gabbard
   & Sarah Bowman - REM/JFB]
   17 Dec., 1860, <u>Jackson</u>   (M-J; TCS; 1870-8,
   WP w/them)

(Baker cont.)

**BAKER (cont.)**

GEORGE "GOOTIE" (c24 b.KY)    [1851-1919;
   s/o Mary Baker - JTB]
   SUSANNAH BAKER (c22 b.KY)   [1852-1895; d/o
   Andrew Baker & Margaret Riley - 1870; TCS;
   JTB]
   c1875        (1880-4; TCS)  [H-remd]
GEORGE (c50 2nd b.KY)  [m1 Susannah Baker abv]
   MARY A. [nee _____] _____ (c34 2nd? b.KY)
   [m1 _____]
   1898/9       (1900 m-1, W-10/4 ch. age 16-6,
   then H-son 12; NL M-J/R; NL 1910Sx)
GRANVILLE ["MUCKER"] (R.Ows. 33 S b.Ows.) P/NC
   & -- [s/o John Hammonds "Mucker Jack"
   Baker & Lucinda Amis - REM; TCS]
   REBECCA WOOD (R.Ows. 22 S b.Ows.) P/Clay
   [d/o John C Wood & Levina Bowling - B-O]
   31 Dec., 1874, Ows., @ Jno. C. Woods'
   [R.Owsley 1880-1890-1900; wid. Rebecca
   1910-1920]
GRANVILLE (R.Br. 22 S b.Ows.)  [1861-1941; s/o
   Andrew Jackson Baker & Margaret Riley -
   1880; JTB]
   ELIZABETH [nee BURTON] DEAN (R.Br. 22 3rd
   b.Br.)  [m1 _____; m2 _____ Dean]
   [1864-1913; d/o Rev. Robert Burton & W1
   Polly Gay - TS-TCS JTB 1870-B; sgl. 1880-B]
   19 Oct., 1884, <u>Breathitt</u> @ George Riley's,
   by John C. Riley; wits. Geo. Riley & George
   Tary (M-B 3:201; TCS; 1900-B-1/86; 1910-B)
HENRY (c33 2nd tailor b.KY)  [m1 c1830 _____
   _____ - 1850-19]
   HENRIETTA _____ (c26 b.KY)
   c1844        (1850 ch. 19, 5 & 1)
HENRY (c20 S b.Buck Cr.)  [1870-1943; s/o
   Josiah Baker & Caroline Price - 1880;
   TS-TCS]
   MARY A. ROWLAND (c17 S b.KY)  [1873-1898;
   d/o Abraham Rowland & W1 Holly Addison -
   1880; LNG; TS-TCS]
   c1890        (1900-2/91 H-remd-1; Mary d.
   1898 - TS-TCS; LNG)

(Baker cont.)

**BAKER (cont.)**

HENRY (c30 2nd b.Buck Cr.)  [1870-1943; widr/o
   Mary A. Rowland above]
      CATHERINE ROWLAND (c16 S b.Buck Cr., Ows.)
      [1882-1957; d/o Abraham Rowland & W1 Holly
      Addison - LNG; TS-TCS; ob-W BE-7/18/57]
      1899         (1900-1910-1920; B-O ch.; LNG)
      [NOTE: W1, Mary, was sis/o Cath., W2.  On
      her deathbed, Mary asked Cath. to marry
      Henry & raise her ch. - DGM's GM Emily, who
      was s-sis/o Cath. & Mary]
IRA (c22 b.Grayson Co., VA)
      MATILDA (nee ABNER) BAKER (c24 2nd b.KY)
      [wid/o Wm. Baker - TCS]  [d/o Elisha Abner
      & Nancy Loving - 1850]
      c1851      (1860-8; B-O ch.; REM; TCS)
ISAAC (R.Ows. 30 S b.Ows) P/Bunc., NC & Clay
      [s/o John H. "Mucker Jack" Baker & Lucinda
      Amis - 1870; M-C; TCS]
      MARGARET PETERS (R.Ows. 20 S b.Ows.) P/Clay
      [d/o Elijah Peters & Margaret Woods - B-O]
      8 Jan., 1874, Ows., @ Elijah Peters
      [R.Jackson Co. 1880-1900]
ISAAC (c19 b.KY)  [s/o Andrew Jackson
      Baker & Margaret Riley  - 1880]
      MARY JANE HELTON (___ b.___)
      c1886         (TCS; widr. Isaac 1900-B-2/87;
      NL M-B)  [H-remd.]
ISAAC (c35 2nd b.KY)  [m1 Mary J. Helton abv.]
      MAHALA "HAILEY" DEATON (c18 b.KY)
      1900/1         (TCS; 1910-B m-9 H-2nd; 1920;
      NL M-B)
ISAAC (R.Ows. 21 S b.Powell) P/Pow.
      LULA PETERS (R.Ows. 15 S b.Ows.) P/Ows.
      [d/o Elisha Peters & Louisa Young - 1900]
      13 Jan., 1910, Ows.    [R.Owsley 1910]
ISIAH - see JOSIAH
JACK - see ANDREW JACKSON
JACKSON - see ANDREW JACKSON
JAMES WILSON (c20 S b.KY)    [1830-1916; s/o
      Andrew Baker & Rachel Wilson/Woods -TS-TCS]
      SARAH ["SALLY"] DAVIDSON (c16 b.KY)  [d/o
      John Davidson & Vina Griffith]
      25 Feb., 1850, Clay Co.    [DIV. 1875-8]
      (M-C; 1850-C; B-O ch.; 1870; 1880 div.;
      DC ch-1932)   [H-remd.]
(Baker cont.)

JAMES "BIG JIM" (c24 b.KY) [1838-1918; s/o
     John H. "Mucker Jack" Baker & Lucinda Amis
     - TS-TCS; JTB]
     CHARLOTTE BOWLING (c20 b.KY) [d/o Wm.
     Bowling & Debbie Duff - TCS]
     c1864      (1870-5; 1880-13; TCS)
JAMES [TODD] (24 S b.Ows.) P/-- Clay [1854-
     1907; s/o John BAKER & Mary BAKER - TCS;
     HTB]
     ELIZA ABNER (R.Br. 24 S b.Ows.) P/-- Clay
     [1852-1914; d/o Willis Abner & Elmira Baker
     - TCS; HTB]
     29 Dec., 1874 Breathitt (M-B; B-B; 1880;
     1900-B; photo-H N-C 11/96 HTB)
JAMES H. [WILSON] (R.Ows. 48 2nd b.KY) P/KY-NC
     [div/f Sarah Davidson above]
     SARAH [nee EVERSOLE] AMIS (R.Br. 41 2nd b.
     KY) P/KY     [m1 John Amis - M-Br. 1856]
     [d/o Wm. Eversole & Barbara Chappell - MT]
     23 Nov., 1877, Ows.     [appar. DIVORCED]
     [R.Owsley 1880-1900]     [H-remd.]
JAMES N. (___ b.Gabbard)
     CALLIE BOWMAN (___ b.Eversole)
     pre-1908          (B-O ch.; NL 1910Sx)
JAMES WILSON (c77 3rd b.KY) [m2 Sarah Eversole
     above]
     SARAH E. (nee CORNETT) HUFF (c48 2nd b.KY)
     [m1 _____ Huff]
     1906/7      (1910, Huff s-d; 1900 James &
     W2 Sarah Eversole together, Sarah a/L as
     "wid" in next fam. w/2 sons, appar.
     separated around this time; Sally Cornett,
     42, hired girl w/James & W2 1900)
JAMES W. (c25 b.Ows.) [1884-1961 Dayton, OH
     nursing home; s/o Andrew J. Baker & Eliz.
     Amis - ob-H&S BE-11/23/61, OCN-8/14/58;
     1900]
     ADDIE HAZEL BOWMAN (c19 b.KY) [1890-1968
     Cin. hosp.; d/o Major Wm. Simpson Bowman
     & Mary Stephens - F/P-CW; 1900; ob-W&S BE-
     5/2/68, OCN-1/31/57]
     c1910          (1920-8; W-NL w/P 1910;
     NL 1910Sx; R.Boonev. 1925 F/P-CW; Boonev.
     1957-1961)

(Baker cont.)

**BAKER (cont.)**
JASON (c18 b.KY) [1875-1902; s/o George Baker
   & W1 Susannah Baker - 1880; JTB]
   ELIZA SANDLIN (c14 b.KY)
   1892/3        (1900; JTB) [ELIZA m2 Louis
   Sizemore (1841-1914); ELIZA m3 c1915, Jim
   Mosley - JTB; 1920]
JEFFERSON (c19 b.KY)
   MELINA/MAXALINE _____ (c14 b.KY)
   c1864        (1870-5; 1880-C-15; NL M-C;
   W/as Melina & Maxaline)
JERRY (c19 S b.Ows/Br.) [1887-1955; s/o Elijah
   Baker & Rebecca   - ob-H OCN-12/1/55]
   ARMILDA "MILDA" MOSLEY (c20 S b.Cortland)
   [d/o Jim Mosley & Eliz. Hornsby - TCS 1900
   BBG]
   1905/6        (1910; B-O ch.; ob-H; BBG;
   1920, SiL Mosley)
JESSE FULLER (c23 S b.Clay)
   EMILY BISHOP (c21 S b.Clay) [1868-1938 Ows;
   d/o Will Bishop & Annie Carmack - DC]
   22 June, 1892, <u>Jackson</u> @ Thee Gay's, by H.
   C. Hughes, JPJC; wits. Thee & Wm. Gay
   (M-J; TCS; B-O ch.; 1910-1920; NL 1900)
JOHN (R.Buffalo; 20 S b.Clay)
   MARTHA BEGLEY (R.Ows. 17 S b.Per.)
   1 May, 1854, Ows.  (listed 2x, H/17,
   W/R.Per., age uk; rest same)
JOHN (c19 b.NC)
   MARY _____ (c22 b.KY)
   c1868        (1870-L-1)
JOHN (c19 b.Proctor, Ows.)
   JOSEPHINE PHIPPS (c15 b.Clay) [d/o Samuel
   Phipps & Mary   - B-C 7/52]
   c1869        (1870 no ch.; B-O ch.; NL M-C)
JOHN (___ b.___)
   EMALINE REYNOLDS (c14-20 b.KY) [d/o Wesley
   Reynolds & Nancy Moore - 1860]
   1864-70        (W-NL w/P 1870; H-NL 1870;
   REM; NL M-C/Pul.)
JOHN "RED JOHN" (c34 b.KY) [s/o Andrew Baker
   & Mary Abner - 1850; 1870]
   SUSAN COON/BEGLEY(?) (c40 b.KY)
   late 1870      (1880-9; H-sgl. 1870; TW)
   [NOTE: Because of her age, this may be a
   2nd mg. for Susan]   [H-remd.]
(Baker cont.)

**BAKER (cont.)**
JOHN L. (c16 b.KY) P/KY
    MARY J. _____ (c15 b.KY)
    c1873        (1880-6)
JOHN A. (c57 2nd b.KY) [widr/o Susan Coon/
    Begley? above]
    MARY A. _____ (c27 b.KY)
    1891/2      (1900, ch. Jesse 13, Rachel 6
    & Paulina 3; 1910 dau. Purlina w/Aunt
    Purlina (Baker) Gabbard; NL 1910Sx)
    [NOTE: a JOHN BAKER md. POLLY JANE/ANN
    EVERSOLE 8/8/92 Per. @ Thos. Eversole's;
    wits. James & Link Eversole; sur. James
    Eversole - M-P G:102; NL 1900-P]
JOHN H. (c23 S b.KY)
    JOSEPHINE "JOSIE" SHEPHERD (c20 S b.KY)
    [d/o Col. Shepherd & Lucinda Price - 1880]
    10 Aug., 1900      (TCS; 1910-R m1-10; BC
    1911-1917-R; NL M-R)
JOHN "HUNGRY JOHN" (c17 S b.KY) [1878/85-1943;
    s/o Bige Baker & Amy Sizemore - TS-JTB]
    MALINDA "LINDA" MOSLEY [RILEY] (c20 S b.KY)
    [wid/o Stephen Riley - M-P; wid. w/P 1900]
    [1881-1963; d/o Jim Mosely & Elizabeth
    Hornsby - 1900; JTB]
    1901/2      (1910; BBG; ob-ch. BS-1/22/98)
JOHN R. ["FLAT BELLY"] (R.Boonev. 47 2nd
    jailor b.Ows.) P/Clay -- [m1 _____]
    [s/o Andrew Baker & Margaret Riley - mg.]
    NELLIE SIZEMORE [_____] (R.Beattyv. 30 2nd
    b.Clay) P/Clay [m1 _____]
    [d/o Hugh Sizemore & China Roberts - mg.]
    16 May, 1907, Lee @ Hugh Sizemore's, by J.
    F. Sutton, LCJ; wits. Clk(?) Hogg & Lula
    Sizemore (M-L)    [JOHN m3 c1912, Sarah
    (nee Sandlin) Bowling (wid/o Isaac) - 1920]
JOSEPH (c22 S b.KY) [1867-1951; s/o James
    Baker & W1 Sarah Davidson - TS-TCS]
    DARCUS [DOROTHY] COTRELL [COTTONHILL] (c16
    b.KY)
    29 March, 1890, Clay (M-C; 1900; TCS)
    [H-remd.]


(Baker cont.)

**BAKER (cont.)**

JOSEPH (R.Ows. 36 2nd b.Ows.) P/Ows.  [m1
    Dorothy Cottonhill above - TCS]
    LINDA HUFF (R.Ows. 21 S b.Ows.) P/Ows.
    [1879-1965; d/o John Wesley Huff & Mary J.
    Burch - TS-TCS]
    2 Dec., 1903, Ows.  [R.Owsley 1910-1920]
JOSIAH (c25 b.KY)
    CAROLINE PRICE (c21 b.KY)  [d/o Adam Price
    & Holly    - 1850; REM]
    c1857        (1860-1; B-J ch-1858; wid.
    Caroline 1870 w/P & 1880-1900)
JULIUS (R.Ows. 24 S b.KY) P/KY   [1851-1912;
    s/o Andrew Baker & Polly Abner - 1860; JTB]
    ARMINDA SANDLIN (R.Ows. 20 S b.KY) KY & TN
    [d/o James Sandlin, Delitha Fox - TCS; WGO]
    19 July, 1878, Ows.  [R.Owsley 1880]
    [JULIUS m2 c1884 Miranda Gay (1864-1917) -
    TCS; JTB; 1900-1910-B]
JULIUS (c21 b.KY)   [s/o "Red Bob" Baker
    & Margaret Baker - 1880]
    SUSAN A. _____ (c17 b.KY)
    1888/9        (1900)
LEANDER "LEE" (c20 S b.KY)  [1877-1942; s/o
    Geo. Baker & W1 Susan Baker - 1880; JTB]
    LUCY J. GABBARD (c20 S b.KY)  [1877-1961 -
    JTB]
    1897        (1900 m-3; 1910 m-12; 1920; B-O
    ch-1909 H/mistakenly listed as Riley,
    W/as Baker; ob-ch. BS-1/29/98)
LEWIS (R.Ows. 19 S b.Clay)
    MARIAH ABNER (R.Ows. 19 S b.Clay)
    18 Dec., 1856, Ows.
MARION (c29 S B'smth st-mill; b.KY)
    MARY J. (nee _____) YOUNG (c31 2nd b.KY)
    [wid/o _____ Young]
    1899/1900        (1910 m-10 W-2nd, Young
    s-ch.; NL 1900)
MORRIS M. (c26 b.KY) [s/o John Baker & Hannah
    Morris - TCS; 1860-70-C]
    MARY A. F. _____ (c29 b.VA)
    c1869        (1870-C, Morris & son Benj.,
    5 mos., w/HP, H-NL; 1880-10; TCS; NL M-C/J)


(Baker cont.)

**BAKER (cont.)**

RILEY (c18 S b.Cortland) [s/o Geo. Baker
   & W1 Susan Baker - 1900 w/F & s-M]
   CATHERINE SIZEMORE (c18 S b.Per.) [d/o
   Lewis Sizemore - TCS]
   1905/6          (1910-1920; BC 1911-1915-
   1919; B-O ch-1909, wf listed on wrong line)
ROBERT R. "RED BOB" (c20 b.KY) [s/o Andrew
   Baker & Mary Abner - 1850]
   MARGARET BAKER (c18 b.KY) [1841-1899; d/o
   Adoniram Baker & W2 Nancy Sandlin - TCS;
   JTB; NL w/P 1860]
   1860          (H-sgl. 1860; 1870-9; TCS)
ROBERT "BLACK BOB" (c32 b.KY) [1833-1881;
   s/o John H. "Mucker Jack" Baker & Lucinda
   Amis - MT; JTB]
   MARY "POLLY" GABBARD (c20 b.KY) [1845-1929;
   d/o Wilson Gabbard & Susan Abner - MT; JTB]
   c1866          (1870-3; B-O ch.; 1880-12;
   wid. Mary 1900-1910-1920)
ROBERT (c21 b.KY) [s/o James W. Baker & Sarah
   Davidson - TCS; 1880 w/M]
   VIRGINIA "JENNIE" COLE (c20 b.KY) [d/o
   Lewis Cole & Susan Coleman - 1870-1880]
   c1880          (TCS; ob-ch. BE-9/1/66, Alice
   b.1881 Ows., bro. Robt.; DC dau. Alice;
   1900 dau. Alice svt. w/Alred Eversole; 1900
   son Robt. b. 12/84 w/uncle Joseph Baker;
   NL 1900Sx - poss. dead; NL M-P)
ROBERT R. (c22 S b.Ows.) [1864-1956; s/o
   Andrew Baker & Margaret Riley - TCS; JTB;
   NSB]
   EMALINE BAKER (c14 S b.Ows.) [1871-1958;
   d/o Black Bob Baker & Mary Gabbard - 1880;
   JTB; NSB]
   1885/6          (1900-1910-1920; TCS;
   M-B ch-1914)
ROBERT H. "SHARPER" (c17 S b.KY)
   LAURA GILBERT (c12 S b.Ows.) [1876-1957 OH;
   d/o John Gilbert & Nancy Smith - TCS; ob-W
   OCN-4/18/57]
   1891/2          (1900-10/94 m-8; 1910-15 m-16;
   1920 WF w/them; BBG; TCS; R.Cincinnati, OH
   1957; ob-ch. BS-12/31/87)

(Baker cont.)

33

**BAKER (cont.)**
ROBERT (c19 S b.Ows.)
   RACHEL HACKER (c17 S b.Clay)  [d/o Julius
   Hacker & Sylvia     - TCS]
   1894      (1900 m-5; 1910 m-16; B-O ch.;
   NL M-C)
ROBERT (c24 S b.KY) [neph/o Joseph Baker -TCS]
   MARY E. _____ (c17 S b.KY)
   1909/10     (1910; 1920-C; NL M-C/J)
STEPHEN (c22 S b.Br.)  [s/o James Wilson Baker
   & W2 Sarah Eversole - 1880-1900)
   JUSTINA "TINA" FIELDS (c17 S b.KY)  [d/o
   Silas Fields & W1   - 1900]
   1900/1     (1910-Clk m1-9 both; BC
   1916 Boone & 1919 Pow.; NL M-B/Clk)
T. G[ARRETT] (c18 b.KY)  [s/o Andrew J. Baker
   & Nancy Allen - TCS; cons/o A. J. Baker]
   [THEO] CORDELIA STRONG (c23 b.KY)  [d/o
   Alex Strong & Anna Wilson - JCH; 1860;
   TCS cons/o Ann Strong]
   11 Sept., 1869, Clay  (M-C; TCS; JCH)
THEO (___ b.___)
   LUVERNIA (nee CLARK) _____ (c19 2nd b.Ows.)
   [m1 _____]  [d/o Anderson Clark
   & Lucy   - 1900; ob-WS OCC-2/21/36]
   1908/9     (1910 W-m2-1, H-NL, w/WM;
   ob-WS; NL 1920Sx-KY/OH; R.Miamisburg, OH
   1936)
W. H. (R.Ows. 35 3rd b.Per) P/Per [m1 _____;
   m2 _____]
   AMANDA [nee _____] HUNDLEY (R.Ows. 28 2nd
   b.Ows) P/Ows.  [m1 _____ HUNDLEY]
   25 April, 1908, Ows.
WALTER (c24 b.KY) [1882-1928; s/o James Wilson
   Baker & W2 Sarah Eversole - TS-TCS; 1900]
   JULIA SEBASTIAN (c20 b.KY) [1887-c1914 Br.;
   d/o Elisha Sebastian & Malinda Turner -BJE]
   c1908    (TCS; 1910-B-1; BJE 1st ch.3/09;
   NL M-B)  [WALTER m2 c1915, Martha Herald
   (1900-1972 d/o Tom Herlad & Esther Turner)
   - BJE 1st ch.8/16; ob-son Everett; TCS;
   1920-10]


(Baker cont.)


34

**BAKER (cont.)**
WILLIAM (c21 b.KY)  [s/o Robert "Boston"
  Baker & Sarah Rogers - N-C-6/95]
  MATILDA ABNER (c16 S b.KY)  [d/o Elisha
  Abner & Nancy Loving - 1850]
  c1843/4         (1850, Matilda Baker, wid.,
  23, w/P; WGO; N-C-6/95 Willard Thomas
  McHone)   [MATILDA m2 Ira Baker]
WILLIAM (c28 b.KY)  [s/o Adoniram Baker
  & Nancy Sandlin - 1850-C]
  NANCY [nee CORNETT/COMBS] ROBERTSON (c28
  2nd b.KY)  [m1 Charles Robertson - M-C
  1/6/49; 1850-C]
  16 Sept, 1855 Clay (M-C; 1860 ch. Margaret
  10, Susan 8, Matilda 3, & Mary 2; B-C dau.
  Polly 2/58 M/Cornett; 1870; widr. Wm. 1880-
  C; 1850-C H1 Chas. & Nancy w/dau. Margaret;
  W/1st M-C to Chas.Robertson as Nancy Combs)
WILLIAM A. (c21 b.Ows.)  [s/o Andrew J. Baker
  & Eliz. Amis]
  JOYCE BAKER (c17 b.Ows.)  [d/o Jim Baker -
  BBG]
  1898/9       (1900; B-O ch; wid. Joyce 1910;
  wid. Rejoicey 1920; ob-ch. BS-6/26/97)
**BALES/BAILS/BAYLS**
HAWKINS (c14 b.KY)
  ELIZABETH _____ (c20 b.TN)
  c1848         (1850-1)
JAMES (c23 b.KY)
  SARAH A. "SALLY" ROBERTSON (c18 b.NC)
  20 Feb., 1844, Clay (M-C; 1850-6;
  1860-1870-1880-J)
**BALL**
BISHOP (___ b.___)
  MARTHA SHEPHERD (c19 S b.KY)  [d/o Riley
  Shepherd & Nancy Morris]
  c1896          (1910, GD Letha Ball 13,
  w/Riley & Nancy Shepherd; VKD/Shepherd
  Family by Moffitt)  [MARTHA m2 1899,
  Lee Blake]
JAMES C. (c25 S b.Lee,VA)  [s/o Enoch Ball
  & Ellen Coldiron - 1910; TCS]
  MARY J. "MOLLIE" McDANIEL (c14 S b.Clay)
  1878        (1880 no ch.; 1880MS 1st ch-
  1879; B-O ch.; 1900; 1910 HM w/them; 1920;
  ob-ch. BS-9/11/86-10/28/93)
(Ball cont.)

**BALL (cont.)**
WILLIAM (c21 b.KY)   [1872-19__; s/o Enoch Ball
   & Ellen Coldiron - 1900]
   _____ BURCH(?) (___ b.___)   [poss. d/o
   Jasper Burch & Rhoda Morris who had GD
   Dazie BALL b.1894 w/them 1900-10]
   c1893         (1900 widr. Wm. w/HP)
WILLIE (c21 S b.KY)
   LOTTIE MILLION (c21 S b.Jack.)   [c1883-1967
   Beattyv.; d/o Ben Million & Lucinda McQueen
   - TCS; ob-W BE-2/16/67]
   1905/6         (1910-1920; TCS; BBG;
   R.Conkling 1964 - ob-WS BE-9/3/64; ob-ch.
   BS-10/15/92)

**BANKS**
ANDREW JACKSON (c18 b.KY)   [s/o John FERGUSON
   & Martha Jane "Jenny" BANKS - ARS]
   NANCY JOSEPHINE GARRETT (c17 b.KY)   [d/o
   Britton Garrett & Susan Bowman - 1880; ARS]
   22 Dec., 1896         (ARS; 1900, WM w/them;
   PWB)
HENRY CLAY (c20 b.KY)   [s/o Andrew J. Banks
   & Eliza Jane Cornett - ARS; 1870; 1880-C]
   NANCY A. LEWIS (c19 b.VA)
   1881/2         (ARS; 1900-J m-18; NL M-J)
HENRY - see WM. HENRY
JOHN RILEY (c22 S b.Mt. Pleasant)   [1870-1931;
   s/o Solomon FRAZIER & Martha Jane "Jenny"
   BANKS - ARS; TS-TCS]
   LUCY JANE BOWMAN (c18 S b.KY)   [1875-1916;
   d/o Henry Bowman & Eliz. McVey -ARS TS-TCS]
   1892         (1900 m-7; B-O ch-1909; 1910
   m-18; ARS; ob-ch. OCN-1/19/51)
   [JOHN RILEY md. 2nd c1917, Linda (nee Pace)
   Caudill (1882-1918; d/o Richmond Pace &
   Talitha Fox - DC; MLJ) (wid/o Clinton
   Caudill, who d. 1907) - MLJ; ARS; widr.
   John 1920; BC-son 1918; their son w/his
   aunt Emma Pace Elkins 1920)
JOHN BAXTER (c39 2nd b.KY)   [m1 _____]
   [s/o Lansford Banks, Druscilla Kelly -1880]
   SUSIE BOTNER (c29 S b.KY)   [d/o Ransom
   Botner & Armina Ketchum]
   1906/7         (1910, w/WF; M-L ch-1942)

(Banks cont.)

## BANKS (cont.)

LANSFORD (c19 2nd b.Per.) [Div/f Virginia "Jane" Miles, d/o Anderson & Rhoda Miles, on 11/24/64 Clay - ARS; TCS] [s/o Anderson FIELD & Casandra BANKS - ARS]
DRUSELLA [DRUSCILLA] KELLY (c20 b.Clay) [d/o Wm. Kelly & Ala Allen - TCS; ARS]
1 Dec., 1864, Clay (M-C; ARS; 1870-C-5; 1880-14, HM w/them; TCS) [LANSFORD m3 11/24/85 Clay, Harriett Delitha Hunter - P-CW ARS]

LANSFORD - see RICHARD LANSFORD

PHILIP (c22 b.KY) [s/o John HALL & Martha Jane "Jenny" BANKS - ARS]
NANCY ELIZABETH SHORT (c22 b.KY) [d/o John B. Short & Lucretia Reese - ARS; 1880]
25 May, 1885 (ARS; 1900)

RICHARD LANSFORD (c23 b.Ows.)
REBECCA SHORT (c22 b.Ows.) [d/o John B. Short & Lucretia Reese - 1880]
1887/8 (1900; BC-dau.; NL 1910-1920Sx; NL M-J)

SOLOMON (c21 b.KY) [s/o _____ PACE & Martha Jane "Jenny" BANKS - ARS]
NANCY ANN BOWMAN (c20 b.KY) [d/o Henry Bowman & Eliz. McVey - ARS]
1892/3 (1900) [After Nancy d., SOLOMON m2 in OK to Maude Griffin; SOLOMON m3 Martha Pearlie Ritchie]

WILLIAM HENRY "HEN" (c34 2nd b.Let.) [m1 Aileen _____ in NC - ARS] [s/o ____ ISOM & Martha Jane "Jenny" Banks - ARS]
MARY GILBERT (c27 S b.NC)
c1892 (1900-6/93 m-11, but this must be W1; 1910-14 m-15, H-2nd; 1920; B-O ch.; H/as Henry & W. H.; Wm. Henry "Hen" - ARS)

## BARGER

ABRAM (R.Per. 23 S b.Perry)
ARMILDA HACKER (R.Clay 19 S b.Clay)
28 Dec., 1855, Perry (M-P; 1860-4; 1870-C)

JACKSON (c23 b.KY)
MANDA _____ (c12 b.KY)
1891/2 (1900; NL M-J)

(Barger cont.)

## BARGER (cont.)

JESSE G. (c20 S b.KY)
   SUSAN BAKER (c18 S b.KY)
   1887/8     (1900-11 m-12; 1910 m-24; BBG;
   ob-ch. HJN-4/30/98; NL 1920Sx; NL M-J)
JOSEPH (c18 b.KY) [s/o Jesse Barger - TCS]
   NICY McINTOSH (c18 b.KY) [d/o Levi
   McIntosh & Peggy   - TCS]
   c1870     (1880-9; NL 1870; TCS; NL M-J)
WILLIAM D. (c23 b.KY)
   SCEALLIE _____ (c18 b.KY)
   1892/3     (1900; NL 1910Sx; NL M-J)
WILLIS (c22 S b.Per.) [1865-1920 Ows.; s/o
   Samuel Barger & Mary Callahan - DC]
   DELILAH "LILY" GILBERT (c22 S b.KY) [d/o
   Henry Gilbert & Marinda   - 1880-P]
   7 April, 1887, Perry @ Marinda Gilbert's,
   by Rev. G. C. J. Barger; wits. Jesse Barger
   & Wm. Bishop (M-P H:12; 1900-4/90, "m-17";
   1910 "m-21"; 1920)

## BARKER

ANDREW JACKSON "JACK" a/k/a JOHN (c29 S mcht
   b.Ows.) [1878-1967 Ows.; s/o Martin Barker
   & Malvery Becknell - MAR; 1880-1900; ob-H
   BE-9/7/67]
   NANCY MAE WILSON (c19 S b.KY) [1887-1964;
   d/o Alford Wilson & Eliza Flannery - TCS;
   ob-WM&S BE-6/20/35-12/25/58-2/26/59]
   6 June, 1907    (MAR/FB; 1910-1920; TCS;
   ME-3/18/04, R. W. Becknell uncle of A. J.
   Barker; H/as John, Andrew J. & A. J.;
   R.Trav. Rest 1935-1959)
DAN (c22 b.KY)
   MATILDA _____ (c23 b.KY)
   1889/90    (1900)
JACK - see ANDREW JACKSON
MARTIN VAN BUREN "MART" (c28 S b.Morg.) [1832-
   1917; s/o John Barker & Nancy   - MAR/FB,
   DC & 1850-Morg.; P-CW]
   MALVERY BECKNELL (c18 S b.Trav.Rest) [1852-
   1922; d/o Wm. Thornberry Becknell & Sarah
   Wilson - NVP; PWB; MAR P-CW]
   22 Dec., 1870, Ows., @ bride's home, by
   Sylvester Isaacs, JPOC; wit. J. H. Herd
   (P-CW MAR; 1880-5; 1890; 1900-1910; H-sgl.
   1870; NVP; JSG; wid. Malvera 1920)
 (Barker cont.)

## BARKER (cont.)

SAMUEL (c49 prob. 2nd b.VA) [m1 _____]
   CHRISTINA (nee _____) BAKER (c28 2nd b.KY)
   [m1 _____ Baker - 1860 wid. Christina)
   c1863      (1870-C, 1st ch. under 10 is
   6; NL 1880Sx; NL M-C)
WILLIAM (c22 barkeeper b.KY) [s/o Wm. Barker
   & Margaret Cotton - TCS]
   _____ (___ b.___) [appar. d. 1858/9]
   c1856      (1860-3, W-NL)

## BARNETT

WILLIAM (R.Ows. 21 S b.Ows.)
   SCYNTHA PHIPPS (R.Clay 20 S b.Lau.) [d/o
   Samuel Phipps & Mary Hash - 1850-C]
   1 March, 1855, Clay (M-C mf)

## BARRETT

ANDERSON (c21 S b.KY) [s/o Wm. Barrett
   & Margaret Vires - 1880-L; 1900-B]
   LULA SHOUSE (c16 S b.KY)
   1900/1      (1910-1920; ob-ch. BS-1/28/99;
   NL M-B)
ANDREW (R.Mid.Fk. 20 S b.Mid.Fk, Br.) [1835-
   1917 Br.; s/o James Barrett & Matilda Neal
   - DC; 1850-B]
   NANCY JOHNSON (R.Mid.Fk. 17 S b.Longs Cr.,
   Br.) [d/o Jesse Johnson & Polly   - WGO]
   - June, 1854, Breathitt, by Samuel Smith
   (M-B mf; a/L M-P 5/19/54, H-23, W-19; B-B
   ch.; 1860-B; M-L ch-1915) [H-remd.]
ANDREW (c30 b.KY)
   SERENA "RENA" COUCH (c16 b.KY) [d/o Elijah
   Couch & Serena   - BJN]
   c1864 Breathitt      (1870-B; 1880 W-md,
   N-NL; M-L ch-1916)
ANDREW (c37 2nd b.KY) [m1 Nancy Johnson abv.]
   MARY "POLLY" KING/TERRY (c21 b.KY)
   c1871      (1880-L, 1st ch under 10 is 8;
   BJN; H-remd. 1910-B; DC ch-1960 M/King; DC
   dau. 1949 M/Terry; NL M-L)
ANDREW (c55 3rd b.KY) [m2 Mary King above]
   [1835-1917 Br.; s/o James Barrett & Matilda
   Neal - DC]
   LETISHA "TISH" BREWER (c20 b.KY)
   1889/90      (1910-B m-20; wid. Tish
   1920-B; DC-ch. 1925-1975; NL 1900Sx;
   NL M-B)
(Barrett cont.)

**BARRETT (cont.)**

ARCH (22 S b.Br.) [s/o Pealy Barrett & Emaline
   Spencer - 1900-B w/HP]
   [LUCINDA] SINDY LYNCH (18 S b.Ows.)
   2 June, 1900, <u>Breathitt</u>, @ James Johnson's,
   by James Johnson, JP; wits. B. Gabbard &
   A. McIntosh  (M-B 8:571; 1900-B w/HP; 1910-
   9, m-9; B-O ch.; M-L ch-1926; ob-ch. BS-
   3/28/85-1/22/87)
BRICEN (c21 b.Ows.)     [s/o James Barrett
   & Keziah Allen - TCS]
   MINERVA ABNER (c21 b.Ows.)  [d/o Lacy Abner
   & Cyntha Combs - 1860]
   c1867       (1870-2; B-O ch.)
BRISON "BRICE" (c17 S b.Ows.)  [s/o Jesse
   Barrett & Susan Abner - TCS]
   ANNIE BARRETT (c24 S b.KY)
   1893/4        (1900-1910-1920; DC ch-1983)
ELBERT - see ELBERT <u>COMBS</u>
G. B. (R.Ows. 23 S b.Harl.) P/Br-Harl.  [s/o
   Jeptha Barrett & Jula Hall - mg.]
   DORA [nee BOWMAN] PALMER (R.Ows. 18 2nd/H1-
   d. b.Ows.) P/Ows. [m1 1903 John Palmer]
   [1890-1908; d/o Major (Wm.) S(impson)
   Bowman & Mary Stephenson - mg.; 1900; TCS]
   3 Oct., 1907 Ows. [rec. Lee] @ Major S.
   Bowman's, by M. C. Taylor, MG; wits.
   Anderson Butler Murell(?) & others  (M-L;
   mf has <u>2</u> Oct.)  [H-remd.]
G. B. (R.Ows. 25 2nd b.Harl.) P/Harl  [m1 Dora
   Bowman above]
   [FANNIE M RADFORD] (R.Ows 17 S b.Ows) P/Ows
   [poss. d/o John Radford & Nannie    - 1900]
   25 June, 1909, Ows. [NL 1910Sx]  [NOTE:
   There was an error in this & several other
   mgs., wherein the bride was listed on the
   wrong line. W/listed as ARMINIE EDWARDS;
   line above was FANNIE RADFORD]


(Barrett cont.)

## BARRETT (cont.)

GEORGE (R.Tallega 20 S b.Lee) P/Br-Lee [1886-
1970; s/o Andrew Barrett & Margaret Angel -
mg.; 1900-L; ob-H BE-2/5/70]
HULDA BOWMAN [PALMER] (R.Ows. 21 2nd/Div b.
Ows.) P/Ows -- [Div/f John Palmer] [1886-
1981; d/o Major Wm. S. Bowman & Mary Ann
Stephens - mg.; 1900; ob-W&S BS-11/19/81-
10/10/68, OCN-1/31/57]
25 May, 1907, Ows. (rec. Lee) @ Major
Bowman's by E. Spencer; wits. Bill Murrill
& Green Bowman (M-L; R.Lone 1957-68; wid.
R.Scottsburg, IN 1981 - ob-W]
GRANVILLE (c18 S b.KY)
SARAH JANE LITTLE (c20 S b.KY) [d/o James
Little - BJN]
1903/4 (1910; BJN from GD/o Sarah)
HARRISON (c18 b.Br.) [s/o James Barrett &
Martha Matilda Neal - 1850-B; DC/sib P/M-C]
LEVISA COUCH (c14 b.Br.)
1860/1 (1870-1880-1900-L; B-L ch.;
M-L ch-1920; ob-ch BE-2/29/68)
HENDERSON PEE (c15-21 S b.KY) [1863-1937 Lee;
s/o Andy Barrett & Nancy Johnson - DC]
_____ (__ b.__)
c1878-84 (H/2nd mg.) [H-remd.]
[HENDERSON PEE] PEALEY (22 2nd b.KY) P/KY
[m1 _____ above]
[AMERICA] MERICA BARRIETT [BARRETT] (22 S
b.KY) P/KY
11 May, 1885, Breathitt, by J. T. Chadwick;
wits. Alfred & Clayborn Spencer (M-B 3:183;
1900-L m-15) [H-remd.]
HENDERSON PEE (c38 3rd b.KY) [m2 America
Barrett above] [1863-1937 Lee]
SARAH FREEMAN (c27 b.KY)
1902/3 (1910 H-m3-7, NL/wf or fam.;
1920-B Pee & Sarah & ch.; M-L ch-1929-1931;
M-B ch-1923-1926; 1920-B]
JAMES (R.Clay 32 widr. b.Clay) [widr/o Kizey
Allen - M-C 4/3/43 - 1850-C; TCS] [poss.
s/o Jesse Barrett, Sr. of Clay - TCS]
ISABELLE (nee BURNS) CARMACK (R.Ows. 32
wid. b.Ows.) [wid/o John Carmack] [d/o
Wm. Burns & Rachel Asher - TCS]
25 Aug., 1856, Ows. [NL 1860/C]
(Barrett cont.)

**BARRETT (cont.)**

JAMES (c22 b.KY) [s/o Thos. Barrett & Barbara
Gabbard; d. Rockc.]
NANCY HENSLEY (c16 b.KY) P/KY [d/o Theo.
Hensley & Elenor Murray; d. Rockc. - WTM]
c1879          (1880 no ch.; NL M-C) [JAMES
m2 10/20/87 Ladocia Davidson - WTM; M-C]
JAMES (c20 S b.KY) [s/o John Barrett & Lucinda
Moore - 1880, w/M & GP; TCS; LNG/Lawrence
Barrett]
MARTHA HICKS (c23 S b.KY) [d/o Wm. Hicks
& Rachel Bowman - TCS; ob-WS OCN-12/6/56;
1880 w/wid. mom]
1898/9          (1900 N#L, 2/1 ch, WM w/them;
1910 m-11; TCS 1920; R.Ows. 1956)
JEFF (R.Ows. 28 S b.Ows.) P/Lee -- [s/o
Andrew Barrett, Nancy Johnson - TCS 1880-L]
MARY BARRETT (R.Br. 15 S b.Br.) P/Ows-Harl.
18 Sept., 1908, <u>Breathitt</u> [rec. Owsley]
[listed 1910 as <u>Jeptha</u> 32 & Mary 15, m1-1,
Bo. w/Wm. & Margaret Moore. NL M-B]
JEPTHA  - see JEFF
JESSE (c26 S b.Per.) [s/o James Barrett & W1
Kezzia Allen - 1870]
SUSAN K. ABNER (c24 S b.Ows.)
late 1870          (1880-8; TCS; 1900 m-31,
but H-sgl. w/P 1870; 1910 m-40; wid. Susan
w/son James 1920)
JOHN (R.Middle Fk. 19 S b.Clay) [c1837-1874;
s/o James Barrett & Martha Matilda Neal -
D-B; DC sib; P/M-C 1833]
ANN COUCH (R.Middle Fk. 18 S b.Br.) [d/o
Elijah Couch          - WGO]
12 Sept., 1856 <u>Breathitt</u>, by Wm. A. Barrett
(M-B; 1860; 1870-B; ch. 1880-L)
JOHN (c19 b.KY) [s/o Thos. Barrett & Barbara
Gabbard - 1880]
LUCINDA MOORE (c20 b.KY) [d/o Madison
Moore & Luzanne Stepp]
c1879          [DIV.] (1880-1/80, W-md. w/P;
Lucinda MOORE w/Barrett son 1900) [H-remd.]
JOHN (c22 2nd b.KY) [Div/f Lucinda Moore
above - LNG]
ESTHER SMITH (c20 S b.KY)
1881/2          (1900 m-18; 1910 m-22; TCS;
LNG; M-L ch.; FH-dau.; NL M-C)
(Barrett cont.)

## BARRETT (cont.)

JOHN B[ELL] (R.Lee 18 S b.Br.) P/Br.  [alive
     1943 - ob-ch.]
     FANNIE BOWMAN (R.Lee 16 S b.Ows.) P/Ows. --
     [c1868-1937; d/o Wilburn Bowman & Mary
     McPherson - ob-W BE-1/20/38; 1880]
     26 Aug., 1885, Lee @ Wilburn Bowman's, by
     J. M. Roberts; wits. Edw. Roberts & Stephen
     Bowman  (M-L 2:566; 1900-1910-L; ob-W;
     ob-ch BE-7/15/43)
JOHN (R.Lee 26 S b.Lee) P/Br-Lee  [poss. s/o
     Wm. Barrett & Mary A.     - 1900]
     MABLE SPENCER (R.Ows. 18 S b.Ows.) P/Br.
     [d/o Preston Spencer & Polly Barrett -1910]
     7 Sept., 1910, Ows.
     [MABLE m2 pre-1945, Mr. Huckba - MRS]
JORDAN (c24 b.KY)  [s/o Wm. Barrett & Margaret
     Vires - 1880-L]
     MARTHA _____ (c14 b.KY)
     1888/9          (1900-B m-11)
JOSEPH (c22 b.Ows.) [1868-1908 Mad., s/o Thos.
     Barrett & Barbara Gabbard - 1880; WTM]
     CHARLOTTE BARRET (c13 b.Clay)  [1877-1960
     Mad.; d/o Wm. Barrett & orlena Bowling -
     WTM]
     26 June, 1890, Clay  (M-C; MT; 1900-C)
LEANDER (R.Ows. 37 S b.Ows.) P/Ows.  [s/o
     Jesse Barrett & Susan Abner - 1900]
     LAURA BISHOP (R.Ows. 28 S b.Ows) P/Clay
     18 Aug., 1910, Ows.
LEWIS (c21 2nd b.KY)  [m1 _____]
     [s/o Wm. Barrett & Margaret Vires - 1900-B]
     ARIZONA "ZONA" SHOUSE (c14 b.KY)  [d/o
     Calvin Shouse & Aggie Mullins - 1900-B]
     1903          (1910-6, m2-6 both; 1920-B;
     BC-1919-Br.; NL M-B)  [NOTE: Even though
     1910 lists W-2nd, I believe it must be an
     error because she is so young]
MATHIAS (c19 S b.KY)  [1862-1919; s/o Thomas
     Barrett & Barbara Gabbard - LNG; TS-TCS]
     [ELIZ.] ALICE "ALLIE" COLLINS (c14 b.KY)
     [d/o Anderson Collins & Margaret Rasner -
     LNG; 1870-80 as Eliz.]
     c1881          (LNG; MT; H-remd. 1900;
     NL M-C)

(Barrett cont.)

**BARRETT (cont.)**
MATHIAS (c29 2nd b.KY)   [widr/o Eliz. Alice
    Collins above - MT]
    SARAH M. COLLINS (c19 S b.Clay) [1870-1961;
    d/o Anderson Collins & Margaret Rasner -
    1880; LNG; TS-TCS; ob-W BE-1/26/61]
    25 Sept, 1889 Clay  (M-C; LNG; 1900-6 m-11;
    1910 m-18; MT; ob-ch BE-9/24/59 R.Clay)
MOSES (R.Lee 22 S lab. b.Lee)  [s/o Wm. Barret
    & Mary Ann (Roberts) - mg.]
    [AGATHA] GATHA TREADWAY (R.Lee 16 S b.Lee)
    [d/o G(eo.) W. Treadway & Eliza    - mg.;
    1900-L]
    17 March, 1904, Ows. (rec. Lee) @ Wm.
    Barrett's, by Eld. G. W. Miller; wits. Wm.
    Barrett & wf & Patric Begley, etc.
    (M-L 7:53; a/L M-B 10:555 as 3/14/1904,
    W/Agatha 18, md. @ Wm. Cole's, rest same;
    1910-L)
RICHARD D. (c18 S b.Br.)  [1866-1955; s/o Wm.
    Barrett & Margaret Vires - TCS; ob-H OCN-
    8/18/55; 1870; 1880-L]
    FRANCES "FANNIE" MOORE (c14 S b.KY) [1870-
    1939; d/o Nicholas Moore & Lucinda McQueen
    - 1880; ob-W OCC-8/18/39]
    c1884       (ob-H&W; 1900-1/85 N#L; 1910 m-
    29 = 1880/1, but W would only be 10; 1920;
    M-L ch-1919; ob-ch. BE-9/20/73, BS-3/2/95)
    [RICHARD m2 1/24/41 Ows., Mary (nee
    Barrett) Stepp (60 wid. b.Clay; d/o Jim
    Barrett & Esther) wid/o Robert Lee Stepp -
    M-O; ob-H]
ROBERT (R.Ows. 21 S b.Ows.) P/Ows. [1889-1968;
    s/o John Barrett & Easter Smith - LNG; WTM;
    1900; ob-H BE-10/17/68]
    LOU[VENA] ABSHEAR (R.Ows. 18 S b.Ows) P/Ows
    [1891-1967 London hosp. - ob-W BE-12/7/67;
    NL DC]
    1 April, 1910, Ows.  [R.Owsley 1910-1920;
    W/also listed as Louetta (1910), Louane
    (1920) & Lovena (ob-ch. BS-1/7/88)]
SHELBY (c19 S b.Br.)  [1877-1960 Les.; s/o
    Andrew Barrett & Polly King - DC]
    LAURA B. HOSKINS (c19 S b.Les.)
    1896/7             (1910; B-O ch.; NL 1900;
    NL M-B/Les.)
(Barrett cont.)

## BARRETT (cont.)

STEPHEN (c18 b.Clay) [1871-19__ Mad.; s/o
   Thomas Barrett & Barbara Gabbard - 1880;
   WTM]
   MARY A. [OLLIE] BARRETT (c15 b.KY) [c1874-
   c1909/10 - WTM]
   28 Feb., 1889, Clay (M-C; MT; 1900-C,
   widr. Stephen, no age, 4 ch., 1st b. 8/95)
   [STEPHEN m2 6/8/1911 Mad., Rosa Collins -
   WTM]
THOMAS (c19 b.KY) [c1828-1882; s/o Murrell
   Barrett & Betsy Price - WTM; LNG]
   BARBARY GABBARD (c18 b.KY) [d/o Mathias
   Gabbard & Sarah Peters - MT]
   30 Dec., 1847 (ML) Clay (M-C; 1850-1860-C;
   1870-1880; wid. Barbara 1900-C)
WILEY C. (20 S b.Yancy Co., NC)
   NANCY STAPLETON (21 S b.Ows.) [prob. d/o
   Wm. Stapleton & Eliza Combs - 1850; LNG]
   20 June, 1858, Laurel (M-Lau.)
WILLIAM (c23 b.KY) [s/o James Barrett & Martha
   Matilda Neal - 1850-B; DC sib; P/M-C 1833]
   MARGARET VIRES (c21 b.KY) [d/o Fleming
   Vires & Mary Johson - 1860-B]
   c1864      (1870-5; 1880-L; wid. Margaret
   1900-B; TCS; ob-ch. OCN-8/18/55)
WILLIAM (c21 S b.Br.)    [1859-1939; s/o John
   Barrett - ob-H OCC-4/21/39; 1860]
   MARY ANN ROBERTS (c17 S b.Br.) [1864-1938
   - ob-W OCC-8/19/38]
   1881      (ob-W; 1900 m-19; 1910-L m1-28
   both; M-L ch-1910-1921)
WILLIAM (c20 S b.Br.) [1865-1945 Lee; s/o
   Andrew Barrett & Serena Couch - 1870-B;
   ob-H BE-12/13/45]
   _____ (___ b.___)
   1885/6      (H-remd. 1900, H/m-14, W2/m-11,
   so m-14 is prob. W1; 3rd M-L; NL M-B)
WILLIAM (c23 2nd b.Br.) [m1 _____ above]
   AMERICA FOX (c29 b.Ows.) [d/o John Fox
   & Sarah Johnson - 1860]
   1888/9      (1900-5/80, H-m-14, W/Marica
   m-11, 8/8 ch., all 8 listed; 1880-B America
   Fox & 2 ch.; M-L ch. 1910-1912; widr. Wm.
   1910-L; NL M-B)    [WILLIAM m3 9/14/16,
   Kansas (nee Lawson) Brown) - M-L]
(Barrett cont.)

**BARRETT (cont.)**

WM. M. (R.Ows. 22 S b.Ows.) P/Clay [1890-1942;
s/o Jesse Barrett & Hannah Estridge - DC]
DAISY PARKER (R.Ows. 16 S b.Ows.) P/Ows.
[d/o Wm. Parker & Nannie Gay - 1900]
12 Aug, 1909, Ows.   [R.Owsley 1910-1920]
[DAISY m2 _____ Byrd - ob-WM OCN-12/16/54]

**BEARD**

ABNER (c26 S b.KY)  [1880-1962 Boonev.; s/o
Robert Beard & America Allen - ob-H BE-
4/5/62]
MARGARET RILEY (c19 S b.KY)  [d/o James
Riley & Rhoda Riley - TCS; ob-WS BE-3/9/72]
1906/7      (1910-1920; TCS; widr.
R.Boonev. 1962-72)
DANIEL (c25 S b.Major, Ows.)  [1876-1909; s/o
John Beard & Susan Brock - D-O; 1900]
SUSIE SMITH (c20 S b.Br.)  [d/o Samuel
Smith & Elizabeth Allen - LM]
c1902      (1910-7, wid. Susie; B-O ch-
1908; wid. Susan 1920)
JOHN (R.Ows. 23 S b.Lee,VA) P/Lee,VA  [s/o
Daniel Beard & Eliza Jane     - 1870]
SUSAN BROCK (R.Ows. 18 S b.Br.) P/Br.  [d/o
Amon Brock & Mahala Patrick - 1870-B]
27 Aug., 1874, Ows., @ Aaron Brock's
[R.Owsley 1880-1900-1910-1920]
ROBERT (R.Ows. 20 S b.VA) P/VA  [s/o Daniel
Beard & Eliza     - 1870]
AMERICA ALLEN (R.Ows. 20 S b.KY) P/KY  [d/o
Abijah Allen, Susan York - 1870; TCS]
18 Feb., 1878, Ows. @ James Brock's [Min.]
ROBERT (c23 S b.Ows.)   [s/o William Beard
& Margaret Riley - 1880]
LUCINDA MORRIS (c21 S b.Morris Fk., Br.)
[d/o Robt. Morris & America Sizemore - BJE]
c1899      (PWB; BJE/Martha Volterman, d/o
Robt. & Lucinda; 1910-B; NL 1900Sx; NL M-B;
1920)
WILLIAM (R.Ows. 23 S b.Lee,KY [VA]) P/-- Ows
[s/o Daniel Beard & Eliza     - 1870]
MARGARET RILEY (R.Ows 18 S b.KY) P/KY-Per
28 July, 1874, Ows., @ James Riley's
[poss. DIVORCED, because Margaret remd. as
Riley] [R.Owsley 1880]   [MARGARET m2 1900
Thomas Johnson & R.Breathitt 1900]

## BEATTY

DECATUR (c24 miner b.KY) [s/o Samuel Beatty
   & W1 Patsy Baxter - M-E; REM]
   EMILY JANE AKERS (c19 b.KY) [d/o John
   Akers & Patsy McGuire - M-E]
   6 June, 1846, Ows. (JFB; 1850) [H-remd.]
DECATUR (c36 2nd b.KY) [widr/o Emily Jane
   Akers above]
   ARTHINA YATES (c37 b.KY)
   c1857        (B-O ch-11/53 by W1; B-O ch-
   6/58 by Arthina; 1870-L)
FRANCIS DECATUR - see DECATUR
[JAMES MADISON] "JASPER" M (c30 Law b.Franklin
   Co, MO) [1836-1915 Lee; s/o Samuel Beatty
   & W2 Patience Kelly - ob-H BE-12/17/15;
   art. BE-9/27/70]
   CAROLINE McGUIRE (c20 b.Ows.) [c1845-1877;
   d/o James McGuire & Evaline Trimble - D-L]
   20 Sept., 1865, Ows. (JFB; B-L ch.; 1870-L;
   ob-H has md. 9/20/<u>66</u>; ob-ch BE-1/6/44;
   photo of James BE-8/27/70)
   [JAMES m2 2/6/79 Lee, Josephine Carr Blount
   (1855-1942; d/o James F. Blount) - 1900-
   1910-L; ob-W OCC-3/6/42; ob-H]
JOHN (c37 <u>Blk</u> boat builder b.KY)
   MARGARET _____ (c16 <u>Blk</u> b.KY)
   c1867     (1870-L-2)
LENY (c25 <u>Blk</u> c.miner b.KY)
   ALMIRA _____ (c15 <u>Mul</u> b.KY)
   c1866     (1870-L-3; NL 1880Sx)
MILO, JR. (c24 b.KY) [1882-1965; s/o Milo
   Beatty Sr. & Fannie Sewell - 1900-L; ob-H&S
   BE-7/22/65-6/20/35-2/23/39; P/M-L 1872]
   NANNIE MAY BREEDING (c19 b.KY) [d/o John
   Breeding & Perlina Hogg - 1900; ob-WF&S
   OCC-5/28/37-1/28/38, BE-11/7/35]
   26 Dec., 1906, Boonev., @ John Breeding's,
   the f/o the bride, by Rev. S. K. Ramey;
   wits. John & Ruth Breeding & others
   (M-O; obits; 1910-L; TCS; BC 1915-L;
   NL 1920Sx; R.Beattyv. 1935-1939; wid. in
   Beattyv. 1965)

## BECKNELL

CURTIS C. (c20 S b.Island City)  [s/o Sam
    Becknell & Nancy Hamilton - B-O]
    ALMILDA HUFF (c17 S b.Jack.)  [d/o John W.
    Huff & Mary Jane Burch - B-O as b.Jack.]
    6 June, 1895, Clay (TCS; 1900-1910-1920;
    B-O ch.; M-O ch-1962)
HENRY L. "BUD" (c22 b.Sturg.)  [1867-1949; s/o
    Wm. Thornberry Becknell & Sarah Wilson -
    PWB; ob-H OCN-7/29/49]
    LUCINDA BOWMAN (c15 b.KY)  [1874-1906;
    d/o Elihu COUCH & Nancy (nee Morris), wid/o
    Robt. BOWMAN - PWB; JSG]
    24 Dec., 1889        (ob-H; 1900 m-9; JSG;
    ob-ch. BS-5/24/90)  [H-remd.]
HENRY L. "BUD" (c40 2nd b.Sturg.)  [widr/o
    Lucinda Bowman above]    [1867-1949]
    MARTHA "MATTIE" (nee BALL) _____ (c25 2nd
    b.Conkling, Ows.)    [m1 _____]
    [d/o James Ball & Mary J. Gabbard]
    22 June, 1907        (ob-H; B-O ch.;
    1910-1920; JSG)
JAMES (c21 b.KY) [s/o Sam Becknell & W1 Nancy
    Hamilton - 1880; neph/o R. W. Becknell -ME]
    MAGGIE MOYERS (c21 S b.IN)
    June, 1901, @ home of Zack Bowman on Fish
    Creek, on a Sat.  (ME-7/5/01; ME-12/15/04,
    soon to move to Ham.,OH; 1910Sx-OH, Maggie,
    Div., R.Cin,, svt. w/Walter Hutchinson)
JOHN LAZARUS (c20 S b.KY)  [s/o Sam Becknell
    & Nancy Hamilton - 1880]
    SARAH HUNDLEY (c18 S b.KY)  [d/o Claiborne
    Hundley & Sarah E Hamilton -1880 w/M & s-F]
    1889        (1900 m-10; 1910 m-21; TCS;
    wid. Sallie 1920)
JOHN W. (c30 S b.KY)  [1861-1932; s/o Wm.
    Thornberry Becknell & Sarah Wilson - 1880;
    PWB; TS-TCS]
    JERUSHA ALICE EVANS (c23 S b.Ows.)  [1868-
    1957; d/o James Evans & Margaret Allen -
    1880; ob-W OCN-9/5/57]
    1890/1        (1900-1910-1920; TCS; JSG;
    ob-ch. OCC-7/12/40; R.Sturgeon 1957)
LAZARUS - see JOHN LAZARUS

(Becknell cont.)

48

**BECKNELL (cont.)**

LEONARD (c20 S b.Ows.) [1887-1959; s/o Robert
    W. Becknell & Mary J. Evans - 1900; TS-TCS;
    ob-H BE-4/30/59]
    MARY BRANDENBURG (c16 S b.KY) [d/o Arch
    BBurg. & Lucy Duff - TCS ob-WM OCC-6/15/34]
    1906/7      (1910-1920; TCS; R.Boonev.
    1934; ob-ch. BS-1/30/92)
ROBERT (c24 S b.Ows.) [1858-1913; s/o Wm.
    Thornberry Becknell & Sarah Wilson - PWB;
    TS-TCS]
    MARY JANE EVANS (c18 S b.Ows.) [1863-1945;
    d/o James Evans & Margaret Allen -1880 TCS]
    1881/2          (1900 m-18; ME-3/18/04 moved
    to Wilmore, Jess., KY; ME-12/15/04 R. W. of
    Wilmore compaigning for BiL R. E. Evans;
    1910 m-27; B-O ch.; NVP; JSG; M-L ch-1918;
    ob-ch. BE-4/30/59 & 3Fks-12/30/98)
ROBERT [W.] (c28 mcht b.KY) [s/o Sam Becknell
    & Nancy Hamilton - 1880]
    [MINTIE] MINNIE BINGHAM (c18 b.KY) [d/o
    John Bingham & Eliza J.      - 1880-J]
    5 May, 1892, Jackson Co. @ John Bingham's,
    by Robt. Bingham; wits. W. J. Bingham &
    Robert Rice; sur. Jasper Huff   (M-J 1:255;
    TCS; 1900 m-8; H-remd. 1910)
ROBERT W. (c34 2nd mcht. b.KY) [widr/o
    Mintie Bingham above]
    MATTIE BURCH (c24 S b.KY) [poss. d/o
    Jasper Burch & Rhoda Eliz. Morris - 1900]
    1904/5          (1910; 1920-Fay.; BC-1915-
    1919 Fay.; NL M-J)
SAMUEL (c21 b.Andrew Co., MO)   [s/o Wm.
    Thornberry Becknell & Sarah Wilson]
    NANCY HAMILTON (c21 b.Hawk.,TN) [d/o
    Curtis Hamilton & Sylvester Smith]
    11 July, 1867, Ows. (JSG; NVP; PWB; 1870-2
    w/WP; B-O ch.; 1880)    [H-remd.]
SAMUEL (c47 2nd b.Andrew Co., MO) [widr/o
    Nancy Hamilton above]
    MARY (nee OLDHAM) BEGLEY (c20 2nd b.KY)
    [wid/o ____ Begley] [1870-1937 Sturg.; d/o
    Lewis Oldham & Rhoda Hamilton - DC; 1870]
    1889/90          (1900, s-s Begly b.6/87;
    JSG; REM; wid. Mary 1910-1920)

(Becknell cont.)

49

**BECKNELL (cont.)**

T[HOMAS] A[NDREW] (R.Ows. 23 S b.Ows.) P/NC-
   Jack. [1886-1957; s/o Wm. Becknell & Nancy
   Kidd - 1910; ob-H OCN-5/9/57]
   GRACE CAMPBELL (R.Ows. 16 S b.Ows.) P/Per.
   [d/o Edward Campbell & Hannah Campbell -
   1910; ob-WS OCN-9/4/53]
   15 May, 1910, Ows. [R.Owsley 1920 & 1950 -
   OCN-5/19/50 their 40th anniv.; Boonev.
   1953-1968 - ob-WS BE-11/7/68]
WILLIAM (c21 S b.KY) [1864-1926 Ows.; s/o Wm.
   Thornberry Becknell & Sarah Wilson - 1880;
   PWB]
   NANCY C. KIDD (c27 S b.KY)    [d/o Thomas
   Kidd & Mary Virginia Stanfield - 1880]
   1884/5         (1900-1910-1920; PWB;
   ob-ch. OCN-5/9/57)
WILLIAM, JR. (c22 S b.Ows.) [s/o Sam Becknell
   & Nancy Hamilton - 1880]
   ELIZABETH "LIZZIE" HOSKINS (c18 S b.Ows.)
   [d/o Wm. Hoskins & Margaret Robertson -
   ob-WS BE-12/8/60]
   1898/9         (1900-1910; B-O ch.; R.Richmond
   1960; ob-ch. BE-10/17/68, M/Lizzie alive)
WILSON (c20 b.KY)    [1871-1907; s/o Wm.
   Thornberry Becknell & Sarah Wilson - 1880;
   PWB; TS-TCS]
   [MALINDA] CARY BURCH (c16 S b.Ows.)   [d/o
   Newton Burch & Mary Hamilton - B-O]
   26 Nov., 1891, Ows.   (ME-12/4/91 as Wilson
   & Cary; JSG; 1900 as Wilson & Linda; TCS;
   wid. Malinda 1910)  [MALINDA m2 c1913 Dan
   Rowland - TSC; 1920, Becknell s-ch.; ob-H
   OCN-2/29/52; ob-ch. BS-6/17/93]

**BEGLEY**

ALBERT (c20 b.KY)  [s/o Swinfield Begley
   & Mary Davidson - TCS]
   MARY WARREN (c19 b.KY)   [prob. d/o George
   J. Warren & Eliza J.       - 1860-1870]
   c1875         (1880-5, w/Matthew & Susannah
   Warren, Mary listed as GD; M-L ch. 1914)
AUGUST (R.Ows. 22 S b.Ows.) P/Ows.  [s/o
   James G. Begley & Adda      - 1900]
   CLAUDA DUNN (R.Ows. 17 S b.Ows.) P/Lee
   [d/o John Dunn & Amazon Young - 1910]
   19 May, 1910, Ows.
(Begley cont.)

50

**BEGLEY (cont.)**
BALLARD - see also W. BALLARD
BALLARD (c17 S b.Ows.)    [s/o Albert Begley
   & Sarah Roberts - 1900-L; ob-HF]
   LAURA BOWMAN (c17 S b.Ows.)    [1887-1967
   Pow.; d/o John Bowman & Rachel Crawford -
   DC; 1900-L]
   1904/5          (1910; B-O ch.; 1920Sx-Pow.,
   Clay City; Clay City, Powell 1939)
   [H/John Ballard - TCS]
BALLARD "SHRIMP" (c21 S b.Lee)    [s/o Perry
   Begley & Margaret Warren - TCS]
   AGNES "POLLY" UNDERWOOD (c21 S b.Lee)
   1907/8          (1910-1920; B-O ch.; BBG)
BRADLEY (c20 b.Per.)    [s/o John R. Begley & W1
   Judy Davidson - ACB]
   EDITH "EDY" EVANS (c20 b.Ows.)    [d/o Hiram
   Evans & Mary Stamper - TCS; ACB]
   1864/5          (1870-4; 1880; 1900-L m-35; M-L
   ch-1909)
ELIJAH (c22 b.KY)    [s/o Henry Begley & Eliz.
   Roberts - TCS]
   MARY COMBS (c17 b.KY)    [d/o Samuel Combs
   & Nancy Cornett - TCS]
   c1850          (1860-9; REM)
GEORGE (c23 S b.Jack.)    [1878-1961 Ida Mae;
   s/o James Grant Begley & Adaline Fulks -
   1900; ob-H BE-8/17/61; DC]
   MILLIE GUM (c20 S b.Ows.)    [1881-1968 Ida
   Mae; d/o Stephen Gum & Sarah Gross - 1900;
   ob-W BE-2/22/68]
   1901/2          (1910; B-O ch.; M-L ch-
   1930-1931; wid. R. Ida Mae 1961-1968)
GRANT - see JAMES GRANVILLE
GRANVILLE - see JAMES GRANVILLE
HIRAM (c20 b.KY)
   LUCINDA EVANS (c17 b.KY)    [1875-1938; d/o
   Wm. Evans & Mary Jane Newman - ob-W OCC-
   6/24/38; 1880-L]
   1891/2          (ob-W; 1900-L; NL M-L; ob-ch.
   OCN-8/7/58)


(Begley cont.)

## BEGLEY (cont.)

JACKSON (c21 b.Per.) [poss. s/o Russell Begley
& Elizabeth Roberts - 1850-P]
   ELIZABETH BOWMAN (c23 b.Ows.) [d/o Elisha
   Bowman & Mahulda Phillips - JFB; ME-6/9/10]
   c1867         (1870 no ch.; 1870MS ch. d.
   9/69 age 1; B-O ch.; 1880; wid. Eliz. 1900-
   1910-1920)
JAMES GRANVILLE "GRANT" (c33 b.MO) [1840-1916
Wild Dog, Ows.; s/o John S. Begley & Jane
Hignite - 1860-P; DC-P/NL]
   ADALINE FULKS (c24 b.KY)
   1873         (1880-L-6; 1900 m-26; DC son
   Geo. b.1878 Jack.; M-L ch-1907; H/as Grant,
   James G. & Granville; NL M-J/L)
JAMES (R.Lee 22 S b.Ows.) P/Per-Clay [poss.
s/o Swimfield Begley & Mary Davidson -
1880-L]
   AMANDA BRANDENBURG (R.Lee 16 S b.Lee) P/Ows
   [d/o Henry BBurg. & Eliz. Roberts - 1880]
   27 Nov, 1890, Lee @ Henry Brandenburg's, by
   James E. Dunagin; wits. Nath Rader & Pin
   Begley     (M-L; 1900-L)   [JAMES m2 Jane
   Wilson - TCS]
JOHN R. (c52 3rd b.Per.) [m1 Judy Davidson -
ACB, VDK; m2 Lucy Eversole - B-P ch-1853,
D-O 1877 son, P-CW 2nd mg. may not have
been legal] [c1815-1892; s/o Henry Begley
& Betsy Roberts - REM; P-CW]
   CATHERINE "KATE" SANDLIN (c29 b.Br.) [1837-
   19__; d/o James Sandlin & Zilpha Baker -
   1850; VDK; NL w/P 1860-B]
   22 May, 1867, Ows., @ John Begley's, by
   George W. Miller (P-CW; 1860 John Div/f W1;
   1870, 1st ch. under 10 is 9; REM; 1880;
   wid. Katie/Cath. 1900-1910) [NOTE: Because
   3 ch. b. betw. 1860-67, poss. md. earlier]
JOHN (___ b.Ows.)
   LAURA TREADWAY (___ b.Ows.)
   pre-1904         (B-O ch. b/d 3/04;
   NL 1910Sx)
JOHN BALLARD - see BALLARD


(Begley cont.)

52

## BEGLEY (cont.)

JOHN R. (c22 S b.Boonev.)  [s/o Jackson Begley
  & Eliz. Bowman - 1880]
  EMMA MOORE (c17 S b.Boonev.)  [d/o Henry
  Moore & W2 Mary Hobbs - 1900; ob-WS OCC-
  9/3/37 & OCN-11/13/53]
  1900/1     (1910-1920; B-O ch.; R.Boonev.
  1937; Lebanon, OH 1953)
MAJOR S. (c18 S b.KY)  [s/o Jackson Begley
  & Eliz. Bowman - 1880]
  DOCIA MURRELL (c20 S b.KY)  [d/o Wiley
  Murrell & Catherine Smith - 1880]
  1889     (1900 m-11; 1910 m-20; REM)
PERRY (c22 b.KY)  [s/o Swimpfield Begley
  & Mary Davidson - 1880-L]
  MARGARET WARREN (c20 b.Ows.)  [poss. d/o
  George Warren & Eliza  - 1870-1880]
  1883/4   [appar. DIV. c1900]  (1900
  H/m-16, W-NL; 1900-L-6/86 W/m-19, H-NL; M-L
  ch-1909; BE-5/20/10, Perry moved to NM from
  Trav. Rest for his health)  [MARGARET m2
  1910-20, James G. Moore, widr/o Mary
  Becknell - 1920 Begley s-ch.; BBG]
SAMUEL "SAM" (c17 b.KY)
  AMANDA "MANDY" McINTOSH (c14 b.Ows.) [1886-
  1976; d/o Elisha McIntosh & Minerva Jane
  Fox - FH; ob-WS OCN-4/19/56; LNG/Bible]
  c1900    (1900, w/WP, Sam listed as md.
  SiL, but Amanda, 14, NL as md; NL 1910Sx;
  1920 as Sam & Mandy, 34; M-L ch-1933;
  R.Beattyv. 1969 - ob-WS BE-10/9/69)
SWIMPFIELD (R.Per. 26 S b.Per.)  [s/o Henry
  Begley & Eliz. Roberts - 1850-P]
  MARY DAVIDSON (R.Clay 18 S b.Clay)
  15 Dec., 1855, _Perry_  (M-P; 1860; B-L ch.;
  1870-1880-1900-L; M-L ch-1946)
W. BALLARD (c21 b.KY)  [1866-1944; s/o John
  Begley & Lizana Felckner - 1870-P; TS-TCS]
  _____ (___ b.KY)  [d. 1890-2]
  c1887    (H-remd-7 1900, 1st 2 ch-5/88
  & 6/90, W2 2/2 ch-12/97 & 8/99)
W. BALLARD (c26 2nd b.KY)  [widr/o _____
  above]  [1866-1944]
  MALVINA GIBSON (c19 S b.KY) [1874-1918; d/o
  Larkin Gibson & Eliz. Moore - 1880; TS-TCS]
  1892/3    (1900 m-7; 1910 "m-15"; TCS)
(Begley cont.)

**BEGLEY (cont.)**
WILSON ["WID"] (R.Lee 20 S b.Lee) P/Per-Clay
[1879-19__; s/o Swimpfield Begley & Mary
Davidson - 2nd mg.; 1900-L]
[IRENE] RENA DAMEREL (R.Lee 17 S b.Lee) P/
Ows. [1883-1943 Richmond, IN; d/o John
Dameral & Elizabeth Angel - PWB]
14 April, 1899 (ML) <u>Lee</u> (to be md. @ Eliz.
Dameral's) (MC-NFI) (M-L; 1900-L m-1, w/HP;
1920-L; M-L ch-1929) [WILSON (R.Hlbg. 67
widr. b.Lee) m2 6/22/46 Lee, Mary L (Eliz)
(BBurg.) McIntyre (67 wid. b.Ows. - d/o
Jackson BBurg. & Martha Callahan) (Mary E.
1874-1958 Fay. - DC; FH; poss. m1 Thomas
Marcum??; m2? _____ Rowland; m3? 6/11/38
Ben McIntire - M-O) - M-L; widr. Wilson
R.Beattyv. 1958; Hlbg. 1961]
**BEHIMER/BEHYMER**
GEORGE W. (c26 b.OH) P/OH    [1849-19__]
MARY B._____ (c14 b.KY) P/TN [c1862-c1890]
c1876        (1880-3)
GEORGE (c42 2nd b.OH) [widr/o Mary _____ abv]
LENORA "NORA" (nee DAY) HACKER (c34 2nd KY)
[m1 Hogan Hacker - TCS] [1855-1928 - TCS]
1891        (1900-J m-9, ch-8/90 & twins
4/92; 1910 m2-7 both, ch. 18 & twins 16;
1920; TCS; NL M-J/R)
**BELCHER**
JASPER (c21 b.KY) P/KY [s/o George Belcher
& Elizabeth    - 3rd M-B]
ELIZA _____ (c19 b.KY) P/KY
c1879        (1880 no ch.; prob. P/o child
b.& d. 3/80, 1880MS) [JASPER (39 2nd) m2
3/24/98 Br., Mary Johnson (39 2nd) - M-B
8:29; JASPER (42 3rd b.Per.) m3 6/1/1901
Br., Lula Campbell (20 S) - M-B 9:231]
**BELL**
LAZARUS (c20 b.Boonev.) [s/o Marcus C. Bell
& Martha Flanery - 1880; ME-4/8/04]
MARY ROWLAND (c19 b.KY) [1871-1901; d/o
Ira Rowland & Eliz. Tyra - 1880; ME-7/5/01]
1889        (1900-2/90, m-10; TCS; ob-ch.
BS-12/31/87 W/as <u>Eliz.</u> Rowland) [H-remd.]


(Bell cont.)

54

## BELL (cont.)

LAZARUS M. (c34 2nd b.Boonev.) [widr/o Mary
   Rowland above]
   MOLLIE METCALF (c32 S b.Maulden, Clay)
   1903/4        (1910-1920; B-O ch.; ob-ch
   HJN-12/89; NL M-C)
THOMAS - see WM. THOMAS
WILLIAM THOMAS "TOM" (c35 S b.Ows.) [1860-
   1911 Ows.; s/o Marcus Bell & Martha Flanery
   - 1880; DC]
   FANNIE (nee BAILEY) SMITH (c40 2nd b.KY)
   [wid/o Houston Smith - TCS] [1853-1938
   Ows.; d/o Hiram Bailey & Sarah Paris - DC;
   LNG; 1910]
   1893/4        (1900-6 m-4; 1910-15, m-16, WM
   w/them; wid. Fannie 1920 w/son Mark; ME-
   2/1/01 Tom Bell shot by Lennie Smith;
   M-O ch-1970)

## BELOMY

ROBERT (c20 b.VA)
   MALINDA _____ (c19 b.KY)
   c1866        (1870-L-3)

## BENNETT

JAMES RICHARD (c28 b.Est.) [s/o Thos. Bennett
   & Malinda Bird - TCS; P/M-E]
   SARAH _____ (c20 b.KY)
   1859/60        (1860-MWY) [H-remd.]
JAMES RICHARD (c34 2nd wagon maker b.Est.)
   [widr/o Sarah _____ above]
   AGNES "AGGY" (nee BURTON) CHARLES (c24
   b.Est.) [wid/o _____ CHARLES] [d/o Sam
   Burton & Eliza     - TCS]
   21 Jan., 1866, Estill (TCS; 1870-L, oldest
   Bennett ch. age 3, s-ch. McCHARLES; B-L
   ch.; 1880-L, s-ch. CHARLES; her son listed
   as CHARLES 1900-L)
JOHN (c25 b.KY)
   SUSAN BURTON (c16 b.KY) [d/o Sam Burton
   & Eliza     - TCS]
   c1855        (1860-4; 1870; B-O ch.; TCS;
   W/as Sarah 1x & Susan 2x)
RICHARD - see JAMES RICHARD
WILLIAM (R.Ows. 20 S b.Est.)
   NANCY PITTMAN (R.Ows. 19 S b.Ows.) [d/o
   Micajah Pittman - 1850]
   26 July, 1855, Ows.

**BIGGS**
WILLIAM W. (c30 shoemaker b.TN)
   HARRIET (BIGGS?) (___ b___)
   c1852      (NL 1850; B-O ch-6/53, W/as
   BIGGS)  [H-remd.]
W[ILLIAM] W. (c33 2nd shoemaker b.TN) [widr/o
   Harriet (Biggs?) above]
   PHOEBE BARRETT (c28 b.KY)
   c1856      (1860, W/Phoebe, ch-6, 3, 2, &
   11 mos.; B-O ch-6/53 by W1, so ch. age 6
   1860 is by W1)
WILLIS (R.Ows. 18 S b.Jack.) P/Ows-Clay
   SARILDA [SHRILDA] GIPSON (R.Ows. 15 S b.
   Ows.) P/TN-Ows.  [d/o Newton Harvey Gibson
   & Sally McGeorge - 1900; ob-WS OCN-6/4/54-
   10/14/54 & BE-1/5/55]
   8 Aug., 1908, Ows.  [R.Owsley 1920; Sturg.
   1954-1955]
**BINGHAM**
B[EN] F. (R.Jack. 33 S b.Jack.) P/Jack.
   HALLY ROWLAND (R.Ows. 34 S b.Ows.) P/Ows.
   [1861-1939 Ows.; d/o Alfred Rowland &
   Thursey Jane Rice - 1880; DC/M as Hally
   Jane Price]
   9 June, 1904, Ows.  [R.Owsley 1910-1920]
**BIRCH**
see BURCH
**BIRCHFIELD**
ADAM (R.Ows. 18 S b.Br.) [s/o John Birchfield
   & Polly      ]
   PHEBE S. [JANE] SPARKS (R.Ows. 18 S b.Est.)
   [c1838-1861; d/o James Sparks & Tempy
   Spencer]
   28 Aug., 1856, Ows.    [R.Morgan 1860]
   [ADAM m2 c1865 Eliz. _____ - 1870-W; ADAM
   m3 3/10/80 Br, Mrs. Caroline Stufflebeen
   (32 2nd) - M-B; ACB]
**BIRD**
see BYRD
**BISHOP**
ARCH (c19 b.KY)  [s/o Perry Bishop & Levisa
   Baker - 1880]
   ELIZA _____ (c13 b.KY)
   1884/5      (1900 m-15, 1st ch-3/84,
   next ch-2/96; NL 1910Sx; widr. Arch w/son
   1920 Clay; W-NL DC Inx; NL M-J)
(Bishop cont.)

BRICE (R.Ows. 25 S b.Ows.) P/Ows.
   JOANA [nee FIELDS] McINTOSH (R.Ows. 25 2nd
   b.Per) P/Per.   [m1 Levi McIntosh - 1900]
   [d/o James Fields & Susan Sizemore - TCS,
   but NL w/P 1880]
   20 Aug., 1904, Ows.   [R.Owsley 1910-1920;
   see NOTE under Levi McIntosh]
DAVID (c21 S b.Ows.)   [1884-1968 Dayton, OH
   hosp.; s/o John Bishop & Lucy Cole - 1900;
   ob-H BE-5/2/68]
   MARY REED (c17 S b.Br.)   [1889-1966 Lex.
   hosp; d/o Wiley Reed & Lydia Mason - 1900;
   ob-W&S BE-10/20/66-1/31/63]
   1906/7      (1910-1920; B-O ch.; R.Ricetown
   1963; widr. David R.Ricetown 1966)
GEORGE (c21 b.KY)   [s/o Perry Bishop & Levisa
   Baker - 1880]
   MAXALINE _____ (c16 b.KY)
   1891/2      (1900; NL 1910; 1920)
IRVINE (R.Clay 18 S b.Clay) P/Clay   [s/o
   Perry Bishop & Levisa Baker - TCS]
   AMANDA J. ABNER (R.Ows. 16 S b.Ows.) P/Ows.
   [d/o Lacy Abner & Cintha Combs - 1860]
   31 Oct., 1874, Ows., @ Absalom Murrell's
   [R.Owsley 1880-1900]
ISAAC (c22 b.KY)
   REBECCA DAY (c12 b.Harl.)   [1851-1939 Ows.;
   d/o John Day & Susannah       - TCS; DC]
   12 Aug., 1877, Clay  (M-C; TCS; 1900)
JAMES (c16 b.KY)   [s/o Wm. Bishop & Susan
   Barrett - TCS]
   RHODA CARMACK (c17 b.TN)   [d/o Isaac
   Carmack & Comfort Hall - VKD]
   c1867        (1880-10; NL 1870; TCS;
   B-O ch.; VKD 1st ch. b.5/68; NL M-C)
JAMES (c22 S b.Clay)   [1873-1954; s/o John
   Bishop & Lucy Kath. Cole - TS-TCS]
   LUCY NICKELS (c17 S b.Clay)
   1895/6        (1900-1910; B-O ch.; NL M-C)
J[NO.] N. (R.Ows. 23 S b.Lee,VA)
   ELIZ. CAROL [HAMILTON] (R.Ows. 28 2nd b.
   Lee, VA)   [wid/o Wm. Hamilton - D-O 1852]
   [d/o Thomas Carroll & Sarah Hamilton - TCS]
   1 Aug., 1859, Ows.  [R.Owsley 1860, 1870,
   wid. Sarah Carroll w/them]
(Bishop cont.)

## BISHOP (cont.)

JOHN (c21 S b.Clay)  [s/o Abraham Bishop
& Nancy Robertson]
[LUCY] CATHERINE COLE (c21 S b.Clay)  [d/o
Charles Cole & Eliz. Robertson]
6 March, 1869, <u>Clay</u>  (M-C; TCS; 1870-C-1;
1880; 1900 m-28; 1910 as m-36; B-O ch.;
wid. Katherine 1920; W/as Cath/Kath. & Lucy
K/C.)

JOHN (___ b.KY)
MARY ELLEN "ELLA" KELLY (c16 S b.Clay)
[1878-1956; d/o Francis Kelly & Fanny
Sparks - ob-W/as Wilson OCN-5/31/56; 1880-C
M-C P]
30 March, 1893, <u>Clay</u>; Halcomb Bishop
signed  (M-C; W-remd-4 1900, Bishop s-ch-
4/94; B-O ch. by H2)     [ELLA m2 John T.
Wilson - ob-W]

LEANDER "LEE" (c18 b.Ows.)  [1886-1957; s/o
Perry Bishop & Levisa Baker - 1880; ob-H
OCN-5/30/57]
NANCY JANE SANDLIN (c20 b.Ows.)  [1874-
1956; d/o Will Sandlin & Martha Peters -
DC; 1880]
1894/5     (1900; VKD; R.Upper Buffalo
1957)

LUTHER (c21 S b.Clay)
LUCY J. MORRIS (c20 S b.Ows.)  [d/o Henty
Morris & Sarah F. Strong - 1900]
1905/6     (1910, w/WM; B-O ch.; NL M-C)

MacHENRY (c22 b.KY)  [1866-1904]  [s/o Wm.
Bishop & Susan Barrett - TCS; 1900Sx]
ALCY ANN DEAN (c22 b.Clay)  [1867-1949; d/o
Ezekiel Dean & Kezziah Barrett - 1880; ob-W
OCN-7/8/49 as Tirey]
1888/9     (1900-C m-11, HM w/them;
ob-W; PWB; NL M-C)     [ALCY ANN m2 1910,
Richard Tirey - M-O; 1920]

ROBERT G. (c17 b.KY)  [poss. s/o John Bishop
& Lucy Cath. Cole - 1880]
DELPHIA GABBARD (c14 b.KY)  [d/o George
Gabbard & W2 Mary Eliz. Shook - TCS ob-WS]
1896/7     (1900; TCS; ob-WS OCC-6/12/42;
R.Oneida, KY 1942)

(Bishop cont.)

## BISHOP (cont.)
SQUIRE (c19 b.Clay) [s/o Wm. Bishop & Susan
   - VKD]
   SARAH BURNS (c16 b.Ows.) [d/o Wm. Burns
   & Rachel Asher - 1860]
   c1861         (1870-8; B-O ch.; NL M-C)
## BLAKE
GIDEON "GID" (c21 S b.KY)    [1884-1966 Cov.
   Nur-H; s/o Wm. Blake & Margaret J. Wolfe -
   VKD; ob-H BE-11/3/66; 1900]
   SARAH ELLEN McQUEEN (c21 S b.Jack.) [1884-
   1956 Lex. hosp.; d/o John McQueen & W2
   Mollie Rains - ob-W OCN-6/28/56; TCS]
   1905/6          (1910-1920; VKD)
JAMES T. (19 S b.Conkling, Ows.) [s/o Wm.
   Blake & Margaret J. Wolfe - 1900; ob-HS BE-
   11/3/66]
   MARY ANN SHEPHERD (c20 S b.Conkling, Ows.)
   [d/o Riley Shepherd & Nancy Morris - 1900]
   31 Aug., 1900          (VKD; 1910 m-10; B-O
   ch.; 1920; R.Ham.,OH 1966; ob-ch. Rich.IN;
   ob-ch. HJN-7/8/96)
JOHN D. W. (c21 b.KY)    [1875-1916 Ows.; s/o
   Wm. Blake & Caroline Wolfe - 1880; DC]
   BETTY DAY (c25 b.KY)
   1895/6          (1900; VKD)
JOHN ( ___ b. ___ )
   BERTHA "BERTIE" CARMACK (c19 b.KY)
   [1891-1985 Br.; d/o Isaac Carmack & Rhoda
   Thomas - 1900; DC/Edwards]
   c1911          (TCS; dau. Mabel b. 9/22/12
   VKD; Mabel Blake, age 6, gd/o Isaac Carmack
   1920)    [BERTIE remd. Mr. Edwards - TCS;
   ob-WS-5/19/66]
LEANDER "LEE" (c20 S b.KY)   [s/o Wm. C. Blake
   & Margaret Jane Wolfe - VKD]
   MARTHA "MATTIE" (nee SHEPHERD) BALL (c22
   2nd b.KY)   [m1 Bishop Ball]   [d/o Riley
   Shepherd & Nancy Morris - 1880]
   7 April, 1899          (VKD/Shepherd Family
   by Moffitt; 1900 m-2; 1910 m-10; REM; 1920;
   ob-ch. HJN-3/12/97-1/26/99)
SILAS A. (c18 S b.KY) [s/o Wm. Blake
   & Caroline Wolfe - VKD]
   SARAH MOORE (c17 S b.KY)
   1900          (1910 2x, m-9 & m-10; VKD)
(Blake cont.)

## BLAKE (cont.)

WM. (R.Ows. 20 S b.TN) P/TN  [s/o Eliz. Blake, raised by his uncle Wm. Blake & wf Caroline - VKD]
MARGARET J. WOLFE (R.Ows 15 S b.TN) P/TN [d/o Emmanuel Wolfe & Caroline Wolfe - VKD]
4 Sept., 1877, Ows., @ Wm. Blake's
[R.Owsley 1880-1900-1910-1920]

WILLIAM (c25 S b.KY) [s/o Wm. Blake & Caroline Wolfe - 1880]
THEODOSHIA DAY (c24 S b.KY)  [d/o Lloyd Day & Emily Jane Allen - ob-WS BE-1/21/65]
1897       (1900 m-2; 1910 m-13; VKD; TCS; ob-H OCC-9/18/36; 1920; R.Cincinnati, OH 1965)

WILLIAM (c59 3rd b.TN)  [widr/o Caroline Wolfe - VKD]
STACY (nee SMITH) MOORE (c52 2nd b.KY) [wid/o John W. Moore]   [d/o Robert Smith & Henrietta     - TCS]
1901/2       (1910, Moore s-d.; TCS)

## BLANTON

GROVER C. (R.Jackson, Br. 22 S [b.KY])
EVA TREADWAY (R.Jackson, Br. 22 S [b.KY]) [d/o Winfield Scott Treadway & Martha Lou Flanery - 1900]
29 June, 1907, Jackson, <u>Breathitt Co.</u>, by W. H. Setzer, Paster; wits. J. L. Stidham & Emma Clark  (M-B 13:99; ob-W OCC-5/9/41; 1910-B m-2, no ch.)

## BLEVINS

ELI (R.Ows. 24 S b.Claiborne Co., TN) [s/o Joseph Blevins & Mary    - TCS; 1850-E]
MILLY HUBBARD (R.Est. 20 S b.Clay)
5 Sept., 1856, Ows.   [R.Owsley 1860; wid. Milly 1870]

ROBERT (c23 b.TN)  [c1831-1855; s/o Joseph Blevins & Mary    - D-O]
MINERVA BOWMAN (c21 b.Clay) [d/o Elisha Bowman & Mary Mahala Phillips - TCS]
c1854       (D-O hus.; NL M-C; M-O 1857 Minerva Blevins, wid., to James Lynch; 1860 James Lynch & wf Minerva & her dau. Mahulda Blevins, 5)

## BLOUNT

CHARLES J. (c29 tchr b.VA) [s/o Charles Blount
   & Jane       - 1850]
   SARAH W. CORNETT (c22 b.TN)  [d/o John
   Cornett & Hetty    - TCS]
   30 Oct., 1851, Ows.  (JFB; B-O ch.; 1860;
   1870-1880-L)
GEORGE (c31 boatman b.VA)  [s/o Charles Blount
   & Jane      - 1850]
   ALICE GALE (c19 b.KY)    [d/o Joseph Gale
   & Eliz. Coyle - 1850-Frk; 1870]
   c1859        (NL 1860; 1870-L-10; their
   ch. w/rel. 1880-L; NL M-J/Frk.)
GUSTAVUS A. (c23 b.KY)  [s/o Charles Blount
   & Jane     - 1860]
   LUCY ANN GALE (c16 S b.Frankfort)  [1849-
   1937; d/o Joseph Gale & Eliz. Coyle - 1850-
   Frk; ob-W OCC-4/9/37 as Twyman]
   11 May, 1865, Ows.  (JFB; W-remd. 1870-L;
   B-L ch. by H2)  [LUCY m2 Broadus Twyman]
JAMES F. (R.Proctor 32 S b.Bedford Co., VA)
   [s/o Charles Blount & Jane      ]
   CLARINDA BARKER (R.Ows. 22 S b.Bedford,
   "KY") [c1830-1860's]
   22 Jan., 1853, Ows., by G. S. Williams
   [R.Owsley 1860; widr. James Lee 1870-1880]
W[ILLIAM] H. (c29 carp. b.KY)   [s/o Charles
   Blount & Jane   - 1850; TCS]
   [NANCY] MARGARET BOTNER (c21 b.VA) [d/o
   James Botner & Mary Eliz. Nunley - 1860;
   DC/sib-1918; LNG]
   3 July, 1863, Ows.  (JFB; 1870-L-6; their
   dau. w/Wm. & Mary Cornelius 1880-L as
   niece; DC-1918 lists Mary Cornelius as d/o
   James Botner)  [NANCY BLOUNT (R.Lee 29 2nd)
   m2 2/12/1872 Lee, Thomas Sewell (69 2nd)]

## BOGGS

JAMES (R.Haz. c23 Dr. b.KY)  [s/o Jesse Boggs
   & Sarah     - ME; 1880-P]
   SARAH EVERSOLE (c19 S b.KY)  [d/o George
   Eversole, late JPC, who moved to Ows. - ME]
   Aug., 1896, Ows., @ G. W. Eversole's,
   near Boonev.  (ME-8/14/96; 1900-P)

## BOLES
see BOWLES

## BOLING
see BOWLING

## BOND/BONDS

_____ (___ b.___)
MARY McINTIRE (___ b.___)
pre-1893            (TCS; VKD)
[MARY m2 John "Buster" Bowman - TCS; VKD]
_____ (___ b.___)
SUSAN CATHERINE GIBSON (c14-24 b.KY)  [d/o
Newton Harvey Gibson & Sarah McGeorge -
ob-WS OCN-6/4/54 & 10/14/54; 1880]
1890-1900          (ob-WS; W/NL w/P 1900;
R.East Bernstadt 1954)
FLETCHER (c19 b.Clay)  [s/o Wm. Bond & Sarah
Truett - TCS]
LEAH JEAN WILSON (c19 b.Clay)  [d/o
Rebecca "Beck" Wilson - TCS]
c1850          [DIVORCED] (1860-9, WM w/them;
B-O ch; 1870; "wid" Leah 1880; NL M-C)
[FLETCHER m2 12/30/83 Rockc., Sophia (nee
Noe) Browning - M-R; TCS; 1900Sx-R]
HARVEY HALL (c23 b.KY)  [s/o Oliver Bond
& Lucinda Gum - 1880]
SARAH "SALLY" McINTIRE (c17 b.KY) [d/o Alex
McIntire & Mary Kelly - 1880]
1884/5          (TCS; 1900-C; NL M-C/R)
JOHN C. ["BRECK"] (R.Ows. 19 S b.KY) P/KY
[s/o Oliver Bond & Lucinda Gum - B-O]
[EVALINE] MARRAGET WARREN (R.Ows. 17 S
b.Ows.) P/VA-TN    [d/o Burgoyne Warren
& Priscilla Anderson - TCS; 1860-1870]
1 Nov., 1876, Ows.  [R.Clay 1900 W/as
Evaline; ME-2/19/04 R.Clay]
JOHN WILSON (c20 S b.KY)  [s/o Fletcher Bond
& Lear Wilson - 1880]
MARY ANN HOLCOMB (c18 b.KY)  [d/o Wm.
Holcomb & Eliz. Christian - 1880]
1882/3          (TCS; 1900-R; NL M-R)
[JOHN m2 Susan Barnett; JOHN m3 Sadie
Stewart - TCS]
NATHAN (c18 b.KY)  [s/o Fletcher Bond & Leah
Wilson - 1880]
MARY I[SABELLE] BULLOCK (c15 b.KY)  [1875-
1971 Rockc.; d/o John C. Bullock & Nancy L.
Kinser - TCS]
23 July, 1890 Rockc. @ J. C. Bullock's, by
Dillard Rankin?, MG; wits. F. M. Ponder &
Robt. Buster  (M-R 48:19; TCS; 1900-R)
(Bond cont.)

**BOND (cont.)**

OLIVER (c23 S b.KY) [s/o Wm. Bond & Sarah
    Barwick - 1880; TCS]
    LUCINDA GUM (c20 S b.KY) [d/o Stephen Gum
    & Betsy Cornelius - TCS]
    1855/6        (1860-1870; B-O ch-3/57;
    1880, HP w/them; 1900; wid. Lucinda 1910)
OLIVER P. (R.Ows. 22 S b.Ows) P -- [1851-1904;
    s/o Fletcher Bond & Leah Wilson - 1860; ME-
    3/18/04]
    [LUANNA] LUVENIA BROWNING (R.Ows. 17 S b.
    Harl.) P --    [d/o Sophia Browning - 1870]
    11 Nov., 1877, Ows., @ Sophia Browning's
    [NOTE: poss. s/b md. 187<u>6</u>, as they had ch.
    d. 9/77, which was NL as illegit.; dau.
    Sarah w/HP 1880; W/as Luvenia & Louanna]
ROBERT (c17 S b.KY) [s/o Fletcher Bond
    & Leah Wilson - 1880]
    MARTHA J. TIREY (c18 S b.KY) [d/o Richard
    Marcellis Tirey & Margaret Allen - TCS]
    1893/4        (1900-1910-1920; TCS)
STEPHEN [GUM] (c22 b.KY)    [1866-1939; s/o
    Oliver Bond & Lucinda Gum - 1880; TS-TCS]
    LUCY [ANN] WILSON (c14 b.KY) [1873-1935;
    d/o Alford Wilson & Martha Hamilton - 1880;
    TS-TCS]
    26 Jan., 1888, <u>Clay</u>  (M-C; TCS; 1900-C;
    ME-2/19/04 R.Clay)
WILLIAM A. (c18 S b.KY)  [s/o Oliver Bond
    & Lucinda Gum - 1870]
    NANCY McINTIRE (c15 b.KY) [d/o Alex D.
    McIntire & Polly Kelly - TCS]
    1877/8        (1900; H-NL w/P 1880;
    H-NL 1880)   [H-remd.]
WILLIAM A. (R.Ows. 49 2nd b.Ows.) P/Ows.
    [m1 Nancy McIntire above]
    SARAH BOWMAN (R.Ows. 45 2nd b.Ows.) P/Ows.
    [m1 _____; nee _____]
    15 July, 1909, Ows. [widr. Wm. R.Ows. 1910,
    1920 w/son Alex]

**BOONE**

M[ILTON] R[HODES] D. (R.Proctor 28 S b.Fay.)
    PATSY J. AKERS (R.Ows. 21 S b.KY Riv.)
    [d/o John Akers & Patsy McGuire; d. 1860's]
    9 Feb., 1853, Ows., by G. S. Williams
    [widr. Milton in Lee 1870-1880; Milton
    Rhodes per ob-ch. BE-4/8/43]

## BOOTH/BOOTHE
MATHIAS (c24 b.VA)
    DOLLY _____ (c22 b.KY)
    c1859       (1860, no ch.)
WILLIAM, JR. (c22 b.VA) [1828-1908 - TS-Wlf]
    ELIZABETH "LIZZIE" SHOEMAKER (c17 b.KY)
    [1829-1902 - TS-Wlf]
    1849/50     (1850-MWY; 1870-1880-1900-W;
    DC son-1918)

## BOTNER/BODNER
BENJAMIN (R.Ows. 23 S b.Wash.,VA) [1830-1927;
    s/o James Botner & Eliz. Nunley - REM; TS-
    TCS]
    PHEBA JAMERSON (R.Ows. 18 S b.Est.)
    14 Dec., 1855, Ows.     [Ben R.Owsley 1860,
    no family]   [H-remd.]
BENJAMIN (c34 2nd b.Wash.,VA)     [widr/o Phebe
    Jameson above] [1830-1927]
    MARGARET PATRICK (c17 S b.KY) [1847-1934;
    d/o James Patrick & Mary McGuire - TS-TCS;
    ob-W BE-7/19/34]
    14 Jan., 1865, Ows. (JFB REM; 1870-1880-L;
    to Trav. Rest c1894 ob-W; 1900 m-36; 1910
    m-47; 1920; ob-ch. OCN-9/20/56)
BURGOYNE - see THOMAS BURGOYNE
ELIAS JR. (c25 b.VA) [s/o Elias Botner, Sr.
    & Matilda     ]
    MARY CLARK (c23 b.KY) [d/o Anderson D.
    Clark & Emily B. Murphy - TCS; ME-6/18/97
    says she is cuz/o Judge A. H. Clark]
    c1867     (1870-2; 1880 w/HP)   [MARY m2
    1897 John H. Brandenburg - ME-6/18/97]
GEORGE (25 S Rev. b.Lee) [1880-1972 Lex. V.A.
    hosp.; s/o Ransom Botner & Armina Ketchum -
    P-Sp.Am.; 1900; DC]
    FANNIE JACKSON (c17 b.KY) [1889-1967; d/o
    Rufus Jackson & Margaret Isaacs - 1900;
    TCS; ob-W&F BE-7/13/67, OCN-12/4/53]
    8 March, 1906, Trav.Rest, Ows., by Rev. J.
    B. Rowlett; wits. Palmer Scott & John
    Botner (P-Sp.Am., 1st ch-9/07; ob-WS OCC-
    4/9/37; NL 1910Sx, poss. in OH; M-L ch-
    1926, dau. b. c1909 OH; DC-ch.; R.Lee 1931;
    Idamay 1937; Beattyv. 1953; widr. George
    R.Beattyv. 1972; ob-ch. 3Fks-2/25/98)

(Botner cont.)

**BOTNER (cont.)**

HIRAM (c25 S b.KY) [1873-1928; s/o Ben Botner
   & Margaret Patrick - TR; TS-TCS]
   SUDIE SMITH (c17 S b.KY) P/KY [1882-1940
   - ob-W OCC-12/27/40]
   1898          (1900-8/99, m-1; 1910 m-11;
   1920; ob-W)
ISAAC (26 S b.Lee,VA)     [s/o James Botner
   & Eliz. Nunley - M-Lee,VA; 1850-H]
   SARAH HARBOUR (17 S b.Lee,VA)  [d/o Elias
   Harbour & Eliz.      - M-Lee,VA; 1850-Lee,VA]
   21 Jan., 1858, Lee Co, VA, by V. A. Woodard
   (M-Lee,VA; B-O ch-12/58 Lee,VA; 1870-1880-
   1890; 1900 m-43 crossed out & m-1 put in
   its place; 1910 m1-54, both)
JOHN C. (c20 S b.KY) [1861-1932; s/o James
   Botner - TS-TCS]
   LAURANDA WARREN (c25 S b.VA) [1856-1945;
   d/o Thomas Burgoyne Warren & Priscilla
   Anderson - 1860-1870-1880; TS-TCS]
   1881          (1900 m-18 WF w/them; 1910 m-29;
   ob-ch. OCN-1/19/51]
JOHN E. (c24 S b.Lee) [1870-1961 Boonev.; s/o
   Ben Botner & Margaret Patrick - TR; TS-TCS;
   ob-H&M BE-10/26/61-7/19/34]
   LULA SMITH (c14 S b.KY)  [1881-1922; d/o
   Henry Smith & Mary Roberts - 1900; TS-TCS]
   27 April, 1895, Ows.  [DIV.]  (ME-5/10/95,
   John B Botner & Lucy Smith; 1900 W-md w/P,
   H-NL, son Clyde, 4; ME-7/17/01, John Botner
   s/o Benj. of Trav. Rest shot, has wf & 1
   ch.; 1910 H-remd-8, son Clyde 14; TCS;
   NL M-C)  [LULA m2 Sam Metcalf - TCS]
JOHN H. (R.Trav.Rest; c28 S b.Ows.)  [1869-
   1955; s/o Isaac Botner & Sarah Harber -
   TCS; ob-H OCN-7/14/55]
   BERTHA BOTNER (c16 S b.KY) [1882-1905; d/o
   John Botner & Laurinda Warren - TCS ME-
   12/24/97-ME-6/1/05-6/8/05]
   16 Dec., 1897, Ows. (Thurs.)  (ME-12/24/97;
   1900; TCS; R.Vincent when wf d.)  [H-remd.]


(Botner cont.)

**BOTNER (cont.)**

JOHN E. (c30 2nd b.Lee) [Div/f Lula Smith
   above - TCS] [1870-1961 - TS-TCS]
   MARTHA "MATTIE" McQUEEN (c18 S b.Ows.)
   [1883-1917; d/o Samuel McQueen & Phoebe
   Parsons - TS-TCS]
   1901         (1910 m-8 H-2nd, 1st ch. under
   10 is 8, WF w/them; B-O ch.; TCS; ob-ch.
   HJN-8/91-7/92)    [JOHN m3 c1919, Della
   (nee Lynch) Price - TCS; TR; 1920; ob-H]
JOHN H. (c34 2nd b.Ows.) [widr/o Bertha
   Botner above] [1869-1955]
   CORA FOX (c16 S b.Ows.) [1888-1963; d/o
   Harvey Fox & Sarah BBurg. - TCS; 1900; ob-W
   BE-8/1/63]
   1906/7         (1910-1920; B-O ch.; W-d.
   Trav.Rest)
RANSOM (25 b.VA) [s/o James Botner & Eliz.
   Nunley - 1860]
   ARMINA "ARMY" KETCHUM (23 b.KY) [1851-
   1909 - TS-TCS]
   11 July, 1873, Lee (M-L; 1880-L; 1900
   m-27; TCS; widr. Ransom 1910)
THOMAS BURGOYNE (21 S b.Trav.Rest) [1884-
   1951; s/o John C. Botner & Laurinda P.
   Warren - ob-H OCN-1/19/51]
   NELLIE S. BRANDENBURG (16 S b.Buck Cr.)
   [1889-1965 Lex. hosp.; d/o Wm. B. BBurg. &
   Josephine Glass - TS-TCS; ob-W BE-5/20/65]
   28 Dec., 1905    (ob-H; 1910-1920;
   B-O ch.; ob-ch. BE-3/12/59, BS-4/1/93)
WALLACE (c22 b.Lee,VA) [s/o Isaac Botner
   & Sarah Harber - 1880]
   MARTHA J. _____ (c19 b.KY)
   1881         (1900-L m-19; 1910 m-28; 1920)
WESLEY A. (c24 b.TN) [s/o Elias Botner
   & Matilda      - TCS]
   CYNTHIA E. MINTER (c29 b.VA) [1839-1895;
   d/o Wm. P. Minter & Mary Bailey - TS-TCS]
   c1869         (1870-1880 no ch.; TCS;
   NL M-C; W/as Syntha & Cinda) [H-remd.]


(Botner cont.)

## BOTNER (cont.)

WESLEY A. (c52 2nd b.TN)  [widr/o Cynthia E.
   Minter above - 1880]
   SUSAN A. GABBARD (c28 b.Ows.)  [d/o Hiram
   Gabbard & Hannah Million - 1880]
   c1897      (1900-2/98, widr. Wesley; MT)
   [H-remd.]
WESLEY A. (c58 3rd b.TN)  [widr/o Susan
   Gabbard above]
   AMERICA BURCH (c32 b.KY)  [d/o Newton
   Burch & Mary Hamilton - TCS]
   c1903      (MT; 1910 wid. America; BBG;
   TCS)   [AMERICA m2 James D. Combs - TCS;
   1920]
WILLIAM (c20 b.KY)  [s/o Elias Botner
   & Matilda      - 1870]
   SARAH EVANS (c15 b.KY)  [d/o John Evans
   & Mary Ann Smith - TCS]
   c1870      [DIVORCED]  (H-sgl. 1870;
   Sarah Div. 1880, 1st ch. age 9; TCS)
WILLIAM (c21 b.KY)  [s/o Isaac Botner
   & Sarah Harber - 1880]
   LOUVISA (a/k/a LOUISA) CAUDILL (c13 b.KY)
   [1870-1955; d/o Alford Caudill & Jane
   Simpkins - TCS; CRC; ob-W OCN-6/9/55 as
   Brewer]
   1883/4      (1900; B-O ch. H2)  [LOUVISA
   m2 1909 Joshua Henry Deeds - M-O; 1910;
   LOUVISA m3 Valentine Brewer - 1920; ob-W]

## BOWLES/BOWLS/BOLES

ANDERSON (c21 b.KY)
   EMILY MUNCY (c16 b.IN)
   c1844      (1850-5; B-O ch.; B-J ch-1858;
   1860; 1870-J; widr. Anderson 1880-J; TCS)
ARTHUR (c19 S b.So. Fk.) [s/o Elisha Bowles
   & Catherine Thomas - 1900]
   REBECCA J. (nee SIZEMORE) HUTCH (c32 2nd
   b.So.Fk, Ows.)  [wid/o _____ Hutch]
   [d/o Henderson Sizemore & Nancy J. Gabbard]
   1905/6      (MT; 1910, Hutch s-d; B-O
   ch-1909; 1920; ob-ch. BS-9/25/86-8/12/93)
CHARLES (c31 S b.Jack.)  [see *]
   LIZZIE (nee WILLIAMS) FLANERY (c28 2nd
   b.Jack.)  [m1 _____ Flanery]
   1903      (1910 m-6, Flanery s-d; B-O ch.
   1904; 1920; TCS; NL M-J)  [H-poss. remd.]
(Bowles cont.)

## BOWLES (cont.)

CHARLES (___ 2nd? b.Jack.) [poss. m1 Lizzie
   Williams above] *[1869-1943 Vincent, Ows.;
   s/o Wm. Bowles & Susie Phillips - DC]
   JEMIMA ELIZ. (nee BOWLES) _____ (___ 2nd?
   b.Ows.) [1876-1943/66; d/o Jedediah Bowles
   & Nancy Mary Brewer - ob-WM OCC-8/5/38;
   1880; B-O; NL ob-WS BE-2/17/66; no DC on
   file]
   pre-1938          (ob-WM; R.Vincent 1938;
   wid. Eliz. R.Vincent 1943; NL M-J)
*[NOTE:  Even though this mg. prob. took place
after 1910, I have included it, because I have
been unable to find a 1st mg. for Jemima Eliz.
& it is poss. that there were 2 Charles Bowles
about the same age--one who md. 1903 Lizzie
Williams Flanery & one who md. pre-1900 Jemima
Eliz. Bowles.  My belief is that both Charles
Bowles are the same person, because I find NL
for Charles & Jemima/Mima/Elizabeth in 1910-
1920Sx.]

DANIEL GARRARD (c24 b.KY)  [s/o Wm. Bowles
   & Elizabeth          - 1850]
   MARGARET J. BURNS (c19 b.KY)
   c1857          (1860; MS son d. 1859, age 1;
   REM; B-O ch.; 1870-1880-J; NL M-J)
DAVID (c21 b.KY)  [poss. s/o Elbert Bowles
   & Nancy Hurley - 1880-J]
   LEONA "LONEY" BEGLEY (c17 b.KY)  [d/o
   Granville Begley & Adaline Fulks - 2nd M-L]
   1897/8          (1900; M-L ch-1921;
   NL M-J)  [LONEY (R.Lee 26 b.Ows.) md. 2nd
   8/2/1907 Lee, Elbert Gibson - M-L; 1910-L,
   Bowles s-ch.]
ELISHA (c21 b.Ows.)  ⌊s/o James Bowles
   & Jemima Thomas - 1880]
   MARY CATHERINE THOMAS (c18 b.Ows.)  [d/o
   Elisha Thomas & Eliz. Bowman - TCS]
   1882/3          (1900; B-O ch.; TCS; 1920, H/as
   Elihu; M-L ch-1909; NL M-J)


(Bowles cont.)

**BOWLES (cont.)**

FINLEY (c24 S b.Ows.) [1878-1971 Boonev.; s/o
    Jedediah Bowles & Nancy Brewer - 1880 as
    John; ob-H&M&S BE-1/7/71 as <u>Frank</u> Finley;
    OCC-8/5/38, BE-2/17/66; REM]
    [MARY "LIZZIE"] ELIZ. GRAY (c29 S b.Clay)
    [c1876-1969; d/o Gustavus Gray & Jennie
    Jackson - TCS; ob-W BE-5/1/69]
    17 May, 1905, <u>Clay</u> (M-C file 33; 1910 m-5;
    1920 WM w/them; R.Major 1938, Boonev. 1966;
    widr. R.Boonev. 1969; H/Finley most rec.)
FRANK FINLEY - see FINLEY
GEORGE (c27 S b.Egypt, Jack.) [1861-1951 Lau.;
    s/o Elbert Bowles & Nancy Hurley - TCS;
    ob-H OCN-4/13/51]
    EMILY ABEE MORGAN (R.Jack. c19 S b.Trav.
    Rest) [1870-c1934 - ob-H]
    28 March, 1889, <u>Clay</u> (M-C; 1900-1910-1920;
    B-O ch.; R.Trav. Rest, Ows. until c1941,
    then moved to Laurel Co. - ob-H)
JAMES [DANIEL] (R.Ows. 23 S b.Est.)  [s/o Wm.
    Bowles & Lucy Thomas - 1850]
    LYDIA WILLIAMS (R.Ows. 20 S b.Hawk,TN) [d/o
    Moses Williams & Nancy Wilder - 1850]
    6 March, 1856, Ows.  [R.Owsley 1860-1870]
JAMES M. (R.Sturg. 23 S b.Sturg.)  [s/o Elbert
    Bowles & Nancy Lair - 1850]
    JEMIMA THOMAS (R.White Oak; 17 S b.White
    Oak) [d/o Joseph Thomas & Anna Couch - LNG]
    13 Jan., 1853, Ows., by J. Ward  [R.Owsley
    1860-1870-1880]
JEDEDIAH H. (c19 S b.Ows.) [1855-1932; s/o
    James Bowles & Jemima Thomas - REM]
    NANCY MARY BREWER (c19 S b.Ows.) [1856-
    1938; d/o Wm. Brewer & Elizabeth Cole -
    ob-W OCC-8/5/38]
    1874          (1880-4; 1900 m-25; 1910 m-36;
    B-O ch.; REM; 1920; NL M-J)
JOHN (c23 b.KY)  [s/o Elbert Bowles & Nancy
    Lair - 1850-1860]
    SYLVANIA PHILLIPS (c17 b.KY)  [d/o Bright
    Phillips & Mary Gum - 1850-E; 1860-J; TCS]
    c1865          (1870-E-4; 1880-14; TCS;
    NL 1900Sx; NL M-E/J)
JOHN FINLEY - see FINLEY

(Bowles cont.)

69

**BOWLES (cont.)**
JOHN (c25 2nd lister st-mill b.KY)  [ml _____
  _____]
  ROSE (nee BECKLEY) MASON (c25 2nd b.KY)
  [ml _____ Mason]
  1909/10          (1910, Mason s-ch.; BC
  ch-1911-1919 Jeff.; NL 1920Sx; NL M-J)
NATHAN (R.Ows. 21 S b.Ows.) P/Ows. [1888-1966;
  s/o Jedediah Bowles & Nancy Brewer - 1900;
  ob-H&M BE-2/17/66, OCC-8/5/38]
  CORA [BELLE] BLAKE (R.Ows. 18 S b.Ows.) P/
  Ows. [d/o Wm. Blake & Margaret J. Wolfe -
  1900; VKD]
  1 June, 1908, Ows. [R.Owsley 1910-1920;
  Franklin, OH 1938-66 when H-d.]
THOMAS (R.Ows. 22 S b.Est.) [s/o Wm. Bowles
  & Lucy Ann Thomas - 1850]
  ANN HEDRIX [HENDRICK] (R.Ows. 17 S b.uk)
  [d/o John Hendrick & Tempy Cooper - TCS]
  1852 (no date), Ows. [NOTE: md. early in
  year, because son b. 12/52; R.Jackson Co.
  1860; B-J ch-1859 W/as Hendricks]
WILLIAM T. (c19 b.KY)
  SUSAN PHILLIPS (c16 b.KY) [c1832-1869
  Jack.]
  c1848          (1850-1; 1860-11; TCS; BC
  son Charles b. 4/1869 Jack.) [H-remd.]
WILLIAM T. (c40 2nd b.KY) [widr/o Susan
  Philips above]
  MARY [nee WOODS] SPARKS (c44 2nd b.KY)
  [wid/o Robert Sparks] [c1825-1870's]
  1 Feb., 1870 (ML), Jackson Co.; bm. groom &
  J. H. Bowles (MC-NFI)  (M-J 2:329; 1870-J,
  Sparks s-ch.; widr. Wm. 1880-J)
WILLIAM (c21 b.Ows.) [James M. Bowles
  & Jemima Thomas - 1870]
  RHODA SMITH (c17 b.Clay) P/TN-KY
  c1875          (1880; B-O ch-3/76; NL M-C/J)
**BOWLING/BOWLIN/BOLIN/BOWLAIN**
ALBERT (R.Benge; 21 S b.Clay) P/Br-Clay
  CALLIE SPICER (R.Annville; 22 S b.Jack.)
  21 March, 1901, Jackson @ E. Pennington's
  (M-J BB 11:424; TCS; 1910; 1920; ob-ch.
  Rich.,IN 6/1/97)

(Bowling cont.)

**BOWLING (cont.)**

ALFRED (c22 S b.KY)   [1858-1937; s/o Eli
    Bowling & Ibby Baker/Woods - TS-TCS]
    LUCY JANE EDWARDS (c23 S b.KY) [1857-1942;
    d/o Jackson Edwards & Nancy Combs - TS-TCS]
    late 1880      (1900 m-19; 1910 m-30; TCS;
    H-sgl w/Abel Gabbard 1880; 1920)
ANDREW J. (20 S b.KY) [1873-1923; s/o Wm.
    Bowling & W2 Sarah Jane Baker - 1880;
    TS-TCS]
    SUSAN BAKER (18 S b.KY) [d/o Black Bob
    Baker & Mary Gabbard - TCS; NSB]
    11 Dec., 1893, <u>Breathitt</u> @ Mary Baker's,
    by John B. Lewis; wits. Wm. Eversole &
    M. Baker  (M-B 6:261; HTB; 1900 m-6; 1910
    m-"18")
BUCHANAN - see JAMES BUCHANAN
ELI (c18 b.KY) [s/o Eli Bowling Sr. - TCS]
    ISABELLE "IBBY" WOODS a/k/a BAKER (c22
    b.KY) [d/o wid. Rebecca (nee Wilson)
    WOODS, prob. by Andy "Pandy" BAKER - JFB;
    NVP]
    24 July, 1851      (MT; TCS; Ibby WOODS,
    sgl. 1850; B-O ch-6/52, W/as Ibby BAKER;
    1860; wid. Ibby 1870-1880-1890; NL M-C)
ELI (R.Ows. 25 S b.KY) P/KY   [d/o Wm. Bowling
    & W1 Edith Woods - 1860 w/F]
    CATHERINE HORNSBY (R.Ows 26 S b.KY) P/KY
    [d/o Job Hornsby & Cath. Gabbard -1860-70]
    25 Jan., 1879, Ows.   [R.Owsley 1880;
    moved to Ham.,OH - HTB]
FINLEY - see FRANK FINLEY
FRANK FINLEY (c22 S b.Ricetown) [1873-1942;
    s/o Thomas BARRETT & Ibby (nee Baker/Woods)
    wid/o Eli BOWLING - 1880; LNG]
    LOU ANN PALMER (c15 S b.Eversole) [1881-
    1959; d/o Andy Palmer, Nancy Reynolds -LNG]
    1895/6        (1900-L; 1910-1920; B-O ch.;
    MT; LNG's H-GP; ob-ch.BS-3/17/88, HJN-4/94,
    Rich,IN-11/19/96; H/as Finley in most
    records)
GRAHAM (c22 b.KY)
    NANCY HACKER (c18 b.KY)
    11 Sept., 1848 (ML) <u>Clay</u>  (M-C; 1850)


(Bowling cont.)

71

## BOWLING (cont.)

GREEN A. (R.Tallega, Lee ___ mcht. b.___)
ETTA BELL ROSE (R.Meadow Cr., Ows. c18 S
b.KY) [d/o Green B. Rose & Jane Cawood -
TCS; ME-12/10/97; ob-WS BE-12/20/60]
2 Dec., 1897, Ows., @ home of G. B. Rose,
Meadow Cr., near Boonev., by Bro. C. S.
Markin    (ME-12/10/97; NL 1900/L;
R.Lancaster, Garrard Co. 1960)

ISAAC (c31 b.KY) [1871-1908; s/o Wm. Bowling
& W2 Sarah Jane Baker - 1880; TCS; D-O]
SARAH SANDLIN (c21 b.KY)
1891/2      (1900; wid. Sarah 1910; TCS;
ob-ch. BS-9/11/86-9/17/92-11/11/93)
[SARAH m2 c1912 John "Flat Belly" Baker -
1920; BBG]

ISAAC (c20 S b.KY) [1873-1942; s/o James
Buchanan Bowling & Elizabeth Barrett -
1880; TS-TCS]
LULIE B. HUFF (___ b.KY)
c1894      (H-remd-1 1900-5, 2 ch. listed,
W2 1/1 ch.; TCS)

ISAAC (c22 2nd b.KY) [widr/o Lulie B. Huff
above]    [1873-1942 - TS-TCS]
LIEDORA "DORA" MARSHALL (c27 S b.KY) [1871-
1959; d/o Joseph Marshall & Rebecca Thomas
- ob-W BE-4/16/59; 1880]
1899      (1900 m-1; 1910 m-10; TCS;
1920; ob-ch. BS-11/20/86-1/4/90)

JAMES BUCHANAN (c18 b.Ows.) [1854-1900 Ows.;
s/o Eli Bowling & Isabelle Baker/Woods -
MT; WTM]
ELIZABETH BARRETT (c15 b.Clay) [d/o
Thomas Barrett & Barbara Gabbard - TCS]
c1872      (TCS; 1880-5; B-O ch.; "wid."
Eliz. 1900; NL M-C)   [ME-2/21/02: Bolin
paroled from prison for the killing of Luke
Callahan c1884; staying w/bro. Lincoln @
Eversole, in poor health]

JAMES (c25 b.Ows.) [s/o Wm. Bowling & W1 Edy
Woods]
MARY ANN BAKER (c28 b.Clay) [1845-1901;
d/o John Baker & Lucinda Amis - 1850; JTB]
c1873      (1880-6; B-O ch.; NL M-C)
[JAMES m2 Charlene Couch - HTB; 1910-P]

(Bowling cont.)

**BOWLING (cont.)**
LEANDER "LEE" (c19 b.KY) [s/o Alfred Bowling
   & Lucy Jane Edwards - 1900]
   MARY BELL PALMER (R.Lymonds Cr., Lee c16 S
   b.KY) [d/o Andrew Palmer & Sarah "Nannie"
   Reynolds - 1900-L; ob-WM OCC-2/16/40]
   July, 1902      (ME-7/18/02; 1910-L;
   R.Lone 1940)
LINCOLN (c23 S b.KY) [1866-1929; s/o Ibby (nee
   Woods/Baker) wid/o Eli Bowling - 1880; TCS]
   MARGARET "MAGGIE" REYNOLDS (c19 S b.KY)
   [1869-1947; d/o John S. Reynolds & Eliz.
   Gabbard - TS-TCS]
   1888/9      (1900 w/WP; MT; ME-2/21/02;
   1910 WF w/them; 1920; OCC-2/16/40)
MACK - see McCOY
McCOY "MACK" (c23 S b.Br.)
   PATSY GILBERT (c20 b.KY) [d/o Aquilla
   Gilbert & Susan Mann - 1870-L; TCS]
   16 Nov, 1870, <u>Lee</u>  (M-L) [H-remd.]
[McCOY] MACK (R.Br. 30 2nd b.Br.) P/--
   [widr/o Patsy Gilbert above]
   SARAH JANE FREEMAN (R.Br. 22 S b.Br.) P/
   Clay-TN [1857-1918 Ows. - TS-TCS]
   22 Dec., 1877, <u>Breathitt</u>  (M-B; 1880-B;
   1900 m-21; ob-ch. OCN-6/5/58; FH-ch-1967)
WM. M. "OLD SPECK" (c19 S b.Clay) [1828-1895;
   s/o Eli Bowling & Nancy Herd - TS-TCS]
   EDITH WOODS a/k/a BAKER (c18 b.KY) [c1828-
   1854; d/o Rebecca (nee Wilson) Woods, prob.
   by Andy "Pandy" Baker - NVP; D-O M/as
   Rebecca WOODS]
   c1846      (1850-3; widr. Wm. 1860; NL M-C)
   [H-remd.]
WILLIAM M. "OLD SPECK" (c42 2nd b.Clay)
   [widr/o Edy Woods/Baker above] [1828-1895]
   SARAH JANE BAKER [RILEY] (c25 2nd b.Ows.)
   [m1 Granville Riley - LM; DC-ch.] [1845-
   1931; d/o John Hammonds "Mucker Jack" Baker
   & Lucinda Amis - 1860; JTB]
   c1870      (1880, last Baker ch-11, next
   Bowling ch-9; DC ch-1954, Maxaline Riley
   b. 1866 Ows.; photo N-C-11/96 HTB; NL M-C)
   [SARAH m3 1910, Enoch Abner - REM; HTB]

(Bowling cont.)

**BOWLING (cont.)**
WILLIAM B. (c21 S b.KY)  [1875-1968; s/o
    James Bowling & Eliz. Barrett - 1880; TCS;
    ob-H BE-8/8/68]
    MALINDA "LINDA" MARSHALL (c21 S b.KY)
    [1877-1972; d/o Jos. Marshall & W2 Rebecca
    Thomas - TCS; 1880; ob-WS BE-8/12/65-
    5/30/68-4/16/59]
    1898/9        (1900 m-10, but s/b m-1 or m-0,
    no ch.; 1910 m-11; 1920; R.Ricetown 1959;
    R.Boonev. 1965-68; ob-ch. BS-4/14/88)
**BOWMAN**
    _____ (___ b.___)
    ELIZABETH ROSS (c14 <u>Mul</u> b.KY)  [d/o Levi
    Ross (<u>Mul</u>) & Sarah Burns (white) - 1870,
    Eliz. age 4]
    c1870          (1880, 2 Bowman Gch. w/Levi
    & Sarah, John F. 7 <u>Mul</u> 7 & Cora 4 <u>w</u>)
    [NOTE: census show Levi & Sarah's daus. to
    be Mary J. (c1843), Eliz. (c1856), Lucy Ann
    (c1859), & Sarah M. (c1862).  The only 2
    poss. are Mary & Eliz.  The other 2 are too
    young & @ home 1870-80. TCS & B-O ch. have
    Mary md. Bonaparte Pritchard, thus Eliz.
    md. Bowman by process of elimination.]
    _____ (___ b.___)
    MELISSA NEWMAN (c14-24 b.KY)  [d/o Daniel
    B. Newman & Sarah Minerva Venable - ob-WM
    OCN-2/17/50; 1880]
    1890-1900          (ob-WM; W-NL w/M 1900;
    R.Lebanon, OH 1950)
ABSALUM (c22 b.KY)  [s/o Thomas Bowman, Sr.
    & Mary Moore - REM]
    MARIAH HUNT (c20 b.TN)
    c1844          (1850-5; WGO)
A[DDISON] D. (c31 S b.KY)  [s/o Thomas Bowman
    & Mariam Morris - TCS]
    LINDA MORRIS (___ b.___)
    15 Oct., 1884, <u>Jackson</u>; groom & John Farmer
    Jr., bm.  (M-J BB 5:195; TCS) [H-remd.]
ADDISON (c40 2nd b.KY)  [m1 Linda Morris abv.]
    KATE MOORE (c21 b.KY)
    1893/4          (1900-1910-1920; TCS)
ALBERT - see WM. ALBERT

(Bowman cont.)

## BOWMAN (cont.)

ANDREW JACKSON (c19 b.Br.) [1843-1916; s/o
   Joseph Bowman & Cynthia Crawford - 1860-B;
   art. BE-3/29/62]
   NANCY JANE EVANS (c18 b.Br.) [d/o Henry
   Evans & Lucinda Hanks - JSG; art. BE-3/62]
   1862, poss. <u>Breathitt</u> (MNC; moved to Bear
   Creek after their mg. - art. BE; 1870-
   1880-L; B-L ch.; 1900-L m-38; 1910-L m-47;
   ob-ch. OCC-12/24/37)
A[NDREW] J[ACKSON "JACK"] (c27 S b.KY) [1848-
   1940; s/o Thomas Bowman & Mariam Morris -
   TS-TCS]
   PAULINA WITT (c16 b.KY) [d/o Robert Witt
   & Polly         - 1860-1870-E]
   10 Dec., 1875, <u>Estill</u>, bm. groom & Robt.
   Witt (M-E; 2nd M-O 1878; TCS) [H-remd.]
ANDREW J[ACKSON "JACK"] (R.Ows. 30 2nd b.KY)
   P/KY [widr/o Pauline Witt above]
   NANCY J. MARSH [LANE] (R.Ows. 33 2nd b.TN)
   P/TN [wid/o John LANE - D-O 1877]
   2 Dec., 1878, Ows. [R.Owsley 1880-1900]
BENT - see GARRETT BENTON
CARTER - see LANDON CARTER
CHARLES SUTTON (c16 S b.KY) [1875-1916; s/o
   Major Wm. Simpson Bowman & Mary Stephens -
   1880; ob-W; killed by a horse - LNG & SE]
   MARGARET COOMER (c17 S b.KY) [c1874-1955;
   d/o Isaac Newton Coomer & Christina
   Hollingsworth - LNG; ob-W OCN-2/24/55 as
   Bowman]
   1891/2 Ows. (1900-1910; LNG; wid. Margaret
   1920; ob-ch. BS-3/31/88; M-O ch-1931)
   [MARGARET m2 Thomas Gabbard; MARGARET m3
   Chesley Young - LNG SE]
CHARLEY (R.Ows. 25 S b.Ows.) P/Ows-VA [s/o
   Wilburn Bowman & Mary McPherson - ob-HS BE-
   1/20/38]
   IDA FOX (R.Lee 20 S b.Ows.) P/Br-TN [d/o
   James Fox & Elizabeth Gilbert - TCS]
   14 Aug., 1899, <u>Lee</u> to be md. @ James B.
   Fox's (M-L 5:425; 1900 N#L, 0 ch.; 1910
   m-11; TCS; M-L dau. 1918; R.WV 1938)


(Bowman cont.)

**BOWMAN (cont.)**
CHRISTOPHER COLUMBUS (c20 b.KY) [s/o Thos.
    Bowman & Mariam Morris - KAS]
    MARTHA B. LANE (c14 b.KY) [d/o John Lane
    & Nancy Marsh - 1880 w/M & s-F]
    Dec., 1886 (ML), Ows. (ME-1/14/87; TCS;
    H-remd-0 1900)
CHRISTOPHER COLUMBUS (c33 2nd b.KY) [m1 Martha
    B. Lane above]
    MELISSA (nee DALTON) HANDY (c24 2nd b.KY)
    [wid/o J. W. Handy - ME] [poss. d/o Sam
    Dalton & Sarah Clark - TCS]
    1899/1900       (1900, s-s HANDY-9/97; TCS;
    ME-3/8/01 C C. Bowman of Cross Roads, who
    lately returned from Ark. & md. wid/o J. W.
    Handy, took his departure last week for
    Lex., where he joined regular army & will
    soon be off for Phillipines)
CLIFTON (R.Ows. 24 S b.KY) P/KY [s/o Henry
    Bowman & Eliz. Roberts - B-O]
    MARY ANN SAWYERS (R.Ows. 26 S b.KY) P.NC-KY
    13 March, 1878, Ows. [R.Owsley 1880]
    [CLIFTON m2 5/12/89, Mary Lee Philpot -
    M-C; 1900-C m-11]
CORNELIUS ["CROSS EYED NEAL"] (R.Ows. 28 S
    b.Clay) [s/o John Bowman & Eliz. McCollum
    - 1850]
    MAHALA PENNINGTON (R.Ows. 23 S b.Br.) [d/o
    James Pennington & Catherine    - TCS]
    6 Aug., 1857, Ows. [R.Owsley 1860-1870]
CORNELIUS "NEAL RAIL-SPLITTER" (c23 b.Ows)
    [1846-1927; s/o Wm. Bowman & Nancy Boles -
    ARS; TS-TCS]
    SARAH McVEY (c23 b.Knox) [d/o Hiram McVey
    & Mary A. Powell - ARS]
    Oct., 1869       (1870; 1880-J; 1900; B-O
    ch.)   [H-remd.]
CORNELIUS "NEAL RAIL-SPLITTER" (c55 2nd b.
    Ows.) [widr/o Sarah McVey above]
    SARAH F. (nee ROWLETT) FLANERY (c39 2nd
    b.KY) [wid/o R. P. Flanery] [1865-1942;
    d/o Jesse B. Rowlett & Eliza Jane Jones -
    1880; OCC-7/31/36 W-71st Bday; TS-TCS]
    1903/4       (1910, Flanery s-ch; 1920; ARS;
    wid. Sarah Flanery 1900; OCN-5/8/52; TCS)

(Bowman cont.)

**BOWMAN (cont.)**
CURTIS - see LOWELL CURTIS
DANIEL (c22 b.KY) [s/o Thomas Bowman & Mariam
   Morris - TCS; 1850]
   ELIZABETH J. FLOYD (c21 b.TN)
   1867/8        (1870 no ch.; TCS; 1880-J;
   1900, Floyd SiL w/them; W/as Isabella &
   Elizabeth 2x)
DAVID "GRAY DAVE" (22 2nd b.Ows.) [m1 _____
   Chandler - TCS] [1845-1911; s/o Julius
   HACKER & Eliz. (nee McCollum), wid/o John
   BOWMAN - MJC]
   MARTHA ANN BOWMAN (18 b.Ows.) [1848-1935;
   d/o Squire Felix Bowman & Rhoda Morris -
   MJC]
   15 July, 1867, Ows. (TCS; 1870-3; 1880;
   B-O ch.; MJC; NL M-J)
DAVID (c21 b.KY) [s/o Robert Bowman & Nancy
   Morris - 1870]
   SILVANIA THOMAS (c13 b.Blake, Ows.) [d/o
   Levi Thomas & Eliz. Sizemore - 1880]
   1883/4        (1900; widr. David 1910, HM
   w/him; widr. David 1920)
DAVID BROWNLOW (c24 S b.KY)
   MINERVA JANE BOTNER (c18 S b.KY)
   1905/6        (1910-1920 as David & Janie;
   BC 1918 W/as Janie; TCS)
ELIHU (c22 S b.KY) [s/o Henry Bowman & Rachel
   Plummer - 1860; JSG; REM]
   MARY JANE WOODWARD (c25 S b.VA) [d/o Martin
   B. Woodward & Louisa Marcum - TCS; 1860]
   1864/5        (1870-3; 1880-1900-1910-L;
   TCS; JSG)
ELISHA B. (c19 b.Ows.) [s/o Elisha Bowman
   & Mahulda Phillips]
   SALLY HOGG (c19 b.KY)
   c1875        (1880-4, w/HP; TCS)
ELISHA (c16-25 b.KY) [s/o Wm. Bowman
   & Margaret Murrell - 1880]
   ANGELINA _____ (___ b.___)
   1891-1900    (TCS; H-NL w/P 1900;
   NL 1900Sx; H-remd-2 1910, no ch. over 10)


(Bowman cont.)

**BOWMAN (cont.)**

ELISHA (R.Lee 30 "S" Tmbr; b.Lee) P/Ows.
  [widr/o Angelina _____ above]
  [MARTHA] JANE BARRETT [McINTOSH] (R.Lee 23
  2nd b.--) P/-- [m1 Presley McIntosh - M-O
  1904] [c1885-1957 Ows.; d/o Peeley Barrett
  & Emeline Vires - ob-W OCN-2/21/57; DC]
  12 April, 1908, Lee @ S. McIntosh's (M-L;
  1910 McIntosh s-s 4; TCS; BC 3/11; 1920-L
  W/as Martha; M-L ch-1938; ob-ch. BE-
  12/11/69, BS-9/19/91)

ENOCH (c26 S b.TN) [s/o John Bowman & Mary
  Wilmont - TCS]
  MALVINA JUDD (c21 b.NC) [c1828-1855; d/o
  Rowland Judd & Fanny Johnson - TCS; D-O]
  c1849         (1850-5 mos.; B-O ch.; their
  dau. Melvina 4, w/Judd GP 1860; TCS; W/as
  Alviney, Malinda, & Malvina 2x)
  [ENOCH m2 Margaret Estes; went to MO - TCS]

GARRETT BENTON "BENT" (c26 S b.Ows.) [s/o Levi
  L. Bowman & Eliz. Turner - 1880; 3rd M-O]
  TELERY J[ULIA] CRANK (c20 b.KY) [c1875-
  1901; d/o James R. Crank & Martha J.
  - 1880]
  1894/5        (1900 w/HM; TCS; ME-12/27/01
  Mrs. Julia Bowman W/o Bent of Bowman Br.,
  died, leaving 2 sm. ch., bur. near Boonev.
  - 1910 shows Telery left 2 sm. ch.)
  [H-remd.]

GARRETT BENTON ["BENT"] (R.Ows. 33 2nd b.Ows.)
  P/Ows. [widr/o Telery Crank above]
  JULIA [nee MORRIS] WARREN (R.Ows. 48 2nd
  b.Ows) P/Ows. [wid/o Matt Warren - 1900]
  [d/o John Morris & Julia Phipps - TCS]
  22 Nov., 1903, Ows. [R.Owsley 1910-1920]
  [G. B. (59 widr. b.Ows.) m3 11/25/1931,
  Sarah M(argaret) Hartsock (26 S b.Ows.;
  d/o Millard Hartsock & Louisa) - M-O]

GEORGE (c22 b.KY)
  MARY BOND (c17 b.KY) [d/o Fletcher Bond
  & Lear Wilson - 1880]
  1883/4         (REM; Mary NL w/M 1900;
  NL 1900Sx for Geo.; 1910-Rockc. m1-26;
  NL M-Rockc.)

(Bowman cont.)

**BOWMAN (cont.)**

GEORGE - see GREENBERRY GEORGE
GRANT (c18 b.KY) [1875-1968 - ob-H BE-6/6/68]
   LUCY WILSON (c24 b.Ows.) [1869-1937; d/o
   Robt. Wilson & Martha Eversole - ob-W OCC-
   2/12/37; 1880]
   1893/4          (1900; ob-W)
GREEN (c22 b.Ows.) [s/o Henry Bowman & Rachel
   Plummer - 1860]
   ELIZABETH JONES (c17 b.Ows.) [d/o Matt
   Jones & Eliza Jane Estes]
   c1866          (1870-L-3; B-L ch.)
GREENBERRY GEORGE (c25 S b.Wlf) [1877-1957;
   s/o Major Wm. Simpson Bowman & Mary Stevens
   - 1880; ob-H OCN-1/31/57]
   SUSAN YOUNG (c17 S b.Ows.) [c1895-1969
   Nursing Home, Richmond - ob-W BE-12/4/69]
   1901/2          (1910-1920; B-O ch.)
HARVEY (c32 b.Ows.)
   MELISSA J. MOORE (c20 b.KY) [d/o Hardin
   Moore & Polly Ann Gabbard - 1880]
   c1880          (1880 has Harvey Bowman, 32,
   lab., w/WP, Melissa Moore, 20, listed after
   Harvey. I suspect they were md. around the
   time this census was taken; M-L ch-1911,
   son Hardie b. c1886 Lee; NL 1900/L)
HENRY CLAY (c26 b.Clay) [c1825-1865 CW; s/o
   Nicholas Bowman & Isabelle Moore - MNC]
   MARY [POLLY ANN] LAWSON (c24 b.Morg.)
   [1827-1895 Lee; d/o John Lawson & Mary
   - JAB]
   21 Dec., 1851, _Morgan_ (M-Morg.; 1860)
HENRY (24 S b.KY) [1845-1919; s/o Wm. Bowman
   & Nancy Boles - TS-TCS]
   ELIZABETH JANE McVEY (19 S b.KY) [1850-
   1913; d/o Hiram McVey & Mary A. Powell -
   ARS; TS-TCS]
   22 Nov., 1869, Ows. (TCS; 1870; 1880-1890-
   1900-1910; ARS)


(Bowman cont.)

79

**BOWMAN (cont.)**
HENRY (c19 S b.Ows.) [s/o Cornelius Bowman
   & Sarah McVey - TCS]
   MARTHA MATHIS (c19 S b.KY) [d/o James
   Mathis & Nancy J. Lamb - TCS; 1880]
   1895/6     (1900-1910-1920; TCS; ob-ch.
   BS-6/8/95-12/17/98; ob-ch. BS-11/17/88 as
   Martha <u>Mathew</u>)   [HENRY (R.Sturg. 64 widr
   b.Ows.) m2 6/12/41 Lucy (Turner) Woods (37
   wid. b.Ows.) d/o Jesse Turner & Lou (Spivy)
   - M-O]
ISAAC (c21 b.Ows.) [s/o Squire Bowman & Rhoda
   Morris]
   MARY J. HENSLEY (c23 b.KY) P/NC
   c1874     (1880-5; B-O ch.; TCS)
JACK - see ANDREW JACKSON
JACKSON - see ANDREW JACKSON
JACOB (c17 b.KY) [s/o Jacob Bowman & Eleanor
   Evans - JSG]
   ELIZABETH PHILLIPS (c16 b.KY)
   c1845     (1850-4; B-O ch.; moved to
   Grant Co., KY in 1850's - JSG)
JACOB "JAKE" (c20 S b.KY) [1882-1950; s/o
   Robert S. Bowman & Dicey Jane Peters - ob-H
   OCN-8/18/50]
   EMILY McGUIRE (c<u>36</u> S b.Lee) [1866-1937;
   d/o Arch McGuire & Helen Treadway - 1880;
   ob-W&S OCC-5/5/37 & JT-3/24/22]
   20 May, 1902    (ob-H; 1910-1920; MT; BBG;
   R.Endwell, Ows. 1922 & 1938; ob-ch. BS-
   8/6/87-11/12/87)
JAMES (21 S b.Ows.) [s/o James Bowman & C.
   - mg.]
   MILDRED KIRK (21 S b.Lee,VA) [d/o Leroy
   Kirk & Catherine    - mg.; 1850-Lee,VA]
   22 Sept., 1864, <u>Lee Co., VA</u>, by James
   Shelbourne   (M-Lee, VA)
JAMES "BLUING RAG" (c26 S b.KY) [s/o Thomas
   Bowman & Mariam Morris]
   HANNAH BLAKE (c15 S b.TN) [d/o Wm. Blake
   & W2 Caroline Wolfe - VKD; 1880]
   1882     (1900 m-18; 1910 m-27; VKD;
   TCS/James' GD)


(Bowman cont.)

## BOWMAN (cont.)

JAMES A. (c20 S b.KY)  [s/o Andrew Jackson
    Bowman & Nancy Marsh - 1880]
    FRANKIE KELLY (c19 S b.KY)  [d/o Francis
    Kelly & Fanny Sparks - ob-WS OCN-5/31/56;
    TCS; P/M-C]
    21 Aug., 1899, <u>Clay</u>  (M-C; 1900 m-0;
    1910Sx-J; ob-ch. BS-7/30/92)
JEREMIAH M. (R.uk 40 S b.uk)
    MATILDA PARNEL (R.Ows. 36 wid. b.Mad)
    15 April, 1852, Ows.
JESSE (28 S b.KY)  [s/o Wilburn Bowman & Mary
    McPherson - TCS; ob-HS BE-1/20/38]
    HAZEL WOODWARD (14 S b.KY)  [d/o Steven
    Woodward & Nancy Catherine Woods - ob-WS
    OCN-6/20/57]
    Jan/Feb., 1900          (1900 m-4 mos.;
    1910 m-10; TCS; R.Hlbg. 1938; Cincinnati,
    OH 1957)
JOHN ["BUSTER"] (R.Ows. 20 S b.Ows) P/Ows.
    [s/o Levi Bowman & Eliz. Turner - 1870]
    EMILY FOREMAN (R.Ows. 19 S b.Ows) P/-- [d/o
    Jos. Foreman & Malinda Hollingsworth -1870]
    16 June, 1874, Ows., @ Joseph Foreman's
    [John w/P 1880]      [H-remd.]
JOHN [H.] (R.Ows. 20 S b.KY) P/--
    SARAH E. BOWLES (R.Ows. 18 S b.Ows.) P/Clay
    [d/o Dan Bowles & Margaret Burns - B-O]
    25 Jan., 1876, Ows., @ Daniel Bowles'
    (a/L 1/2<u>8</u>/187<u>7</u>, HP/KY, W&P/KY, @ D. G.
    Bowles', rest same)    [R.Owsley 1880-2]
    [H-remd.]
JOHN (c26 b.Ows.)  [s/o Henry Bowman & Eliz.
    Roberts - 1880]
    SARAH PENDERGRASS (c22 b.KY)  [d/o Corda
    Pendergrass & Minerva Thompson - 1880;
    ob-WS OCC-7/2/37]
    1886/7        (1900 HF w/them; TCS; M-L ch-
    1911; R.Delvinta 1939)
JOHN R. S. "BUSTER" (c31-44 2nd b.Ows.)
    [m1 Emily Foreman above]
    MARY (nee McINTIRE) BOND (___ 2nd b.___)
    [m1 _____ Bond - TCS]
    1880-93      (TCS; BBG; John w/P 1880,
    age 31)    [H-remd. 1900]

(Bowman cont.)

**BOWMAN (cont.)**

JOHN P. (c18 S b.KY)   [s/o Wm. Bowman
   & Margaret Murrell - 1880; 2nd M-O]
   EMILY OSBORNE (c16 S b.KY) [d/o Andrew
   Osborne & America Moore - 1880]
   1889        (1900 m-11; 1910 m-20; TCS;
   their dau. Maggie w/Osborne GP 1900)
   [JOHN (R.Lone 66 widr. b.Ows.) m2 4/22/37
   Elora (Murrell) Roberts (45 wid.) - M-O]
JOHN R. S. "BUSTER" (c45 3rd b.KY) [m2 Mary
   McIntire above]
   CHALISTA NEWMAN (c20 b.Lee) [d/o Henry
   Harrison Newman Jr. & Mary Pardington -
   TCS; REM; 1880]
   c1894        (BBG; 1900; TCS; REM)
JOHN (c41 2nd b.KY)  [widr/o Sarah E. Bowles
   above]
   MARTHA (nee _____) _____ (c25 2nd b.KY)
   1896/7        (1900 m-3 W-4/4 ch., youngest
   4 were: 9, 7, 3 & 7 mo.; NL 1910Sx)
JOHN T. (37 S b.Boonev.)  [1860-1938; s/o
   Robert Bowman & Mary Turner - 1880; ob-H
   OCC-3/18/38]
   SALLY ANN ABSHEAR (c27 S b.Boonev.)  [d/o
   Isaac Abshear & Mary Eagle - 1880]
   9 Oct., 1897        (ob-H; B-O ch.; 1900-
   1910; ob-ch. BS-7/9/87 & HJN-2/92)
JOHN H. (c26 S b.Boonev.)  [s/o Major Wm.
   Simpson Bowman & Mary A. Stephens - 1880]
   MINERVA J. MASON (c16 S b.Br.)  [d/o David
   Mason & Amy Little - ob-WS BE-12/14/61]
   1897/8        (1900-1910-1920; B-O ch.;
   M-O son 1960; R.Boonev. 1961)
JOHN HIRAN (c17 S b.Ows.)  [1882-1971; s/o
   Henry Bowman & Eliz. McVey - 1900; ob-H&S
   BE-4/1/71-3/4/65]
   NANNIE BOTNER (c18 S b.KY) [d/o Ransom
   Botner & Armina Ketchum - TCS]
   1900        (H-sgl. 1900; 1910-5, m-10;
   1920; TCS; R.Ham.,OH 1965; ob-ch. BS-
   4/21/88, HJN-10/91-2/9/98)


(Bowman cont.)

**BOWMAN (cont.)**

JOHN [B.] (R.Ows. 24 S b.Ows.) P/Ows. [1879-
1938; s/o Robert S. Bowman & Dicey Jane
Peters - MT; 1900; TS-TCS]
MARY E[LLEN] BOWMAN (R.Ows. 18 S b.Ows.)
P/Ows. [1886-1965; d/o Henry Bowman & Eliz.
McVey - ARS; TS-TCS; ob-W BE-3/4/65]
10 Dec., 1903, Ows. [ML 12/03 - ME-1/15/04;
R.Owsley 1910-1920]
JOHN S. (c59 2nd b.KY) [m1 _____]
SARAH (nee _____) _____ (c51 2nd b.KY)
[m1 _____]
1907/8          (1910)
JOSEPH W. (c21-38 S b.KY)  [s/o Thomas Bowman
& Mariam Morris - TCS]
_____ (___ b.___)
1880-96          (H-remd. 1900-1910)
JOSEPH W. (c39 2nd b.KY) [widr/o _____
above]
MARTHA BOWMAN (c21 S b.KY)  [d/o Wilburn
Bowman, Mary McPherson -ob-WS BE-1/20/38]
7 Aug, 1897 <u>Lee</u> @ bride's home; wits. H. S.
& J. B. Barrett  (M-L; 1900 m-2; 1910 m-14;
R.IN 1938)
LANDON CARTER (c19 S b.KY)  [1865-1955 Ows;
s/o Henry Bowman & Rachel Plummer - BBG;
1880; ob-H OCN-6/16/55]
LOU ELLEN MOYERS (c21 S b.KY)  [1864-1910;
d/o Owen Moyers & Lucy Stewart - BBG 1880]
7 Jan, 1886     (BBG from Landon's GD Ella
Bowman Addison; 1900-1910; TCS; ob-H)
[LANDON m2 3/21/12, Jane Hartsock (1871-
1957) - BBG from his GD Ella Bowman
Addison; 1920; ob-W OCN-2/7/57]
LETCHER - see LEVI LETCHER
LEVI (c19 S b.KY)  [s/o Cornelius Bowman
& Eliz. Moore]
ELIZABETH TURNER (c18 S b.KY)  [d/o John
Turner & Tempy Reynolds]
c1845          (1850-4; B-O ch.; 1860-1870;
wid. Eliz. 1880-1900-1910)


(Bowman cont.)

83

**BOWMAN (cont.)**

LEVI LETCHER (c28 S b.Boonev.) [s/o Levi
Bowman & Eliz. Turner - 1880]
   SARAH ELLEN CRANK (c17 S b.KY) [d/o James
   R. Crank & Martha   - 1880]
   1885      (1900 m-14; 1910 m-25; B-O ch.;
   M-L ch-1915)
LOWELL CURTIS (c34 b.KY) [s/o Henry Bowman
   & Rachel Plummer - 1870]
   MARY E. CRAWFORD (c24 b.KY)
   1887/8      (1900 SiL Crawford; TCS)
MAJOR WM. SIMPSON (c25 S b.Ows. [then Clay])
   [1841-1925; s/o Elisha Bowman & Mary
   Mahulda Phillips - P-CW/DC; 1860]
   MARY J. (nee HUGHES) BREWER (c22 2nd b.KY)
   [wid/o Milton Brewer - TCS; M-J 12/6/58;
   BBG] [c1844-c1867 Jack.; d/o Meredith C.
   Hughes & Eliz. Phillips - P-CW; TCS; 1850]
   c1866      (P-CW; BBG/JFB they were
   1st cuzs; Mary & her ch. d. childbirth;
   lived Ows., except for a short time in
   Jack. & Wolfe; NL M-J; H-remd. 1870)
MAJOR WILLIAM SIMPSON (c26 2nd b.Clay) [widr/o
   Mary J. Hughes above - P-CW] [1841-1925]
   MARY ANN STEPHENS (c18 S b.KY) [1854-1919;
   d/o Geo. Stephens & Susan Blevins - P-CW;
   TCS; LNG/Ivory Jewell]
   21 April, 1870, Boonev., by Rev. Corda
   Pendergrass (P-CW; 1870-1880-1890-1900-
   1910; B-O ch.; R.Boonev. 1915-1921; widr.
   M.S. w/dau. 1920; TCS; BBG/JFB; ob-ch. OCN-
   1/31/57)
NEAL - see CORNELIUS
PLEASANT (c39 b.Ows.) [s/o Levi Bowman & Eliz.
   Turner - MT; 1880]
   CATHERINE PETERS (c35 b.KY) [d/o John
   Peters & Margaret Bowman - 1880]
   c1890      (MT; 1900-4/91, wid. Catherine,
   3/3 ch.; 1910-1920)
ROBERT STURGIS (c24 b.Clay) [1819-1909; s/o
   Cornelius Bowman & Elizabeth Moore - OCN-
   4/20/51; MT; TS-TCS]
   MARY TURNER (c19 b.KY) [d/o John Turner
   & Tempy Reynolds - MT]
   2 Feb., 1843, <u>Clay</u> (M-C; 1850-1860-1870-
   1880-1900; B-O ch.)
(Bowman cont.)

**BOWMAN (cont.)**

ROBERT (c26 b.KY)  [s/o John Bowman & Eliz.
  McCollum - JFB; 1860]
  NANCY (nee MORRIS) ROBERTSON (c24 2nd b.KY)
  [wid/o Wm. Robertson - TCS]      [d/o Wm.
  Morris & Margaret Sandlin - 1860]
  5 July, 1864          (TCS; wid. Nancy
  1870-12, 7 & 1; B-O illegit. ch/o Nancy;
  wid. Nancy 1880-1900-1910-1920; NL M-C/J)
ROBERT STURGIS "BUD" (c25 S b.KY)  [1842-1917;
  s/o Henry Bowman & Eliz. Roberts - TS-TCS]
  DICEY JANE PETERS (c21 S b.KY)  [1846-1923;
  d/o Andrew Jackson Peters & Sarah Williams
  - TS-TCS]
  5 March, 1868 Ows. (TCS; 1870-1; 1880; 1900
  m-33; MT; 1910 m-42; BBG; ARS; DC ch-1911;
  wid. Dicie Jane 1920; ob-ch. BE-11/12/59;
  W/as Dicey or Jane in all rec. except 1910
  as Mattie J.)
SIMPSON - see MAJOR WM. SIMPSON
SQUIRE F. (c21 b.KY)  [s/o Thomas Bowman
  & Mary Moore - WGO]
  RHODA MORRIS (c23 b.Clay)
  c1847          (1850-2, w/HP; B-O ch.;
  wid. Rhoda 1870-1880; NL M-C)
STEPHEN (c20 b.Ows.)  [s/o Liberty Bowman
  & Phoebe McPherson - 1870 w/wid. mom]
  LEVISA ROBERTS (c17 b.KY)
  1878/9          (1880 no ch.; 1900-B m-21;
  1910-B; M-L ch-1909-1910; NL M-C)
THOMAS (c21 b.Clay)  [s/o Jacob Bowman
  & Eleanor Evans - DB]
  MARGARET BRANDENBURG (c21 b.Est.)  [c1822-
  1891; d/o Joseph BBurg. & Delilah Vasser -
  DB]
  25 March, 1843, <u>Estill</u>  [DIV. c 1871 - DB]
  (M-E; DB; 1850-1860-1870-E; Margaret "md"
  w/sis. 1880-L)


(Bowman cont.)

**BOWMAN (cont.)**

THOMAS (R.Ows. 56 2nd b.KY) P/-- VA  [m1
    Mariam Morris - M-C 1839]  [s/o Thomas
    Bowman & Polly Moore - MT]
    MARY [nee NANTZ] MORGAN (R.Ows. 53 2nd
    b.Harl.) P/"Harley" [Harlan?] & TN  [wid/o
    Adrian Morgan - B-O ch; 1860; 1850-P]
    [d/o Clement Nantz & Sarah       - TCS]
    27 Nov., 1876 @ Fred Nantz's, Owsley
    [H-remd.]
THOMAS (c59 3rd b.KY)  [m2 Mary Nantz above]
    SARAH (nee CAMPBELL) DALTON (c47 2nd VA)
    P/VA  [sis/o John Campbell - 1880]
    1879/80        (1880-MWY, Dalton s-ch.,
    Campbell BiL; TCS)    [H-remd.]
THOMAS (R.Ows. 68 3rd [s/b 4th] b.Ows.) P/--
    [m3 Sarah Campbell Dalton above - 1880]
    REBECCA [nee PORTER] HOUNSHELL (R.Lee 36
    2nd b.Ows.) P/--    [m1 8/12/86, Jacob
    Hounshell - M-L] [d/o Thomas Porter
    & Mary Bawlden - 1870-L]
    21 Nov., 1889 Lee, by Wm. P. Page; wits.
    Pal & Felix Cole    (M-L 3:519)
THOMAS (c22 S b.Boonev.)  [1877-1961; s/o Wm.
    Bowman & Margaret Murrell - TS-TCS; ob-H
    BE-3/9/61]
    ADELINE "ADA" BOWLING (c19 S b.Br.)  [d/o
    McCoy Bowling & Sarah Jane Freeman - 1880-
    B; ob-WS OCN-6/5/58]
    1898/9        (1900-1910-1920; B-O ch.;
    R.Lerose 1956; wid. Addie Lerose 1961)
TIPTON (c23 b.KY)  [s/o Henry Bowman & Eliz.
    Roberts - 1860]
    ELIZABETH CORNETT (c18 b.KY)  [d/o James
    Cornett & Minerva       - TCS]
    c1868        (1870-7/69; JFB)
WALKER (c20 S b.Ows.)  [1888-1969 Cin.; s/o
    Wm. Bowman & Margaret Murrell - 1900;
    TS-TCS; ob-H&S BE-5/15/69; 3/9/61]
    ALICE STEPP (c19 S b.KY)  [1890-1927 Ows.;
    d/o John Stepp & Martha Moore - TCS; DC]
    1907/8        (1910-1920; TCS; Walker
    R.Cin., OH 1961-1969)


(Bowman cont.)

86

## BOWMAN (cont.)

WILBURN (c29 2nd b.KY)  [widr/o _____]
  [s/o Elisha Bowman & Emily Isaacs - 1900]
  MARY E. McPHERSON (c23 b.VA)  [1843-1903 -
  ME-9/4/03]
  c1866        (1870-3; 1880; 1900 N#L; ob-ch.
  BE-1/20/38; ob-SiL John Bell Barrett who
  md. Fanny; M-L ch-1915)    [H-remd.]
WILBURN (c71 3rd b.KY)  [widr/o Mary E.
  McPherson above]
  NANCY KATHERINE (nee WOODS) WOODWARD (c56
  2nd b.KY)  [wid/o Stephen Woodward - 1880;
  wid. Nancy C. 1900-L]  [poss. d/o Paul
  Woods & Margaret Thomas, who had dau. Cath.
  7 VA 1860]
  1906/7        (1910 H-3rd W-2nd; TCS; NL M-L)
WILEY (c22 S b.KY)  [1868-1936; s/o Wm. Bowman
  & Margaret Murrell - 1880; TS-TCS]
  CORNELIA "NEALIE" TAYLOR (c17 S b.KY)  [d/o
  Minor Clint Taylor, Barsheba Rappitoe-1880]
  1890/1        (1900-1910-1920; TCS)
WILLIAM (c22 b.KY)
  SARAH _____ (c20 b.KY)
  c1859        (1860, no ch.)
WILLIAM (c20 b.Ows.)  [s/o Elisha Bowman
  & Mahulda Phillips - TCS]
  MARGARET MURRELL (c17 b.Per.)  [s/o Thomas
  Murrell & Mary      - TCS]
  6 Dec., 1866, Ows. (TCS; 1870-2; 1880; 1900
  m-32; B-O ch; M-L ch-1908)
WM. SIMPSON - see MAJOR WM. SIMPSON
WILLIAM (c22-31 S b.KY)  [s/o Thomas Bowman
  & Mariam Morris - 1880]
  MOLLY BOWMAN (c15-24 b.KY)  [d/o Nancy
  BOWMAN & unknown - 1880]
  1884-93        (TCS; H-remd. 1900; NL M-J)
WM. ALBERT (c21 S b.KY)  [s/o Levi Bowman
  & Eliz. Turner - 1880]
  MARY McGEORGE (c16 S b.KY)  [d/o Dan
  McGeorge & Sarah Peters - 1880]
  1887        (1900 m-13; 1910 m-22; TCS;
  H/as Albert & Wm. A.)


(Bowman cont.)


87

**BOWMAN (cont.)**
WILLIAM (c32 2nd b.KY) [widr/o Molly Bowman
   above]
   DORA _____ (___ b.KY?)
   1893/4      (1900, wf's data unreadable)
   [WILLIAM m3 Mary Wilson - TCS]
WILLIAM (c22 S b.KY) [s/o Wilburn Bowman &
   Mary McPherson - 1880; ob-HS BE-1/20/38]
   BELLE TAYLOR (c18 S b.KY) [1879-1955 OH;
   d/o James Taylor & Nancy       - ob-W OCN-
   2/3/55]
   1895/6          (1900-L; 1910; NL M-L;
   BC 1917-1921-L; 1920Sx-L; R.Oil 1938)
WILLIAM T. (c23 S b.KY) [s/o James S. Bowman
   & Hannah Blake - TCS]
   LAURA J. CRANK (c21 S b.KY) [d/o Wm. Gillis
   Crank & Emily Amazon Wilson - 1900; JCH]
   1906/7      (1910 each listed w/respective
   par. both m-3; ob-ch. HJN-8/9/98 ch.b.1915)
   [Wm. md. 4x]
WILLIAM (c30 S b.Buck Cr.) [1877-1959 Dayton,
   OH; s/o Robt. S Bowman, Dicey Jane Peters -
   TS-TCS; ob-H BE-12/12/59]
   HATTIE PENDERGRASS (c20 S b.Sturgeon) [d/o
   Ben Pendergrass & Nancy Bell - ob-WS OCC-
   7/28/39; w/Bell GP 1900]
   1906/7          (1910-1920; B-O ch.; MT;
   1900 H-sgl.; BBG; BC 1913)
ZACHARIAH "ZACK" (R.Ows. 22 S b.KY [Ows.]) P/
   KY  [1856-1932; s/o Henry Bowman & Rachel
   Plummer - MT; TS-TCS]
   ELISABETH BOWMAN (R.Ows. 20 S b.KY) P/KY
   [d/o John Bowman & Susan Moore - TCS]
   28 Nov., 1878, Ows.   [R.Owsley 1880]
   [H-remd.]
[ZACHARIAH] ZACK (c31 2nd b.KY) [widr/o Eliz.
   Bowman above]  [1856-1932]
   [REBECCA] SUSAN MOYERS (c32 S b.KY) [1854-
   1933 d/o Owen Moyers, Lucy Stewart -TS-TCS]
   Dec., 1886 (ML) Ows.  (ME-1/14/87; 1900-
   1910-1920; TCS)

## BRANDENBURG/BRANDENBURGH

[ABRAHAM] GUNDA (R.Ows. 21 S b.Est.)   [s/o
    George H. Brandenburg - 1850]
    MARY [ANN] COOMER (R.Ows. 22 S b.Lee, VA)
    18 April, 1859, Ows.  [R.Owsley 1860; Lee
    1870]

ACE (c21 S b.Lee)   [1872-1941 Lone; s/o
    David Brandenburg & Nancy BBurg. - KAS;
    1880-L; ob-H BE-5/15/41]
    ALICE COLE (c17 S b.Ows.)   [1876-1938 Lee;
    d/o Lewis Cole & Martha Cooper - 1880; DC]
    1893/4         (ob-W OCC-12/16/38 & DC;
    1900-1910-L; B-L ch.; ob-ch. BS-6/24/98;
    H/Ace & Asa; his gs says Ace/LNG)

ALBERT (c25 S b.Boonev.)   [1870-1939; s/o
    Ancil D. BBurg. & Levisa Cecil - 1880; ME-
    10/1/97; TS-TCS]
    FLORENCE ELLEN MINTER (c24 S b.Clay Co.)
    [d/o Wm. Minter & Maggie Gilbert - 1880]
    1895/6         (1900-1910-1920; B-O ch.; NL
    M-C; So. Boonev. 1897 - ME)

ALFRED (R.Ows. 18 S b.Ows.) P/Ows-Jack.
    MINNIE LOWE (R.Lee 18 S b.Ows.) P/uk.
    24 Nov., 1887 Lee @ James Snowden's, by G.
    W. Arnold; wits. John N. Smith & Eugene
    Dickerson    (M-L)

ALGON (c21 b.KY)   [s/o Jackson Brandenburg
    & Margaret Evans - 1880-L]
    EMILY TREADWAY (c17 b.Ows.)   [d/o Wm.
    Wallace Treadway & Mary Mainous - 1880]
    1896/7         (DB; 1900-L)

ANCIL DANIEL (c28 S b.Est.)   [1840-1913 Mad.;
    s/o John Henson BBurg. & Deborah Bowman -
    DC P-CW]
    LEVISA ANN CECIL (c20 b.VA)   [c1849-1901
    Mad.; d/o Madison Cecil & Mary Taylor -
    REM; JFB; ME-4/11/01; P-CW has 4/1900]
    16 Sept., 1869, Boonev., Ows., by Rev.
    Elias Botner   (P-CW; 1870, no ch.; DB; REM;
    1890; moved to Mad. 1896 - ME-3/27/96; Mad.
    1896-d.)


(Brandenburg cont.)


89

ANCIL DANIEL (c65 2nd b.Est.)  [m1 Levisa Ann
    Cecil above - P-CW]
    ELIZA [nee _____] PRATHER (c46 2nd b.KY)
    [m1 Edgar S. Prather, who d. 1900 Pul. -
    P-CW]
    24 Aug., 1905, <u>Madison</u> @ Brassfield, by
    Robt. L. BBurg., MG; wits. C. A. Quillen,
    J. B. Adams & T. G. Moberly (P-CW)
ANDREW JACKSON (c23 S b.Est.) [s/o Joseph
    Brandenburg & Rhoda Hamilton - 1850; DB]
    AMANDA ARNOLD (c18 S b.Lee,VA)  [d/o
    Lorenzo D. Arnold & Mary    - 1860]
    1866/7        (1870-L-1; 1880-1900-L;
    1910-L m1-43; B-L ch.; ob-ch. BE-4/10/47)
ANDREW JACKSON (c22 b.KY)
    MARGARET EVANS (c17 b.KY)  [d/o Hiram
    Evans & Nancy Stamper - TCS; ACB]
    c1867        (1870-L-1; 1880-L-12)
ARCHIBALD B. (20 S b.Ows.)  [1861-1942; s/o
    Sam Brandenburg & Mary Smith - 1880; ob-H
    OCC-2/27/42]
    LUCY DUFF (19 S b.Ows.)  [1862-1934; d/o
    Elijah Duff & Polly Eversole - 1880; ob-W
    OCC-6/15/34; art. BE-9/7/72; DC]
    24 Nov., 1881, Ows.  (ob-H&W; 1900 w/HP;
    1920; Yest.; M-L ch-1912)
ASA - see ACE
CASH & CASTRO - see JAMES CASTRO
CHARLES WILSON (c22 S b.Buck Cr.)  [s/o Wm. B.
    BBurg. & Josephine Glass - 1880]
    FRANCES "FRANKIE" BOTNER (c18 S b.Trav.
    Rest, Ows.) [d/o John C. Botner & Laurinda
    P. Warren]
    1899/1900        (1900-1910-1920; DB; B-O
    ch.; M-L ch-1936)
CHARLES (23 S b.KY)
    DAISY McINTOSH (16 S b.KY)  [d/o Thomas
    McIntosh & Susan Bowling - ob-WS BE-
    12/16/48; 1900]
    3 Jan., 1901, Lee @ Miles McIntosh's, by J.
    M. Roberts; wits. Kenos BBurgh. & Grant
    Cole  (M-L; 1900-L m1-10; M-L ch-1922)

(Brandenburg cont.)

## BRANDENBURG (cont.)

CHARLES [H.] (R.Ows. 29 S b.Ows.) [1875-1958;
s/o Hardin BBurg. & Sarah Ann Hall - 1880;
ob-H OCN-2/20/58; d. Lex. hosp.]
ALICE STERNBURG (R.Lee 21 S b.Lee) [1884-
1966 Boonev.; d/o Samuel Sternberg & Mahala
Robinson - FH; ob-W&S BE-1/5/67-2/15/34-
5/10/45; w/bro. 1900-L]
3 Nov., 1904, Lee, @ Hall's Chapel, by R.
T. Baker; wits: Hamm & R. L. BBurg. (M-L;
1910, Sternburg SiL w/them; 1920; R.Boonev.
1934; Beattyv. 1940-41; Ham.,OH 1945; wid.
Beattyv. 1958; ob-ch. BE-8/7/35)
CLAY - see also HENRY CLAY
CLAY (R.Ows. 25 S b.Ows.) P/Ows. [s/o Henry
Brandenburg & Eliz. Roberts - DB]
CALLIE HAMILTON (R.Ows. 17 S b.Ows.) P/Ows.
[d/o John Hamilton & Emma        - TCS; 1900]
14 May, 1909, Ows.    [R.Owsley 1910]
DANIEL (___ b.___)
MARTHA ANN BRANDENBURG (16 S b.Ows) [c1858-
1876; d/o Samuel BBurg. & Mary Smith - DB]
c1874        (DB & TCS)
DANIEL GARRETT (c18 S b.Ows) [s/o Thos. BBurg.
& Nancy Thomas - 1880; ob-H&S OCN-7/25/52,
BE-3/29/34]
SARAH MARGARET NOLAND (c16 S b.KY)
16 March, 1892, Lee, @ Wm. BBurg.'s; wits:
Henry S. & Green BBurg. & Arch Isaacs
(M-L; 1900-1910-1920; ob-H; R.Stay 1934)
DAVID (c16 b.KY)   [s/o Joseph Brandenburg
& Nancy Snowden - 1850 w/wid. mom]
NANCY BRANDENBURG (c15 b.KY)   [d/o Geo.
Brandenburg & Sally Thomas - TCS]
1851        (1860-6; 1880-1900-L; B-O ch.)
DAVID [G.] (R.Ows. 25 S b.Ows) [1878-1963 Lee;
s/o Jackson BBurg. & Martha Callahan -
1900; ob-H&S BE-12/5/63, OCN-6/26/58]
CLARKIE FARMER (R.Lee 15 S b.Lee)
13 Oct., 1904 Lee, @ bride's res., by A. J.
Marcum, Min.; wits. Wm. Gray & Scott Farmer
(M-L; 1910-1920; B-O ch.; R.Beattyv. 1958;
wid. R.Beattyv. 1963)


(Brandenburg cont.)


91

## BRANDENBURG (cont.)

DAVID P. (R.Lee 20 S b.Lee) P/Ows. [1888-1973
- LNG-TS]
[FRANCES] FANCY McINTOSH (R.Ows. 20 S b.
Ows.) P/Br. [1888-1942; d/o Elisha McIntosh
& Minerva Fox - ob-W BE-2/26/42; LNG-TS &
Bible of Icey, d/o David & Fancy]
1 Oct., 1908, <u>Breathitt</u> [rec. Ows.; R.Lee
c1909/10 - M-O ch-1926-1967; R.Lower
Buffalo 1942; ob-ch. 3Fks-3/25/98]

DAVID PRYSE (c40 b.KY) [s/o James K. Polk
BBurg. & Mary Ann Day - DB; 1910-L]
DEMA ASBELL (c30 b.KY) [d/o Samuel Asbell
& Mary Evaline Gourley - 1880-L; ob-W OCN-
10/19/51]
c1910, Ows. (DB; ob-W; W-sgl. 1900-L)

ELISHA (21 S b.Ows.) [s/o Jas. Hamilton
BBurg. & Mary A Thomas]
DEAMY DUNAWAY (19 S b.Ows.)
5 Aug., 1881, <u>Lee</u> (M-L; DB; M-L dau.
1899 cons/o P; 1910-L)

FELIX (c23 b.KY) [1848-1902; s/o "Yankee
Joe" Brandenburg & Rhoda Hamilton - 1870;
ME-3/14/02]
MARTHA TAYLOR (c18 b.TN) [d/o Orville P.
Taylor & Hannah Harvey - 1870]
1872/3 (1880-6; 1900; DB; M-O ch-1919;
ob-ch. OCC-4/9/37, BE-6/21/51, BS-6/17/93;
ch-87 Bday BS-10/30/86)

FRANKLIN (24 S b.Ows.) [s/o James Hamilton
BBurg. & Mary Ann Thomas]
ELIZA ANN ANGEL (16 b.KY) [d/o Wilburn
Angel & Marilda Mays - 1880-L]
26 May, 1881, <u>Lee</u> (M-L; DB; 1900-1910-L)

FRANKLIN B. "FRANK" (c26 S tchr b.Boonev.)
[1872-1942; s/o Hardin BBurg. & Sarah Ann
Hall - TS-TCS; 1880; ob-H&S OCC-5/8/42]
CRESSIE HEIDENRICH (c20 S b.KS) P/Germ.
[1879-1977 - ob-W BS-8/24/77; TS-TCS]
1898 <u>Oklahoma</u> (1900-1910-1920; DB; B-O ch;
Boonev. 1940-1; ob-H; M-O ch-1932; ob-ch.
BE-5/19/49; Yest.; art. on Cressie OCN-
11/7/52 says she met Frank in Kyle, TX)

(Brandenburg cont.)

## BRANDENBURG (cont.)

GEORGE HENSON (c49 2nd b.Clk) [widr/o Sally
   Thomas - M-E 1829] [s/o Samuel BBurg.
   & Sarah Henson]
   MARGARET (nee MOORE) COLE (c30 2nd b.Clay)
   [Div/f Oliver Cole - REM; M-C 1841; 1850,
   Margaret Cole] [d/o Wm. Moore & Deborah
   Bowman]
   c1851 (DB; MNC; 1860-8; Margaret
   1880; NL M-C)
GEORGE H. (R.Lee 21 S b.KY) P/KY-VA [s/o
   John W. BBurg. & Nancy J. Palmer - 1870]
   LUTISHA "LETTIE" PORTER (R.Ows. 21 S b.Ows)
   P/TN-NC [d/o Eli Porter & Mariah Judd -
   1860-1870; TCS; REM; art. BE-2/3/72]
   19 Dec, 1876 Ows. @ Widow [Mariah] Porter's
   (a/L 12/18/76 H-24, HP/KY, LUTITIA "PETERS"
   WP/KY; @ Mariah "Peters"; rest same)
   [R.Lee 1880-1900-1910]
G[EORGE] W. (R.Jess. 26 S mcht b.Ows.) P/Ows.
   DEMA HYDEN (R.Ows. 30 S b.Ows.) [1877-1966
   Lex. hosp.; d/o Allen C. Hyden & Juriah
   Mainous - 1900; ob-W&M&S BE-11/17/66, OCN-
   2/14/57, BE-12/1/38]
   13 July, 1909, Ows. [R.Scoville 1957;
   Booneville 1966]
GREEN (c30 2nd b.KY) [m1 _____]
   CUSHENBERRY WILSON (c21 S b.KY) [d/o Robt.
   Wilson & Caroline Combs - 1880; LNG]
   1892/3 (1900-1910-L; NL M-L; 1920;
   M-L ch-1912; ob-ch. OCN 6/30/55)
GUNDY/GUNDA - see ABRAHAM
HARDEN [KAGER] (R.Ows. 23 S b.Est.) [s/o
   John H. BBurg. & Deborah Bowman - 1850]
   MARTHY SPIVEY (R.Ows. 17 S b.Jack.)
   1 June, 1858, Ows. [R.Owsley 1860; Lee
   1870-1880] [NOTE: B-L ch. list W/as
   b.John.,TN]
HARDEN (c24 S b.Ows.) [1838-1906; s/o Yankee
   Joe BBurg. & W1 Rhoda Hamilton - REM; TCS]
   SARAH ANN HALL (c19 S b.Ows.) [1843-1924;
   d/o Harvey Hall & Mary Bowman - REM TS-TCS]
   1862/3 (1870-5; 1880-1900; wid.
   Sarah 1910; 1920 wid. Sarah w/son; ob-ch.
   OCC-2/21/41; DC ch-1947)

(Brandenburg cont.)

## BRANDENBURG (cont.)

HARVEY G. (c25 S b.Ows.) [s/o Jno. BBurg.
& Paulina Roberts - 1880]
SOPHIA SMITH (c26 S b.KY) [d/o Wm. Smith
& Lucy Ann Gibson - 1880; ob-WM OCC-
3/16/34]
1894/5, Ows. (1900; DB; ME-7/3/03, Miss
Minnie Smith sis/o Mrs. H. G. BBurg.;
R.Yale, OK 1934)

HENRY (c22 b.Ows.) [s/o Samuel BBurg. & Sally
BBurg. - TCS]
ELIZABETH ROBERTS (c12 b.Ows.) [d/o Wm.
Roberts & Celia Phillips - TCS]
c1868 (1870-9/69; 1880-10; B-O ch.)

HENRY (c18 b.KY) [s/o Thomas BBurg. & Nancy
Thomas - 1880; ob-HS BE-3/29/34-1/16/64]
THERESA SEALE (c22 b.Ows.)
1890/1 (1900; M-L ch-1913-1914;
H-remd. 1910-L)

H[ENRY] S[IMPSON] (26 S b.KY) P/Ows-VA [s/o
Jackson BBurg. & Amanda Arnold - 1870-80-L]
[GEORGE] ELLA HALL (16 S b.KY) P/Ows. [d/o
Harvey Hall & Sarah J. Thomas - 1880-L]
21 Dec., 1895, Lee @ Fish Creek Church
House, by Geo. Kincaid; wits. W. E. Evans &
R. L. Brandenburg (M-L; DB; 1900-L as
"Simm" & "George E.") [H. S. (37 2nd) m2
3/8/06, Sarah Mahaffey (31) - M-L]

HENRY CLAY (c25 b.Ows.) [s/o Jno. BBurg.
& Perlina Roberts - 1880; BBG; ob-HS OCN-
5/15/58]
LUCY ANN CREECH (c23 b.KY) [d/o Alexander
Creech & Agnes Sageser - TCS; BBG; 1900;
ob-WS OCC-4/9/37]
14 Feb., 1901 (BBG, Lucy sis/o BBG's
GF; DB; 1910-L; 1920; R.Berea, Mad. 1937 &
1958)

HENRY (32 2nd b.KY) [m1 Theresa Seal above]
JULIA FARLEY (23 S b.Pebworth, Ows.) [1881-
1972 Lex. Nur.H; d/o Sheridan Farley
& Patsy Pennington - 1900; ob-W BE-1/27/72]
9 April, 1905, Lee @ D. B. Pendergrass', by
Wm. Robinson; wits. G. B. Pendergrass &
Carter Brandenburg (M-L; 1910-L H/m2-N#L,
W/m1-N#L; 1920-6, WP w/them; R.Beattyv.
1934-1964 - ob-HS BE-3/29/34-1/16/64]
(Brandenburg cont.)

HOUSTON (c19 S b.KY)    [s/o Wm. Brandenburg
   & Armelda Winkle - 1880]
   MARGARET MAYS (c20 S b.KY)
   1892/3         (1900-1910; BC 1911, 1918-L;
   wid. Margaret 1920)
JACKSON - see also ANDREW JACKSON
JACKSON (c22 S b.Clay) [1843-1928 Ows.; s/o
   Joseph BBurg. & Nancy Snowden - DC; REM]
   MARTHA CALLAHAN (c15 S b.Jack.)  [d/o
   Ezekiel Callahan, Mary Herd - TCS; P/1850]
   1865         (1870-L-4; 1880-14; 1900 m-35;
   1910 m-44; 1920; B-O ch.; DB; TCS; N-EM
   ch.; M-L ch-1904-1946; ob-ch. OCN-6/26/58 &
   BE-9/20/73; NL M-C)
JACKSON - see also ANDREW JACKSON
JACKSON - see also WM. JACKSON
[JAMES HAMILTON] "JASPER" (c23 b.Est.)  [s/o
   Joseph BBurg. & Rhoda Hamilton - 1850]
   MARY [ANN] THOMAS (c22 b.Clay)  [d/o Joseph
   Thomas & Anna Jemima Couch - TCS]
   18 April, 1853, Ows.  (OCN-3/16/51, mgs.
   compiled by JWFW as 4/18/43; 1860; B-O ch-
   1/54; B-L ch.; M-L ch-1907)
JAMES CASTRO "CASH" (c22 b.KY)  [s/o James
   Cook BBurg. & Nancy Thomas - 1850]
   SARAH G. MOORE (c19 b.KY)  [d/o James Moore
   & Lucinda Evans - TCS]
   1859/60       (1860-MWY; 1870-E; Sarah w/HF
   1880-L; TCS; ob-ch. OCN-11/24/50 & BE-
   9/17/53; H/as C.C. 2x, Castro, James Cash,
   & Cash/Kash 3x; W/as Sarah Moore in 2 obits
   & Sarah Thomas in 1)
JAMES K. POLK (c21 b.KY)  [s/o James Cook
   Brandenburg & Nancy Thomas - 1860]
   MARY ANN DAY (c22 b.TN) P/TN
   1866/7    (1870-L-2, wf mistakenly listed
   as Nancy; 1880-1900-1910-L; TR; both sgl.
   1860, Mary A. w/HP as domestic)


(Brandenburg cont.)

**BRANDENBURG (cont.)**

JAMES ["COOK"] (R.Sturg. 84 2nd b.KY) [widr/o
   Nancy Thomas - M-E 1837]  [1808-1896; s/o
   Joseph BBurg. & Delilah Vesser - DB]
   ELIZABETH [nee RADER] ADKINS (60 3rd b.KY)
   [m1 Aquilla White - M-O 1855; m2 Seth
   Adkins - 1880-L]  [1826-1917; d/o George
   Rader & Mary Ambrose - 1850]
   8 June, 1892, <u>Lee</u>  (M-L; ME-6/24/92, James
   of Sturg. got ML to marry)
JAMES S. (23 S b.KY) [1877-1937 Low.Buff.; s/o
   Felix BBurg. & Martha Taylor - 1880 TS-TCS;
   ob-H OCC-4/9/37]
   AMANDA JUDD (21 S b.Lee) [d/o James Roland
   Judd & Nancy Palmer - 1880-L]
   19 July, 1900, <u>Lee</u> @ J. R. Judd's, by W. H.
   Bowman, JPLC; wits: Jos. Cole, Willie Judd
   & G. A. BBurg.  (M-L; 1900 H-sgl.; ob-ch.
   BS-9/19/85; BE-10/17/35)
JAMES (R.Lee 21 S b.Lee) P/Lee
   JANE FOX (R.Ows. 17 S b.Ows.) P/Ows.
   9 April, 1908, Ows.
JASPER - see JAMES HAMILTON
JESSE (c20 S b.Ows.)  [1865-1947; s/o Jno.
   Brandenburg & Paulina Roberts - 1880; ob-H
   BE-6/5/47]
   NANCY CLARK METCALFE (c20 b.KY)  [d/o
   Norris Metcalfe & Henrietta    - 1880]
   27 Aug., 1885, Travelers Rest, Ows.
   (DB; 1900; M-E ch. 1913; to Est. c1920)
J[ESSE] S. (R.Lex. 27 S b.Clk) P/Clk
   ADA YORK (R.Ows. 20 S b.Ows.) P/Ows.
   31 Dec., 1909, Ows. [R.Lex., Fayette 1920,
   W/as <u>Asa</u>, WS Belle York w/them]
JOEL (c20 b.Ows.)   [s/o Joseph Brandenburg
   & Rhoda Hamilton]
   SARAH PLUMMER (c20 b.Br.)  [d/o Samuel
   Plummer & Elizabeth    ]
   c1860      (1870-L-9; 1880-L; B-L ch.)
JOEL (___ b.___)
   MARY E. MOORE (c18 b.Ows.) [d/o Elijah
   Sutton Moore & Amanda Bowman - 1880; ob-W
   OCC-7/24/42]
   c1884     (TCS; ob-W; NL 1900Sx)

(Brandenburg cont.)

## BRANDENBURG (cont.)

JOEL (c20 S b.Lee) [1870-1928; s/o James H.
BBurg. & Mary Ann Thomas - 1880-L; TS-TCS]
MARTHA ANN SMITH (c20 b.KY) [1871-1950; d/o
Asa Smith & Sophia BBurg. - TS-TCS; ob-W&S
OCN-10/20/50 & BE-8/5/43]
1889/90, Ows. (DB; 1900-1910-L; ob-W; ob-
ch. BS-6/7/40; R.Stay 1943; NL M-L)

JOEL [C.] (R.Ows. 23 S b.Ows.) P/-- [1881-
1967; s/o Felix BBurg. & Martha Taylor -
1900; TS-TCS; ob-H&S BE-11/30/67-6/21/51,
OCN-8/25/55, OCC-4/9/37]
FRANCES JUDD (R.Lee 17 S b.Lee) P/--
[1887-1971; d/o James Rowland Judd & Nancy
Palmer - 1900-L; ob-W BE-11/18/71]
4 March, 1905, Lee @ Rolen Judd's, by J. M.
Roberts; wits. Sherman Cooper & Green Rose
(M-L; 1910-1920; TCS; R.Stay 1937; Owsley
1951-55; R.Stay 1964-5 ob-HS BE-9/10/64-
12/16/65; wid. R.Stay 1967)

JOHN S. (c22 b.KY) [1827-1917 Est; s/o Joseph
BBurg. & Nancy      - 1850; BE-11/8/51 art.]
MARTHA "PATSY" WHITE (c20 b.KY)  [d/o
Aquilla White & Sally Shanks - REM]
c1851      (1860-8; B-O ch.; 1870-L)
[JOHN m2 Helen _____ - 1880-L;
supposedly md. 2x more - TCS]

JOHN W. (c24 b.KY) [s/o George Brandenburg
& Sally Thomas - TCS]
NANCY JANE PALMER (c19 b.VA) [d. 1877-9]
c1854      (1860-5; B-Ows.)
[JOHN m2 1877-9, Sarah - 1880-L]

JONATHAN (c20 S b.KY) [s/o Samuel Brandenburg
& Sally Brandenburg]
PERLINA ROBERTS (c17 S b.KY)  [d/o Wm.
Roberts & Celia Phillips - TCS]
8 Jan., 1861, Ows. (TCS; 1870-L; 1900-
1910-1920; DB; REM; ob-ch. OCN-5/15/58)

JOHN W. ["MAJOR"] (21 S b.Ows.) [s/o Henry
Brandenburg & Eliz. Roberts - 1880]
EMILY [EMMA] HAMILTON (15 b.Ows.) [d/o
John Hamilton & Martha Isaacs - DB]
16 May, 1889, Lee (M-L; M-L ch. 1914-1977
lists F. as Major BBurg.; DB; 1900-L;
ob-ch. BE-11/4/71)

(Brandenburg cont.)

**BRANDENBURG (cont.)**

JOHN H. (R.Millers Cr. c52 b.KY)    [prob. md.
    previously - NL 1880-E]
    MARY (nee CLARK) BOTNER (c53 2nd b.KY)
    [wid/o Elias Botner - ME]  [d/o Anderson
    D. Clark & Emily P. Murphy - TCS; ME says
    cuz/o Judge A. H. Clark]
    10 June, 1897 (Thurs.)        (ME-6/18/97;
    1900-E m-2)
JOHN (20 S b.KY)  [s/o Jackson BBurg. & Amanda
    Arnold - TCS]
    LOUISE ["ELIZA" (nee PENDERGRASS)] MAYS (40
    2nd b.KY)  [wid/o _____ Mays - 1900-L;
    NL M-L]   [d/o Cordy Pendergrass & Minerva
    Thompson - 1880]
    5 April, 1902, Lee @ her res., by A. J.
    Marcum; wits. A. B. Marcum & James Burns
    (M-L; 1910-L)
[JNO.] MARION (R.Ows. 24 S b.Ows.) P/Ows.
    [s/o Jno. BBurg. & Perlina Roberts - 1880]
    DOLLY CREECH (R.Ows. 18 S b.Ows.) P/Ows-Lee
    [d/o Henry Creech & Laura        ]
    31 Oct., 1903, Ows.  [R.Owsley 1910 w/HP &
    1920 H/as Marion]
JOSEPH "YANKEE JOE" (c61 2nd b.Clk)  [widr/o
    Rhoda Hamilton - D-O; M-C 5/7/28; wdr 1860]
    [s/o Jos. Brandenburg Sr. & Delilah Vesser]
    MARY JANE (nee _____) GORDON (c49 2nd b.VA)
    [wid/o Kennedy Gordon] [1816-1891 - TS-TCS]
    c1865        (DB; 1870 wf Mary; REM; art. on
    him ME-11/6/95)
JOSEPH B. (24 b.KY) P/KY   [s/o James Hamilton
    BBurg. & Mary A. Thomas]
    NANCY ANN BRANDENBURG (21 b.KY) P/KY
    30 Jan., 1879, Lee  (M-L; 1880-5/80; TCS)
JOSEPH WILSON (c23 S b.Hlbg., Lee) [1877-1949
    WV; s/o James K. P. Brandenburg & Mary Ann
    Day - ob-H BE-1/6/49]
    JOSEPHINE "JOSIE" KENDRICK (R.Pine Grove
    c19 b.KY)  [1879-c1922; d/o James Kendrick
    - DB; ob-H]
    2 March, 1899, Ows.  (ob-H; DB; 1900-L m-1;
    moved to WV; NL M-L)  [JOSEPH m2 Mrs.
    Martha BBurg. of Sturgeon - ob-H]

(Brandenburg cont.)

98

**BRANDENBURG (cont.)**

JOSEPH (R.Lee 23 S b.Lee) P/Lee-Br. [s/o David
  BBurg. & Lourana Vires - TCS; 2nd M-O]
  JALIA FOX (R.Ows. 16 S b.Ows.) P/Ows. [d/o
  Harvey Fox & Sarah A. BBurg. - 1900]
  3 May, 1904, Ows.   [R.Lee 1910; M-O ch-
  1931, age 18 b.Lee; R.Low.Buff. 1931]
  [JOE (R.Lee 50 widr. b.Lee - s/o Dave &
  Louraine) m2 6/26/31 Lee (rec. Ows.), Anna
  BBurg. (19 d/o Jesse & Emma) - M-O]
JOSEPH (c32 S b.Lee) [s/o Jackson BBurg.
  & Martha Callahan - 1880-1900]
  CORDIA _____ (c15 S b.KY) [NL DC]
  1902/3          (1910-E m1-7; TCS)
KASH - see JAMES CASTRO
LEVI (R.Lee 26 S b.Br.) P/Br. [s/o Samuel
  BBurg. & Eliz. Gillespie - 1900-L]
  [LILLIE TACKETT (c18 b.Ows.) P/Ows.] [d/o
  Joseph N. "Little Joe" Tackett & Susan
  Begley - BBG; 1900]
  10 July, 1909, Ows.   [NOTE:  There was a
  marriage error in this & several other
  marriages, wherein the bride was listed on
  the wrong line.  Bride listed as VIRGINIA
  NEECE (R.Ows. 28 S b.Harl.) P/VA-Ows.
  line above was "JULIA" TACKETT.  Levi's wf
  was LILLIE TACKETT - BBG & 1910-L]
LEWIS (R.Ows. 25 S b.Ows.)
  MARY SEALE (R.Ows. 16 S b.Caloway Co, MO)
  18 Sept., 1856, Ows. [NOTE: Lewis went
  off to Civil War & never returned - TCS]
LEWIS F. (c20 S b.KY) [s/o Jno. BBurg.
  & Paulina Roberts - 1880]
  _____ (___ b.KY)
  c1883          (DB; 1900-12/84, W2 wid.;
  H-2nd M-L; NL M-L)
LEWIS F. (R.Lee 28 2nd b.Ows.) P/Mad-Est.
  [widr/o _____ above]
  MARY M. PETERS (R.Lee 28 S b.Ows.) P/NC-IN
  [prob. d/o James Peters & Eliz. Hughes -
  TCS]
  24 May, 1890, Lee @ Lewis BBurg.'s, by
  James E. Dunigan; wits. Liza Peters & Henry
  Underwood (M-L; DB; 1900-12/84, wid. Mary,
  age 38)

(Brandenburg cont.)

**BRANDENBURG (cont.)**

LEWIS L[OGAN] (R.Lee 22 S b.Ows.) P/Est.
    NANCY ELLEN COUCH (R.Lee 21 S b.Ows.) P/--
    & Ows. [1874-1962 Lee; d/o Andrew Couch
    & Lourana Maloney - TCS; ob-W BE-5/10/62]
    2 Dec., 1891, <u>Lee</u> @ Sam Brandenburg's; by
    J. M. Roberts; wits. Joel & Keen BBurg.
    (M-L; 1900; 1910-L; 1920; TCS)
MAJOR - see JOHN W.
MARION F. (c21 S b.KY) [1868-1937; s/o Thomas
    BBurg. & Nancy A Thomas - 1880; ob-HS BE-
    3/29/34-1/16/64; ob-W]
    CLARINDA "CLARA" HOLCOMB (c21 S b.Ows.)
    [1868-1948 OH; d/o Wm. Holcomb & Eliz.
    Christian - 1880; ob-W BE-3/4/48]
    2 May, 1889      (ob-W; DB; 1900; 1910-L;
    M-L ch-1924-1934; R.Congleton 1934; wid. in
    Ham.,OH 1947-1948; ob-ch. BS-12/13/84)
MARION - see JNO. MARION
PATRICK (c19 b.KY) [s/o Joseph BBurg.
    & Rhoda Hamilton - 1850-1860]
    MARY JANE GORDON (c21 b.KY) [d/o Kennedy
    Gordon & Mary J.      - TCS]
    1868      (1870-L-10/69; 1880-L; 1900-L
    m-31; 1910-L m1-42; B-L ch.; M-L ch-1920)
PRYSE/PRICE - see DAVID PRYSE
ROBERT G. "FANCY BOB" (c24 S b.Lee) [s/o
    Jackson BBurg. & Martha Callahan - 1880]
    MARY JANE STRONG (c18 b.KY) [d/o Phillip
    Strong & Sarah Frances Freeman - TCS]
    1896/7      (1900-J; TCS; their ch. w/GM
    Fanny Strong 1910; NL M-J)    [H-remd.]
ROBERT G. "FANCY BOB" (c33 2nd b.Lee) [md.
    1st Mary J. Strong above - TCS]
    MATTIE "DUDE" RICE (c18 S b.Ows.) [d/o
    Wm. Rice & W1 Elizabeth Smith - BBG]
    1905/6      (1910; B-O ch.; BBG; ACB;
    BC 1912; ob-ch. HJN-8/8/97)


(Brandenburg cont.)

## BRANDENBURG (cont.)

ROBERT (c35 b.KY)  [s/o Harden BBurg. & Sarah
    Ann Hall - 1880; ob-HS OCC-8/2/40]
    NORA C. NOLAND (c30 b.KY)  [ob-W BE-2/23/39
    no dates; d. Richmond, IN]
    c1906          (DB; H-sgl. w/P 1900; HP/NL
    1910; NL 1910Sx-KY/IN/GA; in GA c1913-16
    per birthplaces of ch. 1920; 1920-Ohio Co.,
    KY; Rich.IN 1940; NL M-L)
SAMUEL S. (c16 b.KY)  [1825-1900/10; s/o Jos.
    Brandenburg & Nancy Snowden - TCS]
    SALLY PHILLIPS (c14 b.KY)  (1826-19__]
    2 Feb., 1842, <u>Clay</u>  (M-C; 1850-6; 1860;
    1870-1880-1900-L; wid. Sallie 1910-L;
    M-L ch-1912-1923)
SAMUEL (c70 2nd b.Hampshire Co, VA)
    [widr/o _____]   [s/o Mathias
    Brandenburg & Hester Wohlgemuth]
    MATILDA BARNES (c18 S b.KY)
    c1844          (DB)
SAMUEL (c25 S b.KY)  [1832-1913; s/o Yankee
    Joe BBurg. & W1 Rhoda Hamilton - TS-TCS]
    MARY ANN "PAT" SMITH (c18 S b.KY)  [1838-
    1920 - TS-TCS]
    11 June, 1857          (TCS; 1900-1910;
    B-O ch-3/58; 1860-1870-1880; NL M-J)
SAMUEL DOOLEY (c61 2nd b.Clk)  [Div/f Sally
    Brandenburg 1855 - DB; M-E 7/7/39; TCS]
    [s/o Joseph BBurg. & Delilah Vesser]
    LUCY HOOVER (c22 S b.Lee,VA)  [d/o George
    Hoover      - DB]
    c1861          (DB; 1870-L-8; 1880-L; B-L ch.)
SAMUEL (c34 S b.Ows.)  [s/o James Hamilton
    Brandenburg & Mary Ann Thomas]
    SURILDA JANE SMITH (c21 S b.Ows.)
    1888          (1900-L m-12; 1910-L m-21;
    ob-ch. BE-2/26/70)
SIDNEY BARNES (22 S b.Beattyville, Lee)  [s/o
    Archibald B. Brandenburg & Lucy Smith]
    JANE MARCUM (c21 S b.Earnestv., Ows.)  [d/o
    Thomas Marcum & Mourning Warren]
    1896, Earnestville, Ows. (DB; 1900)


(Brandenburg cont.)

SIMPSON (c27 b.KY)   [s/o Yankee Joe BBurg.
   & W1 Rhoda Hamilton - REM]
   LEAH SMITH (c22 b.VA)    [d/o Elkanah Smith
   & Jane Thomas - REM]
   c1869        (1870, no ch.; DB; REM; 1880-L;
   wid. Lean 1900-L; M-L ch-1906-1935)
SIMPSON ["SIMMIE"] (19 S b.Lee)  {1868-1946;
   s/o David BBurg. & Nancy BBurg. - BE-
   12/5/46]
   [EMALINE] EMILY J. MOORE (19 S b.Ows)  [d/o
   Elijah Sutton Moore & Amanda Bowman - 1880]
   24 March, 1887, Lee  (M-L; B-L ch.; 1900-L;
   M-L ch-1919)    [SIMMIE (R.Low.Buff 66 widr.
   b.Lee) m2 4/3/1933 Lee, Farinda (Spencer)
   Johnson (43 wid. - d/o Alfred Spencer &
   Eliz. McIntosh; m1 Granville Johnson);
   SIMMIE (R.Beattyv. 70 widr/div. b.Lee)
   m3 7/12/40 Lee, Margaret (Gay) Deaton (62
   wid.) - M-L]
SIMPSON - see also HENRY SIMPSON
THOMAS (c22 b.Est.)  [1844-1900/10; s/o Joseph
   Brandenburg & Rhoda Hamilton]
   NANCY ANN THOMAS (c17 b.Ows.)   [d/o Isaac
   Thomas & Eliz. Rankin - REM]
   1865/6        (1870-L-2; B-L ch.; 1880-12;
   1900-L m-34; Lee deed heirs of Isaac Thomas
   - LNG; wid. Nancy 1910-L; M-L ch-1911)
THOMAS (c20-26 S b.Ows.)  [s/o Jackson BBurg.
   & Martha Callahan - 1880-1900; 2nd M-L]
   LEATHY _____ (___ b.___)
   1900-6        (TCS; H-sgl. 1900; H-remd.
   1907; NL M-L)
THOMAS F. (R.Ows. 27 2nd brakeman b.Ows.) P/
   Lee-Jack.  [m1 Leathy _____ above - TCS]
   LULA UNDERWOOD (R.Lee 16 S b.Lee) P/Lee
   [d/o Henry Underwood & Margaret Smith -
   mg.; M-L 1885; Lula listed as A-d/o
   Ephraim & Susan Angel 1900-L; WS Luther
   listed as G-GS/o Sarah BBurg. 1900-L]
   28 Sept., 1907 Lee @ bride's house, by A.
   J. Marcum; wits. Jackey Smith & Neal Farmer
   (M-L 8:177; TCS; 1910-L, WM, Margurite
   Smith & WS Luther & Taulbee Underwood
   w/them)

(Brandenburg cont.)

**BRANDENBURG (cont.)**

THURMAN (c18 b.KY)    [1892-19__; s/o Felix
    Brandenburg & Martha Taylor - 1900]
    ALICE _____ (c16 b.Lee)
    c1910              (H-sgl. w/bro. Arch 1910;
    1920-10, 4 & 2)
TRIG C. (R.Ows. 20 S b.Ows.) P/Lee-Ows.  [s/o
    Wm. B. BBurg. & Josephine Glass - ob-HS BE-
    5/20/65]
    ABBIE ISAACS (R.Ows. 17 S b.Ows.) P/Ows.
    [d/o Henry Isaacs & Alpha Scott - 1900;
    ob-WS BS-9/4/80]
    1 Oct., 1908, Ows.   [R.Owsley 1920;
    Whitesville, KY 1965-72; their 63rd anniv.
    BE-10/28/71; ob-WS BE-5/18/72]
WALKER - see WILLIAM WALKER
WALTER CHILDS (c22 S b.Boonev.)  [1875- 19__;
    s/o Ancel BBurg. & Levisa Cecil - 1880]
    MARTHA COMBS (c22 S b.Peb.)  [1876-1968
    Lex. hosp.; d/o Andrew J. Combs & Eliz.
    Burke - 1880; ob-W&S BE-5/2/68-12/11/47-
    1/20/55-12/1/60, OCN-11/8/56]
    1897/8       (1900-1910; B-O ch.; R.College
    Hill 1947-1960; wid. R.Richmond @ d. 1968)
WILBURN (c20 b.KY)  [s/o Wm. BBurg. & Armelda
    Winkle - 1880]
    ELSIE FIELDS (c27 b.KY)
    1899/1900         (1900; NL 1910Sx; 1920-J;
    ob-ch. Rich.IN-4/21/96)
WILLIAM (c20 b.Ows.)  [s/o Samuel Brandenburg
    & Sally Phillips]
    ALMEDIA WINKLE (c17 b.Est.)  [d/o James
    Winkle & Polly       - 1880 & 1880MS]
    1864/5       (1870-L-4; 1900 m-35; B-L ch.;
    ob-ch. BE-3/2/61)
WILLIAM BOWLES (c27 mcht b.KY)  [s/o James
    Brandenburg & Nancy Thomas - TCS]
    JOSEPHINE GLASS (c18 b.VA)  [d/o Wilson H.
    Glass & Martha Minter - Yest.]
    1870/1       (1880-8; 1900 m-29; ME-3/29/95,
    Mrs. BBurg. visits F., Dr. W. H. Glass, So.
    Boonev.; ME-6/21/95, Mrs. Dr. W. H. Glass
    & dau., Mrs. W. B. BBurg. left to visit VA)


(Brandenburg cont.)

## BRANDENBURG (cont.)

WILLIAM MARTIN (c18 b.KY) [s/o Andrew Jackson
    Brandenburg & Amanda Arnold - DB]
    MANDA STEEL (c16 b.KY) [d/o Burrell Steel
    & Sarah E. Payne - 1880]
    1891/2       (1900-L m-8, H/Martin; DB)
WILLIAM JACKSON (c21 S b.Lee) [1871-1945 Lee;
    s/o Patrick BBurg. & Mary Jane Gordan - ob-
    H BE-1/25/45; 1880-L]
    LOUISA "LOU" TREADWAY (c20 S b.Ows.) [d/o
    Wm. Wallace Treadway & Mary Mainous - 1880]
    1892/3       (DB; 1900-1910-L; M-L ch-1913;
    ob-H he was former member KY House of
    Representatives)
WILLIAM WALKER (c27 S b.Ows.) [1869-1946; s/o
    Henry BBurg. & Eliz. Roberts - 1880; FH]
    MARY ANN CREECH (c24 S b.Ows.) [1872-1964
    - BE-4/23/64]
    1896/7, Ows.   (1900-1910-1920; DB; BBG;
    ob-ch. BS-4/2/92)
WILSON - see CHARLES WILSON

## BREEDING

JOHN (c24 b.KY) [s/o Preston Breeding & Polly
    Collins]
    PERLINA HOGG (c16 b.Whitesburg, Let) [1850-
    1935 Lee; d/o Hiram Hogg & W2 Mary Roark -
    ob-W BE-11/7/35]
    13 Dec., 1866 Letcher (M-Let.; ob-W;
    1870-Let.; Boonev. c1871-1917; 1880-1890-
    1900; R.Winchester 3 yrs., then Beattyv.;
    ob-ch. BE-5/27/37)
JOHN B. WILGUS (c28 b.Boonev.) [1873-1940 CA;
    s/o John Breeding & Perlina Hogg - 1880;
    ob-H&M&S OCC-2/2/40; BE-11/7/35-5/27/37]
    MABLE LOYST (c21 b.CA)
    1899/1900 CA   (ob-H; ME-6/2/04 Wilgus, who
    R.CA last 5 yrs. & who has md. & has 2 ch.,
    visiting HF, John Breeding; 1910-Saratoga,
    Santa Clara, CA, m-10; R.Saratoga, CA 1935-
    1940)
THOMAS (c20 b.KY)   [s/o Mary Breeding - 1900]
    DOVIE ISAACS (c16 b.Ows.) [1882-1963 Berea
    hosp.; d/o Elijah Isaacs & Mary Etta Eden -
    ob-W BE-4/18/63]
    4 March, 1900   (OCN-3/24/55 55th anniv.;
    1900; R.Ida Mae 1955)
WILGUS - see JOHN B. WILGUS

**BREWER(?)**
JEREMIAH (R.Br. 17 S b.Br.)
   SARAH F. FAULKINS (R.Ows. 19 S b.Pike)
   16 April, 1857, Ows. [possibly in
   Breathitt 1860]
**BREWER**
_____ (___ b.___)
   ELIZ. BOWLING (c16 b.KY) [c1834-1852; d/o
   George Bowling & Phoebe    - D-O]
   1850/1      (W-sgl. 1850; D-O wf)
_____ (___ b.___)
   SARAH C. ST JOHN (c17 b.KY) [d/o Lloyd
   St John & Lucinda Tirey - 1900]
   c1899      (wid. Sarah 1900, no ch., w/P)
_____ (___ b.___)
   _____ CREECH (___ b.KY) [d/o John Creech
   & Sarah A. Griffin - possibilities are:
   NANCY (b. c1870; md. pre-1900), MARTHA C.
   (b. c1872; md. pre-1900) & EMILY (b. c1882;
   md. 1900-10)
   pre-1901      (1910, Myrtle Brewer, 9,
   GD/o John Creech; NL M-J)
BLEVINS (c24 S b.KY) [s/o Nicholas Brewer &
   Mary Hutson - 1880; art. OCN-9/29/50 &
   10/20/50 photo; ob-HS OCN-12/23/54-7/11/57]
   EMMA B. PETERS (c21 S b.KY)
   1897/8      (1900-1910-1920; TCS;
   R.Sturg. 1950-1957)
DANIEL P. MORRIS (c20 b.Hawk,TN) [s/o Howell
   S. Brewer & Polly Wolfe]
   LUCY ANN WILSON (c17 b.Ows.) [d/o Alfred
   Wilson & Anna Bowman - REM]
   c1866      (1870-3; B-O ch.; 1880-13;
   NL 1900Sx)
DANIEL (c23 S b.KY) [s/o Wm. Brewer & Mary
   Neeley - 1880]
   MATTIE ISAACS (c20 S b.KY) [d/o Wm. Isaacs
   & W2 Nancy J. Cole - 1880]
   6 Oct., 1898      (TCS; 1900-1899, m-1;
   1910 m-12; TCS; 1920; NL M-J)

(Brewer cont.)

## BREWER (cont.)

DANIEL P. M. (c24 S b.Ows.) [1877-1967 Cin.
Nur.H; s/o Nicholas Brewer & Mary Hutson -
1900; TS-TCS; art. OCN-9/29/50 & 10/20/50
photo; ob-H&S BE-10/19/67; OCN-12/23/54-
7/11/57]
SARAH ELIZ. "LIZZIE" PETERS (c19 S b.KY)
[1882-1960 Ows.; d/o Hardin Peters & Mary
J. Hoskins - TCS; 1900; ob-W BE-6/16/60]
1901/2        (1910-1920; BC 1914-1917-1919;
R.Sturgeon, Ows. 1950-1954; W/as Sarah &
Lizzie in BC)

FRANK F. (c16-38 b.KY) [s/o Daniel P. Morris
Brewer & Lucy Wilson - 1880]
STELLA BARTSFIELD (___ b.___)
1888-1910?        (TCS; NL 1900-1910Sx;
NL M-C/J)

HARLAN (c23 S b.Ows.) [1872-1942 Ows.; s/o
Nicholas Brewer & Mary Hutson - 1900;
ob-H BE-5/20/43]
FLORA MARCUM (___ b.KY)
16 July, 1896, Clay (M-C; 1900 m-4, W-NL,
w/HP; TCS; ob-ch. BE-7/3/47)        [H-remd.]

HARLAN (c33 2nd b.Ows.)        [m1 Flora Marcum
above - TCS]        [1872-1942 - ob-H]
BERTHA E. SPENCE (c19 S b.Ows.) [1886-1965
Lee; s/o John Spence & Martha Napier -
1900; ob-W BE-6/24/65]
1904/5        (1910-1920; B-O ch.; R.Sturg.
1942; ob-ch. OCN-3/29/56 & BS-6/25/92-
6/29/95-6/2/97)

HENRY C. (c18 S b.KY) [s/o Nicholas Brewer
& Mary Hutson - 1900]
MARTHA B. PETERS (c19 S b.KY) [1882-1915
Ows.; d/o Robt. E. Peters & W1 Lucy Bowman
- DC]
1900/1                (1910; BC-1913; NL M-J)
[HENRY m2 c1916, Fannie (nee Lane) Pearson
- TCS; wid. Fannie 1920 w/BiL Harlan, ch.
under 10 are 8, 6 & 2; BC-10/1917]

HOWELL, JR. (c28 2nd? b.TN)  [m1 _____]
MARY ANN THOMAS (c28 b.KY)
c1849        (1850, ch-6 & 4; 1860 lists
these 2 ch. last, which usually means they
were ch. from a prev. mg., other ch-6, 5, 2
& 3 mo.; B-O ch.; REM)

(Brewer cont.)

## BREWER (cont.)

HOWELL C. (c23 b.KY) [s/o Valentine Brewer
   & Sarah Wilson - 1880; ob-HS OCN-5/18/51-
   5/14/54-7/11/57 & OCC-2/14/41]
   MOLLIE SPENCE (c21 b.KY)
   1894/5       (TCS; 1900Sx-M, Berea;
   College Hill, KY 1941-51; Richmond 1954-7)
HOWELL COBB (c18 S b.KY) [1885-1954; s/o
   Nicholas Brewer & Mary Hutson - 1900; art.
   OCN-9/29/50 & 10/20/50 photo; ob-H OCN-
   12/23/54]
   AMERICA SPARKS (c18 S b.Ows.) [c1886-1971
   Lex. hosp. - ob-W BE-6/17/71]
   1 July, 1903, Clay (M-C; 1910-1920; TCS;
   R.Clarksville, OH 1950-54)
JAMES (c28 b.TN)
   SARAH _____ (c24 b.TN)
   c1867      (1870-12/69; 1870MS ch. d.
   7/69, age 11 mo.)
JAMES H. (c23 b.KY)
   EMMA WHITE (c23 b.KY) [d/o Oliver BOND
   & Margaret (nee Gross) WHITE, wid/o Shelton
   White - TCS]
   1894/5      (1900, next to WM; TCS)
   [H-remd.]
JAMES (R.Maulden; 23 b.Maulden, Jack.) [s/o
   Wm. Brewer & Polly Neeley - mg.; TCS]
   ANNIE WOLFE (R.Maulden; 28 S b.Jack.) [d/o
   Wm. Alvis Wolfe & Orpha Brewer - mg.; TCS]
   10 Nov., 1904, Jackson Co. @ Henry
   Metcalfe's (M-J; 1910)
JAMES H. (R.Ows. 39 2nd b.Scott) P/TN-Scott
   [widr/o Emma White above]
   SUSAN [nee _____] COLE (R.Ows. 39 2nd
   b.Ows.) P/Ows. [m1 _____ Cole]
   28 July, 1910, Ows.
JEFFERSON (R.Br. 15 S b.Br.)
   SERRILDA HAYS (R.Ows. 17 S b.Br.) [d.
   1861-4; d/o Edward Adrian Hayes & Eliz.
   Cockrell - 1850-B; M-P]
   30 July, 1858, Ows. (a/L 13 Oct, 1858 Br.)
   [JEFFERSON m2 c1865, Gilly Ann Childers -
   1870-W; 1880-B]
JEREMIAH - see BREWER(?)

(Brewer cont.)

## BREWER (cont.)

JOHN TYLER (c29 b.Hanc,TN)  [s/o Howell S.
   Brewer & Polly Thomas - JFB]
   MARTHA JANE COULTON (c18 b.Ows.)  [1851-
   1895; d/o Wm. Culton & Martha Collier -
   TS-TCS; P/1850; ME-10/4/95]
   18 March, 1869, Ows.  (TCS; 1870, no ch.;
   B-O ch.; 1880-9)
JOHN C. (c21 S b.Ows.)  [s/o Wm. Brewer
   & Eliz. Cole - 1860]
   NANCY VENABLE (c18 S b.Lee,VA)  [c1855-
   1951; d/o Joseph Venable & Lucy Ann
   - 1870; TS-TCS; ob-W OCN-6/2/50]
   1874/5           (1900-1910-1920; NL 1880;
   B-O ch-1878; ob-W)
JOHN F. (c23 S b.KY)    [s/o Nicholas Brewer
   & Mary Hutson - 1880; art. OCN-9/29/50 &
   10/20/50 photo; ob-HS OCN-12/23/54-7/11/57]
   MARTHA J. PETERS (c21 S b.KY)  [d/o Wm. T.
   Peters & Emily Morris - 1880]
   1890           (1900 m-10; 1910 m-19; JFB;
   R.Pheba, MS c1918-1950; Clay Co., MS 1954-
   1957)
LAFAYETTE - see MARCUS LAFAYETTE
L[UCIAN] B. (R.Ows. 21 S b.Ows.) P/TN  [1886-
   1954; s/o Valentine Brewer & Sarah Wilson -
   1900; ob-H&S OCN-5/14/54-5/18/51; OCC-
   2/14/41]
   MAUD M. HUGHES (R.Ows. 18 S b.Ows.) P/Ows.
   [d/o Meredith Hughes & Nancy Bowles]
   5 Jan, 1909, Ows.  [R.Owsley 1910 w/HP;
   Ows. 1916 - ob-ch. HJN-9/92; lived much of
   his life in CA & Ark.; R.Danville, Ark.
   1941-1951]
MARCUS LAFAYETTE (c20 S b.Buck Cr.)  [s/o Wm.
   Brewer & Mary Neeley - 1880]
   LUCY EMILY GIBSON (c14 S b.Sturgeon) [1872-
   1954; d/o Newton Harvey Gibson & Sarah
   McGeorge - 1880; ob-W OCN-6/4/54]
   1886/7        (B-O ch.; 1900-1910-1920)
MORRIS - see DANIEL P. MORRIS


(Brewer cont.)

## BREWER (cont.)

MORRIS D[ANIEL] (R.Ows. 33 S b.Ows.) P/TN-KY
[1877-1951 Louisville hosp.; s/o Valentine
Brewer & Sarah Wilson - 1880; ob-H&S OCN-
5/18/51; OCC-2/14/41]
RACHEL MAHAFFEY (R.Ows. 26 S b.Ows.) P/VA
[d/o Jesse Mahaffey & Lucy Ann Bowles - TCS
ob-H]
10 March. 1910, Ows. [ob-H says md. 4/10/
1910 & moved to OR; returned to KY c1912;
went to IN c1916; R.Gilford, IN 1941]

NEWELL (c25 S b.KY) [s/o Wm. Brewer & Mary
Neeley - TCS; 1900]
SARAH ISAACS (c35 S b.KY) [d/o Wm. Isaacs
& W1 Mary J. - 1880]
1906/7 (TCS; 1910-L)

N[ICHOLAS] W. M. (c24 b.Claiborne Co, TN)
[s/o Howell Brewer & Polly Wolfe - JFB]
MARY A[NN] HUDSON (c17 b.Clay)
19 Jan., 1864, Clay (M-C; 1900 m-36;
1870-5; B-O ch.; 1880-15; ME-6/26/96 birth
ch. Sturgeon; ob-ch. OCN-7/11/57)

NICHOLAS SHERMAN (c22 S b.Sturg) [c1880-1969;
s/o Nicholas Brewer & Mary Hutson - 1880;
art. OCN-9/29/50-10/20/50 photo; ob-H&S BE-
8/21/69, OCN-12/23/54-7/11/57]
LILLIE WILSON (c20 b.KY) [d/o Robert S.
Wilson & Mary J. Combs - TCS; 1900]
c1903 (H-remd-4 1910-6; TCS)

NICHOLAS SHERMAN (c25 2nd b.Sturgeon)
[widr/o Lillie Wilson above]
MYRTLE "MIRTIE" PRICE (c17 S b.Sturg) [d/o
Nelson "Bug" Price & Maggie Gibson - TCS;
ob-WS OCN-1/30/53]
1905/6 (1910-1920; B-O ch.; R.Sturg.
1950-1957; R.Boonev. 1967 - ob-HS BE-
10/19/67; R.Loveland, OH 1967 - ob-H/ch.
BE-12/7/67; wid. R.Booneville 1969)

PATRICK B. (c21 b.KY) [s/o Wm. Brewer & W3
Mary Neeley - 1880]
SARAH E[LLEN] SPIVEY (c14 b.KY) [d/o
Russell Spivey & Mary Jane Lynch - TCS]
7 Dec., 1887 (bond), Jackson Co.; bm. groom
& W. H. Clark (M-J 6:372; TCS; 1900-J m-12)

(Brewer cont.)

**BREWER (cont.)**

SHERMAN - see NICHOLAS SHERMAN
VALENTINE (c22 S b.Hanc/Hawk.,TN) [1842-1935;
    s/o Howell Brewer & Polly Wolfe - DC]
    SARAH J. WILSON (c20 S b.Ows.) [1844-1913;
    d/o Col. Alfred C. Wilson & Anna Bowman -
    Yest.; TS-TCS]
    11 May, 1865          (Yest.; TCS; 1870-4;
    1880; 1900-1910; B-O ch.)   [VALENTINE m2
    1914 Louvisa (nee Caudill) Deeds (d/o
    Alford Caudill & Jane Simpkins) (Louvisa m1
    Botner, m2 Deeds) - Yest.; TCS; 1920, s-d
    Deeds; DC/H]
VALENTINE (c16-31 b.Ows.)   [s/o Daniel P.
    Morris Brewer & Lucy Wilson - 1880]
    BERTHA JUDD (___ b.___)
    1895-1910          (TCS; HP/NL 1900;
    NL 1910Sx; NL M-J)
WILLIAM (c16-22 S b.Hawk., TN)   [s/o Howell
    Brewer - REM]
    _____ (___ b.___)
    1846-52          (H-2nd M-O 1853 listing Wm.
    as widr.; Wm. NL 1850)   [H-remd.]
WILLIAM (R.Buck Cr. 23 widr b.Hawk,TN)
    [widr/o _____ above]
    ELIZABETH A. COLE (R.Buck Cr. 14 S b.Clay)
    [c1839-1863; d/o John Cole & Margaret
    Higginbottom - TCS; REM]
    19 July, 1853, Ows., by Rev. J. Ward
    [R.Owsley 1860]   [H-remd.]
WILLIAM (c36 3rd b.Hawk, TN) [widr/o Elizabeth
    Cole above - 1860]
    MARY (nee NEELEY) _____ (c20 2nd b.VA)
    [wid/o _____]   [d/o Harrison J.
    Neeley & Jane Bishop - TCS]
    c1865          (1870, 1st ch. under 10 is 4;
    1880, same ch-14; TCS; wid. Polly 1900-
    1910; NL M-J)
WILLIAM [M.] (R.Ows. 34 S mcht b.Ows.) P/Ows.
    [s/o Valentine Brewer & Sarah Wilson -1900]
    [LUCY] EMMA WILSON (R.Ows. 23 S b.Ows.) P/
    Ows.   [d/o Hardin Wilson & Minerva Hurst -
    TCS; 1900 as Lucy E.; ob-WS OCN-1/12/56]
    2 Dec., 1909, Ows.   [R.Owsley 1910-1920;
    Trav.Rest 1956]

(Brewer cont.)

## BREWER (cont.)

WM. H[ENRY] (R.Ows. 22 S b.Ows.) P/Ows. [s/o
   Lafayette Brewer & Lucy Gibson - 1900]
   DORA BOTNER (R.Ows. 18 S b.Ows.) P/Ows.
   [1893-1923; GD/o Isaac & Sarah Botner - RW;
   1910]
   10 Oct., 1910, Ows. [R.Owsley 1920; H/as
   Wm. Henry - ob-ch. JT-6/15/95]
WILSON G[LASS] (R.Ows. 29 S b.Ows.) P/Ows.
   [1880-1957; s/o Valentine Brewer & Sarah J.
   Wilson - TS-TCS; ob-H&S OCN-7/11/57-
   5/18/51-5/14/54 & OCC-2/14/41]
   MARY LANE (R.Ows. 18 S b.Ows.) P/Ows. [d/o
   John Lane & Rhoda Peters - 1900]
   14 Oct., 1909, Ows. [M-O adds: md. Island
   City, by W. A. Bowman, Bapt. Min.; wits.
   Norman Brewer, D. B. & Maggie Peters - rec.
   11/56] [R.Owsley 1910-1920; Sturg. 1941-
   1954]

## BREWSTER
see BRUSTER

## BROCK

_____ (__ b.KY)
   MARTHA BAKER (c18 b.Ows.) [d/o Sarah Jane
   Baker & unknown - HTB]
   c1884/5      (W-remd. 1900, 1st Brock ch-
   10/85; M-B ch-1916) [MARTHA remd. Wm.
   Fields - 1900]
ALEXANDER (R.Ows. 20 S b.Br.) [s/o Amon
   Brock & Mahala Patrick - 1880]
   MAXLINE RILEY (R.Br. 17 S b.Br.) P/Br.
   [1866-1954 Let; d/o Granville Riley
   & W1 Sarah Jane Baker - DC; LM]
   24 Sept., 1884, Breathitt @ Granville
   Riley's, by Robert Burton; wits. A. J.
   Baker & Abner Allen [DIV. pre-1900 - LM]
   (M-B 3:202; W-remd. 1900)
   [MAXALINE md. 2nd James Smith - LM]
AMON (c20 b.Harl.) [s/o Amon Brock Sr & Mary
   Osborne - TCS]
   MAHALA PATRICK (c18 b.Per.) [poss. d/o
   Alexander Patrick - TCS]
   1844/5, Breathitt (1850-H; 1860-1870-B;
   1880-1900; TCS]

(Brock cont.)

**BROCK (cont.)**
ENOCH (c21 b.KY)
  LUCY _____ (c15 b.KY)
  c1851        (1860-8)
THEOPHILUS (R.Ows. 20 S b.KY) P/KY-TN    [s/o
  Amon Brock & Mahala Patrick - TCS]
  NANCY POWEL (R.Ows. 17 S b.KY) P/--
  25 Nov., 1878, Ows.   [R.Owsley 1880 H-md.,
  W-NL]
**BROGINS/BROGAN**
JOHN (R.Ows. 42 2nd b.TN) P/Ire-TN   [m1 _____
  _____]
  NANCY BOWMAN (R.Ows. 33 S b.Ows.) P/-- Clay
  [d/o John Bowman & Eliz. McCollum - JFB]
  28 Feb., 1876, Ows. @ Nancy Bowman's
**BROWN**
ANDY J. (c32 2nd; fore st-mill; b.Morgan)
  [m1 _____]
  GRACE PETERS (c15 S b.Earnestv) [1890-1956;
  d/o James Elisha Peters & Louisa Young -
  ob-W&S OCN-12/6/56-6/7/54; 1900]
  1905/6        (1910-1920; B-O ch.; NL for
  Andy & W1 1900; R.Muncie 1956)
BRAZIL   (___ b.___)
  EMADATHA (nee SHACKELFORD) MOORE (c35 2nd
  b.KY) [wid/o Wm. Moore - REM 1850-B] [d/o
  Abner T. Shackelford & Nancy Gossett - TCS;
  ACB]
  c1855        (Emadatha MOORE on TL 1852-4;
  1860, wid. Emadatha BROWN, w/3 Moore ch. &
  2 Brown ch., ages 4 & 2, her Moore MiL with
  her; TCS; REM; 1870 Emmadeth Brown w/daus.
  18 & 12 & Judah Moore, MiL)  [EMADATHA
  poss. m3 John Stamper]
**BROWNING**
CALEB B. (c21 S b.Gray Hawk, Jack.)  [s/o
  Robt. Browning & Martha Edwards - TCS]
  MARY BURCH (c17 S b.Island City, Ows.)
  [d/o Jasper Burch & Rhoda E. Morris - TCS]
  1901/2        (1910-1920; B-O ch.)
JOHN (c26 b.KY)
  ALSEY BISHOP (c23 b.KY)
  c1849        (1850, all ch. appar. belong
  to Lois, age 40, who was w/them; B-J ch-
  1858; 1860-J-11)

(Browning cont.)

**BROWNING (cont.)**
ROBERT (c26 b.Laurel) P/KY
    MARTHA EDWARDS (c17 b.Ows.) P/NC  [d/o
    George Edwards & Margaret    - 1870-J]
    late 1870       (1880-6; 1900 m-30; H-sgl.
    w/Elias Moore 1870-J; NL M-J/Lau.)
**BRUSTER/BREWSTER**
SKILLEN M. (c20 b.VA)
    MARY McDANIEL (c17 b.KY)
    11 May, 1860, <u>Clay</u>  (M-C; 1860-MWY)
**BRYANT/BRIANT**
ARTHUR (c19 S b.KY)  [s/o David Bryant
    & Laura Gabbard - BBG]
    AMANDA "MANDY" J. HOSKINS (c15 S b.KY)
    [d/o Wm. Hoskins & Margaret Robertson
    - ob-WS BE-12/8/60]
    1902/3       (1910; TCS; ME-9/18/03,
    "once parted now united are Arthur &
    Amanda Bryant"; R.Lex. 1960)
CHARLIE (R.Lee 20 S b.Lee) P/Br.
    NANNIE McINTOSH (R.Ows 18 S b.Ows) P/Br.
    [d/o Elisha McIntosh & Minerva Jane Fox -
    ob-WS OCN-4/19/56; LNG/Bible of niece Icey]
    14 Oct., 1909, <u>Breathitt</u> [recorded Owsley]
    [NOTE: Nannie listed w/P 1910]
    [R.Lothair 1956]
DAVID (R.Ows. 20 S b.VA) P/NC  [s/o John
    Bryant & Rachel Surrat - MT]
    LAURA GABBARD (R.Ows. 22 S b.KY) P/KY
    [d/o Wyatt Gabbard & Sarah White - 1860]
    17 Dec., 1876, Ows. @ Wyat Gabbard's
    (a/L 12/<u>19</u>/76, H-26, HP/SC, W-21, md. @
    Wesley Botner's; rest same)  [R.Owsley
    1880 w/HP; 1900]   [LAURA m2 Henry Price]
JAMES MORGAN (c22 b.Buck Cr.)  [1877-19__; s/o
    David Bryant & Laura Gabbard - 1880-1900]
    MAUDE JANE PETERS (c18 b.Island City)
    [1883-1939 Jack.; d/o Peter Miller Peters
    & Margaret Scoonover -  DC; 1900]
    1900/1       (B-O son Miller 1908; 1910-J
    m1-9; BC 1916-1918-J; 1920-J; DC/W; widr.
    Morgan R.Gray Hawk, Jack. 1939; NL M-J)

(Bryant cont.)

## BRYANT (cont.)
JOHN (c38 S b.KY)
    SUSAN GABBARD (c21 S b.KY)
    1902/3        (1910 2x, once as m-7 & once
    as m-10 = 1899/1900; BBG)
MORGAN - see JAMES MORGAN
SIMMON [SIMON] (R.Ows. 27 Div. b.Br.)
    LUCINDA SANDERS (R.Ows. 17 S b.Wlk,NC)
    [d/o Hiram Sanders & Susan Jenkins - 1850
    surname as "Sandler"]
    16 June, 1857, Ows.  [R.Owsley 1860]
STEPHEN (c20 b.VA)   [s/o John Bryant & Rachel
    Surrat - 1870]
    MARGARET A. WHITE (c15 b.KY)  [d/o Shelton
    White & Margaret Gross - TCS]
    c1873        (1880-6; TCS)
WALTER (c20 b.KY)  [s/o David Bryant & Laura
    Gabbard - 1900]
    ELLEN VENABLE (c16 b.KY) [d/o Thos. Venable
    & Mary M. Shanks - TCS; 1900]
    1900/1       (D-O puts ch. b. 1901/2; TCS;
    1920)

## BULLOCK
WM. BUTLER (c47 2nd Law. b.KY)  [m1 Nancy
    Wilson - M-C 5/11/71; TCS] [1849-1915; s/o
    John Clark Bullock & Isabella Bowman - KAS;
    TS-TCS]
    MARY [ANN "POP"] EVANS (c34 S b.KY)  [1862-
    1939 Lee; d/o Huram Evans & Nancy Stamper -
    1880; ME-7/15/98; TCS; ob-W BE-4/13/39]
    15 April, 1896 Ows. (Sat.), @ res. of bride
    by Eld. Stump  (ME-4/24/96; ME-7/15/98 Mrs.
    Hiram Evans, Pleasant Grove. visiting dau.,
    Mrs. W. B. Bullock, Boonev.; 1900 m-4; 1910
    m-13 H-2nd, Evans SiL w/them; wid. Mary
    w/sis Nancy Combs 1920; wid. d. Hlbg. 1939;
    H/as W. B., Wm., & W. Butler)

## BUNDY
BENJAMIN (c58 b.VA) P/KY
    EADY(?) _____ (c22 b.KY)
    c1869        (1870 no ch.; widr. Ben 1880-9)

## BURCH/BIRCH/BERCH
BLAINE - see JAMES BLAINE


(Burch cont.)

114

## BURCH (cont.)

CHARLES M. (c22 S b.Island City, Ows.) [s/o
Jasper Burch & Rhoda Morris - B-O]
SYLVANIA EDWARDS (c15 S b.Island City) [d/o
Robt. Edwards & Martha Sizemore - TCS]
1896        (1900 m-4; 1910 m-13; B-O ch.;
ob-ch. BS-4/13/95)

CURTIS W. (c20 S b.KY) [1879-1952; s/o Newton
Burch & W1 Mary Hamilton - 1880-1900; ob-H
OCN-8/29/52]
SHRILDA/SARILDA HUDSON (c16 S b.Ows) [1884-
1961; d/o John Hudson & Eliz. Davidson -
1900; ob-W&S BE-5/4/61, OCN-8/4/55]
1900        (1910 m-10; both sgl. 1900;
BBG; ob-H; 1920; wid. R.Ows. 1952-55;
Boonev. 1961; NL M-J; NL P-Sp.Am.)

FRANK (R.Ows. 22 S b.Ows.) P/Ows.  [1886-1969;
s/o Jasper Burch & Rhoda Morris - 1900;
2nd-3rd M-O; ob-H BE-7/17/69]
IDA PETERS (R.Ows. 15 S b.Ows.) P/Ows.
[d/o Jacob Peters & Mary Moore - MT]
30 March, 1908, Ows.  [R.Owsley 1910-1920]
[FRANK R. (R.Ows. 46 widr. b.Ows.) m2
10/26/32, Mattie Stacy (R.Ows. 30 S b.Ows.)
d/o James Stacy & Susan (Campbell) - M-O;
FRANK (R.Ows. 73 widr. b.Ows.) m3 5/5/59,
Sally (Morris) McIntosh (R.Ows. 75 wid.
b.Br.) d/o Berry Morris & Martha - M-O;
wid. R.Boonev. 1969]

ISAAC ["IKE"] (c25 S b.Ows.) [1883-1967 Sturg;
s/o Newton Burch & W2 Rhoda Madden - 1900;
ob-H&S BE-9/14/67-12/18/58, OCN-5/22/58]
RUTH [nee] NEELEY ROBERTS (c20 2nd b.Ows.)
[wid/o _____ Roberts]  [1888-1960; d/o
Elias Neeley & Eliza Peters - 1900; will-F;
ob-W BE-10/20/60]
7 Aug., 1907, Sturgeon, Ows.; by W. A.
Bowman, Bapt. Min.; wits. Blaine Burch &
Zack, Sarah & Mary E. Bowman  (M-O filed
12/56; OCN-8/15/57 their 50th anniv.; 1910
m-2 W-2nd; TCS; 1920; R.Sturg. 1957; Ows.
1958; ob-ch. BS-1/10/85)

(Burch cont.)

## BURCH (cont.)

[JAMES] BLAINE (c23 S b.KY)  [1884-1958; s/o
Newton Burch & W2 Rhoda Madden - 1900;
ob-H OCN-5/22/58]
EMMA [EMILY] SINGLETON (c28 S b.KY) [1881-
1978 Clay; d/o Eli Singleton & Eva Byrd -
DC; ob-W&S BS-3/20/78 & OCN-12/29/55]
10 March, 1910, Clay  (M-C MT; 1910 m-0,
w/HP; TCS; 1920 & ob-HM; R.Sturg. 1955-
1958; H/as James B. & Blaine)
JASPER (c20 S b.Claiborne Co., TN)  [s/o Wm.
Burch & Malinda Mays - 1860]
RHODA ELIZABETH MORRIS (c16 S b.Ows.)  [d/o
Hardin Morris & Sarah Anderson]
1865        (1870-3; 1880-1890; 1900-6/66,
m-34; B-O ch.; 1910 m-47; REM; wid. Rhoda
1920 w/dau.)
JASPER (c21 S b.Sexton Cr.)
EMILY "EMMA" OLDHAM (c15 S b.KY)
1889/90        (1900-1910-1920; B-O ch.)
JOHN (R.Ows. 28 2nd b.TN) P/TN [m1_____]
[s/o Wm. Burch & Malinda Mays - 1880]
MARGARET M. CARROLL (R.Ows. 18 S b.KY) P/KY
[c1860-1879 - 1880MS]
- Sept., 1878, Ows.  [widr. John in Owsley
1880]    [JOHN m3 10/27/81 Jack., Elizabeth
Johnson - TCS]
LEONARD (c22 S b.Ows.)  [1885-1970 Lex. Nur.H;
s/o Wm. Burch & Mary Brewer - 1900]
MINNIE MAHAFFEY (c18 S b.KY)  [d/o Jesse
Mahaffey & Lucy Ann Bowles - 1900]
1906/7        (1910)
NEWTON (c25 S b.Claiborne Co., TN)  [s/o Wm.
Burch & Malinda Mays - 1860]
MARY HAMILTON (c20 b.Ows.)  [d/o Curtis
Hamilton & Sylvestus Smith - 1860]
c1866        (1870-J; 1880-13, widr. Newton
w/WP; B-O ch.; TCS; NL M-J; ob-ch. BE-
12/18/58)    [H-remd.]
NEWTON (c40 2nd b.Claiborne Co, TN)
[widr/o Mary Hamilton above]
RHODA A. MADDEN (c20 S b.KY)  [1862-1952;
d/o Isaac Madden & Mary Slocess - TCS;
ob-W OCN-1/18/52]
1881/2        (1890-1900-1910-1920;
ob-W; ob-ch. OCN-5/22/58)
(Burch cont.)

**BURCH (cont.)**
NEWTON (R.Clay 26 S b.Clay) P/Clay
    LULA SAYLOR (R.Ows. 22 S b.Clay) P/Clay
    [prob d/o Jesse Saylor, Emily Peters -1900]
    20 Sept., 1904, <u>Clay</u>  (M-C mf)
WILLIAM (c18 b.KY)  [s/o Jasper Burch
    & Rhoda E. Morris - TCS; 1880]
    MARY BREWER (c19 b.KY)  [d/o Valentine
    Brewer & Sarah J. Wilson - 1880; ob-WS
    OCC-2/14/41 & OCN-5/18/51-5/14/54]
    1884/5       (1900 TCS; R.Muskogee, OK 1941;
    Quapaw, OK 1951; Baxter Springs, KS 1954)
**BURK/BURKE**
GEORGE W. (c24 2nd b.VA)    [1855-19__]
    [m1 _____]
    LETITIA (nee PENDERGRASS) MAYS (c25 2nd
    b.VA) P/VA   [Div/f Pealy Mays - REM]
    [1851-19__; d/o Corda Pendergrass & Minerva
    Thompson - ob-WS Patsy Farley]
    1878         (1880-1; 1900-L m-21; 1910-L
    m2-32 both; REM; ob-WS)
LAYFATT [LAFAYETTE] (R.Ows. 23 S b.Lee,VA)
    ELIZ. PENDERGRASS (R.Ows. 18 S b.Lee, VA)
    [d/o Corda Pendergrass & Minerva Thompson -
    1850-Lee,VA]
    5 May, 1859, Ows.   [R.Owsley 1860, 1880-
    1900-1910; widr. Lafayette 1920]
**BURNETT**
JOHN (c19 b.KY)
    SUDIE _____ (c16 b.KY)
    1893/4       (1900)
**BURNS**
_____ (___ b.___)
    LUCINDA GILBERT (c16-25 b.KY)  [d/o John
    Gilbert & Nancy Smith - 1880]
    1880-8       (1910, wid. Lucinda w/WF &
    s-M, 7/7 ch., 2 @ home ages 10 & 8)
ABIJAH B. (c29 b.Ows.)  [1839-1905 Lee; s/o
    John Burns & Louisa Combs - ME-4/13/05]
    MARY J. WEBB (c18 b.KY) P/KY
    1867/8       (1870-2; 1880-11; B-O ch.;
    1890; 1900; R.Proctor when H-d.)
BRICE - see BRISON


(Burns cont.)


117

BRISON (c23 b.KY) [s/o John Burns & Louisa
    Combs]
    BELINDA "MILLY" NEWNAM (c20 b.Ows.) [d/o
    Henry Harrison Newnam & Belinda "Milly"
    Tincher - LP; newspaper art. LNG/LHS]
    1869        (1870 no ch.; 1880-L-9; 1900-L
    m-30; M-L ch-1887; ob-ch. BE-5/18/49-
    11/2/50; fam. photo BE-7/23/70) [H-remd.]
[BRISON] BRICE (R.Lee 57 2nd b.Ows.) P/--
    [widr/o Milly Newnam above]
    ADA ANN SMITH [_____] (R.Lee 45 2nd b.Ows)
    P/--   [m1 _____] [poss. d/o Richard
    Smith & Margt. Evans - 1870-L]
    22 Dec., 1904 <u>Lee</u>, @ Jack Smith's, by James
    E. Dunagin; wits. Mat Smith, Davy Goocy &
    Finley Cornett(?)    (M-L; 1910)
CHESTER W. (R.Ows. 18 S b.Ows.) P/Ows-Clay
    [s/o John S. Burns & Armina       - 1900]
    ELLA MORRIS (R.Per. 23 S b.Per.) P/Per.
    [d/o John Morris & Sarah McIntosh - 1900-P;
    ob-WS BE-4/16/59
    28 Nov., 1909, Ows.  [R.Owsley 1910;
    Buckhorn 1959]
FRANCIS "FRANK" (c20 b.KY) [s/o Wm. Burns
    & Rachel Asher - TCS]
    MARY J. BARNETT (c18 b.KY)
    c1868        (1870-6/69; 1880; TCS)
FRANKLIN "FRANK" (c23 S b.KY) [s/o John Burns
    & Malinda Bowling - 1880]
    LUCY BARRETT (c21 S b.KY) [d/o Irvin
    Barrett & Polly Allen - TCS]
    1893        (1900 m-7; 1910 m-16; TCS;
    1920; ob-ch. OCN-6/13/57 & BS-5/26/88)
GEORGE (c22 S b.KY)
    HANNAH [MATILDA] BARGER (c20 S b.KY)
    28 Feb., 1883, <u>Clay</u>  (M-C; 1900 m-15; 1910
    m-27; W/as Hannah & Matilda)
GEORGE (c21 b.Buck Cr.) [s/o Abijah Burns
    & Mary Webb - 1880]
    LUCY JANE YORK (c21 b.Boonev.) [1875-1960
    OH; d/o Thompson Zacharias York & Elzira
    "Sis" Murphy - PWB/FB]
    24 Jan., 1897, Ows. (Sun.) @ Co. Judge's
    office, by Rev. Stump    (ME-2/5/97; 1900
    m-3; B-O ch-1909)
(Burns cont.)

**BURNS (cont.)**
GREEN (c18 S b.KY)
   CATHERINE "CATTIE" DEAN (c16 S b.KY) [d/o
   Ezekiel Dean & Kezziah Barrett - 1900;
   ob-WS OCN-7/8/49; ME]
   about July, 1903     (ME-1/8/04, they
   were md. some 5 mos. ago & R.Snake Br.;
   1910-7, m-10 = 1900; W-sgl. 1900; PWB;
   1920-16, wid. Cattie BURNS a/L as Cattie
   DEAN; R.IN 1949; NL M-C)
   [CATTIE m2 _____ Barrett - M-O ch. 1929
   W/as Cattie Burns Barrett - M-O]
JACKSON (c16 b.Clay) [s/o Washington Burns
   & Matilda Davidson - TCS]
   LUCIND[A] BURNS (c13 b.Clay) [d/o Granville
   Burns & Nancy Begley - TCS]
   1 Aug., 1867, <u>Clay</u> (M-C; TCS; 1880-11;
   B-O ch.)
JAMES (c26 b.KY)
   MERTIE ISAACS (c17 b.KY) [d/o James
   Isaacs & Sarah E. Flanery - ob-WS OCN-
   6/19/58; 1900)
   c1908     (1920-11; VDK; ob-WS;
   ob-ch. BS-10/15/98; R.Cin.,OH 1958)
JEREMIAH "JERRY" (c23 b.KY) [s/o Wm. Burns
   & Mary Smith]
   EMILY MORRIS (c21 b.KY) [d/o John Morris &
   Sarah McIntosh - 1880-P; ob-WS BE-4/16/59]
   1894/5    (1900; ob-WS; R.Richmond 1959)
JOHN "DANDY" (c30 b.Clay) [s/o Wm. Burns
   & Rachel Asher - TCS]
   MALINDA BOWLIN[G] (c19 b.Clay) [d/o
   Pallas Bowling & Mary Cornett - TCS]
   22 Feb., 1866, <u>Clay</u> (M-C; 1870-3; B-O ch.;
   1880; TCS)  [H-remd.]
JOHN "DANDY" (c51 2nd b.Clay) [widr/o Malinda
   Bowling above]
   MARGARET KETCHUM (c22 b.KY)
   22 Feb., 1887   (MT; 1900; LM; 1910
   wid. Margt. w/s-s Frank; NL M-C)

(Burns cont.)

**BURNS (cont.)**

JOHN S. (c24 S b.Ows/Per.) [1863-1946; s/o
   Wm. Burns & Mary Smith - TS-TCS]
   ARMINA "MINEY" ALLEN (c19 S b.Clay) [1866-
   1948; d/o Irvine Allen & _____ Byrd - DC;
   TS-TCS]
   1888        (1900 m-12; 1910 m-21; M-O ch.,
   John b.Ows.; TCS; B-O ch-1909, John b.Per.;
   1920; NL M-C; W/as Armina, Minnie & Miney)
JOSEPH (___ b.___)
   LUCY ANN ROSS (c21-41 b.KY) [d/o Levi Ross
   (Mul) & Sarah Burns (w) - 1880; TCS; PWB]
   1880-1900        (EERS; NL 1900-1910Sx)
PERRY A. (R.Ows. 24 S b.Ows.) [prob. s/o
   Wm. Burns & Rachel Asher - 1850; P/M-C]
   SARAH DAVIDSON (R.Clay 14 S b.Clay) [prob.
   d/o James Davidson & Rachel Allen - 1850-C;
   P/M-C]
   7 Jan., 1852, Clay  (M-C mf)
PERRY D. (c23 S b.KY) [1856-1918; s/o Wm.
   Burns & Mary Smith - TS-TCS]
   LUCY BISHOP (c16 S b.Ows.) [1862-1932; d/o
   Wm. Bishop & Nancy Baker - DC]
   1879/80        (1880-MWY; 1900 m-20; 1910
   m-32; wid. Lucy 1920)
SAMUEL (c19 S b.Lee) [1877-1950; s/o Brice
   Burns, W1 Milly Newnam - ob-H BE-11/2/50]
   MARY MAYS (c17 S b.KY) [d/o George Mays
   & Elizabeth Eden - TCS]
   1894/5        (1900-L; 1910-1920; TCS)
WILEY (c29 b.KY) [s/o Wm. Burns & Rachel
   Asher]
   RACHEL BISHOP (c17 b.KY) [poss. d/o Wm.
   Bishop & Susan    - MT]
   8 Dec., 1865, Clay  (M-C; LM; 1870-C)
   [WILEY poss. m2 Lucinda Barrett - TCS]
WILEY (c17 S b.KY)  [s/o Washington Burns
   & Matilda Davidson - TCS]
   MALLISSA ["MASSIE"] BURNS (c16 S b.KY)
   [d/o Granville Burns & Nancy Begley - TCS]
   5 May, 1872, Clay  (M-C; TCS; 1880-6; 1900
   m-25; 1910 m-37; W/as Mallissa, Masfurline;
   Massar & Massie) [WILEY m2 Emily _____ -
   TCS; 1920]

(Burns cont.)

120

**BURNS (cont.)**
WILLIAM (R.Per. 21 S b.Clay) [c1832-1907; s/o
   Wm. Burns & Rachel Asher - RP]
   [MARY] POLLY SMITH (R.Per. 18 S b.Per.)
   [1838-1894 Ows.; d/o Jeremiah Smith & Eliz.
   Jones - RP]
   11 Aug., 1853, <u>Perry</u> (M-P; 1860-Lau.;
   1870-14; 1880) [WILLIAM poss. m2 Betty
   Fields - TCS]
WILLIS (c29 S b.KY) [s/o Wiley Burns & Massie
   Burns - 1880]
   JULIA _____ (c17 S b.KY)
   1902/3          (1910)
**BURRIS**
JAMES M. (c45 2nd b.IN) [widr/o Catherine
   Bennett - B-O ch.]
   MINERVA FLANERY (c25 b.VA) [prob. d/o
   Thomas Flanery & Nancy Lock]
   1879/80        (1880-MWY, FLANERY s-ch. ages
   8 & 2; TCS)
**BURROWS**
CHARLES (R.Br. 32 S b.uk.)
   DEMERIAS HIERONYMOUS (R.Ows. 23 S b.Mad.)
   [d/o Samuel Rector Hieronymous & Sally
   White - REM]
   11 Sept., 1855, Ows. (a/L 8 May, 1855 Br.)
**BURTON**
DANIEL (R.Morg. 22 S b.--)
   MATILDA SEBASTIAN (R.Frozen, Br. 15 S b.
   Floyd)    [d/o Wesley Sebastian & Milly
   Birchfield]
   25 Dec., 1857, <u>Breathitt</u>, by Wm. Likins
   (M-B; 1860; NL 1870/B/L)
JOHN (c24 b.KY)
   NANCY (nee _____) MORRIS (c26 2nd b.KY)
   [m1 _____ Morris - TCS]
   c1848          (1850-1; TCS)
ROBERT (R.Br. 28 widr. b.Hanc.,TN) [Rev.]
   [widr/o Mary Ann Gay - D-B 1853] [s/o John
   Burton - JTB]
   SUSAN BAKER (R.Buffalo; 25 S b.Clay) [d/o
   John H. "Mucker Jack" Baker & Lucinda Amis;
   d. 1867]
   - Nov., 1854, Ows. (a/L <u>10/14</u>/54 Br. - M-B)
   [R.Breathitt 1860]    [ROBT. m3 c1868 Br.,
   Ella Hacker]

**BUSH**

HARVEY [GEORGE] (c40 2nd b.KY) [m1 _____]
    MARGARET SNOWDEN (c23 b.KY) [d/o David
    Snowden & Margaret McGuire - REM]
    21 June, 1846, Ows. (JFB; REM; TCS)
JEFFERSON - see THOMAS JEFFERSON
[THOS. "JEFF"] JEFFERSON (R.Wlf 24 S b.KY) P/
    KY [1850-1942; s/o Llewellyn Bush & Martha
    Townsend - ob-H OCC-3/13/42; 1860; 1870-W]
    CHRISTIANA [ANN] PLUMMER (R.Ows. 24 S b.KY)
    P/KY [d/o John Plummer & Celia Turner - TR
    ob-WS BE-1/31/35 M/as Lutes, but B-B sib &
    ob-WS 2/26/43 list M/as Turner]
    13 Dec., 1877, Ows. @ John Plummer's
    [R.Wolfe 1880-1900-1910; Torrent 1935]

**BUTCHER**

FRANKLIN (c24 <u>Mul</u> S b.Clay) [s/o Isaac
    Butcher & Phereby   - 1850]
    _____ (___ b.KY)
    c1872    (H-remd. 1880, ch-7, 4 & 9 mos;
    1900-1910-L w/W2; 1910-L H-2nd) [H-remd.]
FRANKLIN (c27 <u>Mul</u> 2nd b.KY) [m1 _____ abv]
    SURRENA "RENA" GODFREY (c15 <u>Mul</u> S b.Br.)
    1874/5    (1880, ch-7, 4 & 9 mos.;
    1900-L m-25; 1910-L m-33, H-2nd = 1876/7;
    M-L ch-1906)
ISAAC (c24 <u>Mul</u> b.Ows.) [s/o Isaac Butcher
    & Phereby   - 1850]
    REBECCA _____ (c15 <u>white</u> b.Jack.) P/KY
    c1872    (1880-7; NL 1900/J/L)

**BYRD/BIRD**

CRIT (c20 S b.KY)
    ELLEN BEGLEY (c17 S b.KY) [d/o Ballard
    Begley & Malvery Gibson - 1900]
    14 July, 1907 @ E. Spencer's, Ows., by E.
    Spencer, Min.; wits: James Stidham, A. J.
    Spencer & Walter Gibson (M-P J:101; 1910
    w/WP)
FRANK (c21 b.Teges, Clay Co.)
    NANCY ANN COMBS (c16 b.Teges, Clay)
    30 July, 1904, <u>Clay</u> (M-C; MT; B-O ch-
    1908; 1910-C-4, m1-7 both)
GEORGE (R.Clay 21 S b.Clay) P/WV-Clay
    RHODA JANE McDANIEL (R.Ows. 21 S b.Clay) P/
    Clay [d/o Frank McDaniel, Eliz. Baker-1900]
    16 June, 1904, Ows.
(Byrd cont.)

**BYRD (cont.)**
JOHN (c20 2nd b.TN) P/TN  [m1 _____]
   JANE MINTER [_____] (c20 2nd b.Benge,Clay)
   [m1 _____]
   1880       (NL 1880Sx; 1900-Lau. m-20;
   1910 m2-29 both; B-O ch-1908; NL M-C)


**CABLE**
CASPER (R.Ows. 25 S b.TN)  [1826-1886; s/o
   Joseph Cable & Rebecca Pierce - ACB; NC]
   MARTHA DRAKE (R.Ows. 21 S b.Taz., VA) [d/o
   Wm. Drake & Jane Stinson - ACB]
   7 Feb., 1856, Ows.  [R.Owsley 1860; Wolfe
   1870-1880]
CONRAD (R.Ows. 23 S b.John.,TN) [s/o Conrad
   Cable & Mary Whitehead - REM; ACB]
   SARAH BAKER (R.Ows. 23 S b.John.,TN)  [d/o
   Ben Baker & Polly   - 1850]
   25 Feb., 1857, Ows.  [R.Owsley 1860; Wolfe
   1870-1880]
JOSEPH EREALIS (c26 b.Lee,VA/TN)  [1824-1901
   MO; s/o Joseph Cable & Rebecca Pierce - NC]
   MARGARET ELLEN HAMMOND (c23 b.KY)
   13 Nov., 1851     (NC; 1860-7; B-O ch.;
   ACB; moved to Linn Co., MO)
STEPHEN (R.Ows. 25 S b.John.,TN]  [s/o Joseph
   Cable & Rebecca Pierce - ACB; 1850-Lee,VA]
   AMANDA JANE WYATT (R.Ows. 21 S b."With" Co,
   VA)  [Wythe Co., VA]
   18 Jan., 1855, Ows.  [R.Owsley 1860; Wolfe
   1870, 1880 HF w/them, 1900; Lee 1910]
**CAIN/CANE**
DANIEL (c20 b.KY) P/KY
   MARY F. _____ (c20 b.KY) P/KY
   c1879     (1880, no ch.)
WILLIAM (R.Est. 18 S b.Est.)
   MARY ANN GRAY (R.Ows. 17 S b.Ows.)
   27 April, 1855, Ows. [R.Jackson Co. 1860-
   1870 & 1875 B-J ch.; Lee 1900; widr. Wm.
   R.Lee 1910]
WILLIAM (c29 b.KY)
   AMERICA A. ELIZABETH WARD (c25 b.KY)  [d/o
   Wm. Ward & Nancy BBurg. - 1880]
   1899/1900    (ob-ch. HJN-10/89, b.
   3/1/1900 Ows.; 1900-L m-0)

**CALDWELL/COLWELL**
ELISHA (c17 b.KY)   [s/o Susan Colwell - 1870]
   MARY _____ (c13 b.KY)
   c1872       (1880-7)
FREELAND (R.Ows. 22 S b.Ash Co., NC)
   ELIZBETH SHOEMAKER (R.Ows. 22 S b.Lee,VA)
   17 Jan., 1857, Ows.   [R.Owsley 1860; wid.
   Elizabeth R.Lee 1870]
**CALLAHAN/CALLIHAN/CALIHAN**
ALBERT (R.Ows. 22 S b.Ows.)  [1879-1961; s/o
   Daniel Callahan & Emily Lewis - 1880; ob-H
   BE-3/16/61]
   MARY GABBARD (R.Lee 16 S b.Ows.)  [1883-
   1952; d/o Julius Gabbard & Cath. Thomas -
   1880; ob-W OCN-9/20/52]
   31 March, 1900, Lee @ Robt. Angel's, by L.
   H. Wright, MG; wits. David Toler & James
   Cole   (M-L; 1900-1910-1920; B-O ch.; MT)
BASCOM (21 S b.KY)  [s/o Jeremiah Callihan
   & America Wilson - 1880]
   MAGGIE ROSE (16 S b.KY)  [d/o  Ezekiel Rose
   & Cynthia Jett - 1880]
   10 Dec, 1892 Breathitt, by Eugene P Nickel,
   Min.; wits. John Rose & Sam Stidham   (M-B
   6:69; 1900 m-7)    [H-remd.]
BASCOM (c30 2nd b.KY) [widr/o Maggie Rose abv]
   ORLENA "LENA" MURRELL (c19 S b.KY) [d/o
   Wiley Murrell & Cath. Smith - 1900]
   1904/5      (1910; TCS)
CHARLEY (R.Ows. 21 S b.Ows.) P/Ows.  [s/o
   Jeremiah Callihan & W2 America Wilson]
   CAROLINA BRYANT (R.Br. 16 S b.Br.) P/Br.
   [d/o Geo. Bryant & Sarah - D-O 1908]
   11 Feb., 1904, Ows.   [R.Owsley 1910, HM
   w/them]    [H-remd.]
CHARLES (R.Ows. 24 2nd b.Ows) P/Ows. [widr/o
   Carolina Bryant above]
   [JULIA MASON] (R.Ows. 17 S b.Ows) P/Ows.
   [d/o John Mason & Mary McIntosh - ob-WS BE-
   8/8/63-3/9/67; OCN 4/17/58]
   17 June, 1909, Ows. [R.Ows. 1910; Norwood,
   OH 1958; Cin., OH 1963-67] [NOTE: There
   was an error in this & several other mgs.,
   wherein bride listed on wrong line.  Bride
   as ELIS ESTEP; line above was JULIA MASON.
   W/JULIA MASON per B-O ch., 1910, & ob-WS]
(Callahan cont.)

CALLAHAN (cont.)
DANIEL (c22 S b.Ows.) [1854-1931; s/o Jer.
   Callihan & Esther Moore - B-O TCS; 2nd M-O]
   EMILY C. LEWIS (c23 S b.KY) [1854-1928;
   d/o Felix Lewis & Jane Smith - 1870-P; TS]
   1877          (1880-2; 1900 m-23; 1910 m-32;
   1920; B-O ch)   [DAN m2 8/11/1929 Armina
   McIntosh Wilson (wid/o Wm. Wilson) - M-O]
EDMAN [EDWARD "MACK"] (c19 b.NC)
   LUCY ANN SPIVY (c13 b.KY) [d/o Zadock
   Spivey & Susannah Robertson - TCS]
   22 Aug., 1840, Clay (TCS; M-C; 1850-1;
   B&D-Lau. ch-1853 b/d.Ows.; B-J ch-1858;
   1860-1870-J; widr. Edmond 1870-J)
EZEKIEL (c33 b.NC) [s/o Wm. Callahan
   & Celia Cockrell(?) - TCS]
   [MARY] POLLY HERD (c16 b.Clay) [d/o Wm.
   Herd & Rebecca Hudson - TCS]
   1 March, 1846 (ML) Clay (M-C; 1850;
   B-Lau. ch-1852) [POLLY m2 John Farmer]
ISAAC (R.Clay 25 S b.Clay) P/Clay [s/o Wm.
   Callahan & Matilda Gibson - TCS]
   CENA [SENA] WHITE (R.Ows. 24 S b.Ows.) P/
   Ows. [d/o Ben White & Margaret Gross - TCS]
   10 Aug., 1904, Ows.   [R.Owsley 1910]
JEREMIAH (R.Ows. 25 S b.Clay) [s/o Wilson
   Callahan & Sarah York - TCS]
   ESTHER MOORE (R.-- 20 S b.Clay) [d/o
   Elias Moore & Celia Reynolds - TCS]
   -- Aug., 1852, Ows.   [DIV. 1868/9]
   [Esther R.Owsley 1870-1880-1900] [H-remd.]
JEREMIAH (c38 2nd b.KY) [Div/f Esther Moore
   above]
   AMERICA WILSON (c22 b.KY) [d/o Philip
   Wilson & Mary Moore - 1870]
   c1872          (1880-7; NVP; 1890; wid.
   America 1900)
JERRY (c24 S b.Gabbard) [1883-1969; s/o Dan
   Callahan & Emily Lewis - 1900; TS-TCS; ob-
   H&S BE-7/24/69-3/16/61]
   DORA MARSHALL (c18 S b.Gabbard) [1889-1966;
   d/o Abijah Marshall & Rhoda Abshear - 1900;
   TS-TCS; ob-W BE-5/12/66]
   1907/8          (1910-20; B-O ch; Boonev.
   1961; widr. R.Ricetown 1966)

(Callahan cont.)

125

**CALLAHAN (cont.)**
LEANDER "LEE" (c20 S b.Ows.) [1878-1958; s/o
   Jeremiah Callihan & W2 America Wilson -
   ob-H OCN-4/17/58]
   LUCINDA "LUCY" COLE (c16 S b.KY) [1883-
   1958; d/o James Cole & Malinda Combs - BBG;
   TS-TCS]
   1898/9      (1900-1910-1920; TCS; BBG;
   Indian Creek, Ows. 1958)
MACK - see EDWARD MACK
RANDALL - see WM. RANDALL
ROBERT (c18 S b.Ows.) [s/o Jeremiah Callihan
   & W2 America Wilson]
   REBECCA ROSE (___ b.KY)
   c1893      (1900-6/94, widr. Robt.; DC
   dau. 1964)      [H-remd.]
ROBERT (c25 2nd b.Ows.) [widr/o Rebecca Rose
   above - widr. 1900; DC ch.]
   BELLE TAYLOR (c17 S b.Ows.) [c1882-1956;
   d/o Pendleton Taylor & Minerva Jennings -
   TCS; ob-W&S OCN-10/4/56-12/8/55]
   1900      (1910 m-10; B-O ch.; wid.
   Belle 1920; R.So. Fk. 1955; ob-ch. BS-
   3/27/86-7/19/90-9/9/93-10/12/95)
WILLIAM (c20 b.KY) [s/o Jeremiah Callahan
   & Esther Moore]
   MARGARET WILSON (c19 b.KY) [d/o Philip
   Wilson & Mary Moore - NVP]
   c1877      (1880-2; TCS; NL M-J/R)
W[M.] R[ANDALL] (R.Welchburg c23 b.KY) P/KY
   [poss. m1 9/8/92 Lucinda J. Baldwin - M-J]
   [SUSAN] ANNIE FLANERY (c25 S b.Ows.) [d/o
   Joel P. Flanery & Susan Bailey - 1880; ME]
   18 May, 1895, Ows., by Rev. Geo. W. Johnson
   of Annville      (ME-5/24/95; ME-8/28/96 Anne
   Calahan of Jack. visit dad, J.P. Flanery;
   1900-J; 1910 W-remd-2 Farler, Callihan s-s
   12; H/as W. R., Wm. R., Randall - TCS)
   [SUSAN m2 1909 Addison Farlor]
WM. (R.Ows. 23 S b.Ows.) P/Ows [1880-1959; s/o
   Dan Callahan & Emily C. Lewis - 1900; TCS]
   LUTICHA [TISH] MARSHALL (R.Ows. 18 S b.Ows)
   P/Ows [1888-1973; d/o Abijah Marshall &
   Rhoda Abshear - 1900 TCS; ob-WS BE-5/12/66]
   16 Aug., 1904 Ows.      [R.Owsley 1910-1920;
   R.Lawrenceburg, IN 1966]

## CAMPBELL

ABNER (c27 S b.KY) [s/o Hardy Campbell & Sally
   Duff - 1880]
   LENORA GILBERT (c27 S b.KY)  [d/o John R.
   Gilbert & Ann Judith Minter - 1880; TCS]
   1894/5       (1900 W-GF Gilbert w/them;
   1910-1920; NL M-J)
DANIEL (c34 b.KY) [s/o Wm. Campbell
   & Hannah       - TCS]
   SARAH (nee CAMPBELL) McINTOSH (c37 2nd b.
   KY) [m1 _____ McIntosh - 1850-P]  [d/o
   Elijah Campbell & Rebecca       - TCS]
   4 June, 1865, Perry  (M-P; 1870-P; 1880, HF
   w/them; 1890-1900)
EDWARD (c24 b.KY)
   SARAH JACKSON (c17 b.KY) [d/o James Jackson
   & Nancy Napier - TCS]
   20 Feb., 1864, Perry  (M-P B:315; 1870-5;
   Sarah "md" w/bro. Geo. Jackson 1880; TCS)
EDWARD (c18 S b.KY)  [1856-1921; s/o Hiram
   Campbell & Susan Eversole - TS-TCS]
   HANNAH CAMPBELL (c20 b.KY)  [c1854-1896;
   d/o John Campbell & Sarah Lewis - 1860-
   1870-P; ME-5/29/96]
   c1874 Ows.  (BE-8/19/71; 1880-P-5; 1900-
   1/78, H-remd.; TCS; NL M-P)
EDWARD (R.Boonev. c40 2nd b.KY)  [widr/o
   Hannah Campbell above]  [1856-1921]
   MARTHA "MATTIE" M. McCOLLUM (R.Conkling;
   c21 S b.KY)  [1875-1946; d/o Dan McCollum
   & Emily Brewer - 1880; TS-TCS]
   May, 1897, Ows. (ME-6/11/97; 1900 m-3, his
   oldest ch-1/78, HM w/them; 1910 m-11; 1920
   TCS; their photo BE-8/19/71)
ELIJAH (c25 S b.Per.)  [1865-1937; s/o Dan
   Campbell & Sarah Campbell - 1880; TS-TCS]
   HANNAH LOUISE NEELEY (c20 S b.Boonev.)
   [1870-1957; d/o Andrew J. Neeley & Eliz.
   Collier - ob-W OCN-4/18/57; TCS; 1910;
   1870 as Hannah L.]
   1890/1       (1910 WF w/them; NL 1900;
   B-O ch.; TCS; 1920; BC 1915; M-L ch-1916;
   ob-ch. BS-9/16/93; W/as Louise most rec.,
   also as Lulla & Hannah L.)

(Campbell cont.)

127

**CAMPBELL (cont.)**

GARFIELD (c23 b.Per.)  [s/o Edw. Campbell
   & W1 Hannah Campbell - Yest; 1900; TCS]
   CALLIE BECKNELL (c17 b.Sturg. [d/o Robert
   Becknell & Mary Evans - 1910; ob-WS BE-
   4/30/59]
   c1906      (1910-2-1/2 wid. Callie w/P;
   B-O ch.; 1920 wid. Callie; R.Haz. 1959)
HARDEN "HARDY" (c24 b.Per.)
   SARAH DUFF (c15 b.Per.)  [d/o Colson Duff
   & Eliz. Gilbert - TCS]
   c1861      (1870-8; 1880; TCS; widr.
   Hardin 1900; M-L ch-1916)
HENRY (c23 S b.Br.)  [s/o Hardy Campbell
   & Sarah Duff - 1880]
   JANE MOORE (c26 S b.Br.)  [d/o Edw. Moore
   & Rebecca Gabbard - 1880]
   1893      (1900 m-6; TCS; 1910 m-17;
   M-O ch.; 1920 Jane as "wid", but Henry
   w/dau. Dora)
HENRY (R.Ows. 23 S b.Per.) P/Per.  [1887-1961;
   s/o Edward Campbell & Hannah Campbell - TS-
   TCS; ob-HS OCN-9/4/53]
   [MAGGIE] DAISY MOYERS (R.Ows. 17 S b.Ows)
   P/Ows.  [d/o Isaac Anderson Moyers & Martha
   Combs - TCS; 1910]
   2 Oct., 1910, Ows.  [R.Owsley 1920; Boonev.
   1953]
HIRAM (c17 S b.KY)  [s/o Ed Campbell & W1
   Hannah Campbell - 1880-P; Yest.]
   REBECCA JANE FELTNER (c17 S b.KY) [d/o
   James Feltner & Sarah Campbell - 1880-P]
   1 Dec., 1891, <u>Perry</u> @ James Feltner's, by
   Samuel Williams; wits. E. Campbell & Thos.
   Pennington   (M-P MB F; 1900 m-8; 1910,
   WS w/them; 1920)
JAMES D. (c18 S b.Boonev.)  [1888-1946; s/o
   John Campbell & Eliz. Bowman - TS-TCS]
   MARY THOMAS (c17 S b.Boonev.)  [1889-1967
   Lex. hosp.; d/o Elijah Thomas & Lucy
   Carmack - TS-TCS; ob-W BE-10/19/67]
   1904/5      (1910-1920; B-O ch.; wid. Mary
   R.Boonev. 1959 - ob-WS BE-2/19/59-6/30/60;
   wid. R.Boonev. @ d. 1967; ob-ch. BS-1/2/86-
   11/4/86-4/30/87 & 3Fks-7/8/98)

(Campbell cont.)

**CAMPBELL (cont.)**

JOHN (c23 b.KY) [s/o Frank Campbell & Margaret
    Williams - KAS]
    EMILY JANE BOWMAN (c21 b.KY)   [d/o Thomas
    Bowman & Mary Moore - TCS]
    c1849        (1850 no ch.; WGO; TCS; B-Lau.
    ch-1855; 1860-1870-C; 1880 John w/BiL
    Thomas Bowman as md, W-NL)   [EMILY JANE m2
    1894, Joseph Reynolds - TCS; M-L]
JOHN B. (c26 S b.KY) [1840-1915; s/o Wm.
    Campbell & Hannah Frye - TS-TCS]
    ELIZABETH BOWMAN (c23 S b.KY)  [1844-1929
    Ows.; d/o Robert Sturgis Bowman & Mary
    Turner - DC; TCS]
    1866/7        (1870-P; 1880-12; 1890; 1900
    m-33; 1910 m-45; wid. R.Ows. @ d. 1929;
    NL M-J/P; NL P-CW)
JOHN E. (c27 S b.Per.) [c1865-1949; s/o Edward
    Campbell & Sarah     - TCS; 1870; ob-H OCN-
    11/4/49]
    SOPHIA HACKER (c18 S b.Clay)  [c1877-1963;
    d/o Jameson Hacker & Tabitha Davidson -
    TCS; ob-W BE-2/7/63]
    1894/5        (NL 1900; 1910-1920; TCS;
    B-O ch-7/09; ob-ch. BS-6/3/93-1/29/97, son
    Frank b. c1899 Ows.; M-O ch.; NL M-C/P)
JOHN M. (R.Boonev. c27 S b.KY)  [s/o Edward
    Campbell & W1 Hannah Campbell - TCS]
    NANNIE [JANE] ROSE (R.Ows c19 S b.KY)  [d/o
    Leander Rose & Emma Cawood - TCS; ME; ob-WS
    OCN-4/6/34; W-photo BS-2/6/78]
    April, 1905, Ows. (on a Sunday), by Bro.
    S. K. Ramey     (ME-5/4/05; 1910; TCS;
    R.Winchester 1963 - ob-WS BE-5/9/63; ob-ch.
    BS-12/2/93)
LEWIS (c25 S b.Per.)    [1847-1901; s/o William
    Campbell & Hannah Frye - TS-TCS; ME-7/5/01]
    ELIZABETH "BETTY" EVERSOLE (c19 S b.Per.)
    c1871        (1880-8; wid. Eliz. 1910, ch.
    Charlie 22 & Laura 15; BC dau. Laura b.
    1895 Ows.; NL H&W 1900Sx; M-L ch-1901;
    NL M-J)

(Campbell cont.)

**CAMPBELL (cont.)**
SAM (c25 S Lum. b.Per)  [s/o Lewis Campbell
   & Betty Eversole - ME; 2nd mg.]
   ELLEN BINGHAM (c18 b.KY)  [d/o Bennett
   Bingham, decd.; Gd/o Rev. Robt. Bingham of
   Jack. - ME; 1900-J w/her GF]
   Feb., 1902, Ows., So. Boonev. (Sat.), by
   Rev. S. K. Ramey  (ME-3/7/02)  [H-remd.]
SAM E. (R.Lee 31 [2nd] Wl d.; Lum. b.Per) P/
   Per.  [widr/o Ellen Bingham above]
   RACHEL FRY (R.Lee 21 S b.Clay) P/VA-Clay
   [d/o Dave Fry & Lizzie Evans - mg.]
   20 June, 1908, Lee @ L&A Depot, by J. F.
   Sutton, Co. Judge; wits. J. W. Brandenburg
   & Wm. Ross   (M-L)
STEPHEN (R.Ows. 23 S b.Ows.) P/Per-Ows. [1884-
   1960; s/o John Campbell & Elizabeth Bowman
   - ob-H BE-12/29/60; 1900]
   EDITH KINCADE (R.Ows. 15 S b.Ows.) P/Ows.
   [1893-1966; d/o Thos. Jefferson Kincaid &
   Helen Mainous - 1900; ACB; ob-W BE-3/3/66]
   16 May, 1908, Ows.  [R.Owsley 1910 w/HP;
   1920; wid. R.Booneville 1960]
THOMAS (c30 b.VA)  [poss. s/o John Campbell
   & Emily Jane Bowman - 1860-1870-C]
   ALAFAIR _____ (c21 b.KY)
   1880/1         (1900; NL 1910Sx; NL M-J)
**CARDWELL**
ISAA[C] N (R.Ows. 28 S b.Whitley) [Law.- KY-H]
   [s/o John Cardwell & Araminta Watkins]
   JOANAH GALE (R.Ows. 15 S b.Franklin Co.)
   [d. July, 1881 - KY-H]
   25 Dec., 1855, Ows.  [R.Boonev.; then Lex.;
   then Est.; moved to Winchester 1884 - KY-H]
   [ISAAC m2 11/82 Frankfort, Jennie Todd -
   KY-H]
**CARMACK**
ABRAHAM JASPER (c23 S b.Jack.)  [s/o Isaac
   Carmack & Rhoda Thomas - 1880]
   MATTIE HOSKINS (c18 S b.Ows.)  [1882-1960;
   d/o Wm. Hoskins & Mary Margaret Robertson -
   TCS; ob-W BE-12/8/60]
   1901/2         (1910-1920; B-O ch; TCS; wid.
   d. Boonev. 1960; ob-ch. BS-3/1/90-10/26/95;
   H/as Jasper, A. J. & J. S.; NL M-J)

(Carmack cont.)

**CARMACK (cont.)**

AMBROSE (c22 b.Jack.)  [s/o John Carmack
    & Sarah       - TCS]
    EMMA HOSKINS (c18 b.Ows.) [d/o Wm. Hoskins
    & Mary Margaret Robinson - 1900; TCS; ob-WS
    BE-12/8/60]
    1906/7        (B-O ch.; 1910-1920; R.Ham.,
    OH 1960)
ANDREW (c17 b.KY) [GS/o Jacob & Lydia Carmack]
    _____ (___ b.___)
    1898/9       (1900 H-md. w/GP, W-NL;
    NL 1910Sx)
ELIHU (R.Ows. 23 S b.Ows.) P/Ows.  [s/o Levi
    Carmack & Mary Baker - 1900]
    SALLY B[ELLE] McINTOSH (R.Ows. 23 S b.Br.)
    P/Br. [d/o James McIntosh & Eliz.
    Caudill - ob-WF OCN-4/11/57]
    10 March, 1910, Ows.
EZEKIEL (R.Ows. 22 S b.Ows.) P/TN-Ows.  [1887-
    1966 Ows.; s/o Isaac Carmack & Rhoda Thomas
    - 1900-1910; ob-H BE-5/19/66]
    MINNIE BECKNELL (R.Ows. 18 S b.Ows.) P/Ows.
    [d/o Henry L. Becknell & Lucinda Bowman -
    TCS; PWB]
    15 July, 1910, Ows.   [R.Owsley 1920; wid.
    R.Owsley 1966]
ISAAC (c18 S b.TN)   [s/o Abraham Carmack
    & Alcy Dean - MT; 1870]
    JANE BARRETT (c19 S b.KY)  [1850/1-1919
    Ows.; d/o Thomas Barrett & Barbara Gabbard
    - TCS; 1870; DC/Stamper]
    late 1870      [DIVORCED]   (MT; H-remd-
    22 1900; NL M-J)   [JANE m2 c1872 Martin
    Deaton - TCS; DDN; JANE m3 Lewis Stamper]
ISAAC (c26 2nd b.TN)  [m1 Jane Barrett above]
    RHODA THOMAS (c25 S b.KY) [1852-1934 Ows.;
    d/o Joseph Thomas & Anna Jemima Couch -
    TCS; DC]
    1877      (1880-J ch. 3, 1 & 10; 1900
    m-22; MT; ME-11/10/04 in Jack.; 1910, HF
    w/them; 1920; NL M-B/J/L/P/R)


(Carmack cont.)

**CARMACK (cont.)**

JACOB (R.Claiborne Co., TN; 25 "S"; b.VA)
[widr/o Sarah J. Fultz, whom he md. 2/4/51,
Claiborne Co., TN - MT] [s/o Levi Carmack
& Eliz. Peters - MT]
LYDIA BURNS (R.Buffalo; 21 S b.Buffalo)
[d/o Wm. Burns Jr. & Rachel Asher - TCS]
23 Aug., 1854, Ows.    [R.Owsley 1860-1870-
1880-1900-1910]
JAMES (c18 S b.KY)  [1866-1963; s/o Jacob
Carmack & Lydia Burns - TS-TCS]
MARTHA FLANERY (c16 S b.KY)
1893/4        (1900 m-6; 1910 m-19; TCS)
JASPER - see ABRAHAM JASPER
JOHN (c23 b.VA)
ISABELLE ["IBBY"] BURNS (c17 b.KY)  [d/o
Wm. Burns Sr. & Rachel Asher - TCS]
23 Feb., 1843, <u>Clay</u>  (M-C; 1850)
[IBBY m2 James Barrett]
JOHN (c23 b.Ows.)  [s/o Jacob Carmack & Lydia
Burns - 1870]
SARAH J. BIGGS (c20 b.KY)  [d/o Wm. Biggs
& Phoebe Barrett - TCS; 1870]
c1879        (1880, no ch.; NL 1900-Sx;
NL M-J)
LEVI (c20 b.KY)  [s/o Jacob Carmack & Lydia
Burns - 1870]
MARY BAKER (c18 b.KY)
5 Jan., 1880, <u>Clay</u>  (M-C; 1880-MWY; TCS;
1900)
WILLIAM (c27 b.Ows.)  [s/o John Carmack
& Ibby Burns - TCS]
MARY BOWLING (c18 b.Clay)
11 Sept., 1873, <u>Clay</u>  (TCS; B-O ch.;
1880-C-6)

**CARROLL/CARROL/CARRELL**

BEN P. (c35 S b.KY)
MARY BECKNELL (c<u>35</u> S b.KY)  [d/o Samuel
Becknell & Nancy Hamilton - 1900]
1906/7        (1910 m1-3, W-2/2 ch--Jno.
19 & Henry 14; 1900 Mary Becknell w/P as
m-1, 2/2 ch., Jno. 9 & Henry 4; NL M-C/J/R)

(Carroll cont.)

## CARROLL (cont.)
GEORGE W. (c27 2nd/3rd? b.KY)  [Div/f unknown
   - George, Div., w/P 1880]   [s/o Benjamin
   Carroll & Luvisa      - 1880; 1870-Knx]
   LYDIA EVERSOLE (___ b.___)
   15 July, 1880, Clay  (M-C; H-remd. 1900-J)
GEORGE W. (c36 4th b.KY) [md. prev. Lydia
   Eversole above]
   MARY F. (nee _____) _____ (c30 2nd b.KY)
   [m1 _____]
   c1889         (1900-J-10/90, m-12; 1910
   m-20 H-4th W-2nd; NL M-C/J/R)
JOE (R.Ows. 24 S b.Clay) P/Clay   [s/o George
   Carroll & Mary F.     - TCS]
   LULA COLE (R.Ows. 19 S b.Clay) P/Clay
   15 April, 1909, Ows.
WILLIAM (R.Ows. 18 S b.Lee,VA)  [s/o Noland
   Carroll & Druscilla Booth - TCS; 1850]
   MARY ANN WHISMAN (R.Ows. 21 S b.Br.) [d/o
   Michael Whisman & Isabelle Spencer - ACB]
   17 Nov., 1859, Ows.  [R.Wolfe 1870-1880;
   wid. Mary A. w/son 1900 Wolfe]

## CARTER
CHARLES R. (c25 b.VA)
   JEMIMA _____ (c28 b.VA)
   c1859       (1860-J-5 mos.; NL M-J)
   [JEMIMA m2 1864 David R. Neeley - M-J; TCS]
JAMES M. (c24 b.NC)  [d. C.W.]
   CYNTHIA WYATT (c24 b.KY)
   c1856       (1860-3; TR; Rom.Lee; ob-ch.
   BE-3/29/51)  [CYNTHIA m2 Joseph Durbin]

## CASH
CALEB (R.Morg. 27 S b.Morg.)
   DORCAS CAMPBELL (R.Ows. 17 S b.Per.)
   4 Sept., 1856, Ows.

## CASSITY
DAVID (R.Proctor 28 S b.Morg.)
   MARY [ANN] NORMAN (R.Ows. 20 S b.Ows.)
   24 Feb., 1853, Ows., by G. S. Williams
   [R.Breathitt 1860-70; Lee 1880; Breathitt
   1900]

## CASWOOD
WALL (c26 blk b.VA)
   HANEY _____ (c25 blk b.VA)
   c1869       (1870, no ch.)

## CAUDILL/CAUDEL

ALEXANDER (c21 S b.KY) [1871-1956; s/o Lewis
Caudell & Fannie Barret - MT; CRC; TS-TCS]
REBECCA WILDER (c18 S b.KY) [d/o Ewell
Wilder & Lucinda Hornsby - MT]
1892          (1900 m-7; MT 1st ch-1892;
1910 m-20)

ALFRED (c18 b.Br.) [1849-1925; s/o Henry
Caudill & W1 Lucy Couch - TCS; CRC]
JANE SIMPKINS (c18 b.Br.) [1848-1935; d/o
Eli Simpkins & Polly Tyree - TCS; CRC]
1866/7 Breathitt (1870-B; 1880-1900;
B-B ch.) [JANE m2 a Simpkins - TCS]

ALLEN (R.Br. 18 S b.KY) P/VA-KY [s/o Syria
COMBS & Mary CAUDILL - LNG]
POLLY SMITH (R.Ows. 15 S b.KY) P/KY [d/o
James Smith & Emily Gum]
- July, 1877, Ows., @ James Smith's, Ows.
[R.Owsley 1880-1900-1910-1920]

CLINTON (c23 S b.KY) [1883-1907; s/o Allen
Caudill & Polly Smith - 1900; TS-TCS;
killed in a gun fight - MLJ]
LINDA PACE (c25 S b.KY) [1882-1918; d/o
Richmond Pace & Talitha Fox - DC; MLJ; svt.
w/Palmer fam. 1900-L]
c1906          (1910, Linda w/HP, "wid-4",
1/1 ch., age 3)    [LINDA m2 c1917, John
Riley Banks - MLJ]

GREENBERRY (c19 b.Br.) [c1868-1950; s/o
Alfred Caudill & Jane Simpkins - 1880; CRC;
ob-H OCN-3/17/50]
JANE DEEDS (c21 b.Ows.) [1866-1950; d/o
Henry Deeds & Amanda Warren - ob-W OCN-
3/17/50]
6 Aug., 1887, Breathitt @ Dave Warren's
(CRC; 1900; ob-H&W)

HENRY (c40 2nd b.KY) [widr/o Lucinda Couch -
1860-B] [s/o John Caudill & Nancy      ]
ELIZABETH "LIZZIE" (nee BURNS) SLONE (c30
2nd b.Clay) [wid/o Jesse Slone - M-O 1854;
D-O 1859; wid. Eliz. Slone 1860] [c1834-
1874; d/o John Burns & Jane E.     - D-B]
c1864, poss. Breathitt (1870-B; B-O ch. by
Slone; M-L ch-1915)    [HENRY m3 Jane
McIntosh - M-B 1876]

(Caudill cont.)

134

<u>CAUDILL (cont.)</u>
HENRY C. (c29 S b.KY)  [1858-1935; s/o Moses
    Caudill & Sarah Simpkins - 1880-B; B-B sib;
    TS-TCS]
    ANGELINE COMBS (c20 S b.KY)  [1869-1913;
    d/o Mason Combs & Viann Angel - TS-TCS]
    1888/9        (1900-1910; TCS; ob-ch. 3Fks-
    1/3/96)
JAMES IRVINE (R.Lee 17 S b.Lee) P/KY
    EMILY LITTLE (R.Br. 17 S b.Br.) P/Br.
    24 Aug., 1904, Ows.  [R.Lee 1910]
LEWIS (c20 S b.KY)  [1849-1931; s/o Henry
    Caudill & Lucinda Couch - TS-TCS; CRC]
    FANNIE BARRETT (c20 S b.KY)  [d/o James
    Barrett & Matilda Neal - KCM; DC 1928]
    26 June, 1869, <u>Breathitt</u> (P-CW KCM; 1870-
    1880-B; 1900 m-29; 1910 m-40)
    [NOTE: With them 1910 is Cath. RILEY, sgl.,
    78, "MIL", but Fannie was a BARRETT per
    P-CW & DC-H]    [LEWIS m2 Ludema (Riley)
    Gilbert wid/o Keenis Gilbert - KCM]
LEWIS (R.Br. 50 2nd b.Br.) P/Br.  [m1 *NOTE]
    FANNIE CAUDELL (R.Br. 50 2nd b.Br.) P/Br.
    [m1 *NOTE]
    22 Jan., 1904, <u>Breathitt</u> [rec. Owsley]
    [*NOTE:  I believe this may be Lewis &
    Fannie nee Barrett above; poss. div. &
    remd.]
PLEASANT (20 S b.KY)  [s/o Moses Caudill &
    Sarah Simpkins - 1880-B; CRC]
    EASTER DEATON (18 S b.KY)
    1 May, 1900, <u>Breathitt</u> @ Jett's Cr., by
    W. R. Salyers, Min.; wits. M. C. McIntosh
    (M-B 5:1; CRC; 1900) [PLEASANT m2 1/2/1919
    Br., Chloe Dale]
PRESTON (R.Br. 21 S b.Br.) P/Br.  [s/o Henry
    Caudill & Elizabeth Burns - CRC]
    MARTHA JANE GROSS (R.Lee 17 b.Lee)  [d/o
    Simon Gross & Eliz.      - KAS]
    30 May, 1888, <u>Lee</u> @ Simeon Gross', by Moses
    Roberts, JPLC; wits. Wm. H. Bowman & Wm.
    Napier  (M-L; 1900-L; B-O ch., both P/as
    b.Boonev.)    [PRESTON m2 12/10/18 Jack.,
    Elsie Holland - CRC]

(Caudill cont.)

ROBERT (c23 b.KY)  [1836-19__; s/o James
    Caudill & Jane Gilley - EVR)
    NANCY (nee _____) MADDEN (c31 2nd b.KY)
    [m1 _____ Madden - 1850-Let. Nancy Madden
    & ch. w/Samuel Sexton & wf]
    c1859        [DIVORCED 1860-70] (1860-Let.,
    s-s Samuel H. Madden, age 10; NL M-Let.)
    [NANCY m3 Henry Vincel - 1870-W Henry &
    Nancy & Samuel H. Madden 20; 1880-W, Henry
    & Nancy, Samuel H. Madden next to them]
    [H-remd. below]
ROBERT (c32 2nd  b.KY) [m1 Nancy (nee_____)
    Madden above]
    NANCY (nee PENNINGTON) LEWIS (c32 2nd b.KY)
    [wid/o Henderson Lewis - M-P 8/18/56; 1860-
    P]  [1836-1884; d/o Ephraim Pennington
    & Matilda Fields - EVR]
    c1868        (EVR; 1870-C-1, Lewis s-ch.;
    1880-11; NL M-C/Let/P)
ROBERT (c48 3rd b.KY)  [m2 Nancy Pennington
    Lewis above]
    NANCY (nee HUFF) FORD (c36 b.KY)  [wid/o
    _____ Ford - EVR]     [d/o Daniel Huff &
    Peggy Fields - EVR]
    24 Oct., 1884     (EVR; 1900-Lau.; NL M-C)
SANFORD ASHER (c17 S b.Br.)  [1876-1960; s/o
    Alfred Caudell & Jane Simpkins - 1880; CRC;
    OCN-2/29/52 H-76th Bday; ob-H&S BE-7/14/60,
    OCN-6/9/55]
    MARTHA DEEDS (c18 S b.Br.)  [1873-1951; d/o
    Henry Deeds & Amanda Warren - TCS; CRC;
    ob-W&S OCN-8/3/51-3/17/50]
    1892        (1900 m-8; 1910 m-17; 1920; TCS;
    CRC; ob-H&W; ob-ch. BE-6/10/37) [SANFORD m2
    Vina Holcomb (d/o Ira Holcomb) - TCS ob-W
    OCN-2/27/53]    [SANFORD m3 1953-60, Mollie;
    R.WV 1955; Trav. Rest 1960 - ob-HS&H]
SIDNEY B. "SID" (c18 S b.KY)   [s/o Alfred
    Caudell & Jane Simpkins - 1880; CRC]
    MOLLIE CREECH (c18 S b.KY)
    1890        (1900 m-10; 1910 m-19; BC
    1913-Pow.; R.Dry Branch, WV 1960 - ob-HS
    BE-7/14/60)

(Caudill cont.)

**CAUDILL (cont.)**
STEPHEN P. (c26 S tchr b.KY)  [poss. s/o
  Alfred Caudill & Jane Simpkins]
  MINNIE CECIL (c23 S b.KY)  [d/o Samuel M.
  Cecil & Molly Watts - 1900; ob-W&B OCN-
  11/23/51 & OCC-1/22/37]
  1905/6          (1910; ob-W; moved to
  Morehead, KY c1926)
WILLIAM (c20 b.Ows.)  [1879-1958; s/o Allen
  Caudill & Mary Smith - 1880; ob-H OCN-
  7/3/58]
  MARGARET WILSON (c16 b.KY)  [1880-1971; d/o
  Ezekiel Wilson & Sarah BBurg. - TS-TCS;
  ob-W BE-4/15/71]
  1899          (1900 m-1, no ch.; 1910 m-10;
  TCS; B-O ch. W/as Sally; BC 1916-1918;
  wid. Margaret in Lerose 1958)
**CAWOOD/CAYWOOD/KEYWOOD**
[ALONZO LEE] LONNIE (R.Ows. 28 S b.Ows.) P/
  Harl-Br.  [1881-1964; s/o Henry Bascomb
  Cawood & Nancy Jett - 1900; TS-TCS; ob-HS
  OCN-6/28/58 as "Lon"]
  OLLIE SEALE (R.Ows. 23 S b.Ows.) P/Ows.
  [d/o Joseph Seale & Belle Goodman - 1900;
  ob-WS BE-3/8/73]
  1 Jan., 1909, Ows.  [R.Owsley 1910-1920;
  Booneville 1958-73]
BASCOMB - see HENRY BASCOMB
CALVIN (c23 b.KY)
  POLLY A. _____ (c15 b.KY)
  c1860          (NL 1860; 1870-9)
ENOCH (c26 Blk b.KY)
  EMILY BRITTON (c21 Mul b.KY)
  c1861          (1870-8; M-L ch-1922)
GEORGE (R.Ows. 23 S blk b.Ows) P/VA-Ows.
  [poss. s/o Enoch Cawood & Emily Britton]
  SUSAN COUCH (R.Ows. 21 S Mul b.KY) P/--
  [1876-1937 Beattyv.; d/o Eli Couch & Mary
  Combs - DC]
  9 May, 1897 (ML), Lee (MC-NFI)  (M-L,
  oath that Susan is of mixed race, one par.
  being mixed w/Negro; 1900 m-2)
  [SUSAN KEYWOOD (R.Beattyv. 37 2nd b.Per) m2
  John B. Scribner (43 2nd) - M-L; 2 Caywood
  s-ch. Georgia B. 6 & Sister? 4, all Mul -
  1910-L]
(Cawood cont.)

[HENRY] BASCOMB (R.Ows. 22 S b.Harl.) P/-- TN
   [1852-1922 Ows.; s/o Moses Cawood & Emily
   Maddy - 1870; JFB]
   NANCY JETT (R.Br. 15 S b.Br.) P/Clay-Est.
   [d/o Curtis Jett & Nancy Bryant - MT]
   25 Aug., 1875, <u>Breathitt</u>  (M-B 1:178;
   1880-2; 1900-1910-1920; ob-ch. BS-4/26/92)
LONNIE - see ALONZO LEE "LONNIE"
WILLIAM (R.Ows. 31 S b.KY) P/KY-TN  [s/o Moses
   Cawood & Emily Maddy - 1870 JFB]
   HENRIETTA MINTER (R.Ows. 22 S b.KY) P/VA-TN
   [d/o John Minter & Sarah Eliz. Hampton]
   16 Oct., 1878, Ows. [R.Ows.1880-1900-1910]
WM. (c20 S <u>Blk</u> b.Boonev.) [1867/8-1942 Ows.;
   s/o Wm Cawood & Emily Britton -DC; M-L sib]
   MELISSA HOLLAND (c15 S <u>blk</u> b.Lee) [1875-
   1949 Rich.,IN; d/o Talton Holland & Chaney
   Hampton - 1880-L; ob-W OCN-11/11/49]
   19 April, 1889, <u>Breathitt Co.</u> @ Talton?
   Holland's, by Elisha Johnson, Min; wits.
   Samuel & Nancy Jett  (M-B 4:453; 1900 m-<u>6</u>,
   1st ch-2/93; 1910 m-20; 1920; B-O ch.; wid.
   d. Richmond, IN 1949) [NOTE: H/DC lists W/
   as Elizabeth]
**CECIL/CICEL**
ANDREW J. "ANDY" (c21 S b.Ows.)  [1878-1963;
   s/o Samuel M. Cecil & Mary J. Watts - 1880;
   ob-H&S BE-7/4/63, OCN-10/23/58]
   DOROTHY "DOTTIE" VENABLE (c14 S b.Ows.)
   17 May, 1903, Ows. @ Bill Minter's, Trav.
   Rest, by Rev. J. B. Rowlett; attendants
   Charlie Cecil & Miss Matilda Minter; wits.
   John McGuire & M/M Clay Smith (OCN-5/15/53
   their 50th anniv.; ob-H; 1910 m-7; B-O ch.;
   R.Hlbg. 1913-c1948; Ravenna 1958-63)
CHARLES B. (R.Ows. 25 S b.Ows) P/VA-Knx [1877-
   1958; s/o Sam Cecil & Mary Jane Watts -
   1900; ob-H OCN-10/23/58]
   MATILDA E MINTER (R.Ows 21 S b.Ows) P/VA-KY
   [1882-1966; d/o Chas. Minter & Eliza Botner
   - 1900; ob-W&S BE-12/29/66, OCN-3/20/53]
   5 Dec., 1903, Ows.  (a/L ME-12/11/03 W/as
   Miss Matilda <u>Botner</u>, but this is WM/maiden
   name; ME-1/5/04 ML, C. B. Cecil & Matilda
   Minter) [R.Ows.1910-1920; Trav. Rest.1953]
(Cecil cont.)

**CECIL (cont.)**
GRANT - see ULYSSES GRANT
JAMES G. (R.Ows. 18 S b.Pike)
   LOUISA SPIVEY (R.Ows. 21 S b.Clay)
   22 July, 1858, Ows.  [R.Clay 1860]
JOHN (c20 b.KY) [s/o Samuel Cecil & Mary J.
   Watts - 1880]
   REBECCA M. _____ (c18 VA)
   1895/6      (1900, w/HF & s-M; art-s-M
   BE-5/13/37 R.Morehead)
JOHN (R.Ows. 18 S b.Clay) P/Clay
   LUCINDA NEELEY (R.Ows. 18 S b.Ows.) P/Ows.
   [d/o Armon Neeley & Perlina Price - 1900]
   10 Feb., 1904, Ows.  (a/L ME-2/17/04)
   [R.Owsley 1910; wid. Cinda 1920 Owsley]
SAMUEL M. (R.Ows. 23 S b.Taz,VA) [s/o Madison
   Cecil & W1 Cynthia Whitten - D-O; M-Lee,VA
   1850-Lee,VA]
   EMILY E HOBBS (R.Lee,VA 16 S b.Lee,VA) [d/o
   Job Hobbs & Susan Flanary - M-Lee,VA; ACB]
   2 Dec, 1858, Ows. (a/L M-Lee,VA as 12/2/<u>59</u>,
   by Robert Wynn, H-22, W-18, rest same)
   [R.Owsley 1860; 1900 H-remd-42, but this
   was W1; ob-ch. OCC-11/22/40]
SAMUEL M. (c26 2nd b.Taz.,VA) [widr/o Emily
   Hobbs above - 1860]
   MARY JANE WATTS (c17 b.Knox)
   c1868      (1870 ch-7, 4, 2 & 11/69;
   1880 shows 1st ch. whose M. b. KY was Wm.,
   b. 1869; B-O ch.)
SAMUEL M. (R.Ows. 61 3rd b.VA) P/VA [widr/o
   Mary Jane Watts above]
   PATTIE ANN [nee WILLIAMS] HAMMONS (R.Lee
   44 2nd b.Ows.) P/-- [wid/o John Hammonds,
   who d. 1890 - M-L 12/24/85; REM]  [d/o
   George Williams & Ermine Akers - 1880-L;
   art-W BE-5/13/37]
   2 April, 1899 <u>Lee</u> @ John Bowman's, by James
   Warner; wits. Ben Botner & D. H. McDonal
   (M-L; 1900 Sam m-42, but this was W1,
   Hammonds s-s b.10/86, WF w/them; poss. Mrs.
   P. A. Cecil 58 1910-L)  [PATTIE m3 James
   Holman of Bowen - art-W; NL M-O]


(Cecil cont.)

## CECIL (cont.)

[ULYSSES] GRANT (c25 S b.KY) [s/o Samuel
   Cecil & W2 Mary J. Watts - 1880]
   RHODA MAYS (c24 S b.KY) [d/o David Mays
   & Surena Richardson - 1880-L]
   15 March, 1894, <u>Lee</u> @ David Mays'; wits.
   Wm. Ross & C. C. Cornett  (M-L; 1900 m-6;
   1910 m-15; wid. Rhoda 1920)
WILLIAM W. (c22 b.VA) [s/o Madison Cecil
   & W2 Mary Taylor - 1850-Lee,VA; 1860]
   HETTY A. CATRON (c19 b.KY) [1848-1922 Knx;
   d/o Francis Catron & Rhoda Jones - DC]
   1866/7        (1870 w/HP, ch-8, 2 & b.4/70;
   1880-Knx 1st ch-12; 1900-Bell m-33)
   [NOTE: Since there was a ch. age 8 in 1870,
   one of them may have been md. prev.]
WM. THOMAS (c36 S Engr.RR b.Ows.) [1869-1937;
   s/o Samuel M. Cecil & Molly Watts - 1880;
   ob-H OCC-1/22/37]
   EDNA BBURG. (c23 S b.KY) [d/o Wm. BBurg.
   & Josephine Glass - ob-WS BE-5/20/65]
   1905/6          (1910; wid. R.Bluefield, WV
   1937-65)
ZACHARIAH THOMAS (c25 b.VA) [prob. s/o Madison
   Cecil & W1 Cynthia Whitten - TCS]
   MARTHA PARSONS (c21 b.Lee,VA) [d/o John
   "Jackie" Parsons & Mary Simmons - TCS]
   c1856         (1860-3; B-O ch.; TCS)

## CHADWELL

CEPHUS MONROE (c24 b.KY) [s/o _____ COLLINS
   & Catherine CHADWELL - 1880]
   MARY _____ (c16 b.KY)
   1899/1900        (1900, HM w/them; NL M-J)
DAVID WILLIAM (c17 S b.Taz.,TN) [1870-1953;
   s/o Solomon WEDDLE & Catherine CHADWELL -
   TCS; 1880; ob-H OCN-8/21/53]
   LOU EMILY (a/k/a EMMA LOU) BOWMAN (R.Island
   City c17 b.KY)
   1890, Ows.  (ob-H; 1900; TCS; ob-ch. OCN-
   6/7/56; R.Island City) [H-remd.]
DAVE [WM.] (R.Ows. 38 2nd b.Per) P/Br-Per.
   [widr/o Emily Bowman above]
   NANNIE McDANIEL (R.Ows. 30 S b.Ows.) P/Ows.
   [d/o Franklin McDaniel & Eliz. Baker - TCS]
   18 March, 1909, Ows.   [R.Owsley 1910, HM
   w/them; Island City - ob-H]
(Chadwell cont.)

140

**CHADWELL (cont.)**
MONROE - see CEPHUS MONROE
WM. DAVID - see DAVID WM.
**CHAMBERS**
GIDEON (c19 b.TN)  [b. 12/24/1824; s/o Elijah
   Chambers b Rachel Morrow - MT]
   MARY ANN ROSE (c17 b.KY)  [d/o Robt. Rose
   & Mary Esther Moore - MT]
   23 Dec., 1843, <u>Morgan Co.</u>  (M-Morg.; 1850;
   B-O ch.; MT)
WM. MARTIN (c18 b.KY)   [s/o Elijah Chambers
   & Rachel Morrow - MT]
   REBECCA ROSE (c17 b.KY)  [d/o Robt. Rose
   & Mary Esther Moore - MT; ME]
   c1845      (1850-4 w/WP; MT; 1860-Morg.;
   1870-W; 1880-L; 3Fks-4/27/88 mentions Est/o
   Wm. M. Chambers, decd; wid. Rebecca 1900-L;
   ME-2/26/04 Rebecca, Lower Twin Cr., Middle
   Fk. 14 miles from Boonev., raised in Ows.
   d/o Old Bob Rose, Ows. pioneer; NL M-Morg.)
**CHANDLER**
ANDREW (c24 b.KY)  [1862-1925; s/o Larkin
   Chandler & Margaret Herd - TS-TCS]
   MALINDA LEWIS (c18 b.KY)  [1868-1951; d/o
   Felix Lewis & Jane Smith - TS-TCS]
   c1886      (1900-7/87, m-12 = 1887/8,
   W-4/4 ch., all 4 listed; NL 1910)
ANDREW (c24 2nd b.Ricetown) [m1 _____]
   [s/o Wm. Chandler & Levina Baker - TCS]
   LIZZIE BELL (nee SMITH) _____(c15 2nd
   b.Boonev.)  [wid/o _____]
   1900/1      (1910 m2-9, both; B-O ch.
   H/as Anderson)
LARKIN (c21 b.Yancy Co., NC) P/NC
   MARGARET ["PEGGY"] HERD (c18 b.Clay)  [d/o
   Wm. Herd & Rebecca Hudson - TCS]
   23 July, 1843, <u>Clay Co.</u>  (M-C; 1850-1860;
   B-O ch.; 1880-1890; KY-Exp. 9/94 JJDD)


(Chandler cont.)

**CHANDLER (cont.)**
MARION (c26 S b.Ricetown)  [s/o Wm. Chandler
   & Levina Baker - 1880-1900]
   ELIZA HORNSBY (c20 S b.Boonev.)  [1883-1951
   Ows.; d/o Geo. Hornsby & Eliz. Woods - TCS;
   1900; ob-W OCN-4/7/51]
   1903/4          (1910-1920; B-O 4/26/08 son
   John)  [NOTE: B-O also has John b. 5/10/08
   s/o Meredith & Lizzie Chandler. This couple
   NL 1910Sx, so poss. repeat of abv. couple.]
NOAH (c20 b.KY)  [s/o Larkin Chandler
   & Margaret Herd]
   RACHEL J. PETTIT (c18 b.TN)  [d/o Geo.
   Pettit & Sarah J.          - TCS]
   c1869          (1870-1/70; TCS)
ROBERT (c31 Blk coal miner b.Br.)
   MATILDA _____ (c23 Blk b.KY)
   c1869          (1870-L, no ch.)  [H-remd.]
ROBERT (R.Proctor, Lee 40 2nd b.Br.) P/Woodf.
   [Blk - 1880-L]  [m1 Matilda _____ above]
   HANAH BURNSIDE (R.Br. 22 2nd b.Lee) P/Clay-
   NC  [Mul. - 1880-L]
   15 Aug, 1877, Breathitt @ S. P Chandler's,
   by S. P. Chandler, MMES; wits. G. W. Calmes
   & Mariam Puckett (M-B; 1880-L; 1900-L Thos.
   Jett Bo. w/Hannah Chandler)  [HANNAH (48
   2nd) m2 10/17/03 Lee, Thomas Jett, his 2nd]
WILLIAM (c25 S b.Lau.)  [1846-1912; s/o Larkin
   Chandler & Margaret Hernd]
   LEVINA BAKER (c21 S b.Clay) [1852-1932 Ows;
   d/o James Baker & W1 Sarah Davidson - DC;
   1870]
   1872/3          (1900 m-27; 1910 m-32 =
   1877/8; 1880-5; B-O ch-6/74; wid. Viney
   1920; wid. R.Cow Cr. 1932; NL M-C/Lau/R)
**CHESTER**
W[YTHE] B. (28 b.KY)
   MATTIE G. EAGER (22 b.KY)  [d/o Wm. Eager
   & Laura Treadway - 1880; ob-WS BE-5/20/43-
   1/18/45]
   17 July, 1901, Lee, @ Wm. Eager's, by R. A.
   Irvine, Presbyterian; wits: W.T. Eager,
   S.T. Birch, M.J. Treadway  (M-L; REM;
   H-sgl. 1900-L; ME-9/29/04 Laura Eager &
   dau., Mrs. Mattie Chester of Beattyv.,
   visiting Ows.; R.Ark. 1943; Little Rock,
   Ark. 1945)

## CHILDERS

EPPERSON - see RICHARD APPERSON

JAMES MADISON (c24 b.VA)  [s/o Wm. Childers
    & Winnie Breeding - WGO]
    NANCY LOVELACE (c21 b.KY)  [d/o Jeremiah
    Lovelace & Phoebe Lipps - WGO; ACB]
    c1843, <u>Breathitt</u> (1850-B-5; 1860-16;
    1870-W; B-O ch.; B-W ch.)

JOSEPH (26 b.Russell Co, VA) [s/o Wm. Childers
    & Winnie Breeding]
    LAVINA COOK (19 b.Morgan)
    24 June, 1847, poss. md. <u>Breathitt</u>  (MT;
    1850; 1860-B; 1870-W; 1880-Law.; B-O ch.)

RICHARD A[PPERSON] (R.Ows. 22 S b.Per.)  [s/o
    John Childers & Mary Cook - MT; 1850]
    [SARAH] MARGARITE CABLE (R.Ows. 19 S b.TN)
    [d/o Joseph Cable & Rebecca Pierce - NC]
    6 Nov., 1856, Ows.  [R.Owsley 1860]
    [R. A. m2 1889 Lee, Jane (Combs) Curry,
    wid/o George D. Curry - M-L; KAS]

## CHILDS

HANNIBAL "HAN" (c24 S b.Clay)  [s/o James L.
    Childs & Sarah S. Evans - TCS; ob-HM]
    MAIMIE McCOLLUM (c16 S b.Garrard)
    1905        (1910-4, m-4; B-O ch-1910;
    BC 1916; R.San Antonio, TX 1936; W/as
    Maimie 2x & Mary 1x)

JAMES (R.Clay 21 S b.VA) P/VA --  [s/o _____
    Childs & Betsy       - TCS]
    SARAH EVANS (R.Ows. 16 S b.Ows) P/-- [1858-
    1936; d/o Jack Evans & Rebecca Nantz -
    1870; ob-W OCC-5/15/36]
    29 Oct., 1874, Ows., @ Rebecca Evans
    [R.Owsley 1910 WF w/them; W-d. Ham., OH]

J[OHN] D. (R.Ows. 21 S b.Clay) P/Clay  [s/o
    James L. Childs & Sarah Evans - ob-HM&S
    OCC-5/15/36, OCN-11/16/51]
    MINNIE STRONG (R.Ows. 19 S b.Ows.) P/Jack-
    Ows.
    2 March, 1904, Ows.  [R.Owsley 1910-1920;
    BC 1911-1923 W/<u>Vickers</u>; BC 1919 W/Strong;
    R.Rockcastle 1923; Berea 1936; Rockc. 1951]

(Childs cont.)

143

## CHILDS (cont.)

WILLIAM H. (c25 S b.Clay) [c1877-1951 Lex.
hosp.; s/o James Childs & Sarah Evans - ob-
H&M OCN-11/16/51, OCC-5/15/36]
JESSIE BELL PRICE (c17 S b.KY) [1885-1953
London hosp.; d/o Nelson Price & Maggie
Gibson - ob-W OCN-1/30/53]
1901/2          (1910 m-8; 1900 Belle BO
w/James & Polly Neeley; R.Sturg. 1936-53)

## CHOUSE
see SHOUSE

## CHRISMAN

WILLIAM YEARY (c34 b.VA)
SARAH S. HOBBS (c26 VA) [d/o Wm. Zion
Hobbs & Mary Spencer - 1850-Lee,VA]
c1849, prob. VA  (1850-Lee,VA w/WP; B-O ch.
b. 4/58 Lee,VA; 1860; NL 1870/L/W; 1880-W)

## CLARK

ANDERSON (c26 S b.KY) [s/o Wm. Clark
& Tabitha Evans - TCS]
LUCY DAY (c19 S b. VA)
c1869          (1870-1/70; 1880-10; 1890;
wid. Lucy 1900-1910; TCS)
ANDREW H. (c34 Law. b.Ows.) [s/o Wm. Clark
& Tabitha Evans - TCS; REM]
LEVINIA RAINES (c21 b.Lee,VA) [d/o Benj.
Raines & Martha Wilson - TCS]
24 Dec., 1867, Clay (TCS; 1870, no ch.; B-O
ch.; 1880-9; ME-6/5/96, C.C. Reins visiting
sis, Mrs. A. H. Clark)
BILL - see WILLIAM
C[ELUCIUS] C. (c20 S b.MO)
[MINNIE] BELLE WILSON (c20 b.KY) [1879-
1907; d/o Alford Wilson & Martha Hamilton -
1880; TCS]
8 Sept., 1898, Clay (M-C; TCS; 1900-J)
[C.C. m2 1909/10 Leah Davidson - 1910-C-10,
H-m2-0, W-18 m1-0; BC 1915-1917; NL 1920Sx]
E[LHANNON] W. (R.Ows. 38 widr b.Clay) [widr/o
Rachel Evans - 1850; M-C 6/7/1834] [s/o
Henry Clary & Jane Lundy - TCS]
NANCY METCALF (R.Lau. 22 S b.uk)
[30]- Nov., 1852, Ows. (a/L M-Lau. mf as
11/30/52; Elhannon 40; Nancy 35 b.Lau.)
[R.Jackson Co. 1860]

(Clark cont.)

**CLARK (cont.)**

HENRY (c28 b.Ows.) [s/o Wm. Clark & Tabitha
   Evans - 1850-1860]
   EMILY JONES (c19 b.LA)
   c1869        (1870, no ch.; B-O ch.)
[HENRY] JACKSON (R.Jack. 19 S b.KY) P/KY
   [s/o Joseph Clark & Eliza Sandlin - TCS]
   NANCY J. BOWMAN (R.Ows. 18 S b.KY) P/KY
   [s/o Squire Bowman & Rhoda Morris - TCS]
   23 Aug., 1877, Ows. @ J. A. Bowman's
JACKSON - see HENRY JACKSON
JAMES W. (c30 2nd b.KY) [poss. m1 12/29/98
   Nancy Creech - M-C]
   MATTIE SPARKS (c18 S b.KY)
   1909/10       (1910, son Frank, age 11,
   from H-1st mg.; TCS)
JESSE (c18 b.KY) P/VA
   MELISSA JANE LYNCH (c17 b.KY) [d/o Wm. R.
   Lynch & Nancy Catherine Salyers - 1870]
   1879        (ECP; 1880-MWY; 1900 H-remd-
   21, but this is W1)
JESSE (35 2nd b.KY) [widr/o Melissa Jane
   Lynch above]
   SOPHIA HUNDLEY (28 S b.KY)
   3 Feb., 1898, <u>Lee</u> @ Pep Hamilton's; wits.
   Samuel Farmer & Jos. Isaacs  (M-L; 1900
   m-21, but this is W1, md. to Sophia; 1910
   m-12, 1/1 ch.; TCS)
JESSE (c23 S b.KY) [s/o Nathan M. Clark
   & Ibby Wilson - TCS]
   MINTY PIERSON (c22 S b.Ows.) [d/o James
   Pierson & Catherine Bowman - TCS]
   10 Jan., 1900            (TCS; NL 1900;
   1910 w/WP; NL M-C/J/R)
MACK - see NATHANIEL
NATHANIEL MACK "NASH" (c22 b.KY) [s/o Henry
   J. Clark & Patience Bledsoe - TCS; 1870-J]
   ISABELLA "IBBY" WILSON (c19 b.KY) [d/o
   Jesse Wilson & Betsy Strong - JCH; 1870]
   10 Nov., 1870         (TCS; NVP; ob-WS
   OCC-4/13/34; 1870-1880-1900-J; B-J ch-1876
   W/as Alla)
PINKNEY (c23 furniture maker b.VA)  [s/o Wm.
   Clark & Rebecca          ]
   AMANDA _____ (c19 b.KY) P/VA
   c1879        (1880, no ch.)
(Clark cont.)

**CLARK (cont.)**

SAMUEL P. (c24 b.VA)  [s/o Wm. M. Clark
  & Rebecca        - TCS]
  MARTHA J. BELL (c21 b.VA)  [d/o Chas. Mark
  Bell & Martha Flanery - TCS]
  1884/5      (1900; TCS)
WILLIAM "BILL" (c20 S b.Clay)  [s/o Tom CLARK
  & Esther (nee BARRETT) GIBSON, W/o George
  GIBSON - TCS]
  NANCY MALITHA "MATTIE" RILEY (c21 S b.KY)
  1896      (1900 m-3, Esther Gibson w/them
  as "MiL" but she was really HM; 1910 m-14;
  1920; B-O ch-1909; BC 1916-1919; NL M-B;
  ob-ch. BS-10/28/93; W/as Nancy, Maletha,
  Matilda, Mattie)

**CLAY**

HENRY (c27 <u>blk</u> b.KY)  [d. 1899]
  PRISCILLA BELL MADDOX (c17 <u>Mul</u>; b.KY)
  1864/5      (1870-1880-L; 1900-L, wid.
  listed as m-35; B-L ch-6/74; W/as
  Priscilla, Cilla & Bell)

**CLEM**

LEONARD - see W. LEONARD
LEWIS (R.Harl. 22 S b.Harl.) P/Harl.  [1864-
  1952 - ob-H OCN-7/25/52]
  MARY JANE KING (R.Harl.; 16 S b.Harl.) P/
  Harl.  [d/o Woodard P. King & Eliz. Harris
  - TCS]
  21 Oct., 1886, <u>Harlan</u> @ Woodard P. King's;
  bm. groom & M. G. Bailey   (M-H 6:368;
  1900-1910-1920; ob-H)
W. L[EONARD] (c18 S b.KY)  [s/o Lewis Clem
  & Mary J. King - 1900; TCS; ob-HF]
  MILLIE HARRIS (c16 S b.KY)  [c1891-1985;
  d/o Albert Harris & Rachel King - ob-W
  BS-4/18/85]
  17 Aug, 1907, <u>Harlan</u> @ her house, by Garrit
  King, MG; wits. Wm. Stanton & Tom Middleton
  (M-H 18:80; 1910-1920; TCS; BC 1912-1915-
  1917-1920)

**CLONTZ**
JEFFERSON (c49 b.NC)
   MAGGIE (nee GIBSON) PRICE (c45 2nd b.TN)
   [m1 Nelson Price - 1880]  [d/o John Gibson
   & Phoebe Seaborn - TCS]
   1892/3     (1900, Price s-ch. w/them;
   Maggie w/Price in-laws 1880; wid. Maggie
   1920 w/dau.)

**COCKERHAM**
JAMES H. (c20 b.NC)  [s/o Wm. Cockerham
   & Elizabeth     ]
   EMILY STAMPER (c16 b.KY)  [d/o Joel Stamper
   & Polly    - TCS]
   1842     (1850-7; 1860; 1870-1880-L;
   1900-L m-57; B-O ch.; M-L ch. 1918)

**COCKRELL**
_____ (\_\_\_ b.\_\_\_)
   JULIA WHITE (c33 b.KY)  [c1813-1852; d/o
   Whitfield White & Julia - 1850; D-O]
   c1846     (1850-3, wid. Julia w/P; D-O)

**COFFEE**
WILEY J. (R.Ows. 22 S b.TN) P/TN
   ELIZABETH McGUIRE [ALLEN] (R.Ows. 25 2nd
   b.NC) P/NC  [m1 c1872 \_\_\_\_\_ Allen - NL M-J]
   2 Aug., 1877, Ows. @ James Brock's [Min.]
   [R.Jackson 1880, s-s Martin Allen 7]

**COLDIRON**
WILLIAM "WILLIE" (c22 b.KY)  [s/o Taylor
   Coldiron & Mary Wells - TCS]
   EMILY "EMMA" J. MOORE (c23 b.KY)  [1866-
   1952 OH; d/o Joseph Moore & Sally Ann
   Gabbard - 1880; LNG]
   1890     (TCS; 1900-C-6/91, m-9;
   LNG; NL M-C)

**COLE/COAL**
BARTON "BART" (c20 b.KY)  [s/o Wm. Cole &
   Martitia Crawford]
   EMILY EVANS (c17 b.KY)  [d/o Henry Evans]
   c1846     (1850-3; B-O ch.; 1860; 1870-
   1880-L; 1900-L wid. Emily; ob-ch. OCC-
   8/29/41, BE-12/30/48)


(Cole cont.)

<u>COLE (cont.)</u>
BARTON, JR. (c26 b.KY)
    SARAH _____ (c27 b.KY)
    c1869     (1870-L-2/70)
BEN - see JOHN BEN
BURDYNE B. (c24 b.Est.) [s/o James Cole
    & Levica Tipton - 1850-E; M-E 1830 TCS]
    NANCY A. CRAWFORD (c20 b.Br.)
    c1866     (1870-L-3; B-L ch.)
CHARLES G. (c19 b.KY) [c1842-1870; s/o John
    Cole & Margaret Higginbottom - 1860]
    MARGARET ELIZABETH CECIL (c15 b.VA) [d/o
    Madison Cecil & Mary Taylor - 1860; 1850-
    Lee,VA]
    c1861     (wid. Eliz. 1870-8; 1880;
    ob-ch. OCN-8/8/52)
FRANKLIN - see WILLIAM FRANKLIN
GRANT (c30 S b.KY) [1872-1941; s/o Lewis Cole
    & Martha Cooper - 1880 TCS ob-H BE-2/27/41]
    ADA MOORE (c24 S b.KY) [d/o Elijah Sutton
    Moore & Amanda Bowman - 1880]
    1901/2     (1910-1920; TCS; BC 1916;
    ob-ch. BS-6/11/92; W/as Ada & Addie; their
    photo BE-8/27/70)    [GRANT m2 Emma (nee
    Bailey) Cole, his SiL, wid/o Wm. - TCS;
    ob-WS OCC-7/15/38]
HENRY C. (c20 S b.Ows.) [s/o James Cole
    & Malinda Combs - TCS; 1880]
    ELLA BEGLEY (c20 S b.KY) [d/o Jackson
    Begley & Eliz. Bowman - TCS; 1880]
    1897/8     (1900-1910; TCS; BC 1911-
    1915-1920)
JAMES [M.] (21 S b.VA)
    SARAH ANN ["SALLY"] SMITH (23 S b.Clay)
    1 Aug, 1852, <u>Laurel</u> (M-Lau. mf; B-Lau. ch-
    1857; 1860-7; B-O ch.; REM)
JAMES (c22 S b.Knox) [c1844-1896; s/o Lewis
    Cole & Susan Coleman - P-CW; REM]
    MALINDA COMBS (c18 S b.Br.) [1846-1922;
    d/o Samuel Combs & Nancy Cornett - P-CW]
    10 Jan., 1867, Ows., @ house of Samuel
    Combs, by Sylvester Isaacs, JP; wits. A. H.
    Clark & Wm. Isaacs    (P-CW; 1870-2; B-O ch;
    1880; 3Fks-6/1/88 James Cole, Ows.,
    recently drew a pension; 1890; wid. Malinda
    1900-1910-1920)
(Cole cont.)

JEROME (R.Ows. 22 S b.VA) [1832-1904 Jack.;
s/o John Cole & Margaret Higginbottom - ME-
2/26/04; TCS]
RHODA MOORE (R.Ows. 17 S b.Ows.) [c1837-
1889; d/o James Moore & Matilda Cunnigan -
ME-2/26/04; TCS]
11 Dec., 1854, Ows. [R.Owsley 1860-1870;
Jackson 1880] [JEROME m2 1/13/90, Nelly
Jane Byrd - 1900-J anot.; ME-2/26/04]

JESSE H. (c37 b.Est.) [s/o William Cole
& Martitia Crawford - TCS]
RACHEL ANN BOWMAN (c21 b.Ows.) [c1846-
c1869; d/o Elisha W. Bowman & Evaline
Isaacs - TCS]
c1867          (1870-L-2, widr. Jess w/dau.
"Leoni"; 1880, "Senna" Cole w/Bowman GP;
ME-7/29/81 funeral preached over graves of
Rachel Ann & L. L. Cole, wf & s/o Jesse H.
Cole of Beattyv.; M-L ch-1886; 3Fks-
5/18/88, Mrs. Elisha Bowman of Ows.
visiting GD, Mrs. Leni L. Crawford of Lee;
1890; widr. Jesse 1900-L w/neph.)

JOHN (R.Ows. 28 S b.Est.) [c1823-1889 Lee;
s/o Wm. Cole & Martitia Crawford -REM P-CW]
ELIZABETH McGUIRE (R.Ows. 18 S b.Est.)
[1832-1917; d/o Ben McGuire & Diadema Mann
- REM P-CW]
4 Nov., 1852, Ows. [P-CW adds that they
were md. @ Benjamin McGuire's, by Elisha
Wright; wits Timothy & Sally A. Johnson]
[R.Owsley 1860; Lee 1870-1880; wid. Eliz.
1900 Lee]

JOHN HENRY (c20 S b.KY) [s/o Oliver Cromwell
Cole & Margaret Moore - KAS]
ELIZABETH PALMER (c16 S b.TN) [d/o Austin
Palmer & Celia Kilburn]
1863/4          (1870-L-2 mo.; 1880-1900-
1910-L; ob-ch. BE-12/25/47-2/5/58)

JOHN G. (c24 S b.KY) [1872-1950; s/o James
Cole & Malinda Combs - TS-TCS; 1880]
EMMA BEGLEY (c21 S b.KY) [1874-1972; d/o
Jackson Begley & Eliz. Bowman - TCS; 1880]
1895/6          (1900-1910-1920; TCS; BC 1911-
1913)

(Cole cont.)

## COLE (cont.)

JOHN B[EN] (R.Lee 18 S b.Lee) P/Ows. & --
LUCY BEGLEY (R.Lee 18 S b.Lee) P/Per-Br.
[d/o Albert Begley & Sarah J. Roberts -
P/1900-L]
9 Aug., 1899 (ML), Lee, to be md. @ Albert
Begley's (M-L, MC-NFI; 1900-L, next to WP;
ob-ch. 3Fks-8/4/93)
[LUCY appar. m2 a Brandenburg]

JOHNNY (c21 S b.KY)
LIZA D. ROSS (c17 S b.KY)  [d/o Huram Ross
& Sarah Burns - 1900]
1904/5      (1910, WM w/them)

JOSEPH (___ b.___)
FANNY HOLCOMB (c24-44 S b.KY)  [d/o Wm.
Holcomb & Eliz. Christian - 1880]
1880-1900         (TCS; NL 1900Sx;
W/NL w/P 1900)

JOSEPH (c24 S b.KY)  [s/o Jim Cole & Polly
Hammons - 2nd M-L; 1870-1880-L]
MARTHA BARRETT (c16 S b.KY)
1891      (1900 m-9; 1910 m-18; 1920; TCS;
BC 1911)   [JOE (57 widr. b.Ows.) m2
5/12/1922 Lee, Mary (Jewell) Harris (27
Div. - d/o Bill Jewell & Betsy Collins) -
M-L - ob-H/ch. BE-1/25/68 listing half-
sibs]

JOSEPH (c20 S b.Boonev., Ows.)
EDNA ROSS (c18 S b.Buck Cr.)   [d/o John D.
Ross & Stella Venable - TCS]
1902/3      (1910; B-O ch.)

LEWIS (c23 grocery kpr. b.NC)
SUSAN COLEMAN (c17 b.KY) [c1827-1876 Ows.;
d/o Samuel Coleman & Phoebe - NOTE:  Though
D-O 1876 has her as d/o Samuel Black &
Phoebe, REM, FH-dau. & BS-6/27/85 ltr. to
ed all list her as COLEMAN]
c1844         (NL 1850; 1860-15; 1870 WM,
Phoebe Colman, w/them; widr Lewis 1880)

LEWIS (c23 b.Knox)  [1845-1921; s/o James Cole
& Polly Hammonds - P-CW]
MARTHA COOPER (c23 b.Ows.)  [c1848-1894 Ows;
d/o Wm. Cooper & Nancy Smith - P-CW]
14 Sept., 1871, Lee, by M. C. Taylor  (M-L;
P-CW; 1880-6; R.Boonev. 1888; 1900 m-28
crossed out, widr. Lewis)  [H-remd.]

(Cole cont.)

150

COLE (cont.)

LEWIS (c23 b.KY) [1870-1904; s/o James Cole
    & Malinda Combs - TS-TCS; D-O; ME-4/22/04]
    EMMA REYNOLDS (c18 b.KY) [d/o Meredith
    Reynolds & Eliz. Morris - TCS]
    1892/3        (1900; 1904; TCS)
    [EMMA m2 William Reynolds]
LEWIS (R.Low.Buff. c58 2nd b.Knox) [widr/o
    Martha Cooper above - P-CW]
    STELLA C. [nee VENABLE] ROSS (R.Buck Cr.
    c48 2nd b.Lee,VA) [wid/o John D. Ross -
    P-CW; wid. 1900] [1854-1937 OH; d/o Leroy
    Venable Sr. & Rachel Ann McQueen - P-CW]
    8 Oct., 1902, Ows. @ Stella Ross', by Rev.
    L. Clem Roberts; wits. Wm. Ross, Sarah
    Taylor, etc. (P-CW; ME-10/24/02; 1910 m2-7
    both; 1920; wid. Stella St. Helens 1921; wf
    d. S. Lebanon, OH 1937)
OLIVER C. (___ b.___)
    MARGARET MOORE (c22 b.KY) [d/o Wm. Moore
    & Deborah Bowman - MNC]
    19 March, 1841, Clay [DIVORCED - REM]
    (M-C; MNC) [MARGARET m2 George Henson
    Brandenburg]
ROBERT (R.Lee 21 S b.Ows) P/Knx -- [s/o Lewis
    Cole & Martha Cooper - 1900; ob-HS BE-
    2/27/41]
    [MARGARET] MAGGIE MOORE (R.Ows. 26 S b.Lee)
    P/Ows. [d/o Elijah Sutton Moore & Amanda
    Bowman - TCS]
    11 April, 1908, Ows. [R.Owsley 1910-1920;
    Stay 1941-1962 - ob-HS BE-9/6/62]
SAMUEL (R.Ows. [c26] S mcht b.Ows.) P/-- [s/o
    Lewis Cole & Susan Coleman - 1860]
    MARANDA E[LIZABETH] CARDWELL (R.Br. 16 S b.
    Br.) P/Williamsburg, KY & Br. [d/o Thomas
    P. Cardwell & Ellen South]
    10 Dec., 1874, Breathitt (M-B; 1880;
    1900-B; M-B ch-1901)
SAMUEL (31 b.KY) [1868-1945; s/o James Cole
    & Malinda Combs - TS-TCS]
    MARY SMITH (c18 b.KY) [1881-1909; d/o
    Henry Smith & Sarah Taylor - 1880; TS-TCS]
    1898/9        (1900; widr. Sam 1910, HM
    w/him; 1920; TCS)

(Cole cont.)

COLE (cont.)

SPEED C. (c28 S b.Ows.) [s/b Est.] [s/o Orsen
    Cole & Perlina Bennett - 1850]
    AMERICA SNODGRASS (c20 b.Wash.,VA) [d/o F.
    K. Snodgrass & Jane      - 1860]
    c1866      (1870-3; B-L ch.; 1880-L;
    widr. Speed 1900-L; ob-ch. OCN-5/21/54)
THOMAS J. (c23 minr b.KY) [s/o Orsen Cole
    & Perlina Bennett - 1860]
    RHODA A. PHILLIPS (c22 b.Ows.) [c1847-1874;
    d/o B. F. Phillips & Susan Bennett - D-L;
    P/M-E]
    c1868/9      (1870-L; 1870MS-L, ch. d. 1/70,
    age 1 mo.)
THOMAS (c27 S b.Clay) [1872-1959; s/o David
    C. Cole & Charlotte Reed - TCS; ob-H BE-
    5/21/59]
    LAURA (nee HOWARD) HIGNITE (c27 2nd b.KY)
    [wid/o _____ Hignite] [d/o _____ Howard
    & Eliz. Spence - TCS]
    1899/1900      (1900, Hignite s-s b.6/94;
    1910 W-2nd; 1920; TCS)
WILLIAM (R.Ows. 22 S b.Est.) [s/o Orsen Cole
    & Perlina Bennett - 1850; M-E]
    MARY BISHOP (R.Clay 18 S b.Clay)
    22 Aug., 1855, Ows. (a/L M-C mf as 8/2_6_/55,
    H-23 b.Ows., W/as Polly) [R.Owsley 1860;
    widr. Wm. 1880-1900-L]
WILLIAM F[RANKLIN] (R.Ows. 21 S b.Clay)
    [s/o John Cole & Margaret Higginbottom -
    1850; 1870, his dau. w/HP]
    ELIZABETH THOMAS (R.Ows. 19 S b.Clay)
    [d/o Joseph Thomas & Anna Couch - LNG/WT]
    24 Dec., 1857, Ows. [R.Owsley 1860]
    [H-remd.]
WILLIAM FRANKLIN (c29 2nd b.Clay) [widr/o
    Elizabeth Thomas above - 1860]
    MARY GARRETT (c18 b.VA) [poss. d/o George
    W. Garrett & Sarah Thompson]
    1865/6      (1870; B-J ch.; 1880-J;
    1900-J m-34)

(Cole cont.)

## COLE (cont.)

WILLIAM FRANK (c23 S b.Ows.)  [s/o Lewis Cole
& Susan Coleman - 1880]
SARAH M. PRITCHARD (c20 b.KY)  [c1866-1889;
d/o Bonaparte Pritchard (w) & Mary Jane
Ross (Mul) - 1880; TS-TCS]
c1886          (1900, Donna Cole, b. 1887,
w/GP Bonaparte & Mary J. Pritchard; H-remd.
1900; 1910 H-m2-19)
WM. FRANK (c27 2nd b.Ows.) [m1 Sarah Pritchard
above]     [alive 1943]
MARY ANN SMITH (c22 S b.Ows.)  [1869-1943
Est.; d/o Asa Smith & Sophia Brandenburg -
1880; TS-TCS; ob-W BE-8/5/43]
1890/1          (1900-1910; B-O ch.; DB)
WILLIAM (c24 S b.Ows.)  [1875-1923; s/o Lewis
Cole & Martha Cooper - TS-TCS]
EMMA BAILEY (c15 S b.Ows.)  [1885-1966 NC;
d/o Green Bailey & Eliz. Reynolds - TCS ob-
W&S BE-5/5/66, OCC-5/17/40, OCN-1/27/55]
1899/1900          (1900 N#L, no ch, w/HP;
1910 m-10; 1920; TCS)     [EMMA m2 Grant
Cole, her BiL - TCS; ob-WS OCC-7/15/38;
R.Ashville, NC 1955; W-d. NC 1966]

## COLEMAN

JOHN B. (c22-37 b.KY)
SALLIE _____ (c16-31 b.KY)
1855-70          (1870, no ch.;
NL 1860/B/C/E/J/P; NL 1880-1900Sx)

## COLLIER/COLYER

D[AVID] G[RANT] (R.Welchburg; c26 Law. b.KY)
[s/o Geo. Collier & Sarah     - 1880-J]
FANNIE J. MINTER (R.Green Hall, Ows.; c22
tchr. b.KY)
3 March, 1895, Jackson Co. (Sun.); bm.
groom & W. W. Riggs     (ME-3/8/95; M-J
9:232 ML 3/1/95; 1900-J m-5)
JAMES R. (c25 b.KY) [s/o Geo. Collier & Sarah
- 1880-J]
KATE BRANDENBURG (c18 b.KY) [d/o Wm. Bowles
BBurg. & Josephine Glass; GD/o Dr. W. H.
Glass - ME]
1890/1          (ME-8/2/95 Mrs. J. R. Collier
visiting GP, Dr. W. H. Glass & wf of Ows.;
ME-5/22/96 Miss Jennie Brandenburg visiting
sis Mrs. Collier in Welchburg; 1900Sx-Lau.;
NL M-J/Lau.)

## COLLINS

AARON (R.Clay 21 S b.KY) P/KY
   RACHEL DAVIDSON (R.Ows. 22 S b.KY) P/KY
   [d/o Perry Davidson & Eliz. Burns - 1870]
   26 Oct., 1878, Ows. [R.Leslie 1880]
ALFORD (c20 b.VA) P/TN-KY
   SARAH E. VAUGHN (c26 b.Ows.) P/NC-VA [d/o
   Christopher Vaughn & Jane   - 1870 w/wid.
   mom]
   c1872      (1880-7; B-O ch.)
ALEXANDER (c21 b.KY) [s/o Anderson Collins
   & Margaret Rasner - 1880]
   MARY J. NEELEY (c17 b.KY) [d/o John Neeley
   & Eliza Ann Bowles - TCS; 1880]
   1883/4     (1900; TCS)
ANDERSON D. (c25 b.KY) [s/o Wm. Collins &
   Lytha Powell - TW; LNG; 1850-C; P/M-Lee,VA
   1832]
   MARGARET J. (nee RASNER) COTTONGIN (c24 2nd
   b.KY) [wid/o James Cottongin] [d/o John
   Rasner & Jane Redmand - TW]
   25 Aug., 1861, <u>Clay</u> (M-C; 1870-12, next
   ch. 7; 1880 shows 1st ch. Cottongin W/dau.,
   next ch-18; 1900-C as m-42) [ANDERSON poss.
   m2 9/25/1903 Clay, Agnes Reed - M-C; 1910-L
   m2-8]
BIRDINE (24 b.Let.) P/NC [s/o Bryant Collins
   & Mary    - 1850-1860-Let.]
   LEVINA WARREN (c22 b.Lee,VA) [d/o Geo.
   Jordan Warren & Eliza    - 1860-1870]
   c1871     (1880-8; B-O ch.)
CHARLEY (R.Br. 21 S b.Br.) P/Ows. [s/o Wm.
   Collins & Martha Freeman - 1900]
   ORLENA RILEY (R.Br. 23 S b.Br.) P/Br.
   11 Jan., 1910, Ows.
FIELDING (c24 b.KY) [s/o Bryant Collins
   & Mary    - 1850-1860-Let.]
   ANNA BOWMAN (c29 b.KY) [d/o John Bowman
   & Susan Moore - TW]
   c1869     (1870, no ch.; 1880 W-md, H-NL,
   dau. Martha age 12)

(Collins cont.)

**COLLINS (cont.)**

FRANCIS M[ARION] (c26 b.Ows.) [s/o Howard
  Collins & Nancy Dunnigan - 1880-L]
  ELIZABETH "BETTIE" (nee STEPP) SHORT (c30
  2nd b.Ows.) [m1 _____ Short - ME] [d/o
  John Stepp & Martha Moore - ME; 1880-L]
  13 Feb., 1897, Ows., Meadow Creek (Sat.), @
  res. of bride's F, John Stepp, by Bro.
  Taylor [appar. DIVORCED] (ME-2/19/97; 1900
  "wid." Eliz. Collins 6/5 ch., svt., & dau.
  Lillie 2, w/Green B. Rose; M-L ch-1913)
  [F. M. m2 unknown; m3 1904/5 Lizzie _____
  (c19) - 1910-L; NL M-B/L 2nd or 3rd;
  F. M. (40 Div. b.Lee; s/o Howard & Nancy)
  md. 2/9/1918 Br., Mary (Robinson) Barnett
  (25 wid); F. M. (51 widr. b.Lee; s/o Howard
  Collins & Nancy) md. 2/12/21 Br., Alice
  Gabbard (30 wid.) (Alice m1 Oscar Eastes;
  m2 James Gross) - M-B]

HAZEL (R.Jack. 19 S b.TN) P/TN
  SARAH COLLINS (R.Ows. 24 S b.TN) P/TN
  26 Nov., 1874, Ows. @ Henry Clark's
  [R.Letcher Co. 1880]

HENRY (c27 b.VA) [s/o Birdine Collins & Mary
  Morgan - 1850-1860-Let.]
  CLARINDA "CLARA" ANN BOWMAN (c18 b.KY)
  [d/o Elisha Bowman & Mary Mahulda Phillips
  - 1850 as Ann 9; 1860 as Cary Ann 16 svt.
  w/H. M. Lutes]
  1863, Ows. (1870-1880-Let.; B-L ch.; W/as
  Clarinda, Clara, Clary)

HENRY (c21 S b.Br.) [s/o Rural Collins
  & Caroline Smith - 1880]
  ALABAMA GIBSON (c19 S Mul b.Br) [d/o Maston
  Gibson (Mul) & Esther Smith (white) - 1880]
  1887/8         (1900-7/94, m-12; 1910 m-15;
  B-O ch.)

HOWARD R. (c20 b.Clay) [1842-19__; s/o John
  Collins & Mary J.       - 2nd M-L]
  NANCY DUNNIGAN (c14 b.Lee,VA) [1848-
  1900/10]
  1861/2         (1870-L-3; B-L ch.; 1880-L;
  1900-L m-38; widr. Howard 1910-L)
  [HOWARD (67 2nd b.Clay) m2 7/26/1910 Lee,
  Mary (nee Butler) Sutton (26 2nd b.Br.; d/o
  Jack Butler & Nancy) - TCS; M-L]

(Collins cont.)

155

**COLLINS (cont.)**

HUGH (c22 b.Let.) P/NC  [s/o Bryant Collins
    & Mary    - 1850-1860-Let.]
    MARGARET BOWMAN (c19 b.Ows.)  [d/o John
    Bowman & Susan Moore - 1870]
    c1871    (1880-8; TW; went to KS c1884,
    where wf d.; ME-9/10/97, returned to Ows.)
NICHOLAS (c25 <u>Mul</u> b.TN)  [1828-1912 Ows.; s/o
    John Collins & Jane McGaffey - P-CW; DC]
    MAHALA (nee RUSSELL) _____ (19 <u>Mul</u> 2nd? b.
    KY) [m1 _____]  [1834-1901; d/o Matt
    Russell & Polly    - 1870-80; ME-6/21/01]
    1854/5    (NL 1860 because Mul.; 1870
    w/WP; 1880 WP w/them, 2 JONES s-Gch, 9 & 7,
    so appar W-2nd mg.; 1890; 1900) [H-remd.]
NICHOLAS (c71 <u>Mul</u> 2nd b.TN)  [widr/o Mahala
    Russell above]
    TALITHA (nee FOX) HOBBS (c48 4th b.KY)
    [appar. m1 1876 James Fox; m2 Richmond
    Pace; m3 1894 Simeon Hobbs, who d. c1896/7
    - P-CW; M-J] [poss. 1854-19__; d/o Isaac
    Fox & Almarinda Griffith - 1860-1870;
    NL DC/W]
    4 Nov., 1901, Ows., @ G. B. Rose's, by Clem
    Roberts; wits. John Smith & Eliz. Baley
    (P-CW; 1910 m2-10 = 1900; Talitha R.Ows.
    1916; 1920 "Tabitha" Collins w/SiL & dau.
    Emma Elkins; M-O & B-O 1904 show Emma PACE
    md. Green B. Elkins; Talitha md. as PACE to
    Simeon Hobbs)
RURAL (R.Long Cr., Br. 21 S b.Clay)  [s/o Wm.
    Collins & Polly    ]
    CARLINE [CAROLINE] SMITH (R.Br. 18 S b.Br.)
    [c1836-1905; d/o Whitley Smith & Elizabeth
    Maynard - 1850-B; ob-W ME-11/16/05]
    25 Sept., 1855, <u>Breathitt</u>, by James Gun
    (M-B; 1860-C; 1870-80; wid. Caroline 1900;
    wf d. Sugar Camp Br.)
WILLIAM (c17 b.KY)  [s/o Rural Collins
    & Caroline Smith]
    MARTHA _____ (c18 <u>Mul</u> b.KY) P/KY-TN
    1878/9    (1880, no ch.; 1900)
**COLWELL**
see CALDWELL

156

## COMBS

_____ (___ b.___) [TCS thinks H/WM. b.
1884 KY s/o Daniel Combs & Melissa Tirey]
NELLY M. BOWLES (c13-17 b.KY) [1892-1984
Lee; d/o Jedediah H. Bowles & Nancy Mary
Brewer - 1880; DC; ob-WM&S OCC-8/5/38, BE-
2/17/66-8/25/66-1/7/71]
1906-10          (ob-WM&S; NL 1910/L;
R.Beattyv. 1938 & 1966-71; Lee 1984;
NL M-B/L)
ALBERT - see ELBERT
ANDREW JACKSON (c27 b.KY)
MARTHA REYNOLDS (c19 b.KY) [d/o Wesley
Reynolds & Nancy Moore - 1860]
c1862          (NL 1870; 1880-16; ob-ch.
OCC-6/11/37 Tarlton b.1863/4 Ows.)
ANDREW J. (c26 S b.Ows.) [s/o Samuel Combs
& Nancy Cornett - N-E.KY; 1880]
ELIZABETH "BETTY" BURKE (c18 S b.KY)
[d/o _____ Burke & Mary P. Herndon who
later md. Wm. Combs - 1860 w/M & s-F as
Eliz. Burke -TCS]
1867/8          (1870-1; 1880 HP & "BiL" Allen
Edwards w/them, but Allen Edwards was s/o
Jackson Edwards & Nancy Combs, decd., & was
actually Andrew's nephew; 1900 N#L; M-L ch-
1909; 1910 m-42; 1920; ob-ch. BE-12/11/49,
1st ch. b.10/68 Ows.; ob-ch. BE-12/1/60-
3/8/73)
ANDREW (21 S b.KY)
NANCY REYNOLDS (18 S b.KY) [d/o Henderson
Reynolds & Anna Moore - 1880]
5 March, 1889 Breathitt @ Granville Noble's
by W. R. Salyer's; wits. John Caudill & J.
A. Noble (M-B 4:429; son Harlan b. c1893
Ows. per M-L; 1900 Nancy COMBS 24 "sgl"
w/Sherman & Susan Freeman, her COMBS ch.
Julie A. 2 & Charlie 2 mos.)
[NANCY m2 Wm. Duff - TCS; 1910 Nancy DUFF,
38, m2-4, 6/4 ch., Harlan COMBS 21 & Julia
COMBS 15 & Ellen DUFF 2]
ANDREW - see also JACKSON


(Combs cont.)

**COMBS (cont.)**

ARCH G. (R.Beattyv. 27 S mcht. b.Ows.) P/Ows-
    VA  [1881-1973 Lee; s/o Andrew Combs
    & Eliz. Burke - mg.; ob-H BE-3/8/73; 1900]
    NANNIE C. SMITH (R.Beattyv. 20 S b.Lee) P/
    Est-Ows.  [d/o J. N. Smith & Margaret E.
    Snowden - mg.]
    12 Aug., 1909 Lee @ J. R. Smith's, by J. F.
    Sutton, Judge; wits. Wm. Goocey & J. R.
    Smith  (M-L 8:583)  [ARCH m2 Belva Warner
    - ob-H]
BILL - see WILLIAM
BRACK - see JOHN BRECKINRIDGE
BRECKINRIDGE - see JOHN BRECKINRIDGE
DANIEL (c23 S b.KY)  [s/o Wm. Combs
    & Mary P. Herndon - TCS]
    MELISSA TIREY (c15 S b.KY)  [d/o John Wm.
    Tirey & Juliann Blevins - TCS]
    early 1879      (1880-12/79; 1900-L
    m-21; 1910-1920; M-L ch-1910; NL M-J)
DECORSEY - see JAMES DECORSEY
EDWARD (c18 b.Ows.)  [s/o Wm. Combs & Eliz.
    Stapleton - 1850, age 1; P/M-C 1835; 1880-
    Pul.]
    MARTHA E. EGAN (c18 b.Scott Co., VA)
    c1869      (B-Lau. ch-1875-1876; 1880-
    Pul-10, HP w/them; NL M-Pul.)
ELBERT (c20 S b.KY)  [1880-1928; s/o Roger
    Combs & Nancy A. Murrell - TS-TCS]
    MELDA HALL (c21 S b.KY)  [d/o Clinton
    Hall & Nancy J. Noble - TCS; ob-WS OCN-
    7/17/58]
    1900/1      (1910-1920; BC 1911-1913-
    1915-1917-1919; TCS; R.Morristown, OH 1958)
ELBERT [a/k/a ELBERT BARRETT] (R.Lee 21 S b.
    Ows.) P/--  [s/o uk Combs & Armina - bride
    can't state F's name, d. when bride was an
    infant - mg.  (see 2nd mg. for par.)]
    DORA BARRETT (R.Lee 18 S b.Ows.) P/Br-Ows.
    [1887-1906/7; d/o Wm. Barrett & America
    (Fox) - mg.; 1900]
    15 Feb., 1906 Lee @ Wm. Barrett's, by Eld.
    S. E. Wilson; wits. Wm. Barrett & James
    Begley; WF appears & states bride is over
    21  (M-L 7:475; H-remd. 1910)

(Combs cont.)

## COMBS (cont.)

ELBERT [a/k/a ELBERT <u>BARRETT</u>] (R.Lee 23 2nd/
W1-d. b.Ows.) P/-- Ows.   [widr/o Dora
Barrett above]   [s/o Talt COMBS & Armina
BARRETT - mg.; 1900-L w/M & s-F Treadway as
Elbert <u>Barrot</u>]
ALICE FOX (R.Lee 27 S b.Ows.) P/Br-Lee
[d/o Buck Fox & Bettie Taylor - mg.]
10 Oct., 1907, <u>Lee</u> @ John Shoemaker's, by
M. M. Wright, MG; wits. C. C. Treadway &
Thomas BurkHart  (M-L & B-O ch. as COMBS;
1910 as BARRETT)   [NOTE:  John Shoemaker
is H2/o Armina Barrett & s-F/o Elbert]

GEORGE BURKE (c42 b.Ows.)  [1868-1947 Lee;
s/o Andrew Combs & Eliz. Burke - ob-H BE-
12/11/47; 1900]
SADIE MARTIN (c30 b.Lee)  [1879-1943 Lex.
hosp.; d/o Elisha Martin & Nannie Eliz.
Robinson - DC]
fall, 1910        (ob-H W/as <u>Mar</u>; ob-ch.
3Fks-8/21/96 W/as <u>Martin</u>; Lee 1920 when
son Andrew b.; widr. George R.Lee 1943)

GRANVILLE (c16 S b.KY) [s/o Jack Combs, Jr.
& W2 Eliz. Hunt - MT]
MARY CARMACK (c13 S b.Ows.)  [d/o John
Carmack & Ibby Burns]
1857/8        (NL 1860/C; 1870-6; 1880;
1900 m-42; B-O ch.; 1910 m-47)

HARVEY (R.Ows. 60 2nd b.KY) P/SC-KY  [a/k/a
Harvey <u>HUNDLEY</u>] [widr/o Eliz. Parsons - D-O
1876] [s/o James HUNDLEY & Sally Combs,
who later md. Claybourn COMBS - MT]
LUCRETIA [nee SMITH] MOORE (R.Ows. 47 2nd
b.KY) P/KY   [wid/o John Moore]      [d/o
Thomas Smith - TCS]
12 Jan., 1877, Ows., @ H. Combs'  [R.Owsley
1880; wid. Lu w/dau. 1900]

HARVEY (c25 b.KY)  [s/o James H. Combs & Nancy
Burns - TCS; 1880]
MARY HUNDLEY (c18 b.KY)   [d/o Kenneth
Hundley & Angeline Mattingly - TCS; 1880-J]
19 June, 1889, <u>Jackson Co.</u>; sur. Kenneth
Hundley  (TCS; NL 1900/J; NL 1910Sx under
Combs, Hundley or Hunley)


(Combs cont.)


159

**COMBS (cont.)**
HARVEY(?) (c26 b.KY)
    RYER J. _____ (c15 b.KY)
    1889/90          (1900; NL 1910Sx)
JACKSON - see also ANDREW JACKSON
JACKSON G. "JACK" (c24 Hot-kpr. b.KY)  [s/o
    Jackson Combs & Martha Crank - TCS]
    SARAH CATHARINE RAISNER (c18 b.KY)  [c1852-
    1885; d/o Claiborne Raisner & Genira Combs
    - 1870; ME-11/25/85]
    27 Jan, 1870          (1870; ME-11/25/85 has
    md. 1/27/71, but md. 1870; TCS; 1880 BiL
    Raisnor; W/as Cath. & Sarah)     [H-remd.]
JACKSON G. "JACK" (c49 2nd jailer b.KY)
    [widr/o Sarah Catherine Raisner above]
    NANCY J. EVANS (c37 b.KY)  [d/o Huram Evans
    & Nancy Stamper - 1880]
    c1893          (1900 wid. Nannie, s-s Henry &
    Richard, 1/1 son Wilson 6; wid. Nancy 1910,
    1920 WS Mary Bullock w/her; ob-ch. OCN-
    4/13/51)
JAMES H. (c22 b.KY) [s/o Harvey COMBS a/k/a
    HUNDLEY & W1 Eliz. Parsons - MT; 1850]
    NANCY BURNS (c21 b.KY)  [d/o Wm. Burns
    & Rachel Asher - REM]
    c1863          (1870-6; B-O ch.; 1880)
JAMES SLAUGHTER "HUNDLEY" (24 S b.Boonev.)
    [1846-1935; s/o Wm. Jos. SEAL & Artemesa
    COMBS - TS-TCS; 1870; REM; MT; LNG; ob-H
    BE-7/18/35]
    MARY CATHERINE HANDY (20 S b.KY)  [1850-
    1940; d/o Stephen Handy & Sarah Ann Peoples
    - TS-TCS; ob-W OCC-11/29/40]
    27 Dec, 1870 Ows. (ob-H; 1880-7; 1900 m-30;
    1910 m-40; 1920; REM; ob-ch. 3Fks-12/14/94)
JAMES B. - see JOHN BRECKENRIDGE
JAMES D. (c21 b.Ows.)  [1867-1950 Jack.; s/o
    Tinsley Logan Combs & Sarah Ellen Goosey -
    1880; N-P 4/98 MGS]
    MARTHA ISAACS (c19 b.Ows.) [d/o Henderson
    Isaacs & Letitia Margaret Neeley - 1880;
    N-P 4/98 MGS]
    23 Feb., 1888, Jackson Co.; sur. Wm. Isaacs
    (TCS; 1900-J)    [JAMES m2 1910-20, America
    (Burch) Botner, wid/o Wesley Botner - wid.
    Botner 1910; TCS; James & Martha 1920]
(Combs cont.)

**COMBS (cont.)**

JAMES O. (c25 b.KY)
   EMILY J. "JENNIE" BOLIN (c17 S b.KY) [d/o
   Robt. H. Bolin & Cath.      - 3Fks.; 1880]
   5 March, 1888, <u>Perry</u>; sur. I. J. Davidson
   (M-P; 3Fks-5/18/88, Mr. R. H. Bolin gone to
   Haz. to reconcile w/dau. Jennie, who eloped
   w/James Combs some 2-3 mos. ago; 1900-P)
JAMES [JESSE "LONG JIM"] (28 S b.Ows.) [1860-
   1941; s/o Wm. Combs & Mary Herndon - 1880;
   ob-H OCC-2/7/41]
   NANNIE BRANDENBURG (20 S b.KY) [1869-1948
   Danville - ob-W BE-10/28/48]
   3 Sept., 1888 <u>Breathitt</u>, by Eugene Nickel,
   Min.; wits. W. T. Hogg & J. Harvey (M-B
   4:351; 1st ch. b.Ows., ob-ch. BE-1/1/59;
   ob-H; 1900-9/89 N#L; 1910 m-21; M-L ch-
   1912-1914; 1920; to Mad. c1928)
[JAMES] "G" D[ECORSEY] (R.Ows. 26 S b.Lee)
   P/Per. [s/o Squire Combs & America
   Anderson - TCS; 1900]
   EMMA MOORE (R.Ows. 24 S b.Ows.) P/Ows.
   [d/o Henry Moore & Artemise Combs - 1900-
   1910; TCS]
   10 Dec., 1910, Ows. [R.Owsley 1920]
JASPER (c19 b.Ows.)
   SUSAN CATHERINE HUNLEY (c15 b.Ows.) [d/o
   Samuel Hunley & Elizabeth Combs - 1860-70]
   1871         (B-Lau. ch-9/75; 1880-J-8;
   1900-J m-28; 1920-J; NL M-J)
JERRY (R.Clk 38 2nd b.Per) P/Per. [m1 _____
   _____]
   MARY [nee _____] PETERS (R.Ows. 27 2nd b.
   Ows.) P/Ows.    [m1 _____ Peters]
   30 Sept., 1903, Ows.
JOHN & CASSEY BISHOP - see SAM & CASSIE BISHOP
JOHN ["BLACK JACK"] (R.Ows. 21 S b.Ows.) [s/o
   Jack Combs, Jr. & Rebecca Combs - MT]
   RACHEL BAKER (R.Clay 17 S b.Clay) [d/o
   Adroniam Baker, Nancy Sandlin - TCS; P/M-C]
   26 April, 1855 (ML) <u>Clay</u> (M-C, listed mf
   as 4/<u>1</u>6/55; 1860; MT; 1900-C m-45)


(Combs cont.)


161

**COMBS (cont.)**

[JOHN C.] "JAMES" B[RECKINRIDGE] (R.Clay 21 S
   b.KY [Clay]) P/KY [1856-1920's; s/o Samuel
   Combs & Casandra Bishop - TCS; 1860-1870-C]
   NANCY J[ANE] FROST (R.Ows. 18 S b.KY) P/TN-
   VA   [d/o Robt. Frost & Susan Miller - B-O;
   TCS; 2nd M-O]
   6 Dec, 1877, Ows. @ Squire Combs' [R.Owsley
   1880-1900-1910 H/as John; 1920 as Brack]
   [NANCY JANE (R.Ows. 62 wid. b.Ows.) m2
   3/13/1930, Samuel Hill (67) - M-O]
JOHN C. B. (c23 S b.Conkling)   [s/o James
   Combs & Nancy Burns - TCS]
   AMERICA GAY (c16 S Conkling)   [d/o Russell
   Gay & Eliza Williams - ob-WS OCN-12/16/54]
   1893         (1900 m-6; 1910 m-17; B-O ch.;
   R.Mildred 1954)
JOHN (R.Ows. 18 S b.Ows.) P/Ows.  [1889-1933;
   s/o John Combs & Nancy Frost - 1900; TCS]
   LUCINDA REYNOLDS (R.Ows. 18 S b.Ows) P/Ows.
   [d/o Aaron Reynolds & Mary A Wilson - 1900]
   7 Sept, 1908, Ows.   [R.Owsley 1910-1920]
KENNETH (c19 b.Br.)   [s/o Claiborne Combs
   & Sarah Combs - 1850]
   LUCRETIA McGEE (c17 b.TN)   [d/o Robt. McGee
   & Esther      - 1850; MT]
   c1852         (1860-C-4 b.Ows.; B-O ch-5/54
   & 6/55)
LARKIN (c19 b.KY)
   MARGARET _____ (c36 b.KY)
   c1856         (1860-3; NL 1880-1900Sx)
LEE C. (c18 S b.KY)   [s/o John Combs & Nancy
   Frost - TCS]
   LYDIA M. (nee GABBARD) DAVIDSON (c19 2nd
   b.KY)  [wid/o Marion Davidson - B-O ch.]
   [d/o Geo. W. Gabbard & W2 Mary Eliz. Shook
   - TCS; 1900; ob-WS OCC-6/12/42]
   1905/6         (1910, Davidson s-s; TCS; B-O
   Davidson ch.; 1920; Covington, KY 1942)
LOGAN - see also TINSLEY LOGAN


(Combs cont.)

## COMBS (cont.)

LOGAN WESLEY "BUD" (c26 S b.Ows.) [1875-1953;
   s/o James Combs & Mary Cath. Handy - 1880;
   ME; ob-H&F&S BE-12/3/53-7/18/35, OCN-
   4/21/50]
   DORA B. FARLER (19 S b.Per.) [1882-1957;
   d/o Talton Farley & Martha Branson - TS-TCS
   1900; ob-W&F OCN-1/10/57, OCC-12/5/41]
   31 July, 1901 Ows., @ home of Talton Farley
   (ME-8/16/01; ob-H has md. 7/25/01; 1910
   m-8; 1920; B-O ch.; R.Cross Roads 1935;
   Pebworth 1950-52; ob-ch. BE-8/7/52)
LOGAN (R.Ows. 21 S b.Ows.) P/Ows.
   LOTTIE GULLET (R.Jess. 21 S b.Ows.) P/Ows.
   9 June, 1910, Ows.
MASION (___ b.Terry, Br.) [poss. MASON b.
   c1872 s/o Talton Combs & Patsy - 1880-B;
   NL w/P-1900-B]
   ESIBELL McINTOSH (___ b.Terry, Br.) [poss.
   ISABELLE b. c1878 d/o Moses McIntosh
   & Ellis Griffith - 1880-B; NL w/P-1900;
   NL M-B to 1915 for any Isabelle/Esibelle/
   Ibby/Belle McIntosh]
   pre-1909        (B-O dau-8/09; NL 1900/B/L;
   NL 1910Sx; NL M-B)
MERIDA/MEREDITH (c20 b.KY) [1872-19__; poss.
   s/o Jackson Combs & Martha Reynolds - 1880]
   MINERVA JANE REYNOLDS (c18 b.KY) [1874-
   19__; poss. d/o Henderson Reynolds & Anna
   Moore - 1880]
   1891/2        (1900-L; 1910-B; M-B ch-1917
   b. Ows. 1897; DC ch-1975)
MEREDITH (c29 S b.Ows.) [s/o Squire Combs
   & America Anderson - 1900]
   SUSAN ELIZ. WOODS (c16 S b.Ows.) [1883-
   1967; d/o J(eff.) D. Woods & Lizzie (Combs)
   - 2nd M-O; BE-2/16/67 as Gentry]
   1899/1900        (1900 w/HP; 1910-1920;
   B-O ch.; M-L ch-1934)    [SUSAN m2 9/16/29
   M. L. Gentry - M-O; M-L ch-1934]
NAPOLEON B. (c23 S b.Ows.) [s/o Bonaparte
   Combs & Susan Isom - 1880]
   AMANDA BRANDENBURG (c18 S b.Ows.) [d/o
   Hardin BBurg. & Sarah Ann Hall - 1880]
   1886/7        (1910-1920; NL 1900; B-O ch.)

(Combs cont.)

## COMBS (cont.)

PRESTON PROCTOR (c20-25 S b.Br.)
_____ (___ b.___)
1880-5        (1910 H-remd-13; H-sgl. 1880;
NL M-B/C)

PRESTON PROCTOR (c26 2nd b.Br.) [m1 _____
_____ above]
MARY BAILEY (c19 S b.Ows.) [d/o Green
Bailey & Eliz. Reynolds - 1880]
1886/7        (1900-1910; B-O ch.)

RICHARD (c26 S U.S. mail carrier b.Boonev.)
[1880-1953; s/o Jackson G. Combs & Sarah
Cath. Rasner - TCS; ob-H OCN-8/7/53]
NANCY L. SHEPHERD (c19 S b.Boonev.) [d/o
Silas Shepherd & Florence Minter - TCS]
1 July, 1906        (VKD; 1910; B-O ch.;
wid. R.Boonev. 1969 - ob-ch BE-4/24/69)

ROGER (c21 b.KY) [s/o Talton Combs & Jemima
Spicer - WGO; JSG]
NANCY A. MURRELL (c19 b.KY) [d/o Larkin
Murrell & Nancy        - WGO]
9 Dec., 1876, Breathitt @ Robt. Burton's,
by Robt. Burton; wits. G. Hatton & Nancy
Bohn  (M-B 1:332; 1880-5/80, W-md. w/son,
H-NL; H 1880-1900-B)

SAMUEL (R.Clay 22 S b.Ows.) [s/o Jack Combs
& Rebecca Combs - MT]
CASSANDRA ["CASSIE"] BISHOP (R.Clay 25 S
b.Clay) [poss. d/o Stephen Bishop & Sarah
Noble - 1850-C; P/M-C]
14 Dec, 1852, Clay (M-C file 10) [a/L M-O
as John (R.Ows. 23 S b.Per) & Cassey Bishop
(R.Clay 22 S b.--) 1852] [a/L M-C mf as
12/22/52] (B-O ch-10/55; 1860-C-7; 1870-C)

SAMUEL P. (c25 b.KY) [1869-1957 OH, bur. Ows.
- ob-H BE-12/5/57]
MARTHA MARCELLA "MATTIE" THOMAS (c15 b.KY)
[1879-1957 OH - ob-W OCN-3/14/57]
1894/5        (1900; ob-W; M-L ch-1923-
1933; R.Midltwn, OH 1957)

SAMUEL B. (c18 S b.Ricetown) [s/o James Combs
& Nancy Burns - 1880]
MAHULDAH HOBBS (c18 S b.Eversole)
1895        (1900-8/94, m-4, W-2/2 ch.;
1910 m-15; 1920; B-O ch.; ob-ch. HJN-12/89)

(Combs cont.)

## COMBS (cont.)

SAMUEL (c27 S b.Ows.)  [s/o Squire Combs
   & America Anderson - TCS]
   SARAH JANE WOODS (c15 S b.KY) [d/o Jeff.
   Woods & Eliz. Combs - 1900; TCS; JC]
   c1900      [DIVORCED] (both remd. 1910-9,
   H-2nd; W-2nd M-O 1908)   [SARAH JANE m2
   Nathan Eversole - 1910 W/m2-1, Eversole
   ch.]
SAMUEL (c23 S b.Ows.)  [s/o John Combs & Nancy
   Frost - TCS]
   MARY BELL BOWMAN (c16 S b.Ows/Lee) [c1887-
   1962; d/o Harvey Bowman & Melissa Moore -
   TCS; ob-W BE-5/31/62]
   1904/5      (1910-1920; B-O ch.; ob-ch.
   BS-3/5/92)
SAMUEL (R.Ows. 31 2nd b.Ows.) P/Ows.  [Div/f
   Sarah Jane Woods above - TCS]
   KIZZIE BISHOP (R.Ows. 17 S b.Clay) P/Clay-
   Ows.
   23 March, 1909, Clay [rec. Owsley]
   [R.Owsley 1910, H-m2-1, W-NL, 3 ch, 9, 6 &
   4; 1920 Sam & Kizzie]
SIMPSON KELLY (c21 S b.KY) [s/o Tinsley Logan
   Combs & Sarah Ellen Goosey - 1880; N-P 4/98
   MGS]
   SUSIE _____ (c18 S b.KY)
   1890/1     (1910; NL 1900)
SQUIRE (c31 mcht b.Clay) [s/o Jack Combs, Jr.
   & Elizabeth Hunt - MT]
   AMERICA ANDERSON (c19 b.Ows.)  [d/o Frank
   Anderson & Jane        ]
   1869/70      (1900; 1870-1880; MT)
TARLTON (c17 b.Br.) [s/o Syra Combs & Mary
   Roberts - TCS; 1850-1860-B]
   MARY A. "POLLY" WILLIAMS (c15 b.KY) P/VA
   c1864, prob. Breathitt (1870-E, ch. 4, 3, 6
   mo. & Lewis Caudle 7; 1880, ch. 14, 13, 10,
   8, 3 & Lewis 18 as "son", thus it appears
   that Lewis was s/o Talton Combs & a
   Caudill; ob-ch. BE-9/26/46, b. c1865 Br.)


(Combs cont.)

**COMBS (cont.)**

TARLTON (c25 b.Ows.)    [s/o Jackson Combs &
    Martha Reynolds -1880 TCS ob-H OCC-6/11/37]
    LENILCOTI STEWART (c16 b.KY)  [d/o Dan
    Stewart & Matilda Johnson - 1880; TCS]
    13 July, 1889          (TCS; 1900-J; ob-H
    lists ch. by W1; NL M-J/R; BS-12/5/91 ch-
    Flora 100 Bday, M-d. & 6 ch. divided among
    neighbors until F sold Jack. farm & moved
    to Berea)  [TALTON m2 Jennie (nee _____)
    Howard - TCS; 1910-M m2-5 both]
TINSLEY LOGAN (c26 b.Ows. [then Clay])  [1839-
    1902 Ows.; s/o Claiborne Combs & Sarah
    Combs - LP; MT; ME-10/3/02]
    SARAH ELLEN GOOSEY (c18 b.Ows.)  [c1848-
    1928 Ows.; d/o David Goosey & Susan Roach;
    N-P 4/98 MGS]
    3 May, 1865, Ows. @ the cross roads by Geo.
    Miller  (REM P-CW; N-P 4/98 MGS; 1870-L-4;
    B-L ch; 1880-13; 1900 m-35; wid. Sarah
    1910-20)
WALTER (R.Ows. 22 S b.Ows) P/Ows. [s/o Tinsley
    Logan Combs & Sarah E. Goosey - 1900; ob-HS
    BE-2/18/60]
    MARY PRICE (R.Ows. 20 S b.Ows.) P/Ows. [d/o
    Stephen Price & Lucinda Riley - 1900; ob-WS
    BE-4/8/65]
    15 Jan, 1909, Ows.   [R.Owsley 1910-1920;
    Owsley 1960; Vincent 1965]
WILEY (c23 b.KY)    [s/o Samuel Combs & Nancy
    Cornett - ACB; 1850-B]
    ELIZA J. COMBS (c15 b.KY)  [d/o Bonaparte
    Combs & Susan Isom - MT; 1850-B]
    c1850, Breathitt [cousins]  (1860-9, both
    sgl. 1850-B; MT; 1870; B-O ch.; 1880-B)
WILEY (c21 b.KY)
    CELIA COMBS (c16 b.KY)
    c1869       (1870-L, no ch.; B-B ch.,
    W/Combs; 1880-B; 1910 widr. Wiley)
WM. (c33 2nd b.KY) [widr/o Letha Begley - TCS]
    [s/o Sam Combs & Nancy Cornett - TCS]
    MARY P. (nee HERNDON) BURKE (c33 2nd b.VA)
    [wid/o _____ Burke]
    c1855     (TCS; 1860 Burke ch-13, 10, Combs
    ch-13, 11, 6, 4 & 3 mos.; 1870-1880; JFB;
    DC dau-1938)
(Combs cont.)

**COMBS (cont.)**
WILLIAM (c24 b.KY) P/KY
   TABITHA EDWARDS (c21 b.KY) P/KY
   24 Aug., 1878, <u>Perry</u>; sur. Jesse Fields
   (M-P; 1880 no ch.; NL 1900Sx)
WILLIAM -"BILL" (c23 S b.KY)
   SARAH KATHERINE COMBS (c23 S b.Ows) [1872-
   1963 Lee; d/o James S. Combs & Mary Cath.
   Handy - 1880-1900 as Sarah C.; ob-W&S BE-
   10/3/63, OCN-4/21/50, BE-12/3/53 as Kath.]
   1900/1          (1910-L m1-9; ob-WS; 1920-17,
   wid. Katherine; ob-ch. BE-4/28/66 b. c1905
   Ows.; R.Pebworth 1950-1953; Lee 1964)
WM. (R.Ows. 20 2nd b.Ows.) P/Ows. [m1 _____
   _____]
   NANNIE VENABLE (R.Ows. 15 S b.Ows) P/--
   [d/o Thomas Venable & Mary M. Shanks - TCS]
   20 May, 1908, Ows.    [R.Owsley 1910]
**CONGLETON**
HILL (c19 b.Ows.)  [1873-1964 Lee; s/o Isaac
   Congleton & Paulina Asbell - 1880-L; ob-
   H&s-M BE-10/29/64, OCC-11/12/37; 2nd M-L]
   FRONIA CATHERINE STEPP (c20 b.Ows.) [1873-
   1942 Lee; d/o Wm. SEALE & Lucinda (nee
   STEPP), who was Div/f Hardin Moore - LNG;
   ob-W BE-9/7/44]
   19 April, 1893, <u>Lee</u> @ Asa Smith's; wits.
   Lilly Ann Congleton, Ada Cornelius, Emily
   Brewer   (M-L; TCS; 1900-1910-L; M-L ch-
   1923; R.Rocky Hill greater part of mg.,
   then Beattyv. - ob-H SiL BE-8/3/44;
   R.Beattyv. 1941-44; ob-ch. BE-12/11/41)
   [HILL (R.Beattyv. 71 widr. b.Ows.) m2
   4/27/45 Lee, Baltie (nee Martin) Kincaid
   - ob-W2 BE-2/7/63; M-L]
ISAAC G. (21 S b.Ows.) [1846-1921 Lee; s/o
   Isaac Congleton & Delilah BBurg.- 1860 MCA]
   PAULINE CATHERINE "KATE" ASBELL (21 b.Est.)
   [1845-1880 Lee; d/o Henry Asbell a/k/a
   Beatty & Eliza Jane Johnson/Bennett - TCS;
   MCA M/as Bennett; 1880MS-L]
   24 Sept., 1867, Ows. (MCA; N-Lee; B-L ch.;
   1880MS-L; M-L ch-1945)   [ISAAC m2 1/10/81
   Nancy Dunigan a/k/a Thomas (1856-1937) -
   M-L; 1900-1910-L; ob-W OCC-11/12/37]

(Congleton cont.)

167

**CONGLETON (cont.)**
JAMES "JIM" (R.Est. c29 S b.KY)
   [SARAH] ANNA MARCUM (R.Ows. c27 S b.KY)
   [d/o James Marcum & Cynthia Combs - ob-WM&S
   OCC-3/19/39-5/5/39]
   1 Jan., 1897     (Fri.)   (ME-1/22/1897;
   1900-M; 1910-M m1-13 both; BC 1911-E; W/as
   Annie/Anna in all rec. except 1880 W/as
   Sally A. w/P)
JOSEPH S[AMUEL] (R.Est. 19 S b.Est.) P/Ows-
   Est.
   CARLISTA A. "CALLIE" MARCUM (R.Ows. 20 S
   b.Ows.) P/Ows.   [d/o James M. Marcum
   & Cynthia A. Combs - 1900; MJC]
   23 Dec, 1903,  Ows. (ML 12/03 - ME-1/15/04)
   [NOTE:  ob-WM&S list her as Mrs. <u>Sam</u>
   Congleton; R.Est. 1912-1916 - BC]
LEE (c20 b.KY)   [1871-1930; s/o Isaac
   Congleton & Paulina Asbell - 1880-L MCA]
   MARY FRANCES BREWER (c19 b.Jack.)  [1872-
   1944 Barbourville; d/o John Tyler Brewer
   & Martha Culton - TCS; MCA; ob-W BE-8/3/44]
   7 Oct., 1890, Sturgeon  (MCA, which has
   their photos; ME-3/13/96 says Lee Congleton
   moved from Lee to his FiL's, J. T. Brewer,
   on Sturgeon; 1900; 1910-L m1-19; wid. d.
   Barbourville 1944)
PRYSE (c20 b.Lee)  [1868-1939 OH; s/o Isaac
   Congleton & Paulina Asbell - TCS; MCA; ob-
   H&s-M OCC 6/16/39-11/12/37]
   SARAH MARGARET FLANERY (c22 b.Ows.)  [1866-
   1944 Ross, OH; d/o Hampton Flanery & Nancy
   BBurg. - 1880; MCA; ob-W BE-5/18/44]
   19 May, 1889, Ows.  (MCA; DB; 1900-L m-11;
   ob-H; in OH by 1939)
SAMUEL (R.Est. 29 S) [b.KY]  [s/o Isaac
   Congleton & Delilah BBurg. - TCS; 1860]
   EFFARILLA ["EFFY"] ALEXANDER (R.Est. 16 S)
   29 Jan., 1878, <u>Estill</u>; bm. groom & James
   Alexander (M-E; WJM; TCS; NL 1880/E/L)
   [H-remd. 1900-E]
SAMUEL (c39 2nd b.KY)   [m1 Effy Alexander
   above - TCS]
   MARY COMBS (c38 S b.KY)  [d/o Bonaparte
   Combs & Susan Isom - 1880]
   1888/9     (1900-E m-11; WJM; TCS)
SAMUEL - see JOSEPH SAMUEL

**CONNER**
WILLIAM (___ b.VA)
    PERMELIA SPENCE (c28 b.VA)   [d/o Jno.
    Spence & Mary Holmes - 1870]
    c1865        (1870-4, Permelia & ch. w/WP;
    1880 W-remd.; EERS)    [PERMELIA m2 Henly
    Hurst - TCS]
**CONRAD/CONRID**
ALFORD (R.Sturg., Ows. 24 S b.Jack.)   [s/o
    Jeff Conrad & Polly Marcum - mg.]
    ROSA BELLE FREEMAN (R.Green Hall, Jack. 21
    S b.Lee) [F/uk; M/"Luvicy" Freeman 1st
    Wallace - mg.; M/as Louisa Freeman 1900-J;
    1910]
    11 Oct., 1901 Jackson Co., to be md. @
    Elisha Isaacs  (M-J 12:53; 1910 W-m-10, H-
    NL, WM w/her)
ALEXANDER FRANKLIN (c24 b.KY)  [s/o Wm. Jeff.
    Conrad & Ellen Strong - 1900]
    JULIE HARTSOCK (c17 b.KY) [d/o Sam Hartsock
    & Rosa Standifer - 1900; ob-WM&S OCC-
    5/15/36, BE-3/10/60-3/12/64]
    1909/10        (1910 m-0, next to WP; ob-WM;
    R.Portsmouth, OH 1960-64)
ANDERSON "ANCE" (c22 b.KY) [GS/o Franklin
    Conrad & Polly Marcum - 1900]
    SOPHIA McQUEEN (c22 b.KY) [d/o John McQueen
    & Martha Robinson - w/F & s-M 1900]
    1905/6        (1910 m-4; BC 1911; B-O ch-
    1909, H/Anderson CARMACK & wf listed on
    wrong line)   [ANCE m2 c1918, Maggie May
    Banks - 1920; BC 1919-1921; W/as May &
    Maggie]
FRANCIS (c57 b.MO) P/OH-IL
    LUCY ANN FLANERY (c32 b.KY)  [d/o Hampton
    Flanery & Nancy Ann BBurg. - 1880; ME]
    1897/8 Texas   (1900-Grayson Co., TX,
    Flanery s-ch. b.9/81-12/94, b. KY, MO & TX,
    1st Conrad ch. b.11/98 TX; ME-9/8/04, Mrs.
    Lucy A. Conrad of Texas visiting father,
    Hampton Flanery of Levi)
FRANKLIN - see J. FRANKLIN
FRANKLIN - see ALEXANDER FRANKLIN


(Conrad cont.)

**CONRAD (cont.)**
[JEREMIAH] FRANKLIN (R.Ows. 23 S b.uk) [b.NC]
   MARY [POLLY] MARCUM (R.Ows. 22 S b.Morgan,
   IN) [d/o James Marcum & Eliz. Parker -1850]
   13 Aug., 1856, Ows. [R.Owsley 1860; Jackson
   Co. 1870; Owsley 1880-1900; H/as J.F.,
   Jeremiah, Frank & Franklin]
JAMES (c23 b.KY) [prob. s/o Frank Conrad
   & Mary Marcum - 1860]
   MARTHA _____ (c31 b.TN)
   1881      (1900-5/82, m-18)
JEFFERSON - see WM. JEFFERSON
JOHN (c28 S b.Jack.) [s/o Frank Conrad & Mary
   Marcum - 1880]
   MARY (nee McQUEEN) HIGNITE (c22 2nd b.
   Garrett) [wid/o _____ Hignite - 1900]
   1900/1    (1910 Hignite s-ch; B-O ch-1910)
LEWIS (c42 3rd b.Ows.) [m1 _____;
   m2 _____ - NL M-J] [poss. s/o Frank
   Conrad & Mary Marcum - 1880; NL w/P 1900]
   [MARTHA ELIZ.] LIZZIE LORTON (c20 S b.VA)
   17 Jan., 1902, <u>Jackson Co.</u> @ Dan Lorton's,
   by W. H. Anderson; wits. Wm. Simpson,
   Butler McCalf & Sam Judd  (M-J 2:129; TCS;
   1910-1920; B-O ch.; NL for Lewis & prev.
   wives 1900Sx.)
LEWIS (c21 b.Ows.) [1884-1949 New Hope; s/o
   Wm. Jefferson Conrad & Ellen Strong - 1900;
   ob-H OCN-11/25/49; DC]
   CYNTHIA HARTSOCK (c19 b.Ows.) [1887-1964
   OH; d/o Samuel Hartsock & Rosa Standifer -
   1900-1910; ob-W&S&M BE-3/12/64-3/10/60,
   OCC-5/15/36]
   1905/6     (1910 WP w/them; 1920; wid.
   R.Ham.,OH 1960-64)
WM. JEFFERSON (c24 b.Green Hall) [s/o Frank
   Conrad & Mary Marcum - 1880]
   ELLEN STRONG (c16 b.Sturgeon) [d/o Alex.
   Strong & Eliz. Wilson - TCS]
   1883/4    (1900; B-O ch.; DC son)
**CONWAY/CONAWAY**
SOLOMON (c21 b.KY)
   MELISSA _____ (c17 b.KY)
   1894/5    (1900)

## COOK

A[NDREW] K. (R.Ows. 22 S tchr b.KY) P/KY
    LAURA DISHMAN (R.Knox 21 S b.KY) P/KY
    15 Dec., 1874, <u>Knox</u>  (M-Knx mf; 1880-Lau.)
EDWARD (c21 b.Williamsburg, Whitley Co.)
    [1871-1959 Conklin; s/o Quinton Cook
    & Sarah - ob-H BE-4/30/59; TS-TCS]
    DELILAH "LILLIE" TAYLOR (c20 b.Clay) [1869-
    1955; d/o Pendleton Taylor & Minerva
    Jennings - 1880 ob-W&S OCN-12/8/55 & OCC-
    8/22/41]
    1892/3        (1900-1910-1920; B-O ch.; ob-
    ch. BS-11/7/85)
LEWIS MARTIN (c27 b.TN) [s/o Joab Cook & Polly
    Mason - 1860-J)
    SARAH STRONG (c21 b.KY)  [d/o Daniel Strong
    & Rebecca Wilson - JCH; 1860]
    1866/7           (REM; JCH; NL 1870/C/E/L/J;
    1880-J-12; 1900-J m-33; ob-ch. OCC-3/24/39)
MARTIN - see LEWIS MARTIN
WILLIAM (c22 S b.Sturg) [s/o Lewis Martin Cook
    & Sarah Strong - TCS; ob-HS OCC-3/24/39]
    MARY ELLA GABBARD (c18 S b.Trav.Rest)  [d/o
    Hiram Gabbard & Mahala Wilson - TCS]
    1892/3           (1900-J m-7; 1910-1920; B-O
    ch.; ob-ch. BS-11/27/97-12/31/98; NL M-J)

## COOMER

GEORGE TYLER (c19 b.Lee,VA) [s/o Perrin Coomer
    & Sarah Palmer - TCS; 1860]
    MARTHA WELLS (c22 b.Lee,VA)
    c1868        (1870-L-9/69; B-L ch.)
HENRY - see JAMES HENRY
ISAAC NEWTON "NEWT" (c17 b.VA) [1844-19__; s/o
    Perrin Coomer & Sarah Palmer - LNG; TCS;
    1860]
    PRISCILLA "CILLA" STEPP (c17 b.KY) [c1845-
    1871/2; d/o Bob Stepp &  Rachel Moranda
    Seahorse - LNG]
    c1862        (1870-L-7; JWFW; M-L ch. 1887;
    ob-ch. BE-8/2/45)    [H-remd.]

(Coomer cont.)

**COOMER (cont.)**

[ISAAC] NEWTON (R.Lee 31 2nd b.Lee,VA) P/NC
[widr/o Priscilla Stepp above]
[CHRISTINA] CRISTIENER [nee _____]
HOLLINGSWORTH (R.Lee 18 2nd b.Clay) P/Clay
[1854-1877/8]
26 Nov., 1872 (ML) Lee @ Asa Smith's
(M-L; LNG)    [H-remd.]
[ISAAC] NEWTON (R.Lee 31 3rd b.Lee,VA) P/Lee,
VA    [widr/o Christina Hollingsworth above]
RACHEL PORTER (R.Lee 28 S b.Ows.) P/-- [d/o
Thos. Porter & Mary Bawlden - LNG]
1 Feb., 1879, Lee @ John Hammons, by Marion
Gillem; wits. John Hammons, O. M. Tyry, &
E. Hammons    [DIVORCED 10/82 Lee - LNG]
(M-L; 1880-L; LNG; Rachel Porter 1900-L)
[H-remd.]
[ISAAC] NEWTON (R.Lee 37 4th b.VA) P/VA
[div/f Rachel Porter above]
EDITH ROACH (R.Lee 23 S b.Ows) P/uk [c1860-
1888; d/o Thomas Roach & Mary Pebworth -
LNG; mg.]
12 Oct., 1883, Lee @ WM's, Mary Roach, by
J. Roberts; wits. Asa Smith & John Tewart
(M-L; LNG; Lee deed 12/87 heirs of Thomas
Roach, filed 4/88, LNG)    [H-remd.]
[ISAAC] NEWTON (R.Lee 39 5th b.Lee,VA) P/Lee,
VA    [m4 Edith Roach above]
SARAH NOE (R.Lee 24 S b.Mag.) P/Harl-Ows.
[d/o Martin Noe & Mary Paris - LNG 2nd M-L]
16 Aug., 1888, Lee @ Lafayette Noe's [WS],
by J. M. Roberts; wits. Lafayette Noe &
Cornelius Thomas    (M-L; 1900-L)    [SARAH
(R.Proctor 39 2nd b.Lee) m2 6/30/11,
Brownloe Fike (39 2nd b.Lee) - M-L; LNG]
JAMES HENRY (c23 b.Lee,VA)
ELIZABETH JANE VANDERPOOL (c21 b.Ows.)
[c1845-1884; d/o Abr. Vanderpool & Amanda
Estes - 1850; BE-3/26/70 repr/o 3Fks-
6/4/1884]
c1866        (1870-L-2; B-L ch.; 1880-L-13;
TCS)    [H-remd.]


(Coomer cont.)

## COOMER (cont.)

JAMES H[ENRY] (R.Lee 40 2nd b.Lee, VA) P/Lee,
VA [widr/o Eliz. Jane Vanderpool abv.]
[1840-19__]
MARGARET [nee _____] GILBERT (R.Lee 44 2nd
b.Ows.) P/uk-Est. [m1 _____ - poss.
Margaret Gilbert 30 who lived w/Wm. Maloney
1870-L] [1838-19__]
20 Dec., 1884, Lee @ H. H. Thomas Sr.'s;
wits. Robt. Davidson & Evans Bryant
(M-L; 1900-1910-L)
LEANDER (c18 b.Adair)
ELLEN MARSHALL (c19 b.Stokes Co., NC) [d/o
David Marshall & Charlotta     - TCS]
1868      (1870-L-1; B-L ch.; 1880-L;
1900-L m-31)    [LEANDER appar. m2 12/25/05
Lee, Zannie Bowman - M-L]
NEWTON - see ISAAC NEWTON
PATTON (c19 b.VA)
MARY _____ (c15 b.KY)
c1865      (1870-L-4) [PATTON m2 1875/6,
Lourana Emaline Smith - 1880-1900-L; appar.
wf started div. proceedings, but didn't
follow through - BE-11/27/08, Lee Ct, L. E.
Coomer vs. Patton Coomer; together 1910-L,
H-m2-34; W-m1-34]
TYLER - see GEORGE TYLER

## COOPER

ALFRED (R.Lee 23 S b.Ows.) [s/o Wm. Cooper
& Nancy Smith - 1860]
MARTHA E[LLEN "PATSY"] COLE (R.Lee 21 S
b.Ows.)
24 July, 1875, Lee (M-L; 1880; 1900 H-md.,
W-NL; widr. Alford 1910; M-L ch-1912-1927;
DC ch-1935)
JOHN (c26 b.KY) [s/o Wm. Cooper & Nancy Smith
- 1860]
RACHEL ANN CHAMBERS (c20 b.KY) [d/o Gideon
Chambers & Mary Rose - TCS]
c1867      (1870-2; 1880-L; REM; ob-ch.
OCN-1/2/58, BE-4/8/37-10/7/48; both poss.
d. 1893-1900, as all ch. listed w/John G.
below 1900)


(Cooper cont.)

**COOPER (cont.)**

JOHN G. (c29 b.KY)  [s/o John Cooper & Rachel
   Chambers - 1880-L; ob-HS BE-4/8/37]
   ELMA TAYLOR (c22 b.Levi)  [1884-1941; d/o
   Orville P. Taylor & Sarah Ellender Hamilton
   - ob-W&S OCC-1/31/41, BE-8/15/35; 1900]
   1906          (H-sgl. 1900; ob-W; ob-ch.
   BE-3/2/39; R.Congleton, Lee c1905-1941)
SHERMAN T. (R.Low.Buff.Cr., Ows. c34 S mcht b.
   Boonev.)   [1873-1970 Richmond hosp.; s/o
   John Cooper & Rachel Chambers - TCS; ob-H&S
   BE-7/23/70-4/8/37-10/7/48; H-89 Bday BE-
   4/20/61]
   MINNIE HERD (R.Boonev. c33 S tchr b.Trav.
   Rest)   [1871-1927; d/o Andrew/Robt. Herd
   & W2 Mary Eliz. Searsy - 1880; TS-TCS]
   Nov., 1905, So. Boonev., Ows. (on a Thurs.)
   @ home of bride, by Bro. S. K. Ramey  (ME-
   11/23/05; BE-11/27/08 R.Buffalo near Lee
   Co. line; 1910-1920; B-O ch.; TCS)
   [SHERMAN m2 Grace Rowland - ob-H; R.Stay
   1937-48; wid. R.Beattyv. 1970; NL M-L]
[THOMAS WAYNE] TOM WAIN (c26 S b.KY) [1877-
   1957; s/o John Cooper & Rachel Chambers -
   1880-L; w/HS John 1900; TS-TCS; ob-HS BE-
   4/8/37-10/7/48]
   [CECILIA] JANE JUDD (19 S b.Lee)  [1885-
   1961 OH; d/o James Rowland Judd & Nancy
   Palmer - ob-W BE-10/19/61; TCS; 1900-L]
   15 Aug., 1903, Ows. (ME-9/4/03; 1910-L m-6;
   TCS; R.Stay 1937-1948; wid. d. Dayton, OH
   1961)
WILLIAM (R.Ows. 22 S b.Ows.) P/Ows-Lee  [s/o
   Alford Cooper & Martha Cole - TCS; 1900]
   [SARAH] SALLY McINTOSH (R.Ows. 20 S b.Ows.)
   P/Br.   [1891-1969 Lex. hosp.; d/o Elisha
   McIntosh & Minerva J Fox - TCS; ob-W BE-
   10/9/69]
   1 Sept., 1910, Ows. [R.Owsley 1920; wid.
   R.Beatty 1967 - ob-ch. BE-3/16/67] [SALLY
   m2 1967-9, _____ Bowman - ob-W as Bowman]
**COPE**
LUTHER J. (c21 S b.KY)
   MAGGIE EDWARDS (c18 S b.KY)  [d/o John
   Wesley Edwards & Nancy E. Burch - TCS]
   1908/9          (1910; TCS)
(Cope cont.)

## COPE (cont.)
NATHAN (c27 S b.KY)     [a/k/a Nathan HICKS]
   [1877-1965 - TS-TCS as COPE]
   [VIRGINIA] JENNIE [nee WELLS] ALLEN (c25
   2nd b.KY)   [m1 Elijah Allen - MT]   [1882-
   1931 - TS-TCS]
   16 April, 1907, <u>Clay</u>  (M-C MT; 1910 m-3,
   Nathan COPE, Allen s-s; 1920 Nathan HICKS;
   TCS; BC 1912-1917-1922 as COPE)

## CORNELIOUS/CORNELIUS/CORNELISON
SIDNEY (c22 b.KY)   [1873-1954 OH; s/o Wm.
   Cornelius & Mary A. Botner - 1880-L; ob-H
   OCN-6/25/54]
   MARTHA E. ROWLAND (c23 b.KY) [d/o John
   Rowland Sr. & Sarah Campbell - 1880; ob-WS
   OCN-2/29/52 & BE-6/6/35]
   1894/5          (EERS; 1900-L; R.Osborne,
   OH 1935; Dayton, OH 1952; Fairborn OH 1954)
WILLIAM (c20 b.KY) P/KY
   MARY ANN BOTNER (c25 b.Wash,VA) [1837-1918
   Lee; d/o James Botner & Eliz. Nunley - LNG/
   WT; 1860; TCS; DC lists M/as Mary A.]
   1863/4          (NL 1870/L; R.Lee 1875 when
   son b. - ob-ch. BE-11/23/44; 1880-L, Blount
   niece w/them, d/o Wm. Blount & Nancy
   Botner; 1900-L; NL M-J)
WM. JR. (c23 S b.Lee)  [1883-1959 Lee; s/o Wm.
   Cornelius & Mary A. Botner - 1900-L; ob-H&S
   BE-5/14/59-11/23/44, OCN-6/25/54; TS-LNG]
   ELIZABETH A. "LIZZIE" COMBS (c20 S b.KY)
   [1886-1990; d/o James S. Combs & Mary Cath.
   Handy - 1900; ob-WS&F OCN-4/21/50 & BE-
   12/3/53-10/3/63-7/18/35; TS-LNG]
   1905/6          (1910-L; ob-WS; R.Congleton
   1935; Beattyv. 1950-54; wid. R.Beattyv.
   1959-63)

## CORNETT
CLARK (R.Ows. 40 2nd b.Br.) P/Br.  [m1 c1868
   Br., America _____ - 1870-1880-B]
   REBECCA HORN (R.Br. 29 S b.Ows.) P/Ows.
   [prob. Rebecaa <u>Hornsby</u> d/o Job Hornsby
   & Catherine Gabbard]
   1885, <u>Breathitt</u> (no date, 188_)   (M-B
   3:197; 1900-14, m-23 = 1876/7)

(Cornett cont.)

175

**CORNETT (cont.)**

JAMES (21 S b.KY) [s/o Sam Cornett & Nancy
   McIntosh - 2nd M-B; 1880]
   TABITHA KILBURN (16 S b.KY)
   25 Aug., 1897, <u>Breathitt</u> @ Stephen
   McIntosh's, by Nathan L. Arrowood; wits.
   John & J. R. Arrowood  (M-B 7:485; 1900-B,
   dau. Lillie b. 4/1900; H-remd. 1910)
JAMES (30 2nd b.KY) [m1 Tabitha Kilburn above]
   JULIA BRYANT (21 S b.KY) [d/o Huram Bryant
   & Julia Ann Jett - 1900-B; mg. says d/o
   Hugh Bryant]
   3 Nov., 1905, <u>Breathitt</u> @ Edward Turner's,
   by John B. Lewis; wits. Wm. Cornett &
   Martha Turner  (M-B 11:453; 1910 m-4, 1st
   ch. Lillie, 10, by W1)
[JOHN] HIRAM (c21 b.Clay) [s/o Hiram Cornett
   & Charity Ann Rice - TCS; 1850-C]
   MARANDA STRONG (c24 b.Br.) [d/o Alex
   Strong & Anna Wilson - JCH; 1850]
   5 Aug., 1859, <u>Clay Co.</u> (M-C; 1860-C; JCH;
   TCS; NL 1870/C/L/Let/P/Wlf)
JOHN BLACKSON (c21 b.KY) [s/o James Cornett
   & Minerva? McKnight - 1860; TCS]
   MARGARET THOMAS (c20 b.KY) [d/o Joseph
   Thomas & Anna Jemima Couch - JGN; LNG]
   c1869      (1870-2/70; TCS)
PATRICK (c23 S b.KY) [1861-1913; s/o Eli
   Cornett & Jane Roberts - LNG; SE; DC has
   M/as Martha Ross, who was HS - D-L 5/77]
   MARY EVANS (c24 S b.KY)  [c1860-1901]
   28 Aug., 1884, <u>Lee</u>  (LNG; SE; 1900-L;
   M-L ch. 1912 & 1924)    [H-remd.]
PATRICK (c41 2nd b.KY)   [m1 Mary Evans above]
   VASHTI (nee NEWNAM) EDWARDS (c35 2nd b.KY)
   [wid/o Allen David Edwards - wid. 1900;
   TCS; LNG & SE] [1867-1942; d/o Richard
   Morris Newman & Lucinda Steele - LNG & SE]
   1902       (H/1910-L m2-8, W-NL & W/1910
   m2-8, H-NL, Edwards ch.; LNG, TS son b.
   1903; SE; TCS)
SAMUEL (c15 b.KY)
   MARGARET WILSON (c19 b.KY) [d/o Phillip
   Wilson & Christine Rogers - TCS]
   12 Oct., 1844 (ML) <u>Clay</u>  (M-C; 1860-14;
   NL 1850; 1870-P; TCS)
(Cornett cont.)

**CORNETT (cont.)**
SAM (___ b.___)
   CORDELIA WILSON (c16-26 b.KY)  [d/o Philip
   Wilson & Jane Strong - 1860]
   1860-70       (TCS; NL 1870/Br/C/L/Let;
   W-remd. 1880-R)  [CORDELIA m2 Harry
   Rhiner/Riner - TCS; 1880-R]
SAMUEL (c21 S b.KY)    [1876-1962 - TS-TCS]
   MARY "POLLY" (nee MOORE) _____ (c20 2nd
   b.KY) [m1 _____] [1878-1949; d/o
   Edw. Moore & Rebecca Gabbard - 1880 TS-TCS]
   1898/9      (1900-1910; TCS; ob-ch. OCN-
   2/21/57)
SAM[SON] C(ARLISLE] (c26 b.KY)  [s/o Wm. H.
   Cornett & Elizabeth Crawford - MT]
   [MARY] BELLE GABBARD (c18 b.KY)  [d/o
   Michael Gabbard & Mary Ann Mangan - MT;
   1900]
   5 July, 1910, <u>Perry</u> @ Hazard, by A. S.
   Petrey, MG; wits. D. Y. & Mary Combs
   (M-P J:191; BE-7/13/72 their 62nd anniv.
   - R.Boonev.)
WILLIAM (c23 S b.KY)
   ELIZABETH "LIZZIE" GILBERT (c17 S b.KY)
   [d/o Kenus Gilbert & Loudema Riley - TCS]
   1902/3     (1910-1920; TCS; BC 1912;
   R.Covington 1969 - ob-WS BE-1/16/69)

**CORUM**
WILLIAM (c18 b.KY)
   PERLINA WHITE (c17 b.KY)  [sis/o Robt.
   White - 1880-L]
   c1852       (1860-7; 1870-L; wid.
   Paulina 1880-L)

**COUCH**
_____ (___ b.___)
   FERILEY _____ (c14-32 b.KY) P/KY
   1861-79    [DIV. pre-1880] (1880,
   Feriley, Div., no ch., w/Ansil D. BBurg.
   as housekeeper)
ABIJAH (c20 S b.Ows.)  [s/o Elijah Couch
   & Elizabeth Estep - TCS]
   NANCY COUCH (c24 S b.Br.)
   1895/6    (1900 m-4; 1910 m-12; B-O
   ch.; BC 1912-1915-1919-P; NL 1920-P)

(Couch cont.)

**COUCH (cont.)**

ANDERSON (c23 b.Per.)  [s/o Thomas Couch
    & Eliz. Campbell - TCS]
    ELIZABETH ANN COMBS (c15 b.MO)
    14 Aug., 1865, <u>Perry</u>; sur. Wm. Hoskins
    (M-P B:351; 1870-P; 1880-14)
ANDREW "BUCK" (c18 b.KY) [s/o Eli Couch - ACB]
    LOURANA (nee MALONEY) HOLLOWAY (c20 2nd b.
    Ows.)  [ml L. Church Holloway]  [1845-1915
    Ows.; d/o Wm. Maloney & Permelia Rhodes]
    c1869        (1870-L, 1st ch. was by
    Holloway; 1880-11; 3Fks-3/30/88, Andrew
    "Buck" Couch arrested, charged w/stealing
    2 mules; wid. Lourana 1900-1910)
ANDREW J. (R.Lee 18 S b.Lee) P/Br.  [poss.
    s/o Peter Couch & Margaret Smith - 1900-L]
    MANDA COLE (R.Ows. 23 S b.Br.) P/Br.
    28 Oct., 1909, Ows.   [R.Lee 1910]
BIGE - see ABIJAH
ELIJAH (R.Clay c21 S b.Per.)  [c1838-1921; s/o
    Wm. Couch & Daugherty    - 1850; TS-TCS]
    ELIZ. ["BETTY"] EASTEP (R.Clay c21 S b.Per)
    [d/o Joseph Estep & Sarah    - 1850-C]
    7 May, 1859, <u>Clay</u>  (M-C; a/L M-C mf as
    5/<u>19</u>/59; B-O ch; 1860-P ch. Jesse 4,
    Rebecca 2, Wm. 2 mos., 1st 2 ch. poss. rel.
    or illegit. ch. of one of them; 1870-14,
    12, 11, etc.; NL 1880Sx; 1900 m-40, 12/12
    ch., none @ home; 1910 ml-50 both; DC-ch.
    1925)
ELISHA (c17 S b.Ows.)  [s/o Elijah Couch
    & Eliz. Estep - TCS]
    SOPHIA SANDLIN (c15 S b.KY)  [d/o Willis
    Sandlin & Martha A. Peters - TCS]
    1895        (1900-3/97, H-m-5, W-m-3; 1910
    m-14; TCS; BC 1914-1916-C & 1921)
EZEKIEL - see HENRY EZEKIEL
FARMER (23 S b.Clay)
    PATIENCE JAMISON (19 S b.KY)  [d/o John
    Jamison & Sarah Spencer - 1880-L]
    30 Aug, 1894 <u>Lee</u> @ home of John D. Jameson
    wits: Willie Jameson, Rilda Jameson
    (M-L; 1910; NL 1900; B-O ch.; B-L ch.)


(Couch cont.)

## COUCH (cont.)

HENRY (c20 b.KY)   [poss. s/o William Couch
   & Daugherty        - 1850; 1860-C]
   CATHERINE _____ (c20 b.KY)
   c1866        (1870-3 w/HP; NL M-C)
HENRY (c21 b.Per.)   [s/o James Couch
   & Louisa Rice - 1860-B; B-C sib.]
   ANN MARSHALL (c17 b.Lee,VA)   [d/o Wm.
   Marshall & Sarah E. Thompson - TCS; 1860]
   1867/8        (1870-1; B-L ch.; 1880-1900-L;
   wid. Annie 1910-L; M-L son 1908)
HENRY [EZEKIEL] (c20 b.Ows.)   [1872-1925 Ows.;
   s/o Elijah Couch & Eliz. Eastep - DC/Henry]
   ALABAMA BARGER (c21 b.KY)   [d/o Joseph
   Barger & Nicy McIntosh - TCS; 1880]
   1891        (1900 m-8 as Henry & Anna B.;
   TCS; 1910 Henry remd-19; M-O son 1930, as
   Henry & Alabama)
HENRY - see also HENRY CREECH
HENRY [EZEKIEL] (R.Ows. 37 S b.Ows.) P/Ows.
   [widr/o Alabama Barger above]  [1872-1925]
   [MARGARET] MAGGIE COLWELL (R.Ows. 25 S b.
   Br.) P/Br.
   4 Nov., 1909, Ows.  [R.Owsley 1910, H-m-19,
   but this is W1; widr. Henry Owsley 1920-5;
   H/as Henry & Ezekiel]
JAMES (c26 b.KY)
   SARAH "SALLY" CALDWELL (c22 b.KY)
   1897/8        (1900, near Elijah & Eliz.;
   1910, next to Elijah & Eliz.; M-O ch. 1929;
   ob-ch. BS-5/23/85)
JAMES - see JAMES CREECH
JEFFERSON D. (23 S b.KY)   [s/o Andrew Couch
   & Lourana Maloney - 1880]
   ELIZA JANE BAKER (17 S b.KY)
   6 Nov., 1895, Breathitt, @ Elijah Combs',
   by M. H. Bowman, JP; wits. Eli Miller & C.
   Bowman  (M-B 7:49; 1900Sx-Les.)
   [NOTE:  TCS has W/as Eunice Baker]
JOHN (c17 2nd crp b.KY)  [m1 _____]
   MARGARET _____ (c18 S b.KY)
   1893/4        (1900 m-6; 1910 m-17, H-2nd;
   NL 1920Sx)
JOHN (R.Ows. 24 S b.Ows.) P/Ows.
   SALLIE DAVIDSON (R.Clay 25 S b.Clay) P/Clay
   15 Sept., 1904, Clay  (M-C mf)
(Couch cont.)

**COUCH (cont.)**
JOSEPH A. (c17 b.KY)
   SARAH _____ (c24 b.KY)
   1878/9        (1900; NL 1880)
JOSEPH (c22 S b.Ows.)   [s/o Elijah Couch
   & Elizabeth Estep - TCS; 1870]
   MARGARET SANDLIN (c16 S b.Ows.)  [poss.
   d/o Willis Sandlin & Martha Peters - 1880]
   1889       (1900-5/90, m-8 = 1891/2;
   B-O ch. W/as Couch; 1910 m-20 = 1889/90;
   BC-1913; DC-ch.)
OWEN (c27 b.Les.)
   VIRGINIA EDNA McPHERSON (c20 b.Ows.)  [d/o
   Stephen McPherson & Rebecca Pendleton -
   1900; ob-WS OCC-12/28/34]
   8 May, 1903     (TCS; BC-dau. Effie 12/04
   Taft, Ows.; NL 1920Sx-OH; R.Ham.,OH 1934;
   W-alive 1944; NL M-J)
PETER/PELEY "PETE" (c19 b.Br.)  [s/o Patrick
   HOWARD & Sally COUCH - 2nd M-O; w/GP Elijah
   & Serena Couch 1870-L]
   MARGARET SMITH (c19 b.Ows.) [1859-1904 Lee;
   d/o Elcannah Smith & Jane Thomas -D-L 1870]
   1877/8, Ows.  (1880-1; LNG; 1900-L m-22;
   M-L ch. 1899; M-L ch. 1904-1910-1918-1919-
   1945-1960; M-O ch-1946; H/as Peter, Peeley
   & Pete)  [H-remd.]
[PETER] PELEY (R.Lee 45 2nd b.Br) [m1 Margaret
   Smith above]
   LULA MULLINS (R.Ows 21 S b.Ows) P/TN-Ows.
   [d/o Mart Mullins & Luiza Gibson - mg]
   10 Jan, 1907 Lee @ CH, by D.B. Pendergrass,
   CLCC; wits. Sally & Nancy Roberts  (M-L
   8:29; 1910-L as Peter & Louisa H/m2-3, W/
   m1-3)  [PETE m3 1910-12, _____;
   PETE (52 4th b.Br.) m4 1/14/13 Mary Bailey
   (48 2nd b.VA) - M-L; PETE (R.Lee 59 widr.
   b.Br.) m5 10/8/18, Mary (nee Shoemaker)
   Pelfrey (48 wid. b.Lee) - M-L; LNG]
RILEY - see WM. RILEY
SAMPSON (c20 b.Per.)  [s/o Wm. Couch &
   Daugherty      - 1850-1860-C]
   NANCY [nee _____] WEST (c26 2nd b.Per.)
   [m1 Isaac West - 1850-C; NL M-C]
   1 Nov., 1855, Clay (M-C; 1860-C w/HP, W's
   son Zach. w/them; 1870)
(Couch cont.)

COUCH (cont.)
SAMPSON "SAM" (c17 b.KY)   [s/o Elijah Couch
   & Eliz. Estep - 1870; TCS]
   NANCY M. _____ (c16 b.KY)
   1880/1              (1900)
WILLIAM [RILEY] (R.Ows. 21 S b.Ows.) P/uk-Ows.
   [a/k/a Wm. Riley HOLLOWAY] [1876-1947 Lee;
   s/o L. Church Holloway & Louisa Maloney;
   raised by s-F, Andrew COUCH - 1880; ob-H
   BE-8/14/47 as Riley W. HOLAWAY]
   JOSEPHINE ["JOSIE"] BRANDENBURG (R.Lee 15
   S b.Lee) P/Ows-Br.  [1876-1939 Oil; d/o
   George BBurg. & Lourana Vires - TCS; ob-W
   BE-8/31/39 as HOLLOWAY]
   5 March, 1890, Lee @ Huston BBurg.'s, by J.
   M. Roberts; wit. Johnnie & Wm. BBurg. (M-L;
   ACB; 1900 m-10 H/Wm. R. COUCH; 1910-L as
   HOLLOWAY; M-L ch-1915 Holloway; ob-ch. OCN-
   1/23/58, 3Fks-3/25/98; all obits HOLLOWAY)
COULTON/CULTON
WILLIAM (___ b.KY)
   IDA HOGG (c23 S b.Boonev.) [1873-1956 Mad.;
   d/o Hiram Hogg & Virginia Caroline Snyder -
   1880; DC; ob-W&S OCN-12/13/56, BE-4/29/43]
   1896/7            (1910 Ida w/P m-13, H-NL;
   1920 Ida & ch. w/WM; NL 1900Sx; DC-ch.;
   Ida R.Beattyv. 1943; ob-ch. BE-3/2/72)
COX
E[LISHA] R[OBT.] W[INN] (c23 b.Lee,VA) [1827-
   19__; s/o Elisha Cox & Mary Virginia
   Crabtree - N-E 12/97 Herbert D. Estes]
   SUSAN [JANE] PITMAN (c18 b.Est.)  [1833-
   1884; d/o Micajah Pittman & W1 Naomi
   Johnson - 1850; N-E 12/97 Herbert D. Estes]
   8 April, 1852, Ows. (JFB; 1870-1880-L; B-O
   & B-L ch.; ob-ch. OCC-4/12/37, BE-2/11/37;
   art. BE-8/27/70 H/Ethelbert Robt. Winn Cox,
   his photo)   [H-remd.]
ELISHA R[OBERT] W. (R.Lee 55 2nd surveyor b.
   Lee,VA) P/Lee,VA & Wash,VA   [m1 Susan Jane
   Pitman above]
   MARY W. CRABTREE (45 S b.Lee,VA) P/Lee,VA
   [d/o Jacob Crabtree & Polly     - 1880-L]
   8 June, 1884, Lee @ Elkanah J. Crabtree's;
   by Thos. Robbins, MG, wits. Charlie Powell
   & Edward Combs  (M-L; 1900-L)
(Cox cont.)

**COX (cont.)**

GEORGE W. (c44 2nd b.TN) [poss. m1 10/17/77,
as G. W. (20 S b.TN) to Nancy Beams -
M-Lau.; NL 1880-Lau.)
BARBARA MARGROVES (c24 S b.TN) [d/o Wm.
Margroves & Louisa    - ob-WS BE-1/21/60]
1896/7      (1900 m-12, H-2nd; 1910-1920;
R.Lex. 1960)

JOEL [S.] (30 S b.Ows.) [s/b R.Ows. b.NC -
1850-1860] [s/o Braxton Jason Cox & Lydia
- mg.]
NAOMI C. [nee REASOR] HOBBS (25 wid. b.Lee,
VA) [m1 Aaron S. Hobbs - M-Lee,VA 11/6/56]
[d/o Peter Reasor & Rebecca      - mg.;
1850-Lee,VA]
24 May, 1866, Lee Co., VA, by Joshua M.
Redwine      (M-Lee,VA; 1870-1880-W)
[JOEL m2 April, 1888, Phoebe Jane Shoemaker
- 3Fks-5/4/88; 1900-W]

ROBERT - see ELISHA ROBERT W.

**CRABTREE**

ABRAM (c26 b.VA) [s/o Jacob Crabtree & Polly
- 1850-E]
MINERVA _____ (c22 b.KY)
c1859      (1860, no ch.)

DAVID SIMPSON (c25 b.Lee,VA)    [s/o Jacob
Crabtree & Polly      - 1850-1860-E; TCS]
MARY ELIZABETH WILSON (c20 b.Lee,VA)
1864/5 (poss. VA)    (R.Lee,VA 1867 ob-ch.
BE; 1870-L-3; 1880-L-13 VA; 1900-L; 1910-L
m1-45; ob-ch. BE-5/24/62; H/as Simpson in
census & David S. in B-L ch.)

GEORGE (c30 b.Lee,VA) [s/o Jacob Crabtree
& Polly    - 1850-E]
ELIZA ROGERS (c17 b.Est.)
c1867      (1870-L-2; B-L ch.)

SIMPSON - see DAVID SIMPSON

**CRANK**

CARRIGAN T. (c22 b.KY) [s/o James R. Crank
& Martha J.   - TCS]
NANCY BAILEY (c21 b.KY) [d/o Samuel Bailey
& Eliz. Combs - B-O; TCS]
1895      (1900; wf a/L w/F 1900 as
md. w/2 ch., 1st ch-6/96)

GILBOUS or GILLIS - see WILLIAM GILLIS

(Crank cont.)

**CRANK (cont.)**
JAMES (R.Ows. 29 S b.Jack.) P/--
    EVA HENSLEY (R.Ows. 18 S b.Ows.) P/Harl --
    [d/o Jack Hensley & Rachel Bowman - 1900-L]
    26 Sept., 1908, Ows.
JOHN E. (c25 b.KY)
    ORPHA _____ (c22 b.TN)
    c1867       (1870-J; 1880-12; NL M-J)
WILLIAM GILLIS (c22 S b.KY) [s/o James Crank
    & Martha    - 1880]
    EMILY AMAZON WILSON (c22 S b.KY) [d/o
    Philip Wilson & Jane Strong - 1880; JCH]
    1880/1    (1900 HF w/them; 1910-1920;
    JCH)

**CRAWFORD**
ALBERT (26 b.Bear Cr., Est) [s/o Arch Crawford
    & Peggy Brown - MNC]
    EMILIA BRAWNER (17 b.KY) [d/o Luther
    Brawner & Mariah Garrard - MNC]
    16 Oct., 1852, Ows. [moved to TX - MNC]
CALLOWAY (R.Wolfe 21 S tchr b.Br.) P/Br.
    LENI L. COLE (R.Lee 18 S b.Ows.) P/Est-Ows.
    [d/o Jesse H. Cole & Rachel Ann Bowman -
    1870-L widr. Jesse & dau. "Leoni"; 1880
    "Senna" w/Bowman GP]
    1 Dec., 1886, Lee, Beattyville (were to be
    md. @ Jesse H. Cole's), by C. H. Lockwood,
    Presb. Min.; wits. Walker Jameson & Rebecca
    Jones    (M-L; 3Fks-5/18/88, Mrs. Elisha
    Bowman of Ows. visits GD, Leni L. Crawford)
ELIHU (c21 b.Est.) [s/o Joseph Crawford
    & Nancy Gray - 1850; TCS]
    ELIZABETH SPARKS (c13 b.Est.)    [d/o
    Barnett Sparks & Mary Muck - TCS]
    5 Aug., 1856, Ows. (TCS; NL 1860;
    1870-L-10; B-L ch.; 1880-L)
GEORGE WASHINGTON (c30 widr b.KY)
    [widr/o Martha - 1850-M; D-O 7/52]
    ELIZABETH MARCUM (c21 b.KY) [poss. d/o
    Thomas Marcum & Polly Wilson]
    1853    (1860-E; B-O ch-4/54)


(Crawford cont.)

## CRAWFORD (cont.)

JAMES GRIFFIN (c20 b.Br.) [s/o Claiborne
    Crawford & Susan Jett - 1860-B; MNC]
    AMERICA PLUMMER (c18 b.Br.) [d/o Sam
    Plummer & Rachel Evans - 1860-B]
    c1867, poss. Breathitt (1870-L-2; B-L
    ch.; 1880-L)
JOHN W. (c33 b.GA) [NOTE: B-Lau. ch. has
    him b.Ows. & KY]
    MARIAH WEAVER (c19 b.KY) [d/o Joseph
    Weaver & Fanny Powell Bledsoe - TCS]
    28 Dec., 1848, Laurel (PWR; 1850-8 mos.;
    B-Lau. ch-1853 b.Ows; B-Lau-1855-1856-
    1857; wid. Mariah 1880-Lau.)
LINDON (c25 b.KY)
    ELIZABETH _____ (c17 b.KY)
    c1849          (1850, no ch.)
MARCUS (c18 b.Ows.) [s/o Joseph Crawford
    & Nancy Gray - 1860; TCS]
    LETHA FOWLER (c17 b.Est.) [d/o Jeremiah
    Fowler & Mary     - TCS]
    31 Aug., 1864, Jackson Co. @ Jeremiah
    Fowler's, by John Murphy; wits. Easter
    Fowler & George Sparks (M-J; TCS; 1870-L-2;
    B-L ch.)
PIERCE (R.Lee 16 S b.Lee) P/Lee
    CALLIE CAWOOD (R.Lee 15 S b.Ows) P/Ows.
    8 Oct., 1909, Ows. [R.Lee 1910 as Mul.]
SIMPSON (c25 b.KY) [d. 1908 TX; s/o Arch
    Crawford & Peggy Brown - MNC; JSG]
    ELIZABETH EVANS (c17 b.KY) [d.1858 TX -
    JSG]
    c1849          (1850 no ch.; MNC; WEB; moved
    to TX)    [SIMPSON m2 6/12/1862, Mary (nee
    Tarkingon) Brown - JSG]
WASHINGTON - see GEORGE WASHINGTON
WILLIAM (c32 b.KY) P/KY
    EMILY ELLEN [ASHCRAFT?] (c21 b.MO) P/KY
    c1866          (1870-L-3; 1880-L; an Eliza
    b. c 1885 d/o W. H. Crawford & Ellen
    Ashcraft - ob-ch. BE-7/23/59;
    NL 1900-B/E/J/L/W]
WILLIAM (c23 blk b. KY)
    ELIZABETH _____ (c18 blk b.KY)
    1894/5 [poss. s/b c1892]          (1900-3/93,
    m-5)

## CREECH

ALEXANDER (c23 b.Ows.)   [s/o Elijah Creech
& Nancy Brandenburg - TCS]
  AGNES E. SAGESER (c21 b.KY)
  1875/6            (1900; NL 1880; BBG; wid.
  Agnes 1920; NL M-J; ob-ch. OCC-4/9/37)
ANDREW J. "SHERIFF ANDY" (c23 b.KY)   [1882-
1964; s/o Enoch Creech & Mary Tackett -
1900 TS-TCS]
  MARY C. CREECH (c15 b.KY)   [1890-1948; d/o
  Alex Creech & Agnes Sageser - TS-TCS; ob-WS
  OCC-4/9/37]
  c1905            (BBG, they were md. 17 years
  before they had a ch., b/d 3/8/22; NL 1910;
  1920 no ch.; R.Boonev. 1937)
A[NDY] F. (R.Ows. 28 S b.Ows.) P/Ows-Clay
[1879-1968; s/o John Creech & Sarah Griffey
- mg.; 1900; ob-H BE-6/13/68]
  ELLEN ["ELLA"] FARMER (R.Lee 18 S b.Lee)
  P/Lee --   [d/o John Farmer & Margaret Gray
  - mg.]
  1 May, 1909, Lee @ John Farmer's, by D. B.
  Pendergrass; wits. E. L. Creech & Levi
  BBurg. (M-L; 1910-1920; B-O ch.; wid.
  R.Beattyv. 1968)
ARTHUR (R.Fay. 20 S oil wkr. b.Lee)   [s/o
Alex. Creech & Agnes Sageser - 1900; ob-HS
OCC-4/9/37]
  LOUDITH FARMER (R.-- 20 S b.Lee)   [poss.
  d/o John Farmer & Perdilla      - 1900-L]
  18 Nov., 1905, Lee @ J. E. Farmer's, by G.
  B. Bowman, MG; wits. S. D. BBurg., A. J.
  Creech & A.J. Gabbard (M-L; 1910; B-O ch.)
  [ARTHUR m2 c1916 Leah Hall - BBG; Arthur
  R.Metamore, IN 1937]
ARTHUR (R.Ows. 21 S b.Ows.) P/Harl-Owen   [s/o
Sam Creech & Serena Marion - TCS]
  MARTHA E. GABBARD (R.Ows. 15 S b.Ows.) P/
  Ows.  [d. 9/1911 childbirth; d/o Henry
  Gabbard & Jane Bryant - TS-BBG]
  16 April, 1910, Ows.
BLAINE (c21 S b.KY)
  LOUELLEN _____ (c21 S b.KY)
  1906/7      (1910; NL 1920Sx)
CLINTON - see DEWITT CLINTON

(Creech cont.)

185

**CREECH (cont.)**
DEWITT CLINTON "CLINT" (c23 b.Lee,VA)
   MATILDA SPENCER (c19 b.Ows.) [d/o Goolman
   Spencer & Phoebe Shoemaker - 1860]
   1867/8      (1870-L-1; 1880-1900-L; B-L
   ch.; widr. Clint 1910-L)
ELIJAH (c48 2nd b.KY) [Div/f Nancy BBurg.
   - TCS; BBG; M-E 7/3/40; 1850]
   LOUISA ["ELIZA" PORTWOOD?] (c38 b.KY)
   [poss. d/o Solomon Portwood & Eliza   -
   850; TCS; BBG]
   c1858      (1860 W/Louisa, last ch. by
   W1 b. 2/55 - B-O; TCS; BBG)
ELIJAH GREEN (c25 b.VA)
   MARGARET JANE McGUIRE (c21 b.KY) [d.1870's;
   d/o Jack McGuire & Elizabeth Smallwood]
   c1861      (1870-L-8; MMH; widr. Elijah
   1880-1900-1910-L)
ENOCH (c28 S b.KY) [1854-1922; s/o John Creech
   & Nancy Minerva Farmer - 1870; ob-W]
   MARY FRANCES TACKETT (c24 S b.Ows.) [1858-
   1941; d/o Oliver Tackett & Nancy Hall -
   1870; ob-W OCC-12/12/41]
   26 Feb., 1883, Jackson Co. (TCS; liv.
   together, but not md. 1880, w/dau. age 2;
   Trav. Rest c1890; 1900 m-21; 1910 m-30;
   Enoch listed as "widr" 1920, but wf alive;
   ob-W; art. on dau.'s 96th Bday BS-12/20/79)
FRED (c17 S b.Jack.) [s/o Joseph Creech
   & Sarah Gabbard - TCS; 1900]
   MAGGIE CREECH (c18 S b.Ows.)
   1905/6      (1910; B-O ch. wf CREECH)
GILBERT (c23 b.KY)
   REBECCA _____ (c23 b.KY)
   c1843      (1850-6)
GREEN - see ELIJAH GREEN
HARVEY (R.Ows. 23 S b.Harl.) P/Ows-KY
   CARMELIA A. EVANS (R.Ows. 16 S b.Ows.) P/--
   [d/o James Evans & Margaret Allen - 1860]
   15 Jan., 1874, Ows. @ James Evans'
   [R.Owsley 1880]


(Creech cont.)

**CREECH (cont.)**

HENRY (c22 b.Harlan)  [1850-1908; s/o John
    Creech & Nancy Minerva Farmer - 1870 D-O]
    ELIZ. BECKNELL (c20 b.Ows.) [d/o Wm. Thorn-
    berry Becknell & Sarah Wilson - 1870; PWB]
    1873        (1900; 1880-6, s-d age 9;
    D-O puts ch. b. Oct/Nov. 1873; B-O ch.; D-O
    1908 Henry; wid. Bettie 1910)
HENRY (R.Lee 21 S b.Ows.)  [s/o Elijah Creech
    & Nancy L. Brandenburg - B-O]
    MARY F[RANCES] BRANDENBURG (R.Lee 19 S
    b.Ows.)  [d/o John Brandenburg & Patsy
    White - B-O]
    31 April, 1876, <u>Lee</u>  (M-L; TCS; 1880-L)
HENRY (26 2nd b.KY)  [m1 Mary F. Brandenburg
    above - TCS]
    LAURA SMITH (22 b.KY)  [d/o Richard Smith
    & Margaret Evans - 1880-L]
    28 April, 1881, <u>Lee</u>  (M-L; 1900; TCS)
HENRY (c18 S st-mill b.KY)  [poss. s/o Henry
    Creech & Laura Smith - 1900]
    EVA _____ (c15 S b.KY)
    1907/8      (1910 as <u>Couch</u>)
HEZEKIAH (c32 b. KY)
    SARAH A. BECKNELL (c20 b.KY)  [d/o Wm.
    Thornberry Becknell & Sarah Wilson - NVP;
    JSG; PWB]
    c1867      (1870-2; NVP; JSG)
HEZEKIAH C. (c21 S b.Trav. Rest)  [s/o John
    Creech & Nancy Minerva Farmer - 1870]
    ELIZ. BEGLEY (c17 S b.Trav.Rest) P/KY
    [d/o John R. Begley - 1870]
    early 1880      (1880-MWY W-md. w/P,
    H-NL; 1900 m-20; 1910 m-29; B-O ch-1908)
JAMES H. (R.Ows. 19 S b.Harl.) P/Harl.  [s/o
    John Creech & Nancy Minerva Farmer - 1870]
    ARAMINTA HALL (R.Ows. 20 S b.KY) P/KY
    [poss. d/o John Hall & Polly    - 1860]
    25 Oct, 1874, Island Cr. Church House, Ows
    [James 1880 Ows. w/P, W-NL; together 1900]


(Creech cont.)

**CREECH (cont.)**

JAMES (R.Ows. 18 S b.Ows) P/Ows. [NOTE: listed as <u>COUCH</u> in marriage] [poss. GS/o John Creech & Minerva Farmer - 1900]
  MIRTIE SMITH (R.Ows. 17 S b.Ows) P/Lee-Ows. [d/o Kirby Smith & Martha "Katie" Creech - 1900; BBG; ob-WM OCN-6/29/51]
  2 April, 1909, Ows. [R.Owsley 1910 w/WP, listed as <u>Creech</u>; ob-WM as <u>Creech</u>; R. Manchester, MI 1951]
JOE BOB - see JOSEPH A.
JOHN (c21 b.Ows.) [s/o Elijah Creech & Nancy Louisa Brandenburg - TCS]
  SARAH ANN GRIFFEY (c18 b.Clay) [d/o James Griffey & Eliz. Herd - TCS]
  1865/6      (1870-C-2; 1880-10; 1900; BBG; TCS; M-L ch-1909; widr. John 1910-1920; DC ch-1919; NL M-C)
JOSEPH A. "JOE BOB" (c27 S b.KY) [s/o John L. Creech & Minerva Farmer - TCS]
  SARAH GABBARD (c24 S b.Ows.) [d/o Hiram Gabbard & Mary J. Freeman - B-O]
  1879      (1880-5/80, Sarah & son w/WP; MT; 1900 m-21; 1910 m-30; M-L ch. 1923)
LUTHER (R.Ows. 18 S b.Jack) P/Harl-Ows. [s/o Joe Bob Creech & Sarah Gabbard - 1900]
  FLORA BOWLES (R.Ows. 17 S b.Jack) P/Clay-Ows. [d/o Geo. W. Bowles & Emily A. Morgan - 1900]
  22 Feb, 1909 <u>Jackson Co.</u> [recorded Owsley] [R.Owsley 1910, wife <u>Laura</u>]
OATER B. (R.Ows. 17 S b.Ows.) P/Ows. [s/o Samuel Creech & Serena Marion - 1900; TCS]
  DELLA BOWLES (R.Ows. 18 S b.Ows) P/Ows. [d/o Geo. W. Bowles & Emily Morgan - 1900; ob-WF OCN-4/13/51]
  24 Dec., 1908, Ows. (a/L 2/22/1909 <u>Jack.</u> - M-J TCS) [R.Owsley 1910-1920; London 1968 - ob-HS BE-10/10/68]


(Creech cont.)

PEALY (c24 S b.Sturg.)  [s/o John Creech
   & Nancy Minerva Farmer - 1880]
   SARAH C. MARCUM (c17 b.KY)  [d/o Phillip
   Marcum & Eliz. Vickers - TCS]
   30 Dec., 1891, Jackson @ Phillip Marcum's,
   by George L. Davis, Bapt.; wits. Henry &
   America J. Marcum; sur. Silas Creech
   (M-J; TCS; 1910 H-remd-14)
PEALY (c29 2nd b.Sturg.)  [m1 Sarah C. Marcum
   above - TCS]
   LULA BOWMAN (c16 S b.KY) [d/o Cornelius
   Bowman & Sarah McVey - TCS]
   1895/6      (1900-1910-1920; B-O ch.;
   BC 1911-1915; W/as Louisa, Lou, & Lula)
PERRY L. (c19 S b.Trav. Rest)  [s/o John
   Creech & Nancy Minerva Farmer - 1880]
   MINNIE F. BOWMAN (c19 S b.Sturg.)
   1893/4      (1900 m-6; B-O ch.; 1910 m-14
   = 1895/6; 1920; ob-ch. BS-1/22/87 & HJN-
   10/89)
SAMUEL [B.] (c23 S b.KY)  [s/o John Creech
   & Nancy Minerva Farmer - 1870]
   SERENA MARION [_____] (c22 2nd b.KY)
   [m1 _____] [d/o Anderson Marion
   & Sarah     - TCS]
   8 Aug., 1883, Jackson Co., @ Anderson
   Marion's, by J. B. Rowlett, Elder; sur.
   Enoch Creech; wits. John S. & Riley Creech
   (M-J; TCS; 1900 m-15; 1910 m-24 W-2nd;
   1920)
SAMUEL H. (c18 b.KY)  [1881-1909 Ows.; s/o Joe
   Bob Creech & Sarah Gabbard - ME-11/18/09;
   TS-TCS; BBC/Dora's niece]
   DORA B. GABBARD (c21 b.KY)  [1887-1942;
   d/o Henry Gabbard & Eliza Jane Bryant -
   TS-TCS; BBG]
   c1908      (BBG; wid. Dora w/P 1910, no
   ch.)  [DORA m2 1910 Wm. Floyd Hunley]
SILAS W. (c21 b.KY)  [s/o Enoch Creech
   & Patience Kelly]
   BARBARA NANTZ (c20 b.KY)  [d/o Frederick
   Nantz & Sarah Chappell]
   c1864     (1870-5; HC)

(Creech cont.)

CREECH (cont.)
SILAS WOODSON (c18 b.KY)    [s/o John L. Creech
    & Nancy Minerva Farmer]
    SALLY RADER (c14 b.Jack.)   [d/o Frederick
    Rader & Nancy BBurg. - 1880]
    1879/80         [DIVORCED]   (1880-MWY, WM
    w/them)    [SALLY m2 1894 Lee, Wm. Mays]
    [H-remd.]
SILAS WOODSON (c29 2nd b.KY)   [Div/f Sally
    Rader above - 1880]
    MARTHA E. PETERS (c24 b.KY) [d/o James E.
    Peters & Eliza L. Hughes - 1880]
    1 July, 1891, Jackson Co.; sur. John B King
    (TCS; 1900-J "m-13", ch. 10, 5 & 8 mo.)
TILFORD (c27 S b.KY)  [s/o Alex Creech & Agnes
    Sageser - BBG; 1900; ob-HS OCC-4/9/37]
    CYNTHIA E. GABBARD (c22 S b.KY)  [d/o Henry
    Gabbard & Eliz. Bryant - BBG]
    25 Aug., 1906        (BBG; 1910-1920; BC
    1911-1917-1919; R.Earnestville 1937)
WILLIE O. M. (c22 b.Trav. Rest)  [1883-1909;
    s/o Joe Bob Creech & Sarah Gabbard - BBG,
    "W.O.M." on TS; MT; 1900]
    ZINADA FLORENCE FLANERY (c21 b.Trav. Rest)
    [1884-1968; d/o Mike Flanery & Emaline
    Gabbard - BBG; 1900 as Zinada F.]
    c1905       (1910-4 wid. Florence; B-O ch.;
    TS-BBG has son Major b. 1906; M-O ch. 1929)
    [FLORENCE m2 c1920, James Pryse - BBG]
CRESS
    _____ (___ b.___)
    EMILY COLLINS (c16-25 b.KY)  [d/o Rural
    Collins & Caroline Smith - 1880]
    1890-99        (1900, wid. Emmer Cress
    w/M, no ch. listed)
    [EMILY m2 Joseph Moore - B-O ch.]
CRITZER
LEANDER (c28 B'Smth b.Loudon/Nelson Co., VA)
    ALMEDIA PITT (c24 b.Montgomery Co.)
    c1852        (1860-8; B-O ch.; B-L
    ch.; 1870-1880-L; TR)
CULTON
see COULTON
CUMMINGS/COMMINGS
FRED (c36 2nd sawyer b.PA) [m1 _____]
    ANNIE _____ (c28 S b.KY)
    1900/1        (1910 m-9 H-2nd; NL 1900)

## CUNDIFF

WILLIAM (c38 3rd b.Pul.) [m1 Eliz. Jett - JSG
dau. Eliz.'s DC; m2 5/17/42 Ann H. Reid -
Div. - JSG; M-C]
ANGELINE VIRGINIA WHITE (c17 b.Anderson)
c1848, poss. Breathitt (1850-15, 14, &
Eliz. 11, from H-1st mg., next ch-1; B-O
ch.; B-B ch.; 1860-B; 1870-W)

## CUNNIGAN

SAMUEL (c24 b.KY) [s/o James Cunigan & Nancy
Roberts - TCS]
SARAH "SALLY" GUM (c19 b.KY) [d/o Stephen
Gumm & Eliz. Cornelius - TCS]
c1844 (1850-5; B-O ch.; 1860;
1870-1880-J; TCS)

## CURRY

ANDREW (c21 b.VA) [s/o Wm. Curry & Ellen
- 1860-E]
MARGARET _____ (c18 b.KY)
c1867 (1870-L-2)
[ANDY m2 10/27/72 Lee, Nancy Ann Belomy]
GEORGE (c18 b.Lee,VA) [s/o Wm. Curry & Ellen
- 1850-E]
_____ (___ b.KY) [appar. d. 1866-9]
c1865 (1870-L-4, W-NL; B-L ch. by W2)
[GEORGE m2 4/26/72, Eliza Jane Combs - M-L;
1880-L]

## DAILEY/DAILY/DALEY

CHARLES (c37 b.KY) [1856-1902 Jack.; s/o Sam
Dailey & Virginia B. Minter - TS-TCS; ME-
7/4/02; 1880-J]
FANNIE R. MINTER (c22 S b.KY)
28 May, 1893, Ows., @ ME Church, Green Hall
(ME-6/2/93, says they plan to move to KS;
1900)
HAMPTON H. (c22 b.VA) [s/o Samuel C. Dailey
& Virginia B. Minter - TCS; 1860]
SOPHIA WILLIAMS (c21 b.KY) [1852-1934; d/o
John L. Williams & Catherine        - 1870;
ob-W OCC-10/5/34]
2 Jan., 1873 (ob-W; 1880-J-6; 1900-J,
m-27; NL M-C/J)
(Dailey cont.)

**DAILEY (cont.)**
TROY (c22 b.KY)   [s/o Hampton Dailey & Sophia
    Williams - 1900-J]
    LOU PENDERGRASS (c19 b.KY)   [d/o Ben
    Pendergrass & Nancy Bell - TCS; w/Bell GP
    1900; ob-WS OCC-7/28/39]
    1902/3          (ob-WS; 1910-R m1-7; B-J
    ch-2/04; NL M-J)
W[ILSON] G. (c26 Dr. b.KY)   [s/o Samuel Dailey
    & Virginia Miner - 1880-J; TCS]
    BIRDIE SANDERS (c17 b.KY)   [d/o Prof.
    Sanders of Union City, TN - ME]
    5 Nov., 1886, Boonev., Ows. @ M. E. Church
    (ME-11/5/86; ME-7/15/92, Mrs. Prof. Sanders
    of Union City, TN visits daus. Mrs. Harris
    & Mrs. Dailey of Boonev.; 1900-B m-13)
**DALE**
HENRY (c22 S b.Br.)   [1884-1966 Lee; s/o Henry
    Dale Sr. & Mary        - FH; BE-10/6/66]
    LUCY E. ROSS (c23 S b.KY)   [d/o Hiram Ross
    & Sarah Burns - 1900, w/wid. mom]
    1906/7          (1910 w/Wm. Ross & wf Ida as
    BiL & sister; widr. Henry d. Beattyv.)
**DALTON/DAULTON/DOLTEN**
BENJAMIN H. (c27 b.TN)
    NANCY E. HURST (c18 b.KY)   [d/o James Hurst
    & Mary Rucard - 1870]
    16 Jan, 1879, Jackson Co.; sur. J. W. Baker
    (TCS; REM; 1880-J-2 mo.; NL 1900Sx)
ISAAC (R.Ows. 20 S b.VA) P/VA   [s/o Thomas
    Dalton & Cath. Hollingsworth - 1870; M-Lee,
    VA; B-O sib]
    REBECCA BELL (R.Ows. 18 S b.VA) P/VA   [d/o
    Marcus C Bell & Martha Flanery - 1870]
    28 Nov., 1876, Ows. @ M. C. Bell's
    [R.Owsley 1880]
SAMUEL (c27 S b.KY)
    ELIZA JANE SHOOK (c14 S b.KY)   [d/o Lucinda
    Shook, who md. Richard Reynolds - 1900]
    1864/5          (1870-1880, no ch.; 1890;
    1900, MiL Lucinda Reynolds w/them; 1910)


(Dalton cont.)

**DALTON (cont.)**
SAMUEL (R.Ows. 22 S b.Lee,VA) P/TN-VA [s/o
    Thomas Dalton & Cath. Collinsworth - 1870;
    M-Lee,VA]
    SARAH C. CLARK (R.Ows. 19 S b.VA) P/--
    [d/o Wm. Clark & Rebecca      - 1870]
    31 Dec., 1874, Ows., @ Widow Clark's
SAMUEL P. (c21 b.TN)  [d. 1895 - ME-8/30/95]
    [MARY?] REBECCA FLANERY (c19 b.KY)  [prob.
    d/o Elcannah Flanery & Amanda Mainous (who
    remd. David Spivy) - TCS; TR; P/1860-J no
    ch.; 1870-J as Mary B(ecca?) age 9]
    19 Oct., 1879, <u>Jackson Co.</u> @ Davis Spivy's,
    by Cornelius Moore; wits. Cyrus Powell &
    Lazarus Minter  (TCS; 1880-MWY; W-remd.
    1900)   [REBECCA m2 John Holcomb]
THOMAS (c22 b.TN)  [s/o Timothy Dalton & Susan
    Kelly]
    CATH. COLLINSWORTH (c17 b.VA)  [d/o Thomas
    Collinsworth & Esther A.     - 1850-Lee,VA]
    20 Sept., 1851, <u>Lee Co., VA</u>  (M-Lee,VA; B-O
    ch.; 1870; 1880-Lau.)
**DAMERAL/DAMREL**
JOEL (R.Ows. c16 b.Br.)  [s/o Samuel Dameral
    & Sarah Stamper]
    PHOEBE WRIGHT (18 b.Let.)  [d/o Hiram
    Wright & Susan Roark - TCS]
    12 July, 1861 <u>Wolfe</u> (M-W; 1870-L; B-L ch.)
JOHN (c20 b.Br.)  [1836-1892; s/o Sam Dameral
    & Sarah Stamper]
    ELIZABETH ["LIZZIE"] ANGEL (c15 b.Ows.)
    [1841-1934; d/o Ephraim Angel & W2 Susan
    Ingram - LNG; ob-W OCC-12/7/34]
    28 March, 1862, Ows., @ Davis Mayes, by S.
    Isaacs, JPOC; wits: Isaac Botner & David
    Mayes  (ML PWB; AB; WN; 1870-L-8; B-L ch.;
    1880-L; wid. Eliz. 1900-1910-L; M-L ch-
    1925; ob-ch. BE-1/26/50)
**DANIELS/DANIEL**
BRADLEY (R.Ows. 22 S b.Clay) P/Br-Clay [1887-
    1969; s/o George Daniels & Lucy Allen -
    1900; ob-H BE-4/17/69]
    ELLEN ABNER (R.Ows. 17 S b.Ows.) P/Ows-Clay
    28 April, 1910, Ows.

(Daniels cont.)

**DANIELS (cont.)**

CHARLIE (c<u>13</u> S b.KY) [prob. s/o George Daniel
   & Lucy Allen - TCS]
   ROSA NOLAND (c<u>20</u> S b.KY)
   1900        (1910-9, m-10; 1920; TCS)
GEORGE W. (c39 Law. b.KY) [s/o John Marcus
   Daniel & Louisa Daniel - 1850]
   SALLIE A. _____ (c27 b.KY)
   July, 1869     (1870)
GEORGE W. (c17 S b.Clay)
   LUCY ALLEN (c17 S b.Clay)
   1872      (1880-C-5, ages <u>36</u> & <u>21</u>; 1900
   m-27, both age 44; 1910 m-38, both 54;
   1920, both 64; rec. of sons; DC-son;
   NL M-C)
IRVIN (R.Ows. 18 S b.Ows.) P/Clay [s/o Geo.
   Daniel & Lucy Allen - 1900]
   LOTTIE GAY (R.Ows. 23 S b.Ows.) P/Ows.
   [d/o Henry Gay & Nancy M. Bishop - TCS]
   25 Aug., 1910, Ows. [R.Owsley 1920]
ISAAC (c20 S b.KY) [s/o Geo. Daniel & Lucy
   Allen - TCS; 1900; ob-HS BE-9/23/71]
   FLORENCE BAILEY (c19 S b.KY)
   1900/1    (1910; TCS; BC 1912, 1921-H;
   R.London, KY 1969-71 - ob-HS)
JOHN MARCUS (c35 2nd Dr. b.KY) [widr/o Louisa
   Daniels - M-E 5/11/30] [c1810-1880's;
   s/o Beverly Daniel & Jane Hiatt - TCS]
   MARY FRILEY (c26 b.KY) P/VA
   7 Dec., 1845, <u>Estill</u> (appar. div.) (M-E;
   1850-1860; REM; "wid" Mary w/dau. 1900-L)
   [H-remd.]
JOHN H. (R.Clay 18 S b.Br.) P/Clk-Clay
   ELIZABETH BAKER (R.Ows. 16 S b.Clay) P/Clay
   15 Jan., 1874, Ows.
JOHN MARCUS (c50's 3rd Dr. b.KY) [m1 Mary
   Fraley above]
   _____ (___ b.___)
   1861-75    (H-4th M-L 1/75; NL M-J)
   [H-remd.]
JOHN MARCUS (59 4th Dr. b.KY) [m3 _____
   above] [c1810-1880's]
   HARRIET JACKSON (18 b.KY)
   3 Jan., 1876, <u>Lee</u> (M-L; 1880-L)

(Daniels cont.)

## DANIELS (cont.)

KENIS (R.Ows. 24 S b.Clay) P/Clay  [s/o George
Daniel & Lucy Allen - 1900]
LULIE GAY (R.Ows. 18 S b.Ows.) P/Ows-Clay
[d/o Henry Gay & Nancy M. Bishop -     1900]
20 Aug, 1908, Ows.  [R.Owsley 1910-1920]
MARCUS - see JOHN MARCUS
QUINTUS C. ([c22] b.Lee)  [s/o Dr. John Marcus
Daniel & W2 Mary Fraley - 1860]
J. F[RANCES] COMBS (___ b.Ows.) [d/o Daniel
Garrett Combs & Rachel Turner - Yest.]
11 June, 1874, <u>Breathitt</u> @ D. G. Combs, by
Wm. M. Jones; wits. Henry Combs & J.
Sebastian  (M-B 1:54; H-sgl. 1870; B-O ch-
4/77; NL 1880Sx)
SCOTT - see W. SCOTT
THOMAS JEFFERSON (c29 Dr. b.KY)  [s/o John
Marcus Daniel & W1 Louisa Daniel - 1860]
[ANNA] FRANCES McGUIRE (19 S b.Ows.)  [d/o
Arch McGuire & W3 Cath. Brandenburg]
28 June, 1865, Ows.  (JFB; DB)
W[INFIELD] SCOTT (c19 s-mill b.Ows.)  [s/o
John Marcus Daniel & W2 Mary Fraley - 1860]
MATILDA ROBINSON (c16 b.Ows.)
1868/9        (1870-L, no ch.; B-L ch.;
1880-1900-L)

## DAUGHERTY

FRANCIS (c32 c.minr; b.Donnegal Co, Ire.)
MARTITIA COLE (c22 b.Est.)  [d/o Orson Cole
& Perlina Bennett - 1860; 1880-L; P/M-E]
c1862        (1870-L-7; B-L ch.)

## DAULTON

see DALTON

## DAVIDSON

ALLEN (c21 S b.KY)
NANCY A. MOORE (c19 S b.KY) [1861-1885; d/o
James R. Moore & Cynthia Warford/Walton -
TS-TCS; DC-sib.]
1880/1              (TCS; H-remd. 1900)
ALLEN (c27 2nd b.KY)  [widr/o Nancy Moore abv]
AMANDA MOORE (c20 S b.KY)  [d/o Andrew
Moore & Margaret Gabbard - MT]
1886/7        (1900-2/88, m-19, but this is
W1; W1 d. 1885; 1910 m-23; MT)

(Davidson cont.)

## DAVIDSON (cont.)

CARLO (c19 S b.KY)  [c1874-1949 - ob-H OCN-
   11/4/49]
   MARTHA B. ALLEN (c21 S b.KY)  [d/o Job
   Allen & America Sizemore - TCS]
   1898/9      (1910, Aunt Sylvania Sizemore,
   sgl., w/them; 1920; TCS; NL 1900; Carlo
   w/DiL @ Taft when he died)
HANSFORD (c18 b.KY)  [s/o James A. Davidson
   & Rachel Allen - P/M-C 1827]
   REBECCA "BECKY" HACKER (c16 b.KY)  [d/o
   Samuel Hacker & Chaney Roberts - TCS]
   c1846      (1850-3; SD; 1870-1880-C)
JASON WALKER (c18 b.Clay)  [s/o Perry Davidson
   & Eliz. Burns - 1860-C]
   MARY "POLLY" GAY (c17 b.Per.)  [d/o Nelson
   Gay & Hannah Barger]
   1867, Ows.  (1870-2; 1880; SD; B-O ch.;
   LNG; to Arkansas; OK 1907-19)
JOHN (c20 b.Clay)  [s/o Perry Davidson & Eliz.
   Burns - TCS; 1860-C]
   NANCY ROBERTS (c24 b.Clay)  [d/o Wash.
   Roberts & Malinda Lewis/Cole]
   4 Dec., 1873, Clay  (M-C; TCS; 1880-5; B-O
   ch.)
MARION (___ b.Br.)
   LYDIA M. GABBARD (c16 S b.Ows.)  [d/o Geo.
   W. Gabbard & Mary Shook - 1900]
   c1903      (B-O ch-1904; 1910 W-remd-4,
   Davidson s-s)  [LYDIA m2 Lee Combs - 1920]
RAY (c20 S b.KY)  [s/o Allen Davidson & Amanda
   Moore]
   EMMA MOORE (c22 S b.KY)  [d/o Wm. Moore
   & Eliza Reynolds - TCS]
   1907/8      (1910; TCS)
ROBERT (c18 b.KY)  [s/o James A. Davidson
   & Rhoda Morris]
   NANCY HACKER (c19 b.KY)  [d/o Samuel Hacker
   & Chaney Roberts - TCS]
   20 Jan., 1842, Clay  (M-C; 1850 1860-C; SD)
   [ROBT. m2 11/13/62 Clay, Melissa Helton -
   TCS]


(Davidson cont.)

**DAVIDSON (cont.)**
SAMUEL (c19 b.Ows.) [s/o Perry Davidson
    & Eliz. Burns - TCS; 1860-C]
    SARAH FIELDS (c18 b.KY) [d/o Jeremiah
    Fields & Eliza Eversole - TCS]
    8 Sept., 1866, Clay [appar. DIVORCED]
    (TCS; 1870-3)
SAMUEL (c23 b.Clay) [s/o Morgan Davidson
    & Mary Stidham - SD; 1860-C]
    SYLVANIA CHANDLER (c14 b.KY) P/NC-KY
    22 Dec, 1870 Clay (M-C; 1880-8; SD)
WALKER - see JASON WALKER
W[ILLIAM] M. (R.Ows. 22 S b.Clay) P/Clay-Ows.
    [s/o Perry Davidson & Eliz. Burns - 1870;
    1860-C]
    RACHEL DEAN (R.Ows. 18 S b.Ows.) P/TN-Clay
    [d/o Ezekiel Dean & Kezziah Barrett - 1870]
    31 Dec, 1874, Ows. @ Ezekiel Dean's
    [R.Owsley 1880; wid. Rachel 1900 & 1920]
**DAVIS**
CHARLES (c21 b.KY) [c1845-1864 C.W. in
    Anderson, GA - ob-ch. BE-4/2/43]
    NANCY HIERONYMOUS (c15 b.KY) [1829-1908;
    d/o Sam Hieronymous & Sally White - 1850]
    14 May, 1846, Ows. (REM; 1850-4, w/WP; B-O
    ch.; VH; 1860; M-L ch. 1926; ob-ch. BE)
    [NANCY m2 Claiborne Duff - 1870-W; TCS]
**DAY**
ASHLIN (c29 b.KY)
    MARTHA _____ (c16 b.KY)
    1893/4          (1900)
BEATTY (R.Ows. 65 3rd b.Harl.) P/-- [m1 _____
    _____; m2 1/3/72 Sarah A Davenport - M-H;
    1880-H; widr. Beatty 1900]
    MARGARET MORRIS (R.Ows. 45 S b.Ows.) P/Ows-
    Lee,VA [d/o Theo Morris & Letitia    - TCS]
    28 May, 1908, Ows.   [R.Owsley 1910; wid.
    Margaret 1920]
BERRY - see N. BERRY


(Day cont.)


197

**DAY (cont.)**

EWELL (c17 S b.Mt.Pleasant, Harl.) [1881-1969;
    s/o Lloyd Day & Emily Jane Allen - TCS; ob-
    H&S BE-1/1/70-1/21/65]
    ARMINA "MINIE" HATTON (c16 S b.KY)
    1897/8        (1900-1910-1920; B-O ch.; BC
    1912-1916; ob-ch. BE-4/2/70 & BS-8/20/87-
    9/22/94; R.Boonev. 1965; wid. R.Boonev.
    1969-70; NL M-H; W/as Armina, Mina, Mainie)
IRA (c23 b.Lee,VA)
    ELIZA _____ (c18 b.Harl.)
    c1862         (1870-L-6; 1880-L-17; B-L ch.)
JEROME (45 S b.VA)
    NANCY LEWIS (c20 S b.KY) [d/o Mathias
    Lewis & Chaney Fields - TCS]
    c1880         (1880 liv. in Adultery; NL
    1900Sx) [NOTE: They might not have md.]
JOHN (c42 b.VA)
    SUSANNAH _____ (c20 b.KY)
    c1860         (NL 1860; 1870-9)
MINTER (c21 S b.Harl.) [1881-1965 Lee; s/o
    Lloyd Day & Emily Jane Allen - TCS; 1900;
    ob-H BE-1/21/65]
    MARTHA VENABLE (c19 S b.KY) [d/o Thomas
    Venable & Mary J. Shanks - TCS]
    1901/2        (1910; TCS; 1920 HM w/them;
    BC 1911)
N. B[ERRY] (R.Ows. 25 S b.VA) P/VA-Harl.
    LETHY COUCH (R.Ows. 19 S b.--) P/--
    11 Oct., 1908, Ows. [R.Whitley 1910 H/as
    m2-1; R.Perry 1924 - BC]
NEWBERRY (c24 miner b.Lee,VA) [appar. s/o
    John Day - 1860]
    DIANA JAMERSON (c19 b.Est.) [poss. d/o
    Mordica Jamerson]
    22 Oct., 1849, Estill; sur. Mordica Jamison
    (M-E; 1850-1860; B-O ch.; B-L ch.; 1870-
    1880-L; wid. Diana 1900-L; 1910-L w/son)
WILLIAM V. (c22 b.KY) [s/o Beatty Day &
    W2 Sarah Davenport - 1900]
    BELLE _____ (c21 b.KY)
    1899/1900        (1900 w/HF)

**DEAN/DEANE**
BRICE - see BRISON
BRISON "BRICE" (c23 S b.KY) [1872-1957; s/o
    Ezekiel Dean & Keziah Barrett - TS-TCS;
    ob-HS OCN-7/8/49]
    ARRA/IRIE/IRA DANIELS (c17 b.KY) [d/o
    George Daniel & Lucy Allen - TCS; 1880-C]
    1894/5        (1900; ob-ch. OCN-9/1/50 & BS-
    6/25/98 M/Ira Daniels; NL M-C/J) [H-remd.]
BRISON "BRICE" (c33 2nd b.KY) [m1 Arra/Irie
    Daniels above]
    MARY ELLEN RICE (c25 S b.Ows.) [1876-1956
    - ob-W OCN-1/19/56]
    1904        (1910 m-5, ch. 12, 10, 5, 4 &
    4 mos., dau. age 5 is Mary Ellen's - ob-W;
    1920; ob-ch. BS-12/10/98; R.Boonev.1949-50)
DANIEL BOONE (c19 S b.Ows.) [1879-1962; s/o
    Ezekiel Dean & Kezziah Barrett - TS-TCS]
    _____ (___ b.___) [d. pre-1900]
    c1899        (1900, widr. Dan, no ch.; TCS;
    NL M-J)    [H-remd.]
D[ANIEL] B[OONE] (R.Ows. 27 2nd b.Ows.) P/Lee-
    Clay    [widr/o _____ above]
    IDA NEECE (R.Ows. 26 S b.Ows.) P/Ows. [d/o
    Wm. Neace & Martha J.        - 1900; ob-WF
    OCC-12/25/36]
    2 Dec., 1909, Ows. [R.Owsley 1910-1920;
    Scoville, Ows. 1949 - ob-HS OCN-7/8/49;
    Boonev. 1969 - ob-WS BE-12/4/69]
EZEKIAL (R.Clay c23 b.VA)
    KEZZIAH BARRETT (R.Clay c20 S b.Clay)
    [d/o Jesse Barrett & Polly Asher]
    6 Aug., 1859 Clay (M-C & mf; 1860-C;
    1870-1880-1890-1900; B-O ch.)
GEORGE (c23 S b.KY) [1878-1951; s/o Ezekiel
    Dean & Keziah Barrett - 1900; ob-H&S OCN-
    5/4/51-7/8/49]
    MARTHA GAY (c21 S b.Ows.) [1879-1968; d/o
    John Gay & China Barker - TCS; 1900; ob-W
    BE-3/7/68]
    1900/1        (1910-1920; TCS; R.Mistletoe,
    Ows. 1949)
JESSE (c21 S b.Teges, Clay) [s/o Ezekiel Dean
    & Kezziah Barrett]
    JANE RILEY (c15 S b.Gabbard)
    1896/7        (1900 m-3; 1910 m-11; B-O
    ch.; 1920)

**DEATON**

BROWN - see CHARLES BROWN

[CHARLES] BROWN (c24 S b.KY) [1882-1970 Jack;
s/o James Deaton & Sophia Abner - 1900;
DDN]
LULA (nee GAY) LEDFORD (c20 2nd b.KY)
[m1 _____ Ledford - DDN] [d/o Russell
Gay & Eliza Williams - ob-WS OCN-12/16/54]
1905/6          (1910, her son Oscar, age 9,
no other surname listed; 1920-J, son Oscar
Ledford - DDN; R.Tyner, Jack. 1954)

DAVID (c19 S b.Ows.) [1880-1964 Ows.; s/o
James Deaton & Sophia Abner - DDN; 2nd M-O]
MARTHA SIZEMORE (c16 S b.KY) [d/o Wm.
Sizemore & Polly Gabbard - TCS]
1899/1900          (1900; TCS; DDN; 1910, BiL
Logan Sizemore, 23; BC 1914; 1920; ob-ch.
BS-1/7/93)          [DAVID m2 8/11/40 Ows.,
Artemecia Griffith d/o Miza Griffith - DDN]

GARDNER (c20 b.KY) [s/o Wilson Deaton & Nancy
Ann Aikman - JEM; DDN]
TISHA McINTOSH (___ b.___)
13 July, 1901, Sebastian, Ows. [rec. Perry]
by H. H. Rice, JPPC; wits. W. S. Herndon &
Mary Rice     (M-P G:122)

JAMES (c22 S b.Ows.) [1855-1921 Ows.; s/o
Isaac Deaton & Nancy Smith - B-O; DDN]
SOPHIA ABNER (c27 S b.Ows.) [1849-1910 Ows;
d/o Wm. Abner & Jane Baker - DDN]
1877          (1880-2; 1900 m-22; B-O ch; 1910
m-36; DC ch.)  [JAMES m2 c1911, Sarah Woods
(1888-1965; d/o Magoffin Woods & Nancy
Elizabeth Deaton, who m2 John Eversole) -
1920; DDN; JC; DC-W; ob-ch. BS-10/24/91-
2/27/97; SARAH remd. 11/20/26 Ows., Willie
Roberts (1889-1968) - ob-W&H BE-4/22/65-
11/28/68]

JASON (c22 2nd b.KY) [m1 _____]
[s/o Thos. Deaton & Eliz. Little -1880-B]
ISABELLE BAKER (c19 b.KY) [d/o Andrew
Jackson Baker & Margaret Riley - 1880]
20 July, 1891, Perry @ Thomas Deaton's,
by Rev. A. A. Morris; wits. C. B. Baker &
John Deaton     (M-P H:35)

(Deaton cont.)

**DEATON (cont.)**
JERRY (c17 S b.Gabbard)
_____ (14 b.__)
12 Sept., 1897          (ME-9/17/97, Jerry
Deatone, a young man charged with detaining
a girl about 14 yrs. old in this Co. &
bound over to answer at the next term of
the court last night beat his case by
taking the girl & marrying her; NL M-J)
[H-remd.]
JERRY (c28 2nd b.Gabbard) [m1 _____ above]
ROSA MULLINS [a/k/a GIBSON] (c16 S b.
Boonev.) [appar. d/o Minerva Gibson (wid/o
Anderson Mullins - M-O 12/74) & unknown -
1900 as Rosa B. Mullins, b. 12/91, Ni/o
Larkin Gibson]
11 Aug, 1908, <u>Breathitt</u> @ Robt. Callahan's,
by R. C. Roberts; wits. A. B. Marshall & B.
Callahan   (M-B 13:503, info NFI; TCS; 1910
m-1; B-O ch-8/09; BC 1911-1918 DDN; M-B ch-
1927; H/as Jerry 3x, as <u>Charlie</u> B-O; W/as
Gibson B-O, as Mullins BC 2x)
JOHN (c23 S b.KY) [1886-1966; s/o James Deaton
& Sophia Abner - 1900; DDN]
DORA HILL (c19 S b.KY)   [1889-1913; d/o
David Hill & Nancy Combs - DC]
1908          (1910-1, m-1; TCS; BC 1911-
1912)   [JOHN m2 c1919, Sarah (nee Smith)
Peters, d/o Marion Smith & Levina Evans,
wid/o Wm. Peters - TCS; 1920; DDN]
MARTIN (c30 2nd b.Bunc., NC)   [widr/o Calista
Hammons - 1870MS; 1860-J; M-J mf 12/25/59]
[s/o Isaac Deaton & Nancy Smith - DDN]
JANE (nee BARRETT) CARMACK (c20 2nd b.KY)
[Div/f Isaac Carmack - TCS]   [1850/1-1919
Ows.; d/o Thomas Barrett & Barbara Gabbard
- TCS; 1870; DC/Stamper]
c1872          [DIVORCED]   (DDN; TCS; Jane's
H1 Carmack; remd-22 1900)   [MARTIN m3
9/25/79 Clay, Mary Hensley - DDN; M-C;
1880-1900-C]   [JANE m3 5/89 Clay, Lewis
Stamper - DDN]

(Deaton cont.)

## DEATON (cont.)

NATHAN (c22 b.NC)  [s/o Isaac Deaton & Nancy
    Smith - CED; DDN]
    MALVINA GILBERT (c18 b.KY)
    9 Jan., 1868        (CED; 1870-1)
THOMAS [R.] (R.Br. 20 S b.Br.) P/Br.  [s/o
    Alex Deaton & Eliz. Richardson - 1880-B;
    DDN]
    ELLEN BAKER (R.Ows. 18 S b.Ows.) P/Ows.
    [NOTE: JTB says her name is actually ELAH;
    d/o Andrew Jackson Baker & Margaret Riley
    - 1880]
    1 Oct., 1885, Breathitt, by J. W. Cardwell
    (M-B 3:223; DDN; 1900-1910-B; wid. Ellen
    1920-B)
WILLIAM (c17 S b.KY)   [s/o Isaac Deaton
    & Nancy Smith - DC]
    SUSAN [nee COMBS] FREEMAN (c28 2nd b.KY)
    [wid/o Sylvester Freeman - 1890]  [d/o
    Harvey Combs & Eliz. Parsons - TCS]
    1868         (1870 ch-James 16, Jos. 8,
    Nancy E. 1; 1880 lists Jos. as Freeman &
    s-s/o Wm., a/L w/Harvey Combs as GS; 1890
    Susan Deaton f/w/o Sylvester Freeman; 1900
    m-31; 1910 W-m2-37)

## DEEDS

DAVID ["BUD"] (R.Ows. 40 S b.Ows) P/VA-Harl.
    [1864-1946; s/o Henry Deeds & Amanda Warren
    - 1880; TS-TCS]
    FRANKIE PETERS (R.Ows. 27 S b.Ows.) P/Jack-
    Ows.  [d/o James Elisha Peters & Louisa
    Young - 1900]
    12 March, 1909, Ows.  [R.Owsley 1910-1920]
    [FRANCES m2 _____ Wilson - ob-WS OCN-
    6/7/56]
HENRY - see JOSHUA HENRY
JOSHUA HENRY (c22 b.Lee,VA)   [1840-1912;
    s/o _____ Deeds & Polly      - TS-TCS]
    AMANDA WARREN (c21 b.Lee,VA)  [1841-1908;
    d/o George Jorden Warren & Eliza      -
    1850-H; TS-TCS; D-O]
    1862/3         (1870-5; 1880-16; 1900, HM
    w/them; B-O ch. by W2)   [H-remd.]


(Deeds cont.)


202

## DEEDS (cont.)

[JOSHUA] HENRY (R.Ows. 66 2nd b.VA) P/VA
[widr/o Amanda Warren above]
LUVIN [LOUVISA nee CAUDILL] BOTNER (R.Ows.
39 2nd b.Br.) P/Br. [wid/o Wm. Botner]
[1870-1955; d/o Alford Caudill & Jane
Simpkins - TCS; ob-W OCN-6/9/65 Brewer]
15 Feb., 1909, Ows. [R.Owsley 1910]
[NOTE: maiden name from B-O ch.]
[LOUVISA m3 Valentine Brewer - 1920; ob-W]

## DICKERSON

HENRY C. (c28 cabinet maker b.VA)
SERENA HOWERTON (c26 b.KY) [d/o James
Jacob Howerton & Rebecca Williams - TCS]
c1855        (1860-2; D-O puts 1st ch. b.
1856; B-O ch.)

## DOOLEY/DOOLY

BASCOMB (c20 b.KY) [s/o John Dooley & Virginia
Hughes - ob-HS BE-8/19/43, which lists
sibs, but not par.; bros. par. per TCS]
VIRGINIA "JENNIE" CORNETT (c21 b.KY)
c1899        (NL 1900-1910Sx; 1920 1st
ch-20, all ch. b.KY; R.Boonev. 1943; ob-
ch. BS-7/15/93 b.c1912 Ows.; ob-ch. BE-
12/20/84 b.c1915 Per. & BS-6/4/98; NL M-P)
CHESTER A. (c20 S b.KY) [s/o John Dooley
& Virginia Hughes - TCS; ob-HS BE-8/19/43;
1900-L as neph/o John Fraley & wf Susan]
LILLIE PRICE (c20 S b.KY) [1886-1915; d/o
Elias Price & Martha Cecil - 1900; TS-TCS]
1907/8        (1910; TCS)    [CHESTER m2
Virginia Bond - TCS; R.West Carrollton, OH
1943]
MELVIN - see WILLIAM MELVIN
WILLIAM MELVIN (c19 S b.VA) [1872-1947 Lee;
s/o John Dooley & Virginia Hughes - TS-TCS;
ob-H&S BE-1/23/47 & 8/19/43]
REBECCA JOSEPHINE "JOSIE" HAMILTON (c16 S
b.Boonev.) [1875-1949; d/o Alex. Hamilton
& Cath. Pendleton - TCS; ob-W OCN-7/8/49]
18 Feb., 1892, Ows. (ob-H; TCS; 1900-1910-
1920; B-O ch.; H-d. Lee; ob-W; ob-ch. BS-
11/15/84)

**DORTON**
FRANKLIN (c22 b.VA)
   MAHALEY [STRONG?] (c17 b.KY)  [poss. d/o
   John Strong & Marinda Wilson - 1880]
   1886/7          (1900; NL 1910Sx; NL M-J)
**DOUGHERTY**
see DAUGHERTY
**DRAKE**
JOHN (R.Taz.,VA 19 yrs, 5 mos. b.Taz.,VA)
   [1835-1877; s/o Wm. Drake & Jane Stinson -
   ACB; D-W]
   CHARLOTTE STEEL (R.Taz,VA 21 S b.Taz, VA)
   8 Sept., 1854, Ows.  [R.Owsley 1860; Wolfe
   1870; wid. Charlotte 1870 Wolfe]
LARKIN (c23 b.KY)    [s/o Wm. Drake & Jane
   Stinson - ACB]
   MALINDA "LINDY" LESTER (c20 b.KY)  [c1834-
   1858 - TS-Wlf]
   c1854          (B-O ch-7/55; H-remd. 1860)
LARKIN (c30 2nd b.VA)  [widr/o Malinda J.
   Lester above]
   MARGARET J. _____ (c22 b.KY)
   1859/60          (1860-MWY; 1870-W-9)
PATTON - see WM. PATTON
WILLIAM T. [PATTON] (R.Ows. 20 S b.Taz., VA)
   [s/o Wm. Drake & Jane Stinson - ACB]
   MARTHA JANE HERD (R.Morg. 18 S b.Lee,VA)
   8 March, 1859, Morgan [rec. Owsley]
   [R.Owsley 1860; 1870 Wolfe; H/as Wm. both
   times]
**DUCK**
NATHAN W. (c27 crp b.KY)
   RACHEL McCOLLUM (c21 b.KY)  [d/o Daniel
   McCollum Sr. & Lydia Johnson - TCS]
   c1859          (1860-1870 no ch.; REM)
**DUFF**
CLAIBORNE (c42 2nd b.VA)  [m1 _____]
   NANCY (nee HIERONYMOUS) DAVIS (c39 2nd
   b.KY)  [wid/o Charles Davis - 1850-60]
   [1829-1908; d/o Samuel Hieronymous & Sally
   White - 1850 W&H1 w/WP]
   c1869          (1870-W, Davis s-ch.; wid.
   Nancy 1900-L; TCS; NL M-J)


(Duff cont.)

**DUFF (cont.)**

DANIEL (c23 S b.Ows.) [s/o James Duff
   & Lucinda Frost - 1900 M/as Wilder]
   JULIA REYNOLDS (c19 S b.Ows.) [d/o Malon
   J. Reynolds & Malinda Abner - TCS]
   1908/9       (1910; B-O ch.)
ELIJAH C. (c25 b.KY) [1835-1927; s/o John
   Duff & Polly Combs - TS-TCS]
   MARY EVERSOLE (c21 b.Per.) [1839-1909;
   d/o Wm. Eversole & Betty Bowling - TS-TCS]
   20 Oct., 1860, <u>Perry</u>; sur. Jesse Combs
   (M-P B:191; 1870-P-8; 1880-1890; 1900 N#L;
   widr. Elijah 1910-1920)
JAMES (c26 S b.Per.) [1856-1930 s/o Colson
   Duff & Eliz. Gilbert - TS-TCS; B-P]
   LUCINDA "BABE" FROST (c18 b.KY) [d/o Robt.
   Frost & W2 Susan Miller - TCS; 1880]
   c1884      (wf wid/o H2 1900, as Lucinda
   WILDER, ch. a/L as WILDER but s/b DUFF, ch.
   Daniel 14, Eliz. 12, Etta 9, Albert 5 &
   Goramandra 3; wid. Lucinda DUFF 1910, w/SiL
   & dau. Lizzy 21, ch: Herbert WILDER 9,
   Garamandra DUFF 12 & Albert DUFF 15) [BABE
   m2 _____ Wilder - 1900; BABE m3 John Noble
   - TCS]
JOHN (c30 b.VA)
   LUCINDA _____ (c20 b.VA)
   c1869      (1870-L, no ch.)
LOGAN (c37 b.Per.) [1854-1943; s/o Colston
   Duff & Eliz. Gilbert - 1880; TS-TCS; B-P]
   MARY BAKER (c16 b.KY) [1875-1908; d/o James
   W. Baker & Sarah Davidson - 1880; D-O]
   1891/2      (1900; D-O wf; widr. Logan
   1910-1920)
WILLIAM (c29 b.KY) [1858-1932; s/o Colston
   Duff & Eliz. Gilbert - 1880; TS-TCS]
   RACHEL MOORE (c19 b.KY) [1868-1903; d/o
   Andrew J Moore & Margaret Gabbard - TS-TCS]
   1887/8      (1900; TCS; ob-ch. BS-8/25/88)
   [H-remd.]


(Duff cont.)

**DUFF (cont.)**

WM. "BILL" (c18 S b.Ows.) [1878-1970 Oneida
    Mt. Hosp; s/o Logan Duff & unknown - ob-H
    BE-8/6/70; MT]
    JALIE GABBARD (c18 S b.Ows.) [1879-1958;
    d/o Geo. W. Gabbard & W2 Mary Eliz. Shook
    - ob-W&S OCN-11/6/58-1/9/58, OCC-6/12/42]
    1897/8        (1910-1920; NL 1900; MT;
    BBG; NL M-J/R.; R.Ricetown, Ows. 1942-1958;
    ob-ch. BS-2/6/86-5/29/97-5/29/97)
WILLIAM (c47 2nd b.KY) [widr/o Rachel Moore
    above] [1858-1932 - TS-TCS]
    NANCY (nee REYNOLDS) COMBS (c34 2nd b.KY)
    [m1 c1889 _____ Combs - wid. Nancy Combs -
    1900-J-4/90; NL M-J]    [d/o Henderson
    Reynolds & Anna Moore - 1880; TCS]
    1905/6       (1910 W-m-4, H-NL, Combs s-ch.
    & Duff dau.)

**DUKE**

JOHN (c18 b.KY)
    MARGARET _____ (c17 b.KY)
    c1849        (1850 no ch.)
JOHN (c24 b.Campbell Co., TN)
    EMILY E. DURBIN (c23 b.Est.)
    c1856      (1860-3; B-O ch.) [EMILY m2
    1865/6, John Townsend - TCS; 1880-L]

**DUNAGIN**

see DUNIGAN

**DUNAWAY**

DAVID (c56 b.VA) [s/o Ben Dunaway & Spicy
    Chamberlain - D-L; P/M-E)
    PRISCILLA McGUIRE (c51 b.VA) [d/o James
    McGuire & Diadema Mann - D-L; 1850]
    c1858        (1860 no ch; W-sgl. @ age
    50, JJDD)
DAVID (25 S b.Lee [Ows.]) [s/o Wm. Dunaway
    & Angeline Brandenburg - LNG; ob-H OCC-
    8/21/36]
    ELIZABETH BRANDENBURG (24 b.Lee [Ows.])
    2 Sept, 1880, Lee (M-L; LNG; 1900-L; M-L
    ch-1908-1912-1920-1930)    [H-remd.]


(Dunaway cont.)

**DUNAWAY (cont.)**
DAVID (c46 2nd b.KY)   [widr/o Eliz. BBurg.
   above - LNG]
   REBECCA GABBARD (c29 S b.Ows.)   [d/o Julius
   Gabbard & Catherine Thomas - 1880; LNG;
   ob-WS OCN-9/20/52]
   c1903, Ows.  (MT; 1910-L-6, H-m2-4, W m1-4;
   Rebecca was great-aunt of LNG; ob-H)
JOHN M. (c22 b.KY)
   PERLINA SPARKS (c18 b.KY)   [d/o Isaac
   Sparks & Jemima Jane Maloney - TCS; ACB]
   c1844         (1850-4; 1860; TCS; ACB)
PINK - see WILLIAM "PINK"
THOMAS (R.Ows. 23 S b.Ows.)   [c1832-1875; s/o
   Benjamin Dunaway & Spicy Chamberlain - D-L;
   P/M-E]
   ELIZABETH DUNAGIN (R.Ows 20 S b.VA) [c1835-
   1877; d/o Isaac Dunagin & Nancy      - D-L;
   1850-Lee,VA]
   11 Oct., 1855, Ows.  [R.Owsley 1860; Lee
   1870; ch. in Lee 1880 w/Thomas' sister]
WILLIAM ["PINK"] (R.Proctor 26 S b.Ows.) [s/o
   Ben Dunaway & Spicy Chamberlain - 1850]
   ANGELINA BRANDENBURG (R.Ows. 17 S b.So.Fk)
   [d/o George H. BBurg. & Sally Thomas - 1850
   w/F; P/M-E]
   3 Feb, 1853 Ows, by G. S. Williams  [R.Ows.
   1860; Lee 1870-1880-1900; widr. Wm. 1910-L]
**DUNIGAN/DUNAGAN/DUNAGEN**
   _____ (___ b.___)
   SUSANNAH HOLCOMB (c19-39 S b.KY)   [d/o Wm.
   Holcomb & Eliz. Christian - 1880]
   1880-1900         (TCS; W-NL w/P 1900;
   H-NL 1900Sx; NL M-J)
BERRY (c20 b.Lee,VA) P/NC  [s/o Isaac Dunigan
   & Nancy      - 1850-Lee,VA; D-O HF]
   MARTITIA BRYANT (c24 b.Br.) P/VA
   c1863         (1870-L-5; 1880-L-16; B-L ch.;
   KAS; TCS; NL 1900Sx)
EWING - see JAMES EWING
JAMES EWING (c22 b.Ows.)
   AMANDA SPENCE (c26 b.Lee,VA)   [d/o Jno.
   Spence & Mary Holmes - 1860]
   1868/9         (1870-L-11/69; 1880-1900-L;
   B-L ch.; wid. Amanda 1910-L)

(Dunigan cont.)

## DUNIGAN (cont.)

JESSE (c21 b.VA)  [s/o Isaac Dunigan
   & Nancy       - 1850-Lee,VA; D-O WF]
   SUSAN MALONEY (c20 b.KY)  [d/o McKinley
   Maloney & Malinda Landsaw]
   5 May, 1865          (FB; 1870-L; NL 1880-
   1900Sx)
JOHN (c22 b.IN)  [s/o Jesse Dunigan & Sally
   Wilson - 1870 w/wid. mom]
   JOSEPHINE WILSON (c19 b.KY)  [c1854-1877;
   d/o Philip Wilson & Jane Strong - JCH;
   1870; D-O 1/77]
   c1873          (both sgl. 1870; D-O wf;
   JCH; NVP; NL widr. John 1880/L; NL M-J)
   [JOHN appar. md. 2nd pre-1880, Mary _____
   - 1880-Jeff. w/ch. Sally 6 & Wesley 4]
WILLIAM (c19 b.Lee,VA)  [poss. s/o Isaac
   Dunigan & Nancy, who lived 1850-Lee,VA]
   AMERICA COUCH (c16 b.Br.)  [d/o James Couch
   & Louisa Rice - TCS; 1860-B]
   Nov., 1869          (1870-L; B-L ch.; 1880-L)

## DUNN/DONE

DILLARD (c24 S b.KY)   [s/o _____ Dunn
   & Martha       - TCS]
   MARY MULLINS (c13 S b.KY)
   6 March, 1898, Jackson, by W. H. Templeton;
   wits. Alex Carmack & Enoch Longsworth
   (M-J; 1900-J m-1; 1910 m-13; TCS)
JOHN P. (c21 S b.KY)
   LARINDA (nee _____) JOHNSON (c31 3rd b.KY)
   [m1 _____ Gabbard; m2 _____ Johnson]
   1878/9          (1880, 1st Done ch-6 mo.,
   Gabbard s-s 13, Johnson s-ch-7 & 3;
   NL 1900Sx)
JOHN H. (c22 S b.KY)  [s/o Wm. Dunn & Eliz.
   Stevens - TCS]
   AMAZON YOUNG (c15 S b.KY)  [d/o Reese Young
   & Nelly Collins - TCS; 1880]
   1893          (1900 m-7; 1910 m-16; widr.
   John 1920; TCS)
WILLIAM (c19 b.Mad.)
   ELIZABETH STEVENS (c16 b.Jack.)  [d/o Mary
   Stevens & unknown - 1880]
   1867/8          (1880 WM w/them; NL 1870/J;
   1900; NL M-J)

## DURBIN/DURBAN
AMBROSE (R.Ows. 22 S b.Est.)    [Joseph Durbin
   & Margaret       - 1850]
   MARY J. FRAILEY (R.Ows. 15 S b.Est.)
   27 July, 1858, Ows.
AMBROSE (c29 b.KY)  [s/o John Durbin & W1
   Nancy Wagers - 1850; P/M-E 1814]
   DELITHA _____ (c30 b.KY) P/KY
   1863/4        (1870-L-3; 1880-1900-L; H-sgl
   w/sis 1860; W/as Delitha & Talitha)
AMOS (c23 S b.KY)     [s/o Francis Durbin
   & Margaret Ashcraft - REM; 1860]
   NANCY J. REYNOLDS (c18 S b.KY)  [d/o Joseph
   C. Reynolds & Esther Morris - TCS; 1870]
   1874/5        (1900-1910; TCS; NL 1880/E/L;
   NL M-J)
ELIHU (c27 b.KY)  [c1841-1885/8; s/o John
   Durbin & W2 Juda Mann - 1880-L; 1860]
   SARAH A. NEWTON (c15 b.Ows.)  [1853-1940;
   d/o Allen Newton & Rachel Isaacs - 1860;
   ob-W BE-8/29/40 as Howard]
   c1868        (1870-L-1; 1880-L; M-L ch-
   1911; ob-W)   [SARAH m2 11/29/88 John S.
   Howard - M-L; ob-W; 1900-L wid. Sarah
   Durbin, Durbin & Howard ch.]
FRANCIS "FRANK" (c19 b.Est.)  [poss. s/o John
   Durbin & W1 Nancy Wagers -M-E 1814; 1830-E]
   MARGARET ASHCRAFT (c16 b.Est.)  [d/o Amos
   Ashcraft - M-cons.]
   23 Nov., 1848, Estill  (M-E; 1850-E;
   1860-10; B-O ch.)
JAMES H. (c20's b.KY)  [s/o Joseph Durbin
   & Margaret       - 1850]
   DIADEMA DUNAWAY (c20's b.KY)  [d/o Ben
   Dunaway & Spicy Chamberlain - TCS; 1850]
   1850's        (both sgl 1850; W-NL w/F
   1860; NL 1860/B/E/E/J; 1870-L no ch.;
   NL M-J)
JOHN, JR. (c19 b.Est.)  [poss. s/o Joseph
   Durbin & Margaret       - 1830-E]
   [SARAH] SALLY ANN HALL (c15 b.Rockc.)  [d/o
   James Hall - M-cons.]
   29 Feb., 1844, Estill; sur. Joseph Durbin
   (M-E; 1850; B-O ch.; 1860-E HPH; D-L ch.)
   [JOHN m2 2/13/74 Lee, Malinda Hamilton -
   M-L; 1880-L]
(Durbin cont.)

**DURBIN (cont.)**
JOSEPH (R.Ows. 22 S b.Est.)   [s/o Joseph
    Durbin & Margaret        - 1850; TCS]
    ZERILDA DURBIN (R.Ows. 19 S b.Est.)   [d/o
    John Durbin & Wl Nancy Wagers - 1850]
    25 Nov, 1852 Estill, by Geo. Williams   (M-E
    mf; TCS; B-O ch.; 1860; 1870-1880-L; ob-ch.
    BE-7/24/52 has M/as Shrillida Wagers)
JOSEPH (c70 2nd b.KY)   [d. 1870's Lee]
    [ml Margaret _____ - 1850]
    CYNTHIA (nee WYATT) CARTER (c44 2nd b.KY)
    [wid/o James M. Carter]
    c1869, Ows. @ Est/Ows. Co. line, by Squire
    George Stubblefield Williams   (ML in Est.;
    md. in Ows. - Rom.Lee; 1870-L, Carter ch.
    12, 8, & 5; TR; wid. Cynthia 1880-1900-
    1910-L)
WILLIAM (R.Missouri c25 b.KY)   [s/o Francis
    Durbin & Margaret Ashcraft - 1860]
    EMMA REYNOLDS (R.Ows. c25 S b.KY)   [d/o
    Joseph Reynolds & Esther Morris - 1870]
    Dec., 1879 Ows., @ res. of Joseph Reynolds,
    by Rev. S. K. Ramey   (ME-2/6/80, no date,
    but other mgs. in this column took place
    Dec., 1879 per M-L; 1880 no ch.)
**DURHAM**
JOSEPH (c21 b.KY)   [s/o Isaac Durham & Eliz.
    - 1850]
    MARTHA ANN WITHE (c22 b.KY)
    c1849        (1850 w/HP; B-O ch. W-NL;
    B-J ch-1858; 1860-J-10; wid. Martha 1880-J)
**DUVALL**
WILLIAM (c19 b.NC)
    MARTHA _____ (c17 b.VA)
    c1865        (1870-L-4; NL M-J)


**EAGER/AGER**
JOHN WESLEY (c26 b.VA)   [s/o John Eager
    & Levina Alford - REM]
    MARY TINCHER (c26 b.KY)   [d/o Wm. Tincher
    & Margaret Smallwood - 1850]
    9 Jan., 1853, Ows.   (REM P-CW; 1860-5;
    B-O ch.)

(Eager cont.)

**EAGER (cont.)**

PRICE (R.Lee 25 S tmstr b.Lee) [1870-1945;
  s/o Wm. T. Eager & Laura Treadway - 1880;
  ob-H&S BE-7/18/45-5/20/43]
    LINDA FLANNERY (20 S b.Jack.) [1875-1950;
    d/o Silas Flanery & Deborah    - 1880-J;
    ob-W BE-3/23/50]
    18 Dec., 1895, Lee, @ Silas Flannery's
    wits: David Evans & Martha Flannery
    (REM; M-L; 1900-J; 1910-L; R.Beattyv. 1943-
    1945)

ROBERT T. (28 b.Ows.) [s/o Wm. T. Eager
  & Laura Treadway - B-O]
    ELLEN ROBERTS (19 b.KY)
    20 Aug., 1902, Lee @ T. T. Roberts, by R.A.
    Irvine; wits. Mrs. T. T. Roberts, W. B.
    Chester & M. F. Clayton  (M-L; REM)

WILLIAM THOMAS (c25 S crp b.Lee,VA) [s/o John
  Eager & Levina Alford - REM]
    LAURA MARSH TREADWAY (19 S b.Ows.) [d/o
    Wm. W. Treadway & Margaret Bowman; ob-ch.]
    2 March, 1865, Ows. (REM P-CW; 1870-L-2;
    B-O ch; 1890; 1900-L m-35; ME-10/26/05 Mrs.
    Laura Eager of Beattyv. visiting dau, Mrs.
    Mollie Flanery of Levi; 1910-L m1-45; ob-
    ch. BE-5/20/43-1/18/45)

**EARLEY**

FRANK[LIN] (28 S b.KY [s/b b.Lee,VA]) P/KY
    JULIA F. STAMPER (17 S b.KY [b.Lau.]) P/KY
    29 Jan., 1874, Laurel (M-Lau. mf; 1880-5;
    B-O ch. W/as Julie Standiford; NL 1900Sx)

**EATON**

JAMES L. (R.Whit. 19 S b.Whit.) P/Whit.
    EVALINE McFARLAND (R.Whit. 21 S b.Whit.)
    P/Whit.
    20 Jan., 1874, Whitley @ James Eaton's
    (were to be md. @ Wash. McFarland's), by
    John B. Lewis, MG; wits. A. C. McFarland &
    C. C. Gray  (M-Whit.; B-Lau. ch-9/75 W/as
    Evaline CRAWFORD b.Ows.; 1880-Whit.)

**EDENS**

WILLIAM (R.Br. 21 S b.Wilkes Co., NC)
    ANN BAILY (R.Br. 18 S b.Harlan)
    30 Dec., 1853, Ows., by Wm. Barret

## EDWARDS

[ADDISON NIRAM] ANDY (c24 S b.KY) [s/o James
   Edwards & Mary Austin - 1870; 1880; TCS]
   RHODA BOWMAN (c15 S b.KY) [1885-1969 Clay;
   d/o David Bowman & Martha Bowman - DC]
   2 Feb, 1900, <u>Clay</u>    (M-C MT; 1900 m-0;
   1910-C m-10; 1920-C; TCS; H/as Niram 1870,
   Addison N. 1880, Andy all other recs.)
ALLEN DAVID (c32 S b.KY) [1851-1895; s/o
   Jackson Edwards & Nancy Combs - TS-TCS;
   w/Uncle Andrew J. Combs 1880, mistakenly
   listed as BiL]
   VASHTIE NEWNAM (c17 b.KY) [1867-1942; d/o
   Richard Morris Newnam & Lucinda Steele -
   TS-TCS; 1880]
   16 Oct., 1884      (LNG SE TCS; M-L ch-1918;
   1900-1/86 wid. Vashti; 1910 Vashtie CORNETT
   m2-8 w/EDWARDS ch.; ob-ch. BE-4/21/49)
   [VASHTI m2 Patrick Cornett - LNG SE]
ANDY - see ADDISON NIRAM
D. B. (___ b.Boonev.)
   MANDA COLLINS (___ b.Boonev.)
   pre-1908      (B-O ch-4/1908 dau. Minerva;
   NL 1910-1920Sx; didn't find P/1880-1900;
   NL M-J)
DANIEL B. (c18 S b.KY) [s/o Wm. Edwards
   & Sally Bailey - 1880]
   MALVERY CAUDILL (c17 S b.KY) [d/o Lewis
   Caudill & Fannie Barrett - KCM]
   1891/2      (1910; NL 1900; KCM; BC 1915)
DAVID - see ALLEN DAVID
GEORGE T. (c16 S b.KY) [1873-1956; s/o
   James Edwards & Mary Austin - 1880; TCS;
   ob-H&S OCN-10/4/56-8/18/55]
   MARTHA ELLEN BURCH (c15 S b.KY) [1874-
   1958; d/o Newton Burch & W1 Mary Hamilton
   - TS-TCS; ob-W&S&s-M BE-12/18/58, OCN-
   5/22/58-1/18/52]
   1889/90      (1900-1910; TCS; BC 1911-
   1913-1917; R.Taft 1955-1958)


(Edwards cont.)



212

**EDWARDS (cont.)**

GEORGE (R.Lee mcht 25 2nd b.Ows.) P/NC & TN or
    VA [m1 _____] [poss. s/o Wm.
    Edwards & Sarah Bailey - 1870-1880]
    CAROLINE [nee MOORE] STAPLETON (R.Br. 25 S
    b.Ows.) P/uk [Div/f Jeff. Stapleton - LNG]
    [c1865-1938; d/o Nicholas Moore & Lucinda
    McQueen - LNG; TS-TCS]
    23 Sept, 1892 Lee @ James Taylor's, by Wm.
    P. Page, Min.; wits. Nancy Taylor & Eliza
    Johnson    (M-L 4:165; LNG; wid. Caroline
    1900-1910 w/P, no surname; M-O ch-1931)
HUGH (c20 S b.KY) [1888-1962; s/o Robt.
    Edwards & Martha Sizemore - TCS; TS-WE]
    SUSAN "SUDA" SINGLETON (c20 S b.KY) [1889-
    1955; ob-W OCN-12/29/55]
    1908/9        (1910; EDS; BC 1914-1916-1918)
JAMES (R.Clay 25 S b.Yancey Co., NC) [1834-
    1896?; s/o George Edwards & Margaret Allen
    - TCS; TS-WE]
    MARY ["POLLY"] AUSTIN (R.Clay 18 S b.Yancey
    Co., NC) [c1840-1908; d/o Robert Austin -
    TS-WE]
    22 Sept., 1859, Clay    (M-C & mf; 1860-C;
    1870-1880-1890; wid. Polly 1900)
JOHN WESLEY (c17 S b.Ows.) [1872-1955; s/o
    James Edwards & Mary Austin - 1880; TCS;
    ob-H OCN-8/18/55]
    NANCY E. BURCH (c16 S b.KY) [1873-1943; d/o
    Jasper Burch & Rhoda E Morris - TCS; TS-WE]
    1889        (1900-6/90; 1910; TCS)
JOHN H. (c20 b.Ows.) [s/o Robert Edwards
    & Martha Sizemore - 1880]
    RHODA BURCH (c19 b.Clay)
    1894/5        (1900; B-J 1904-1909/10; BC
    1915-J; 1920Sx-J)
ROBERT (R.Ows. 20 S b.Clay) P/NC [1855-1929;
    s/o Geo. Edwards & Margaret Allen - TCS;
    TS-WE]
    MARTHA SIZEMORE (R.Ows. 19 S b.Ows) P/--
    [1856-1929; d/o Smith Sizemore & Matilda
    Hudson - B-O; TS-WE]
    26 Nov., 1874, Ows., @ Smith Sizemore's
    [R.Owsley 1880-1900-1910]


(Edwards cont.)

**EDWARDS (cont.)**
WILLIAM (c21 b.Lee,VA)  [s/o wid. Martha
    Edwards - 1850-H HC]
    SARAH ANN BAILEY (c17 b.Harl.)
    c1853, prob. Breathitt  (1860-B; B-B ch;
    1870-1880; B-O ch)
WILLIAM H. (c19 S b.KY)  [1868-1927; s/o James
    Edwards & Mary Austin - 1880; TCS; TS-WE]
    WINNY BISHOP (c17 S b.KY)
    29 Sept., 1887, Clay  (M-C; TCS; 1900 m-12;
    1910 m-20; 1920)

**ELKINS**
GREEN B. (R.Ows. 19 b.Ows.) P/VA-Ows.  [s/o
    Moses Elkins & W1       - 1900]
    EMMA PACE (R.Ows. 18 S b.Ows.) P/Ows.
    [d/o Richmond Pace & Talitha Fox, who remd.
    Simeon Hobbs & Nicholas Collins - 2nd M-O;
    listed as A-d/o Elias Palmer 1900-L]
    4 Feb., 1904, Ows.  [R.Owsley 1910, 1920
    WM w/her; M-L son M/Emma Elkins Caudill]
    [EMMA ELKINS (R.Ows. 43 wid. b.Ows.) m2
    10/4/30 Ows., H. J. Caudill (57 widr.);
    EMMA CAUDILL (55 wid.) m3 9/12/41 Ows.,
    Henry Green (65 widr.) - M-O]  [ob-ch. BE-
    2/23/67 M/Emma Pace Elkins of Beattyv.]
MOSES (c24 S b.VA)
    _____ (___ b.___)
    c1884       (1900-6/85 H-remd-13; NL M-J)
MOSES (c27 2nd b.VA)  [m1 _____ above]
    MARY ANN WILSON (c37 S b.KY)  [d/o Alford
    Wilson & Deborah Moore - TCS]
    1886/7      (1900 m-13; 1910 m-20 =
    1889/90; 1920; TCS)

**ENGLE**
B[ENJAMIN] F[RANKLIN] (R.Ows. 26 S b.Knox)
    ELIZABETH HAYES (R.Knox 23 S b.Knox)
    19 Sept., 1854, Ows.  [R.Jackson Co. 1860-
    1870-1880; widr. Ben 1900]

## ESTEP/ESTEPP
JAMES (R.John.; 23 S b.John.) P/VA
    AMANDA McCARTY (R.John.; 20 S b.John.) P/VA
    [1856-1945; d/o Lydia McCarty - TS-TCS & M-
    cons.]
    11 May, 1876 <u>Johnson Co.</u> @ Lydia McCarty's,
    by Robert Calboren; wits. Frank & John
    Senters (M-John.; 1900-23 N#L, McCarty BiL
    w/them; 1910 m-34; NL 1880Sx; ob-ch. OCN-
    2/6/53)
JOHN R. (c24 b.John) [prob. s/o James Estep
    & Amanda McCarty]
    FRANCES COMBS (c16 b.Ows.) [d/o Jasper
    Combs & Susan C. Hensley - TCS]
    c1903       (B-O ch-10/04; H-sgl. 1900;
    TCS)
ROBERT (R.Per. 23 S b.Per.) P --
    LINDA JOHNSON (R.Per. 16 S b.Lau) P/Per.
    30 April, 1874, Ows., @ Wm. Barker's
SAMPSON (R.Br. 20 S b. Harlan)
    SARAH BUSH (R.Br. 20 S b.Clay)
    16 Oct., 1855, Ows. (a/L M-C mf as <u>9/13</u>/55,
    H-R.Ows. 18 b.Clay; Sally R.Clay 18 b.Per.)
## ESTES/ESTIS/EASTES
ANCIL D. "DOC" (c21 minr b.Est.) [s/o Robert
    Estes & Sarah Graves]
    CELIA NEWMAN (c21 b.Clk) [d/o John Newnam
    & Leah Scholl - REM]
    c1848       (1850-1; B-O ch.; 1860;
    1870-1880-L)
[ASBERRY] GREENBERRY (R.Ows. 22 S b.Est)
    [1836-1918 Est.; s/o Robt. Estes & Sarah
    Graves - FJR]
    MARGARITE [JANE] MAYES (R.Ows. 20 S b.Clay)
    [d/o Wm. Mays & Mary Gross - 1850]
    28 Dec., 1856, Ows. [R.Owsley 1860; Lee
    1870-1880-1900-1910]
ASBERRY (c22 b.Est.) [1843-1941 Lee; s/o
    Chas. Estes & Sarah Hatton - 1860; P-CW]
    [ISABELLE] IBBY NEWTON (c18 b.Est.) [1836-
    1914; d/o Allen B. Newton & Rachel Isaacs -
    P-CW]
    23 March, 1865, <u>Estill</u>, @ Alan Newton's,
    by Elijah Gabbart, Bapt. Min. (M-E; P-CW;
    N-E-10/81; B-L ch.; CC; 1870-1880-1900-L;
    ob-ch. OCN-4/12/56)
(Estes cont.)

**ESTES (cont.)**

BERRY - see ROBERT BERRY & ASBERRY

BRAZIL (c48 2nd b.Est.)  [m1 _____]
  [1820-1910 Grainger Co., TN; s/o Charles
  Estes & Sarah Hatton - 1860; FJR]
  AMANDA BURNS (c25 b.TN)
  c1869, <u>Tate Springs, TN</u>   (1870, no ch.;
  ECP; FJR)  [BRAZIL m3 c1876, Grainger Co.,
  TN, Sally Steadman; BRAZIL m4 _____]
CHARLES (27 b.KY)  [s/o Charles Estes & Sarah
  Hatton - 1860]
  DIANAH NEWTON (22; b.KY)  [d/o Allen Newton
  & Rachel Isaacs - 1860]
  9 Dec., 1864, <u>Estill</u>, @ Allen Newton's,
  by Enoch Wakefield  (M-E; N-E-9/92, CC;
  1870-L; 1900-E)
FIELDING (c22 b.KY)  [1824-1909; s/o Chas.
  Estes & Sarah Hatton - M-cons.; FJR; BE-
  11/19/09]
  EMILY JANE ESTES (c16 b.KY)
  9 Sept., 1846 (bond) <u>Estill</u>   (M-E; FJR;
  1850; 1860-E; 1870-1880-1900-L)
GREENBERRY - see ASBERRY
HIRAM (24 b.Ows.) [s/b b.Est.]  [1836-1933;
  s/o Chas. Estes & Sarah Hatton - 1860]
  NANCY NEWTON (c19 b.Ows.) [s/b b.Est.]
  [d/o Allen B. Newton & Rachel Isaacs]
  19 Feb., 1861, Ows.  (N-E-1/82; B-L ch.;
  N-EM ch.; FJR)
JESSE (c22 c.minr b.KY)
  REBECCA J. _____ (c21 b.VA)
  c1859/60        (1860, 1 ch. age 10, prob.
  a rel.; 1870-L-9)
JOHN (c28 b.KY)  [s/o Ancil D. Estes & Celia
  Newman - 1860]
  MILLIE NEWMAN (c11 b.KY)  [d/o Wm.
  Crittendon Newman - REM]
  1883        (1900 m-17; 1910-L m1-26; REM)
MASON ["MACE"] (R.Lee 21 S b.Ows) P/-- Clk
  [s/o Ancel Estes & Celia Newman - 1860]
  [MARSHA] MARTHA NEWNAM (R.Ows. 19 S b.Ows)
  P/Clk --    [d/o Henry Harrison Newnam
  & Susan Mays - REM]
  6 Feb., 1874, Ows., @ Byson Burns' [R.Lee
  1870-1880; W/as Marshal, Marshoney, Martha,
  Mashal, & Marsha in recs.; Marsha - REM]
(Estes cont.)

**ESTES (cont.)**
MOSES (R.Proctor 21 S b.Ows.[Est.]) [s/o
   Robt. Estes & Sarah Graves]
   RACHEL FRALEY (R.Ows. 22 S b.Ows.[Est.])
   29 June, 1853, Ows., by G. S. Williams
   [R.Owsley 1854-5; Breathitt 1859-60]
PLEASANT (c22 b.Orphy) [s/o John Estes
   & Millie          - 1900]
   MAGGIE GRIFFEE (c14 b.Orphy) [d/o Elijah
   Griffee & Nancy Stamper]
   c1906          (1910-3, wid. Maggie w/WF;
   B-O ch-1908; 1920 w/WF)
ROBERT BERRY (c25 b.KY)
   MARGARET (nee MAYS) DAMRELL (c25 2nd b.
   Ows.) [m1 _____ Damrell] [1864-1938
   Idamae; d/o Giles Mays & Polly Isaacs -
   1880; ob-W OCC-12/16/38 ]
   1890          (ob-W; 1900-L-10/90, s-s
   Damrell; M-L ch-1919; H/as Robt. B. &
   Berry)
**EVANS**
_____ (___ b.___)
   JULIA ROSE (c14-34 b.Ows.) [1866-1956; d/o
   Ezekiel Rose & Cynthia Jett - ob-W&S OCN-
   7/26/56-4/11/52; 1880; DC]
   1880-1900          (ob-W; NL 1900/B/J/L;
   W-NL w/P 1900; R.Booneville 1952; NL M-J)
ALFRED (R.Ows. 22 S b.Claiborne Co., TN)
   REBECCA JANE BAKER (R.Ows. 15 S b.Giles
   Co., VA)
   12 July, 1854 Ows.   [R.Jackson Co. 1860]
FREDERIC (R.Ows. 21 S b.KY) P/TN-KY   [s/o
   John Evans & Rebecca Nantz - 1870]
   ELANDER STRONG (R.Ows. 21 S b.KY) P/KY
   [d/o John Strong & Marinda Wilson - TCS]
   8 Sept., 1878, Ows.   [R.Owsley 1880]
GEORGE (c19 b.Ows.) [1878-1944 Trimble; s/o
   Wm. Evans & Mary Jane Newman - DC; 1880-L;
   ob-HS OCC-6/24/38]
   MYRA JUDD (c16 b.Ows.) [c1881-1951; d/o
   Thomas Judd & Annie Thomas - ob-W OCN-
   6/29/51 sis/o Arch & Ed Judd; P/1880]
   1896/7          (1900; R.Louisville 1938;
   wid. R.Bedford, Trimble Co., 1951; ob-ch.
   3Fks-2/19/97)

(Evans cont.)

**EVANS (cont.)**

GREEN (c46 b.Per.) [1857-1944 Lee; s/o _____
Evans & Polly Farler - ob-H BE-5/11/44; DC]
MOLLIE MAYS (___ b.___)
Jan., 1903, Ows. [DIV. pre-1910] (H-sgl.
w/M 1900; ME-3/20/03 Green Evans, who md.
Mollie Mays @ the Jan. term of Cir.Ct. to
avoid criminal prosecution for seduction
was arrested last week, sued by wf, charged
w/abandonment; H-Div. w/M 1910)
[GREEN m2 1920-37 Julia Pendergrass - ob-WS
Patsy Farley; not md. 1920, but Julia next
door. Julia & Green had at least one son
together before they md. - DC son Grover
Cleveland Pendergrass; ob-H; M-L 1925]
[HARRISON] HARRY (R.Ows. 19 S b.Ows) P/Per-Lee
[1888-1950; s/o Joe Evans & W2 Kansas Cole
- 1900; ob-H OCN-2/24/50]
HATTIE PRICE (R.Ows. 21 S b.Ows) P/Ows.
[d/o Elias Price & Martha B.    - 1910]
25 Aug., 1909, Ows.   [R.Owsley 1910 W-md.,
H-NL]     [HARRISON m2 Millie Spicer of Old
Landing, Lee Co.; went to GA c1940/2 & d.
there - ob-H]
HARVEY (c19 S b.Ows.) [1859-19__; s/o Huram
Evans & Nancy Stamper - TCS; ACB; ob-HS BE-
11/4/43; F/P-CW]
CATHERINE "KATE" ROWLAND (c21 S b.Ows.)
[d/o Martin Rowland & Martha Ann Evans -
TCS   (Kate d. 1912-20)]
1879          (1880; 1900 m-20; 1910 m-30;
R.Major 1912; widr. Harvey 1920; R.Br.
1943)
HENDERSON (R.Ows. 18 S b.Ows.)   [s/o Jesse
Evans & Edie Smith - TCS]
LYDIA MOORE (R.Ows. 22 S b.Ows.)   [d/o
Elias Moore, Sr. & Celia Reynolds - TCS]
5 July, 1853, Ows., by J. Ward   [R.Owsley
1860]    [LYDIA m2 8/18/1890 Jack., Alex
McDaniel - TCS]
HENRY SIMPSON (c27 b.KY)   [s/o Jesse Evans
& Edie Smith - TCS]
NANCY PLUMMER (c27 b.KY)
c1864          [DIVORCED 1871-80]   (1870-5;
1880-15, Nancy div.)

(Evans cont.)

**EVANS (cont.)**

HIRAM (c21 b.KY) [s/o Jesse Evans & Edie
   Smith]
   POLLY STAMPER (c22 b.KY) [poss. d/o Wm.
   Stamper & W1 Resina Kidwell]
   c1844          (1850-5; B-O ch.; 1860-1870-
   1880)
HIRAM (c19 b.KY) [1847-19__; s/o Huram Evans
   & Nancy Stamper - 1850-1860; REM; F/P-CW]
   MARY ANN STEELE (c19 b.KY) [d/o Andrew J.
   Steele & Nancy King - TCS]
   1866/7      [appar. DIV. 1900-10] (1870-2;
   TCS; 1880-11; B-O ch.; 1900; M-L ch. 1908;
   Mary "div." 1910-L; ob-ch. BE-6/10/48)
HURAM (c22 S b.Clay) [1825-1906; s/o Jesse
   Evans & Edie Smith - TS-TCS]
   NANCY STAMPER (c17 S b.KY/OH) P/NC-OH
   [1829-1904; poss. d/o Wm. Stamper & W1
   Resina Kidwell - TS-TCS; MMH]
   18 Jan., 1846, Ows., by L. J. Robison
   (P-CW; 1850-2; B-O ch.; 1860-1870-1880;
   1900 m-52; M-L ch-1909; ob-ch. BE-2/14/52)
JACK - see JOHN & JACKSON
JACKSON "JACK" (c21 S b.Ows.) [1869-1943 Ows.;
   s/o Huram Evans & Nancy Stamper - 1880;
   ACB; ob-H BE-11/4/43]
   MINERVA (nee McPHERSON) ENGLISH (c24 2nd b.
   Lee,VA) [m1 ____ English - BBG; TCS] [1867-
   1934; d/o Stephen McPherson & Rebecca J.
   Pennington - TCS; ACB; ob-W OCC-12/28/34]
   10 May, 1890      (obits; 1900-1910-1920;
   BBG; ACB) [JACK (R.Levi 67) m2 4/2/36 Ows,
   Julia Ann Rose (R.Boonev. 66) - TCS; ACS;
   OCC-4/12/36; R.Pleasant Grove 1943 - ob-H]
JAMES (R.Ows. 25 S b.Claiborne Co., TN) [s/o
   Wm. Evans & Mary Stone - TCS]
   MARGARITE ALLEN (R.Ows. 24 S b.Clay) [d/o
   Job Allen, raised by a Phillips - TCS]
   16 Dec., 1855, Ows. [R.Owsley 1860-1870-
   1880-1900-1910]


(Evans cont.)

**EVANS (cont.)**

JAMES C. (R.Ows. 26 S b.Ows.) P/VA  [s/o Sam
  Evans & Mary Matilda Russell - 1880]
  LOU EMILY PEARSON (R.Ows. 19 S b.Ows) P/Ows
  [d/o Sam Pearson & Rachel Strong - 1900;
  ob-WS OCC-5/3/40, OCN-1/29/54-11/21/57]
  9 March, 1904, Ows.    [R.Owsley 1910-1920;
  Ham.,OH 1954-1957]
JESSE (R.Ows. 23 S b.Clay)  [1833-1903 Lee;
  s/o Jesse Evans, Sr. & Edy Smith - 1850;
  TCS; D-L & ME-9/18/03]
  ELIZABETH J. GORDAN (R.Ows 18 S b.Smith Co,
  VA)   [1837-1917; d/o Kennedy Gordan & Mary
  - REM; TS-TCS]
  8 Nov., 1855, Ows.   [R.Owsley 1860; Lee
  1870-1880-1900; wid. Elizabeth 1910-L]
JESSE (R.Ows. 22 S b.KY) P/KY   [s/o Hiram
  Evans & Polly Stamper - B-O; ACB]
  ELIZABETH [LIZZIE] HALL (R.Lee 18 S b.KY)
  P/VA-KY  [d/o Harvey Hall & Mary Bowman -
  TCS]
  19 June, 1877 <u>Lee</u>  (M-L; 1880; 1900-L m-23;
  ob-ch. OCN-3/24/55, BE-6/25/59; FH ch-1960)
JOB A. (c23 S b.KY)   [s/o James Evans
  & Margaret Allen - 1880; TCS]
  REBECCA J. STRONG (c16 S b.KY)  [d/o John
  Strong & Marinda Wilson - 1880]
  1884            (1900 m-16, 7/4 ch. ch. 11
  Ark., 9, 6 & 1 KY; 1910-L m1-25 both; TCS)
JOHN (R.So.Fk. 25 S b.So. Fork)  [1829-1876;
  s/o Jesse Evans & Edie Smith - TS-TCS]
  MARY [ANN] SMITH (R.So.Fk. 17 S b.Harl.)
  [1836-1914; d/o Robert Smith & Polly     -
  TS-TCS; 1850]
  21 Dec., 1853, Ows., by Judge A. Pennington
  [R.Owsley 1860-1870; wid. Mary/Polly 1880-
  1890-1900-1910]
JOHN "JACK" (c26 b.TN)  [s/o Wm. Evans & Mary
  Stone - REM]
  REBECCA NANTZ (c14 b.Harl.)  [d/o Frederick
  Nantz & Sarah Chappell - 1850-C]
  c1853          (1860-J-6; B-J ch-1859;
  1870-1880; REM; JO)


(Evans cont.)

## EVANS (cont.)

JOHN (c30 b.KY)  [1856-1929; s/o Jesse Evans
   & Elizabeth Gordon - TS-TCS; 1880-L]
   ARDENIA ROBINSON (c19 b.KY)  [1867-1912;
   d/o Squire Robinson & Emaline Tincher -
   TS-TCS; 1870]
   1886/7        (1900-L; TCS)
JOHN H[ARVEY] (R.Beattyv, formerly of Pleasant
   Grove, Ows.; c29 S Dr. b.KY)  [1873-1951;
   s/o Joseph Evans & Mary Hamilton - ob-H
   OCN-2/2/51; 1880]
   JULIA McGUIRE (22 S b.KY)  [d/o Arch
   McGuire & W3 Catherine Davis - 1880-L]
   Nov/Dec., 1902, <u>Lexington</u> (Thurs.)  (ME-
   12/12/02; H-sgl. 1900-L; 1910-L m1-6,
   Bo. w/H. L. Wheeler)
JOSEPH "JOE" (c20 b.Per.)  [s/o John Evans &
   Polly Farley - 1880; TCS; ob-H OCC-7/3/36]
   MARY HAMILTON (___ b.VA)
   c1873       (1880-6 H-md, W-NL, Farlor
   aunt w/him; ob-ch. John H.)  [H-remd.]
[JOSEPH "JOE"] "JOSIAH" (R.Ows. 31 2nd b.Per.)
   [m1 Mary Hamilton above]
   KANSAS L[EE] COLE (16 S b.Ows.) [1866-1947;
   d/o Speed Cole & America Snodgrass - 1880-L
   ob-W BE-4/3/47]
   4 Jan., 1883, <u>Lee</u>  (M-L; 1900-15, m-24, but
   this is W1; 1910 m-26 1920; ob-H & his son;
   ob-ch BE-7/22/48; FH-ch.1970; H/as Joseph
   in all obits)
LEWIS (c23 b.KY)  [1873-1937; s/o Wm. Evans &
   Mary J. Newman - 1880-L; ob-H OCC-6/18/37]
   MARY CATHERINE "KATE" SMITH (c18 b.KY)
   [1878-1960; d/o Breckenridge Smith & Eunice
   Jones - 1880-L; ob-H; ob-W BE-2/11/60]
   5 May, 1897      (ob-H; 1900-L m-3;
   NL M-L)
ROBERT S. (20 b.KY)  [s/o John Evans & Mary
   Smith - 1880]
   LOUISA BLOUNT (19 b.KY)  [d/o Wm. Blount
   & Nancy Botner - 1870]
   27 March, 1883, <u>Lee</u>  (M-L; 1900)

(Evans cont.)

**EVANS (cont.)**

ROBERT E. (c30 S b.Sturgeon) [s/o James
    Evans & Margaret Allen - 1880]
    MARZENA COUCH (c25 S b.Les.)
    1896        (1900 m-3, w/HP; 1910 m-14;
    B-O ch.; 1920)
ROBERT - see SAMUEL ROBERT
SAMUEL D. (c24 S b.Claib., TN) [s/o Wm. Evans
    & Mary Stone - REM]
    MARY MATILDA RUSSELL (c18 S b.Gray., VA)
    [d/o Sam Russell & Susan    - TCS]
    1866        (1870-3; 1880-13; 1900 m-32;
    1910 m-43; REM)
SAMUEL ROBERT (c27 S b.KY) [s/o Samuel D.
    Evans & Mary Matilda Russell - 1880-1900
    as Samuel R.]
    CATHERINE [PEARSON?] (c24 S b.KY) [poss.
    d/o George Pearson & Mary Dunigan - 1880-
    1900; NL DC/W]
    1900/1        (1910; 1920-J, H/as
    Robert S.; NL M-J)
SIMPSON (c23 b.KY)
    NANCY _____ (c22 b.KY)
    1859/60        (1860-MWY)
SYLVESTER (c19 b.KY) [s/o Jesse Evans & Edie
    Smith - TCS]
    LUCINDA MOORE (c21 b.KY) [d/o Elias Moore
    & Celia Reynolds - TCS; REM]
    14 March, 1850        (TCS; 1850-MWY;
    B-O ch; 1860-1870-1880)
W[ALTER] C. (R.Ows. 24 S b.Ows.) P/Ows-Harl.
    [1871-1931; s/o John Evans & Mary Ann Smith
    - 1880]
    SILADETH LUTES (R.Lee 20 S b.Lee) P/--
    [d/o Wm. Lutes & Serilda Thompson - 1880-L]
    6 March, 1896, Lee @ Wm. Lutes, by J. M.
    Roberts; wits. Wm. Lutes & wf   (M-L 4:605;
    1900-L) [WALTER m2 1916 Lee, Nellie Rasner]
WALTER (R.Lee 24 S b.Lee) P/Ows. [s/o Wm.
    Evans & Mary Jane Newman - 1900-L]
    ALPHA BRANDENBURG (R.Ows. 18 S b.Ows.) P/
    Ows. [1890-1972; d/o Jesse BBurg. & Nancy
    Metcalfe - 1900; ob-W BE-3/30/72]
    13 Nov., 1908, Ows. [R.Jackson 1910 m1-1;
    Richmond 1938; Mad. 1954; widr. Walter
    R.Richmond 1972 - ob-HS OCC-6/24/38-6/4/54]
(Evans cont.)

**EVANS (cont.)**
WILLIAM HENRY (c21 b.Ows.) [1851-1939; s/o
   Sylvester Evans & Lucinda Moore - TS-TCS]
   LUCY ANN REYNOLDS (c21 b.Ows.) [d/o Wesley
   Reynolds & Nancy Moore - TCS]
   c1872      (1880-7; B-O ch.)
WM. (R.Lee 52 2nd b.Ows.) P/Ows. [widr/o
   Mary Jane Newman - 1900-L; TCS]
   [SARAH] MINERVA [nee VENABLE] NEWMAN (R.Ows
   51 3rd b.Ows) P/Ows.   [wid/o Dan Newman -
   TCS; 1880; wid.1900] [d/o Leroy Venable,
   Rachel McQueen - TCS; ob-W OCC-9/18/36]
   2 Jan., 1904, Ows. (ML 12/03 Ows. - per
   ME-1/15/04)   [R.Owsley 1910-1920]
**EVE**
[WM. "WILLIE"] N. J. (R.Lee 24 S mcht b.Knox)
   P/Lee [1884-1965 IN; s/o James Eve & Sarah
   Thomas - ob-H BE-3/4/65; 1900-L; P/M-L]
   MAMIE GABBARD (R.Ows. 19 S b.Ows) P/Ows.
   [d/o John Gabbard & Mollie Herndon - 1900]
   17 Feb., 1909, Ows. [R.Owsley 1910]
   [WILLIE m2 c1915, Kate Evans (d/o Wm. Evans
   & Mary Jane Newman) - TCS; 1920; WILLIE
   m3 Roxie Rowland - ob-H; H-d. Austin, IN]
WILLIAM (R.Proctor 21 S b.Knox)
   SARAH [FRANCES] SMITH (R.Proctor 17 S b.
   Ows.) [d/o John Smith & Lucy Mize - TCS]
   [26] July, 1859, Ows. [26th - REM; TCS]
   [R.Owsley 1860; Lee 1870-1880]
**EVERSOLE**
ABRAHAM, JR. (c25 b.KY) [1837-1872 NE; s/o
   Abraham Eversole, Sr. & Sarah Williams -
   JEW; 1860; TCS]
   ADELIA BEGLEY (c16 b.KY) [d/o John Begley
   & W1 Judy Davidson - 1850-P; 1860]
   8 June, 1862, Ows. (JEW; NL 1870)
   [ADELLA m2 8/27/80 Milton McIntosh - JEW]
ALFRED (c26 S b.KY) [1871-1918; s/o George
   Eversole & Rebecca J. Moore - JEW; 1880]
   MARTHA BARKER (R.Cow Cr. c22 S b.KY) [1875-
   1927; d/o Martin Barker & Malvina Begley -
   JEW; TCS; 1920; PWB; MAR]
   July, 1896, Trav. Rest, @ bride's father's
   (ME-7/24/1896; 1900 m-3; 1910 m-13; TCS;
   wid. Martha 1920 WM w/her)

(Eversole cont.)

**EVERSOLE (cont.)**

CHARLES (c29 S asst.cash. b.Cow Cr.) [1877-
  1967 Est. hosp.; s/o George Eversole
  & Rebecca Moore - JEW; ob-H&S BE-2/9/67;
  OCN-3/31/55-5/8/58]
  IDA McCOLLUM (c27 S b.Conkling) [1879-1938;
  d/o Dan McCollum, Emily Brewer -1880-1900]
  1905/6        (1910-1920; B-O ch.; R.Irvine,
  Est. Co. 1955-1966 - ob-HS BE-3/31/66)
DUTCH - see WOOLERY
GEORGE (23 S b.Per.) [1844-1920 Cow Cr.; s/o
  Wm. Eversole & Barbara Chappel - JEW;
  P-CW/DC]
  REBECCA JANE MOORE (c19 S b.KY) [1849-1931
  Cow Cr.; d/o James Moore & Cynthia Warford
  a/k/a Walton - JEW; P-CW/DC]
  2 Jan., 1868 Ows., Cow Cr. @ James R.
  Moore's, by James W. Baker, JP; wits.
  Joseph Moore & Andrew Baker    (P-CW; 1870-
  1880-1890-1900-1910-1920; wid. Rebecca Jane
  R.Ows. 1927; TCS; ob-ch. OCN-5/8/58)
HARRISON C. (c20 S Law. b.KY) (s/o John C.
  Eversole & Nancy Duff - JEW]
  EMILY MORGAN (c16 S b.KY) P/KY
  1871/2        (1880-6; NL 1900; 1910 m-38;
  JEW)
HIRAM (c17 b.KY) [s/o John Eversole & Betsy
  Judd - TCS]
  MARY "POLLY" CAMPBELL (c17 b.KY)
  c1845         (1850-4; 1860-P; 1870-W;
  1880-L; JEW; NL M-P)
JAMES (c26 b.KY)    [s/o Abraham Eversole
  & Sarah Williams - TCS]
  NANCY ABNER (c21 b.KY)  [poss. d/o Wm.
  Abner & Jane Baker - JC; 1850]
  1859        [DIVORCED 6/29/81 Ows. - N-C]
  (1860-MWY; 1870; 1880, ch. w/Nancy, James
  liv. in Adultery w/Siranda Lewis; N-C-6/95
  JE, P-CW 1st ch. b. 3/60)
JAMES (c49 2nd b.KY) [div/f Nancy Abner above;
  liv. w/Siranda Lewis 1880]
  ELIZABETH ROBINSON (___ b.___)
  4 Oct., 1883, Clay  (M-C; TCS)


(Eversole cont.)

JEFFERSON (c25 2nd b.Ows.)  [m1 8/15/96 Knox,
   Bestina Jackson - Div. by 1898 - N-C-6/95
   JEW]  [s/o James Eversole & Sarah Barrett/
   Hornsby - mgs. N-C-6/95 JEW]
   EMILY BARGER (c17 b.KY)
   24 March, 1899, Leslie  (N-C-6/95 JEW;
   1900; 1910-B; 1920-Butler Co., OH)
   [JEFFERSON m2 9/8/23 Br., Elizabeth (Tharp)
   Evans - N-C-6/95 JEW]
JOHN C. "CASH" (28 S  b.KY)  [1859-1935; s/o
   Wm. Eversole & Barbara Chappel - JEW; TCS]
   AERY TURNER (c14 S b.KY)  [1872-1950; d/o
   Elliott Turner & Sarah Helton - TCS; ob-W
   OCN-4/28/50]
   20 Oct., 1887          (JEW; 1900-1910-1920;
   TCS; BBG)
JOHN (c25 b.KY) [1863-1902; s/o James EVERSOLE
   & Elizabeth ABNER - JC; 1880 w/uncle Robert
   Abner; TS-TCS]
   NANCY ELIZABETH (nee DEATON) WOODS (c20
   2nd b.KY)  [m1 Magoffin Woods - DC-ch.]
   [1868-1950; d/o Wm. Deaton & Susan Combs -
   1880; ob-W OCN-12/15/50 as McKee]
   1888/9          (1900; GD Sarah Woods w/Wm.
   & Susan Deaton 1900, WM Susan 4/2 ch.;
   1900 Nancy & FREEMAN ch. by H1; thus Nancy
   m1 Woods; 1910 GD Sarah Woods still w/Wm. &
   Susan Deaton + GS Willie Eversole, s/o John
   & Nancy - 1900; DC-ch. by H1)
   [NANCY m3 to George McKee - TCS; 1910-Flem.
   m2-2, Eversole s-ch.; 1920 wid. Nancy
   McKee w/son Nathan Eversole; ob-W]
JOHN C. (R.Boonev, formerly Per.; c24 S b.KY)
   [c1865-1950 WA - ob-H OCN-4/28/50-5/5/50]
   ALICE HOGG (R.Boonev; c18 S b.Ows.) [c1870-
   1941 Lex.; d/o Stephen P. Hogg & Sally
   Combs - 1880; ob-W OCC-9/12/41]
   June/July, 1888          (ME-7/13/88 as "md.
   last week"; 1900Sx-Swain Co., NC; ME-
   2/22/01, they returned from NC & settled in
   Boonv.; 1910 WF w/them; R.Boonev., then
   Haz., then Yakima, WA, widr. John in Zilla,
   WA 1950 - ob-H)

(Eversole cont.)

**EVERSOLE (cont.)**

LOGAN (c23 b.KY)  [1854-1941; s/o Wm. Eversole
& Barbara Chappel - JEW; 1860; ob-H OCC-
3/7/41]
MARGARET MOORE (c26 b.KY)  [1849-1904; d/o
Edward Moore & Minerva Evans - REM; TS-TCS]
1876/7       (1880-2; 1900; TCS; NL 1910;
ob-H; ob-ch. BS-5/2/85)   [LOGAN m2 after
1905 Mahala (nee Helton) Sandlin (1861-
1949; d/o Carr Helton & Susie Turner; wid/o
Lewis Sandlin) - TS-TCS; 1920 W-NL]
NATHAN (R.Ows. 20 S b.Ows.) P/Ows.  [1889-1975
Lau.; s/o John Eversole & Nancy Elizabeth
Deaton - 1900 N-C-6/95 JEW]
SARA JANE [nee WOODS] COMBS (R.Ows. 21 2nd
b.Ows.) P/Ows. --   [wid/o _____ Combs]
[1888-1965; d/o Jefferson Woods & Eliz.
Combs - TS-TCS; JC]
10 Nov., 1908, Ows.    [R.Owsley 1910 w/WP;
1920 HM, Nancy E. McKee, w/them; R.Conkling
1965 - ob-HS BE-4/22/65]
ROBERT (c25 mcht b.Per.)  [s/o Wm. Eversole
& Jennie Combs - D-O; 1870]
MARY COMBS (c16 b.Per.)  [1857-1939; d/o
Elijah Combs & Nancy Begley - RW; DC]
c1874       (1880-5 SiL Amanda Moore & sis.
Laura <u>Moore</u>; D-O 1878 Wm.; DC dau. 1959)
[MARY m2 Robert S. Wilson - TCS]
[NOTE:  B-O Wilson ch. list W/as Mary
<u>Sexton</u>; N-C, TCS, & DC have Mary <u>Combs</u>]
ROBT. LEE (c22 S b.Ows.) [1871-1947; s/o James
Eversole & Eliz. Abner - DC; JEW; TCS]
CHINA "CHINEY" TAYLOR (c24 S b.KY)  [1869-
1932; d/o Pendleton Taylor & Minerva
Jennings - 1880; TS-TCS]
1893/4       (1900-1910-1920; JEW)
[ROBT. m2 5/20/1938 Lee, Martha Herald
Wilson - N-C-6/95 JEW]
WILLIAM (29 2nd b.KY)  [widr/o Eliza Bowling -
JEW]  [1814-1897 - JEW]
BARBARA A. CHAPPELL (20 b.KY)  [1823-1899;
d/o Geo. Chappell & Eliza Pace - JEW; TCS]
20 Feb., 1844, <u>Clay</u>  (M-C; 1850-P; 1860-
1870-1880; Cow Cr. 1886 & 1897 - art. OCN-
5/23/52 & ME-12/24/97)

(Eversole cont.)

## EVERSOLE (cont.)

WILLIAM B. (R.Per. 21 S b.Per.) [s/o Joseph
    Eversole & Sally Bowling - TCS]
    [MARY] POLLY LEWIS (R.Clay 21 S b.Clay)
    [d/o John Lewis & Jenny McIntosh - TCS]
    25 Dec., 1856, Clay (a/L md. Perry)
    (M-C; M-P; 1860-1; 1870)
WILLIAM (c19 b.KY) [s/o James Eversole
    & Nancy Abner - JEW]
    NANNIE J. WILDER (c15 b.KY) [d/o Wm. H.
    Harrison Wilder & Levina Miracle - TCS]
    1885/6           (1900; TCS)
    [WILLIAM m2 c1920 Emma Couch - TCS]
WOOLERY "DUTCH" (27 S b.KY) [1862-1949; s/o
    Wm. Eversole & Barbara Chappel - JEW; 1880]
    MARY WILSON (c24 S b.KY) [1865-1918; d/o
    Wm. Wilson & Rebecca Peters - 1880 TS-TCS]
    4 July, 1889        (JEW; 1900 m-11; 1910
    m-20; TCS; BBG; widr. Woolery 1920)


## FARLEY
see FARLOR
## FARLOR/FARLER/FARLEY

ADISON (R.Ows. 47 S b.Per.) P/Ows. [1862-1933;
    s/o Faris Farley & Nancy Combs - TS-TCS;
    2nd M-O]
    [SUSAN] ANNIE [nee FLANERY] CALLIHAN (R.Ows
    30 [s/b c42] 2nd b.Ows.) P/Ows. [m1 _____
    Callihan] [d/o Joel P. Flanery & Susan
    Bailey - TCS]
    15 Jan., 1909, Ows. [R.Owsley 1910, W/as
    Susan A., Callihan s-s] [ADDISON (R.Ows.
    70 widr. b.Per.) m2 11/20/31, Sarah (nee
    Jewell) Jackson (70 wid. b.Ows.) - M-O]
JAMES S. (c19 b.KY) [1873-1927; s/o John
    Farlor & Mary Howell - 1880-L; ob-W]
    MARY BELL VENABLE (c17 b.Ows.) [1875-1950
    Lee; d/o Leroy Venable & Permelia Isaacs -
    1880; ob-W BE-9/14/50]
    1892/3            (ob-W; 1900-1910-L;
    R.Hlbg., Lee c1913-1950)

(Farlor cont.)

**FARLOR/FARLEY (cont.)**
JOHN (c25 b.Per.)  [s/o Alex Farler & Roxanne
   Mullins - 1860-P; P/M-P]
   MARY S. HOWELL (c19 b.IN)  [d/o Guias
   Howell & Mary Tincher - 1860]
   1862/3        (1870-P-5; 1880-1900-L; B-L
   ch.; NL M-P)
SHERIDAN (c30 2nd b.VA)  [m1 _____]
   [1849-1944 Lee - ob-H BE-6/29/44]
   MARTHA "PATSY" ANN (nee PENDERGRASS) NEWNAM
   (c32 3rd b.Lee,VA) [m1 John Malayer - ob-ch
   BE-6/24/43; m2 John Newnam - 1880 D-O 1878]
   [1847-1937; d/o Corda Pendergrass & Minerva
   Thompson - ob-W OCC-7/2/37]
   1880      (1880-MWY, s-s MALAYER 14 & s-ch.
   NEWNAM 5 & 3; 1900 m-19; 1910 m-30; 1920
   w/dau. & SiL BBurg.; REM; ob-W; ob-H Newnam
   s-ch.)
TALTON C. (c20 S b.Per.)  [1859-1941 Lee; s/o
   Farris Farley & Nancy Combs - ob-H OCC-
   12/5/41; TS-TCS]
   MARTHA BRANSON (c19 S b.Let.)  [1860-1939;
   d/o James Walkerson Branson & Sally Howard
   - DC; JMC; TCS; ob-W BE-3/2/39]
   22 May, 1879 Perry @ Sampson Brashear's, by
   John H. Hall; sur. Augusta G. Combs; wits.
   Sampson & Robt.Brashear (M-P D:210; 1880-P;
   1900 m-20; ME-3/18/04 sold farm & moved to
   Beattyv.; 1910-L; 1920; ob-ch.OCN-1/10/57)
WILLIAM (c21 b.KY)
   JANE BALL (c19 b.KY)
   19 Sept., 1878 (ML) Harlan; bm. groom &
   John C. Farler  (M-H; 1880-H-1; 1900 m-20)
**FARMER**
   _____ (___ b.___)
   REBECCA CATH. "KATIE" BRANDENBURG (c14-24
   b.KY)  [d/o Jackson Brandenburg & Martha
   Callahan - 1880]
   1890-1900        (TCS; DB; W-NL w/P 1900;
   NL M-J)
CHARLES E. (c16 S b.KY)  [s/o Cornelius
   Farmer & Louisa Brandenburg - TCS]
   MYRTLE _____ (c16 S b.KY)
   1900/1        (1910-1920)

(Farmer cont.)

## FARMER (cont.)

CORNELIUS ["NEAL"] (R.Ows. 18 S b.TN) [s/o
   John Farmer & W1 Icy Frost - TCS; F & s-M
   1860-J]
   LURINDA [LOUISA] BRANDENBURGH (R.Ows. 15 S
   b.Ows.) [s/o Joseph Brandenburg & Nancy
   Snowden - w/wid. mom 1850]
   10 Aug., 1855, Ows. [R.Owsley 1860; Lee
   1870 W/as Louisa; Jackson Co. 1880-1900]
CORNELIUS NELSON "NEAL" (c21 b.Ows.) [s/o
   James Farmer & Matilda Brandenburg - TCS]
   LETITIA TACKETT (c21 b.Lee,VA) [d/o
   Oliver Tackett & Nancy Hall - 1870; TCS]
   c1873 (1880-6; TCS; 1900-J; M-L ch-
   1907 has M/Letitia <u>Tagget</u> b.TN)
DENTON (R.Ows. 21 S b.Claib., TN) [s/o John
   Farmer & W1 Icy Frost -TCS; F & s-M 1860-J]
   SYLVANIA HERD (R.Ows. 18 S b.Clay) [d/o
   Wm. Herd & Rebecca Hudson - TCS]
   15 June, 1854, Ows. [R.Owsley 1860; W-md.,
   H-NL 1870-1880; Jackson 1900 as Sylvania
   Farmer m-3]
GENERAL [M.] (c21 b.KY) [s/o Denton Farmer
   & Sylvania Herd - 1880; TCS]
   MARGARET TINCHER (c22 b.KY) [d/o James
   Tincher & Nancy - TCS]
   14 May, 1886, <u>Jackson</u>, by Cornelious Moore;
   wits. Ambrose Finley Moore & James Moore;
   sur. John R. King, Jr. (M-J 1:151; TCS;
   1900-J)
GEORGE (R.Lee 23 S b.Lee) P/Ows.
   MARGARET BRANDENBURGH (R.Ows. 19 S b.Ows)
   P/Ows. [1888-1973; d/o Jackson BBurg.
   & Martha Callahan - 1900; ob-W&S BE-
   9/20/73, OCN-6/26/58]
   19 March, 1908, Ows. [R.Beattyville 1958-
   1963 ob-WS BE-12/5/63; wid. Margaret d.
   Beattyv. 1973]
JAMES FRANKLIN (c22 S b.TN) [s/o Wm. Farmer
   & Eliz. Frost - DB; TCS]
   MATILDA BRANDENBURG (c16 b.KY) [c1833-1874;
   d/o Joseph "Squint" Brandenburg & Nancy
   Snowden - D-L; TCS]
   1849 (DB; 1850-5 mo; 1860; 1870-L;
   D-L wf) [H-remd.]

(Farmer cont.)

**FARMER (cont.)**
JAMES F[RANKLIN] (R.Lee 53 2nd b.Hawk,TN) P/--
[widr/o Matilda Brandenburg above]
    LUCY JANE [nee SMITH] BRANDENBURG (R.Lee 26
    2nd b.Ows.) P/-- [m1 Arch BBurg. - TCS;
    M-L 3/25/73] [d/o Richard Smith & Margaret
    Evans - TCS]
    18 Feb., 1877, <u>Lee</u> @ James Brandenburgh's,
    by Harvey P. Hall, MG; wits. James BBurg. &
    Thomas Lynch (M-L; 1880-L)
JAMES FRANKLIN (c64 3rd b.TN) [m2 Lucy Jane
    Brandenburg above]
    SARAH ELIZABETH LYNCH (c25 b.KY) [d/o Wm.
    R. Lynch & Cath. Nancy Salyers]
    1886/7 (ECP; 1900-L; NL M-L)
JOHN (R.Ows. 48 widr b.Harl.) [widr/o Icy
    Frost - TCS] [s/o Stephen Farmer & Nancy
    Russell - TCS]
    MARY [nee HERD] CALLAHAN (R.Ows. 30 wid
    b.Clay) [wid/o Ezekiel Callahan - 1850]
    [d/o Wm. Herd & Rebecca Hudson - TCS]
    28 Jan., 1856, Ows. [R.Jack. 1860-1870,
    Callahan s-d.; 1880] [Mary nee HERD - B-J
    ch-1859]
NEAL - see CORNELIUS
NELSON - see CORNELIUS NELSON
**FARRIS/PHARIS**
LEANDER (c23 b.VA) P/NC
    VELARA _____ (c21 b.KY) P/KY
    c1879 (1880-5/80 as PHARIS; NL M-J)
S. J. (c29 b.KY)
    SALLIE L. McEWAN (c27 b.KY)
    1 Dec., 1885, <u>Fayette</u>, @ Broadway Church,
    by John S. Shouse; wits. Bruce Trimble &
    Eugene Smith (M-Fay.; ME-10/15/86, Miss
    Maggie McEwan of Lex. visiting sis, Mrs. S.
    J. Faris; ME-12/10/86 birth of baby girl to
    W/o S. J. Faris of Boonev.; this child
    listed 1900Sx-Clk-12/86)
**FAULKNER**
see FORTNER

## FELTY/FELTA

DANIEL WEBSTER (21 b.Sexton Cr., Clay) [1858-1941 Jack.; s/o James Felty & W1 Margaret Ailsey Linville - MJC; 1860-C]
AMANDA PARALEE McCOLLUM (15 b.Clay) [1865-1941 Jack.; d/o Richard "Sun" McCOLLUM & Catherine COLE (who later md. John Bishop) - MJC]
11 March, 1880        (MJC/Felty Bible; 1880 no ch.; 1900-C m-20)

JAMES (c78 2nd b.VA) [m1 c1844, Margaret Ailsey Linville (1827-1899 Clay) - MJC; 1850-Wash,VA GLM; 1860-1870-C] [1823-1902 Clay; poss. s/o George Felty & Polly Held - GLM; MJC]
ELIZABETH [nee PACE] NAPIER (77 2nd b.KY) [m1 Patrick R. Napier (1813-1899 Clay) - MJC; 1850-P; 1860-1870] [1824-19__; nee PACE - MJC; TCS]
9 Nov., 1901, Clay  (M-C; MJC; ME-11/29/01, Island City news, W/as P. R. Napier)

JAMES (c18 S b.Clay)  [1888-1958 El Paso, TX; s/o Daniel Felty & Amanda McCollum - MJC]
MOLLIE [JANE nee BOWMAN] SPARKS (c26 2nd b. Ows.)  [m1 5/9/90 Israel Sparks - TCS; MJC; M-C]  [1875-1948 Kenton Co.; d/o David Gray Bowman & Martha Ann Bowman - TCS; MJC]
9 June 1905, Clay @ David Bowman's house, Sexton Cr.   [DIVORCED ca 1919 - MJC]
(MJC; M-C MT; TCS; 1910 m-5, Sparks s-ch. w/them)   [JAMES m2 Alice _____ - MJC]

RILEY [TACKETT] (24 S b.Lau.) P/Clay-Ows. [1879-19__; s/o John Felty & Mary Singleton - MJC; GS/o James J. Felty - 1900-C]
RHODA ALLEN (___ b.___)
17 April, 1903, Clay Co.  (M-C file 31; H-2nd M-O; H-sgl. w/GF 1900-C; NL 1910Sx)

RILEY [TACKETT] (R.Lau. 30 2nd b.Lau.) P/Clay-Ows.  [m1 Rhoda Allen above - M-C]
SARAH BOTNER (R.Ows. 26 S b.Ows) P/Harl-Br. [d/o Ransom Botner & Armina Ketchum - 1900]
4 June, 1910, Ows.  [R.Laurel 1911-12; OH c1915; Lau. 1916 ; OH 1919; Laurel 1920Sx]
[NOTE:  BC 1911-1912 Lau. list W/Sarah Botner & BC 1916 Lau. lists W/Sarah Ross, some people believe Riley m2 Sarah Botner & m3 Sarah Ross - MJC]

**FERRINGTON**
WILLIAM (c29 b.SC)
>PEGGY [MARGARET LEE?] (c17 b.KY)
>c1845        (1850-4; appar. WM&S w/them;
>NL 1870Inx; a Wm. Ferrington & wf Margaret
>Lee had ch: Eliz. 11/57 & Jackson 4/59 -
>B-Lau. ch; NL 1860-Lau/HPH; NL 1880Sx]

**FIELDS**
BROWNLOW (c21 S b.KY)  [s/o Elhannon Fields
>& Rebecca Burns - 1900]
>ALLIE MAE FLANERY (c14 S b.KY)
>1907/8        (1910; BC-1916; 1920Sx-Lau.)

CRIT - see J. J. CRITTENDON
ELHANON (c23 b.KY)  [s/o Hiram Fields & Mary
>Young - TCS; B-P sib]
>REBECCA BURNS (c18 b.KY)   [d/o John Burns
>& Louisa Combs - TCS]
>1880        (1900-2/81, m-21; 1880, both
>sgl, same household; M-L ch-1923)

GEORGE (c25 b.TN) P/TN
>NANCY _____ (c21 b.TN) P/TN
>1879/80        (1880-MWY; NL M-J)

HARRISON - see WM. HARRISON
HENDERSON (c20 b.KY)  [s/o James Fields
>& Susan Sizemore - 1880]
>ELIZA JANE PETERS (c20 b.KY)  [d/o James
>Elisha Peters & Louisa Young - 1880]
>1896/7        (1900 w/WP)

HIRAM (c23 b.Per.)
>MARY "POLLY" YOUNG (c20 b.Per.)
>c1852        (1860-P; NL M-P; 1870-80-L;
>B-L ch-1878 b.Ows.)

J. J. CRITTENDON "CRIT" (c21 S b.Conkling/
>Clay) [1884-1959 Boonev.; s/o John Fields
>& Eliz. Spence - TS-TCS; 1900; ob-H BE-
>6/25/59]
>CHARITY HOWARD (c28 S b.Harl.) P/Harl-Clay
>[1877-1916 Ows.; d/o Anglin Howard & Mary
>Ann Allen - DC]
>1905/6        (1910; B-O ch.; M-O ch.)
>[CRIT m2 Pearl Gabbard (1893-1972), d/o
>John L. Gabbard & Jaley Reynolds - MT; TCS;
>1920; ob-H; ob-W2 BE-5/25/72]


(Fields cont.)

FIELDS (cont.)

JAMES W. (R.Ows. 22 S b.NC)
   MARTHA ENELINE (R.Ows. 18 S b.MO)
   21 Nov., 1855, Ows.
JAMES (c23 b.KY)  [a/k/a JAMES TOLER]
   [s/o _____ TOLER & Chaney FIELDS]
   SUSAN SIZEMORE (c18 b.KY)  [d/o Henderson
   Sizemore & Minerva Combs - TCS]
   Oct., 1869        (1870; 1880-10; 1900; TCS;
   M-L ch-1908)
JESSE (R.Earnestv. 23 S b.Ows.) P/Clay-Ows.
   [s/o James Fields & Susan Sizemore - mg.]
   LUCY FARMER (R.Earnestv. 15 S b.Lee) P/Lee-
   Est. [d/o J. C. Farmer & Perdilla Lynch
   - mg.]
   24 Dec., 1908, Lee @ bride's res., by A. J.
   Marcum; wits. Whitley Mays & Columbus Gray
   (M-L; 1910)
JOHN (c17 b.Per.)  [a/k/a TOLER]  [s/o _____
   TOLER & Chaney FIELDS]
   ELIZABETH THOMAS (c21 b.Ows.)  [1844-1914;
   d/o Jesse Thomas & Martha Combs - TS-TCS]
   c1868        (1870-L-11/69; B-O ch.;
   widr. John 1880)  [H-remd.]
JOHN (c23 2nd b.Per.)  [widr/o Elizabeth
   Thomas above]
   ELIZABETH (nee SPENCE) HARVEY (c27 3rd
   b.VA)  [m1 Robt. Howard; m2 1877 Prior
   Harvey - TCS; 2nd M-O; 1880 wid. Eliz.
   Harvey] [1844-1914; d/o Jno. Spence & Mary
   Holmes - DC; 1870]
   late 1880        (erroneously listed 1900 as
   m-27; 1910 m-30; 1880 widr. John Fields &
   wid. Eliz. Harvey, her son Benton, age 2;
   1900, Benton w/M & s-F; Benton next to
   half-bro. Crit Fields 1910)
MATTHAN A. (c21 b.Sextons Cr.) P/TN-KY
   MARTHA ADDISON (c19 b.Ender)  [d/o Elias
   Addison & Eliz. Clementine Carmack - PWB]
   c1902        (TCS; B-O ch-1908 Eliz.; PWB;
   NL 1910Sx; BC 1913-1915-J & 1918; 1920;
   M-O ch-1930; M-L ch-1938; NL M-J)


(Fields cont.)


233

**FIELDS (cont.)**

SILAS (c24 1st/2nd b.TN)
  ELIZABETH [nee BINGHAM] BURCH (c21 2nd
  b.KY) [m1 _____ Burch - NL M-J] [poss.
  d/o Robt. Bingham & Ailsy    - 1870-J]
  8 March, 1875, <u>Jackson</u>, @ R. Bingham's,
  by Robt. Bingham; wits. J. G. & Mary Ann
  Bingham  (M-J 1:47; BC son Mason-1888;
  1880-C-4; TCS) [H-remd.]
SILAS (c47 3rd b.TN) [m1/2 Elizabeth Bingham
  above]
  ARMITTA ["MINTIE"] ASHER [PETERS] (c31 2nd
  b.KY) [m1 _____ Peters - TCS]
  3 March, 1895, <u>Clay</u>  (M-C MT; 1900-2/79,
  m-5, s-s PETERS b. 3/90; W/as Armilda &
  Mintie) [H-remd.]
SILAS (c58 4th b.TN)  [widr/o Armitta Asher
  above]
  OLLIE [nee JONES] STIVERS (c30 2nd b.TN)
  [wid/o _____ Stivers]
  24 March, 1906, <u>Clay</u>  (M-C MT; 1910 m-4
  H-4th, W-2nd, Stivers s-ch.; B-O ch.;
  1920; BC 1912 W/as Jones)
STEPHEN G. (c19 b.Taft) [s/o Joseph Fields
  & Mary Hignite]
  DORA McQUEEN (c17 b.Trav.Rest)
  1896/7      (1900, w/HM & s-F, John
  Gabbard; B-C sib. as b. Ows. B-O ch.)
WM. HARRISON (c27 b.Logan Co., VA) [s/o
  Chaney FIELDS & unknown - 1850-P]
  JOSEPHINE ROBINSON (c23 b.Clay)
  c1869      (1870-L, no ch.; B-L ch.)
WILLIAM (c27 B'smth b. TN) P/KY-TN
  MARY DAYBERRY (c17 b. NC) P/NC
  c1876     (1880-2; B-O ch-8/77) [H-remd.]
WILLIAM (c40 2nd B'smth b.TN) [widr/o Mary
  Dayberry above]
  MARTHA (nee BAKER) BROCK (c23 2nd b.KY)
  [wid/o _____ Brock] [d/o Sarah Jane
  Baker - HTB]
  1889/90     (1900-8/89 H-ch., s-ch. Brock
  10/85 & 1/89, next ch. b.11/90; 1910 m-20)

**FIKE**
LEOPOLD (c28 b.Germany)   [d. 1850-4]
    CYNTHIA LUCINDA WARD (c19 b.Clay)
    c1843            (1850-6, ch. Henry 6, Ann 3,
    Jos. 9 mo.; 1860 wid. Cynthia, ch. Henry
    16, Rebecca 12, Jos. 10, Elihu 5, Cely 3;
    B-O ch-6/54 Elihu s/o Cynthia, H-NL, so
    appar. Leopold d.; 1870-L wid. Cynthia;
    1880-L lists Rebecca 31 as d/o Cintha, not
    s-d; N-E-1/95 Ralph & Maryanna Barnes; W/as
    Cynthia in all rec. except 1850 as Lucinda)
**FLANERY/FLANNERY**
_____ (___ b.KY)   [d. pre-1900]
    SUSAN _____ (c18 b.KY)
    c1883/4           (wid. Susan 1900-12/84;
    NL M-J)
CHESTER (R.Jack. 21 S b.Jack.) P/Jack.
    EMILY WILSON (R.Ows. 17 S b.Ows.) P/Ows.
    [d/o Theo. Wilson & Martha Rowlett - 1910]
    6 Oct., 1910, Ows.
DAVID (c21 S b.Ows.)   [1868-1940; s/o John M.
    Flanery & Mary Coulton - 1880; ob-H OCC-
    5/17/40]
    EMMA MAHAFFEY (c19 S b.KY)   [d/o Martin
    Mahaffey & Mary Bowles - 1880]
    26 March, 1890, Ows.   (ob-H; 1900 m-10;
    1910-L m1-20, WM w/them; TCS; ob-ch. OCN-
    1/27/55)
DOW - see LORENZO DOW
ED (c26 b.Ows.)   [s/o Thomas Flanery & Lucy
    Searcy - 1900]
    [VIRGINIA] JENNIE MAINOUS (c20 S b.KY)
    [d/o John Tyler Mainous & Ellen Botner -
    1900 w/F & s-M]
    Dec., 1904, Ows. (on a Tues.) (ME-12/29/04;
    NL 1910Sx)
ELCANNAH (c18 b.VA)   [c1841-1865; s/o James
    Flanery & Polly Minter - TR; BS-7/6/78 his
    CW record]
    AMANDA MAINOUS (c19 b.VA)   [d/o Lazarus
    Mainous & Rebecca Flanery - TR; TS-8/17/78]
    26 Jan., 1860, Ows., by WF, Lazarus L.
    Mainous, JP   (TR; 1860-J; BS-8/17/78 art.;
    DC ch-1939)   [AMANDA m2 1869, David Spivy]

(Flanery cont.)

**FLANERY (cont.)**

ENOCH (c24 b.Let.)   [s/o Thomas Flanery
& Nancy Lock - 1870]
NANCY CREECH (c20 b.Harl.) [d/o John L.
Creech & Nancy Minerva Farmer - 1870]
1872/3        (1880-6; B-O ch.; 1900-J m-27;
NL M-J)

FINLEY F. (c22 b.Ows.) [1874-1950 MS; s/o John
Flanery & Mary Coulton - ob-H BE-12/7/50]
FANNIE BREEDING (c19 b.KY)  [1876-1937; d/o
John Breeding & Perlina Hogg - 1880; ME;
ob-W&F BE-5/27/37-11/7/35]
1895/6          (ME-6/27/02, F. F. Flanery of
Beattyv. visiting his FiL John Breeding of
Boonev.; 1900-L m-4; R.Beattyv.; Indianola,
MS 1935-37; then Jackson, MS)

HAMPTON (R.Jack. 24 S b.VA [Scott Co.]) [1838-
1937; s/o James Flanery & Polly Minter -
TR; TS-TCS]
NANCY A[NN] BRANDENBURG (R.Ows. 16 S b.Est)
[1842-1923; d/o James BBurg. & Nancy Thomas
- TS-TCS]
14 Dec., 1858, Ows.    [R.Jackson Co. 1860;
Owsley 1870-1880-1900-1910-1920]

HARVEY - see JAMES HARVEY

JACOB (c23 b.VA)   [s/o Thomas Flanery & Nancy
Lock - 1860]
MARTHA J. _____ (c18 b.VA) P/VA
1860/1          (1870-3; 1880; 1900-J m-39;
NL M-J)

JAMES HARVEY (R.Ows. c20 b.KY)  [1860-1898;
s/o Hampton Flanery & Nancy BBurg. - TS-
TCS; 1880; ob-ch. BE-3/31/66]
RACHAEL EVALINE ["DOLLIE"] VENABLE (c17 b.
Lee,VA)  [1863-1951; d/o Leroy Venable &
Rachel McQueen - 1880 TCS; ob-W OCN-1/4/52]
29 June, 1880, Ows.  (ob-W; OCN-3/16/51 as
6/29/63, but BE-3/29/51 amends that they
were actually md. 6/29/80, per their dau.;
both sgl. 1880; shortly after mg., they
moved to MO; then back to KY; wid. Dolly E.
1900-L; ob-ch. BE-3/31/66]    [DOLLY m2 a
Williams - ob-W]


(Flanery cont.)

236

## FLANERY (cont.)

JAMES H. (c22 S b.Ows.) [s/o John M. Flanery
  & Mary Coulton - 1880; ob-HB BE-12/7/50]
  LOUISA "LULA" BOTNER (c21 S b.Ows.) [1869-
  1940; d/o Elias Botner Jr. & Mary Clark -
  1880; ob-W OCC-2/9/40]
  1891/2        (1900 Botner BiL w/them; 1910;
  B-O ch.; R.Richmond 1950)
JAMES R. (c33 S b.KY) [1862-1930; s/o Joel
  Flanery & Susan Bailey - TS-TCS]
  MATTIE BRANDENBURG (c21 S b.KY)  [d/o Wm.
  Brandenburg & Josephine Glass]
  1895        (1900 m-4; 1910 m-15; TCS; 1920)
JOEL P. (c23 b.VA) [1828-1907; s/o Thomas
  Flanery & Eliz. Parsons - TS-TCS; 1850-
  Lee,VA]
  SUSAN BAILEY (c23 b.KY) [1829-1895; d/o
  Andrew Jackson Bailey & Anna Kelly -1850-H]
  c1852        (appar. Lee Co, VA c1853-55;
  then returned to KY c1856-7; B-O ch-1858;
  1860-7; 1870-1880; widr. Joel 1900; REM;
  NL M-H)
JOHN N. (c19 b.Scott Co., VA) [s/o James
  Flannary & Mary        - TCS]
  MARY M. COULTON (c21 b.KY) [d/o Wm.
  Coulton & Martha Collier - TCS]
  1867        (1870-J-2; 1880-12; TCS; ME-
  4/5/95, John of Sturg. sold farm & moved to
  Rogersville, Mad.; 1900-M m-32; NL M-H/J]
LEONARD (c25 S b.KY) [1871-c1931 KY; s/o
  Robt. M. Flanery & Matilda Botner - 1880-J]
  CORA M. TREADWAY (c22 S b.KY) [1874-1937
  TX; d/o Winfield Scott Treadway & Martha
  Lou Flanery - ob-W OCC-7/2/37]
  1896        (1900 m-3; 1910-L m1-14; BC
  1911-Law; ob-W says moved to Independence,
  KY; then TX; NL M-J]
LORENZO DOW (c21 S b.KY) [s/o Michael Flanery
  & Emaline Gabbard - TCS]
  BARBARA E. EDWARDS (c21 S b.KY) [d/o _____
  Edwards & Alpha Peters - TCS]
  1907/8        (1910, w/HM&S; TCS; BBG;
  1920 WM w/them; BC 1911-E, 1913-1918-1920;
  ob-ch. BS-3/12/81)

(Flanery cont.)

**FLANERY (cont.)**

MARCUS BELL (R.Ows. c28 b.KY) [s/o Wm. Flanery
& W1 Susan Spivey - 1880]
MOLLIE T. EAGER (R.Ows. 22 b.Ows.) [1868-
1942 Mad.; d/o Wm. T. Eager & Laura M.
Treadway - 1880; ob-W BE-5/20/43]
29 Jan., 1890, Ows. (REM; ME-5/3/95, Mrs.
W. T. Eager, Beattyv, visiting dau. Mrs. M.
"P" Flanery of Buck Cr.; 1900; ME-10/26/05
Mrs. Laura Eager of Beattyv. visiting dau.
Mrs. Mollie Flanery of Levi, Ows.; NL M-L;
moved to Mad. 1910, then Berea - ob-W)

MICHAEL "MIKE" (c24 b.KY) [s/o Thomas Flanery
& Nancy Lock - 1880]
EMALINE "EMMA" GABBARD (c22 b.KY) [d/o
Abraham Gabbard & Mary Burris - 1880]
1882/3 (1900; TCS; wid. Emeline
w/son Abr. 1910)

MORGAN MINTER (c22 S b.Ows.) [1868-1949 Ows.;
s/o Wm. Flanery & W2 Margaret Williams -
1880; ob-H&S OCN-12/2/49, B-Ent-6/20/35]
MARY L. HALE (c18 S b.Ows.) [d/o James
Curtis Hale & Susan Razer - 1880]
1891 (1900 m-9; 1910 m-18; B-O ch.;
1920; R.Levi 1935; ob-ch. BS-8/29/85)

PRESTON - see ROBERT PRESTON & WM. PRESTON

ROBERT MARTIN (c26 S b.VA) [s/o James Flanery
& Mary Minter - 1880-J; 1860-J; TR]
MATILDA _____ (c19 b.TN)
c1865 (1870-J-3, wf Matilda; 1880-J
H & W3, ch. 14, 12, 10, 8 & 4 mo.; NL M-J)
[H-remd.]

ROBERT MARTIN (c34 2nd b.VA) [m1 Matilda _____
above]
MATILDA A. BOTNER (c18 b.KY) [c1855-1874;
d/o Elias Botner & Matilda     - 1870;
ME-3/20/74]
c1873 (ME-3/20/74, Mrs. Matilda A.
Flanery W/o Martin Flanery & d/o Rev.
Elias & Matilda Botner d. 2/19/74; 1880-J
H & W3, ch. 14, 12, 10, 8 & 4 mo.; NL M-J)
[H-remd.]

(Flanery cont.)

## FLANERY (cont.)

R[OBERT] M[ARTIN] (c40 3rd b.VA)  [m2 Matilda
   A. Botner above - ME-3/20/74]
   MARGARET E[LLEN] MINTER (c27 b.VA)  [d/o
   Wm. M. Minter & Rebecca J.      - 1870]
   18 Jan, 1879, Jackson Co., by Elias Moore;
   wits. Wm. H. Scott & Wm. E. Minter [her
   bro.]; sur. W. H. Scott   (M-J 1:80; TCS;
   1880-J, HF w/them; 1900-J m-21; 1910-J
   H/m2-31, W/m1-31)
ROBERT PRESTON (c18 b.KY)  [1865-1899; s/o
   Elcannah Flanery & Amanda Mainous - TS-TCS;
   ME-1/20/99]
   SARAH ROWLETT (c18 S b.KY)  [1865-1942; d/o
   Jesse B. Rowlett & Eliza Jane Jones - 1880;
   TS-TCS]
   c1883/4        (TCS; art. OCN-8/8/52; 1900-
   12/84, wid. Sarah; 1910 Sarah m2-6, Flanery
   s-ch. 14 & 12)   [SARAH m2 Cornelius Bowman
   - 1910; OCC-7/31/36 W-71st Bday]
SPENCER (c23 b.VA)  [s/o Thomas Flanery
   & Nancy Lock - 1860]
   ELIZABETH MAYS (c17 b.Ows.)
   c1868        (1880-L-4; D-L ch. 1877, ages 4
   & 8; H NL w/P 1870; REM; widr. Spencer
   1900-L)
THOMAS J. (c22 b.Ows.)  [s/o Wm. Flanery & W1
   Susan Spivey - TCS]
   LUCY K. CIRCY/SEARSEY (c22 b.Ows.)  [d/o
   Charles Searcy & Lucinda      - 1900]
   1874/5        (1880-3; 1900; B-O ch.;
   ME-7/25/02, death Mrs. Searcy, formerly of
   Mad., w/SiL T. J. Flanery, m/o Chas. Searcy
   of Mad., State Rep.)
WHITE H. (R.Jack. 18 S b.KY) P/VA-KY  [s/o
   Black S. Flanery & Lydia      - TCS]
   NELLEY A. COPE (R.Jack. 16 S b.KY) P/TN
   [d/o George W. Cope & Jane      - TCS]
   30 Nov., 1878, Jackson, @ wid. Black
   Flanery's, by Cornelius Moore; wits. Hiram
   & John Moore   (M-J mf & 4:214, 100:77;
   TCS; 1880-1/80)

(Flanery cont.)

**FLANERY (cont.)**

WILLIAM PRESTON (c27 S b.VA)  [s/o Thomas
    Flanery & Eliz. Parsons - TCS]
    SUSAN SPIVEY (c24 b.KY)
    c1851       (1860-8; B-O ch.; TCS)
    [H-remd.]

WILLIAM PRESTON (c42 2nd b.VA)  [widr/o Susan
    Spivey above - 1860]
    MARGARET JANE WILLIAMS (c25 b.VA) P/VA-TN
    1864/5      (1870-1880-1900; ob-ch. ME-
    9/29/82, oldest dau. b. 9/66; TCS; W/as
    Margaret & Jane)

W[M.] L. (c33 S b.KY)  [1860-1938; s/o Joel P.
    Flanery & Susan J Bailey - 1880; TS-TCS]
    CINTHIA MINTER (c23 S b.KY)  [1870-1944;
    d/o Wm. E. Minter & Elizabeth    - TS-TCS]
    8 Nov, 1893, <u>Jackson Co.</u>  (TCS; M-J 8:482;
    1900-1910-1920)

WILLIAM H[ENRY] (c20 S b.Ows.)
    EMMA BOWLS (c15 S b.Jack.)  [d/o Anderson
    Bowles & Emily Muncy - 1880-J; P/1870-J)
    28 Nov., 1887, <u>Jackson Co.</u>, bm. groom &
    James A. Boles; MC/NFI  (M-J 6:362; 1900-J;
    1910-J ml-22; M-L ch-1939; ob-ch. HJN-5/95
    Lula B., b. 1904/5 Ows.]

**FLETCHER**

JOHN (c59 b.VA)
    AMANDA _____ (c36 b.VA)
    c1868      (1870-7/69; NL 1880/L;
    NL M-J)

**FORBES/FORBUS**

ELI G. (R.Lau. 21 S b.Lau.) P/KY-TN
    SARAH [nee TRUITT] PARKER (20 2nd b.Lau.)
    P/--  [NOTE B-Lau. lists W/b.Ows.]
    [ml 1/3/69 Lau., Daniel Parker - M-Lau.
    BB:138]  [poss. d/o Reddin Truett & Eliz.
    Moore - 1850; 1860-J]
    26 Feb., 1871, <u>Laurel</u> @ William Truett's;
    by. groom & John H. Forbus  (M-Lau. E:555;
    B-Lau. ch-10/78; 1880-Lau., s-s Eli Parker
    10, 1st Forbes ch-8)

**FORD**
DAVID ALEXANDER (c21 S b.KY) P/VA-KY    [s/o
    John Ford & Cath. Lewis - 1880]
    LUCINDA MOORE (c20 S b.KY) P/KY  [d/o James
    "Fiddler" Moore & Emily Smith - TCS]
    1877/8          (1880 no-ch., HF w/them;
    1900 m-18, which is wrong; 1910 m-32; TCS)
JAMES M. (c19 b.Per.)  [c1841-1913 Les.; s/o
    John Ford - DC]
    SARAH STIDHAM (c15 b.Per.)  [1846-1948; d/o
    John Stidham & Margaret   - 1860-P; JS]
    1860        (1870-P-2; 1880-12; B-O ch.;
    1900-Les. m-39; 1910-Les. m1-50 both;
    NL M-J/P)
JAMES (R.Ows. 22 S b.Ows.) P/Ows.
    SUSAN BURCH (R.Ows. 18 S b.Ows.) P/TN-Ows.
    6 March, 1908 Ows.  [R.Owsley 1910-1920]
**FOREMAN**
JOSEPH (R.Clay 22 S b.Clay) P/Clay
    FANNIE J. ST JOHN (R.Ows. 18 S b.Ows.) P/
    Ows.
    29 Aug., 1904, Ows.
**FORTNER/FAULKNER**
ABRAHAM (c24 S b.KY)  [s/o Samuel Fortner
    & Margaret Gabbard - 1880]
    MARY JANE OLINGER (c27 b.VA) P/NC
    23 Aug., 1883, Jackson; sur. H. B. Barris
    (TCS; MT; 1900-J, HM Margaret Phillips
    w/them)
SAMUEL (___ b.KY)
    MARGARET GABBARD (c26 b.KY)  [d/o Jacob
    Gabbard & Susan Bowman - 1850]
    c1857/8         (Margaret & son Abr.
    Faulkner, 1, w/WP 1860; Margaret w/P as
    GABBARD 1870, as FORTNER 1880)
    [MARGARET m2 Theo. Phillips - MT; REM]
**FOSTER**
JAMES (c24 Dr. b.KY)
    FRANCES [RECTOR?] (c15 b.NC)  [c1833-1860
    - 1860MS]  [w/them 1850 are Thomas Rector
    23 NC & Mary Rector 19 NC, poss. WS]
    c1848        (1850-1; widr. James 1860;
    1860MS)    [H-remd.]


(Foster cont.)


241

**FOSTER (cont.)**
JAMES (c36 2nd Dr. b.KY) [m1 Frances (Rector?)
    above - 1850; 1860MS; widr. 1860]
    RACHEL CLARK (c21 b.KY) [d/o Wm. Clark
    & Tabitha Evans - TCS; 1860]
    c1860          (1870-Sx-Lau-9; 1880-Lau-17;
    NL B-Lau.; NL M-J/Lau.; NL 1900Sx)
**FOWLER**
ALBERT (c21 S b.Jack.) [1886-1940; s/o James
    Fowler & Lucy Ann Newman - TS-TCS; ob-H
    OCC-7/5/40]
    HATTIE LEE VENABLE (c18 S b.Ows.) [1889-
    1961; d/o Leroy Venable & Permelia Isaacs -
    TS-TCS; art. OCN-9/15/50; ob-W&S BE-
    10/26/61-11/11/43-3/30/61]
    1907          (1910; TCS; wid. Hattie in
    Congleton 1943; Beattyv., Lee Co. 1950-61)
**FOX**
_____ (___ b.___)
    SUSAN PETERS (c19 b.KY) [d/o Elijah Fox
    & Margaret Woods - 1880-J]
    c1879          (Susan Fox w/P 1880-J, H-NL;
    WTM; NL M-J)
BERRY - see WM. BERRY
FOUNTAIN (24 S b.Ows.) [1844-1919 Jack.; s/o
    John Fox & W2 Hannah Riley - TCS; P-CW]
    REBECCA GILBERT (c17 b.KY) [c1851-1883 -
    P-CW]
    10 Sept., 1868, Ows. (a/L Aug., 1865, Ows.
    by John Stevenson) (P-CW; 1870-2; 1880-15)
    [H-remd.]
FOUNTAIN (R.Ows. 38 2nd b.Ows.) P/Ows.  [m1
    Rebecca Gilbert above - TCS]
    SARAH JANE HELTON (R.Ows. 16 S b.Ows.)
    [1869-19__; d/o George H. Helton & Leannah
    - 1880]
    1 Sept, 1883 Breathitt, @ Geo. Helton's, by
    James Riley; wits. Levi Abner & Geo. Helton
    (M-B 3:214; P-CW as 9/17/84 Ows., by Rev.
    John C. Riley, Bapt. Min.; TCS; 1900-C,
    H-m-27 & W-m-17; B-J ch-1900; 1910-J m-24
    H-2nd; R.Annville, Jack. 1912; wid. Sarah
    moved to Ham., OH after Fountain d. & to
    Richmond, IN c1920 - RP)

(Fox cont.)

## FOX (cont.)

GEORGE (R.Jack. 23 S b.Br.) P/-- KY    [s/o
    John Fox & Sarah Johnson - TCS; 2nd M-L]
    MARY J[ANE] REYNOLDS [BAILEY] (R.Ows. 23
    2nd b.Ows) P/Ows.  [m1 _____ Bailey]    [d/o
    Wesley Reynolds & Nancy Moore - 1850]
    13 Sept., 1874 Ows. @ Green Williams   (a/L
    M-B, W/MARY JANE BAILEY, 2nd)    [R.Owsley
    1880-1900-1910]  [GEORGE (R.Ows 65 widr.
    b.Br) m2 8/21/15, Ellen BBurg. (25 S) -
    M-L; TCS; 1920]
GEORGE (c26 b.Ows.)   [1858-1950 Clay; s/o
    Isaac Fox & Almarinda Griffith - TCS;
    BBG/AJ; TS-BBG]
    LUCINDA BISHOP (c19 b.KY)  [1866-1950;
    d/o Perry Bishop & Levisa Baker - TS-BBG;
    1880-P]
    1885/6       (1900; BBG; NL M-B/C)
HARMON FRANCIS (c21 b.Ows.) [1855-1913 OK; s/o
    John Fox & W2 Hannah Riley - RP; 1870]
    SARAH JANE SMITH (c21 b.Per.)   [poss. d/o
    Sylvester smith & Dicey Jones - RP]
    c1877        (RP, 1st ch-5/78 KY; then went
    to Ark.; 1880-John.,Ark. RP)   [HARMON
    (R.Mad, Ark.) m2 5/16/93 John.,Ark., Fannie
    Mason - went to Allen, OK; Indian Terr.
    1900; Pontatoc, OK 1910 - RP]
HARVEY (c26 S b.KY)  [s/o John Henry Fox
    & Sarah Johnson - RP]
    SARAH ANN BRANDENBURG (c18 S b.KY)  [d/o
    Geo. Brandenburg & Emmaline BBurg. - TCS]
    1881/2       (1900-1910-1920; TCS;
    NL M-B/C)
ISAAC ANDERSON (c18 b.Anderson Co., TN)  [s/o
    John Fox Sr. & W1        - TCS]
    ALMARINDA GRIFFITH (c14 b.Br) P/VA-NC
    1849         (1850-MWY, 1st ch-1; B-O ch.;
    1860-1870-1880; 1900-J m-51; NL M-C)
JAMES (R.Br. 18 S b.KY [Br.]) P/NC  [s/o John
    Fox & Sarah Johnson - RP]
    [TALITHA] LYTHA FOX (R.Ows. 23 S b.Ows.)
    P/KY -- [d/o Isaac Fox & Almarinda Griffith
    - 1860-1870]
    14 Dec, 1876, Ows. @ Isaac Fox's [DIVORCED]
    [H-remd.]   [TALITHA m2 Richmond Pace; m3
    Simeon Hobbs; m4 Nicholas Collins]
(Fox cont.)

## FOX (cont.)

JAMES (c20 b.KY)  [m1 Talitha Fox above]
ELIZABETH GILBERT (c19 b.TN) P/TN
1878          (James & W1 has son 12/77 -
B-Ows.; 1880-1; TW; TCS; 1900-L m-22;
1910-L m1-30; NL M-C)

JOHN (c53 2nd b.Stokes Co., NC)  [m1 Nancy
Cox/Cook - RP]
HANNAH RILEY (c16 S b.KY)  [d/o "Gransir"
John Riley & W1 Eliz. Williams - RP 1850-B]
c1843          (1850-6; B-O ch.; 1860-1870;
RP; NL M-C)

JOHN HENRY (c26 b.Anderson Co., TN)  [s/o John
Fox Sr. & 1st wife - RP; TCS; RP]
SARAH JOHNSON (c20 b.KY)
c1848, Breathitt    (1850-B; B-O ch.; 1860;
1870-1880-B; M-L ch-1915; NL M-C)

LEANDER "LEE" (c19 b.Br.)  [s/o John Fox
& Sarah Johnson - 1870-1880-B]
ISABELLA "IBBIE" McINTOSH (c17 b.Br) [1870-
1943 Ows.; d/o Thomas McIntosh & Susan
Bowling - ob-W&S OCC-3/26/43-1/24/41; 1880]
1886/7      (1900-L; B-O ch.; NL M-B/C;
M-L ch-1917-1921-1930; R.Low.Buff. 1941-
1943)

[MADISON] MATISON (R.Br. 17 S b.Br.) P/-- Br.
[s/o John Fox & Sarah Johnson - 1870-B]
MARTHA SHORT (R.Br. 14 S b.Br.) P/Knx-Br.
31 Oct., 1882, Breathitt @ the mouth of
Robert's Fk. of Turkey Cr., by Wm. Terry,
Esq.; wits. Miles & Robt. Terry    (M-B
3:93)    [H-remd.]

MADISON "MATT" (c23 2nd b.KY)  [m1 Martha
Short above]
BELLE ROBERTS (c16 b.KY)
1888          (1900-L-6/89, m-12; 1910 m-21
H-2nd; 1920; M-L ch-1919; NL M-B/C)

MARTIN (c20 b.Ows.)  [s/o John Fox & W2 Hannah
Riley - TCS]
PERMENIA/VERNINA/PERLINA GULLETT (c17 b.
Per.)  [d/o Wm. O. Gullett & Anna       -
1860-P]
c1872          (1880-7, H-md, W-NL; B-O ch-
1877; 1900-C m-26 = 1873/4; NL 1910Sx;
W/as Permenia, Vernina & Perlina; NL M-C/J;
M-P does not have this time period)

(Fox cont.)

**FOX (cont.)**

MATT - see MADISON

THOMAS (R.Br. 25 S b.KY[Br.]) P/TN-KY [1851-
1900 Lee; s/o John Fox & Sarah Johnson -
D-L]
HARRIET TAYLOR (R.Ows. 21 S b.TN) P/TN
[d/o Orville P. Taylor & Hannah Harvey]
6 Sept., 1877, Ows., @ F. Brandenburg's
(a/L M-B as 3/1/77, W-20, rest same)
[R.Owsley 1880; Lee 1900; wid. Harriet 1910
Lee]

WM. BERRY (c21 S b.Br.) [1878-1919 Ows.; s/o
Wm. M "Pet" TERRY & Rhoda FOX - TCS; DC/as
Berry]
MARY BELL PETERS (c23 S b.Ows.) [d/o John
B. Peters & Mary Peters - 1880; TCS]
1900         (Mary FOX "wid.", w/P 1900, no
ch.; MT; B-O ch. 1910; 1910 Berry & Mary
Fox m-9; wid. Mary R.Island Cr. 1919; wid.
Mary 1920; BC 1912; NL M-B/C)

**FRALEY/FRAILEY/FRILEY**

JOHN (c25 b.Est.) [s/o Martin Fraley & America
Freeman - 1860]
NANCY JANE WHITAKER (c17 b.Br.)
c1864, poss. md. <u>Breathitt</u> (1870-B-5;
B-B ch.; IBW; 1880-B)

STEPHEN (16-1/2 S b.Lee) [1878-1947 Lee; s/o
Henry Fraley & Susan Ellen Gum - ob-H BE-
9/11/47]
DORA [nee MALONEY] MALONEY (22 2nd b.Lee)
[wid/o Columbus Maloney - M-L 1890] [1872-
1961 Winchester; d/o Geo. Maloney & Mildred
Blount - 1880-L; ob-W BE-7/27/61]
7 March, 1896, <u>Lee</u> @ Mildred Van Hart's;
wits. Geo. E. & Mildred Van Hart [her M &
s-F]   (M-L; 1900-L; B-O ch-1908 W/as Dora
MOORE; 1910-L H-m1-14, W-m2-14; BC 1918-L
W/as Dora Maloney; R.Lee 1947; ob-ch. 3Fks-
12/20/95-1/10/96 & HJN-11/89)


(Fraley cont.)

**FRALEY (cont.)**
THOMAS (c26 c.minr b.KY)  [c1841-c1893?; s/o
   Martin Fraley & America Freeman]
   CAROLINE [DURBIN?] (c27 b.KY)  [1839-1915
   Lee; d/o John _____ - DC]  [NOTE: I believe
   Caroline may be d/o John Durbin & W2 Juda
   Mann.  Search of 1850 finds only 1 Caroline
   age 10-11.  She is d/o John Durbin.  1860
   finds Caroline w/P family #476 & Thos.
   Fraley, lab., w/family #477]
   c1867              (1870-L-2; 1880-L; wid.
   Caroline 1900-L; 1910-L Caroline listed as
   wid. "m-26", which means prob. md. 26 yrs.
   when Thos. d., putting his death c1893)
THOMAS G[REENBERRY "TOMMIE"] (20 S b.Beattyv.)
   [s/o Henry Fraley & Susan Ellen Gum - ob-HS
   BE-9/11/47]
   CORA MALONEY (18 S b.Beattyv.) [d/o George
   Maloney & Mildred A. Blount - 1880-L]
   18 July, 1892, Lee (M-L; B-O ch-1908, W/as
   Cora MULLINS; 1900-L; BC 1915-B W/as Cora
   Maloney; 1920-B; R.OH 1922-1956 KAS; ob-ch.
   HJN-11/89-12/20/97 as Maloney)
**FRANCE**
LEMUEL (c24 b.Lee,VA)  [s/o Owen France. &
   Mary      - TCS]
   MARY B. STAMPER (c15 b.Let.)  [d/o John W.
   Stamper & Nancy Hogg]
   c1876            (1880-3, Stamper BiL)
LEWIS (c21 b.VA)  [s/o Owen France & Polly
   - TCS]
   GENEVA BOWMAN (c20 b.KY)  [d/o Henry Bowman
   & Rachel Plummer - TCS]
   c1869            (1870-L-1/70; B-L ch.)
**FRANKLIN**
BENJAMIN (c20 b.KY)  [s/o Robt. P. Franklin
   & Eliz.    - TCS; 1880]
   HELEN MAINOUS (c20 b.KY)  [d/o Absalom
   Mainous & Susan Treadway - 1880; TCS]
   c1882            (TCS; NL M-J)  [HELEN m2
   c1885/6, Thomas J. Kincaid - widr. Thomas
   1900]

**FREEMAN**
MIDDLETON (c30 S b.Est.) [s/o Moab Freeman
   & W3 Tennessee Vaughn - PWB; 1850-E]
   BETTIE DANIEL (c20 b.Clay) [1855-1927; poss
   d/o Britton Daniel & Massie Hacker - B-C;
   1860-C; ob-W Pb]
   10 Feb, 1876, <u>Estill</u> (PWB; H-sgl. 1870;
   1880-3) [BETTIE m2 James Bryant - PWB;
   ob-W]
ROBERT (c21 <u>Mul</u> b.KY) [s/o Hiram Freeman
   & Edie Chance - 1870-B]
   MARY _____ (c19 <u>white</u> b.KY) P/KY
   c1870, poss. <u>Breathitt</u> (H-sgl. 1870-B;
   1880-9)
SHERMAN (c20 b.KY) [1864-1922 - TS-Wlf]
   SUSAN HORNSBY (c18 b.KY) [d/o Job
   Hornsby & Catherine Gabbard - 1880 -
   NL DC/Inx.]
   1884/5 (1900 N#L, 1/0 ch.; WTM;
   1910-W both m1-25; 1920-Morg.; NL M-J)
TENNESSEE (c21 S <u>Mul</u> b.KY) [s/o Robt. Freeman
   & Mary - 1880]
   LOURAINE BARRETT (c18 S b.KY)
   1897/8 (1910; NL 1900Sx; NL M-L;
   BC 1911-1913-1917-1920-L; M-L ch.1917-1918)
WILLIAM (c30 2nd b.Mad) [widr/o Patsy _____,
   who d. 1850-60] [s/o Moab Freeman & W1
   Chancy Bentley - PWB]
   NANCY _____ (c31 b.KY)
   c1853 (1860, 1st ch. under 10 is
   age 6; 1880-L) [WILLIAM m3 5/4/93 Lee,
   Ruth Pritchard (36); WILLIAM (R.Lee 70 4th
   b.Lee) m4 8/20/1901 Lee, Susan (nee _____)
   Roberts (45 2nd) - PWB; M-L]
WILLIAM (c38 <u>Mul</u> b.Clay) [s/o Hiram Freeman
   & Edie Chance of Br.]
   MARGARET CORNETT (c19 <u>White</u> b.Let.)
   c1880 (1900 m-26, but liv. in
   adultery 1880, w/2 ch., ages 4 & 2)


(Freeman cont.)

## FREEMAN (cont.)

[WILLIAM] WILLIE (R.Ows. 23 S b.Lee) P/Ows. --
[c1885-1960 Lex.; s/o Moab Freeman & Ebby
Marcum - mg.; BE-7/7/60]
    MARY ROACH (R.Lee 28 S b.Lee) P/Ows. [1875-
1953; d/o Peter Roach & Elizabeth Freeman -
mg.; ob-W OCN-12/11/53]
    6 Nov., 1908, <u>Lee</u> @ J. C. Smallwood's, by
J. C. Smallwood, Min.; wits. Alice Kelley,
Martha Tincher, Kate Daugherty & Mintie
Tincher   (M-L; ob-W says md. 1908 Boonev.;
1910 m-1; B-O ch-9/09; R.Cincinnati, OH
1953)

## FREY
see FRY

## FRIAR
see FRYER

## FROST

A[LBERT] G. (c18 b.KY) P/TN-KY
    MARY A. FARMER (<u>c28</u> S b.KY)  [d/o Denton
Farmer & Sylvania Herd - 1870; 1880 w/WS
Rebecca Gibson]
    5 Nov., 1890 (ML) <u>Jackson Co.</u>; bm. groom &
J. E. Ward  (M-J 7:396; 1900-J m-11, WM
w/them; TCS)

ANDERSON - see JAMES ANDERSON

CORNELIUS S. (R.Clay 24 S b.Hawk.,TN)  [1830-
1902; s/o Simeon R. Frost & Jane    - ME-
5/2/02]
    CATHARINE ["KATE"] GRINDSTAFF (R.Clay 16 S
b.Clay)
    30 Oct., 1854, <u>Clay</u> (M-C ML 10/23; M-C mf
W/as KAT; 1860-1870-1880; widr. Cornelius
1900)

CORNELIUS "NEAL" (c19 S b.Major) [1880-1950;
s/o Thomas Jefferson Frost & Nancy Marshall
- 1900; TS-TCS]
    MARY ELLEN RADFORD a/k/a BOWMAN (c17 S b.
Turin) [1883-1970; d/o Lucinda Bowman, who
md. George Moore - JFB/BBG; TS-TCS; ob-W
BE-5/7/70]
    1900        (1910 m-10; H-sgl. 1900, but
Mary NL w/M & s-F 1900; B-O ch-1908 W/as
RADFORD; 1920; BC 1916-1919 W/as BOWMAN &
1923 as RADFORD)

(Frost cont.)

## FROST (cont.)

ELISHA S. (c21 b.Ows.) [s/o James Anderson
    Frost & Sarah Lucinda Miller - 1880]
    CORA WILDER (c21 b.Ows.) [d/o Ewell Wilder
    & Lucinda Hornsby - MT]
    1899        (MT; 1900-J-5/1900, m-0; went
    to St. Louis, MO - MT)
GILFORD (R.Sturg. 22 S b.Claib., TN)
    NANCY MILLER (R."L.F." Rock, Ows. 23 S
    b.Washington Co., VA)
    2 Jan., 1853, Ows., by Rev. J. Ward
HENRY (c24 S b.KY) [s/o Cornelius Frost
    & Cath. Grindstaff - 1880]
    MAGGIE FREEMAN (c17 S b.Lee) [1881-1959
    Clk hosp. - ob-W BE-6/18/59]
    1898/9       (1900-1910)
JACOB (c21 S b.KY) [s/o James Anderson Frost
    & Sarah Lucinda Miller - 1880]
    HANNAH WILDER (c21 S b.Ows.) [d/o Ewell
    Wilder & Lucinda Hornsby - TCS; 1880]
    1887        (1900 m-12; 1910 m-23; B-O ch.)
[JAMES] ANDERSON "ANCE" (c16 b.KY) [s/o Robt.
    Frost & Eliz. Moore]
    [SARAH] LUCINDA MILLER (c23 b.Lee,VA) [d/o
    John Miller & W1 Susan Baker - w/F & s-M
    1860-J]
    2 April, 1865, Jackson Co. @ John Miller's,
    by Wm. Anderson; wits. Moses Riggs & Jacob
    Miller    (M-J; 1870-4; B-O ch; 1880 Sarah
    "md" w/ch., James A. "md" w/Jane Bowles,
    adulteress; Ance & Lucinda back together
    again 1900-J m-37; widr. J. Anderson 1910]
JEFFERSON - see THOMAS JEFFERSON
JOHN [S.] (R.Ows. 23 S b.TN)
    SUSANAH WARD (R.-- 19 S b.TN) [poss. d/o
    John Ward & Pemelia, who lived next to them
    1860-J]
    15 Oct., 1852, Ows. [R.Jackson Co. 1860-
    1870]
JOHN G. (c22 b.KY) [s/o Cornelius Frost
    & Cath. Grindstaff]
    TEMPERANCE JANE BOWMAN (c25 b.KY) [d/o
    Levi Bowman & Eliz. Turner - 1880]
    1889/90        (1900; TCS)

(Frost cont.)

**FROST (cont.)**

JOHN (c25 b.KY) [1871-1946; d/o James Anderson
   Frost & Sarah Lucinda Miller - TS-TCS 1880]
   NANCY ANN EVERSOLE (c23 b.KY) [1873-1955;
   d/o Geo. Eversole & Rebecca Jane Moore -
   ob-W OCN-3/31/55]
   1895/6          (1900-1910-1920; TCS; BC
   ch-1911-1913; wid. Nancy d. Cow Cr.; ob-ch.
   BS-2/20/86-12/29/88)
MICHAEL (c20 S b.KY)
   NANCY HILL (c20 S b.KY)
   1905/6          (1910; BC 1924-P)
NEAL - see CORNELIUS
ROBERT (c24 S b.TN)   [s/o Simeon R. Frost
   & W1              - TCS]
   ELIZABETH MOORE (c23 b.So.Fk.KY River)
   [c1825-1854; d/o James Moore & Eliz. Morris
   - D-O; TCS]
   c1848          (NL 1850; B-O ch.; D-O wf;
   D-O ch-8/54; H-remd. 1860-11; NL M-C)
ROBERT (c31 2nd b.TN)   [widr/o Eliz. Moore
   above - D-O 7/54]
   SUSAN MILLER (c18 b.VA)
   1855          (1860; B-O ch-5/56; wid. Susan
   1870-80)
SIMEON R. (c48 2nd b.TN)   [m1 _____
   - widr. Simeon 1830-1840-Hawk.,TN]
   JANE _____ (c32 b. NC)
   1849/50          (1850-MWY; 1860)
SIMEON (c58-67 3rd b.TN)   [widr/o Jane _____
   above - 1860]
   RACHEL (nee _____) KILBURN (c44-53 b.VA)
   [appar. wid/o George Kilburn]
   1860-9          (1870; TCS; NL M-J)
THOMAS JEFFERSON (c18 b.Ows.) P/Hawk,TN-Clay
   [s/o Cornelius Frost & Catherine Grinstaff
   - B-O]
   NANCY MARSHALL (c18 b.KY)   [d/o Joseph
   Marshall & W1 Caroline Combs]
   1873/4          (1900; 1880-1; B-O ch.)
THOMAS (c21 S b.Ricetown)   [s/o Robert Frost
   & Susan Miller]
   ALABAMA ["BAM"] DAVIDSON (c18 S b.Ricetown)
   3 Nov, 1883, Clay (M-C; 1900 m-17; 1910-25
   m-25; B-O ch. W/as FROST)

(Frost cont.)

**FROST (cont.)**
WHITE (c19 b. KY) [s/o Robert Frost & Susan
   Miller]
   ELIZA ANN _____ (c15 b.KY) P/KY
   c1879      (1880 no ch.; NL 1900Sx;
   NL M-J)
WILLIAM TANDY (c21 S b.Ows.) [s/o Robert
   Frost & Susan Miller - TCS]
   NANCY BAKER (c14 b.KY) P/KY [c1862-1955;
   d/o James Wilson Baker & W1 Sarah Davidson
   - TS-TCS has 1859-1955, but age 8 1870]
   1877/8      (1880-2; 1900 m-22, but W2
   listed; TCS)   [H-remd.]
WILLIAM (c19 S b.KY) [s/o Cornelius Frost
   & Cath. Grindstaff - 1880]
   ELIZABETH SAWYERS (c33 - b.KY) [d/o wid.
   Martha Sawyers - 1900-C]
   31 July, 1890, <u>Clay</u> (M-C MT; 1900-C m-10,
   WM w/them; 1910 H-remd-8)
WILLIAM TANDY (c36 2nd b.Ows.) [widr/o Nancy
   Baker above]
   SARAH ANN WILDER (c28 S b.KY)
   1892      (1900, Wm. m-22, but this is
   W1, Sarah m-8, 3/3 ch, 4 ch. listed; 1910
   m-17; 1920; TCS)
WILLIAM (c31 2nd b.KY) [widr/o Eliz. Sawyers
   above]
   RACHEL (nee BOWMAN) HENSLEY (c46 3rd b.KY)
   [m1 Wm. Hicks; m2 Jackson Hensley] [1857-
   1929 Ows.; d/o Robt. S. Bowman & Mary
   Turner - DC]
   1901/2      (1910; TCS)
WILLIAM (c23 S b.KY) [s/o Wm. T. Frost
   & Nancy Baker - TCS]
   NANNIE _____ (c21 S b.KY)
   1905/6      (1910 no ch.; NL 1920Sx;
   NL M-J)
**FRY/FRYE/FREY**
_____ (___ b.___)
   ELIZABETH DUNAWAY (c14-31; b.Ows.) [c1846-
   1878 Lee; d/o John Dunaway & Paulina Sparks
   - D-L; TCS; 1850-60]
   1861-77      (D-L wf; WP/NL 1870/E/L;
   NL Frey w/wf Eliz. 1870/B/E/L; NL widr. Fry
   1880/L; NL M-C/J)

(Fry cont.)

## FRY/FREY (cont.)

_____ (___ b.VA)
ELIZABETH EDWARDS (c22 b.KY)  [d/o James
Edwards & Mary Austin - 1880]
c1884          (1900-9/85, wid. Eliz., WM
w/her; TCS)
HILLERY (c27 S b.VA)
DIADAMA BINGHAM (c19 b.KY)  [d/o Robert
Bingham & Alice      - TCS]
2 Sept., 1870 (ML) Jackson Co.; bm. groom
& Robt. Bingham  (M-J 2:375; TCS; 1880-8)
[H-remd.]
HILERY (c57 2nd b.VA)  [widr/o Diadema
Bingham above - TCS]
SARAH _____ (c32 b.KY)
1898/9          (1900; NL M-J)
JOHN [B.] (c19 S b.KY)  [s/o Hilery Fry & Wl
Diadema Bingham - TCS; 1880]
CASSY ELIZABETH BANKS (c17 S b.KY) [d/o
Lansford Banks & Druscilla Kelly - 1880]
11 Sept., 1895 (ML), Jackson Co.; bm. groom
& H. C. Banks  (M-J 9:308; TCS; 1900 m-5,
Banks SiL w/them; B-J ch-1904; 1910 m-14;
1920; W/as Cassy Eliz.; Eliz., & Cassie E.)
MILLARD - see PETER MILLARD
P[ETER] MILLARD (R.Ows. 23 S tchr b.Ows.) P/VA
-KY  [s/o Hilery Fry & Wl Diadema Bingham
- TCS; 1880]
[MARTHA] MATTIE J. GENTRY (R.Ows. 20 S b.
Jack.) P/VA-Ows.  [d/o Hiram D. Gentry &
Araminta Bowman - TCS; 1900; ob-WS OCC-
7/22/38]
14 July, 1904, Ows.  [R.Owsley 1910-1920;
Booneville 1938]

## FRYER/FRIAR

TIMOTHY (c27 b.Per.)
MARY ANN _____ (c22 b.VA)
c1849          (1850-4 mos.; 1860-C 1st 2
ch. b.Ows.; NL M-C)

## FUGATE/FUGITT

JAMES (c31 b.Law.)
ESTHER VICKERS (c16 b.Russell Co., VA)
c1866          (1880-13; NL 1870; NL M-B/C)

**FULKS**
THOMPSON (c24 b.VA) P/VA
    ELIZABETH ROBERTS (c20 b.KY) P/KY
    c1847        (1850-2; B-B ch.; B-O ch.;
    1860-B; 1880-L)
**FULLER**
HIRAM (R.Ows. 21 S b.Owen) P/VA-Ows.
    CORA M. HERD (R.Ows. 20 S b.Ows.) P/Ows.
    [d/o Jesse Herd & Nancy Flanery - 1880;
    TCS; ME]
    30 Nov., 1895, Ows. (rec. Lee) @ W. M.
    Treadway's, by Eld. J. E. Morris; wits. W.
    M. & Geo. M. Treadway    (M-L 4:569; ME-
    12/6/95 says md. 12/1, by Rev. Morris of
    Br.; 1900 w/WP; widr. Hiram 1910-L)
THOMAS C. (c22 S bank cashier b.KY)
    CARRIE BRUCE (c17 S b.KY)
    1897/8        (1910; NL 1900Sx; BC 1911;
    NL M-B/C/J/L)
**FULLINGTON**
FRANKLIN "FRANK" (c23 b.Claib.,TN)
    SUSAN MATHIS (c18 b.Ows.)  [d/o James
    Madison Mathis & Nancy Lamb - 1880]
    1892/3        (1900; NL 1920Sx; Aff/o
    Frank 1943 on BC-ch.; NL M-J)


**GABBARD/GABBERT**
ABEL C. (c25 b.KY)  [1841-1906; s/o Isaac H.
    Gabbard & Jane Isaacs - MT]
    LUCY EVERSOLE (c15 b.KY)  [1851-1917; d/o
    Wm. Eversole & Barbara Chappel - MT]
    c1867        (1870-1; JFB; 1880; 1900 N#L,
    1st ch. b. 1868; wid. Lucy w/son 1910-Les.)
ABEL CARTER (c16 S b.KY)  [1888-1957; s/o Geo.
    W. Gabbard & W2 Mary Eliz. Shook - 1900;
    TCS; BJE; MT; ob-HS OCC-6/12/42]
    REBECCA ROBERTS (c15 S b.KY)  [1889-1954;
    d/o John Roberts & Sarah Thorpe - TCS; BJE]
    1903/4        (1910-1920; TCS; BC 1915-
    1919-1921)

(Gabbard cont.)

## GABBARD (cont.)

ABIJAH B. (c26 S b.KY) [1843-1927; s/o Isaac
   H. Gabbard & Jane Isaacs - MT TS-TCS]
   NANCY J. BISHOP (c21 S b.KY) [d/o Wm.
   Bishop & Susan Barrett - MT; TCS]
   Oct., 1869          (1870; JFB; 1880-1890;
   MT; 1900-M; 1910 m-37)

ABIJAH (c26 b.KY) [1865-1894; s/o Geo. W.
   Gabbard & Eliz. Williams - MT; w/Gabbard
   GP 1880; BBG; TS-TCS]
   ISABELLE "BELLE" (nee BOWLING) McDANIEL
   (c22 2nd b.KY)    [m1 Dan McDaniel - MT]
   [d/o Ibby (nee Baker/Woods) wid/o Eli
   BOWLING & unknown - MT]
   c1891/2           (MT; 1900 W-remd. Moore,
   McDaniel s-s b. 11/89)   [BELLE m3 Charles
   Benjamin Moore - 1900]

ABRAHAM (c31 b.KY) [s/o Jacob Gabbard
   & Susannah Bowman]
   MARY BURRIS (c25 b.Daviess Co., IN) [1835-
   1913 Ows.; d/o Henry Burris & Eliz. Moore -
   MT; DC]
   1859/60          (1860-MWY; MT; 1870; 1880 WM
   w/them; wid. Mary 1900)

ALBERT (R.Ows. 24 S b.Ows.) P/Ows. [1876-1950;
   s/o John Gabbard & Jaley Reynolds - TS-TCS;
   ob-H&M OCN-2/17/50-12/16/49; MT]
   MARY ALICE HICKS (R.Lee 21 2nd b.Rockc.) P/
   -- & Ows. [m1 _____] [1878-1962; d/o Wm.
   Hicks & Rachel Bowman - MT; TS-TCS; ob-WS
   OCN-12/6/56; 1880 w/wid. mom]
   30 May, 1900, Lee @ George Jackson's, by
   Geo. Kincaid; wits. Geo. & Tempa Jackson
   (M-L; MT; 1900 m-0 mo. w/HP; 1910 m-10;
   1920; ob-H; R.Owsley 1956)

ANDREW (c21 b.KY) [1871-c1899; s/o Geo. W.
   Gabbard & W2 Mary Eliz. Shook - TS-BBG
   has 1871-1901, but d. pre-1900]
   SUSAN A. FROST (c15 S b.KY) [d/o Wm. T.
   Frost & Nancy Baker - TCS; MT]
   c1892/3          (1900-12/93, wid. Susan;
   Susan m2-1 1910, Gabbard s-ch.; BBG)
   [SUSAN m2 Robert Reynolds - MT]

BENTLEY - see WM. BENTLEY
BENTON - see C. BENTON & CHARLES BENTON

(Gabbard cont.)

**GABBARD (cont.)**

BLEVINS (R.Teges 27 S b.Ows.) P/Ows. [1882-
1947; s/o Geo. W. Gabbard & W2 Mary Eliz.
Shook - 1900; TS-TCS; ob-HS OCC-6/12/42]
MARY BISHOP (R.Teges, Clay; 15 S b.Clay)
P/Clay
11 March, 1909, Teges, <u>Clay</u> (M-C mf; MT;
1910-2 mo., m-1, DiL Mary a/L w/Geo. & Mary
Gabbard 1910)

C. B[ENTON] (R.Cope's Br.; 25 S b.Ows.) [1877-
1959; s/o Willis Gabbard & Mary Bishop -
mg.; 1880; MT]
SUSAN SHACKELFORD [_____] (R.Cope's Br.
22 2nd b.Harl.) [m1 _____]
[d/o Thomas Shackelford - mg.]
9 March, 1902, <u>Breathitt</u> @ James Johnson's,
by James Johnson, JPBC; wits. James Bryant
& Nancy Johnson (M-B 9:461; MT; 1910-B-7;
1920-B)

CHARLES BENTON (c22 S b.Gabbard) [1873-1949;
s/o John L. Gabbard & Jaley Reynolds - 1880
MT; ob-H&M OCN-7/1/49-12/16/49]
EMMA ROSA MOYERS (c28 S b.Boonev.) [1867-
1925; d/o Owen Moyers & Lucy Stewart -1880;
MT; ob-H]
1895 (1900-4/96, m-4; B-O ch.; 1910
m-14; 1920; MT ob-ch. OCN-1/25/53)
[CHARLES m2 7/16/27 Ows., Lennie Mainous
(1888-1973; d/o Green S. Mainous & Lucinda
Thomas) - M-O; ob-H; TS-TCS]

CHARLES TYLER (c26 S b.Ows.) [1870-1958; s/o
Hiram Gabbard & Hannah Million - 1880; TCS;
MT]
MARTHA JACKSON (c31 S b.KY) [1865-1951; d/o
James Jackson & Malinda Jackson - 1880; MT]
1896/7 (1900 WM w/them; 1910; 1920
WM w/them; MT; BBG; ob-ch. 3Fks-2/27/97)

CHESTER (R.Ows. 20 S tchr. b.Ows) P/Ows.
[ISABELLE] BELLE COMBS (R.Ows. 16 S b.Ows)
P/Ows. [d/o Squire Combs & America
Anderson - 1900; MT; ob-WS OCN-12/18/53]
4 Dec., 1909, Ows. [R.Owsley 1910, WS,
James Combs, w/them]

(Gabbard cont.)

## GABBARD (cont.)

CORNELIUS (c20 b.KY) [s/o Jacob Gabbard
& Susan Bowman - MT]
MARY MOORE (c18 b.KY) [d/o James Moore
& Eliz. Morris - MT]
4 Sept., 1841, Clay (M-C; NL 1850/C;
1860-1870-1880)

CORNELIUS "NEAL" (c18 S b.Ows.) [1877-19__;
s/o Hiram Gabbard & Mahala Wilson - TCS;
MT; H/95th Bday BE-7/13/72]
NANCY J. "NAN" CAUDILL (c18 S b.Br.) [d/o
Alfred Caudill & Jane Simpkins - TCS; CRC;
MT]
1895/6        (1900-1910-1920; TCS; MT; BC
1913)    [CORNELIUS m2 Edna Botner - MT]

DANIEL BOONE (c20 S b.KY) [1875-1953; s/o
Elisha Gabbard & Mary Peters - 1880; MT;
ob-H OCN-7/3/53]
CHANEY HACKER (c17 S b.KY) [1875-1918 -
TS-TCS]
1895/6            (1900-1910; TCS; BBG; LM; BC
1915; widr. Daniel B. 1920)    [DANIEL m2
Esther (nee Million) Sims (1887-1947; d/o
Ben Million & Lucinda McQueen; m1 _____
Sims) - TS-TCS MT. She m3 a Barrett]

DILLARD (c32 2nd b.KY) [m1 _____]
[s/o Wyatt Gabbard & Sarah White - 1880 MT]
MALLIE GAYHEART (c18 b.KY)
26 June, 1907, Knott Co. @ Huey Terry's, by
Huey Terry, JP; wits. Polly & Joseph Terry
(M-Knt 4A:177; MT; H-sgl. Bo w/Henry
Holbrook 1900-B; 1910-Knt H/m2-3 W/Mollie
m1-3)

DOCK - see WILSON

EDWARD DOUGLAS (c23 S b.Ows.) [1866-1928; s/o
Michael Gabbard & Mary Ann Mangan - MT]
MATILDA EVERSOLE (c19 S b.KY) [d/o Geo.
Eversole & Rebecca Moore - 1880; MT]
1889        (JFB; 1900-8/90, m-10; 1910
m-20; 1920; MT)

(Gabbard cont.)

## GABBARD (cont.)

E[DDIE] B. (R.Ows. 22 S b.Ows) P/Ows. [s/o
    John Gabbard & Molly Herndon - TCS; MT;
    2nd M-B]
    HALLY CREECH (R.Ows. 21 S b.Ows) P/Ows.
    [d/o John Creech & Sarah A Griffin/Griffey
    - MT; TCS]
    8 Feb., 1908, Ows. [DIVORCED 1910-17]
    [R.Owsley 1910 as m-2, w/WF]
    [EDWARD (31 Div.) m2 3/26/17 Br., Carry
    Morgan (21 S) - M-B]
    [HALLIE m2 1910-20, Leonard Isaacs - 1920;
    ob-WS BE-6/13/68]
ELIHU "HUGH" (c25 S b.Ows.) [s/o Hiram
    Gabbard & Mary J. Freeman - 1880]
    NANCY M. RICHARDSON (c19 S b.KY)
    1886           (MT; 1900-E m-13; 1910-E
    both m1-24; NL M-B)
ELIJAH (c22 S b.Ows.) [1872-1933; s/o Elisha
    Gabbard & Mary A. Peters - TS-TCS; 2nd M-L]
    AMANDA "AMY" BISHOP (c15 S b.KY)
    1893/4          (1900-1910; TCS; BBG; MT; BC
    ch-1911-1915.)   [ELIJAH (52 widr. b.Ows)
    m2 3/3/24 Lee, Bettie (nee Campbell) Thomas
    (43 wid. b.Br.; d/o Cail Campbell & Sallie
    Barrett; m1 a Campbell) - M-L]
ELIJAH (28 S b.KY) [1869-1940; s/o Claiborne
    Gabbard & Mary Chambers - MT]
    MARY JANE COOPER (R.Ows. c27 b.KY) [d/o
    John Cooper & Rachel Chambers - 1870]
    20 Nov., 1895, Lee by W. H. Bowman, JPLC;
    wits. Lamont Cole & Rachel Gabbard
    (M-L; 1900 m-5; ob-ch. BE-9/14/67-7/3/69)
ELISHA (R.Ows. 21 S b.Clay) [s/o Peter
    Gabbard & Susan Harrison - MT]
    NANCY MOORE (R.Ows. 17 S b.Clay) [d/o
    James "Whitehead" Moore & W1 Isabella
    McQueen - MT]
    14 Aug., 1855, Ows. [R.Owsley 1860;
    Jackson Co. 1870-1880-1900]


(Gabbard cont.)

## GABBARD (cont.)

ELISHA (c22 S b.Ows.)  [1848-1914; s/o Wilson
    Gabbard & Susan Abner - TS-TCS 1870]
    MARY ANN PETERS (c19 S b.Ows.) [1851-1914;
    d/o Elijah Peters & Margaret Woods - TS-
    TCS; WTM]
    late 1870      (1880-9; 1890; 1900 m-29;
    Ows. deed Elisha & Mary to Wilson [their
    son] 10/1902 - OCN-3/31/50; 1910 m-40; B-O
    ch.; MT; H-1870; M-L son 1924)
ELISHA MITCHELL "BUD" (c27 S b.KY)  [s/o
    Michael Gabbard & Perlina Baker - 1880 MT]
    ARKIE GILBERT (c17 S b.KY)
    1906/7          (1910; BBG; MT; ob-ch. has
    P/Mitchell Gabbard & Arkie Angel, but BBG
    said Bud was uncle of her hus. & wf was
    Arkie Gilbert)
GEORGE WASHINGTON (c20 b.Clay) [1830-1910; s/o
    Isaac H. Gabbard & Jane Isaacs - MT]
    ELIZA ANN WILLIAMS (c23 b.KY) [1828-1865;
    d/o Jno. Williams & Eliz. Hunt, who later
    md. Jack Combs - MT]
    7 Aug., 1851      (MT; 1860; B-O ch-5/52;
    JFB; DC ch-1924)        [H-remd]
GEORGE W. (c35 2nd b.Clay)  [widr/o Eliza
    Williams above]
    MARY ELIZABETH SHOOK (c18 b.NC)  [1846-
    1922; d/o David Shook & Lida Lust - DC; MT]
    19 April, 1866, Ows. (JFB; MT; 1870;
    1900-1910; B-O ch.; wid. Mary 1920)
GEORGE (c19 S b.KY)  [s/o Mike Gabbard
    & Paulina Baker - 1880]
    MALVARY GILBERT (c18 S b.KY)
    1896/7          (1900-1910; MT)
GRANT (c23 S b.KY) [1872-1925; s/o Henry Clay
    Gabbard & Rebecca Gabbard - 1880 MT TS-TCS]
    NANCY BAKER (c19 S b.Ows.)  [d/o Red Bob
    Baker & Margaret nee Baker - 1880; MT]
    1894/5          (1900-1910-1920; MT; BC 1920;
    wid. Nancy R.So.Lebanon, OH 1967 - ob-ch.
    BE-5/4/67)
HARRISON - see WILTON HARRISON


(Gabbard cont.)

**GABBARD (cont.)**

HARVEY (R.Ows. 23 S b.KY) P/KY  [1855-1934;
    s/o Hiram Gabbard & Mary Freeman - B-O; MT;
    TS-TCS]
    ELISABETH WEST (R.Jack. 23 S b.KY) P/NC
    [d/o Buford West & Jane Tillery - MT]
    11 Oct., 1878, Ows.  (a/L 10/10/78 Jack. @
    wid. West's, by Eld. J. B. Rowlett; wits.
    Presley & H. Gabbard, Clay & Betsy Roberts
    - M-J 100:77; 1900-E m-21)   [HARVEY m2
    Ella (Jackson) Moore (1870-1949), wid/o
    Martin Moore, d/o James Jackson & Malinda -
    ob-H OCC-8/3/34; MT; TS-TCS]
HECKLIFF - see WILSON HECKLIFF
HENRY CLAY (20 b.Ows.)  [1844-1903; s/o Jacob
    Gabbard & Eliz. Woods - MT]
    REBECCA GABBARD (c26 b.Ows.)   [1838-1901;
    d/o John Gabbard & Margaret Combs - MT; TS-
    TCS]
    1865, Ows.   (MT; 1870; B-O ch.; 1880-1890;
    1900 m-35)
HENRY C. (c19 S b.KY) [s/o Noah Gabbard & Juda
    Moore, who m2 Elcannah Richardson - TCS MT]
    MARTHA NOBLE (c16 S b.KY)  [d/o John Noble
    & Catherine Fugate - MT]
    1883      (1900 m-17; 1910 m-26; TCS)
HENRY "TIP" (c26 S b.Ows.)  [1858-1960; s/o
    Hiram Gabbard & Mary J. Freeman - MT; 1880]
    ELIZABETH JANE BRYANT (c23 S b.VA)  [1860-
    1937; d/o Jno. Bryant & Rachel Surrat -
    1880; MT; TS-TCS]
    1884           (1900 m-16; 1910 m-25; MT;
    BBG; 1920)
HENRY (R.Ows. 21 S b.Ows.) P/Ows. [1888-1977
    Wlf; s/o John Gabbard & Jaley Reynolds - MT
    ob-HM&S OCN-12/16/49-7/1/49]
    [MELISSA "LISSA"] LIZZIE WILSON (R.Ows. 21
    S b.Ows.) P/Ows.  [1888-1977; d/o Sam
    Wilson & Martha Stewart - TCS; MT; ob-W&M
    BS-1/3/78 & OCC-11/11/38]
    24 Sept., 1909, Ows.  [R.Owsley 1910 w/WP;
    Owsley 1915 - BC; 1920; Cow Creek, Ows.
    1949]


(Gabbard cont.)


259

## GABBARD (cont.)

HIRAM (c27 b.Clay) [1824-1905; s/o Jacob
Gabbard & Susan Bowman - BBG; MT]
MARY JANE FREEMAN (c25 b.Est.) [1825-1864;
d/o Moab Freeman & Wl Chancy Bentley - PWB;
MT; 1850-E]
c1851       (1860-11, but 1870 shows this
ch. to be FREEMAN; B-O ch-5/52; DC ch-1930)
[H-remd]

HIRAM (c40 2nd b.Clay) [widr/o Mary Jane
Freeman above] [1824-1905]
HANNAH MILLION (c18 b.Mad.) [1846-1893;
d/o Eli Million & Harriet Freeman - MT;
TS-TCS; BBG]
1865       (MT; BBG; Wl d. 7/64; 1870
lists wf Hannah, ch. under 5 were 3, 1, &
b.6/70; B-O son Wm. erroneously lists W/as
WILSON; 1880; widr. Hiram 1900)

HIRAM (29 b.KY) [1842-1892; s/o Cornelius
Gabbard & Mary Moore - MT]
MAHALA WILSON (25 b.KY) [1846-1906; d/o
Lemuel Wilson & Eleanor Moore - REM]
13 Feb., 1872, Ows. (JFB; MT; ECP)

HIRAM B[RADLEY] (c18 b.KY) [s/o Abraham
Gabbard & Mary Burriss - 1870; BBG] .
NANCY E. MARION (c13 b.TN)
16 Nov., 1880, <u>Jackson Co.</u> on a place of A.
Bowles, by Elder J. B. Rowlett; wits. Henry
Gabbard, M. C. Hughs, etc. (M-J; H-sgl.
w/uncle 1880; 1900-J m-19; ob-ch. OCN-
6/28/56)

HIRAM (c23 S b.Ows.) [1860-1930 Ows.; s/o
Hiram Gabbard & Mary Jane Freeman - 1880;
DC]
MARY BRYANT (c28 S b.KY) [d/o Jno. Bryant
& Rachel Surrat - 1880; MT]
1883       (1900 m-17; 1910 m-26; 1920; MT;
wid. Mary R.Ows. 1930)

HIRAM PRESLEY "PRESS" (c23 b.KY) [1879-1919;
s/o Jacob Gabbard, Sarah Freeman - 1880 MT]
MARY JANE (nee CREECH) METCALF (c24 2nd b.
KY) [Div/f _____ Metcalf - BBG; 1900]
[1877-1919 Ows.; d/o John Creech & Sarah
Griffee - MT; BBG]
c1901/2       (BBG; TCS; MT; H-sgl. 1900;
Mary Metcalf, Div. 1900; NL 1910 or w/P)

(Gabbard cont.)

## GABBARD (cont.)

HOUSTON B. (c25 S b.Ows.)  [1868-1941; s/o
Geo. W. Gabbard & W2 Mary Eliz. Shook -
TCS; MT; 2nd M-J]
MARTHA BAILEY (c23 S b.KY)  [1870-1916; d/o
Samuel Bailey & Eliz. Combs - 1880; MT]
1893, Ows.  (MT; 1910 m-17; NL M-J)
[H. B. (R.Ricetown 48 widr. b.Ows) m2
9/21/16, Ettie (Creech) Farmer (29 wid. b.
Ows - d/o J.B. Creech & Martha) - M-J 17:3;
MT; HOUSTON m3 Edna Marshall - TCS; MT]
ISAAC (c19 b.Ows.)  [1849-1916 AR; s/o Jno.
Gabbard & Margaret Combs - TS-MT]
DRUSCILLA HORNSBY (c19 b.Clay)  [1849-1914;
d/o Jacob Hornsby & Mariah Gabbard; raised
by Job Hornsby & Cath. Gabbard & Gpar.
Mathias & Sally Gabbard - TS-MT]
c1868          (1870-2; MT went to Ark]
ISAAC HUGH "PREACHER IKE" (c24 S b.Ows) [1876-
1967 Boonev.; s/o Michael Gabbard & Mary
Mangan - 1880; MT; OCN-anniv.; ob-H&S BE-
7/20/67, OCN-3/16/58]
ELIZABETH ["LIZZIE"] EVERSOLE (c23 S b.Ows)
[1879-1966; d/o George Eversole & Rebecca
Moore - 1880; OCN-anniv.; ob-W&S BE-
3/31/66; OCN-3/31/55-5/8/58]
30 Nov, 1899 (Thanksgiving) Cow Cr, Ows. by
Rev. Clint Taylor, Meth. Min.  (OCN-12/2/49
50th anniv; LNG; M-O; 1900 m-6 mo; JFB; MT;
B-O ch.; 1910-1920; R.Cow Cr.; Boonev.
c1946-1966)
IKE - see WILSON HECKLIFF
JACKSON (R.Cope Br. 30 S b.Ows.)  [s/o Willis
Gabbard & Mary Bishop - mg.; 1880; BBG; MT]
GILLIANN BARRETT (R.Cope Br. 17 S b.Br.)
[d/o Peter Barrett & Emeline Vires - mg.]
10 May, 1901, Breathitt, @ James Johnson's,
by James Johnson, JPBC; wits. Dal Gabbard &
H. C. Barrett   (M-B 9:227; 1910-B-5; TCS;
BBG; MT; 1920-B)


(Gabbard cont.)

## GABBARD (cont.)

JACOB (c30 b.Wash. Co., VA) [1813-1900; s/o
   Henry Gabbard & Barbara Hunsucker - JFB MT
   ob-H ME-4/20/1900]
   ELIZABETH WOODS (c22 b.Clay) [c1822-1896;
   d/o Samuel Woods, Jr. & Rebecca Wilson -
   1870; MT; ME-5/8/96 art. on Jacob]
   2 March, 1844, Clay Co. (M-C; 1850; ob-H;
   1860-1870-1880)
JACOB (c23 b.Clay) [s/o Isaac H. Gabbard
   & Jane Isaacs - MT]
   ELIZABETH PETERS (c17 b.KY) [1840-1893;
   d/o Elijah Peters & Margaret Wood - MT;
   WTM]
   1858          (MT; 1860-6 mo.; B-O ch.;
   1880-J-18; widr. Jacob 1900-J]
JACOB W. "JAKE BROKER" (c19 S b.Ows.) [1855-
   1928; s/o Jno. Gabbard, Margaret Combs -MT]
   MARY JANE BOWLING (c18 S b.Ows) [1856-1914;
   d/o Eli Bowling & Ibby Baker/Woods - MT]
   1875          (1880; B-O ch-6/76; 1900 m-24;
   1910 m-32; DC-ch. 1914 M/Jane Bowlen; widr.
   Jacob 1920; MT; BBG)
JACOB (c20 S b.Trav.Rest) [1852-1914; s/o
   Hiram Gabbard & Mary Jane Freeman - MT]
   SARAH M. FREEMAN (c16 S Est.) [1853-1914;
   poss. d/o Michael Freeman & Eliz. - TCS MT]
   1876          (1880-2; 1900 m-24; 1910 m-33;
   MT, they were cousins; B-O ch.)
JACOB K. (28 S b.KY) [1866-1934; s/o Henry
   Clay Gabbard & Rebecca Gabbard - 1880; MT]
   MARTHA EVERSOLE (c20 S b.KY) [1875-1914;
   d/o Geo. Eversole & Rebecca Jane Moore -
   1880; MT]
   March, 1895          (MT; 1900-1910)
   [JACOB m2 c1916, Martha Florence Moore
   (1887-1953 TX; d/o Henry Moore & Mary
   Hobbs) - MT; W-sgl. w/sis 1910; 1920; BC
   1917; ob W&S OCN-11/13/53 & OCC-11/9/34-
   9/3/37; obit-ch. BS-5/8/86]
JAMES B. ["BUD"] (R.Indian Cr. 22 S b.Ows.)
   [1832-1859; s/o Isaac H. Gabbard & Jane
   Isaacs - MT]
   ELIZABETH [ANN] FROST (R.So.Fk. 24 S b.
   Hawk.,TN) [d/o Robert Frost - MT]
   1 July, 1854, Ows. [wid. Eliz. R.Ows. 1860]
(Gabbard cont.)

## GABBARD (cont.)

JAMES B. (R.Ows. 22 S b.KY) P/KY [s/o Wyatt
Gabbard & Sarah Ann White - B-O; MT]
RACHEL [IBBY] LYNCH (R.Ows. 13 S b.KY) P/TN
[d/o Wm. R. Lynch & Cath. Nancy Salyers -
ECP; TCS]
18 Aug., 1878, Ows. [R.Lee 1900]
JAMES MADISON "MATT" (c20 b.KY)    [s/o Wm.
Gabbard & Eliz. Johnston - MT]
CATHERINE ANGEL (c16 b.KY) P/-- KY
c1879         (1880-1/80, H-GF w/them;
widr. Madison 1900-L; KAS; NL M-J)
JOHN LIVINGSTON (c21 S b.KY) [1851-1919; s/o
Jacob Gabbard & Eliz. Woods - 1860 MT TCS]
JALEY REYNOLDS (c16 S b.Cow Cr.)   [1855-
1949; d/o Wesley Reynolds & Nancy Moore -
MT; ob-W OCN-12/16/49]
1871         (MT; 1880-6; 1900 m-29; 1910
m-38; BBG; wid. Jaley 1920; R.Indian Cr.
after mg. to her death - ob-W)
JOHN M. (c20 b.Ows.)  [s/o Henry Gabbard
& Mary Woods - MT]
ELENDER STACY (c19 b.Ows.)  [1852-1902; d/o
Ben Stacy & Hannah Young - MT; ME-3/28/02]
1870/1        (B-O ch-6/77; 1880 ch. Martha
10 & Chas. 2, but H-sgl. 1870; 1900-B m-29,
dau. Martha b. 10/73; M-L ch-1903; WF/P-CW;
MT)
JOHN W. (c18-40 S b.KY) [1851-1924 Cow Cr.;
s/o Geo. W. Gabbard & Wl Eliz. Williams -
TCS; MT; 1870; DC]
[LYDIA?] ISAACS (poss. c18 b.KY)
1870-92 (poss. c1876?)              (TCS; MT;
NL 1880; NL M-J) [poss. 1880-J as John 28,
Lydia 22 & ch. Mary J. 3 & Isaac 3 mos.,
but MT says no ch.; 1860-70-J shows a LYDIA
d/o Andrew Isaacs & Lucinda Carpenter -
WP/M-Lau. NL 1900-J. This is NOT the same
couple as John & Lydia (Chambers) - 1880-
1900-L]  [H-remd-9 1900 no Gabbard ch.]
JOHN C. B. (c25 b.KY) [1858-1906; s/o Wyatt
Gabbard & Sarah A. White - MT; TS-TCS]
MARY ELIZ. "MOLLIE" HERNDON (c23 b.Ows.)
[1860-1918; d/o Geo. W. Herndon & Jalah
BBurg. - 1880; TS-TCS]
1883/4        (1900; JFB; wid. Mollie 1910)
(Gabbard cont.)

## GABBARD (cont.)

JOHN (c21 S b.Ows.) [1870-1951 Ows.; s/o
Julius Gabbard & Cath. Thomas - 1880; MT;
ob-H OCN-4/20/51]
   MALINDA CALLAHAN (c24 S b.Ows.) [1866-
   1956; d/o Jeremiah Callahan & W1 Esther
   Moore - 1880; MT; TS-TCS]
   1890          (1900 m-10; 1910 m-19; MT;
   B-O ch.;   1920; ob-ch. BS-12/17/98)
   [JOHN m2 Lennie _____ - ob-H]
JOHN W. (c42 2nd b.KY) [m1 _____ Isaacs
   above - TCS]   [1851-1924 Ows. - DC]
   MARY "POLLY" (nee HIGNITE) FIELDS (c36 2nd
   b.Clay) [wid/o Jos. Fields - 1880-J; TW]
   1890/1          (1900 m-9, Fields s-ch-4/76
   & 2/78; wid. R.Cow Cr. 1924; NL M-J)
JOHN P. (c27 b.Ows.) [1866-1904; s/o Hiram
   Gabbard & Hannah Million - 1880; MT]
   MARY JANE "MOLLIE" WILSON (c26 b.KY) [d/o
   Hardin Wilson & Minerva Hurst - 1880; MT]
   1894          (MT; 1900 m-2; TCS; BBG)
[JOHN] LOGAN (R.Lee 18 S b.KY) [s/o Hiram
   "Top" Gabbard & Mary Bryant - TCS; BBG; MT]
   FLORENCE M. BRANDENBURG (R.Lee 17 S b.KY)
   [d/o Theo. BBurg. & Hannah Jackson - MT]
   21 Nov., 1903, Lee @ Richard BBurg.'s, by
   G. B. Bowman, MG; wits. A. S. Abshear &
   Tilford Creech  (M-L; 1910-1920; BBG; BC
   1913-1915-1917-1919)  [LOGAN m2 Elizabeth
   Cole - TCS]
JULIUS C. (c26 b.KY)   [1842-1898; s/o John
   Gabbard & Margaret Combs - MT; TS-TCS]
   CATHARINE THOMAS (c22 b.KY) [1846-1916;
   d/o Joseph Thomas & Anna Couch - MT;
   LNG/WT; TS-TCS]
   4 May, 1868, Ows.; wits. Henry Thomas &
   John Sizemore   (P-CW LNG; 1870-1; MT;
   1880-11; 1890; wid. Katherine 1900)
LAFAYETTE (c26-36 b.KY) [s/o Abijah Gabbard
   & Nancy Bishop - 1880; 1900-M]
   RACHEL HIGNITE (___ b.___)
   1900-10?          (MT; HP/1900-M; NL 1900Sx;
   NL M-J/P)


(Gabbard cont.)

**GABBARD (cont.)**
LEE (c28 S b.KY)    [s/o Jackson Gabbard - BBG;
  MT]
  ELIZA HOLLON (c19 S b.KY)
  1898          (1900 m-1; 1910 m-12; BBG; MT)
LOGAN - see JOHN LOGAN
MADISON - see JAMES MADISON
MEREDITH C. (c20 S b.KY)  [1849-1925; s/o
  Cornelious Gabbard & Mary Moore - MT 1870]
  MARY "POP" SIMPSON (c24 S b.KY)  [1845/6-
  1937; d/o John Simpson & Jane Browning -
  MT; 1870; TCS]
  late 1870         (1880-J; B-J ch-1874; 1900
  m-30; 1910 m-39; 1920; BBG's GF; NL M-J)
MEREDITH (c25 b.Ows.)  [1878-1966 MI; s/o John
  L. Gabbard & Jaley Reynolds - 1880; MT; ob-
  HS&M 7/1/49-12/16/49]
  LUCINDA "LOU" FLANNERY (c24 b.KY) [d/o Tom
  Flannery & Lucy K. Circy - 1880; MT]
  June, 1904      (MT; ME-6/29/05 R.Ham.,OH
  when twin daus. b.; R.MI 1949)
MICHAEL (c27 b.Clay)  [1837-1902; s/o Isaac H.
  Gabbard & Jane Isaacs - MT; ob-H ME-9/5/02]
  MARY ANN MANGAN (c16 S b.Ire)  [1848-1923;
  d/o Hugh Mangan & Annie McKinley - MT]
  15 Sept, 1864, Ows.  (JFB; 1870-1880-1900;
  MT; wid. Mary 1910; ob-ch. BS-11/20/86)
  [NOTE: ob-H says he was stationed in
  Chicago during Civil War & while there md.
  Mary]
MICHAEL "BUNTY MIKE" (c21 S b.KY)  [1852-1940;
  s/o Wilson Gabbard & Susan Abner - 1870;
  MT; JTB]
  PERLINA BAKER (c21 S b.KY) . [1852-1917; d/o
  Andy "Pandy" Baker & Polly Abner - 1860;
  TCS; MT; JTB]
  1873          (1880-6; 1900 m-26; 1910 m-35;
  MT; BBG; M-L ch-1914)  [MIKE m2 1917-20
  Jane Baker - MT]
MICHAEL (c21 b.Indian Cr.)  [1861-1942; s/o
  George W. Gabbard & W1 Eliza Ann Williams
  - MT; ob-H OCC-6/12/42]
  RACHEL COMBS (c15 b.KY)  [sis/o Martha E.
  Combs Hill - ob-WS OCC-4/29/38]
  24 July, 1884 Ows.  (ob-H; 1900 m-17; later
  moved to Berea; R.Mad. 1938 ob-WS)
(Gabbard cont.)

GABBARD (cont.)
MICHAEL "BUD" (c18 b.KY) [s/o Elisha Gabbard
    & Mary Ann Peters - TCS; MT]
    MARY J. DEAN (c15 b.KY)
    1897/8            (1900; TCS) [H-remd.]
[MICHAEL] MIKE (R.Cope Br.; 22 S b.Ows.) P/Br-
    Clay [s/o Willis Gabbard & Mary Bishop -
    1880; GGB; MT]
    JALEY JOHNSON (R.Athol; 18 S b.Br.) P/--
    12 Oct., 1899, Lee [rec. Br.] @ Whitley
    Johnson's, by W. H. Bowman, JPLC; wits.
    John Jett & G. B. Gilbert    (M-B 8:408; MT;
    1900-B m-1; 1910-B-8, HS w/them; 1920-B)
MICHAEL (___ b.___)
    AMANDA ANGEL (___ b.___)
    7 Feb., 1901, Ows. [rec. Perry] @ Elisha
    Gabbard's, by H. H. Rice, JPPC; wits.
    Elisha & George Gabbard    (M-P G:124;
    NL 1910Sx)
MICHAEL (R.Ows. 29 2nd b.Ows.) P/Ows. [ml
    Mary J. Dean above - TCS]
    ROSA [nee GILBERT] MORRIS (R.Per. 24 2nd
    b.Per.) P/Ows.    [ml _____ Morris]
    [d/o Isaac Gilbert - MT]
    24 Dec., 1910, Ows. [R.Owsley 1920; W/as
    both MORRIS & GILBERT in BC]
MITCHEL (c21 S b.Est.) [1877-1912; s/o Jacob
    Gabbard & Sarah Freeman - TCS; 1880]
    MARY JANE "JENNIE" RADER (c15 S b.Ows.)
    [d/o Nathan Rader & Emeline Gabbard - BBG]
    1898/9        (1900-1910; B-O ch.; TCS; BBG;
    ob-ch. BS-4/23/87)    [JENNIE m2 Melvin
    Madden - TCS; BBG; 1920; ob-ch. by H1
    BE-4/11/63]
MITCHELL - see also ELISHA MITCHELL
NOAH (R.Ows. 23 S b.Clay) [1838-1864; s/o
    Henry Gabbard & Polly Woods - MT]
    JUDITH MOORE (R.Ows. 21 S b.Clay) [1836-
    1917; d/o Edward Moore & Minerva Evans -MT]
    1859 (no date), Ows. [JUDITH m2 Elcannah
    Richardson - MT; 1890 Judah Richardson
    f/w/o Noah Gabbard]


(Gabbard cont.)

## GABBARD (cont.)

PERRY M. (c24 S b.Ricetown) [1873-1936; s/o
  Geo. W Gabbard & Mary Shook - 1880 MT]
  SARAH COMBS (c18 S b.Ricetown) [1880-1945;
  d/o John Breckenridge Combs & Nancy J.
  Frost - 1880; MT]
  1898      (MT; 1900 m-2; 1910 m-12; 1920;
  B-O ch.; BC 1913-1915-1917; ob-ch. BS-
  10/13/88)
PETER B. (c32 b.KY) [1836-1921 OK; s/o Jno.
  Gabbard & Margaret Combs - MT; TCS]
  JEMIMA FORD (c17 b.KY) [d/o Wilse Ford -MT]
  3 Dec., 1868, Ows. (TCS; 1870, no ch; MT;
  TCS; went to AR pre-1880, then OK)
PHILIP (c27 S b.KY) [s/o Wyatt Gabbard & Sarah
  Ann White - 1880]
  LINDA LOVELESS (c16 b.KY)
  1887/8      (TCS; 1900-W)
  [PHILIP (56 widr.) m2 2/17/1918 Br., Ella
  Jane Mullins - M-B]
PLEASANT W. (c23 S b.KY) [s/o Jacob Gabbard
  & Mary J. Bowling - 1880-1900; MT]
  LULU BAKER (c14 S b.KY)
  July, 1900      (MT; H-sgl. 1900; 1910-
  1920; BC 1912-1914-1919)
PLEASANT H. (c24 S b.Ows) [1877-1946; s/o
  Henry Clay Gabbard & Rebecca Gabbard - FH;
  DC; 1900; MT]
  LULA WOODS a/k/a GABBARD (c16 S b.Ows.)
  [1883-1970 Danville hosp.; d/o Pleasant
  GABBARD & Virginia "Jennie" WOODS - DC;
  BBG; MT; W/as GABBARD - FH & DC-H; TS-TCS;
  ob-W BE-2/26/70]
  late 1900      (H-sgl. 1900; 1910 m-10;
  1920; B-O ch.; MT; BBG; BC 1918; wid. Lula
  R.Ricetown 1967 - ob-ch. BE-9/14/67)
PRESS - see HIRAM PRESLEY
SIDNEY (c20 S b.Clay) [1879-1938; s/o Elisha
  Gabbard & Mary Peters - 1880-1900; MT; ob-H
  OCC-11/11/38]
  CHARITY BISHOP (c17 S b.Br.) [1883-1954;
  d/o David Bishop & Mary Bishop - MT; TCS;
  ob-W OCN-8/6/54]
  1900      (H-sgl 1900; 1910 m-10; B-O ch;
  1920 WM w/them; BC 1911-1913; ob-ch. BS-
  3/31/88-5/28/98)
(Gabbard cont.)

## GABBARD (cont.)

STEPHEN ARNOLD (c25 S b.Ows.) [1880-1963 Mad;
s/o Michael Gabbard & Mary Mangan - MT; ob-
WS OCN-3/6/58]
FLORA SEALE (c21 S b.Ows.) [1884-1920; d/o
George Seale & Margaret Evans - MT]
1904/5          (1910; JFB; MT; B-O ch.; BC
ch-1913-1916; 1920; ob-ch. BS-12/3/92-
12/19/91) [STEPHEN m2 1936, Laura B. Moore
- MT; R.Richmond 1958]

TATE - see TAYLOR PRICE

TAYLOR PRICE "TATE" (28 b.Ows.) [1878-1973 AZ;
s/o Michael Gabbard & Mary Ann Mangan - MT;
ob-WS OCN-3/6/58]
AMANDA FRANCES MOORE (23 b.KY) [1883-1954
AZ; d/o Wm. J. Moore & Mary McDaniel - MT;
TCS]
7 June, 1906          (JFB; MT; R.AZ 1958,
Tempe, AZ 1967 - ob-HS BE-7/20/67)

WICKLIFF - see HECKLIFF

WILBURN "TATER WILL" (c23 S b.Eversole) [s/o
Geo. W. Gabbard & W2 Mary E. Shook - TCS;
1870 as Wilburn; MT; ob-HS OCC-6/12/42]
MAGGIE McWHORTER (c16 S b.Jack.)
1889/90          (BBG & MT W/as McWhorter;
1910; NL 1900; B-O ch. W/as Maggie
McCreary; NL M-J; ob-HS; R.Harrison, IN
1942; H/as Wilburn, Wm. & Will; NL M-B)

WILLIAM "BILLY BUCK" (R.Ows. 18 S b.Clay)
[s/o Jacob Gabbard & Susan Bowman - TCS]
MARY GABBARD (R.Ows. 18 S b.Mad.) [d/o
Philip Gabbard & Jane Carpenter - MT]
9 Feb., 1856, Ows. [R.Owsley 1860-1870]
[WILLIAM m2 10/3/1887 Jack., Icy Madden -
TCS; MT; wid. Isa w/son Gentry 1920]

WILLIAM (c26 b.Clay) [1832-1905 Jack.; s/o
Mathias Gabbard & Sally Peters - MT; LNG;
TCS]
[RACHEL] ELIZABETH JOHNSTON (c14 b.Clay)
[1844-1907; d/o Samuel Johnston & Rachel
Pennington - MT; TCS; LNG]
16/19 Dec, 1858, Ows. (P-CW MT; 1860; JFB;
REM; 1860MS has son d. 2/60 @ 1 mo.; TCS/
Rufus J. Bruner)

(Gabbard cont.)

## GABBARD (cont.)

WILLIAM RILEY (19 b.Ows.) [1844-1922 Mad.; s/o
Peter Gabbard & Susan Harrison - MT]
SARAH ANN PETERS (c24 b.Ows) [1949-1916 AR;
d/o Elijah Peters & Margaret Woods -MT]
31 Dec., 1863        (MT moved to Ark., then
back to KY)

WM. BENTLEY (c24 S b.Ows.) [1847-1912; s/o
Jacob Gabbard & Eliz. Woods - TS-TCS]
SALLY BARRETT (c19 S b.KY) [d/o Thomas
Barrett & Barbara Gabbard; w/GP Mathias
& Sarah Gabbard 1860 - MT; TCS]
1871, Ows.        (MT; 1880-1900-1910; wid.
Sally 1920)

WILLIAM M. "BUFFALO BILL" (c22 b.KY)  [s/o
Wilson Gabbard & Susan Abner - MT]
RACHEL PETERS (c21 b.Ows.)  [d/o Elijah
Peters & Margaret Wood - MT; WTM]
c1877        (1880-2; MT; WTM; 1900-B as
m-21 = 1878/9; M-B ch-1904; NL M-B)

WILLIAM A. "TREE BILL" (c26 S b.Ows.)  [1853-
1927; s/o Isaac H. Gabbard & Jane Isaacs -
B-O; MT]
VANETTA LEWIS (c18 S KY) [1861-1948; d/o
Fielding Lewis & Jane Smith - MT]
1878/9        (1880 no ch.; 1900 m-21;
1910 m-31; MT; JFB; 1920)

WILLIAM OWSLEY (23 S b.Gabbard, Ows.) [1869-
1944; s/o Henry Clay Gabbard & Rebecca
Gabbard - MT]
MARTHA HAYES GABBARD (21 S b.Ricetown)
[1872-1942; d/o Michael Gabbard & Mary Ann
Mangan - MT; FH]
28 July, 1893        (JFB; MT; 1900-1910-1920;
B-O ch.)

WILLIAM (c31 S b.KY)
RACHEL _____ (c17 S b.KY)
1894/5        (1910; NL 1900Sx; NL M-B/J)


(Gabbard cont.)

GABBARD (cont.)
WILLIAM B. (c22 S b.Ows.) [1876-1943; s/o
   Hiram Gabbard & Hannah Million - MT; BBG;
   1880; TS-TCS]
   LOUVINA RICHARDSON (c22 S b.KY) [1877-1943]
   11 Feb, 1899, Jackson (TCS; 1900-1910-1920;
   BBG; MT)
WILLIAM [P.] ["BUFFALO BILL"] (c22 S
   b.Sebastian) [s/o Elisha Gabbard & Mary
   Peters - 1880; MT]
   LAURA B[ELL] RICE (c14 S b.Sebastian)
   [1887-1911 Ows.; d/o Henry Rice & Margaret
   Sandlin - MT; DC]
   26 Jan., 1900, Ows. [rec. Perry] @ George
   Miller's, by H. H. Rice, JPOC; wits: Minnie
   Seal & Jas. B. Williams    (M-P G:16; 1900,
   m-6 mos.; 1910 m-6; B-O ch.; MT)
   [WILLIAM m2 Rose Nell Burns - TCS; MT;
   1920; BC 1913-1914-1915-1919; WILLIAM m3
   Bertha Lewis from Hyden - BBG/WOG MT]
WILLIS "TEEN" (c24 b.Ows.) [s/o Wilson Gabbard
   & Susan Abner - MT]
   MARY BISHOP/BAKER (c22 b.Clay)
   c1867         (1870-2; B-O ch.; 1880-12; BBG;
   MT)    [NOTE: MT BBG the GD/o Willis & Mary
   says Mary was actually a Baker; but both
   B-O ch. & M-B of son C. B. list her as
   Mary Bishop]
WILSON "DOCK" (c17 S b.Ows.) [1873-1912; s/o
   Elisha Gabbard & Mary Peters - 1880; MT;
   DC; TS-TCS]
   CLARA BAKER (___ b.KY)
   c1891         (MT, Wilson & Clara's son
   Michael Riley raised by GP; GS Michael b.
   12/93 w/Elisha & Mary Gabbard 1900, but F
   remd. 5/93, so prob. s/b 12/92; GS Riley,
   17, w/Elisha & Mary 1910)
WILSON "DOCK" (c19 2nd b.Ows.)    [m1 Clara
   Baker above - MT] [1873-1912 - TS-TCS]
   MATILDA WILLIAMS (c14 S b.Lee) [1878-1960
   Ows.; d/o Enoch Williams & Eliz. Bishop -
   1880; MT; ob-W BE-6/9/60]
   28 May, 1893        (MT; 1900 m-7; 1910 m-17;
   wid. Matilda 1920; TCS; BBG; LM; B-O ch-
   1908, W/listed on wrong line)

(Gabbard cont.)

## GABBARD (cont.)
WILSON HECKLIFF "IKE" (c16-30 b.KY)  [s/o
   Willis Gabbard & Mary Bishop - 1880; MT]
   REVELLA _____ (___ b.___)
   1896-1910        (MT; BBG/Wilson's niece
   Margaret Gilbert Terry, decd.; HP/NL 1900;
   NL 1900-1910Sx; moved to FL; NL 1910Sx-FL;
   NL M-B/J)
WILTON HARRISON "BUNK" (c21 S b.Ows.) [1879-
   1950 Ows.; GS/o Abe & Mary Gabbard - 1880;
   s/o Emaline GABBARD - BBG/Conley Mainous;
   MT; DC & ob-H BE-11/17/50 have s/o Harrison
   Gabbard & Emma Flanery, but this is in
   error. His mother, Emma Gabbard, later md.
   Mike Flanery.]
   MARY ANN "SISSIE" CREECH (R.Jack. c16 S b.
   Big Sturgeon)  [1883-1980's; d/o Enoch
   Creech & Mary F. Tackett - TCS; MT; ob-WS
   OCN-12/16/54; BS 12/20/79 art.]
   1899        (BS-12/20/79 art.; 1900 m-0,
   Harrison & Mary A.; 1910 m-9, Harrison &
   Sissie, H-GM Mary w/them; 1920; BBG; TCS;
   MT; BC 1913-1914-1916-1920-1924; Trav. Rest
   1950-54; in 1962 Sissie sold farm & moved
   to Connersville, IN, where she R.1979)
WYATT (R.Ows. 22 S b.Ows.[s/b Mad. or Est.])
   [s/o Philip Gabbard & Jane Carpenter - MT]
   S[ARAH] A[NN] WHITE (R.Ows. 16 S b.Ows)
   [d/o Aquilla White & Sarah Shanks - MT]
   10 Aug., 1854, Ows. [R.Owsley 1860-1870-
   1880]
## GAINS
JOSEPH (c19 b.TN)
   SALLIE LUKER (c18 b.Ows/Jack.)
   c1871        (1880-Lau-8; B-Lau. ch-1874-
   1878)
## GALE
LEWIS S. (c20 b.KY)
   LOUISA _____ (c21 b.KY)
   c1858        (1860-1; NL M-J)

**GALLAGER/GALAGER**
DANIEL (24 S b.OH)
    ELIZA J[ANE] PRICE (17 S b.Buck Cr.) [d/o
    Henry Price & Levina Estes - TCS]
    26 June, 1889, <u>Lee</u> (M-L; 1900-L; art. BE-
    1/18/73 says moved to Vincent, Ows. 1902;
    1910-1920; B-O ch.)
    [LIZA JANE (R.Beattyv. 65 wid. b.Lee) m2
    7/31/1937 Lee, Jesse Greer - M-L]
**GARRETT**
ARTHUR - see WILLIAM ARTHUR
BRITTON (c19 b.Lee,VA) [s/o Geo. Washington
    Garrett & Sarah Eliz. Thompson - PWB]
    SUSAN BOWMAN (c25 b.KY) [d/o Wm. Bowman &
    Nancy Bowles - PWB]
    c1869      (1870 no ch.; B-O ch.; wid.
    Susan 1880-1900)
EUGENE C. (c22 S b.KY) [s/o Lafayette Garrett
    & Susan Bell - ob-HS OCN-12/23/49]
    BERTIE COMBS (c16 S b.KY)
    1908/9      (1910; PWB; TCS;
    R.Midltwn.,OH 1949)
GEORGE WASHINGTON (c31 S PM b.Boonev.) [s/o
    Lafayette Garrett & Susan Bell - 1880;
    ob-H&S OCN-9/1/50-12/23/49]
    LUCY SUSAN MOYERS (c20 S b.Boonev.) [d/o
    Isaac Anderson Moyers & Martha Combs - PWB;
    ob-H]
    16 Sept., 1906      (PWB; 1910-1920; ob-H;
    B-O ch.; BC 1919; Richmond, KY 1949-50;
    ob-ch. BS-10/11/90)
LAFAYETTE MARK (c20 S b.Lee,VA) [s/o George W.
    Garrett & Sarah Thompson - 1870; PWB]
    SUSAN WARD BELL (c17 S b.Lee, VA) [d/o
    Marcus C. Bell & Martha J. Flanery - 1870]
    1871      (18880-7; B-O ch.; 1900 m-28;
    1910 m-39; PWB; wid. Susan W. 1920; ob-ch.
    OCN-9/1/50-12/23/49)


(Garrett cont.)

**GARRETT (cont.)**
MARCUS B. (c25 S b.KY)   [1874-1946; s/o
   Lafayette Garrett & Susan W. Bell - 1880;
   ob-W; ob-HS OCN-12/23/49 H/as decd.]
   MINERVA BOND (c16 S b.Ows.) [1883-1961; d/o
   Oliver Bond & Lucinda Gum - 1900; ob-W BE-
   3/16/61]
   11 June, 1899, Ows. (Sun. morning), by Rev.
   J. B. Rowlett  (ob-W; ME-6/23/99; 1900 m-1,
   w/WP; 1910 m-10, WM w/them; PWB; BC 1913-
   1915)
WM. ARTHUR (c24 S b.Buck Cr.)  [1882-1965; s/o
   Lafayette Garrett & Susan W. Bell - 1900;
   ob-H&S BE-3/25/65, OCN-12/23/49-4/24/58]
   MINNIE SMITH (c19 S b.Sturgeon)  [d/o Wm.
   Smith & Lucy A. Gibson - TCS; ob-WM&S OCC-
   3/16/34-10/3/41, BE-1/31/46]
   1906/7        (1910-1920; B-O ch-1908;
   R.Pebworth 1934-1958; wid. R.Pebworth 1965)
**GAY**
CLARK (c26 S b.KY)  [s/o John B. Gay & China
   Jane    ]
   MARY _____ (c16 S b.KY)
   1908/9      (1910 w/HP)
ELIJAH (c51 2nd b.KY)  [widr/o Polly Baker -
   M-C 8/10/1838]
   CATHARINE HENSLEY (c18 b.TN/VA)
   c1862        (1870-6; 1880-17; LNG;
   NL M-J)
HENRY (c20 b.KY)
   HETTY _____ (c14 b.KY)
   c1865        (1870-4)
HENRY C. (c32 b.KY)
   MARY [ELIZABETH] CARMACK (c22 b.KY)  [d/o
   Abraham Carmack & Alcy Dean - 1870 Eliz.]
   14 Dec., 1876 Jackson Co. @ R. D. Gibson's,
   by Elias Moore, Min.; wits. Peely Short &
   Jacob Gabbard   (M-J 1:61; TCS; 1880-J;
   W/as Eliz. & Mary E.)
HENRY (c20 S b.Mistletoe, Ows.) [s/o Russell
   Lewis Gay & Eliza Williams - 1880]
   NANCY M. BISHOP (c17 S b.Clay) [d/o James
   Bishop & Rhoda Carmack - TCS; BBG]
   1884/5       (1900-1910-1920; B-O ch.)

(Gay cont.)

273

**GAY (cont.)**

JAMES B. (c23 b.Clay)   [s/o Elijah Gay
   & Polly Baker - TCS]
   MATILDA WILLIAMS (c18 b.KY)   [d/o James
   Williams & Lucinda Abner - 1860]
   c1861          (1880-18; NL 1870)

JEFF - see THOMAS JEFFERSON

JOB (c24 b.Clay)   [s/o Elijah Gay & W1 Polly
   Baker - LNG]
   LUTICIA "TISH" BOWMAN (c21 b.Ows.)   [1853-
   1936 Ows.; d/o Robt. Bowman & Mary Turner -
   1870; B-O; ob-W OCC-11/27/36]
   1875          (1880-4; TCS; LNG; NL M-J)

JOHN [B.] (c20 S b.KY)   [s/o Nelson Gay
   & Hannah Barger - TCS]
   CHANNY [CHINA JANE] BARKER (c16 S b.KY)
   [d/o Abr. Barker & Armilda Hacker - TCS]
   5 Oct., 1875, <u>Clay</u>  (M-C; TCS; 1880-3;
   1900-1910-1920; W/as China, Jane &
   Chaney/Channy/Chanee)

MACK - see McCOY

MAURICE - see MORRIS

McCOY L. (c23 S b.KY)   [s/o Elijah Gay & W2
   Cath. Anderson]
   MARY McINTOSH (c22 S b.KY)   [d/o Wm.
   McIntosh & Mary J. Harris - TCS]
   8 April, 1887, <u>Perry</u> @ Schoolhouse; wits.
   John Morris & Jno. McIntosh  (M-P G:154;
   1900 m-13; 1910 m-24; BC 1917; wid. Mary
   1920)

MORRIS (c26 b.KY)   [s/o Russell Lewis Gay
   & Eliza Williams - 1880]
   MATILDA MORGAN (c19 b.KY)   [d/o John
   Morgan - BBG]
   1897/8          (1900; BBG; BC 1915)


(Gay cont.)

## GAY (cont.)

ROBT. "BOB" (c24 S b.Br.) [1879-1922; s/o Job
   Gay & Leticia Bowman - 1880-1900; LNG]
   MARTHA MARSHALL (c21 b.KY)   [d/o Green
   Marshall & Rebecca Abshear - 1900; LNG/FiL]
   1902/3           [appar. DIVORCED, though it
   appears they had ch. together after Div.]
   (LNG's FiL, who was neph/o Bob Gay, says W1
   was Martha Marshall; 1910 H-remd-7; ob-ch.
   Nettie Peters lists P/Bob Gay & Martha
   Marshall; 1920 Martha Marshall & ch., inc.
   dau. Nettie; M-O daus. Nettie as Marshall &
   Bertha as d/o Bob "Marshall" & Martha
   Marshall; NL M-B)
ROBERT "BOB" (c27 2nd b.Br.)    [m1 Martha
   Marshall above]
   LENNIE ELIZABETH "BETTY" BOWMAN (c19 S
   b.Eversole)  [d/o Levi Letcher Bowman &
   Sarah E. Crank - TCS; 1900; JFB/BBG]
   c1906          (1910 H-2nd, m-7, but this
   was appar. W1; 1920; B-O ch.; BC 1915-1919;
   LNG's FiL; W/as Lennie E., Betty/Bettie L.
   Bowman; NL M-B)   [BETTY m2 after 1922,
   Leslie Stacy (s/o James & Susan) - LNG]
RUSSELL LEWIS (c22 b.Per.) [s/o Elijah Gay
   & Polly Baker - TCS]
   ELIZA WILLIAMS (c15 b.Ows.)   [d/o James
   Williams & Lucinda Abner -1860]
   c1862          (1870-7; 1880; 1890 Eliza
   wid/o Russell Gay; wid. Eliza 1900; TCS)
THEOPHILUS (c37 b.KY)  [s/o James Gay
   & Matilda Williams - 1880; TCS]
   SUSAN GAY (c32 b.KY)
   8 Oct., 1898, Jackson Co. @ R. P.Gay's;
   wits. R. P. Gay & Geo. Williams  (M-J 2:26;
   1900-J anot.; TCS)
THOMAS JEFFERSON (c23 S b.Ows.) [1867-1949;
   s/o Russell Lewis Gay & Eliza Williams -
   1880; TS-TCS]
   LYDIA TAYLOR (c26 S b.Clay)  [1864-1944;
   d/o Pendleton Taylor & Minerva Jennings -
   1880; ob-WS OCC-8/22/41; TS-TCS]
   1890          (1900 m-10; 1910 m-19; 1920;
   B-O ch.)

(Gay cont.)

**GAY (cont.)**
THOMAS (c24 b.KY)  [s/o Nelson Gay & Hannah
    Barger - LNG]
    JOSEPHINE DAVIDSON (c18 b.KY)
    9 May, 1878, <u>Clay</u>  (M-C; 1880-1; TCS)
WALKER B. (c17 S b.Major)  [1876-1958; s/o Job
    Gay & Luticia Bowman - 1880; LNG; ob-H BE-
    12/11/58]
    REBECCA MOORE (c18 S b.KY)  [d/o Madison
    Moore & Luzanne Stepp - LNG; 1880]
    c1893, Ows.  [DIVORCED]  (LNG; DC ch-1976)
    [H-remd.]  [REBECCA m2 1896, Rev. Bill
    Thomas - LNG; 1910]
WALKER B. (c23 2nd b.Major)  [Div/f Rebecca
    Moore above - LNG]  [1876-1958 - ob-H]
    MARTHA ROWLAND (R.Buck Cr. c17 S b.Major)
    [d/o Abe Rowland & Holly Ann Addison - LNG]
    March, 1899 Ows., by Bro. Bent Bowman
    (ME-4/7/99; LNG; 1900 m-1; 1910 m-11; B-O
    ch.; 1920; BC 1914-1918; R.Major, Ows. 1936
    - ob-HM; ob-ch. BS-12/11/86-8/19/93)
WILLIAM J. (c24 b.KY)  [s/o James Gay &
    Matilda Williams - 1880; TCS]
    MARY FRANCES ISAACS (c23 b.KY)  [d/o
    Linville Isaacs & Ella Asbell - TCS]
    2 Feb., 1892 <u>Jackson Co.</u> @ Lenville Isaacs,
    by H. C. Hughes, JPJC; wits. Thee Gay &
    Irvin Baker  (M-J 1:213; 1900-J anot. m-7;
    TCS)
**GENTRY/JENTRY/JENTREY**
ALEXANDER (R.Ows. 25 S b.Carter Co., TN)
    AMERICA COLLIER (R.Ows. uk S b.VA)  [poss.
    d/o David Collier & Rebecca        ]
    14 Sept., 1858, Ows.  (a/L 9/21/58; W-18,
    b.Lee,VA)  [R.Owsley 1860; Wolfe 1870-1880]
ALFRED (R.Br. 25 S b.TN)
    ESTHER McKINNY (R.Lau. 15 S b.Ows.)
    8 Jan., 1856, <u>Laurel</u>  (M-Lau. mf; B-Lau.
    ch-1857; 1860-2)
CRITTENDEN - see JOHN CRITTENDEN


(Gentry cont.)

GENTRY (cont.)

FRANKLIN G. ["FRANK"] (c25 S b.KY) [s/o Hiram
    Gentry & Araminta Bowman - TCS; 1870-80-J;
    ob-HS OCC-7/22/38]
    [REBECCA] RACHEL STRONG (c16 S b.KY)
    30 Aug., 1890, Jackson; bm. groom & A. L.
    Tincher (M-J 7:350; TCS; 1900-8 m-13; 1910
    m-19, near HP both years; TCS; BC 1912; in
    Jackson 1938; ob-ch. HJN-1/89; W/as Rachel
    & Rebecca R.)
GENERAL J. (c22 S b.Tyner, Jack.) [s/o Hiram
    Gentry & Araminta Bowman - ob-HS OCC-
    7/22/38; TCS; 1870-J]
    MARTHA BROGANS (c16 S b.Island City)
    [d/o Nancy Brogan - 1900]
    1894/5          (1900 m-5 WM w/them; 1910
    m-16; JFB/BBG; B-O ch.; BC 1916; NL 1920Sx;
    R.Chester, PA 1938)
JAMES ["JIM"] (c20 S b.KY) [s/o Alfred Gentry
    & Esther McKinney - TCS; P/M-Lau.]
    MARY FLINCHUM (___ b.___)
    10 Oct., 1889, Jackson, @ wid. Flinchum's,
    by S. E. Johnson, "ELGC"; wits. W. C. &
    Geo. McDaniel; sur. Alfred Gentry
    (M-J 1:181; TCS) [H-remd.]
JAMES "JIM" (c24 2nd b.KY) [m1 Mary Flinchum
    above - TCS]
    WINNIE F. _____ (c24 S b.KY)
    1893/4          (1910; NL 1900Sx;
    NL M-B/C/J)
JAMES THOMAS "TOM" (c29 S b.KY) [s/o Hiram
    Gentry & Araminta Bowman - TCS; ob-HS OCC-
    7/22/38; TCS]
    GARNETT _____ (c21 S b.WV)
    1907/8      (1910 near HP; TCS; R.WV 1938)
JOHN CRITTENDEN (c28 S b.KY) [s/o Hiram Gentry
    & Araminta Bowman - TCS; ob-HS OCC-7/22/38;
    1870-1880-J]
    MARTHA J. BOWMAN (c22 S b.KY) [A-d/o Daniel
    Bowman & Isabelle J. Floyd - TCS; ME-6/5/96
    & 6/26/96]
    1894/5          (1900; 1910, near HP; TCS; BC
    1912; R.Loveland 1938)


(Gentry cont.)

**GENTRY (cont.)**
ROBERT (R.Jack. 19 S b.Est.) P/Est.  [s/o
    James J. Gentry & Ellen Kelly - mg.]
    BERTIE FARMER (R.Lee 18 S b.Lee) P/Lee
    [d/o John Farmer & Margaret Gray - mg.;
    1900-L]
    13 Sept., 1907, <u>Lee Co.</u> @ John Farmer's, by
    Elijah Isaacs; wits. R. H. & S. P. Farmer
    (M-L; 1910-L m1-3; BC-1912-1919; 1920)
THOMAS - see JAMES THOMAS
**GIBSON/GIPSON**
ALBERT (c26 2nd b.Fay.)    [s/o John Gibson
    & Sarah    - 3rd M-O]  [m1 _____ -
    NL M-Fay.]
    RACHEL MOORE (c18 S b.KY)  [1871-1927]
    1892/3         (1900-1910; ob-ch. BS-9/27/90
    & DC-ch-1971; NL M-Fay/J)   [ALBERT (R.Ows.
    66 widr. b.Fay.; s/o John Gibson & Sarah)
    m3 2/9/1929 Ows., Margaret Riley (R.Ows. 44
    wid. - d/o James Riley & Nancy) - M-O]
ARCHIBALD (R.Jack. 18 S b.TN) P/TN
    CYNTHIA COLLINS (R.Ows. 21 S b.Let.) P/--
    Let.
    17 Feb., 1874, Ows. @ Henry Clark's
ELIJAH (c22 b.Ows.) [1876-1965 Clk hosp; s/o
    Wm. Gibson & Lucinda Angel - PWB; 2nd M-L;
    ob-H BE-8/26/65]
    RHODA _____ (c17 b.KY)
    1898/9      [DIVORCED 1900-1921 - 2nd M-L]
    (1900 m-1, no ch.; NL M-J)   [ELIJAH m2
    9/21/1921 Lee, Ethel Stepp - R.Lone 1965 -
    ob-H]
ENOCH (c23 b.KY)
    LYDIA ANN SEE (c17 b.TN)
    c1851         (1860-8; B-O ch.)
EWING (19 S b.Hanc.,TN)  [s/o Charles Gibson
    & Oney    - mg.]
    ELIZABETH GIBSON (19 S b.Hanc.,TN)  [d/o
    Andrew Gibson & Abby    - mg.; D-O as d/o
    Andrew & <u>Evy</u>)
    27 Oct., 1868, <u>Lee Co., VA</u>  (M-Lee,VA;
    1880-9, widr. Ewin; D-O W/as nee GIBSON;
    B-O ch-5/74 W/as <u>Collins</u>)


(Gibson cont.)

**GIBSON (cont.)**
GEORGE (c24 S-mason b.TN)  [s/o David D.
   Gibson - 1860; TCS]
   ESTHER BARRETT (c28 b.KY) P/KY
   c1865          (TCS; Esther Gibson w/dau.
   Josephine 1870, H-NL; 1880 Geo. & Esther
   w/ch: Geo.13, Josephine 11, Grant 10, Mary
   2 & Isaac 9 mo. & s-s Wm. 7.  TCS says s-s
   Wm. was s/o Esther by Tom CLARK while she
   was md. to George Gibson.  1900 has Geo. as
   "widr," dau. Mary w/him, & Esther as "wid,"
   w/son Wm. CLARK; NL M-R)
HARVEY NEWTON  - see NEWTON HARVEY
ISAAC (R.Ows. 24 S b.KY) P/KY-VA
   ELIZA J. "LIZZIE" [nee COLLINS?] COLLINS
   (R.Ows. 29 2nd b.TN) P/KY-TN [ml c1869 VA,
   ____ Collins]  [prob. sis/o Sarah Collins
   who md. Hazel Collins & Cynthia Collins who
   md. Arch Gibson]
   7 Dec., 1877, Ows., @ H. Clark's [R.Leslie
   1880, H/37, W/34, 1st Collins s-ch-10 VA;
   1900-Les. m-23]
JAMES (c17 S b.KY)
   MARTHA _____ (c18 S b.KY)
   1889/90          (1900 m-10; 1910 Martha
   m-22, H-NL; NL M-J)
JESSE (c24 <u>Mul</u> b.VA)   [c1841-1919 Clay; s/o
   John Gibson & Charity   - 1860-Let; P-CW]
   NANCY ROSS (c18 b.KY)  [c1843-c1870; d/o
   Herod Ross & Minerva Woolery - 1850-60]
   c1864          (1870-5; P-CW; NL M-Let.)
   [H-remd.]
JESSE (c31 <u>Mul</u> 2nd b.VA)  [widr/o Nancy Ross
   above - P-CW; 1870]
   MANERVY [MINERVA J] SEXTON (c18 <u>Mul</u> S b.VA)
   [c1853-1922 Jack.]
   25 March, 1871, <u>Clay</u> (M-C; P-CW; 1880, 1st
   ch. under 10 is 7; 1890; B-O ch-4/77; moved
   to Sexton Cr., Clay by 1892)
JOHN (c16 b.TN)  [s/o David D. Gibson - TCS]
   PHOEBE A. SEABORN (c16 b.TN)
   c1852          (1860-7, Phoebe "wid" w/D. D.
   Gibson; TCS; 1870-17, John & Phoebe, <u>both
   alive</u>; 1890 Phebe wid/o John Gibson)

(Gibson cont.)

**GIBSON (cont.)**

JOHN (R.Ows. 20 S b.[KY]) [1882-1980; s/o Wm.
  Gibson & Lucinda Angel - TCS; ob-H BS-
  4/24/80]
    NANCY J[ANE] BARRETT (R.Lee 18 S b.[Br.])
    [1888-1963 Lee; d/o Andrew Jackson Barrett
    & Margaret Angel - 1900-L; P/M-L 1883; DC;
    ob-W BE-6/27/63]
    18 Dec., 1902, <u>Lee</u> @ Jackson Barrett's, by
    M. C. Taylor, MG; wits. James M Barrett &
    Green Kilburn    (M-L 6:437; 1910-1920;
    ob-H; widr. R.Boonev. 1963; Lone 1965)
JORDEN (R.Knox 21 S b.TN)
    MANERVY GIBSON (R.Knox 25 S b.Knox)
    15 Oct., 1855, Ows.
LARKIN (c28 S b.Let.)  [1844-1924; s/o John
  Gibson & Sarah Collins - TS-TCS]
    ELIZABETH MOORE (c24 S b.KY)  [1848-1912;
    d/o John Moore & Lucretia Smith - TS-TCS]
    1872/3        (TCS; 1880-13, then 6, 3 &
    5/80; 1st ch. appar. illegit. or rel.;
    1890; 1900-1910)      [LARKIN m2 c1914,
    Fannie Thomas - TCS; 1920]
LARKIN (18 S b.Hanc,TN)  [s/o David Gibson
  & Rebecca      - mg.]
    [MARTHA] PATSY COLLINS (20 S b.Hanc.,TN)
    [d/o Perry Collins & Anna        - mg.]
    30 Sept., 1869, <u>Lee Co., VA</u>  (M-Lee,VA;
    B-O ch-6/74; NL 1880-1900Sx)
LARKIN (22 S b.Cow Cr.)  [s/o Wm. Gibson
  & Lucinda Angel - LG-art.]
    MARY VAN DYKE HEFLIN (R.Est; __ b.___) [d/o
    Will Edgar Heflin, Katie McKenney - LG-art]
    23 Dec., 1909, <u>Estill</u>  (PWB; LG-art.;
    R.Lexington 1980 - ob-HS BS-4/24/80)
LEWIS (c22 S b.Boonev.) [1880-1956; s/o Larkin
  Gibson & Eliz. Moore - 1900; ob-H&S OCN-
  11/15/56-9/11/53]
    ELIZABETH "LIZZIE" MOORE (c22 S b.Eversole)
    [1879-1948; d/o Wm. Moore & Eliza Reynolds
    - 1900; TS-TCS]
    1902/3         (1910-1920; B-O ch.; BC 1912-
    1915-1920; M-O ch-1935; Boonev. 1953; ob-
    ch. OCN-7/18/57 & BS-1/2/86)

(Gibson cont.)

**GIBSON (cont.)**

MASTON (c32 <u>Mul</u>; S-mason; b.TN)
    ESTHER A. SMITH (c21 <u>white</u> b.KY) [c1847-
    1922 Ows.; d/o Whitley Smith & Eliz.
    Mainous (Maynard) - DC]
    c1868       (1870-1; 1880-11)
MERIDA [MEREDITH] (c26 S b.Br.)
    MILLIE REECE (c17 S b.Jack.) [d/o David
    Thomas Reese & Martha Jane Gum - ob-WF&S
    BE-7/15/37, OCN-8/4/55]
    15 July, 1898, <u>Perry</u>, by Isaac Gibson;
    wits. Frank Barger & Liss ----- (M-P H:68;
    NL 1900Sx; B-O ch-1904; 1910-L both m1-12;
    M-L ch-1918-1921; R.Cressmont 1937;
    OH 1955)
NEWTON HARVEY (c17 S b.Claib. Co., TN) [s/o
    Isaac Newton Gibson & Susan Catherine Biggs
    - 1860; TCS]
    SARAH A. McGEORGE (c17 S b.Ows) [1854-1923;
    d/o Patrick McGeorge & Eliz. York - B-O;
    JDW; TS-TCS]
    1870/1      (1880-1900-1910; B-O ch.;
    ob-ch. BE-1/15/56; H/as Harvey & Newton H.)
PERRY ALFRED (c20 S b.KY) [s/o Newton Harvey
    Gibson & Sarah McGeorge - 1900; ob-HB BE-
    1/15/56]
    MARTHA E. CHILDS (c17 S b.KY) [d/o James
    Childs & Sarah Evans - ob-WM OCC-5/13/36]
    1904/5      (1910; ob-WM; R.Ham.,OH 1936)
SHERMAN (c21 S b.KY) [s/o Larkin Gibson
    & Eliz. Moore - 1880; ob-HS OCN-9/11/53]
    LAURA [MURRELL?] (c22 S b.KY) [poss. d/o
    Wiley Murrell & Cath. Smith - 1880]
    1897/8      (1900-1910; R.Taylorsville,
    KY 1953)
WALTER B. (c23 b.Claib. Co., TN) [s/o John
    Gibson & Phoebe Seaborn - TCS]
    REBECCA J. FARMER (c23 b.Est) [d/o Denton
    Farmer & Sylvania Herd - TCS]
    c1876      (1880; B-O ch-3/77)
WILLIAM (c15 S b.TN)
    ELIZABETH _____ (c15 S b.KY)
    c1848     (1860-11, 8 & 2 mos.; NL 1850)
    [H-remd.]

(Gibson cont.)

**GIBSON (cont.)**
WILLIAM (c30 2nd S-mason b.TN)  [widr/o
  Elizabeth _____ above - 1860]
  ELIZA _____ (c20 b.VA)
  c1867        (1870, ch. under 10 were: 8 &
  2, the oldest is prob. by W1)
WILLIAM (___ b. Hanc.,TN)
  EMALINE COLLINS (c18 b.Hanc., TN)
  c1868        (wid. Emily 1880-J-11;
  B-O son Willoughby 4/74 Jack.; NL M-J)
WILLIAM (R.Ows. 21 S b.KY) P/VA    [s/o John
  Gibson & Sarah Collins - LG-art.]
  [LU]CINDA ANGEL (R.Ows. 21 S b.KY) P/KY
  [d/o Reuben Angel & Cath. Couch - LG-art.]
  9 Aug, 1877, Ows. @ James Johnson's
  [R.Owsley 1880 Mul; 1900 white; M-L ch-
  1921, Wm., Mul. - LNG; went to Clk - LG-
  art.]
WILLIAM (c18 b.KY)  [GS/o John Gibson & Sarah
  Collins - 1900; TCS]
  MARY _____ (c17 b.KY)
  1898/9       (1900 H-GM w/them)
WILLIAM H. (c27 S Dr. b.KY)  [1882-1953; s/o
  Larkin Gibson & Eliz. Moore - TCS; 1900;
  ob-H OCN-9/11/53]
  LENA HAZEL MENEFEE (c21 S b.Geneva,OH) [d/o
  E. P. Menefee    - Yest.; ob-W BE-9/24/70]
  1908         (Yest.; 1910 m-1; 1920; TCS)
**GILBERT**
  _____ (___ b.___) (d. 1878-80)
  LUCINDA (FOX?) (c19 b.KY)  [poss. d/o
  Isaac Fox & Almarinda Griffith]
  c1871        (1880-8, wid. Lucinda;
  NL M-J)
ABRAHAM [a/k/a ABRAM] (c18 b.KY)
  ELIZABETH BAKER (c13 b.KY)
  1887/8       (1900; wid. Eliz. 1910-1920;
  M-O ch-1959; DC ch., W/as "Elive" Baker)
BERRY (c21 S b.Ows.)  [1885-1957 Lex. hosp.;
  s/o Keenis Gilbert & Loudemia Riley - 1900;
  ob-H OCN-2/7/57]
  SUSAN CORNETT (c19 S b.Ows.)  [d/o Sally
  Cornett - TCS]
  1906/7       (1910-1920; B-O ch.)  [BERRY
  m2 Polly _____ - ob-H; in Arnett 1957]

(Gilbert cont.)

## GILBERT (cont.)

CLABE (R.Ows. 22 S b.Ows.) P/Per-Ows.
  EVELINE BAKER (R.Ows. 22 S b.Ows) P/Ows.
  24 Nov., 1909, Ows.
CLABE (R.Ows. 22 S b.Ows.) P/Per-Ows. [1888-
  1913; s/o Abram Gilbert & Eliz. Baker - DC
  M/as "Elive" Baker; 1900-10]
  NANCY A. [nee _____] BURNS (R.Ows. 21 2nd
  b.Ows.) P/Per  [ml _____ Burns]
  23 June, 1910, Ows.
EZEKIEL (c19 b.KY) [s/o Aquilla Gilbert
  & Jane Stewart - TCS]
  JANE McGUIRE (c21 b.KY)
  11 Sept., 1848, Ows.  (JFB; 1850-4 mos.;
  went to KS - TCS]
FRANCIS (c22 b.KY) [s/o Aquilla Gilbert
  & Susan Mann - 1860]
  ELIZABETH _____ (c19 b.VA) P/VA
  c1867        (1870-L-2; 1880-L)
ISAAC (c18 b.KY)
  SCYTHY FREEMAN (c22 b.KY) [d/o Wm. Freeman
  & Margaret      ]
  1893/4       (1900 Scythy w/P as m-6, 3/0
  ch., no surname listed, Isaac Gilbert
  listed next to them as m-6, 3 ch. listed;
  I believe they are md.)
JAMES MICKLEBERRY "MICK" (c23 b.KY)  [poss.
  s/o Aquilla Gilbert & Susan Mann]
  SARAH "SALLY" ANN ESTES (c16 b.Est.) P/KY
  1859          (1860 no ch.; 1870-1880-L;
  1900-L m-40; DC-son; ob-ch BE-4/9/59; H/as
  James, Mick, Mickleberry, Mulberry)
JESSE B. (c27 b.KY) [1872-1906 - TS-TCS]
  LOUETTA GABBARD (c21 b.KY) [d/o Meredith
  Gabbard & Mary P. Simpson - TCS; 1900]
  1898/9         (1900 w/WP)
JOHN (c24 S b.Per.) [1835-1920 Ows.; s/o Isaac
  Gilbert & Rebecca Gabbard - 1850-P; DC]
  NANCY SMITH (c19 S b.Per.) [c1840-1890 Ows]
  11 May, 1859, <u>Breathitt</u> (P-CW; NL 1860/B/P;
  1870-9; B-O ch.; 1880; H-remd. 1900)


(Gilbert cont.)

## GILBERT (cont.)

JOHN R. (c22 b.KY) [s/o Abijah Gilbert
& Martha Gibson - 1860; TCS]
ANN JUDITH MINTER (c21 b.VA) [d/o Wm. P.
Minter & Mary E. Bailey - TCS]
1863          (1870-6; 1900; 1900 their dau.
Lenora Campbell had Gilbert GF w/her; TCS;
wid. Ann J. 1920)

JOHN (c56 2nd b.KY) [widr/o Nancy Smith above
- P-CW]
DARRITY [DAUGHERTY] COUCH (21 S b.KY)
[1870-1937 Ows.; d/o Elijah Couch & Eliz.
Estep - TCS; 1870]
25 Oct., 1891, Ows. @ John Gilbert's, by
A. C. Murrell, Min.; wits. Elisha Colwell &
Eley Fox  (P-CW; 1900 H-remd-45, but this
is wrong, W-m-10; 1910 m-18; W/as Darrity,
Darkis & Daugherty)

JOHN (c20's S b.Ows.) [s/o Robert Gilbert
& Chaney McIntosh - 1910C; 3rd M-B]
_____ (___ b.___)
1900-8        (2nd M-O 1909; NL M-B)

JOHN (R.Br. 29 2nd b.Ows.) P/Per-Br.
[m1 _____ above] [s/o Robert
Gilbert & Chaney McIntosh - 1910; 3rd M-B]
JANE REYNOLDS (R.Br. 26 2nd b.Br) P/Ows.
[m1 _____; nee _____]
22 Nov., 1909, Breathitt [rec. Owsley;
NL M-B] [R.Breathitt 1910, HF w/them]
[JOHN (35 b.Ows.) m3 1/16/1914 Br., Jona
Barrett (27 S) - M-B 17:336]

KENIS (c28 S b.KY) [1854-1924; s/o Jackson
Gilbert & Lydia Fox - TS-TCS; 1880-B]
LOUDEMIA RILEY (c21 S b.KY) [d/o John
Riley & W2 Lydia Rice - TCS]
1881/2        (1900-1910-1920; ob-ch.
OCN-2/7/57; M-O ch-1963; 1880-B Keenas w/F
+ Lucy Riley, svt.; NL M-B) [LOUDEMA md.
2nd 1923, Lewis Caudill - RP; KCM]

MICHAEL (c22 b.KY)
JOYCE _____ (c18 b.KY)
1879/80        (1880-MWY)

MICK - see JAMES MICKLEBERRY


(Gilbert cont.)

## GILBERT (cont.)

NOAH (c25 S b.Cortland)  [s/o John Gilbert
   & Nancy Smith - 1880]
   SARAH J. BEGLEY (c19 S b.Per.)  [d/o Hiram
   Begley & Elizabeth Smith - HTB]
   1896      (1900-11/97 m-4; 1910 m-12;
   1920-P; HTB N-C 11/96; B-O ch-1909 W/listed
   on wrong line)
QUILLER (c21 b.KY)
   NANCY M. FLANNARY (c13 b.KY)  [d/o Jacob
   Flannary & Martha     - TCS]
   13 Aug., 1885, McKee, <u>Jackson</u>; bm. groom &
   Jacob Flannary  (M-J 6:20; TCS; 1900 m-5)
RICHARD (c18 S b.Ows.)  [1889-1969; s/o Kenis
   Gilbert & Loudemia Riley - 1900; TCS; ob-
   H&S BE-1/16/69-9/15/66]
   CATHERINE "KATE" MASON (c20 S b.KY)  [1897-
   1961 Boonev.; d/o David Mason & Amy Little
   - 1900; P/M-B; ob-W BE-12/14/61
   1907/8      (1910-1920; BC-1913-1925;
   M-O ch-1932; R.Boonev. 1966; ob-ch. BS-
   3/20/97-4/24/97)
ROBERT (R.Br. 30 S b.Br.) P/Br.
   CHANEY McINTOSH (R.Br. 32 S b.Br) P/Br.
   [d/o Zachariah McIntosh & W1   - TCS]
   5 Feb., 1878, Jett's Cr., <u>Breathitt</u>, by
   James Johnson, Esq. (M-B 2:24; 1880-2;
   TCS; NL 1900Sx, their son John w/Henry
   McIntosh as svt. 1900-B; widr. Robt. 1910-B
   w/son John)
ROBERT (c21 2nd b.Ows.) [ml _____]
   JOSEPHINE "JOSIE" CUMINS(?) (c18 S b.Ows.)
   1901/2      (1910 Trav.Rest; BC-1913;
   NL 1920Sx; NL M-J)
SIDNEY (c22 b.KY)  [s/o Kenus Gilbert
   & Loudemia Riley - TCS]
   ANN SMITH (c<u>13</u> b.KY)
   1898/9      (1900; BBG/WOG)
SIDNEY (___ b.___)
   LEAN SANDLIN (___ b.___)
   5 ----, 1901, Ows. [rec. Perry] @ Martha
   Sandlin's, by H. H. Rice, JPPC; wits. John
   B. & Martha Sandlin  (M-P)


(Gilbert cont.)

**GILBERT (cont.)**
SIDNEY (c28 2nd b.Br.)   [m1 Ann Smith above -
  TCS; BBG/WOG]
  MARTHA MOSLEY (c15 S b.Br.)   [d/o James
  "Jim" Mosley - BBG]
  1903/4        (1910; B-O ch.; NL M-B)
WALTER T. (c20 S b.KY)   [s/o John Gilbert
  & Ann Judith Minter - 1880; TCS]
  LEVINA CAMPBELL (c22 S b.KY)   [1870-1960;
  d/o Daniel Campbell & Sarah Campbell - TCS]
  1891/2        (1900-1910-1920; TCS)
ZEBEDEE "ZEB" (19 S b.KY)   [1876-1966 Beattyv;
  s/o Isaac Gilbert & Polly Smith - BJN; ob-H
  BE-12/15/66]
  MARY JANE GABBARD (18 S b.KY)   [d/o Willis
  Gabbard & Mary Bishop - 1880; BJN]
  20 Dec, 1893, Breathitt @ Willis Gabbard's,
  by Elisha Johnson, Min.; wits. W. Gabbard &
  Chas. Terry  (M-B 6:267; BJN; 1900-B;
  R.Beattyv. 1966)
**GILLESPIE**
HARVEY (R.Morg. 22 S b.Russell Co., VA)
  PHEBE JANE HOLLAND (R.Ows. 18 S b.Br.)
  24 Dec., 1857, Ows.  [R.Owsley 1860]
JAMES (c30 b.KY)   [s/o _____ Gillaspie
  & Rachel Fowler - TCS]
  EMILY J[ANE] LYNCH (c18 b.Lee)   [d/o Thos.
  Henry Lynch & Nancy Brandenburg]
  1 Dec., 1889 Jackson Co., by Wm. Anderson;
  wits. W. R. & John Lakes & Wm. Sparks; sur.
  John Farmer, Jr.  (M-J; TCS; DB)
WILLIAM (c22 b.KY)
  VIRGINIA _____ (c16 b.KY)
  c1868        (1870-Lee-1; NL M-J)
**GILLEY/GILLY**
HIRAM (c21 b.KY)   [s/o Levi Gilley & Malinda
  - TCS]
  LUCY _____ (c20 b.KY)
  1859/60        (1860-MWY; NL M-J)
JOHN (c25 b.KY)   [s/o Levi Gilley & Malinda
  - TCS]
  ELIZABETH _____ (c33 b.KY)
  c1867        (1870-Lee-2; NL M-J)

**GILLOUS**

HOSKIN (R.Lee 25 S b.Lum. b.VA) P/TN
   HESTER BRANDENBURG (R.Ows. 18 S b.Ows.) P/
   Ows.
   24 Aug., 1908, Ows.

**GLASS**

ARCHIBALD McGUIRE (c22 S Dr. b.KY) [1863-
   1916; s/o Wilson H. Glass & Martha Minter -
   1880; TS-TCS; ob-HM ME-11/9/05]
   LUCY HERD (c15 S b.Ows.) [1869-1962 OH; d/o
   Andrew/Robert Herd & W2 Mary Eliz. Searsy -
   1880; TS-TCS; ob-W BE-11/22/62]
   fall, 1885          (Yest.; 1900 m-16; Boonev.
   1905; 1910 m-24; DC-WS; ob-ch. BE-12/27/34;
   wid. Lucy d. Tulsa, OK 1962)

**GODFREY**

JOSEPH (c20 blk c.minr b.KY) P/KY
   MATILDA SMITH (c18 Mul b.KY) P/NC-KY
   1859/60          (NL 1860 because slaves;
   1870-1880-1900-L; widr. Joseph 1910-L;
   M-L ch-1906)

**GODSEY**

see GOODSEY

**GOE**

BENJAMIN T. (c30 b.Clk) [s/o Nathan B. Goe
   & Elizabeth Frame]
   MARIETTA "MARY" FRANCES HOWARD (c20 b.Est.)
   [d/o Phillip Howard & Luvina      - TCS]
   c1862          (1870-L-7; B-L ch.; 1880-L;
   ob-ch. BE-10/1/42 & OCN-9/18/53)

**GOFORTH**

WALTER [PRESTON] (R.Proctor 22 S b.Ows.) P/NC-
   Ows.   [1882-1944 Rockc.; s/o Wm. Goforth
   & Margaret "Dollie" Harvey - mg.; DC]
   ROSY [ANN] [nee GIBSON] MARIAN (R.Beattyv.
   26 [s/b 20] 2nd b.Lee) P/VA-Br.   [m1 1901,
   Frank Marion - M-L]   [1886-1967; d/o Wm.
   Starleton Gibson & Polly Harvey - ob-W BE-
   11/16/67 as Fike; 4th M-L]
   7 Feb, 1906, Lee @ Clerk's office, by J. F.
   Sutton, JLCC; wits. J. N. Lutes & Wm.
   Sturnburg [DIVORCED]   (M-L; 1910)
   [WALTER (38 "widr." b.Ows.) m2 7/13/23,
   Rockc., Cleo Martin (20 S b.Lau) - H/DC;
   M-Rockc.]   [ROSIE m3 Walker BBurg. - LNG;
   m4 1962 Brownlow Fike - M-L]
   (Goforth cont.)

## GOFORTH (cont.)

WILLIAM J. (c26 b.NC)  [s/o George Goforth
   & Margaret Rucker?]
   MARGARET "DOLLIE" HARVEY (c18 b.TN) P/TN
   [poss. d/o Prior Harvey & W1 Perlina Blake
   - 1870]
   1879/80        (1880-MWY; 1900-C, H/m-19,
   W/NL; M-L ch-1907; DC-son; NL M-J)
   [WM. J. m2 9/27/1900, Lizzie (nee _____)
   Hacker - M-C; 1910-L, Hacker s-ch.]

## GOODMAN

JAMES (c21 S b.TN)  [1861-1903; s/o _____
   Goodman & Sarah Taylor - 1880; TS-TCS]
   MARY MARGARET (nee MOORE) SEALE (c37 2nd
   b.KY) [wid/o Robt. Seale] [d/o Presley B.
   Moore & Rachel Morris - 1880]
   1893/4        (1900, 2 s-ch-16 & 13; wid.
   Margaret 1910-1920)

## GOODSEY/GODSEY/GOOSEY/GOOCEY

DAVID (c24 S b.Est/Clay)
   SUSAN ROACH (c17 S b.KY)  [d/o Thomas Roach
   & Sally         ]
   c1847     [DIVORCED 1850-2]  (1850-2; MT)
   [H-remd.]  [SUSAN m2 Wm. Smallwood]
DAVID (c30 2nd b.KY)  [Div/f Susan Roach abv.]
   ARMINA ROACH (c16 b.Est.)  [d/o Thomas
   Roach & Sally         ]
   c1853        (1860-4; B-O ch; B-Lau. ch-
   1854 b.Ows. & D-Lau. ch-1855; B-L ch.;
   1880-L; 1900-L m-43 = 1856/7; wid. Armina
   w/son 1910-L; NL M-J; ob-ch. OCN-12/12/57 &
   OCC-11/27/42)

## GRAHAM

JAMES F. (c22 mechanic b.KY)
   MARY ELIZABETH SMITH (c16 b.KY)
   29 Aug., 1855, Proctor, Ows.  (REM; 1860;
   B-O ch-5/57; 1880-Frk, Belle Point]

## GRAVES

R[ICHARD] C (R.Beattyv. 36 S Engr. b.Woodford)
   P/Woodford-Fay.
   MARTHA FLANERY (R.Br. 23 S b.Ows) P/VA-Ows.
   [1873-1966; d/o Hampton Flanery & Nancy
   BBurg. - 1880; ob-W&S BE-5/26/66-5/18/44-
   4/18/46]
   3 Dec., 1896, Lee @ H. Flanery's; wits. C.
   W. Sales, S.K. Baird, C. L. Dorman & others
   (M-L 5:59; 1900-L; R.Haz. c1936-1966)

## GRAY/GREY
BENJAMIN THOMAS (c34 b.Fay.)  [s/o Thomas Gray
   & Lucy      - TCS; 1850]
    CAROLINE "CARRIE" DUFF (c31 b.KY) P/VA
    c1867     (1870-L-2; wid. Caroline/Carrie
    1880-1900-1910-L; M-L ch-1893; DC-dau. 1931
    Montana; NL M-Fay/J; H/Thomas in all rec.
    except DC-dau. as Benj. T.)
JAMES TURNER (c21 S b.KY)
    CATHERINE "KATE" WARD (c22 S b.KY) [d/o
    James Wm. Ward & Nancy Brandenburg - 1880]
    1900/1     (1910 W-GM, Celia Ward,
    w/them; 1920)
THOMAS - see BENJAMIN THOMAS
## GRAYBEAL
ENOS (R.Lau. 26 S b.NC) P/NC
    ELIZ. BOWMAN (R.Ows. 22 S b.KY) [d/o Elisha
    Bowman & Evaline Isaacs - 1860-70; TCS]
    28 Dec., 1877, Ows. @ E. Bowman's
    [R.Laurel 1880]   [ENOS (53 2nd b.KY) m2
    6/4/04 Matilda Jones (33 2nd) - M-Lau.]
## GREEN
BURNAM (___ b.Mistletoe)
    CATHERINE BURNS (___ b.Mistletoe)
    pre-1908     (B-O ch.; NL 1910Sx; NL M-J)
ELISHA (c27 b.Harl.)
    ROSA ANN MULLINS (c19 b.Ows.)
    c1873     (1880-Lau-6; B-Lau. ch-1876)
ENOCH (c19 b.KY)
    RACHEL H. _____ (c19 b.KY)
    c1866     (1870-3; NL M-J)
LEWIS (c33 2nd B'smth b.VA)  [m1 c1869 _____
    _____ - NL M-C]  [c1839-1902 - ME-5/2/02]
    ELMINA [nee CHANDLER] RADDFORD [HACKER]
    (c32 3rd b.NC) [m1 5/1/58, Richard Radford
    - M-C mf; 1860-C; m2 ____ Hacker]
    [d/o Joseph Chandler & Martha   - 1850-C]
    3 Nov, 1872 Clay (ML) (M-C; 1880 Radford
    s-ch. 18 & 17, Hacker s-s 14, 1st Green ch-
    10 must be by W1; NL 1870/C; 1900 widr.
    Lewis w/s-s Hacker)
LEWIS (___ b.___)
    NANCY CHANDLER (___ b.___)
    Dec., 1886, Ows. (ML) (ME-1/14/87;
    NL 1900Sx; NL M-J)

(Green cont.)

**GREEN (cont.)**
R. W. (R.Ows. 41 3rd b.TN) P/TN   [poss. m1
   Martha _____ (1883-1899) & m2 Gloria _____
   (1870-1903) - both bur. same cem. as R.W.,
   TS-TCS; NL M-J]   [1862-1905 - TS-TCS]
   AMERICA SHORT (R.Br. 32 2nd b.Ows.) P/Ows.
   [m1 _____]
   19 May, 1904, Ows.  [NL 1910Sx]
RICHARD (c18 b.TN)
   MARY BRAY (c22 b.KY)
   1881/2      (1900; TCS)
ROBERT (c26 S b.TN)   [1868-1936 - TS-TCS]
   _____ (___ b.___) [d. pre-1900]
   1893/4      (1900 H-remd-6, but this must
   be W1; NL M-J)
ROBERT (c33 2nd b.TN)  [widr/o _____ above]
   [1868-1936 - TS-TCS]
   CORA (nee BLAKE) REED (c21 2nd b.Ows.)
   [m1 _____ Reed - NL M-J]   [1878-1951; d/o
   Wm. Blake & Caroline Wolfe - 1880 ob-W OCN-
   4/7/51]
   1900        (1900 w/WP, m-6, but these are
   prev. spouses, ch-4/96 & 6/98, but 1910
   shows ch. to be REEDS; 1910 m2-9 both, Reed
   s-s, 12; 1920; TCS; NL M-J)
T[ILMAN] J. (R.Ows. 21 S tchr b.TN) P/TN
   [c1888-1977; s/o Richard Green & Mary Bray
   - TCS; art. BS W-Bday]
   EVA AMIS (R.Ows. 17 S b.Ows.) P/Per-Ows.
   [d/o Robt. Amis & Esther Baker - TCS; art.
   BS-4/5/90 W-98 Bday; ob-WS BE-9/7/72]
   6 Jan., 1910, Ows. (a/L M-O 1:54-A, md by
   R. C. Roberts, Min.; wits. L. G. Moore &
   Laura Reynolds)   [R.Owsley 1910-1920;
   Boonev. 1972]
**GREER/GREEYOR/GREYER**
   _____ (___ b.KY)
   DRUSCILLA "DREW" OSBORNE (c17 S b.KY)
   1885/6        (1900 W-remd. Wm. Peters; Wm.
   m-30, which is W1, Drew m-14, which is
   this mg.; Greer s-ch. ages 12 & 5; TCS;
   NL M-J)    [DREW m2 Wm. Peters - 1900]


(Greer cont.)

## GREER (cont.)

ISAAC (R.Ows. 20 S b.Claiborne Co., TN)
[ELIZABETH] ANNA MAHAFFA [MAHAFFEY] (R.Ows.
22 S b.Yancy Co, NC) [d/o James Mahaffey
& Ella Crawford - REM/BM]
28 March, 1855, Ows. [R.Owsley 1860 WM
w/them; 1870-1880 Owsley; listed as GREEYOR
1880]

JESSE (c22 S b.Ows.) [1865-1941 Proctor; s/o
Isaac Greer & Anna Mahaffey - 1880; 2nd M-
L; ob-H OCC-1/3/41]
FRANCES MOORE (c16 b.KY) [d/o Henry H.
Moore & Mary Hobbs - 1880]
1886/7          (TCS; 1900-1910-L; M-L ch-
1911-1915; NL M-L) [JESSE (R.Tallega 44
2nd b.Ows.) m2 2/12/11 Rachel (nee Roberts)
Barrett (38 2nd) d/o Moses Roberts (& Nancy
Burns) - M-L; LNG: ob-W OCC-2/6/37;
JESSE (R.Beattyv. 71 widr. b.Lee) m3
7/31/1937 Lee, Liza Jane (nee Price)
Gallagher (wid/o Daniel Gallagher)]

ROBERT (c21 b.KY) [s/o Isaac Greer & Anna
Mahaffy - 1870]
MARTHA AMBROSE (c16 b.KY) P/KY
14 April, 1880 (ML) Jackson Co.; bm. groom
& John Farmer, Jr. (MC-NFI)    (M-J 4:432;
1880-MWY)

WILLIAM (c18 b.Ows.) [1856-19__; s/o Isaac
Greer & Anna Mahaffy - B-O]
SARAH A. _____ (c16 b.KY) P/KY
1874/5          (1880-1/80; 1900-P m-25, as
GREYER; 1910-P; NL M-J/P)

## GREY

see GRAY

## GRIFFEE/GRIFFEY

ELIJAH (R.Ows. 32 S b.KY [Clay]) P/uk [1844-
1921 Ows.; s/o James Griffee & Elizabeth
Herd - TCS; 1860 w/wid. M]
NANCY J[ANE] STAMPER (R.Ows. 19 S b.KY
[Ows]) P/KY-VA    [1855-1884 Ows.; d/o Wm.
Stamper & Margaret Alford - B-O; P-CW]
15 March, 1877, Ows., @ Wm. Stamper's
[R.Owsley 1880]    [H-remd.]

(Griffee cont.)

**GRIFFEE (cont.)**
ELIJAH (41 2nd b.Clay) [m1 Nancy Stamper abv.
  - P-CW] [1844-1921 Ows. - P-CW]
  MINERVA LYNCH (c17 b.KY) [1869-1898 Ows.;
  d/o Wm. R. Lynch & Cath. Nancy Salyers -
  1880; P-CW]
  15 Aug., 1886, Ows., by Eld. Jesse B.
  Rowlett (P-CW; ECP; 1890; widr. Elijah
  1900-1910-1920; R.Ows. until his death)
JOHN (c14 b.KY)
  MINIA _____ (c15 b.KY)
  1894/5        (1900-10/97, m-5; NL M-J)
WILLIAM N. (c25 S b.Earnestv.) [1879-19__;
  s/o Elijah Griffey & W1 Nancy Stamper]
  FLORA PENDERGRASS (c19 S b.Ows.) [d/o
  Wash. Pendergrass & Phoebe Flanery]
  1905/6        (1910; B-O ch.)
**GROSS**
ROBERT (R.Ows. 26 S b.Ows.) [1876-1948; s/o
  Devana N. SPENCE & Anna GROSS - B-O; TS-
  TCS]
  MINNIE DAMERAL (R.Lee 20 S b.KY) [d/o Wm.
  Damrell & Emaline Mays, who later md. Allen
  Sams - M-L 6/82 & 4/93]
  19 Oct., 1903, Lee @ Allen Sam's, by James
  E. Dunigan; wits. Mary & Jane Smith
  (M-L; TCS; H-sgl. 1900)
SIMON (c14 S b.Br.) [1849-19__; s/o Henry
  Gross & Louvina Jones/Roberts - 1850-60-B]
  LOUISA "ELIZA" _____ (c18 S b.KY)
  c1863        (1870-L-6; 1880; 1900-L m-31 =
  1868-9; 1910-L m-48 = 1861/2; NL M-J)
**GUESS**
CALVIN (c27 blk B'Smth b.TN) P/TN [c1832-1904
  - ob-H ME-2/5/04]
  MARY RUSSELL (c13 blk b.KY) P/KY
  c1859        (1870-10; 1880, Russell SiL
  w/them; NL 1860 because slaves; 1900, widr.
  Calvin as m-30, which would be 1869/70,
  unless he was m-30 when Mary d.)

(Guess cont.)

**GUESS (cont.)**
HENRY (c23 S <u>Blk</u> b.KY) [s/o Calvin Guess
    & Mary Russell - 2nd M-O]
    NANNIE LOU JETT (c16 S <u>Blk</u> b.KY) [1887-
    1952; d/o Wm. Jett & Margaret Combs - ob-W
    OCN-7/11/52; 1900]
    1902/3      (1910-1920; ob-W; BC 1912-
    1919-1925) [HENRY m2 11/5/55, Lucy
    Crawford (66 Div.) d/o Sim Crawford - M-O]
**GULLETT**
HENRY C. (c20 b.Perry) [s/o Wm. O. Gullett
    & Anna    - 1850-60-P]
    ALCY ANN SIZEMORE (c21 b.Ows.) [d/o Hen.
    Sizemore & Minerva Combs - 1850-1860]
    1867/8      (1870, no ch.; B-O ch.;
    1880-8; 1900-Oldham m-32)
JOHN (R.Ows. 19 S b.KY) P/KY [poss. s/o Wm.
    O. Gullett & Anna    - 1860-P]
    CYNTHIA A. SIZEMORE (R.Ows. 15 S b.KY) P/KY
    [d/o Henderson Sizemore & Minerva Combs -
    1870]
    22 Aug., 1877, Ows., @ H. C. Gullett's
    [R.Owsley 1880]
**GUM/GUMM**
ABRAHAM (c22 b.KY)
    MATILDA SIMPSON (c14 b.KY) [c1834-1896 -
    ME-2/28/96 - poss. gd/o Deborah Simpson]
    c1848      (1850-8 mos.; B-Lau. ch-1853;
    1860-J, Deborah Simpson, 73, w/them; 1870-
    1880-J; Moore's Cr., Jack. 1896; widr. Abr.
    1900-J)
ALEXANDER "MACK" (c20 S b.KY) [s/o Stephen
    Gum & Sarah Gross - 1900]
    MARY "MOLLIE" PRICE (c19 S b.KY) [d/o
    Elias Price, Jr. & Martha Cecil - TCS]
    1904/5      (1910 w/HP; TCS; BBG; 1920;
    BC 1916-1919; ob-ch. BS-7/12/90-10/31/91;
    ob-ch. HJN-7/90) [MACK m2 Minnie _____
    - BBG; Minnie was staying w/their son
    Kenneth & wf Lucille (nee Moore) Gum. Mack
    went to Kenneth's house, where he killed
    both Minnie & Lucille. He returned home &
    killed himself - BBG; TCS; art. OCN-
    8/29/52]

(Gum cont.)

**GUM (cont.)**

DILLARD (___ b.Egypt, Jack.) [poss. DILLARD
    b.1877/8 GS/o Berry Gum & Nancy - 1880-L;
    NL 1900-L]
    MARY MULLINS (___ b.Egypt, Jack. Co.)
    pre-1908      (B-O ch-1908.; NL 1900/J -
    a Mary E. Mullins 39 w/3 ch. 1900-J;
    NL 1910Sx; NL M-J)
ELIAS (c47 b.KY)
    SUSAN ROBERTS (c33 b.KY)
    19 April, 1842, Clay    (M-C; NL 1850; 1860;
    wid. Susan 1870-L)
GREENBERRY (c19 c.minr b.KY)
    EMILY CATHERINE FRAILEY (c14 b.Est) [c1837-
    1855; d/o Ben Frailey & Eliz. Goosey - D-O]
    c1851      (B-O ch; W/D-O; H-remd. 1860-8)
GREENBERRY (c24 2nd c.minr b.KY)  [widr/o
    Emily Catherine Frailey above - D-O 12/55]
    NANCY BAKER (c19 b.VA)
    1856      (1860; B-O ch-1/57; 1870-1880-L)
    [GREENBERRY m3 1/21/96 Lee, Permelia (nee
    Spence) Snowden (m1 Conner; m2 Henly Hurst;
    m3 James Snowden)]
JOHN (c23 b.KY)  [1828-1892 Louisville - WEJ;
    appar. bro/o Wm. B. Gum, who md. Lucinda
    Benton]
    ELLEN DANIEL (c17 b.KY)  [c1832-1857 - WEJ;
    poss. d/o Dr. John Marcus Daniel & Louisa
    Daniel]
    c1849      (1850 no ch.; B-O ch.; moved to
    Louisville, KY 1857; their dau. Caroline
    liv. w/John M. Daniel 1860, poss. her GF)
    [H-remd.]
JOHN (c32 2nd sawyer b.KY)  [m1 Ellen Daniel
    above - WEJ]  [1828-1892 Louisville - WEJ]
    SARAH JANE (nee POWELL) DICKENS (c21 2nd
    b.Est.)  [m1 8/16/53 Est., James M. Dickens
    - WEJ; M-E]  [c1837-1909 Louisville; d/o
    John B. Powell - WEJ]
    25 Feb., 1858, Estill    (WEJ; 1859 moved
    from Louisville to Cottage Furnace, Est.;
    then Ows. until 1861, where he served in
    C.W.; then went to Clay's Ferry, Mad., liv.
    across the river in Cleveland, Fay.;
    1870-M; 1880-Fay., Louisville; wid. Sarah
    1900-Fay., Louisville w/GD.)
(Gum cont.)

## GUM (cont.)

JOHN (c17 b.KY)
   MARY E. WHITE (c13 b.KY) [d/o Shelton
   White & Margaret Gross - 1860]
   c1868     (1870-9/69, WM w/them)
MACK - see ALEXANDER
STEPHEN (c20 S b.KY) [s/o Stephen Gum, Sr.
   & Betsy Cornelious]
   SARAH GROSS (c16 S b.KY) [d/o John Gross
   & Mary Mays - REM]
   c1864/5    (1870-4; 1880-14; 1890;
   1900 m-33, but this puts them md. after
   ch. were b.; 1910 m-49, but this puts
   ages @ c14 & c10, too young; B-O ch.)
STEPHEN, JR. (R.Ows. 26 2nd b.Ows.) P/Ows.
   [m1 _____ - NL M-J]  [s/o Stephen
   Gum & Sarah Gross - 1880]
   ALLIE CAUDILL (R.Ows. 18 - b.Ows) P/Ows.
   [d/o Allen Caudill & Mary Smith - 1900]
   21 Jan, 1909, Ows.  [R.Owsley 1910-1920]
WILLIAM (c20 S b.Trav. Rest) [s/o Stephen Gum
   & Sarah Gross - 1880]
   LURINDA "LUDY" ADDISON (c16 S b.Trav.Rest)
   [d/o Isaac Addison & Cath. Garrett - 1880]
   1893/4    (1900 m-6; 1910 m-14; B-O ch.)

## GURLEY/GOURLEY

MITCHELL (c28 b.Scotland)
   REBECCA _____ (c23 b.KY)
   c1849    (1850, no ch.)

## HACKER

_____ (___ b.NC)
   ELMINA (nee CHANDLER) RADFORD (c28 2nd
   b.NC) [m1 Richard Radford - M-C 1858;
   1860-C]
   c1865    (W-remd. 1880, Radford s-ch
   18 & 17 & Hacker s-s 14) [ELMINA m3 1872,
   Lewis Green - M-C; 1880]
BART (R.Ows. 19 S b.Clay) P/Ows. [1890-1967
   Ows.; s/o Sam Hacker & Polly Burns - DC;
   ob-H&S BE-9/14/67-10/27/60]
   MARTHA McINTOSH (R.Ows. 17 S b.Per) P/
   Per-Br.
   29 Dec., 1909, Ows. [BART m2 Rose Barger
   (b. c 1931) - ob-H BE-9/14/67 shot Rose
   then committed suicide; R.Sexton Cr. 1967]
(Hacker cont.)

**HACKER (cont.)**

B[LEVINS] P. (c29 S b.KY)
   SOPHIA STIDHAM (c37 S b.KY)
   28 May, 1906, <u>Clay</u> (M-C MT; 1910-4, m-4)
DANIEL (c23 b.Clay) [c1883-1960 Is. Cr.; s/o
   Sam Hacker & Polly Burns - DC-bro.;
   ob-H BE-10/27/60]
   MARGARET ALLEN (c19 b.Clay) [d/o George
   Allen & Sarah Baker - TCS; ob-W OCN-
   10/17/57]
   2 Nov., 1904, <u>Clay</u> (TCS; 1910-3 N#L, 3/2
   ch.; 1920; R.Island City 1957)
GRANVILLE (c31 3rd b.KY) [widr/o Sally Hunt -
   M-C 5/23/41] [s/o John Hacker & Massie
   Spread - TCS]
   ANNA NANCE (c23 b.KY)
   29 April, 1849, <u>Clay</u> (M-C; 1850-E; TCS;
   1860-15, 14, 11, 8, 6 & 2)
HOGAN (c26 b.IN) [s/o Granville Hacker & W3
   Anna Nantz - 1860]
   NORA J. DAY (c21 b.Lee,VA) [1855-1928 -TCS]
   c1876      (1880-3; B-O ch.)
   [NORA m2 George Behymer]
ISAAC (c22 b.KY) [s/o Julius Hacker & Margaret
   Herd - TCS]
   EASTER MORRIS (c22 b.KY) [d/o Wm. Morris
   & Margaret Sandlin - TCS; poss. d. 4/96
   Jack: old Aunt Easter Hacker d - ME-5/1/96]
   c1848      (1850-1; B-O ch.; 1860-11;
   wid. Esther 1870)
JAMES (R.Ows. 26 S b.Clay) [s/o Julius Hacker
   & Margaret Herd - N-C]
   SARAH ANN WILSON (R.Clay 21 S b.Clay) [d/o
   Philip Wilson & Christina Rogers - TCS]
   12 May, 1853 <u>Clay</u> (M-C mf; M-C as <u>4/14</u>/53;
   TCS; 1860-6; B-O ch.)
JAMES (c21 S b.KY)
   NANCY _____ (c16 S b.KY)
   1886/7      (1910-1920; NL 1900Sx;
   NL M-B/C/J)
JAMISON a/k/a JAMES (c18 b.KY) [s/o Claiborn
   Hacker & Action Roberts - TCS; P/M-C]
   TABITHA DAVIDSON (c17 b.KY)
   c1847      (1850-C-2; 1860-C; 1870; B-C
   ch.; NL M-C) [JAMISON (58 2nd) m2 12/19/87
   Br., Mahala Cornett (35 -) - M-B 4:237]
(Hacker cont.)

## HACKER (cont.)

JESSE (c23 S b.KY) [poss. s/o Julius Hacker
& Zelpha Burns - 1880]
  NANCY A. FIELDS (c18 S b.KY) [d/o John
  Fields & W1 Eliz. Thomas - 1880]
  1892        (1900-C-5/93, m-7, Henry
  Fields BiL; 1910 m-18; BC 1914; NL M-C)
JOHN (c25 b.KY)
  JANE _____ (c27 b.KY)
  c1849        (1850 no. ch.; B-O ch. W-NL)
JOHN (c26 b.KY) [d/o Julius Hacker & Margaret
  Herd - TCS]
  ELIZABETH MORRIS (c19 b.KY) [d/o John
  Morris & Leah Clark - TCS; 1850-C]
  19 Feb., 1851, Clay (TCS; 1870-C; 1880-J)
JOHN (c20 S b.Ows.) [1876-1955 Cov. Nur-H
  - ob-H OCN-2/10/55]
  LUCY A. WILLIAMS (c20 S b.KY) [1875-1907;
  d/o Lewis Williams & Eliza J. Anderson -
  1880; TS-TCS]
  1895/6        (1900; TCS; ob-ch. BS-7/14/88)
  [H-remd.]
JOHN (R.Ows. 33 2nd b.Ows.) P/-- [widr/o
  Lucy A. Williams above - TCS] [1876-1955]
  VIVIA PENDERGRAS (R.Ows. 17 S b.Ows) P/Per-
  Ows. [d/o Green EVANS & Julia PENDERGRASS
  - TCS]
  26 Dec., 1908, Ows. [R.Owsley 1910-1920]
JULIUS (c19 b.KY) [s/o Granville Hacker & W3
  Anna Nantz - 1860; TCS]
  ZILPHA BURNS (c20 b.KY) [d/o Wm. Burns Jr.
  & Rachel Asher - TCS; 1860]
  c1867        (1870-C, ch. 1 & 9 mo.; 1880-12;
  1900-J m-27 = 1872/3; TCS; NL M-C)
MADISON ["MATT"] (c18 S b.KY) [poss. s/o
  Julius Hacker & Esther Burns - 1870-C]
  ELIZABETH HENSLEY (c16 S b.KY)
  20 Sept., 1888, Clay (M-C; 1900-J m-12;
  B-J ch-12/1900; 1910-J m-21)


(Hacker cont.)

**HACKER (cont.)**
MADISON "MAT" (c22 b.Ows.)  [s/o _____ Hacker
   & Elmina Chandler (who m3 Lewis Green) -
   1880]
   MARY _____ (___ b.Ows.)
   c1888     (widr. Matison 1900-2/89,
   his s-F w/him; M-B ch-1916 Carl s/o Matt &
   Mary, both b.Ows.; NL M-J)
MEREDITH (c15 S b.KY)
   SALLY _____ (c15 S b.KY)
   1889/90     (1910; NL 1900; NL M-C/J)
ROBERT "DUMP" (c24 S b.KY)  [s/o Jameson
   Hacker & Tabitha Davidson - TCS]
   BELLE CROOK (c23 S b.KY)
   6 June, 1881, <u>Clay</u> (TCS 1910-1920; NL 1900)
SAMUEL (c19 S b.KY)  [s/o Jameson Hacker
   & Tabitha Davidson - TCS; 1880]
   MARY BURNS (c21 S b.KY)  [d/o Wm. Burns Jr.
   & Rachel Asher - TCS; 1860]
   1874/5     (1800-C, ch-8, 6, 4, 2 & 1 mo,
   HM w/them, 1st 2 ch. poss. W's; 1900 m-25;
   1910 m-30; TCS; DC-son; NL M-C)
THEOPHILUS (c15 S b.KY)
   NANCY COUCH (c15 S b.KY)  [d/o Elijah Couch
   & Elizabeth Estep - TCS]
   1 April, 1884, <u>Perry</u> @ H. C. Gay's; wits.
   Nelson Barger & Elijah Gay  (M-P G:130;
   1910; NL 1900)
WM. JESSE (c27 b.Ows.)  [1878-1949; s/o Hogan
   Hacker & Nora J. Day - 1880; TS-TCS]
   ELLEN THUMAN (c23 b.KY)
   1903/4     (1910-Linc.; MT/TW;
   NL M-B/C/J)
WM. M. (R.Ethel 28 2nd b.Clay)  [m1 _____
   _____ - NL M-J]  [s/o Julius Hacker
   & Zelpha Burns - mg.; 1880; P/1900-J]
   MARY SMITH (R.Ethel, Jack.; 21 S b.uk -
   thought to be b.Jack.)  [d/o Jasper Smith -
   mg.]
   12 Sept., 1901, <u>Jackson Co.</u> @ Wm. J. Burns,
   by Robt. Bingham; wits. A. B. Burns &
   George Marcum  (M-J 12:27; 1910-C H/m2-9,
   W/m1-9; BC-1911; 1920)

**HADDIX**
JESSE (R.Flat Woods 18 S b.Br.)  [s/o
    Zachariah Haddix & Katherine     ]
    SARAH JOHNSON (R.Flat Woods 22 S b.--)
    14 April, 1853, Ows., by Rev. J. D. Spencer
**HADLER**
JOHN (c20 b.KY)
    LUCY _____ (c20 b.KY)
    1895/6          (1900; NL M-J)
**HALCOMBE**
see HOLCOMB
**HALE**
JOHN P. (c25 S b.KY)    [s/o Elisha Hale
    & Cynthia Hobbs - TCS]
    SARAH JANE ROWLAND (c21 S b.KY)  [d/o John
    Rowland, Sr. & Sarah Campbell - 1880; TCS;
    ob-WS OCN-2/29/52 & BE-6/6/35]
    1896/7          (1900-1910; EERS; R.Hazel Green
    1935; Dayton, OH 1952)
NATHAN (___ Rev. b.___)
    LAURA SEBASTIAN (poss. c16 b.KY) [poss. d/o
    James M. Sebastian & Debora Needham - 1880]
    2 May, 1888, @ Methodist Church, by Rev.
    Coda Pendergrass; attendants Martin Neeley,
    Miss Belle Moore, Mr. Bird of TN, & Miss
    Addie Franklin    (3Fks-4/27/88-5/11/88;
    NL 1900Sx; NL M-J/L)
ROBERT D. (c28 S b.KY)  [1874-1943; s/o James
    Curtis Hale & Susan Razer - 1900; TS-TCS]
    NANNIE C. McPHERSON (c22 S b.KY)   [1880-
    1974; d/o Stephen McPherson & Rebecca Jane
    Pendleton - 1880; TS-TCS; ob-WS OCN-7/8/49
    & OCC-12/28/34]
    1902/3          (1910 m-7; 1920; TCS;
    R.Ham.,OH 1934; Scoville, KY 1949; ob-ch.
    BS-6/13/85; NL M-J)
THOMAS FLOURNEY (c28 S b.Ender, Ows.)   [s/o
    Elisha Hale & Cynthia Hobbs - 1880]
    CHARLOTTE "LOTTIE" ROWLAND (c18 S b.Buck Cr
    Ows.) [d/o Ira Roland & Eliz. Tirey - 1900]
    1901/2          (1910-1920; B-O ch; BC 1917;
    R.Connersville, IN 1962 - ob-HS BE-8/23/62)


(Hale cont.)

**HALE (cont.)**

TILMAN HOWARD "BUD" (c23 S b.Buck Cr.) [1870-
   1957 Berea; s/o Elisha Hale & Cyntha Hobbs
   - 1880; ob-H OCN-12/12/57]
   EMILY HERD (c17 S b.Ows.) [1876-1920; d/o
   Jesse Herd & Nancy Flanery - TCS BBG; 1880]
   1893/4      (1900; B-O ch; 1910, HP w/them;
   1920 WF w/them; BC 1911-1914-1916)
WILLIAM (c28 b.Russell Co., VA)
   MARY JANE HOOVER (c24 b.Lee,VA)
   c1860      (1870-L-9 as Hall; 1880-L as
   Hale; B-L ch-1874; NL 1860)

**HALL**

AARON (c25 b.KY) [s/o Harvey P. Hall, Sr.
   & Betsy Beckett - TCS]
   MARGARET BOWMAN (c18 b.Clay) [d/o Ann
   Bowman who md. James Roberts - M-cons.,
   twin Mary md Harvey Hall, Aaron's bro.- MT]
   4 Aug., 1842, Estill (M-E; 1850; B-O ch.;
   1860-1870-1880; M-L ch.)
AARON (c19 S b.KY) [s/o Harvey Hall & Mary
   Bowman]
   ANNA THOMAS (c20 S b.KY) [d/o James Thomas
   & Mary Ann Roark - REM; 1850]
   1865      (1870-1880-L; 1900-L m-35;
   1910-L m1-44; REM)
AARON, JR. (28 S b.KY) [1856-1936 Proctor; s/o
   Aaron Hall, Sr. & Margaret Bowman - 1880;
   ob-H OCC-8/14/36]
   [LUGENIA] LOGENIUS ANGEL (19 S b.KY) [1867-
   1954 OH; d/o Henderson Angel & Rebecca
   Steel - 1880-L; ob-W BE-4/15/54]
   27 July, 1888, Lee (M-L; 1900-L; Proctor
   1936; wid. Logenia in Summerfield, OH 1954)
BASCOM (c31 S b.Harl.) [1865-1952; s/o Melvin
   Hall & Susan Shook - TCS; ob-H OCN-3/14/52]
   ETTA B. ELKINS (c15 S b.Ows.)
   1896/7      (1900-1910; B-O ch; ob-H;
   NL M-B)
BENJAMIN (c24 S b.Br.) P/WV-KY [s/o John
   Hall & Catherine      - M-O HB 1932]
   _____ (___ b.___)
   1886      (H-remd. 1900-C, oldest ch-
   6/87 listed as Clint CHANDLER "son"; 1910
   Ben & W2 Martha, H-m2-21; NL M-B/J)

(Hall cont.)

**HALL (cont.)**

BENJAMIN (c26 2nd b.Br.) [m1 _____ abv]
  MARTHA MOORE (c20 S b.Ows.)  [d/o Edward
  Moore & Rebecca Gabbard - 1880]
  1888/9       (1900-C m-13, W-6/2 ch--Floyd
  2/93, Luccie 8/98, & Clint CHANDLER 6/87;
  1910 m-21 H-2nd, W-7/3 ch--Floyd 16,
  Melissa 11, Tilman 2; 1920; B-O ch.;
  NL M-B/C)
CHARLES P[ETERSON] (28 S b.Low.Buff.)  [1873-
  1943; s/o Harvey Hall, Jr. & Sarah J.
  Thomas - ob-H BE-5/20/43; 1880-1900-L]
  [MINNEOLA] MINNIE ARNOLD (c27 S b.Lee)
  [1874-1954; d/o George W. Arnold & Mary
  Thomas - ob-W OCN-12/30/54]
  28 April, 1902, Lee @ Mrs. G. W. Arnold's,
  by Wm. Robinson, JLC   (M-L; 1910; B-L ch.;
  M-L ch-1925; ob-H; W/as Minnie 2x, Mennie,
  Mannie, Minneola & Myonie)
CLAY - see HENRY CLAY
CLINTON (R.Ows. 21 S b.KY) P/KY  [1856-1939;
  s/o John Hall & Cath.   - 2nd M-O; TS-TCS]
  NANCY J[ANE] NOBLE (R.Ows. 16 S b.Br.) P/
  Per-Br.   [1860-1929; d/o John Noble
  & Katherine Fugate - 1870; TS-TCS]
  15 Jan., 1876, Ows., @ John Noble's  (a/L
  1/23/77, H-b.Ows; W&P b.KY; rest same; a/L
  M-B 1877)  [R.Owsley 1880, 1900 m-23, 1910
  m-33; 1920]   [CLINT (R.Ows. 75 widr. b.
  Law.,VA) m2 8/5/31 Br. (rec. Ows.) Pink
  South (R.Br. 26 S d/o Green) - M-O]
COLUMBUS QUILLA (c20 b.Harl.)
  FRANCES RIDDLE (c20 b.Ows.)  [d/o Aquilla
  Riddle & Rebecca Smith - 1880]
  c1895/6        (1900-12/96 N#L; BC-ch.1896;
  NL M-B/J) [FRANCES remd. pre-1943, Mr.
  Parsons - Aff/o Frances Parsons, mother,
  BC-ch. 1896]
CRIT (R.Lee 35 2nd b.Ows.) P/Harl-NC [m1 _____
  _____ - NL M-B/C/J]
  LIZZIE CAUDILL (R.Ows. 18 S b.Ows.) P/Br.
  [poss d/o Allen Caudill, Mary Smith - 1900]
  30 June, 1910, Ows. [R.Owsley 1920 H/as
  Crit C.]


(Hall cont.)

301

HALL (cont.)
DANIEL (c25 b.Boonev.) [1853-1923; s/o Aaron
    Hall & Margaret Bowman - 1880; TS-TCS]
    _____ (___ b.___) [d. pre-1880]
    c1878          (1880 Daniel, widr., 25, w/P;
    NL M-B/J)    [H-remd.]
DANIEL (c29 2nd b.Boonev.) [widr/o _____
    above - 1880 widr. Daniel]
    MARY FRANCES FLANERY (c16 b.KY) [1866-1882;
    d/o Wm. Preston Flanery & W2 Margaret Jane
    Williams - ob-W ME 9/29/82; 1880]
    4 July, 1882, Ows. (ob-W; H-3rd M-L 9/86)
    [H-remd.]
DANIEL (R.Ows. 33 3rd b.Ows.) P/VA-Clay
    [widr/o Mary Frances Flanery abv - ob-W ME]
    EMILY THOMAS (R.Lee 22 S b.Ows.) P/Est-
    Nicholas   [1863-1925; d/o Isaac Thomas &
    Eliz. Rankins - TS-TCS]
    3 Sept., 1885, Lee @ Harvey Hall's (M-L
    3:23; 1900-L-6/87; 1910-1920; B-O ch.)
HARVEY [PLEASANT] (c23 b.KY) [s/o Harvey
    Hall, Sr. & Betsy Beckett - TCS]
    MARY BOWMAN (c18 b.KY) [d/o Elisha Bowman
    & Ann Evans (who m2 James Roberts) - REM;
    M-cons.; MT]
    17 Jan., 1843, Estill (M-E; 1850-1860;
    B-O ch.; 1870-1880-L)
HARVEY (c22 b.KY) [appar. s/o Aaron Hall
    & Margaret Bowman]
    MARY JANE McKINNEY (c19 b.KY)
    Dec., 1869      (1870; B-J ch.; 1880-J)
HENRY CLAY (c20 b.KY)   [1875-1910; s/o Zach.
    Hall & Sarah Isaacs - 1880; TS-TCS]
    CORA HAMILTON (c17 b.Ows.) [1878-1896; d/o
    Alex. Hamilton & Catherine Pendleton - B-O;
    ob-W ME, dates below]
    c1895       (1900 H-remd-3, W2-2/2 ch., 3
    listed--5/96, 10/97 & 3/1900; TCS; ME-
    6/5/96 Mrs. Clay Hall d., leaving hus. & 2
    day old infant; ME-6/19/96 Ivy Pendleton d.
    a few days after his GD, Mrs. Clay Hall;
    ME-8/14/96 funeral preached for Mrs. Cora
    Hall; NL M-B)


(Hall cont.)

## HALL (cont.)

HENRY CLAY (c22 2nd b.KY)   [widr/o Cora
    Hamilton above]
    MARTHA MAINOUS (c20 S b.Ows.)   [1877-1950;
    d/o John Tyler Mainous & Ellen Botner -
    1880; ob-W OCN-3/24/50]
    16 Dec., 1896, Ows. (Wed.), @ bride's F's,
    by Elder Stump  (ME-1/8/1897 2x; 1900-3;
    ME-10/16/1903, Chester, Jennie & Matilda
    Mainous visted their sis Martha Hall; R. B.
    Mainous visited BiL H. C. Hall of Vincent
    ME-11/6/03)      [MARTHA m2 1914, Charlie
    Judd - ob-W; 1920]
HEZEKIAH (c22 S b.Harl.)
    REBECCA FARMER (c17 S b.KY)   [d/o Wm.
    Farmer & Elizabeth Frost - JTB]
    9 April, 1847      (JTB; 1850-H)  [H-remd.]
HEZEKIAH (c29 2nd b.KY)  [widr/o Rebecca
    Farmer - JTB; HC; 1850-H]
    ELIZABETH BROWNING (c19 b.KY)
    c1854         (1860, ch. ages 11, 8, 6, 6,
    4, 3, 2, 1, & 2 mo.; B-O ch-12/55 is listed
    as age 3; NL 1870Inx for this Hezekiah;
    1880-B; wid. Eliz. w/dau. Sarah McIntosh
    1900-B)
JAMES M. (c17 b.NC)
    SARAH _____ (c17 b.VA)
    c1858       (1860-1; NL M-J)
JAMES M. (c16 S b.Boonev.)  [s/o Rhodes Hall
    & Mary Eliz. Sandlin - 1900]
    ADA NOBLE (c15 S b.Gabbard)  [d/o John
    Anderson Noble & Julie Reynolds - 1900]
    1900/1       (1910-1920; B-O ch.; TCS;
    NL M-B)
JOHN (R.Ows. 49 widr. b.Harrison Co., VA)
    [widr/o Polly _____ - 1850]
    PHEBE GILLY (R.Ows. 20 S b.Per.)  [d/o
    Levi Gilley & Malinda      - TCS]
    21 Sept., 1856, Ows.  [R.Owsley 1860]
JOHN D. (c40 S b.KY)    [s/o Aaron Hall
    & Margaret Bowman - 1880; TCS]
    FRANCES MOORE (c22 S b.KY)  [c1871-1934 -
    ob-W OCC-9/28/34]
    1892/3       (1910-1920; NL 1900; TCS;
    NL M-B)

(Hall cont.)

303

**HALL (cont.)**

JOHN (c23 S b.Br.)  [s/o Rhodes Hall & Mary
    Elizabeth Sandlin]
    DICEY ROBERTS (c15 S b.Cow Cr.)  [d/o John
    Roberts & Sarah Thorp - 1900, wid. mom]
    1906/7      (1910-1920; B-O ch.; BC 1915-
    1917-1920; moved to IN - BBG; NL M-B)
JOSEPH (c19 b.Ows.)  [s/o Harvey Hall & Mary
    Bowman - 1860; M-E 1843]
    AMERICA THOMAS (c18 b.Clay)  [d/o James
    Thomas & Mary Roark - 1860]
    c1868      (1880-L-11, wf America; B-L
    ch-1875 W/as Mary Thomas; ob-ch. same dau.
    OCN-7/26/56, W/as America Thomas;
    NL 1870/J/L)
RHODES (R.Br. 16 S b.Floyd) P/--  [1860-1940;
    s/o John Hall & Catherine   - ob-H OCC-
    9/27/40; M-O HS 1932 Clint, who is listed
    in ob-H]
    [MARY] ELIZABETH SANDLIN (R.Br. 18 S b.Br)
    P/Clay-TN [poss. d/o James Sandlin &
    Delitha Fox - TCS]
    6 June, 1877, Breathitt  (M-B; 1880-B;
    1900-1910)
RHODES (c21 S b.Br.)  [1881-1963; s/o Clinton
    Hall & Nancy Jane Noble - TS-TCS; ob-HS
    OCN-7/17/58]
    DEPSEY/DEBBIE GREEN (c17 S b.Ows.)  [1885-
    1926; d/o Richard Green & Mary Bray - 1900;
    TS-TCS]
    1902/3      (1910; B-O ch.; NL M-B)
    [RHODES prob. m2 Easter Turner (1897-1966)
    - TCS]
WILLIAM - see WM. HALE & MARY JANE HOOVER
WILLIAM (c23 b.KY)  [1844-19__; s/o Aaron Hall
    & Margaret Bowman - TCS]
    LUCY THOMAS (c17 b.Ows.)  [1850-1938; d/o
    Joseph Thomas & Eliz. Brewer - TCS; ob-W
    2/11/38 PWB]
    1868, Ows.  (LNG; 1870-L-1; 1880-1900-L;
    ob-W; ob-ch. BE-4/29/48, OCN-7/7/55)


(Hall cont.)

**HALL (cont.)**
WILLIAM (c26 b.KY)   [s/o Harvey Hall & Mary
    Bowman - TCS]
    SARAH J. HERNDON (c30 S b.KY)  [d/o George
    W. Herndon & Jalia BBurg. - 1880; TCS]
    Aug., 1893 (on a Wed.), Ows., @ the
    Christian Church, by Bro. Thrasher of
    Louisville; attendants Charles Hogg, Wm.
    McGuire, Miss Mary Duff, & Miss Addie
    Brandenburg (ME-8/18/1893; 1900-L; TCS)
WM. (R.Ows. 24 S b.Ows.) P/Ows-Br. [1885-1958;
    s/o Clinton Hall & Nancy J. Noble - ob-H
    OCN-7/17/58; TCS]
    ELIZ. BOWMAN (R.Ows. 18 S b.Ows.) P/Ows.
    [d/o Wiley Bowman & Nealie Taylor - TCS]
    5 May, 1910, Ows.  [R.Owsley 1920; H-d.
    Cow Cr. 1958]
ZACHARIAH (c19 b.Ows.)  [s/o Aaron Hall
    & Margaret Bowman - 1880; TCS]
    SARAH ISAACS (c19 b.Ows.)  [1854-1876; d/o
    Silvester Isaacs & Martha Brewer - TS-TCS]
    c1873         (1880 widr. Zach. w/P; B-O
    ch-10/74; REM)
**HAMILTON**
ALEXANDER J. (c22 b.Lee,VA)  [s/o Linda
    Hamilton, who was w/them 1880 VA]
    CATHERINE PENDLETON (c21 b.Lee,VA)  [d/o
    Ivy Pendleton & Pheobe Flanery - 1870; ME-
    8/14/96, funeral preached for Mrs. Cora
    Hall; ME-6/19/96 Ivy Pendleton d. a few
    days after his GD, Mrs. Clay Hall]
    c1873         (B-O ch-Wm. 10/76 & Cora 8/78;
    1880Sx-Lee,VA, 1st ch. 6 KY, Wm. & Cora
    listed; NL 1900Sx-VA)
BALLARD (R.Ows. 17 S b.Ows.) P/Ows.  [c1891-
    1972 Cin. hosp.]
    LUCINDA ANDERSON (R.Ows. 17 S b.Ows) P/Ows.
    [1889-1971; d/o Wm. Anderson & Sarah Ford -
    1900; TCS; ob-W BE-3/25/71]
    2 July, 1908, Ows.  [R.Owsley 1910; widr.
    R.Beattyv. 1971-72]


(Hamilton cont.)

## HAMILTON (cont.)

ELISHA B. (c27 b.KY)  [s/o Patrick Hamilton
  & Sally Stivers - 1850; M-M; k. C.W.; REM]
  NANCY SPIVEY (c24 b.KY)  [d/o James Spivey
  & Mary Bowles - TCS; B-O sib]
  26 Jan., 1860, Ows.  (REM P-CW; 1860-MWY)
  [NANCY m2 John Payne - REM]
GENERAL (c17 b.KY)
  ELIZA [DEEDS?] (c18 b.KY)  [poss. d/o Henry
  Deeds & Amanda Warren - 1880]
  1891            (1900-8/91, m-8; NL 1910Sx;
  NL M-J)
HENRY (c30 b.KY)  [s/o Owen Hamilton & Anna
  Roberts - TCS]
  LUCINDA EVANS (c26 b.Ows.) [d/o Huram Evans
  & Nancy Stamper - B-O; TCS; ACS; ob-WS BE-
  11/4/43]
  c1884            (1900-3/85, wid. Lucinda 42;
  TCS; 1910 wid. Cinda; R.Richmond 1943)
JOHN SPEED (c22 b.KY) [c1824-1900; s/o Patrick
  Hamilton & Sarah Stivers - TCS; P-CW]
  LUCINDA MORRIS (c17 b.KY) [c1829-1913 P-CW]
  2 April, 1846, Ows., by Wm. Morris, JPOC
  (P-CW REM; 1850-3; TCS; B-J ch-1859; 1860-
  1870-1880-J; R.McKee, Jack. 1890-98 - P-CW)
JOHN (c27 b.Ows.)  [s/o Thomas Hamilton
  & Polly Burns - 1870-L]
  MARTHA ISAACS (c18 b.Ows.)  [d/o Elijah
  Isaacs & Sarah Bowman - 1870]
  1871/2          (1880-L-6; 1900-L; B-L ch.;
  DB; M-L ch-1908-1914; ob-ch. BE-2/9/50;
  NL M-L)
JOHN SPEED (c17-47 S b.KY)  [s/o Owen
  Hamilton & Anna Roberts - 1880]
  POLLY McQUEEN (___ b.___)
  1880-1910        (REM; NL 1900Sx; NL M-J)
JOHN L. (c22 b.Ows.)  [s/o Speed Hamilton
  & Lucinda Morris - TCS]
  EMMA SMITH (c18 b.Ows.)
  1886/7          (1900; N-EM ch.; M-L ch-1920;
  M-O ch.)
LUTHER (R.Ows. 19 S b.Ows.) P/-- [s/o Henry
  Hamilton & Lucinda Evans - 1900; TCS; ACB]
  GRACIE MAINOUS (R.Ows. 18 S b.Ows.) P/VA
  [d/o Wm. Mainous, Mary Pendleton - TCS ACB]
  7 May, 1908, Ows.
(Hamilton cont.)

OWEN (c22 b.KY) [c1826-1895; s/o Patrick
   Hamilton & Sarah Stivers - REM ME-12/20/95]
   ANNA ROBERTS (c25 b.KY) [c1823-1895; d/o
   Joseph Roberts & Eliz. Wilson - REM; TCS;
   ME-5/17/95]
   7 Sept., 1848, Ows. (REM P-Mex.; 1850,
   no ch.; B-O ch.; 1860-J-7; TCS)
PATRICK (21 b.KY) [s/o Owen Hamilton & Anna
   Roberts - 1870]
   ELLEN BRANDENBURG (15 b.KY)
   7 Aug., 1879, <u>Lee</u> (M-L; 1880 no ch; TCS;
   1900-L m-20; 1910-L m-28)
RANDOLPH SMALLWOOD (c22 b.KY) [s/o Patrick
   Hamilton & Sarah Stivers - 1850; M-M]
   SUSAN SPIVEY (c17 b.KY) [d/o James Spivey
   & Mary Bowles - TCS; B-O sib]
   Nov., 1857, Ows. (REM P-CW; 1860-2 w/HM;
   TCS)
SPEED - see JOHN SPEED
THOMAS (c21 b.KY) [c1819-1897; s/o Patrick
   Hamilton & Sally Stivers - TCS; REM]
   POLLY BURNS (c19 b.Clay) [c1828-1907; d/o
   John Burns - TCS; REM]
   18 June, 1840, <u>Clay</u> (M-C; 1850-1860; B-O
   ch.; 1870-1880-L; ob-ch. OCC-5/22/36, BE-
   5/21/36)
WESLEY (R.Ows. 23 S b.Est.) [s/o Patrick
   Hamilton & Sally Stivers - TCS]
   [DEBORAH] DELILA PHILLIPS (R.--; 19 S b.--)
   [d/o Thomas Phillips & Edy Gum - TCS]
   [4 Nov.,] 1852, Ows. [NOTE: no date; REM,
   P-CW has 4 Nov., 1852] [R.Owsley 1860,
   W/as Deborah; moved to Gallatin Co. - P-CW
   REM]
WILLIAM (c25 b.KY) [c1826-1852; s/o Patrick
   Hamilton & Sarah Stivers - 1850; M-M; D-O]
   ELIZABETH CARROLL (c21 S b.Lee,VA) [d/o
   Thomas Carroll & Sally Hall - TCS]
   c1851        (REM; D-O hus.) [ELIZ. m2
   Jno. Bishop - REM]
WILLIAM C. (c26 S b.Ows.) [s/o Owen Hamilton
   & Ann Roberts - 1880]
   RACHEL WILSON (c18 S b.KY) [d/o Theo.
   Wilson & Minerva Gibson - 1880]
   1881/2        (1900-1910; TCS)
(Hamilton cont.)

## HAMILTON (cont.)

[WILLIAM S.] WILLIE (c22 S b.KY) [s/o Alex.
J. Hamilton & Cath. Pendleton - TCS]
[MARTHA] MATTIE ISAACS (c18 S b.KY) [1879-
1965; d/o Sylvester Isaacs & Martha Brewer
- 1880; ob-W BE-11/18/65]
23 Feb., 1898, Ows. [rec. Perry], @ Joseph
B. Scott's, by Eld. J. B. Rowlett, Bapt.;
wits. Henry Isaacs & D. C. & Samuel Mainous
(M-P G:112; 1900 w/WP; 1910-1920; widr.
R.Vincent 1965)     [WILLIAM m2 Bertie Ross
- TCS; ob-H]

## HAMMOND/HAMMON/HAMMONDS

A. J. (R.Ows. 25 S b.Montg.)
SARAH MOORE (R.Ows. 21 S b.Witt Co., MO)
7 Dec., 1854, Ows.
JAMES (c24 b.KY)
LUCINDA ABNER (c20 b.KY)
c1848      (1850-1; B-O ch.; B-J ch-1858;
1860-J-11)
JAMES (c24 b.KY)
MARTHA _____ (c15 b.KY)
c1848/9      (1850 1 ch. listed, age 9,
poss. rel., unless she s/b 9 mo.)
J[EFFERSON] E. (R.Ows. c25 S druggist w/firm
of Bullock & Hammons; b.KY)
[BELVADORA] BELLE HOGG (R.Boonev. c16 S
b.KY) [c1866-1886 Ows.; d/o Stephen Hogg
& Sally Combs - 1880; ob-W ME-10/1/86]
Sept., 1882, Ows., @ bride's home, by Rev.
C. Pendergrass of ME Church (ME-9/29/82;
1900 H-remd-17, but this is W1)
JEFFERSON E. (c30 2nd druggist b.Knox)
[widr/o Belle Hogg above]
NANNIE R. REINS (c17 S b.Clay) [d/o C.
C. Reins of Madison Co. - ME]
1887/8      (ME-5/29/1896, WF visiting
them; 1900 m-17, but this is W1; 1910
m-22; DC dau. Edna 10/1911)


(Hammond cont.)

## HAMMOND (cont.)

JOHN (R.Proctor 30 S b.Morg.) [1826-1890 Lee;
   prob. s/o Thomas Hammonds & Alice   - TCS]
   ELIZABETH "BETSY" ANN McGUIRE (R.Proctor 15
   S b.Ows.) [1837-1881 Lee; d/o Archibald
   McGuire & Cath. Brandenburg - will-F; ob-W
   ME-7/29/81]
   1 Sept., 1853, Ows., by G. S. Williams
   [R.Owsley 1860; Lee 1870-1880]   [H-remd.]
JOHN (57 2nd b.Morg.) [widr/o Elizabeth Ann
   McGuire above]
   PATSY ANN WILLIAMS (33 S b.KY) [d/o George
   S. Williams & Ermine Akers - art-W BE]
   24 Dec., 1885, Lee   (M-L; 1900 W-remd.,
   Hammonds s-s 13, WF w/them; art-W BE-
   5/13/37) [PATSY m2 1899 Sam Cecil - art-W;
   M-L]

## HAMPTON/HAMTON

ALEXANDER S. (c18 b.TN) [s/o Hamilton B.
   Hampton & Rebecca Flanery]
   CLARINDA WYNN (c17 b.VA)
   c1853, Breathitt   (1860-6; B-B ch.)
ANDREW (R.Middle Fk. 22 S b.Middle Fk.)
   LIDDYAN [LYDIA ANN] CHAMBERS (R.Middle Fk.
   20 S b.Morg.) [d/o Elijah Chambers &
   Rachel      ]
   15 April, 1858 Breathitt, by Wm. Littleton
   (M-B; 1860; 1870-1880-L)
FLOYD (c21 S Blk b.Tallega, Lee) [s/o Wilson
   Hampton & Pender Jett - TCS]
   DELORAS JETT (c21 S Blk b.Boonev.)
   1907/8      (1910; B-O ch.; ob-ch.
   Rich.IN-6/15/96)
JAMES J. (R.Boonev. 22 S b.--) [s/o Hamilton
   B. Hampton & Rebecca Flannary - TCS]
   DRUCILLA P. CAWOOD (R.Ows 16 S b.Harl) [d/o
   Moses Cawood & Emily Madden - TCS/Janette
   G. Nolan]
   27 May, 1859, Ows. [R.Owsley 1860-MWY;
   Lee 1870-1880]
JOSEPH P. (c24 b.TN) [s/o Hamilton B. Hampton
   & Rebecca Flanery - 1860; 1850-Lee,VA]
   HANNAH L. _____ (c21 b.VA)
   1864      (1870-5; NL M-J)

(Hampton cont.)

**HAMPTON (cont.)**
MILOM/MILUM (c27 <u>Blk</u> b.KY)
   JANE _____ (c16 <u>Blk</u> b.KY)
   1882/3    (1900; NL M-J)
SOLOMON (c36 <u>Mul</u> b.John.,TN)
   ARA CRAWFORD (c19 <u>Mul</u> b.Br.) [poss. d/o
   Patsy Crawford]
   1867/8    (1870-L-12/69; B-L ch.;
   1880-1900-L)
THOMAS (c20 b.KY)
   SYLVANIA PROFITT (c19 b.KY) [appar. d/o
   Sarah, who was w/them 1860]
   c1842    (1850-7; B-O ch.; 1860-16;
   NL M-C/E)
WILLIAM A. (___ b.___)
   AMANDA MOORE (c21 b.KY) [1865-1899 -TS-TCS]
   Dec., 1886 (ML) Ows. (ME-1/14/87; TCS)
WILLIAM (c23 S <u>Blk</u> b.Tallega, Lee)
   LIZZIE ROSE (c15 S <u>Blk</u> b.Tallega, Lee)
   1907    (1910; B-O ch-6/1908)
WILSON (24 S [<u>Blk</u> b.Tallega, Lee])
   PENDER JETT (15 S [<u>Blk</u> b.Tallega, Lee])
   - Oct., 1881, <u>Breathitt</u> @ J. T. Chadwick's,
   by J. T. Chadwick (M-B 3:7; 1900-L m-18;
   1910; B-O ch.)
**HANDY**
J. W. (c17 b.KY)
   MELISSA DALTON (c20 S b.KY) [poss. d/o
   Sam Dalton & Sarah Clark - TCS]
   c1896    (ME-3/8/01, C. C. Bowman,
   who is md. to <u>wid/o J. W. Handy</u>; NL M-J)
   [MELISSA m2 Christopher C. Bowman - ME;
   1900; TCS]
**HARALD**
see HERALD
**HARDY**
GEORGE (c18 2nd b.KY) [m1 _____ - NL M-J]
   ISABELLE _____ (c25 S b.KY)
   1889/90    (1910; NL 1900Sx; NL M-J)
LEWIS (c22 b.KY)
   DRUCILLA [poss SIMMS/BISHOP - TCS] (c19
   b.KY)
   1879/80    (1880-MWY; TCS; NL M-C/J)
   [DRUCILLA m2 Wm. Sandlin - TCS; 1900;
   listed 1910 as Druscilla HARDY]

**HARGIS**
KENAZ F. (c22 Law. b.KY) [s/o John Hargis
    & Eliza      - TCS]
    ELIZABETH A. McGLASSON (c17 b.KY)
    19 Feb., 1857      (REM, KY-Hist; 1860-2;
    B-O ch. W/McGap; 1870-1880-L; NL M-J)
**HARRIS**
_____ (\_\_\_ b.\_\_\_)
    _____ SANDERS (\_\_\_ b.\_\_\_) [d/o Prof.
    Sanders of Union City, TN - ME]
    pre-1892      (ME-7/15/92, Mrs. Prof.
    Sanders of Union City, TN visits daus. Mrs.
    Harris & Mrs. Dailey of Boonev.; NL M-J/L)
    [NOTE: 3Fks-3/8/89 mentions Prof. A.
    Sanders of Boonev.]
GILBERT (R.Ows. 21 S b.Ows.) P/Ows. [1883-
    1913/14 - JTB]
    MATTIE RICE (R.Ows. 16 S b.Ows.) P/Ows.
    13 Jan., 1904, Ows.
HENDERSON (c17 b.KY) [s/o _____ Harris
    & Susan      - TCS]
    LEVINA "VINA" FOX (c20 b.KY) [d/o John Fox
    & Sarah Johnson - 1860-O]
    c1869      (1870-B w/WP, no diff. surname
    listed; 1880-B, Vina HARRIS & ch. w/WP;
    M-L ch-1938)    [H-remd. 1880]
HENDERSON (c24 2nd b.KY) [Div/f Vina Fox]
    MIMA _____ (c18 b.KY) P/KY
    c1879      (1880, ch. by W1; NL 1900Sx;
    NL M-B/J)
JAMES T. (\_\_\_ b.\_\_\_)
    FLORA ELLEN CAWOOD (c22 b.Ows.) [1886-
    1964 Fay.; d/o Henry Bascum Cawood & Nancy
    Jett - COJ; 1900; ob-WS OCN-6/26/58]
    c1908      (COJ son b. 10/09; R.Lex. 1958)
STEPHEN (R.Lee 19 S b.Br.) P/Br. [s/o Henly
    JOHNSON & Vina FOX (who m1 Henderson
    HARRIS) - 2nd M-L]
    SUSAN PACE (R.Lee 19 S b.Lee) P/Lee
    17 Jan., 1900 Lee @ John H. Fox's, by J. M.
    Roberts, MG; wits. J. H. & Lee Fox
    (M-L 5:489; 1900-L m-0; 1910 m-11; B-O ch.)
    [STEPHEN (R.Lee 39 widr. b.Br.) m2 6/16/19
    Callie (nee Little) Vires (40 wid. b.Br. -
    d/o Dave Little & Lyddie Johnson) - M-L;
    1920-B]
(Harris cont.)

## HARRIS (cont.)

THOMAS (c18-38 b.KY) [s/o Henderson Harris
& W1 Vina Fox - w/F 1880 & M 1880-B]
MARY "POLLY" JANE BARRETT (c24-44 b.Clay)
[1865-1939 Ham., OH; d/o Thomas Barrett
& Barbara Gabbard - MT]
1890-1910          (MT; NL 1900Sx-KY/OH;
NL M-B/C/J)
WILLIAM (c23 b.KY)
    MAHALA _____ (c25 b.KY)
    c1859          (1860, no ch.; NL M-J)
WILLIAM "WILL" (___ b.___) [NOTE: poss. s/o
Henderson Harris & W1 Vina Fox; b. c1874 -
listed w/F 1880 & w/M 1880-B]
    AMERICA MOORE (c16-36 b.Ows.) [d/o Edward
    Moore & Rebecca Gabbard - TCS; BBG]
    1890-1910          (TCS; NL 1900Sx; NL M-B/J)
WILLIAM M. (c21 S b.KY) [1872-1961; s/o Hiram
Harris & _____ Simpkins - TCS]
    MARY JANE (nee HALL) ROBERTS (c35 2nd b.KY)
    [wid/o _____ Roberts] [1858-1935; d/o
    John Hall & Catherine Harris - TCS]
    1893/4          (1900-B m-6 Roberts s-ch;
    1910-1920; TCS; NL M-B/J/R)     [WILLIAM m2
    Sarah Allen - TCS]
WILLIAM (c24 b.KY)
    LOU EMILY COOPER (c19 b.KY) [1880-1935
    Campbell; d/o Albert (s/b Alfred) Cooper
    & Patsy Cole - DC]
    1897/8          (1900-1910-L; 1920; NL M-J/L)

## HARTSOCK/HEARTSOCK

JOHN WESLEY (c17 S b.KY) [s/o Thomas Hartsock
& Susan E. Warren - TCS]
    ALLIE M. DALTON (c16 S b.KY) [d/o Samuel
    Dalton & Rebecca Flanery - TCS]
    Jan., 1905, Ows. (ME-1/26/1905; 1910 m-5;
    1920; TCS; ob-ch. OCC-5/28/37; BC 1911)
JOHN W. (c18 S fireman on mill; b.KY) [s/o
Peter Hartsock & Martha E. Conner - TCS]
    MARY J. _____ (c20 S b.KY)
    1904/5          (1910; NL M-J)
MILLARD (c20 S b.Ows.) [1881-1940 - TS-TCS]
    MARIAH LOUISA CREECH (c32 S b.Ows.) [c1868-
    1948; d/o John L. Creech & Nancy Minerva
    Farmer - 1870-1880-1900; TS-TCS]
    1901/2     (1910-1920; B-O ch.)
(Hartsock cont.)

## HARTSOCK (cont.)
PETER (c26 S b.VA) [s/o John Hartsock
 & Melissa Napier - 1880; TCS]
 MARTHA E. CONNER (c18 S b.KY) [d/o Wm.
 Connor & Permelia Spence - EERS; 1880 w/M
 & s-F]
 1887      (1900 m-13; 1910 m-22; 1920 EERS)
SAMUEL (c21 S b.Scott Co., VA) [s/o Jno.
 Hartsock & Mary      - TCS]
 ROSA B. STANDIFORD (c18 S b.Lee,VA) [ob-W
 OCC-5/15/36]
 1866      (1870-2; 1880-13; 1900-3/67
 m-33; B-O ch; 1910 w/dau. Cynthia; 1920)
THOMAS (R.Ows. 21 S b.VA) P/VA [s/o John
 Hartsock & Melissa Napier - TCS]
 SUSAN WARREN (R.Ows. 26 S b.KY) P/VA-TN
 [d/o Thomas Burgoyne Warren & Priscilla
 Anderson - TCS; 1850-H; 1860-1870]
 - April, 1878, Ows. [R.Ows. 1880-1900-1910]
THOMAS (c28 b.KY)
 EVLINEY _____ (c23 b.KY)
 1881/2      (1900; NL M-J)
WESLEY - see JOHN WESLEY
WILLIAM (c32 b.KY) [s/o John Hartsock
 & Melissa Napier - 1880]
 LUCY A. BREWER (c26 b.KY) [d/o Valentine
 Brewer & Sarah J. Wilson - 1880; ob-WS
 OCC-2/14/41, OCN-5/18/51-5/14/54]
 1896/7      (1900; B-O ch.; R.Raymore, MO
 1941; Kansas City, MO 1951-4)

## HARVEY
BENT - see HARVEY BENTON
CLAY - see W. CLAY
GEORGE W. (c23 S b.TN) [s/o Prior Harvey &
 W1 Perlina Blake - 1870; TCS]
 FRANKIE BOWMAN (teens b.KY) [d/o Rachel
 BOWMAN & unknown - BBG/JFB; NL w/M & GM
 1860]
 late 1880      (TCS; H-sgl. 1880 w/s-M;
 1900-1/81 H-remd-10; NL M-J)


(Harvey cont.)


313

**HARVEY (cont.)**

GEORGE W. (c33 2nd b.TN)  [m1 Frankie Bowman
   above]
   ISABELLE MOORE (c27 b.KY)  [d/o James
   "Fiddler" Moore & Emily Smith - 1880; TCS]
   1889/90        (1900; TCS; 1920; M-O ch-
   1966; NL M-J)
   [NOTE: a G. W. (R.Blake 80 widr b.grainger
   Co, TN - s/o Spencer Harvey & Carolina -
   instead of Prior Harvey & Perlina Blake)
   md. 9/1/37 Curl (nee Collins) Bowles (72
   wid.; d/o Ance Collins) - M-O]
H[ARVEY] B[ENTON] (R.Ows. 31 S b.Ows.) P/TN-VA
   [1878-1948; s/o Prior Harvey & W2 Eliz.
   Spence - 1900; TS-TCS]
   LUCY PRITCHARD (R.Ows. 32 S b.Ows) P/Ows
   [1877-1942; d/o Bonaparte Pritchard & Mary
   Jane Ross - ob-WS OCC-4/3/36; TS-TCS]
   16 May, 1909, Ows.   [R.Owsley 1910-1920]
ISAAC "IKE" (c17 S b.KY)  [s/o Prior Harvey
   & W1 Perlina Blake - 1880]
   LUCINDA FIELDS (___ b.___)
   c1881/2        (FH-ch. Ida b. 10/82 Boonev;
   NL 1900Sx)
MANUAL (c22 b.TN)
   MARGARET _____ (c25 b.KY)
   1893/4        (1900; TCS)
PRIOR (R.Ows. 45 2nd b.KY) P/TN  [m1 6/26/52
   TN, Perlina Blake, d/o Wm. Blake & Hannah
   - VKD; D-O 1876; M-L ch-1929 has Paulina
   Taylor]
   ELIZABETH [nee SPENCE] HOWARD (R.Ows. 30
   2nd b.VA) P/VA   [wid/o Robert Howard]
   [1844-1914 Ows.; d/o Jno. Spence & Mary
   Holmes - 1870; DC/Fields]
   8 Feb., 1877, Ows. @ Widow Spence's  [wid.
   Eliz. R.Ows. 1880]   [ELIZABETH m3 John
   Fields]
W. CLAY (c22 S b.Blake)  [1882-1958; s/o Wm.
   Harvey & Nancy A. Fields - TCS; 1900; ob-H
   OCN-10/9/58]
   LILLIAN "LILLIE" HARVEY (c22 S b.Blake)
   [d/o _____ Harvey & Frances Wilson - TCS]
   1904        (1910-5, m-5; 1920; B-O ch. &
   BC 1912-1913-1917; ob-ch. BS-2/14/85)

(Harvey cont.)

**HARVEY (cont.)**

WILLIAM (c20 S b.TN) [1858-1908; s/o Prior
    Harvey & Perlina Blake - 1870; TS-TCS]
    NANCY A. LEWIS (c22 S b.KY) [1856-1924
    Ows.; d/o Mathias Lewis & Chaney Combs
    a/k/a Chaney Fields - DC; TS-TCS]
    c1879         (1880, no ch.; 1900 N#L; wid.
    Nannie w/BiL Clay Harvey 1910; wid. Nancy
    1920)

**HAULKMAN**

see HOLCOMB

**HAYES/HAYS**

DAVID (c29 b.TN)
    ZERILDA _____ (c29 b.KY)
    c1869         (1870 no ch.; NL M-J)
ELSBERRY (R.Br. 21 S b.Per.) [s/o Edward
    Adrian Hayes & Eliz. Cockrell]
    MARTHA AN TAULBEE (R.Br. 17 S b.Per.)
    [d/o Wm. A. Taulbee & Polly      ]
    1 Nov., 1855, Ows. (a/L M-B same date)
    [R.Owsley 1860; Breathitt 1870; Wolfe 1880]

**HELTON**

DANIEL (c23 b.KY)
    CATHERINE REED (c19 b.KY) [d/o Wiley Reed
    & Lydia Mason - TCS 1900; ob-WS BE-1/31/63-
    10/20/66]
    c1903         (1920-16; NL 1910Sx; BC 1911-
    1916-1919; ob-ch. HJN-12/94; R.Morrow, OH
    1963-1966)
EPHRAIM (c23 b.KY) [s/o John Helton & Jemima
    Osborn - TCS]
    MARGARET [MARTHA] TAYLOR (c17 b.KY) [d/o
    James Taylor - 1850-H]
    19 Oct., 1857, Harlan @ James Taylor's, by
    Jacob Buckhart (M-H; TCS; 1860 no ch.;
    W/as Martha & Margaret M.; 1880-Les.)
HARRISON - see JAMES HARRISON
JAMES HARRISON (c22 b.KY) [s/o James Helton
    & Matilda Lutes - 1860]
    SARAH SANDLIN (c18 b.KY) [c1851-c1890/2]
    c1869         (1880-10; NL 1870/C/J/L;
    TCS; NL M-C)  [JAMES m2 1/26/1893, Sophia
    Murray - M-C MT; 1900Sx-C]


(Helton cont.)

315

**HELTON (cont.)**
JOHN MILUM (c21 S b.KY)  [s/o Joseph Helton
   & Kate Mason - BBG]
   MARTHA GILBERT (c13 b.KY)  [1883-1906 -
   TS-TCS]
   1896/7          (1900; BBG; B-O ch.; their
   oldest son b. 6/98, alive 1995 - BBG;
   ob-ch. BS-4/16/97; NL M-B)   [H-remd.]
JOHN MILUM (c31 2nd b.KY)  [widr/o Martha
   Gilbert above]
   EASTER REYNOLDS (c24 S b.KY)  [d/o Aaron
   Reynolds & Mary A. Wilson - TCS]
   1906/7          (1910-1920; BBG; TS-TCS W1
   d. 3/1906; BC 1913-1915)
STOKLEY (c21 b.KY]
   LOURANY JANET JOHNSON (c18 b.KY)
   c1847          (1850-3; 1860-J; TR; W/as
   Aurraney & Janet, W/as Lourany - TR)
WILLIAM (R.Ows. --[c21] S b.--)  [s/o John
   Helton & Jemima Osborne - TCS; 1880-Les.]
   MARGARETT GABBARD (R.Ows. 20 S b.Lau.)
   [d/o Peter Gabbard & Susan Harrison - TCS]
   -- June, 1859, Ows.  [R.Owsley 1860; Clay
   1870; Leslie 1880, HP w/them]
WILLIAM (c30 S b.KY)  [s/o George H. Helton
   & Leannah         - TCS]
   ELIZA FREEMAN (c21 S b.KY)
   28 Aug., 1895, Clay (M-C; MT; 1900-B
   m-10 = 1889/90, ch. 6/92, 4/96 & 1/1900;
   1910 m-18 = 1891/2, ch. 17, 12, etc.)
   [NOTE:  It appears that one of them had
   ch. before their marriage]
WILLIAM A. (c19 S b.Br.)
   ELVIRA BRYANT (c16 S b.Cafe)
   1892          (1900 m-7; 1910 m-18; 1920;
   B-O ch.; TCS; M-L ch-1922; W/as Elvira all
   rec. except one B-O ch. as Lizzie)
**HENLEY**
see HUNDLEY
**HENSLEY**
_____ (___ b.___)
   NANCY _____ (c16 b.KY)
   c1858          (1860-1, wid. Nancy)


(Hensley cont.)


316

**HENSLEY (cont.)**
AMOS (c19 b.KY)   [s/o Burton Hensley & Rachel
    Tipton - TCS]
    HANNAH KING (c17 b.Taft)   [c1891-1909; d/o
    Samuel King & Nancy      - D-O]
    c1908        (1910, widr. Amos 21 w/P; D-O
    9/1909 son; NL M-H)      [AMOS m2 c1911,
    Louvada Byrd - TCS; BC]
FIELDING [H.] (c20 S b.Harl.)   [s/o Burton
    Hensley & Rachel Tipton - ob-HS BE-7/27/61]
    NANCY FOWLER (c17 S b.Harl.)
    22 April, 1904, Harlan, @ J. R. Fowler's,
    by E. S. Howard, JP; wits. Wm. Taylor & J.
    R. Fowler   (M-H; 1910 m-6; 1920; B-O ch.;
    R.Berea 1961; H/as Feling 1908 & H. 1910)
H. F. (R.Ows. 29 S b.Ows.)
    LUCINDA JANE BRAWNER (R.Ows. 21 S b.Clay)
    [d/o Luther Brawner & Maria Garrard - TCS]
    27 Oct., 1857, Ows.   [R.Owsley 1860]
JACKSON "JACK" (c21 S b.KY) [s/o _____ Hensley
    & Nancy      - TCS]
    RACHEL (nee BOWMAN) HICKS (c25 2nd b.KY)
    [wid/o Wm. Hicks - M-O 1874]   [1857-1929;
    d/o Robt. Sturgis Bowman & Mary Turner -
    1860; DC/Frost]
    c1882        (TCS; wid. Rachel HICKS 1880;
    wid. Rachel HENSLEY 1900-L-3/88, ch. 10/7;
    1910 W-remd-8 Frost, Hensley s-s 22;
    NL M-L; ob-ch. OCN-12/6/56 b.1/84; NL M-H)
    [RACHEL m3 Wm. Frost - 1910]
JAMES R. (c21 S b.KY)
    [ELIZABETH] BETSY NOE (c22 S b.KY)
    11 April, 1895, Harlan, @ Benjamin Noe's,
    by E. L. Buckhart; wits. John Ledford & Ben
    Noe   (M-H; 1910 m-15; NL 1900/L; BC 1911-
    1913-1916)
JAMES A. (c21 S b.Harl.)   [poss. s/o Burton
    Hensley & Rachel Tipton]
    ELIZABETH "ELIZA" KING (c18 S b.Harl.) [d/o
    Samuel King & Nancy      - TCS]
    1907/8        (1910; B-O ch; widr James 1920)


(Hensley cont.)




317

## HENSLEY (cont.)

JOHN (c22 2nd b.Avendale) [m1 _____]
   [c1879-1961 London hosp.; s/o Burton
   Hensley & Rachel Tipton - ob-H BE-7/27/61]
   PINEY FOWLER (c16 S b.Avendale)
   c1901          (1910 N#L, 6/1 ch.; B-O ch.;
   1920; BC 1912-1914-1915-1918; ob-ch. BS-
   3/20/86)
JOHN (c21 S b.Clay)
   FLORENCE SIZEMORE (c19 S b.Ows.) [d/o Mary
   J. SIZEMORE & unknown - 1910]
   1903/4          (1910 WM w/them; B-O ch.;
   NL M-C)
SNEED (c22 b.TN)
   MAHALA _____ (c21 b.Clay)
   c1856          (1860-C-3, 1st ch. b. Ows.;
   NL M-C/J)

## HERALD/HARALD

JOHN (R.Br. 20 S b.Br.) P/Br.
   MARY ELLEN FROST (R.Ows. 16 S b.Ows) P/Ows.
   [d/o Jacob Frost & Hannah Wilder - 1900]
   28 July, 1904, Ows.
RICHARD (R.Br. 21 S b.Br.) [s/o Alex Herald
   & Elizabeth Turner - 1850-B]
   EMILY COMBS (R.Br. 18 S b.Br.)
   28 Nov., 1853, Ows., by Wm. Barret (a/L
   1/53 Breathitt)   [R.Breathitt 1860-1870-
   1880-1900]
WILLIAM (R.Ows. 24 S b.Br.) P/Br.
   ELLA SANDLIN (R.Ows. 16 S b.Ows.) P/Br.
   [d/o Lewis Sandlin & Mahala Helton - ob-WS
   OCN-2/20/58; 1900]
   17 Nov., 1910, Ows. [R.Boonev. 1958]

## HERD/HEARD/HURD

ANDREW J. a/k/a ROBERT (c20 S b.Clay) [c1830-
   1891 Mad.; s/o Wm. Herd & Rebecca Hudson -
   ME-2/23/1911; P-CW]
   EMILY TURNER (c23 b.KY) [d/o Jesse Turner
   & Cynthia Roberts - ob-WS ME-10/25/95]
   1849/50          (1850-MWY; D-O 1st ch. b.
   1851; Andrew on TL 1849; 1860; REM; H/as
   Andrew J. & Robt.)   [H-remd.]

(Herd cont.)

## HERD (cont.)

ANDREW J. a/k/a ROBERT (c33-37 2nd b.KY)
[widr/o Emily Turner above]
_____ (___ b.___)
1863-7          (P-CW says 1st 2 wives
decd.) [H-remd.]

ANDREW J. a/k/a ROBERT (c37 3rd widr. b.KY)
[widr/o _____]
MARY E[LIZABETH] SEARCY (c20 S b.Mad.)
[c1848-1906; poss. d/o Chas. Searsy &
Lucinda    - 1850-M]
13 April, 1868, Waco, Madison, by Rev. J.
B. Rowlett  (P-CW; 1870; R.Lee 1876; 1880;
1890 Kingston, Mad.; wid. Mary 1891
Kingston, Mad.; 1892-94 wid. Mary in Ows.;
wid. 1900; DC ch.; NL M-J; H/as Andrew J. &
Robert; W/as Eliz. & Mary E.)

CHARLES E. (c25 b.KY)  [s/o Andrew/Robt. Herd
& Mary Eliz. Searsy - 1880]
LAURA _____ (c22 b.KY)
1898/9          (1900-Bell m-1, 1st ch-
11/99; HM 1900; R.Middlesboro, Bell Co.
1947 - DC sib; NL M-Bell/J)

ELIJAH (c23 b.KY)  [s/o Wm. Herd & Rebecca
Hudson - TCS]
NANCY DAVIDSON (c14 b.KY)  [d/o John
Madison Davidson & Eliz.      - TCS]
3 May, 1844 (ML) Clay Co.  (M-C; 1850-
1860; 1870-L; 1880; wid. Nancy 1900,
w/nephew Abner Baker)

GEORGE M. (c24 b.Clay)  [s/o Wm. Herd
& Rebecca Hudson]
LUCINDA YOUNG (c20 b.KY)
6 Aug., 1864, Estill, by Lige Gabbard
(M-E; LNG; 1870-4; 1880-E; 1900-M m-36;
DC ch-1934; W/Lucinda all rec. except 1870
W/Malinda)

JESSE (R.Ows. 22 S b.Ows.) P/Clay-Ows. [s/o
Andrew/Robt. Herd & W1 Emily Turner - 1860]
NANCY FLANARY (R.Ows. 14 S b.Ows.) P/Lee,VA
-Clay [1858-1919; d/o Wm. Flanary & Susan
Spivey - B-O; TS-TCS]
26 Nov., 1874, Ows., @ Wm. P. Flanary's
[R.Owsley 1880-1900; widr. Jesse 1920]

(Herd cont.)

319

**HERD (cont.)**

JOHN D. (c21 S dentist b.Trav. Rest) [1881-
1913; s/o Joseph Herd & Nancy Ellen Wilson
- TS-TCS; 1900; listed as d. ob-M]
   LOUVINA CHILDS (c19 S b.Clay) [d/o James
   Childs & Sarah Evans - ob-WM OCC-5/15/36]
   1903/4    (1910; B-O ch.; TCS; wid. Vina
   1920; R.Louisville 1936)
JOSEPH F. (c20 b.Clay) [1846-1911; s/o Wm.
Herd & Rebecca Hudson - TS-TCS; ob-H ME-
2/23/11]
   NANCY ELLEN WILSON (c20 b.Ows.) [1846-1936;
   d/o John G Wilson & Amelia Bowman - TS-TCS;
   ob-W OCC-5/8/36 lists her b.Grant Co; 1850]
   1866    (ob-W; 1870 no ch.; B-O ch.;
   B-J ch; 1880-7; 1900 m-33, WM w/them; 1910
   m-43; TCS; wid. R.Trav. Rest 1911; wid.
   Nancy 1920; DC ch-1949; W/as Ellen & Nancy
   E.)
ROBERT - see ANDREW J.
ROBERT N. (c22 S b.KY)
   ELIZABETH _____ (c19 S b.KY)
   1889/90    (1910; NL 1900; NL M-C/J)

**HERNDON/HARNDON**

CHARLES TYLER (c34 S b.KY) [1875-1947; s/o
Geo. W. Herndon & Jalah BBurg. - TS-TCS]
   MAGGIE WILSON (c23 S b.KY)
   1909/10    (1910 HM w/them; 1920; TCS;
   BC 1912-1915-1918; ob-ch. 3Fks-3/11/98)
G[EORGE] W[ASHINGTON] (R.Ows. 34 S b.Lee, VA)
   JALAH BRANDENBURGH (R.Ows. 23 S b.Est.)
   [1837-1912; d/o Yankee Joe BBurg. & Rhoda
   Hamilton - 1850; P/M-C; TS-TCS]
   8 Sept., 1859, Ows. [R.Breathitt 1850-54;
   Owsley 1855-1860-1870-1880; wid. Jalah
   1900-1910]
JESSE - see SAM JESSE
JOSEPH [BBURG.] (34 S b.Boonev.) [1871-1939;
s/o Geo. Herndon & Julia BBurg. - TS-TCS]
   [MARTHA] MATTIE HALL (18 S b.Lee) [1887-
   1975; d/o Dan Hall & Emily Thomas - TS-TCS]
   11 Jan., 1906 <u>Lee</u> @ Beattyv., by Rev. C. T.
   Brookshire; wits. Mattie & Rhoda BBurg.
   (M-L; 1910 m-4; 1920; B-O ch; BC 1912-1914)

(Herndon cont.)

**HERNDON (cont.)**
SAMUEL JESSE (c28 b.KY) [1866-1948; s/o
    George W. Herndon & Jalah BBurg. - 1880 ME]
    ALICE F. ROSE (c19 b.KY) [1875-1963 Lee;
    d/o Leander C. Rose & Emma Cawood - 1880;
    ob-W&F&S BE-5/9/63, OCC-4/6/34-5/15/42; ME]
    1894/5        (TCS; ME-6/14/95 Lee Rose & wf
    of Boonev. visiting dau., Mrs. Samuel
    Herndon of Welchburg; 1900-J m-5; P/1900;
    ME-6/14/01, Sam, of Welchburg, visits M &
    FiL; 1920; ob-ch. BS-4/21/88)
**HICKERSON**
WILLIAM M. (c41 b.KY)
    HANNAH F. GABBARD (c19 b.Ows.) [1874-1957
    Lex. hosp.; d/o Wyatt Gabbard & Sarah Ann
    White - ob-W OCN-5/9/57; 1880]
    8 March, 1894, Lee @ Jesse Thomas'; wits.
    R. W. Parks & Martin Clayton   (M-L; 1900-L)
**HICKS**
JOHN (c33 2nd b.KY) [m1 _____ - poss. m1
    12/1/84 Jack, Zilphia Wilder - NL 1900Sx]
    MARY A. _____ (c13 S b.KY)
    1897/8          (1900-11/99, m-2; 1910 m-10,
    H-2nd; NL M-J)
NATHAN - see NATHAN COPE
WILLIAM (R.Clay 21 S b.TX) P/-- KY
    RACHEL BOWMAN (R.Ows. 17 S b.Ows) P/--
    [1857-1929; d/o Robt. Sturgis Bowman & Mary
    Turner - 1860; DC/Frost]
    13 Nov., 1874, Ows., @ R. S. Bowman's
    [wid. Rachel R.Owsley 1880]   [RACHEL m2
    Jackson Hensley; RACHEL m3 Wm. Frost - TCS]
**HIERONYMOUS/HIERONYMUS/HYERONYMUS**
FRANCIS (21 S b.Mad) [1822-1874 MO; s/o Samuel
    Rector Hieronymous & W1 Nancy Elkins -REM]
    ANN BUSH (c17 b.KY) [d/o Harvey Geo. Bush
    & W2 Margaret Snowden - REM]
    8 June, 1864, Ows.  (JFB; REM; R.Franklin
    Co., Ark. 1870)
GEORGE WHITFIELD (24 S b.KY) [1835-1910; s/o
    Samuel Rector Hieronymous & W2 Sarah White
    - REM]
    MARY CATHERINE DUFF (29 S b.KY) P/VA [1830-
    1918 - REM]
    16 May, 1860        (REM; 1860-MWY; 1870-
    1880-1900-1910-L; art. BE-8/27/70)
(Hieronymous cont.)

321

**HIERONYMOUS (cont.)**
TOM [THOMAS FRYE] (24 b.Est.) [1837-1900 Lee;
    s/o Samuel Rector Hieronymous & W2 Sarah
    White - REM; 1860]
    MARGARET T[ANDY] BUSH (15 b.Est.) [1844-
    1931 Lee; d/o Harvey G. Bush & W2 Margaret
    Snowden - REM]
    6 Nov., 1861, Ows. (JFB; REM; 1870-1880-L;
    wid. Margaret 1900-L; wid. Margaret 1910-L
    w/son)

**HIGNITE/HIGNIGHT**
_____ (___ b.KY)
    MARY McQUEEN (c14 b.Garrett Co.)
    c1892        (1900-11/94 wid. Mary, 4/3 ch.,
    a ch. b. 2/93, bur. Ows. poss. hers; TW;
    NL M-C/J)  [MARY m2 John Conrad]
_____ (___ b.KY)
    LAURA HOWARD (c20 S b.KY)  [d/o _____
    Howard & Elizabeth Spence - TCS]
    c1893        (TCS; 1900 W-remd., Hignite
    s-s b.6/94; NL M-C/J)  [LAURA m2 Thos.
    Cole - TCS]
HUGH (c22 b.KY)
    SOPHIA BAKER (c14 b.KY)
    20 Sept., 1888, Clay  (M-C; 1900 m-12)
JOSEPH [JR.] (R.Clay 20 S b.Per.) P/Knx-Clay
    [s/o Joseph Hignite, Sr.]
    MARY E[MILY] BURNS (R.Clay 17 S b.Clay) P/
    Clay  [d/o Perry Burns & Sarah Davidson -
    TW]
    26 July, 1874, Clay  (M-C & mf as 7/25/74,
    W/as Emily; 1880-2)  [JOSEPH m2 Elizabeth
    Burns - TW]
PETER (c22 2nd b.KY) [m1 _____]
    [s/o Joseph Hignite & Sarah Jane     - TW]
    MARY ELIZABETH McINTOSH (c20 b.KY)
    1896/7        (1900 m-3; B-J ch.; 1910-C,
    H/m2-13, W/m?-13; NL M-B/C/J)

**HILL**

DAVID (c21 S b.Ows.)  [s/o Preston Hill
   & Mary        ]
   NANCY JANE COMBS (c12 S b.Ows.) [d/o Squire
   Combs & America Anderson - 1880; ob-WS OCN-
   12/18/53]
   1888          (1900 m-12, HP w/them; 1910
   Nancy J. m-21, H-NL; wid. Nancy Jane 1920,
   HF w/her; B-O ch.)
DAVID (c22 b.KY)  [s/o Hugh Hill & Agnes
   Jane       - 1900-1910]
   [AMANDA] MANDY HUNLEY (c24 b.KY)  [d/o Wm.
   Hundley & Susan Baker - 1900-J anot.]
   23 Nov., 1895 (ML) Jackson Co., bm. groom
   & John Reed  [DIVORCED & remd. again below]
   (M-J 9:346; 1900 David w/HM; 1900-J Amanda
   w/WM as n-5)
DAVID (c31 2nd b.KY)  [m1 same]
   AMANDA HUNLEY (c33 2nd b.KY)  [m1 same]
   Sept/Oct., 1904         [DIVORCED pre-1910]
   (ME-10/20/04, David Hill & Amanda Hunley
   remd. some 2 weeks ago; NL M-J; 1910 David,
   Div., HM w/him; widr. David 1920, HM w/him)
EDWARD (R.Ows. 21 S b.Ows.) P/Ows.  [s/o
   David Hill & Nancy Jane Combs - TCS]
   CALLIE HUFF (R.Ows. 18 S b.Ows.) P/Ows.
   [d/o _____ Huff & Sarah Cornett - 1910 w/M
   & s-F James Baker; TCS]
   22 Dec., 1910, Ows.  [R.Owsley 1920, WM,
   Sarah Baker, w/them]
HUGH (c23 b.TN) P/TN
   AGNES JANE GABBARD (c24 b.TN)  [c1849-1928;
   d/o James Gabbard, Elsie Frost - DC TS-TCS]
   c1873          (1880-6 W/as Jane; wid. Eggie
   1900; wid. Agnes 1910)
JAMES A. (c27 b.Sims, NC)
   ANN F. BEATTY (c26 b.Franklin Co., MO) [d/o
   Samuel Beatty & Patience Kelly - 1860]
   c1868          (1870-L-1; B-L ch.)
JAMES P. (c20 S b.KY)  [s/o Samuel Hill
   & Jennie J. Gabbard - TCS]
   PEARL WHITAKER (c15 S b.KY)  [d/o William
   Whitaker & W1        - TCS]
   1904/5          (1910 w/HS; TCS)


(Hill cont.)

## HILL (cont.)
PRESTON H. "KIT" (c21 S b.TN) [s/o Preston
Hill, Sr. & Mary      - TCS]
MARTHA ELIZABETH COMBS (c19 S b.KY) [1865-
1938 Cov.; d/o ____ Combs & unknown - DC;
ob-W OCC-4/29/38]
16 Sept., 1884      (ob-W; 1900 m-16;
1910 m-20; 1920; DC ch-1957 b.6/90 Ows.;
NL M-M)
SAMUEL (c19 S b.Claib.,TN)  [s/o Preston Hill
& Mary      - MT; 2nd M-O]
JANE GABBARD (c19 S b.KY) [1858-1914; d/o
James B Gabbard & Eliz. Frost - MT; TS-TCS]
1877/8      (MT; 1880 no ch.; 1900 m-22;
1910 m-34; 1920)     [SAMUEL (R.Ows. 67
widr. b.Claib.,TN) m2 3/13/1930 Ows.,
Nancy Jane (Frost) Combs (R.Ows. 62 wid.
b.Ows. - d/o Robt. Frost & Susan Miller -
wid/o John B. Combs - 1880-1900-1910-1920)
- M-O]

## HOBBS
EZEKIEL P. (c26 b.VA)  [s/o Wm. Zion Hobbs
& Mary Spencer - TR/Larry Baker]
ANNE ELIZA OLINGER (c18 b.VA)
16 Oct., 1851, **Lee Co., VA**  (M-Lee,VA; B-O
ch.; 1860)
G[RANVILLE] H[ENDERSON] (26 S b.Lee, VA) [s/o
Job Hobbs & Susan Flanery - mg.; ACB]
JANE MYRES [MYERS] (19 S b.Lee,VA)  [d/o
John Myres & R.      - mg.]
3 Feb., 1857, **Lee Co., VA**  (M-Lee,VA; 1860;
B-O ch-10/58)
HENDERSON - see GRANVILLE HENDERSON
ISAAC S. (c27 b.VA) [1826-1892 Wlf; s/o Wm.
Zion Hobbs & Mary Spencer - TR/Larry Baker]
TEMPERANCE "TEMPY" SHOEMAKER (c17 b.KY)
[1837-1919 Wlf; d/o James Shoemaker
& Phoebe Spencer - 1850; TR/Larry Baker]
c1854      (1860-5; 1870-1880-W; wid.
Tempy 1900-1910-W)


(Hobbs cont.)

**HOBBS (cont.)**
SIMEON (poss. c68 2nd b.KY)  [poss. m1 Mahulda
  Hibbard - M-C 1845; 1860-C; 1870-J]
  [d. c1896/7 - P-CW W/H4]
  [TALITHA] TELLITHA [nee FOX] PACE (c40 3rd
  b.KY) [m1 1876 James Fox - M-O; m2 Richmond
  Pace - DC-ch]  [1854-19__; d/o Isaac Fox
  & Almarinda Griffith - 1860-1870]
  21 Aug., 1894, Jackson; bm. groom & Wm.
  Lynch (M-J 9:104)    [TALITHA m4 1901,
  Nicholas Collins - M-O; 1910; wid.
  "Tabitha" w/dau. Emma (Pace) Elkins 1920]
THOMAS (c26 b. VA)    [1825-1878; s/o Job
  Hobbs & Susan Flanery - ACB]
  MARY CABLE (c30 b.TN)    [1821-1896; d/o
  Joseph Cable & Rebecca Pierce - ACB; NC]
  c1851        (1860; B-O ch-8/52; 1870-W;
  wid. Mary 1880-W; TS-Wlf; ob-ch.BE-2/26/48)
THOMAS (R.Ows. 28 2nd b.Kenton) P/Clay
  [m1 _____]
  MARGARET KEITH (R.Ows. 19 S b.Clay) P/Clay
  1 Sept., 1910, Ows.
WILLIAM ZION (c21 b.Lee,VA)  [1844-1915; s/o
  Wm. Zion Hobbs & Mary Spencer - TR/Larry
  Baker]
  SARAH JANE SHOEMAKER (c15 b.Ows.)    [d/o
  James Shoemaker & Phoebe Spencer]
  1864/5        (1870-1880-1900-L; B-L ch.)
  [W. Z. (R.Fincastle 65 2nd/W1-d. b.Lee,VA)
  m2 7/19/1909, Nancy (nee _____) Carroll -
  M-L; 1910-L]
**HOGAN**
ADAM (58 3rd b.KY)  [m1 1894/5 Sarah _____ -
  1900-L; m2 12/26/1902 Sarah Baker (56 2nd)
  - M-L]
  POLLY J. (nee _____) GIBSON (48 3rd b.KY)
  [poss. m2 Wm. S. Gibson]
  30 Dec., 1905, Lee @ Polly Gibson's; wits.
  Lums Spicer & J. W. Newton  (M-L; 1910)
**HOGG**
EDWARD EVERETT (c26 S Law. b.KY)  [s/o Hiram
  Hogg & Virginia Snyder]
  LOUISA DUFF (c24 S b.KY)  [d/o Elijah Duff
  & Mary Eversole - 1880]
  1888/9        (1900-1910; Yest.; ob-ch.
  BE-12/3/36; art. BE-9/7/72)
(Hogg cont.)

HOGG (cont.)
GEORGE M. "LIT" (c32 S tanner b.IL) [s/o
   Hiram Hogg & Virginia Snyder - 1900]
   MARTHA WILSON (c21 S b.Sturg.) [1879-1950;
   d/o Robt. Wilson & Caroline Combs - 1900;
   ob-W OCN-6/23/50]
   1900/1         (ME-7/26/01, G. M. Hogg left
   Ows. for OK Terr.; 1910 m-9, 1st ch-8 OK;
   B-O ch.; ob-W says R.Louisville, Maysville
   & Cynthiana)
HENRY (c31 dry goods mcht b.KY) [poss. s/o
   Hiram Hogg & Levina Polly - 1850-Let.]
   MARTHA A. _____ (c15 b.KY)
   1866/7         (1870-12/69; 1880-10; 1900-
   Saratoga, Santa Clara Co., CA; ME-6/2/04
   left Ows. 1885 & R.Saratoga, CA, visiting
   relatives in Ows.)
HIRAM H. (c25 S b.Let.) [s/o Hiram Hogg
   & Levina Polly - 1850-Let.]
   VIRGINIA C[AROLINE] SNIDER [SNYDER] (c16 S
   b.VA) [d/o Jacob Snyder & Kernen Davidson -
   REM]
   29 Dec., 1859, Hawkins Co., TN, by James M.
   Bellomy, JP; bm. Joseph Wills (M-Hawk.,TN;
   1860-Let; ob-ch. OCC-6/13/41, b.11/60
   Whitesburg; VA dur. CW, c1865 to IL, then
   Boonev. - ob-ch.; 1870-9; 1880; ME-7/8/83
   d. of Mrs. Snyder MiL/o Hiram Hogg; ME-
   6/26/96 R.Boonev.; 1900 m-41; 1910 m-50;
   B-O ch.; wid. Virginia C. 1920)
STEPHEN P. (c26 dry goods mcht b.Let) [c1832-
   1917; s/o Hiram Hogg & Levina Polly - 1850-
   Let.; ob-H JT-10/26/17]
   SALLIE A. COMBS (c17 b.KY) [d/o Jackson
   Combs & Martha Crank - REM]
   1 Jan., 1859         (REM; 1860-P no ch.;
   1870-7; 1880; NL M-B/Let/P)   [H-remd.]
S[TEPHEN] P. (c62 2nd Law. & Cir.Ct.Clk. b.KY)
   [widr/o Sallie A. Combs above]
   MARTHA (nee _____) COLDIRON (R.Manchester,
   Clay 46 2nd b.KY)   [1848-19__ - 1900-C]
   14 Aug., 1895, Ows. [rec. Clay] [separated
   1900] (M-C file 27; ME-8/30/95, widr. S.P.
   Hogg md. Mrs. Martha Coldiron; 1900 W-NL;
   Marthy Hogg 1900-C, dau. K. P. Coldiron b.
   9/85; 1910 S. P. m2-16, W-NL, w/dau. Alice
   & John C. Eversole; no mention of wf ob-H)

## HOLBROOK

CAMPBELL RICE (c31 Dr. b.Law.) [1830-1923; s/o
   Ambrose Holbrook & Nancy Elam - N-E.KYN]
   MARGARET/MARY ANN WILSON (c18 b.KY) [d/o
   Jesse Wilson & Eliz. Strong - JCH; 1860 as
   Mary Ann; 1850 as Polly]
   19 Jan., 1862          (N-E.KYN, JCH & MT
   W/as Mary Ann; 1870-8, W/as Margaret)
   [H-remd.]
CAMPBELL (c42 2nd Dr. b.Law.) [widr/o
   Margaret/Mary Ann Wilson above]
   NANCY FRANCES "FANNIE" HOLBROOK (c16 b.
   Wilkes Co., NC) [d/o Ralph Holbrook, Jr.
   & Nancy Spicer - N-E.KYN]
   12 Sept., 1872          (N-E.KYN; 1880, 1st
   ch. whose mom b. NC was 6; B-O ch-3/78; to
   OK 1890's - N-E.KYN)
JESSE (27 S b.Ows.) [s/o Campbell Holbrook
   & Margaret/Mary Ann Wilson - TCS; N-E.KYN]
   CHARLOTTE "LOTTIE" EVANS (c24 S b.KY)
   [1870-1959; d/o James Evans & Margaret
   Allen - 1880; ob-W&M BE-4/30/59, OCN-
   9/5/57]
   12 April, 1894, Ows.  (N-E.KYN; 1900-1910-
   1920; ob-ch. BS-11/19/87; R.Elias 1957)

## HOLCOMB/HOLCOMBE/HALCOMBE

EMMERSON - see IRA EMMERSON
ENOCH (c19 S b.Ows.) [1864-1928; s/o Ira
   Holcomb & Mary Creech - TCS]
   LAURA BELLE MINTER (c19 S b.Ows.) [1864-
   1940; d/o Wm. Minter & Cynthia Mainous -
   TCS; ob-W OCC-1/15/40]
   7 Jan, 1884, Jackson Co., @ Ira Holcombe's,
   by John B. King; wits. Rebecca Powell &
   Cassius Johnson  (M-J; B-O ch; 1900-J m-16
   TCS; 1910-1920; ob-W & ch BE-10/19/67)
HENDERSON HENRY (c16-33 b.KY) [s/o William
   Holcomb & Eliza Christian - 1880; TCS]
   MARY _____ (___ b.___)
   1883-1900          (TCS; H-NL w/P 1900;
   NL 1900-1910Sx; NL M-J/R)


(Holcomb cont.)


327

**HOLCOMB (cont.)**

HENRY B. (c37 S b.KY) [1872-1939 Ows.; s/o
   Jesse Holcomb & Amanda Scott - DC; 1910;
   ob-H OCC-10/20/39]
   SUSAN NAPIER (c16 S b.KY)
   1909/10       (1910 w/HP; ob-H;
   NL 1920Sx; wid. R.Boonev. 1939)
IRA (c27 b.Per.) [1833-1911; s/o Hardin
   Holcomb & Susan Cornett - MM; TCS]
   MARY CREECH (16 b.Harl.)   [1847-1912; d/o
   Enoch Creech & Patience Kelly - HC]
   30 June, 1864, Ows. (MM; HC; 1870-6; B-O
   ch.; 1880; AJ)
[IRA] EMMERSON (R.Ows. 22 S b.Garrard) P/Ows.
   [1888-1967; s/o Enoch Holcomb & Laura Bell
   Minter - TCS; ob-H&M BE-10/19/67, OCC-
   1/15/40]
   NELLIE MAINOUS (R.Ows. 19 S b.Ows) P/Ows
   [d/o Green S. Mainous & Lou Thomas - ob-W&S
   OCN-9/2/49 & OCC-2/28/41; TCS]
   17 Dec., 1910, Ows. [R.Owsley 1920; lived
   Ows. until 1923, then moved to IN - ob-H;
   W/d. Connersville, IN; widr. R.Metamore, IN
   1966 - ob-HS BE-12/15/66]
JOHN W. (c23 S b.KY) [s/o Wm. Holcomb & Eliz.
   Christian - 1880; ob-HS BE-3/4/48]
   REBECCA (nee FLANERY) DALTON (c35 2nd b.KY)
   [wid/o Samuel Dalton - 1880; TCS]  [d/o
   Elcannah Flanery & Amanda Mainous - TCS]
   1896       (1900 m-4, but 1st Holcomb ch-
   3/94, 3 Dalton s-ch.; TCS; 1910 m-13;
   R.Scoville 1948; ob-ch. HJN-11/93)  [JOHN
   m2 Myrtle McIntosh; JOHN m3 after 1920,
   Charlena Gibson - TCS; ob-WS OCN-6/4/54
   R.Sturgeon (Charlena m1 Mays; m2 Elbert
   Hurst)]
MILLARD (c32 b.Let.)  [s/o Hardin Holcomb
   & Susan Cornett - TCS]
   EMILY C. NANTZ (c15 b.Clay) [d/o Frederick
   Nantz & Sarah Chappell - TCS; 1850-C; 1860]
   1864/5       (1870-4; B-O ch.; 1900-J)


(Holcomb cont.)

## HOLCOMB (cont.)

MILLARD [MILLER] (c22 S b.Ows) [s/o Wm.
Holcomb & Eliza Christian - 1880; TCS; B-O]
ELIZABETH WILSON (___ b.___)
9 Aug., 1882 (ML) Jackson; bm groom & Ira
Holcomb (MC-NFI) (M-J 5:43) [H-remd.]
MILLARD [MILLER] (c30 2nd b.Ows.) [m1 Eliz.
Wilson above - TCS]
NANCY DAVIDSON (c37 b.KY)
9 Aug., 1890 (ML) Jackson; bm. groom &
Isaac Harrison (MC-NFI) (M-J 7:346; TCS;
1900-J)
NATHAN (c25 b.NC)
SALLY PONDER (c20 b.NC) [d/o Joseph
Ponder & Catherine Holcomb - TCS]
c1849 (1850-1 mo., listed as
HAULKMAN; TCS) [SALLY m2 1/30/54 Clay,
Wm. H. Anderson]
WILLIAM (c20 b.KY) [1832-1915; s/o Hardin
Holcomb & Susan Cornett - TS-TCS]
ELIZABETH CHRISTIAN (c19 b.KY) [1834-1911;
d/o Mary CHRISTIAN & poss. an ABNER - TS-
TCS]
1853/4 (1860-5; B-O ch.; 1870-1880-
1900; 1910 Wm. m1-N#L w/son; Eliz. 1910-L
m1-56, w/dau.; ob-ch. BE-3/4/48)
WILLIAM ABNER (c30 S b.Boonev.) [s/o Wm.
Holcomb & Eliza Christian - TCS; 1880; ob-
HS BE-3/4/48]
FLORA BELL COMBS (c31 S b.Peb.) [1874-1950;
d/o James S. Combs & Mary Cath. Handy -
1880; ob-W&F OCN-4/21/50, BE-7/18/35]
31 Jan, 1906 (ob-W; 1910 m-4 HF w/them;
B-O ch.; BBG; 1920; R.Levi 1935-48; ob-ch.
BE-2/10/49 & BS-1/17/91)

## HOLDANE

GEORGE M. (R.Ows. 23 S tchr b.Scot.) P/Scot.
[MARY P. WILSON] (R.Ows. 23 S b.Br.) P/Br.
[d/o James Wilson & Lucy Carmack - 1900;
ob-WM OCN-9/30/49]
12 June, 1909, Ows. [R.Henderson Co., KY
1910Sx; Huntington, WV 1949] [NOTE: There
was an error in this & several other mgs.,
wherein bride listed on wrong line. Bride
as JULIA MASON; line above was MARY P.
WILSON. JULIA actually md. Chas. Callihan.
George md. MARY WILSON - 1910Sx & ob-WM]

**HOLDER**
MATT (c26 S st-mill b.KY)
   MINNIE PATTON (c16 S b.KY)
   1906/7       (1910; BC-1913 Pow.;
   NL 1920Sx)
**HOLDERLY**
JAMES P. (c60's 2nd SClk b.VA) [widr/o
   Sarah _____ - 1860-Morg.]
   LUCINDA (nee PERKINS) NEEDHAM (c38-45 2nd
   b.NC) [wid/o Christian Needham - 1860-
   Morg.] [1824-1887 - TS-TCS]
   1862-9 [prob. Wolfe] (1870-W, no ch. under
   10; 1880; TCS; NL M-Morg.; NL M-W 1861)
**HOLLAND/HOLLON**
[DANIEL] WILSON (R.Br. 19 S b.Br.) [s/o Wm.
   Holland & Candus Short - JSG]
   LUCINDA HAYS (R.Ows. 14 S b.Br.) [c1844-
   1916 OK; d/o Edward Adrian Hayes & Eliz.
   Cockrell - 1850; JSB]
   2 June, 1858, Ows. (a/L 2/25/1858 Br.)
   [R.Breathitt 1870; wf d. Logan Co, OK -JSG]
ELISHA (c20 b.KY) [1839-1933; s/o Andrew
   Jackson Holland & Sarah Wright - ACB]
   SARAH "SALLY" BRYANT (c18 b.KY) [1840-1929;
   d/o Wm. Evan Bryant & Eliz. King - ACB]
   1859/60      (1860-MWY; 1870-W; ACB)
PATRICK (23 2nd b.Br.) [m1 _____
   - NL M-B] [s/o Alfred Hollon & Polly
   Howard - mg.; 1900-B]
   IDA B. LITTLE (20 S b.Br.) [d/o Mort
   (Morrison) Little & Nancy Gabbard - mg.;
   P/M-B]
   18 July, 1901, Breathitt @ Morson
   [Morrison] Little's, by Daniel Little,
   Min.; wits. Govan Smith & W. Caudill
   (M-B 9:261; 1910 m-9 H-3rd; B-O ch.)
WILSON - see DANIEL WILSON
**HOLLOWAY**
see COUCH
**HOLMAN/HOLEMAN**
JAMES (c23 wagonmaker b.NC/TN)
   RACHEL FRAILEY (c19 b.KY)
   29 March, 1868, Ows. (JFB; 1870-E, Diane
   Fraly 12, w/them; 1880-E)

**HONDLEY**
see HUNDLEY

**HORNE/HORN**
GEORGE (c22 b.KY)
    LOUISA _____ (c34 b.KY)
    c1868        (1870-L-1; NL M-J)
JOHN (c17 S b.KY)
    MARTHA B. _____ (c16 S b.KY)
    1901/2       (1910; NL M-J)
MICHAEL (c26 b.KY)
    MARY ANN _____ (c22 b.KY)
    c1859       (1860-1 mo.; NL M-J)
ROBERT & EMMA - see HORNSBY
THOMAS (R.Hardin 24 S b.Hardin) P/Hardin
    LAURA B. FROST (R.Ows. 18 S b.Ows.) P/Ows.
    9 July, 1908, Ows.

**HORNSBY**
CHARLES (c22 b.KY) [s/o Thomas Hornsby
    & Larky Shields - TCS]
    NANCY VAUGHN (c22 b.KY) [d/o _____ Vaughn
    & Jane    - TCS]
    c1876      (1880-3; TCS; NL 1900Sx)
    [CHARLES poss. m2 5/16/89 Lucinda Harvey,
    her 2nd also - NL 1900-L]
GEORGE (R.Ows. 25 S b.KY) P/KY [1846-19__;
    s/o Job Hornsby & Catharine Gabbard - 1870;
    F/P-CW]
    ELISABETH WOODS (R.Ows. 22 S b.KY) P/KY
    [d/o John Woods & Vina Bowling - MT]
    11 April, 1878, Ows. [R.Owsley 1880-1900-
    1910]
GRANT (___ b.Eversole/Boonev.)
    MOLLIE MURRELL (c19 b.Eversole) [d/o Wiley
    Murrell & Catherine Smith - TCS; 1900]
    c1901      (TCS; B-O ch-1903 b/d, W/as
    Millie) [MOLLIE m2 1905/6 James Walter
    Reynolds - TCS]
JOHN (R.Ows. 18 S b.KY) P/KY [prob. s/o
    George Hornsby & Eliz. Woods - 1900]
    MARTHA B. HICKS (R.Jack. 15 S b.KY)
    July, 1901, Jackson Co. (M-J mf)


(Hornsby cont.)

**HORNSBY (cont.)**
MATHIAS [H. "TICE"] (c19 S b.Ricetown) [s/o
    George Hornsby & Eliz. Woods - 1880]
    ROSE HICKS (c17 S b.Sebastian)
    2 Oct., 1896, Jackson Co., @ Hickry Hicks',
    by G. L. Davis, Bapt.; wits. Wm. Cope &
    Frank Hicks    (M-J; 1900 m-4; 1910 m-13;
    B-O ch.; B-J ch-1904)
ROBERT (c18 b.KY) [s/o Charles Hornsby & Nancy
    Vaughn - 1880]
    EMMA EUNICE STEPP (c18 b.KY)  [d/o John
    Stepp & Martha Moore - TCS]
    1897/8          (TCS; 1900-1910-1920 as HORN;
    BC 1913-1915 as HORNSBY)
TICE - see MATHIAS
**HORTON**
JOHN B. (c24 b.VA)
    ELIZA DRAKE (c29 b.VA) [d/o Wm. Drake
    & Jane Stinson - ACB]
    c1854          (1860; B-O ch. 5/55)
JOHN [WESLEY] (R.Devils Cr. 19 S b.Lee,VA)
    [s/o Wm. Horton & Eliza Jane      - TCS]
    [MARY] POLLY AN SHACKELFORD (R.No.Fk., Br.;
    21 S b.N.Fk, Br.) [1832-1912; d/o Abner T.
    Shackelford & W1 Nancy Gossett - ACB; art.
    BE-8/7/52]
    1 Nov., 1855, Breathitt, by S. P. Chandler
    (M-Br.; 1860)
MICHAEL G. (c31 b.VA)
    CATHARINE F. GARRARD (c28 b.Clay)
    11 Sept., 1850, Clay  (M-C; 1860-C-8, 1st
    ch. b. Ows.; 1870-C)
**HOSKINS**
JAMES B. (c21 b.Harl.)
    SOPHRONIA TAYLOR (c17 b.TN) [d/o Minor C.
    Taylor & Barsheba Rappitoe - 1870]
    1871/2          (B-O ch-1/76; 1900-J m-28;
    NL 1880Sx)
JEFFERSON (R.Ows. 22 S b.Lau.) P/Harl-KY
    EMILY SHORT (R.Ows. 19 S b.Harl.) P/Harl.
    [d/o John B. Short & W1        ]
    8 Oct., 1874, Ows., @ Jno. B. Short's

(Hoskins cont.)

332

**HOSKINS (cont.)**
WILLIAM (R.Ows. 22 S b.KY) P/KY [s/o Levi
   Hoskins & Eliz. Hunter - TCS]
   [MARY] MARGARET ROBERTSON (R.Ows. 18 S b.
   Ows.) P/Clay [d/o Wm. Robertson & Nancy
   Morris - TCS; 1920]
   4 Jan., 1876 [1877], Ows., @ Rhoda Bowman's
   (a/L 1/4/7Z, W&P b.KY; md. @ Wid. Bowman's;
   rest same)    [R.Owsley 1880 no ch.; 1900
   m-22; 1910 m-33; wid. Margaret 1920, WM
   w/her; W/as Mary M. & Margaret]
**HOUNDSHELL/HOUNSHELL**
GEORGE W. (c20 crp b.Wythe Co, VA) [1828-1890;
   s/o John Houndshell & Sarah Powell - TCS]
   MARY SCHOOLCRAFT (c18 b.VA)   [d/o Michael
   Schoolcraft & Martha Fenn(?) - TCS]
   c1848       (REM; 1850-C; TCS; 1860-11 HM
   w/them; TCS; NL M-C)      [H-remd. 1868]
GEORGE W. (c40 2nd crp b.Wythe Co, VA)
   [widr/o Mary Schoolcraft above - TCS]
   CATHERINE (nee JONES) DEZARN (c22 2nd b.KY)
   [m1 11/6/63 Wm. Dezarn - TCS; M-C]   [1844-
   1931; d/o Milton Jones & Malinda Sasser -
   TCS]
   26 March, 1868 Clay (TCS; 1870-1880-C; JEW/
   1894 Clay sch.cen. ch. Jeff. 17 & Steven 13
   w/Geo. Lyttle & son Floyd 11 w/Wm. Dezarn;
   wid. Cath. 1900-C ch. Steve 6/79 & Floyd
   11/81]   [CATHERINE m2 Jerry McCowan - TCS]
JACOB (c31-39 brick mason b.VA)
   ELIZABETH SAMS (c16-24; b.TN)
   1851-9       (H-sgl. 1850-B; 1860 no ch.,
   Aggy Sams b.TN, svt. w/them; 1870-W no ch.;
   1880-L, Sams BiL; NL M-J)
**HOWARD**
CLEMENT (c21 b.KY)
   NANCY ANN DURBIN (c24 b.Est.)
   c1848       (1850-10 mos.; B-E ch-1852;
   M-L ch-1879)   [NANCY m2 c1865, Benjamin F.
   Phillips]
GEORGE (c24 b.KY)
   MARTHA HILL (c19 b.KY)
   23 May, 1843, Estill   (M-E; 1850)
JACKSON (c17 b.KY)
   MARTHA _____ (c15 b.KY)
   c1852       (1860-7)
(Howard cont.)

**HOWARD (cont.)**
ROBERT R. (c23 b.KY)    [poss. s/o Samuel
    Howard & Sarah Pace - JO]
    CHARITY NANTZ (c19 b.KY)  [d/o Frederick
    Nantz & Sarah Chappell - TCS; 1850-C]
    31 March, 1853, <u>Harlan</u>  (TCS; JO; NL 1860;
    1870-13; 1880)
ROBERT (___ b.KY)
    ELIZABETH SPENCE (c23 S b.VA)  [1844-1914;
    d/o Jno. Spence, Mary Holmes - TCS DC 1870]
    c1872         (1880 Eliz. wid/o H2 HARVEY,
    s-d HOWARD 7; TCS)  [ELIZ. m2 1877 Prior
    Harvey - M-O; ELIZ. m3 John Fields - TCS;
    1900-10]
SAMUEL (c19 b.KY)  [s/o Robt. Howard & Charity
    Nantz - 1880]
    HANNAH _____ (c19 b.KY)
    1888/9          (1900 HM w/them)
**HOWELL**
DANIEL (c27 hatter b.VA)
    MATILDA _____ (c18 b.KY)
    c1852          (1860-7)
ELIAS TINCHER (30 S b.Est.)  [s/o Gaius Hastin
    Howell & Mary Tincher - 1860; REM]
    [LEANNAH] LENAH NEWMAN [WHITE] (c20 2nd
    b.Ows.)  [wid/o Francis Marion White - REM]
    [d/o Wm. Newman & Rhoda Tincher - REM]
    5 June, 1868, Ows., @ Rhoda Newman's, by
    Rev. Geo. Miller; wits. John Newman & Elias
    Tincher  (JFB; B-L ch.; REM; NL 1870Inx;
    1880-1900L; ob-ch. BE-8/6/42)
JAMES (c20 b.Lau.) P/KY
    NANCY JANE HOLCOMB (c17 b.Ows.)  [d/o Wm.
    Holcomb & Eliz. Christian - B-O]
    c1875/6          (1880; B-O ch-12/76; wid.
    Nancy 1900; NL M-Lau/R)
    [NANCY JANE m2 Mr. Kelly - ME-11/2/05, Mr.
    Kelly of Livingston, came to Ows. & md.
    Mrs. Nancy J. Howell.  They started for
    Livingston, their future home.]
SAMUEL P. (c21 b.Est.)  [s/o Gaius Howell
    & Mary Tincher - 1860; TCS]
    ELIZA J. TINCHER (c21 b.Est.)  [d/o Wm.
    H. Tincher & Margaret Smallwood - TCS]
    2 Dec., 1863, Ows.  (TCS; JFB; B-L ch.;
    1870-1880-1900-L; ob-ch. BE-11/9/50)

## HUBBARD
BEVE [BEVERLY] W. (R.Ows. c25 S; drummer @
Chas. Hosenheimer & Co. of Louisville b.KY)
[prob. s/o Wm. Hubbard & Lucinda Lunsford -
TCS]
MATTIE [MARTHA] SMITH (R.Ows. c23 S b.KY)
[d/o Wm. A. Smith & Lucy Ann Gibson - ob-
WM&S OCC-3/16/34-10/3/41, BE-1/31/46; 1900]
9 April, 1903, Lexington, Fayette Co., by
F. S. Graves, JP; wits. A. W. O'Neill &
Horace Greer (M-Fay. 8A:148E; ME-4/17/03;
B-Lau. ch-1904; 1910-Lau., m1-7; 1920Sx-
Scott; ob-WM; R.Lexington 1934; Beattyville
1941)
JOHN F[RANK] (c30 S b.Est.)
ROSSE [ROSA] ELIZ. MALICOTE (c20 S b.Jack.)
[d/o W. D. Malicote & Mary      - TCS]
1 Jan., 1889 (ML), Jackson Co.; bm. groom &
John Malicote (M-J 7:20; TCS; 1900-1910;
B-O ch. as John HUBERT & Rosa McIntosh; B-J
ch-1904 as Frank & R. E. Malicoat)
W. A. (R.the White Mts. of NH; ___ b.___)
BETTIE PENDERGRASS (R.White Oak; c24 b.Ows)
[d/o Wash. Bowen Pendergrass & Phoebe
Flanery - 1860-1900; B-O; BS-7/13/78 their
photo, caption says she d. soon after photo
taken]
Oct., 1902 Ows. (ME-10/31/02 plan to R.New
England) [NOTE: There is no 1910Sx for NH
& they are NL 1910Sx-KY; NL 1920Sx-NH/KY]
## HUBERT
see HUBBARD
## HUDSON/HUTSON
BLEVINS (c19 b.KY) [poss. s/o John Hudson
& Eliz. Davidson]
LUCRETIA "CREATY" EVANS (c17 b.KY)
1899/1900      (1900; ob-ch. BS-12/3/87)
JOHN (c20 b.Clay) [s/o Blevins Hudson & Susan
Davidson - TCS]
ELIZABETH DAVIDSON (c15 b.Clay) [poss. d/o
Hansford Davidson & Rebecca Hacker - B-C]
2 Sept., 1869, Clay (M-C; 1870 no ch.;
1880-9; B-O ch.; 1900-1910; wid. Eliz.
1920)

(Hudson cont.)

**HUDSON (cont.)**

THEOPHILUS (c18 S b.KY)  [s/o John Hudson
& Eliz. Davidson - 1880; TCS]
MARTHA SHORT (c15 S b.KY)  [d/o Jackson
Short & Frances    - TCS]
1888          (1900 m-12; 1910 m-21; 1920;
TCS; ob-ch. BS-5/17/90)

**HUFF**

BALLARD T. (c22 S b.Per.)  [s/o Edward Huff
& Polly Thomas - TCS]
MARGARET GABBARD (c20 S b.Gabbard, Ows.)
[1873-1932; d/o Wm. B. Gabbard & Sally
Barrett - 1880; TS-TCS]
1892/3          (ME-7/24/96 R.Gabbard; 1900-
1910-1920; B-O ch.; ob-ch. BS-2/6/92)
IRA (c24 b.VA)  [s/o Isaac Huff & Cath. Lewis
- TCS; 1850-H HC]
PHOEBE PARSONS (c14 b.KY)  [d/o Stephen
Parsons & Eloise Morgan - TCS; HC]
14 Aug., 1851, Lee Co., VA  (M-Lee,VA;
1860; B-O ch.; TCS)
JASPER (c19 b.KY)  [s/o John Wesley Huff
& Mary Jane Burch]
SARAH M. _____ (c16 b.KY)
1890/1          (1900; TCS; NL M-J)
JOHN JR. (c28 b.KY)  [s/o John Huff, Sr.
& Mahala Begley - TCS]
PERMELIA REYNOLDS (c25 b.KY) [d/o Wesley
Reynolds & Nancy Moore - 1860; TCS]
26 May, 1864, Perry (TCS; 1870-P)
JOHN WESLEY (c30 2nd b.Harl)  [m1 Aug., 1856,
Catharine Cope (d. 6/1/66 Clay; d/o Jacob
Cope & Sarah Adams - HPH) - W1/as Cath. &
Julitha P-CW; 1860-H W/Cath.; NL M-C/H/J;
NL 1860/C/J] [John 1836-1910/15; s/o Isaac
Huff & Catherine Lewis - 1850-H HC]
MARY JANE BURCH (c20 S b.Claiborne Co., TN)
[1845-1917; d/o Wm. Burch & Malinda Mays]
7 Sept, 1866 Jackson Co., by Rev. John Ward
(P-CW; TCS; 1870-J, ch. 12, 10, 8, 6, 2 & 2
mo.; 1880-12; R.Is. City, Ows. 6/83; 3Fks-
6/1/88 John W. of Is. Cr. allowed pension;
Sexton Cr, Clay 1898; 1900 m-34; 1910 m-43,
H-2nd; wid. Mary Jane 1915 Ows; NL M-H/J)

(Huff cont.)

**HUFF (cont.)**
ROBERT N. (c21 b.KY) [s/o John Wesley Huff
  & Mary Jane Burch - TCS]
  ELIZABETH HUNTER (c16 b.KY) P/NC-KY
  1 Nov., 1888, Clay (M-C; TCS; 1900; 1920)
WILLIAM "WILL" (c19 S b.Gabbard) [c1875-1964
  - TS-TCS]
  REBECCA JANE GABBARD (c19 S b.Eversole)
  [1875-1926; d/o Wm. B. Gabbard & Sally
  Barrett - 1880; TS-TCS]
  1894           (1900 m-6; 1910 m-15; B-O ch.;
  1920; their photo BS-5/8/80)
WILLIE (c20 S b.Ows.)      [1887-1964 Ows.; s/o
  Buck ROWLETT & Sarah HUFF - DC]
  GERTRUDE "GERTIE" HILL (c19 S b.KY) [d/o
  Samuel Hill & Jennie Gabbard - TCS]
  1907/8      (1910, Hill BiL w/them; BBG)
  [GERTIE m2 James Bryant - TCS]
**HUFFAKER**
HORACE H. (c26 S crp b.TN)
  MARGARET "MAGGIE" SMITH (c21 S b.KY) [d/o
  Richard Smith & Nancy A. Creech - TCS]
  1907/8           (1910; TCS)
**HUGHES/HUGHS**
CAMPBELL (R.Buck Cr. c22 S b.Lee,VA) [s/o
  Walter Hughes & Susie Pruitt - PWB]
  MARY "MOLLIE" BELL REYNOLDS (R.Cow Cr. c22
  S b.Ows.) [1873-1947; d/o Elihu Reynolds
  & Sarah Wilson - 1880; TS-TCS]
  June, 1896, Ows. (ME-7/3/96; 1900 m-4;
  ME-12/15/04 & 12/22/04 d. of ch., who was
  Gch/o Elihu Reynolds of Cow Cr.; 1910 m-13;
  B-O ch.; wid. Belle 1920; ob-WS OCC-2/2/37;
  DC ch-1911)
F[RANKLIN] J. (R.Ows. 19 b.Clay) [s/o
  Meredith C. Hughes & Eliz. Phillips - 1850]
  ELISA LONG (R.Ows. 16 b.TN)
  - March, 1857, Ows. (M-J mf, but Jack. not
  formed until 1858; NL 1860/J)


(Hughes cont.)

337

HUGHES (cont.)
JAMES FRANK (c16-26 b.Ows.) [s/o Newton J.
   Hughes & Jane Anderson - TCS; B-O 1854]
   SOPHIA WILSON (c18-28 b.KY) [d/o Philip
   Wilson & Jane Strong - TCS; 1870]
   prob. 1870-80          (WP/NL 1880/L;
   NL 1880-1900Sx; NL M-J)
JAMES I. (c22 b.KY) [s/o Meredith Hughes
   & Nancy Bowles - TCS; B-O 1878]
   MINNIE SPENCE (c18 b.KY) P/KY
   1899/1900          (1900; TCS)
JASPER - see NEWTON JASPER
JOHN (c17 S b.KY/VA) [s/o Walter Hughes
   & Susie Pruitt - TCS; ob-H OCC-4/8/38 PWB]
   LUCINDA "LUCY" JUDD (c23 S b.KY) [d/o
   Leander Judd & Nancy Moore - TCS; 1880]
   6 April, 1889          (ob-H; 1900-8/92, both
   b. KY; 1910 m-21, both b. VA; 1920; TCS;
   ob-ch. HJN-10/97)
JOHN J. (c21 S b.Sturg.) [s/o Meredith C.
   Hughes & Nancy Bowles - 1900; TCS]
   RHODA J. SPENCE (c18 S b.Sturg.) [d/o
   John Hammet Spence & Martha Napier - TCS]
   1905/6          (1910-1920; B-O ch.)
MEREDITH C. (c20 S b.Clay) [s/o Meredith C.
   Hughes Sr. & Eliz. Phillips - 1850; TCS]
   NANCY BOWLES (c17 S b.Ows.) [d/o Anderson
   Bowles & Emily Muncy - TCS]
   2 Oct., 1867, Jackson Co.     (TCS; 1870;
   B-J ch-1874; 1880-1900-1910-1920; M-L ch-
   1917)     [MEREDITH m2 Etta Lakes - TCS]
NEWTON JASPER (c20 b.Clay) [1833-1863; s/o
   Meredith C. Hughes & Eliz. Phillips - 1850;
   TCS]
   MARY JANE ANDERSON (c18 b.Jefferson Co, TN)
   [d/o Wm. Anderson & Nancy          - TCS]
   c1853          (1860-J-6; TCS; PWB; B-J ch-
   1858)
NEWTON [P.] (R.Jack. 18 S b.KY) P/KY
   MARY WADLE (R.Jack. 17 S b.VA) P/VA
   3 Jan, 1876, Jackson Co.     (M-J mf; PWB/LDS
   chart of dau. Malinda Rowland; 1880-2)


(Hughes cont.)


338

## HUGHES (cont.)

WALTER F. (c37 2nd b.VA) [m1 Susie Pruitt -
PWB] [s/o Isaac Hughes, Sr. & Malvina
- PWB; 1900]
   MARGARET BOND (c22 S b.KY) [d/o Fletcher
   Bond & Lear Wilson - 1880]
   1887          (REM; 1900-L m-12, HM w/them;
   1910-L m-23, H/2, W/1; NL M-L)
WILLIAM (c28 b.KY)
   SARAH _____ (c29 b.VA)
   c1869         (1870-L, no ch., Amanda
   Smith, 11, w/them; NL 1880-1900Sx;
   NL M-J)    [H-remd. possibly]
WILLIAM (c40 2nd? KY) [poss. m1 Sarah _____
   above]
   SARAH BELL WILLIAMS (c19 KY)
   1880/1        (1900-L, W-9/9 ch., 10 listed,
   1st ch. Rosa b.11/79; ob-ch. BE-12/7/39 &
   DC-ch. 1939; NL M-L]
WM. H. (c21 S b.Buck Cr.) [s/o Walter Hughes
   & Susie Pruitt - PWB]
   SUSAN "SUDIE" KINCAID (c16 S b.Buck Cr.)
   [d/o Thomas Jefferson Kincaid & Helen
   Mainous - TCS]
   1905/6        (W-sgl. w/F 1900, 1 of her
   sibs w/Mainous GF; B-O ch.; 1910-Fay., m1-
   4; BC-1913-1916; 1920-13)

## HUNDLEY/HONDLEY/HONLEY/HENDLEY

CLAIBORNE ALABAMA (c21 b.KY) [1839-1871; s/o
Sam Hundley & Eliz. Combs - 1850; TS-TCS]
   SARAH ELENDAR HAMILTON (c18 b.Ows.) [d/o
   Thomas Hamilton & Mary Burns - TR]
   9 March, 1860, Sturgeon's Creek, Ows.
   (TR; 1860-MWY; 1870; B-O ch. by H2)
   [SARAH E. m2 c1877 Orville P. Taylor]
FLOYD - see WM. FLOYD
HARVEY - see HARVEY COMBS
HENRY H[ARGESS] (c17 b.KY [s/o Samuel
Hundley & Elizabeth Combs - 1870]
   LEVINA _____ (c19 b.KY)
   c1876        (1880-J-4; NL M-J)


(Hundley cont.)


339

## HUNDLEY (cont.)

JAMES (R.Ows. 27 [s/b 17] S b.Ows.)  [s/o Sam
   Hundley & Eliz. Combs - TCS; REM]
   ELIZABETH WHITE (R.Ows. 27 S b. Ows.)  [d/o
   Aquilla White & Rachel Ashcraft; REM]
   9 April, 1854, Ows.  [R.Owsley 1860; widr.
   James 1870]
JOHN (c21 b.KY)  [s/o Samuel Hundley & Eliz.
   Combs - 1860]
   MARGARET JANE HAMILTON (c18 b.KY)  [d/o
   Thomas Hamilton & Mary Burns]
   1866          (REM; 1870-L-2, Margaret w/P;
   NL M-C)
KENNETH (c20 b.KY)  [s/o Samuel Hundley
   & Elizabeth Combs - 1860]
   ANGELINE _____ (c21 b.KY)
   c1868          (1880-J-11; NL 1880/C/J/L;
   NL M-J)
THEOPHILUS (c25 b.KY)    [s/o Samuel Hundley
   & Elizabeth Combs - 1860]
   LUCY [MATTINGLY?] (c29 b.KY)
   c1869          (H-sgl. 1860; 1870 no ch.;
   REM; TR; NL 1880-1900Sx; NL M-C/J)
[WM.] FLOYD (R.Ows. 22 S b.Lee) P/Ows.
   DORA [nee GABBARD] CREECH (R.Ows. 22 2nd
   b.Ows.) P/Ows.  [wid/o _____ Creech]
   [1887-1942; d/o Henry Gabbard & Eliz.
   Bryant - 1910; TS-TCS]
   6 Oct., 1910, Ows.  [wid. Dora CREECH
   w/P 1910 Owsley; Floyd & Dora R.Owsley
   1920 w/WP]

## HUNT

JAMES (c18 b.TN)
   NANCY ANDERSON (c18 b.TN)  [d/o Wm.
   Anderson & Nancy    - TCS]
   c1846          (1850-3; TCS; NL 1860/C/E/J;
   NL 1900Sx)
WILLIAM (R.Per. --[c25] S b.--[KY])
   NANCY ABNER (R.Ows. --[c20] S b.Clay)
   25 Nov., 1859, Ows.  [NL 1860/C/E/J;
   R.Owsley 1870-1880-1890; widr. Wm. 1900
   Owsley]

**HUNTER**
NATHAN (c28 b.Bunc.,NC)
   MARGARET HAMILTON (c24 b.VA)
   c1855          (H/sgl. w/Ezekiel Sandlin
   1850; B-J ch-1857 b.Mad.,NC; B-J ch-1859;
   1860-J-4, 1st 2 ch. b.NC; 1870-1880-J;
   NL M-C; NL M-Bunc/Mad.,NC)
WILEY (c24 b.Mad,NC) [s/o George W. Hunter
   & Eliza     - TCS; 1860-C]
   MARY SANDLIN (c15 b.KY) [d/o Ezekiel
   Sandlin & Sarah Clark - TCS]
   22 May, 1867, Clay (TCS; 1870-C; 1880-11;
   1900-C m-32)
**HURD**
see HERD
**HURLEY**
JOHN JAMES (c23 b.Hawk.,TN) [s/o James Hurley
   & Mahala Jane Parker - TCS]
   MARY _____ (c27 b.KY)
   c1866          (1870-L-3; NL M-J)
   [JAMES m2 1876 Lee, Paulina Cole (d/o
   Austin Cole & Paulina) - TCS; 1880-L; M-L
   W/as Hannah Cole]
**HURST**
EDD (c20 S b.KY) [poss. s/o Sevier Hurst
   & Nancy Eliz. Whicker - 1900-J]
   SARAH MARGARET "SALLIE" BREWER (c16 S b.KY)
   [d/o John C. Brewer & Nancy Venable - 1900
   as Margaret; ob-WM OCN-6/2/50; TCS]
   1904/5          (1910; ob-WM; R.Tyner 1973
   - ob-WS BE-3/1/73; NL M-J)
[ELBERT] ELBE (R.Jack 22 S b.Mad) P/VA-Ows.
   [poss s/o Sevier Hurst & Eliz. Whicker -
   1900-J]
   CHARLINA GIPSON [MAYS] (R.Ows 24 2nd b.Ows)
   P/Ows. [wid/o _____ Mays - 1900] [d/o
   Newton Harvey Gibson & Sally McGeorge -B-O]
   25 Feb., 1904, Ows. [R.Owsley 1910-1920]
   [CHARLENA m3 John Holcomb - ob-WS OCN-
   6/4/54; R.Sturgeon 1954]


(Hurst cont.)

**HURST (cont.)**

HENLEY (R.Ows. 53 2nd mech b.TN) P/VA [widr/o
    Celia Stone - 1860; B-O ch.]
    PARMELIA L. [nee SPENCE] CONNER (R.Ows. 42
    2nd b.VA) P/VA    [m1 _____ Conner - wid.
    Permelia 1870 w/P]    [d/o Jno. Spence &
    Mary Holmes - 1870]
    29 Aug., 1878, Ows.    [R.Owsley 1880]
    [PERMELIA HURST (R.Lee 54 3rd) m3 1/22/91,
    James Snowden (widr/o Lucy Thomas) - M-L;
    m4 1/21/96, Green Berry Gumm (m1 Emily
    Catherine Frailey; m2 Nancy Baker) - M-L]
HENRY (R.Jack. 19 S b.Knox) P/-- & Knox
    MARY WHICKER (R.Ows. 19 S b.--) P/--    [d/o
    Zachariah Whicker & Martha Hurst - B-O]
    19 Oct., 1874, Ows., @ Martha Whicker's
    [NL 1880/J]
JAMES K. POLK (c23 S b.TN)    [1843-1918 Ows.;
    s/o Harmon Hurst & Nancy Johnson - NVP; DC
    has M/as "Eliz." Johnson]
    CATHERINE "KITTY" ANN PEARSON (c15 b.TN)
    [d/o Joshua Pearson & Catherine Collins -
    1860; NVP]
    c1866        (1880 ch. 13, 11, & 9 b.TN & 7
    KY; appar. TN 1870; B-O ch-1876) [H-remd.]
JAMES K. POLK (c57 2nd b.TN) [widr/o Catherine
    Pearson above - NVP]
    MINTA HICKS (c19 S b.KY)
    1899/1900        (1900-1910; wid. Minta 1920;
    BC 1914 W/as COPE & 1919 W/as HICKS; ob-ch.
    HJN-12/92 as Minnie HICKS & Hiram Hurst;
    W/as Millie 1x, all other recs. as Minnie/
    Minta/Mintie/Minty)
JOHN (R.Ows. 25 S b.Claib.,TN)
    LOUISA EVANS (R.Ows. 17 S b.Claib.,TN)
    [d/o Wm. Evans & Mary Stone - TCS]
    20 Dec., 1857, Ows.    [R.Owsley 1860]

(Hurst cont.)

**HURST (cont.)**
JOHN [R.] (R.Jack. 24 S b.TN) P/TN-NC    [s/o
    James M. Hurst & Mary Rookard - 1870]
    MELISSA F[RANCES] SEALE (R.Jack. 20 S b.
    Boonev.) P/VA-KY    [1858-1960 Lex.
    @ 101;
    d/o Joseph W Seale & Martha Gilbert - 1870;
    ob-W&S BE-12/18/60; OCC-11/8/40-4/3/42]
    27 Jan., 1878, Jackson Co. (M-J mf only;
    ME-2/22/78 W/as R.Ows.; REM; NL 1880Sx;
    1900-M-3/79 m-"25"; R.WA 1940-1942; wid.
    d. Lex. 1960)
JOHN (c29 S b.KY)
    ELIZABETH "BETTY" CONRAD (c34 S b.Is.City)
    [1865-1942 Ows.; d/o J(eremiah) F(ranklin)
    Conrad & Mary (Marcum) - DC; 1880]
    1900            (1900-J John N. Hurst 29 &
    Bo. Eliz. Conrad 33; 1910 m-10; NL 1920Sx;
    NL M-J)
ROBERT H. (R.Richmond 20 S mcht. b--) P/--
    MITTIE SEALE (R.Ows. 22 S b.Ows.) P/--
    [d/o John Seal & Julia Ann Brown - mg.;
    1880-1900]
    1 Jan., 1902, Lee @ Clerk's Office, by I.
    McGuire, JLC; wits. J. H. Hammons & W. C.
    Lutes (M-L 6:283; BE-2/26/70 reprint of
    BE-1/3/02 adds that Miss Mittie Seale
    R.Boonev.)
THOMAS D. (c26 b.TN) P/VA
    ELIZABETH MAHAFFY (c22 b.KY) [d/o James
    Mahaffey & Ella Crawford - REM/BM]
    1856/7            (1860-2; 1900-R m-43; B-O ch.)
THOMAS (R.Mad. 19 S b.Whitley) P/TN-KY
    EMALINE SMITH (R.Ows. 26 S b.Ows.) P/--
    [d/o Frank Smith & Lucretia Barrett - 1870]
    15 Oct., 1874, Ows., @ Martha Whicker's
    [wid. Emaline w/P 1880 Owsley]
THOMAS HENRY (c22 b.Ows.) [s/o James Hurst
    & Catherine Pearson - 1880]
    SARAH ELIZABETH KIDD (c25 b.Ows.) [c1864-
    1895/9; d/o Thomas Kidd & Mary Virginia
    Stanfield - 1870-1880]
    c1889            (1900 widr. Thomas, 2 ch.:
    Chas. b. 2/90 & Ellie b. 4/95; BC Ellie;
    NL M-C)    [H-remd.]

(Hurst cont.)

**HURST (cont.)**
THOMAS W. (c17 S b.KY)
  SARAH [CATHERINE] MARCUM (c18 S b.KY)
  30 June, 1895, <u>Breathitt</u> @ W. D. Maloney's,
  by W. D. Maloney; wits. S. Roberts & C.
  Maloney (M-B 6:559; TCS; 1910; NL 1900/B)
T[HOMAS] A. [HENRY] (c35 2nd b.KY) [widr/o
  Sarah Eliz. Kidd above]
  MARTHA NANTZ (c27 S b.KY)
  16 April, 1902, <u>Clay</u> (M-C MT; 1910 m-8;
  BC 1913; 1920Sx-J H/as Henry F.)
WILLIAM NELSON (c19 b.Claib.,TN) [s/o James
  M. Hurst & Mary Ruchard - REM]
  DELILAH PERSON (c19 b.Wash.,TN) [d/o
  Joshua Pierson & Cath. Collins - 1860]
  1864/5      (1870-4; B-O ch.; 1880-J;
  1900-M m-35; NVP; TCS)
**HUTCHINSON/HUTCHERSON  (a/k/a HUTCH)**
_____ (\_\_\_ b.KY)
  REBECCA J. SIZEMORE (c28 S b.KY) [d/o
  Henderson Sizemore & Nancy Gabbard - 1880]
  c1902     (MT; 1910 W-remd-4, HUTCH s-d
  age 6; NL M-J) [REBECCA m2 Arthur Bowles -
  1910]
ANDY H. (c26 S b.Ows.) [s/o Isaac Hutchinson
  & Arrilda Stewart - 1880]
  NONA J. THOMAS (c16 S b.Ows.) [poss. d/o
  Elisha Thomas & Eliz.Bowman - listed as
  Lona, age 5, 1880]
  1892/3      (1900-1910; B-O ch.; BC-
  1912; NL 1920Sx; NL M-J; W/as Delora &
  Nona)
ISAAC (c52 b.James River, VA) [NOTE: Because
  of his age, he may have been md. prev.]
  ARRILDA STEWART (c28 b.Lee,VA) [poss. d/o
  James Stewart & Mariah     1850-Lee,VA]
  c1862     (1870-7; 1880; TCS)
JAMES (c20 b.KY)
  RHODA YEARY (c15 b.KY)  [1884-19\_\_; d/o
  John Morgan Yeary & Rhoda Allen - 2nd M-B;
  M-O sibs; P/1900)
  1898/9      (1900; wid. Rhoda 1910;
  NL M-J) [RHODA (32 wid.) m2 9/14/1915
  Br., Jasper N. Morris (43 widr.) - M-B]

(Hutchinson cont.)

## HUTCHINSON (cont.)
JOHN (c23 b.KY)   [s/o Isaac Hutchinson
  & Arrilda Stewart - 1880]
  MINNIE _____ (c17 b.KY)
  1887/8          (1900-P m-12; 1910-P m-22;
  1920Sx; NL M-P)
NORMAN (c16 S b.KY)
  MARY _____ (c15 S b.KY)
  1899/1900        (1910 m-10; NL 1900; ME-
  6/2/04, R.5 miles above Boonev.; NL 1920Sx)
  [MARY poss. m2 _____ Sizemore - M-O ch-
  1932, Mayme b. c1911 Ows., d/o Norman
  Hutchinson & Mary Hutchinson Sizemore]

## HUTSON
see HUDSON

## HYDEN
ALLEN C. (R.Ows. 26 S b.Lee,VA) P/Lee,VA
  [1849-1902; s/o Wilson Hyden & Martha
  Chandler - 1870; TS-TCS]
  JERIAH ["HONEY"] MAINOUS (R.Ows. 20 S b.
  Lee,VA) P/Lee,VA   [1853-1957; d/o Lazarus
  Mainous & Rebecca Flanery - 1860; ob-W&S
  OCN-2/14/57, OCC-7/7/39; W-97-100 Bday OCN-
  12/8/50-12/11/53]
  24 May, 1874, Ows. [R.Ows. 1880-1900; Allen
  killed when a Judge of Ows.; wid. Juriah
  1910-1920 Owsley; R.entire md. life in same
  place, about 5 miles from Boonev.]
E[UGENE] C. (R.Lee 26 S mcht. b.[Ows]) [1875-
  1938; s/o Allen C. Hyden & Jeriah Mainous -
  1880; ob-H OCC-12/2/38, BE-11/24/38]
  SALLIE J. HIERONYMOUS (R.Lee 24 S b.Lee)
  [1877-c1934; d/o George Hieronymus & Mary
  Catherine Duff - ob-H; 1880-L]
  8 Jan., 1902, <u>Lee</u>, @ bride's home, by R. T.
  Moore; wits. G. W., Kitty & C. Hieronymus,
  J.H. Creech (M-L; ob-H; to Br. c1908; 1910-
  1920-B)   [EUGENE m2 Pearl Abner Hurst -
  ob-H; NL M-B]
JACKSON (c18 b.KY)
  ELIZABETH _____ (c15 b.KY)
  c1865          (1870-4; NL M-J)

(Hyden cont.)

**HYDEN (cont.)**
JOHN (R.Clay 44 2nd b.Lee,VA) [m1 1846 Per.
Eliz. McIntosh]
SOPHIA HACKER (R.Ows. 20 S b.Ows.) [prob.
d/o Julius Hacker & Eliz. Wilson - 1850]
8 Feb., 1859, Clay (M-C mf; 1860-1870-C)
**HYERONYUMOUS**
see HIERONYMOUS


**INGRAM/INGRUM**
GARRETT (___ b.___)
NANCY FROST (c18 b.Ows.) [d/o James
Anderson Frost & Sarah Lucinda Miller -
1880; 1900-J]
17 Aug., 1894 (ML) Jackson Co.; bm. groom
& Moses Ingram (M-J 9:102; 1900-J, wid.
Nancy Ingram w/P)
HARDIN (c42 3rd b.Est.) [m1 Debbie Alcorn -
M-E 1845; 1850-E; m2 c1853? Adelia ___ -
1860-E]
MARY PATRICK (c15 b.KY)
10 June, 1865, Estill, by Enoch Wakefield;
wits. James M. Ingrum & James J. Sparks
(M-E; 1870-L, 3 of his sons still sgl. in
Est.; 1880-L H-md, W-NL) [H-remd.]
HARDIN (R.Lee 59 3rd [4th] b.Est.) P/TN-Est.
[m3 Mary Patrick above]
ELIZABETH STAMPER (R.Lee 45 S b.Ows.) P/VA
[d/o Wm. Stamper & W1 Resina Kidwell -
1860-1880]
30 March, 1882, Lee @ Joseph Sparks, by A.
R. Bryant; wits. Joseph & Malinda Sparks
(M-L; wid. Eliz. Ingram w/bro. 1900)
SCOTT - see WM. SCOTT
[WILLIAM] SCOTT (c22 b.KY) [s/o Harden Ingram
& W1 Debbie Alcorn]
ELIZABETH _____ (c22 b.KY)
1868 (1870-L-4, but this is a
niece, as shown in 1880-L; their dau.
Margaret b. 1869; 1900-L)

## ISAACS

B[ALLARD] B[LACKWELL] (R.Ows. 21 S b.Ows.) P/
Ows. [1882-1980; s/o Henry Isaacs & Alpha
Scott - ob-H BS-9/4/80]
MAMIE WINN (R.Ows. 16 S b.Ows.) P/Ows.
[1887-1966 Richmond hosp.; d/o Wm. Wynn
& Susan Combs - 1900; ob-W BE-7/14/66]
8 Jan., 1904, Ows. (a/L ME-1/15/04-1/29/04
H/as Ballard B.) [R.Owsley 1910-1920;
Boonev. 1972 - ob-HS BE-5/18/72]
CORNELIUS (c21 b.Clay) [s/o Fielding Isaacs
& Susan         - TCS; 1850-E]
MARGARET A. PIGG (c22 b.Clay)
c1856          (1860-J-3; 1870-1880-J;
B-J ch.; NL M-C)
ELIJAH (c17 b.Ows.)     [1857-1918; s/o Preston
Isaacs & Rachel Johnson - TS-TCS; 1860]
MARY ETTA EDEN (c17 b.KY) [1857-1936 - TCS]
1874/5         (1880-L; 1900; TCS; NL M-L;
M-L ch. & FH-dau.)
GEORGE (R.Earnestv., Ows. 29 S b.Ows.) P/Ows-
VA [s/o Henderson Isaacs & Luticia Neeley
- mg.]
[MARY EVALINE] EVA GRAY (R.Earnestv., Ows.
22 S b.Lee) P/KY [d/o Elihu Gray & (Mary
Jane) Sissie Isaacs - mg.; 1900-J]
3 Oct., 1901, Jackson, to be md. @ Elihu
Gray's (MC-NFI) (M-J 12:51, a/L mf W/as
Evaline; 1910 m-8; 1920; B-O ch.)
GODFREY, JR. (c21 b.KY) [s/o Godfrey Isaacs,
Sr., & Eliz. Howard - TCS]
LYDIA MORRIS (c24 b.KY) [d/o George Morris
& Eliz. Johnson - TCS]
c1846          (1850-3; 1860-J-14, WM w/them)
GODFREY (c19 b.KY)
EMELINE "EMILY" CRAWFORD (c17 b.KY) [d/o
Joseph Crawford & Nancy Gray - TCS]
c1846          (1850-M-3; B-O ch-1854; 1860-E)
HENDERSON (c19 b.Ows.) [s/o Elijah Isaacs
& Sally Bowman - 1850]
[LETITIA] LETTY M[ARGARET] NEELEY (c20
b.VA) [d/o Harrison J. Neeley & Jane
Bishop - TCS]
1 Feb, 1858 Ows. (REM/JFB; 1860-5 mo; 1870;
M-J ch.)

(Isaacs cont.)

**ISAACS (cont.)**

HENRY (c23 S b.Ows) [1856-1922; s/o Sylvester
    Isaacs & Martha Brewer - 1870; TS-TCS]
    ALPHA SCOTT (c16 S b.KY) [1863-1932; d/o
    Wilkerson W. Scott & Martha Mainous - 1870;
    TS-TCS]
    1879          (1880-MWY; 1st ch-8/80 TCS;
    1900 m-19; 1910 m-30; 1920)
ISAAC (c23 S b.KY) [1848-1926; s/o Elijah
    Isaacs & Sally Bowman - 1850 TS-TCS]
    PERMELIA HALL (c20 b.KY) [1850/1-1872;
    d/o Harvey Hall & Mary Bowman - REM; TCS]
    c1871          (REM; both sgl. 1870-L;
    H-remd. 1880, no ch.; NL M-L]
ISAAC (R.Ows. 29 2nd b.KY) P/KY     [widr/o
    Permelia Hall above]
    PHOEBE SCOTT (R.Ows. 20 S b.VA) P/VA
    [c1857-1937 Ows.; d/o Wilkerson W. Scott
    & Martha J. Mainous - 1860-70; DC]
    26 Sept., 1877 @ L. L. Mainous', Ows.
    [R.Owsley 1880-1900-1910-1920]
ISAAC J. "BUD" (c19 S b.KY) [s/o Wm. Isaacs
    & Wl Mary J.    - 1870]
    SARAH SUSAN "SUSIE" COMBS (c22 S b.KY)
    [1869-1954; d/o Tinsley Logan Combs & Sarah
    Ellen Goosey - 1880; ob-W&S OCN-10/21/54
    & OCC-12/18/36]
    1888          (ob-W; 1900 m-12; 1910 m-22;
    1920; M-L ch-1926-1965; TCS; ob-W&S; W/as
    Sarah S. & Susie)
JAMES B. (c22 S b.KY) [s/o Sylvester Isaacs
    & Martha Brewer - 1880]
    SARAH ELIZABETH "SALLY" FLANERY (c17 S b.
    Jack.) [1862-1939 Ows.; d/o Elcannah
    Flanery & Amanda Mainous - TCS; DC; GD/o
    Lazarus & Rebecca Mainous - 1880]
    1880/1          (1900-1910-1920; TCS; R.Ows.
    1939 when wid d.; ob-ch. BS-2/22/90)
JAMES S. (c20 S b.KY) [s/o Henderson Isaacs
    & Letty M. Neeley - TCS]
    SERILDA _____ (___ b.KY) [d. pre-1897]
    1883/4          (TCS; 1900-10/86, H-m-16
    crossed out & m-2 replaces it, W-m-2, so
    m-16 must be Wl; NL M-J)     [H-remd.]


(Isaacs cont.)

348

## ISAACS (cont.)

JAMES S. (c35 2nd b.KY) [widr/o Serilda
above - TCS]
DORA BRANDENBURG (c19 S b.KY) [d/o Henry
Brandenburg & Elizabeth Roberts - B-O]
2 Sept., 1897, Lee @ Henry Brandenburg's;
wits. Pelis Vickers & J. A. Creech (M-L;
1900, H-m-16 crossed out & m-2 replaces
it, W-m-2; 1910 m-13; TCS)
JOHN D. (R.Jack. 23 S b.Ows.) P/Ows. [s/o
Wm. Isaacs & Nancy J. Cole - 1900]
MADA M. MADDEN (R.Ows. 15 S b.Jack) P/Jack.
1 Oct., 1903, Ows.
LEWIS (R.Ows. 19 S b.Jack.) P/Jack. [1884-
1958; s/o Elisha Isaacs & Luvina Brewer -
TCS; 1900-J; ob-H BE-11/20/58]
IDA NEELY (R.Ows. 19 S b.Ows.) P/Ows.
[1883-1968; d/o Lafayette Neeley & Sophia
Isaacs - 1900; ob-W BE-8/1/68]
19 Oct., 1903, Ows. [R.Owsley 1910-1920;
OCN-11/3/50, their 47th anniv.; wid. Ida
R.Ows. 1966 - ob-ch. BE-10/27/66]
PRESTON (R.Ows. 21 S b.Clay) [s/o Elijah
Isaacs & Sally Bowman - 1850]
RACHEAL JOHNSON (R.Ows. 18 S b.Clay) [d/o
Jesse Johnson, Elender Bowman - TCS]
25 May, 1855, Ows. [R.Owsley 1860]
[RACHEL m2 Samuel Mays - 1890 Rachel Mays
f/w/o Preston Isaacs]
PRESTON (c19 b.KY) [s/o Sylvester Isaacs
& Martha Brewer - 1880]
JOSEPHINE ROWLETT (c15 b.KY) [d/o Jesse B.
Rowlett & Eliza Jane Jones - art. OCN; TCS;
1870]
1882/3 (1900; TCS; art. OCN-8/8/52)
SAMUEL (c24 b.KY) [s/o Godfrey Isaacs & Eliz.
Howard - TCS]
ELIZA CRAWFORD (c15 b.KY) [d/o Joseph
Crawford, Nancy Gray - TCS; art.BS-8/15/85]
15 March, 1847 (TCS; 1850-2; 1860-
1870-1880-J; B-J ch-1858-59)


(Isaacs cont.)

## ISAACS (cont.)

SYLVESTER (R.Buck Cr. 22 S b.Ows) [1831-1916; s/o Elijah Isaacs & Sally Bowman - 1850; TS-TCS]
MARTHA ["PATSY"] BREWER (R.Sturg. 18 S b.Hawk.,TN) [1834-1918; d/o Howell Brewer - TS-TCS]
2 June, 1853, Ows., by Rev. J. Ward [R.Owsley 1860-1870-1880-1890-1900-1910; family photo BE-9/30/71]

WILBURN (c26 b.KY) [s/o Fielding Isaacs & Susannah Bowman - TCS]
AMERICA "MECCA" HACKER (c19 b.KY) [d/o Isaac Hacker & Esther Morris - 1860; TCS]
c1868　　　　(1870-1 w/WM; NL M-J)

WILLIAM (c20 b.Ows.) [s/o Elijah Isaacs & Sally Bowman - 1850-1860]
MARY J. _____ (c15 b.KY)
c1867　　　　(1870-2; NL M-J)

WM. T. (R.Jack. c21 b.Ows) [s/o Godfrey Isaacs & Lydia Morris - ME; B-O; 1860-J]
REBECCA A. GABBARD (c19 b.Ows.) [d/o Jacob Gabbard & Eliz. Woods - B-O; 1860; ME]
1872/3　　　　(B-J ch-1874; 1880-J-6; ME-5/8/96 art. on WF; 1900-J m-27; NL M-J)

WILLIAM (c26 2nd b.Ows.) [widr/o Mary J _____ above - 1870]
NANCY J "SIS" COLE (c18 b.Knox) P/VA-KY
c1873　　　　(1880, ch. under 10 were 8, 3, & 4 mos.; B-O ch-10/74; NL M-J)


## JACKSON

EDWARD (c18 b.KY) [s/o James Jackson & Nancy Napier - TCS]
SOPHIA SANDLIN (c16 b.KY) [d/o Lewis Sandlin & Nancy Abner]
c1872　　　　(1880-7; REM; NL M-J)


(Jackson cont.)

**JACKSON (cont.)**

GEORGE (c23 S b.KY) [1856-1922; s/o James
   Jackson & Nancy Napier - 1870]
   TEMPERANCE J. "TEMPY" BOWMAN (c28 S b.Ows.)
   [1850-1942 Lex.; d/o Robert Sturgis Bowman
   & Mary Turner - 1860-1870; LNG; ob-W&S BE-
   2/12/42, OCC-12/18/36-3/18/38]
   1878/9          (1880 no ch.; B-O sibs;
   ME-8/1/90 & 12/13/95 mention John Bowman &
   sis Tempa Jackson, who killed their cuz
   Henry Bowman; 1900-L m-21; 1910-L m1-30;
   M-L ch-1910 b. c1882 Ows.; R.Beattyv., then
   Lex. - ob-W; both bur. Lee; NL M-L)
GEORGE WASHINGTON (c21 S b.KY) [1873-1955; s/o
   James Jackson & Malinda Jackson - 1880 TCS
   ob-H OCN-2/24/55]
   AMANDA JANE GARRETT (c17 S b.Ows.) [1878-
   1958 Levi; d/o Lafayette Garrett & Susan W.
   Bell - ob-W&S OCN-4/24/58-12/23/49]
   24 Jan., 1894, Boonev., Ows. (ob-H; 1900
   m-5; 1910 m-16; ob-ch. BS-11/26/87; R.Levi,
   Ows. 1949-58)
MOODY - see SHERMAN MOODY
RUFUS (c21 S b.Knox) [1863-1953; s/o Landon
   Jackson & Susie Wilson - ob-H OCN-12/4/53]
   MARGARET ISAACS (c20 S b.KY) [1865-1938;
   d/o Sylvester Isaacs & Martha Brewer -
   1880; ob-W OCC-7/29/38]
   1886          (1900 m-13; 1910 m-24; 1920;
   TCS; ob-ch. OCC-4/9/37)
SHERMAN MOODY (___ b.___)
   MARTHA BELLE MAINOUS (c15-24 b.KY) [1886-
   1954; d/o Daniel Carter Mainous & Mary
   Isaacs - 1900; ob-W&F OCN-4/23/54 & OCC-
   7/7/39; WP/anniv. OCC-4/2/37; will 1:150,
   as Martha Mainous Jackson]
   1901-10          (TCS; ob-W&F; W-NL w/P 1910;
   NL 1910-1920Sx for Sherman/Moody; Ows.
   1937-39; Vincent 1954; NL M-J)
SMITH A. (c25 S b.VA) [1866-1934 Lex. hosp.
   - ob-H BE-11/15/34]
   ROSA BELLE GARRETT (c19 S b.Buck Cr.)
   [1873-1949 Ows.; d/o Lafayette Garrett &
   Susan W. Bell - 1880; ob-W OCN-12/23/49]
   1891          (1900 m-8; 1910 m-19; 1920;
   B-O ch.; PWB; wid. R.Pebworth 1934; ob-W)

## JACOBS

GEORGE W. (R.Est. 22 S b.uk)  [poss. s/o
   Nathan Jacobs of Est.]
     PAULINA V. HAMILTON (R.Est. 19 S b.Est.)
     15 Oct., 1856, Ows.  [NL 1860-E - HPH]

## JAMISON/JAMERSON

JOHN D. (c23 b.Ows.)    [s/o Jno. Jameson
   & Elizabeth Kelly]
     SARAH J. SPENCER (c20 b.Ows.)  [d/o Goolman
     Spencer & Phoebe Shoemaker]
     c1866         (1870-L-3; B-L ch.; NL M-J)
MIDDLETON (c23-33 b.KY)
     EVALINE _____ (c23-33 b.KY)
     1860-9        (H-sgl. 1860; 1870-L no ch.;
     NL 1880Sx; NL M-J)
MORDICA (c40 2nd b.KY)  [widr/o Lucinda Benton
   - REM]
     SARAH WINKLER (c21 b.KY)
     7 Nov, 1844, Estill  (M-E; 1850-E; 1860-13)
ROBERT BEATTY (c29 mcht b.KY)  [1827-1892 Lee;
   s/o Wm. Jameson & Margaret Beatty; raised
   by his uncle, Sam Beatty - TR; sgl. 1850]
     GILLY ANN McGUIRE (c15 b.KY)  [1841-1896
     Lee; d/o John Guyer McGuire & Jane McGuire
     - TR; 1850; ME-3/27/96]
     c1856         (1860-3; TR; 1870-1880-L;
     ob-ch. BE-12/28/50; NL M-J)

## JENNINGS/JENINGS/GENNINGS

HENRY (c22 b.KY)  [s/o Wm. Jennings & Sarah
   Taylor - 1880]
     MARIAH CLARK (c17 b.KY)  [d/o Anderson C.
     Clark & Lucy    - 1880 ob-WS OCC-2/21/36]
     1891/2 [poss. s/b 1889]  (1900-5/90, m-8,
     W-4/4 ch., all 4 listed; NL M-J)
JAMES M. (c19 b.VA)
     MILLY A. GUMM (c21 b.KY)  [d/o Stephen Gumm
     & Eliz. Cornelius - TCS; 1860]
     c1864         (1870-5; wid. Milla 1880; TCS;
     DC ch-1925; NL M-J)
JAMES (c17 b.KY)  [1872-19__; s/o James M.
   Jennings & Millie Gum - 1880]
     _____ (___ b.___)
     1887/8        (H-remd. 1900-W as m-12,
     1st ch-8, W/4 ch., all listed)

(Jennings cont.)

**JENNINGS (cont.)**
JAMES (c19 2nd b.KY)  [m1 _____ above]
    HELEN "ELLEN" _____ (c14 b.KY) [1877-19__]
    c1890       (1900-W, m1-12 = 1887/8, but
    this may be W1; 1910-B, H/2nd m-13 = 1896/7
    but, since all ch. listed as hers, prob.
    md. c1890; 1920-B; M-B ch. lists 1st 2 ch.
    b.Ows., ch/o James & Helen; NL M-B)
RILEY L. (c19 b.Ows.)  [c1865-1925 Per; s/o
    James M. Jennings & Millie Gum - 1880; DC]
    SARAH MORGAN (c17 b.Ows/Per.)  [1866-1948
    Per.; d/o Wilson Morgan & Lucy Lewis - DC]
    1884       (1900-W m-16; 1910-B, m-25;
    1920-B; M-B ch. lists 1st 2 ch. b.Ows.;
    NL M-B; H/as Raleigh L. & Robt. L., but
    most often as R. L. or Riley L.; W/as Sarah
    Jane & Sarah E.)
WILLIAM (c37 S b.TN)  [1861-1930 - TS-TCS]
    SARAH (nee EVERSOLE) SMITH (c30 S b.Cow Cr)
    [wid/o Joseph Smith - TCS]  [1868-1956; d/o
    George Eversole & Rebecca J. Moore - 1880;
    TS-TCS; ob-WS OCN-3/31/55]
    1899       (1900-9/90, m-1, W-3/3 ch.;
    1910 m-10, 2 Smith s-ch. B-O ch. Smith;
    1920; R.Arnett, KY 1955)
**JENTRY/JENTREY**
see GENTRY
**JETT/JET**
ALLEN (c16 <u>Mul</u> S b.Br) [c1847-1908 Per.- P-CW]
    HANNAH A. McKINNEY (c17 <u>Blk</u> b.KY)
    c1863    [DIVORCED] (1870-6; P-CW
    Hannah says md. after CW; he abandoned her
    & she filed for DIV. 1871 & 1873, but no
    decree entered; Allen says DIV. 1867, had 2
    ch. b. 1860 & 1862; these ch. ages 6 & 2
    1870 w/both P/listed; ch. ages 16 & 13
    1880-L w/M & s-F; DC ch-1939 b. 1864 Ows.)
    [H-remd.]    [HANNAH remd. Samuel Minter -
    1880-L]

(Jett cont.)

<u>JETT (cont.)</u>
ALLEN (c27 <u>Mul</u> 2nd b.Br.)    [Div/f Hannah
    McKinney above]
    MARY A. (nee _____) _____ (c33 <u>blk</u> 2nd
    b.Lee) P/VA  [c1840-1900/3 - P-CW]
    c1874         (1880, s-ch. Mariah 15 Mul,
    Martha B. 7 Mul, & s-GD Martha 1 Mul. D-B
    son Alfred 8 Blk, d. 2/27/76 Br, b. Ows, =
    b. c1868.   Alfred's age s/b 8 "mos.";
    1900 m-16 = 1883/4, which prob. s/b "26",
    W-7/1 ch., dau. Mattie B. 19 Blk.)
ALLEN (c47 <u>Mul</u> 3rd b.Br.)  [m1 Mary A. _____
    above - P-CW]
    ELIZABETH COMBS (___ b.___)
    25 June, 1904, <u>Perry</u>, @ Simon Walker's, by
    A. A. Cornett; wits. Simon & Phylis Walker
    (M-P I:98; P-CW as 6/<u>26</u>/1904 Per.)
ARCH (R.Copes Br. 23 S b.Br.) P/Br.  [s/o
    Hercannus Jett & Caroline McQuinn - mg;
    1900-B]
    ALLIE CRAWFORD (R.Oakdale 19 S b.Br.) P/Br-
    Lee  [d/o Dick Crawford & Lucy Bowman - mg]
    10 April, 1901 (ML) <u>Breathitt</u> @ Dick
    Crawford's  (M-B 9:203 MC filled in for
    diff. couple; B-O ch.; 1910-B m1-7 both)
    [ARCH (R.Oakdale 64 widr. b.Br.) m2 4/12/43
    Eliza (Vires) Osborn (50 wid. b.Br.) - M-L]
CHARLES (c21 <u>Blk</u> c.minr b.KY)
    ANN _____ (c17 <u>Blk</u> b.KY)
    c1866         (1870-L-3; Ann in court 3Fks-
    8/1/83)
CHARLEY (R.Lee 25 S [<u>Blk</u>] b.Br.) P/Br.
    JANE JETT (R.Lee 21 S [<u>Blk</u>] b.Ows.) P/Ows-
    Br.
    14 June, 1903, Ows. [rec. Lee]  (M-L; 1910)
CURTIS (c24 S b.Br.)  [1874-1955 Mad.; s/o
    Hiram Jett & Sarah J. Sewell - MT]
    REGINA REYNOLDS (c20 S b.Ows)  [d/o Leander
    Reynolds & Rachel Stewart - ob-WM OCC-
    4/25/41; 2nd M-B]
    1898/9         [appar. DIVORCED 1910-16]
    (1900-B; 1910-B-8 mos., m1-11; NL M-B)
    [REGINIA m2 12/16/1916 Br., Daniel Griffith
    - appar. DIVORCED because she is listed in
    ob-WM 1941 as Regina Jett of Yakima, WA]

(Jett cont.)

**JETT (cont.)**
GEORGE (R.Ows. 24 S [Blk] b.Ows.) P/Ows.
   CLAUDY HAMPTON (R.Ows. 17 S [blk] b.Lee)
   P/Lee-Ows.
   23 April, 1908, Ows.  [R.Owsley 1910]
HYRCANOUS C. (R.Mid.Fk, Br; 18 S b.Mid.Fk, Br)
   [s/o Newton Jett & Eliz. Cloud - 1850-B]
   CAROLINE McQUINN (R.Ows. 16 S b.Morg)
   [1840-1919; d/o Alex. McQuinn & Levisa  -
   ob-W JT-10/24/19; 1850-Morg.]
   15 Feb., 1857, Breathitt, by Joseph Noble,
   Min. Br. Co.  (M-B mf; 1870-1880-1900-B;
   M-L ch-1943)  (a/L M-Morg. ML 2/26/56)
ISAAC (c20 S Blk b.Lee)  [s/o Jeptha Jett
   & W1 Elizabeth      ]
   BETTIE LEVELL (c15 S Blk b.Garrard Co.)
   1886         (1900 m-14; 1910 m-23; B-O
   ch.; NL M-B)
JAMES (R.Ows. 23 S Blk b.Ows.)  [s/o Allen
   Jett & W1 Hannah McKinney - 1880-L, w/M &
   s-F Sam Minter]
   MATTIE JETT (R.Lee 17 S Blk b.Br.)
   12 Aug., 1887, Lee @ America Jett's, by W.
   H. Bowman; wits. America Jett & Samuel
   Minter  (M-L; JEM)  [H-remd.]
JAMES (c27 2nd Blk b.Ows.)  [m1 Mattie Jett
   above]
   MATTIE LOU JETT (c13 S Blk b.Lee)  [poss.
   d/o Isaac Jett & Betty Lovell - TCS; 1900]
   1900/1        (1900, both m1-9, but s/b
   H-2nd; 1920; B-O ch. Robt. 12/04, W/as Lou
   Jett, but Robt. NL 1910; JEM; NL M-B; W/as
   Mattie & Lou)
JEPTHA (24 Blk c.minr b.KY)
   ELIZABETH _____ (c13 Mul b.KY)
   c1864        (1870-L-5)  [H-remd.]
JEPTHA (c33 blk 2nd b.KY) [widr/o Eliz. _____
   above - 1870-L]
   MATILDA FRANCIS (c20 Mul b.Let.)
   c1877      (1880, 1st ch. under 10 is 2;
   B-O ch.)


(Jett cont.)

JETT (cont.)
JOHN (c23 S b.Br.)  [poss. s/o Harcannus Jett
   & Caroline McQuinn - 1900-B]
   LULA REYNOLDS (c17 S b.Cow Cr.)   [d/o
   Henderson Reynolds & Ann Moore; ob-WS OCN-
   3/14/52; 1000]
   1904/5           (1910; B-O ch.; NL M-B)
SIMON (20 S b.Br.)  [s/o Morton Jett & Eliz.
   Crawford - JSG; 1880-B]
   MARY JANE TERRY (18 S b.Br.)  [d/o Miles
   Terry & Louraine Johnson - JSG]
   24 Aug., 1892, Breathitt @ Miles Terry's
   (JSG; M-B 5:442; H-remd. 1910-B-16)
SIMON (c26 2nd b.KY)  [m1 Mary Jane Terry
   above - JSG]
   SOPHIA GABBARD (c28 S b.KY) [d/o Willis
   Gabbard & Mary Bishop - 1880]
   1897/8           (JSG; 1910-B m-12 H-2nd;
   NL M-B)   [SIMON m3 Tymanda (nee Deaton)
   Callahan, wid/o Ed Callahan - JSG]
THOMAS (c17-24 blk b.KY) P/KY
   SARAH _____ (c19-26 Mul b.VA) P/VA
   c1873-9           (appar. DIVORCED pre-1900)
   (1880 no ch.; H-sgl. 1900-L Bo. w/Hannah
   Chandler; H-remd. 1910-L; NL M-B)
THOMAS (R.Lee 47 2nd blk b.KY)  [m1 Sarah
   _____ above]
   HANNAH [nee BURNSIDE] CHANDLER (R.Lee 48
   2nd Mul)  [wid/o Bob Chandler - B-M 1877]
   17 Oct., 1903, Lee @ H. Chandler's, by Wm.
   Robinson, Judge; wits. Wm. Lutes
   (M-L colored book; 1910-L]
WILLIAM (19 S blk b.KY)  [1864-1939 Ows.; s/o
   Allen Jett & Hannah McKinney - 1870; 1880-L
   w/M & s-F; DC]
   MARGARET COMBS (19 S blk b.KY) [1860-1952
   - ob-W OCN-1/9/53]
   20 Oct., 1882 Breathitt, by J. W. Cardwell;
   wits. Wm. Jett & Sam Minter (M-B 3:90;
   1900 m-19; 1910 m-30; wid. Margaret
   R.Boonev. 1939; TCS; ob-ch. OCN-7/11/52)

**JEWELL/JEWEL**
BUTLER (R.Ows. 21 2nd b.Ows.) P/Ows. [m1 _____
_____ - NL M-J] [s/o Wm. Jewell & Bettie
J. Collins - 1900]
    DORA COLLINS (R.Ows. 22 3rd b.Br.) P/Br.
    [m1 _____; m2 _____]
    8 Jan., 1904, Ows. (a/L ME-1/15/04 ML;
    NL 1910Sx) [They went to prison for 2 yrs.
    for housebreaking - ME-5/19/04]
ELBERT (c18 S b.KY)
    LENER _____ (c15 S b.KY)
    1906/7          (1910)
JACOB (___ b.___) [poss. m1 Elizabeth Riley
- poss. 1870-B; 1880]
    MARGARET (nee GROSS) WHITE (c49 2nd b.Ows.)
    [wid/o Shelton White - M-O 1853; 1870-1880;
    P-CW REM] [d/o John Gross & Polly Mays -
    REM]
    c1885          (P-CW Shelton White REM, md.
    betw. 6/4/84 & 5/3/86; 1900 wid. Margaret
    "WHITE" w/son)
LEE (R.Ows. 18 S minr b.Ows) P/Ows. [s/o Wm.
Jewell & Betsy J. Cottongin - 1900]
    MAGGIE PALMER (R.Lee 19 S b.Lee) P/Lee-Ows.
    [d/o Andrew Palmer & Sarah Nannie Reynolds
    - 1900-L w/wid. mom]
    8 Nov., 1909, Ows. [R.Owsley 1910]
WILLIAM (c20 S b.KY)
    ELIZABETH "BETSY" JANE (nee COTTONGIN a/k/a
    COLLINS) _____ (c21 2nd b.KY) [m1 _____
    _____] [d/o James Cottongin & Margaret
    Rasner - 1870 w/M & s-F Anderson Collins;
    MT]
    1879          (1880, s-d age 2 listed as
    JEWELL & ch-4/80; 1900 m-20; 1910 m-30
    W-2nd; M-L ch-1916-1922; M-B ch-1926)
**JOHNSON/JOHNSTON**
_____ (___ b.___)
    CATHERINE _____ (c21 b.KY)
    c1845          (1850-4 wid. Cath.)
_____ (___ b.KY)
    LARINDA (nee _____) GABBARD (c25 2nd b.KY)
    c1872          (1880 W-remd. Done, Johnson
    s-ch. 7 & 3, Gabbard s-s 13) [LAURINDA m3
    1878/9 John Dunn - 1880]

(Johnson cont.)

**JOHNSON (cont.)**
ALBERT (R.Br. 16 S b.Br.) P/Br.
  EMMA WADKINS (R.Br. 16 S b.Br.) P/Br.
  20 April, 1908, Ows. [R.Breathitt 1910]
ALEXANDER (c37 b.NC)
  CLARINDA BOOTH (c20 b.VA) [prob. d/o Wm.
  Booth Sr. & Sarah   - 1850; TCS]
  c1854    (B-O ch-1855; NL 1860;
  1870-L-14)
ALFRED (R.Pow. 25 S b.Montg.)
  MARGARITE KINCAID (R.Ows. 18 S b.Br.) [d/o
  Edw. Wyatt Kincaid & Miriam Plummer - TR]
  24 April, 1856, Ows. [R.Owsley 1860]
ANDERSON (R.Ows. 22 S b.--) [s/o Samuel
  Johnson & Rachel Pennington - 1850]
  MARY DAULTON (R.Ows. 23 S b. TN)
  23 Dec., 1855, Ows. [R.Owsley 1860]
CHARLES (R.Br. 22 S b.Br.) P/Br.
  MARTHA REID (R.Ows. 2 S b.Ows.) P/Ows.
  [d/o Wiley Reed & Lydia Mason - 1900; BBC]
  6 Aug, 1908, Ows. [R.Owsley 1910-1920]
CORNELIUS (R.Ows. 29 S b.Est.) P/VA-Jack.
  MARY G[RACE] BARKER (R.Ows. 25 S b.Br.)
  P/Br. [1883-1928 Lee; d/o Martin V. Barker
  & Malvina Becknell - PWB 1900 MAR]
  19 Feb., 1909, Ows. [NOTE: They are GP/o
  H/o MAR]
ELISHA (R.Br. 20 S b.Br.) P/Br.
  NANIE L. GABBARD (R.Br. 17 S b.Br.) P/Br
  6 Aug., 1908, Ows.
FRANK (___ b.___)
  SARAH JANE (nee HORNSBY) ADAMS (c35-65 2nd
  b.KY) [m1 Freddie Adams - TCS; 1880] [d/o
  Job Hornsby & Cath. Gabbard - TCS]
  1880-1910    (Sarah & H1 1880; TCS;
  NL 1900Sx)  [SARAH m3 Irvine Wooton - TCS]
GEORGE W. (c20 b.KY) [s/o Samuel Johnson
  & Rachel Pennington - WGO; 1850]
  MARINDA CALLAHAN (c17 b.KY) [d/o Wilson
  Callahan & Sally York - WGO]
  c1853    (1860-6; B-O ch.; W/as
  Marinda, Lurinda & Marinda)


(Johnson cont.)

GRANVILLE PEARL (c19 b.Br.)  [1866-1932 Ows.;
    s/o James Johnson & Mary Ellen McIntosh -
    TCS; DC]
    FANNY McINTOSH (c19 b.Br.)  [1866-1910; d/o
    Richard McIntosh, Armina Caudill - TCS CRC]
    1884          (1900-7/85, m-14 H/as Pearl;
    1910 widr. Granville; B-O ch.)  [GRANVILLE
    m2 c1915 Farinda Spencer (d/o Alfred
    Spencer & Betty McIntosh)  - TCS; 1920;
    W/2nd M-L - wid. Farinda R.Cow Cr. 1932]
GRANVILLE (18 b.Per.)  [s/o Robert Johnston
    & Hannah Brewer - AJ]
    PARALIE JANE HOLCOMB (15 S b.Island Cr.)
    [d/o Ira Holcomb & Mary Creech - 1880]
    8 Dec., 1884, Welchburg, Jackson Co., by
    Judge John King     (AJ; 1900-J anot.)
GREENVILLE (c20 b.KY)  [s/o Isaac Johnson
    & Nancy     - TCS]
    MARIAH MATILDA BURNS (c17 b.IN)  [1845-1936
    Lee; d/o Wm. Burns & Sarah Barrett - 1850-
    1860-B.  NOTE: DC has Wm. Johnson & Salley
    Burns, but census & P/M-C show them as abv]
    1862/3, Breathitt (1870-B; 1880-17; 1900-B
    m-37; B-O ch. M/Burris; M-L ch.; H/Green or
    Greenville in all rec. except W/DC as
    Granvil)
HENRY (c21 b.KY)
    JANE _____ (c18 b.KY)
    1897/8          (1900)
[JAMES] ABRAHAM (c19 b.VA)  [s/o James Johnson
    & Elizabeth     - M-cons]
    MARTHA CAIN (c14 b.KY)  [c1831-1852; d/o
    John Cain - M-cons.; D-O]
    5 May, 1845, Estill  (REM; M-E; 1850-5;
    widr. James 1860; H/as Abraham & James A.)
    [H-poss-remd.]
JAMES A. (R.Ows. 36 widr. b.--)  [poss. widr/o
    Martha Cain abv - D-O 5/52; if so Nancy d.
    or they Div. pre-1860, when James was widr]
    NANCY [nee _____] KILBOURN (R.Ows. 30 wid
    b.VA)  [wid/o George Kilburn - 1850]
    11 Aug., 1852, Ows.


(Johnson cont.)

## JOHNSON (cont.)

JAMES [SKINNY JIM] (R.Per. 20 S b.KY) [s/o
    James Johnson & W2 Margaret Gay - WGO]
    NANCY EVERSOLE (R.Per. 19 S b.Per.) [d/o
    Wm. Eversole & Barbara Campbell - TCS]
    15 Oct., 1857, Perry (M-P; B-J ch-1858;
    1860-1; went west to KS & OR - AJ)
JAMES (c26 b.TN) [poss. s/o John Johnson
    & Mary Gentry]
    NANCY LUTES (c16 b.KY) [d/o Charles Lutes
    & Lucinda Plummer]
    1864/5        (1870-L-4; 1880-1900-L; TCS)
JOSEPH H. (___ b.___)
    NANCY ANN BAKER (___ b.___)
    1 Feb., 1900, Ows. [rec. Perry] @ George
    Baker's, by Wm. Baker, MG; wits. Geo. Baker
    & Rod Hall (M-P G:74; NL 1900/J/P;
    NL 1910-1920Sx)
L[EVI P.] (R.Ows. 22 S b.--[Ows.]) [s/o Sam
    Johnson Jr. & Rachel Pennington - TCS]
    REBECCA SMITH (R.Ows. 19 S b.Harl.) [d/o
    Robert Smith & Polly      - TCS]
    9 June, 1859, Ows.  [R.Owsley 1860;
    Jackson Co. 1870; Jackson 1874-75 B-J ch.]
MATT (R.Br. 22 S b.Lee) P/Br. [s/o Anderson
    Johnson & Dolores Gabbard - 1900-L]
    FLORA HERD (R.Lee 21 S b.Les.) P/VA
    11 Nov., 1908, Ows.  [R.Lee 1910; Sewell
    1959 - ob-HS]
PASCHAL (c24 b.KY) [s/o Robert Johnson
    & Rachel      - WJ]
    RHODA ALLEN (c22 b.KY) [d/o Morris Allen
    & Rachel Bishop - TCS]
    c1848, Breathitt (1850-B; B-B ch.; 1860)
PEARL - see GRANVILLE PEARL
ROBERT (R.Br. 19 S b.KY) P/KY [poss. s/o
    Jesse Johnson & Clarissa      - 1870-B]
    DELILAH CURBY (R.Br. 22 S b.TN) P --
    31 Dec., 1874, Ows.
ROBERT (R.Br. 19 S b.Br.) P/Harl-"K" Co.
    DICY EDWARDS (R.Ows. 18 S b.Ows.) P/Clay-
    "C" Co., TN [d/o Wm. Edwards & Sarah
    Bailey - 1870]
    15 Nov., 1875, Breathitt (M-B; 1880 Dicy
    md., H-NL; B-O ch-2/78)

(Johnson cont.)

**JOHNSON (cont.)**

SAMUEL (c27 b.Let.) [c1836-1897; s/o George Washington Johnson & Sarah Frances - BJN/Sam's neph. Sidney Johnson; 1860-Let.; ME-6/25/97]
ZARILDA [FRANCES] McGUIRE (19 b.Ows.) [d/o Arch McGuire & Catharine Brandenburg] 23 July, 1863, Ows. (JFB; B-L ch; 1870-L-6; 1880-L; Boonev. 1897-8; ME-1/28/98 wid. Zarilda)

THOMAS (R.Br. 24 S b.Br) P/Harl-Br. [poss. s/o Isaac Johnson & Nancy -1870-B]
FANNY [nee McINTOSH] SHORT (R.Br. 23 2nd b.KY) [wid/o George Short - 1870-B] [d/o Peter McIntosh & Jane Gross - M-P] 13 Nov., 1874, Ows., @ Joseph Woodward's (a/L M-Br. 1874, mo. & day unreadable]

THOMAS (c31 b.KY)
MARGARET RILEY [BEARD] (c40 2nd b.KY) [ml Wm. Beard - M-O 1874] 27 March, 1900 Sebastian, Ows. [rec. Perry] by Harvey Rice, JPOC; wits. Allen Moses & Sinda Gilbert (M-P G:20; 1900-B m-0; NL 1910-1920Sx)

TIMOTHY (R.Ows. 24 S b.Est.)
SARAH AN PITTMAN (R.Ows. 19 S b.Est.) [d/o Micajah Pitman & Norma - TCS] 11 April, 1854, Ows. [R.Owsley 1860; Lee 1870-1880-1900; wid. Susan w/son 1910 Lee]

WILLIAM (c52 2nd stonemason b.VA)
[widr/o _____]
CATHERINE ROBERTSON (c26 b.TN) c1844 (1850 W/32, ch. ages 19, 15, 5 & 1; B-O ch.; 1860; 1870-W)

WILLIAM (R.Ows. 24 S b.Est.) [s/o Wm. Johnson, Sr. & Cath. Robertson - TCS]
NANCY SPENCER [s/b SPARKS] (R.Ows. uk [19] S b.Est.) [poss. d/o Ephraim Sparks & Sarah ] [8] July, 1858, Ows. (a/L M-B as 7/1/58, W/as SPARKS; B-O ch. & B-W ch. W/as SPARKS)

WILLIAM (R.Ows. 21 S b.Ash Co., NC)
JEMIMAH BOOTH (R.Ows. 21 S b.Lee,VA) [d/o Wm. Booth & Sarah - 1850] 1 Dec., 1859, Ows.

## JONES

C[OSLEY] A. (R.Lee 26 S b.VA) P/VA
   NANCY A. ROBERTS (R.Ows. -[18] S b.KY) P/KY
   [d/o James Madison Roberts & Sarah Steel -
   B-O]
   27 Sept., 1877, Ows., @ J. M. Roberts'
   [R.Lee 1880]
HENRY C. (c24 tailor b.VA)
   ELIZ. BARKER (c14 b.KY)
   c1846          (1850-3; B-O ch.; 1860-12)
ISAAC S. (R.Ows. 28 S b.Knox) [s/o Dutton
   Jones & Rebecca Stewart - TCS]
   NANCY ALLEN (R.Clay 17 S b.Clay)
   10 Dec., 1857, Clay (M-C mf; a/L M-J mf
   as 12/23/57, but Jack. not formed until
   1858, H-27; B-J ch-1858; 1860-70-80-1900-J)
JOHN (c25 b.KY)
   LUCINDA PARSONS (c19 b.KY)  [d/o Stephen
   S. Parsons & Louisa      - TCS]
   17 Nov., 1848, Clay  (M-C; REM; 1860-6, 1st
   ch. b. VA; B-O ch.)
JOHN (c21 b.VA)
   LUCINDA _____ (c18 b.KY)
   c1867          (1870-L-2)
JOHN JAMES (c17 b.KY)
   MINERVA J. NEELEY (c17 b.Scott Co., VA)
   [1851-1920 - P-CW Newnam]
   1867          [DIVORCED 9/19/1895 Ows. &
   Minerva restored to maiden name of Neeley -
   P-CW H2 REM]  (P-CW H2 REM; 1870-1; TCS;
   REM)  [John J. poss. remd below]
   [MINERVA m2 Henry H. "Dump" Newman - P-CW]
JOHN (c23 b.Morg.) [s/o Matt Jones & Eliza
   Jane Estes - 1860]
   NANCY BUCKHART (c21 b.Lee,VA) P/VA
   c1868          (1870-L-1; B-L ch.)
JOHN J. (R.Lee 45 3rd b.Clay) P/TN-KY  [m1
   poss. Minerva J. Neeley above; m2 poss.
   c1895 unknown]
   NANCY JANE KENDRICK (R.Lee 20 S b.--[KY])
   P/-- [poss. d/o Wm. Kendrick & Margaret
   Burns - 1880]
   16 Nov, 1896, Lee @ Geo. Kincaid's, by Geo.
   Kincaid; wits. L. B. Kincaid & Mrs. G. W.
   Gourley (M-L; 1900 H/age 48 crossed out &
   age 32 put in its place)
(Jones cont.)

**JONES (cont.)**
MATTHEW (c24 b.Morg.) [c1820-1859 - D-B]
ELIZA JANE EASTES (c21 b.Fay.) [d/o Robert
Estes & Sarah Graves - FJR]
20 May, 1844, Estill; sur. Robt. Estes
(M-E; 1850; B-B ch.; Br. 1859; wid. Eliza
1860-B; FJR; wid. Eliza w/Owen Crawford
1870-1880-1900-L)
MILLARD F[ILLMORE] (22 S b.Buck Cr., Ows.)
[1861-1935; s/o Joshua Jones & Lutitia
- TCS; 1880-L; ob-H BE-9/19/35]
FRANCES E[MMA] NEWNAM (17 S b.Ows.) [1865-
1949 OH; d/o Elias Newman & Mary Smallwood
- TCS; 1870; 1880-L; ob-W BE-3/17/49]
28 Feb., 1884, Lee (M-L; 1900-L; 1910
m-23; H-d. Haz., bur. Lee; to Ham.,OH)
**JUDD**
ALBERT - see JAMES ALBERT
ANDREW (c24 S b.KY) [1870-1946; s/o Leander
Judd & Nancy Moore - 1880; TS-TCS; ob-HS
OCN-6/9/51]
LULA BOWMAN (c21 S b.KY) [c1874-1946; d/o
Henry Bowman & Eliz. McVey - TS-TCS; 1880]
1893/4        (1900-1910-1920; TCS; in
Metamora, IN 1951)
ARCH (R.Ows. 24 S b.Ows.) P/Ows. [s/o Thomas
Judd & Anne Thomas - 1900; ob-HS OCN-
6/29/51-8/29/57; BE-3/1/73]
LULA WOODS (R.Ows. 15 S b.Ows.) P/Ows. [d/o
Jefferson Woods & Eliz. Combs - 1900; TCS;
JC]
23 Oct., 1909, Ows.  [R.Owsley 1910-1920;
Metamora, IN 1951; IN 1957; Connersville,
IN 1973]
CHARLIE B. (R.Levi c23 S b.Ows.) [1878-1939;
s/o Nathl. Judd & Sarah J. Neeley - 1880;
TCS; ob-W2]
HATTIE B. JUDD (R.Levi c16 S b.KY) [1887-
1914; d/o Daniel Judd & Josephine McPherson
- TS-TCS]
2 Nov, 1904, Ows. (ME-11/10/1904; 1910 m-6;
TCS)   [CHARLIE m2 1914, Martha (nee
Mainous) Hall, wid/o Henry Hall, d/o John
Tyler Mainous & Sarah Ellen Botner - TCS;
1920; ob-W OCN-3/24/50]

(Judd cont.)

**JUDD (cont.)**

DANIEL (c24 b.KY) [1863-1903; s/o Leander Judd
& Nancy Moore - 1880; ME 3/13/03]
 JOSEPHINE "JOSIE" McPHERSON (c18 S b.KY)
 [1869-1949; d/o Stephen McPherson & Rebecca
 Jane Pendleton - 1880; ob-W OCN-7/8/49]
 Dec., 1886 (ML), Ows. (ME-1/14/87; 1900
 m-13; TCS; 1910 W-m2-4; ob-ch. BS-7/1/93)
 [JOSEPHINE m2 Thomas Kincaid - 1910]
HENRY (c31 S b.KY) [1877-1914; s/o James Judd
& Eliza Jane Baughman - 1880; B-O; TS-TCS]
 NELLIE COMBS (c20 S b.KY) [d/o Raleigh
 B. Combs & Amanda Brandenburg - 1920]
 1907/8 (1910; wid. Nell Judd 1920
 w/P)
JAMES "THE SADDLER" (c23 sadl b.Ows) [1850-
1904; poss. s/o Elvira Judd; GS/o Roland
Judd - 1860; REM; ME-12/22/04]
 ELIZ. JANE BAUGHMAN (c29 b.Knox) [1844-
 19__; d/o Thomas Baughman & Eliz. -
 1870]
 1874 (1880-5; 1900 m-25; B-O ch.;
 TCS; wid. Jane 1910 & wid. Eliz. 1920 Bo.
 w/Duff; W/as Eliz. & Jane)
JAMES ELIJAH (c23 b.Ows.) [s/o Leander Judd
& Nancy J. Moore - 1870]
 AMERICA NEELEY (c18 b.KY) [d/o Andrew J.
 Neeley & Eliz. Collier - TCS; 1870]
 1879/80 (1880-MWY; TCS) [H-remd.]
JAMES ELIJAH (c38 2nd b.KY) [widr/o America
Neeley above - TCS]
 MARTHA SPIVEY (c23 S b.Ows.) [d/o David
 Spivey & Amanda Mainous - TCS; 2nd M-O]
 1893/4 (1900 m-6; 1910 m-16 H-2nd;
 TCS; wid. Martha 1920) [MARTHA (R.Ows. 62
 wid. b.Ows.) m2 9/15/32, Robt. Amis (65
 widr.) - M-O]
JAMES ALBERT (c20's b.KY) [1880-1951; s/o
Nathaniel Judd & Sarah Neeley - 1880; TS-
TCS]
 ELLEN WILSON (c14-23 b.KY) [1887-1961;
 d/o Robt. Wilson & Martha Eversole - 1900;
 TS-TCS]
 1901-10 (TCS; W-sgl. 1900;
 NL 1910-1920Sx)

(Judd cont.)

JUDD (cont.)
LEANDER (R.Ows. 35 S b.Lee,VA) [s/o Roland
    Judd & Fanny Johnson - 1850; TCS]
    NANCY MOORE (R.Ows. 16 S b.Ows.) [d/o
    James Moore & Matilda Cunagin - TCS]
    9 Feb., 1852, Ows. [R.Owsley 1860-1870-
    1880-1890-1900]
LEE M. - see N. LEANDER
N. L[EANDER] (R.Ows. 21 S b.Ows.) P/Ows.
    [1886-1961; s/o James Judd & W1 America
    Neeley - 1900; TS-TCS]
    ELLA P. GARRETT (R.Ows. 18 S b.Ows.) P/
    Ows. [d/o Lafayette Garrett & Susan W.
    Bell - 1900; ob-WS OCN-4/24/58, OCN-
    4/24/58, BE-3/25/65]
    11 Dec., 1908, Ows. [DIVORCED 1910-20]
    [R.Owsley 1910; H/as N. L., Lee N. & Lee
    M.] [ELLA m2 Floyd L. Price (1886-1962
    OH; s/o Isaac Price & Mildred Kidd - 1910;
    art. BE-10/21/48, 10/24/57; ob-H BE-
    1/11/62) - TCS; 1920; ob-WS; R.Cleveland,
    OH 1948-1965]
NATHANIEL (c20 b.Ows.) [s/o Leander Judd
    & Nancy J. Moore - 1870; TCS]
    SARAH J. NEELEY (c16 b.KY) [d/o Andrew
    Neeley & Eliz. Collier - 1870; TCS]
    c1875      (1880-4; B-O ch.; ob-ch.
    HJN b.1884 Ows.)    [H-remd.]
NATHANIEL (c37 2nd b.Ows.) [widr/o Sarah J.
    Neeley above - 1880]
    KIZZEY INGRAM (___ b.KY)
    29 July, 1892, Jackson Co. (TCS)
    [H-remd. 1900-1910]
NATHANIEL (R.Ows. 42 3rd b.Ows.) P/VA-Ows.
    [m2 Kizzey Ingram above - TCS]
    MARTHA [nee _____] SMITH (R.Lee 32 2nd b.
    Ows.) P/-- [m1 _____ Smith]
    24 Dec., 1894, Lee @ Price Congleton's, by
    C. Pendergrass, MEC; wits. Price & Geo.
    Congleton (M-L; 1900 m-5; 1910 m-16 H-3rd
    W-2nd) [a MARTHA JUDD (65 wid. b.Ows.) md.
    8/3/1929 Ows., A. H. Obert]


(Judd cont.)

365

**JUDD (cont.)**

ROLAND (c70-79 2nd b.Wilkes Co, NC) [widr/o
    Frances Johnson - 1860; md. 5/28/12 Wilkes
    Co., NC TCS]
    IBBA CAROLINE (nee ROBINSON) TIREY (c38-47
    4th b.NC) [m1 John Tyree - DC ch; m2 _____
    Carter - 1850 wid. Caroline Carter; m3 Ben
    Tirey - TCS, M-C; 1860 wid. Caroline Tyra]
    1860-9          (1870; 1900 wid. Ibba C. w/GS
    Jesse Turner; 1910 wid. Caroline w/dau.
    Jane Turner; TCS; W/as Caroline & Ibba C.)
THOMAS (c20 S b.Ows.) [s/o Leander Judd
    & Nancy Moore - B-O]
    ANNE THOMAS (c21 S b.KY) [d/o Wm. Thomas
    & Eliz. Mays - TCS]
    1877/8          (1880-1900-1910-1920; TCS;
    ob-ch. OCN-8/29/57)
WILLIAM (c22 S b.Ows.) [1876-1965; s/o Nathl.
    Judd & Sarah Neeley - 1880; TCS; ob-H BE-
    3/11/65]
    MARY JANE GROSS (c19 S b.Ows.)    [d/o
    Emeline GROSS & unknown - TCS]
    1897/8          (1900-1910-1920, WM w/them;
    TCS; M-O ch-1963; ob-ch. BS-2/3/94)
WILSON (c19 S b.Ows) [s/o Leander Judd &
    Nancy Moore - 1880; TCS]
    ALPHA HUGHES (c14 S b.KY) [c1876-1935 Levi;
    d/o Walter Hughes & W1 Susie Pruitt - ob-W
    BE-5/16/35 lists sibs & half-sibs; PWB TCS]
    1892          (1900 m-7; 1910 m-18; B-O ch.;
    1920; M-L ch-1919)


**KEE**
see KEY
**KELLER**
ANDERSON (c18 b.Knox) [1869-1911 Ows.; s/o
    Isaac Keller & Sally Gilliam - DC; TS-TCS]
    MALINDA SHOUSE (c17 b.Ows.) [1870-1958;
    poss d/o Wiley Shouse & Rachel    - TS-TCS]
    1888          (1900-11/88, m-11; B-O ch.;
    M-O ch-1967)

(Keller cont.)

**KELLER (cont.)**
JOHN (c18 S b.Knox) [1881-1964 Lee; s/o Ike
  Keller & Sally Gilliam - 2nd M-O; 1900
  w/wid. mom; ob-H BE-12/10/64]
  CAROLINE JEWELL (c18 S b.Boonev.) [d/o Wm.
  Jewell & Betty   - 1900]
  1900         (1910 m-10; B-O ch.; M-L ch-
  1937; ob-ch. 3Fks-6/26/96-12/4/96)
  [JOHN (R.Lone 66 widr. b.Knox) m2 12/10/48,
  Rosa (nee Campbell) Young (64 wid.) (d/o
  Will Campbell & Sally) - M-O]
**KELLY/KELLEY**
DILLENHAM (R.Morg. 26 2nd b.Morg.)
  [widr/o _____]
  TABITHA C. FALCONER (R.Ows. 22 S b.Carter
  [Co.], TN)
  15 July, 1858, Ows.
JAMES (c32 b.KY) [c1813-c1855 - FJR, Guilford
  Estes apptd. Admr/o estate 6/1855]
  NISSINIA THOMAS [a/k/a ESTES] (c22 b.Mad.)
  [1822-1907 KS; d/o Elisha ESTES, Jr. &
  _____ THOMAS - ob-W FJR, wherein she is
  listed as sis/o Scott Estes; B-E ch. by H2
  W/as ESTES; pd. $200 from est/o Elisha
  Estes - FJR]
  3 March, 1845, Ows. (JFB; 1850-E; FJR Est.
  Ct. 9/57 Hiram Kelly [s-F] apptd. gdn/o
  Sina's ch. by James Kelly; Wm. Bowen apptd.
  gdn. 8/65; W/as Lycina, Misina, Sinea,
  Fanny, Vina in various recs.)
  [SINA m2 9/8/56, Hiram B. Kelly (1832-1906
  KS; s/o Samuel Kelly & Rachel) - M-E; FJR;
  B-E ch-1857-1859; 1860-1870-E; to KS c1879;
  in Atchison Co., KS 1880 to death - census,
  deeds, ob-H FJR; FJR found recs. that
  indicate Sina filed for Div. from Hiram
  7/63, but did not go through with it.]
JAMES (R.Clay 21 S b.Clay) P/Clay
  LUCY PETERS (R.Ows. 18 S b.Ows) P/Ows.
  [d/o Hardin Peters & Mary J Hoskins - 1900]
  12 May, 1904, Ows. [R.Owsley 1910; London
  1960 - ob-WS BE-6/16/60]


(Kelly cont.)

**KELLY (cont.)**

MARION H. (R.Ows. 19 S b.Br.)
   LOUISA J. HOLMES (R.Ows. 16 S b.KY) [prob.
   d/o Robert S. Holmes & Nancy      - TCS]
   27 Sept., 1858, Ows.   [R.Owsley 1860]
SMITH (R.Livingston c41 2nd b.KY)
   [m1 _____]
   NANCY JANE (nee HOLCOMB) HOWELL (R.Ows. c44
   2nd b.Ows.) [wid/o James Howell - 1900]
   [d/o Wm. Holcomb & Eliz. Christian - B-O]
   1905, Ows. (ME-11/2/1905 as Mr. Kelly &
   Mrs. Nancy J. Howell, plan to R.Livingston;
   1910-Merc., m2-5, Kelly ch. 16 & 9, Howell
   s-dau. 27)
WILLIAM S. (c31 b.KY)
   NANCY J. GILBERT (c21 b.KY)  [d/o Aquilla
   Gilbert & Mary Baker - TCS]
   4 Oct., 1849, Ows. (JFB; B-O ch.; REM;
   1850-1860; wid. Nancy 1870-1880-1900-L)

**KENDRICK/KENDRIC/KINDRICK**

FLETCHER - see JOHN FLETCHER
JAMES B. (R.Lee 24 S b.Ows.) P/Russ,VA &
   Stokes Co., NC [s/o John Fletcher Kendrick
   & Lucy Seale - 1870-L]
   MARGARET THOMAS (R.Lee 21 S b.Ows.) P/
   Pitts,VA & Mad. [d/o John James Thomas
   & Mary Ann Roark - TCS]
   3 Feb., 1877, Lee @ Wm. Smith's, by James
   M. Roberts; wits. W. M. & Harrison T. Smith
   & Wm. P. Brown   (M-L 1:405; 1880-2;
   H-remd. 1900-L)
JAMES S. (R.Lee 43 2nd b.Ows.) P/VA-NC  [m1
   Margaret Thomas above]
   EMELINE ["EMMA" BARBARA] HOWELL (R.Lee 39 S
   b.Ows.) P/--  [1857-1942 Lee, d/o Guias
   H. Howell & Mary Tincher - B-O; DC; 1860)
   18 April, 1896, Lee @ J. S. Smallwood's (W-
   BiL); by Geo. Kincaid, MG; wits. W. N.
   Tincher & J. S. Smallwood   (M-L; ME-5/1/96
   W/as Mrs. Emma Howell; 1900-L)


(Kendrick cont.)

## KENDRICK (cont.)

JOHN FLETCHER (c31 b.Russell Co., VA) P/VA
[c1817-1888 - ob-H 3Fks-9/21/88]
LUSETTA "LUCY" STEEL (c23 b.Stokes Co., NC)
[d/o Andrew Jackson Steel & Nancy King]
c1848        (1850-1; B-O ch.; REM; 1860;
1870-1880-L; wid. Lucy 1900-L w/son James;
M-L ch-1877-1891; ob-ch. BE-5/12/49)
JOHN (R.Ows. 29 S b.Ows.) P/Ows. [s/o Wm.
Kendrick & Margaret Burns - 1880]
[ARMINE EDWARDS] (R.Ows. 28 2nd b.Ows.)
P/Ows. [m1 c1901 _____]
9 July, 1909 Ows.   [1910-L Armina m2-1, H-
NL, son George 8; NL Armina Edwards 1900/L]
[NOTE: There was an error in this & other
marriages, wherein bride was listed on the
wrong line. Bride listed as JULIA TACKETT;
line above was ARMINE EDWARDS. JULIA
"LILLIAN" TACKETT actually md. Levi BBurg.]
WILLIAM (c23 b.Floyd) [s/o John Fletcher
Kendrick & Lucy Steele - 1870-L]
MARGARET BURNS (c19 b.Ows.) [poss. d/o
John Burns & Lucinda Combs]
1871/2        (1880-7; 1900-L m-28; B-O
ch.; ob-ch. OCN-10/4/56)

## KETCHUM/KETCHAM

JEREMIAH "JERRY" (c22 c.minr b.Br.) P/KY [s/o
George Ketchum & Susan Miller - JSG]
LOUISA LITTLE (c18 b.KY)
c1869        (1870-L-3/70; LNG/Carol
Marcum, Jer's G-G-GD) [H-remd.]
JEREMAH (R.Lee 30 2nd minr b.Br.) P/KY
[m1 Louisa _____ above]
ANNA BENNETT (R.Lee 20 S b.Ows.) P/MO-KY
3 Sept., 1877, Lee @ Wm. Bennett's (M-L &
mf; 1880-L, no ch.)   [H-remd.]
JEREMIAH (R.Lee 36 3rd b.Br.) P/-- [m2 Anna
Bennett above]
MARY FRANCES BOTNER (R.Lee 17 S b.Ows.) P/
VA-Ows.   [1865-1893; d/o Benjamin Botner
& Margaret Patrick - 1880-L; TS-LNG]
30 Jan., 1883, Lee @ V. J. Doty's, by Robt.
Cole, MG; wits. V. J. Doty & Deamy Thomas
(M-L)   [H-remd.]

(Ketchum cont.)

**KETCHUM (cont.)**
JEREMIAH (47 4th b.Br.) [m3 Mary Frances
   Botner above]
   REBECCA STAMPER (38 4th b.Ows.) [m1 _____
   _____; m2 _____; m3 _____]
   17 May, 1894, <u>Lee</u> @ Wm. Porter's; wits.
   Bell Hall & Mary Daugherty (DIVORCED 1897
   Lee - LNG 8:525) (M-L; LNG; NL 1900/L)
   [JEREMIAH m5 Rebecca Porter - LNG/Carol
   Marcum, G-G-GD/o Jer.]
**KEY**
GEORGE T. (c43 wool carder b.VA) [NOTE:
   Because of his age, he may have been md.
   prev.]
   MARTHA ANN BURNS (c23 b.KY) [d/o John
   Burns & Louisa Combs - 1850 as Ann; 1860
   as Martha]
   c1864          (1870-5; 1880-15; B-O ch.)
**KEYWOOD**
see CAWOOD
**KIDD**
ANDREW J. (c27 b.KY) [s/o Robert Kidd
   & Prescovy Peters - 1880]
   MAGGIE MAYS (c18 b.Ows.) [1874-1951; d/o
   Samuel Mays & Rachel Johnson - 1880; ob-W
   OCN-11/9/51]
   25 Aug., 1892          (ob-W; 1900 m-6;
   R.Berea, Mad. 1951-1956; NL M-J)
DAVID JESSE (c30 S b.KY) [1869-1940; s/o Thos.
   Kidd & Mary Virginia Stanfield - 1880; ob-H
   OCC-5/10/40]
   ORLENA SMITH (c25 S b.KY) [1873-1941; d/o
   Wm. Smith & Lucy Ann Gibson - 1880; ob-W&M
   OCC-10/3/41-3/16/34]
   1898          (obits; 1900-6/99, m-1 w/HF;
   1910 m-11; 1920; R.Endee 1934; Ows. 1940-
   1941; H/as D. J., David & Jesse D.; ob-ch.
   BE-7/4/40)
HARDEN - see THOMAS HARDEN
JESSE - see DAVID JESSE


(Kidd cont.)

**KIDD (cont.)**
NEWTON (c19 b.KY)  [s/o George Kidd & Mary
    Watson - 1860]
    SARAH BURCH (c19 b.KY)  [d/o Wm. Burch &
    Malinda Mays - 1870; TCS]
    1867/8              (1880-9, Sarah md., H-NL,
    w/WS; 1900; NL M-J)
ROBERT (c22 b.NC) P/VA-NC  [s/o George Kidd
    & Mary Watson - 1860]
    PRESCOVY PETERS (c20 b.VA)  [d/o Andrew
    Jackson Peters & Sarah Williams - REM]
    1861, Virginia  (REM; AB; 1870-6 VA;
    1880-18 VA; 1900 m-38)
TANDY (R.Ows. 23 S b.Stokes Co., NC)  [poss.
    s/o George Kidd & Mary Watson]
    ELIZABETH CREECH (R.Ows. 19 S b.Harl.)
    1 Dec., 1859, Ows.  [R.Owsley 1860]
[THOMAS] HARDEN (c23 b.KY)  [s/o Robt. G. Kidd
    & Prescovy Peters - TCS; 1880; ob-HS BE-
    12/16/37]
    EMILY PETERS (c20 b.KY)  [d/o Anderson
    Peters & Eliz. Jane Evans - 1880]
    22 May, 1893 (bond) Jackson Co. (M-J 8:410;
    1900 m-7; ME-3/13/03 moved to Mad.; R.Berea
    1937; H/as Harden all rec., except 1880
    w/P as Thomas H.)
**KILBURN/KILBOURN**
ARCHIBALD (c20 b.VA)
    SARAH JANE VIRES (c19 b.Br.) P/VA-KY
    c1866              (1870-3; 1880; TCS)
MARTIN (c20 b.Clay)
    MARY BELLE MOORE (c14 b.Ows.)  [d/o Hardin
    Moore & Polly Gabbard - 1880; LNG]
    1886/7            (LNG; 1900-L m-13; 1910-L
    m-21 = 1888/9; M-L ch-1915; moved to OH -
    LNG/Lillian Dunaway)
**KINCAID**
CHARLES (R.Fincastle 24 S b.Lee) P/Lee-Wlf
    [s/o Edward Kincaid & Sarah Carroll - mg.]
    FLORENCE BARRETT (R.Beattyv. 23 S b.Lee) P/
    Br.  [d/o Wm. Barrett & Mary A. Roberts -
    mg.; ob-WF&M OCC-4/21/39-8/19/38; 1910-L]
    16 June, 1910, Lee @ Wm. Barrett's, by L.
    H. Wright, MG; wits. Elery Williams & Henry
    Edwards  (M-L 9:127; ob-WF&M; 1900)

(Kincaid cont.)

**KINCAID (cont.)**
EDWARD (c25 b.Est.)
 LUVINA GRAY (c25 b.Ows.) [d/o John Gray
 & Mary Dolly Hatton - TCS]
 1860        (1870-8; B-L ch.; 1880-1900-L;
 ob-ch. BE-8/13/53, b.8/61)
GEORGE B. (R.Ows. 40 S b.Est.) [s/o George
 Kincaid & Peggy     - D-L 1875]
 MARGARITE McGUIRE (R.Ows. 25 S b.Est.)
 [d/o Benjamin McGuire & Diadema Mann]
 8 Oct., 1856, Ows. [R.Owsley 1860; Lee
 1870; wid. Margaret 1880-1900 Lee]
HENRY (R.Lee 49 2nd b.Ows.) P/VA-NC
 [m1 _____]
 MARY BELLE ALDER(?) (R.Ows. 36 2nd b.Per.)
 P/Per.   [m1 _____]
 4 Sept., 1908, Ows.   [NL 1910Sx]
JEFFERSON - see THOMAS JEFFERSON
JESSE T[AYLOR] (R.Lee 20 S b.Lee) P/Wlf-Ows.
 [1872-1937 OH; s/o Robt. B. Kincaid & Lydia
 Ellen Stamper - ob-H BE-4/22/37; Rev.]
 ANNAH E. THOMAS (R.Lee 19 S b.Lee) P/Est-
 Lee,VA   [c1873-1897; d/o Henry Thomas
 & Jane Shoemaker - 1880-L; ob-H]
 21 July, 1892, Lee @ Henry Thomas', by M.
 F. Stamper, MG; wits. Joseph Gentry & M. F.
 Cable  (M-L 4:115)   [H-remd.]
JESSE TAYLOR (c26 2nd b.Lee) [widr/o Annie
 Thomas above - ob-H]   [1872-1937 OH]
 MARTHA HALE (R.Ows. c31 b.VA)  [1867-1962
 IN; d/o Elisha Hale & Cynthia Hobbs - 1870-
 1880; ob-WS OCN-12/12/57]
 Aug., 1898       (ob-H; 1900-L m-2;
 R.Beattyv. & Stanton; H-d. Cincinnati 1937;
 W-d. Jeffersonville, IN 1962; NL M-L)
[JOHN] MILES (c25 b.KY) [c1831-1864; s/o Edw.
 Wyatt Kincaid & Miriam Plummer - TR; BS-
 8/17/78 art.]
 MARTHA ANN AKERS (c23 b.KY) [1833-1915;
 d/o Wm. Akers & Perdelia Pitman - ECP]
 20 Feb., 1856, Ows. (JFB; 1860-4; B-O ch.;
 1870-L; wid. Martha A. 1880-L)  [MARTHA m2
 11/6/81, Absolom Mainous - ECP M-L 1900-10]


(Kincaid cont.)


372

**KINCAID (cont.)**
LYCURGUS (c20 b.Est.) [s/o Edw. Wyatt Kincaid
    & Miriam Plummer - TR]
    MALINDA SPENCER (c20 b.Lee,VA) P/VA
    1850          (1850-MWY; 1860; 1870-1880-
    1900-1910-L; TR)
MILES - see JOHN MILES
PLUMMER - see SAMUEL PLUMMER
SAMUEL P[LUMMER] (c30 b.KY) [s/o Edward
    Wyatt Kincaid & Miriam Plummer - TR]
    [DIADEMIA] DEMIS NOLAN (c27 b.KY) [d/o
    Henry Noland & Nancy Snowden - 1850]
    5 Feb., 1864, Ows. (JFB; 1870-L)
SOCRATES (c23 b.Est.) [s/o Edward Wyatt
    Kincaid & Miriam Plummer - TR]
    ELIZ. LUTES (c27 b.KY) [c1822-1852 - D-O]
    c1849          (1850-2 mo; D-O W&ch.) [H-remd.]
SOCRATES (c29 2nd b.Est.) [widr/o Elizabeth
    Lutes above - D-O 9/52]
    CINTHA ANN TRIMBLE (c20 b.Montg.) [d/o
    Isaac Trimble & Mary          ]
    early 1855          (B-O ch-11/55; 1860; B-L
    ch.; 1870-1880-1900-L; ob-ch. BE-5/2/35-
    11/13-47-1/15/48; W/as Ann & Cintha)
THOMAS J[EFFERSON] (20 S b.Ows.) [1860-1932;
    s/o John Miles Kincaid & Martha Akers -TCS]
    POLLY CABLE (20 b.Lee)
    11 March, 1880, <u>Lee</u> (M-L; 1880-L w/HP)
    [H-remd.]
THOMAS JEFFERSON (c26 2nd b.Ows.) [widr/o
    Polly S. Cable - M-L; 1880-L]
    HELEN (nee MAINOUS) FRANKLIN (c24 b.KY)
    [wid/o Benjamin Franklin - TCS]    [d/o
    Absalum Mainous & Susan Treadway]
    c1885/6          (TCS; widr. Thomas 1900, ch.
    b. 11/80, 12/86, 3/89, 1/93, 3/96, 1/99,
    last ch. w/Mainous GF 1900)
THOMAS JEFFERSON (c46 3rd b.Ows.)    [widr/o
    Helen Mainous above]
    JOSEPHINE "JOSIE" (nee McPHERSON) JUDD (c37
    2nd b.Ows.) [wid/o Daniel Judd - 1900]
    [1869-1949; d/o Stephen McPherson & Rebecca
    Jane Pendleton - 1880; ob-W&S OCN-7/8/49
    & OCC-12/28/34]
    1905/6          (1910 m2-4 both, but s/b H-3rd,
    Judd s-ch.; B-O ch.; TCS, H1 d. 1903; 1920
    s-d Judd; R.Ows. 1934; ob-ch. HJN-9/16/95)

**KINDRICK**
see KENDRICK

**KING**

EWELL V. (c17 S b.Taft, Ows.) [s/o Sam King
   & Nancy        - 1910 bro. Jeff. w/Ewell;
   same bro. w/Sam & Nancy 1900]
   NANCY JANE WILSON (c17 S b.Taft, Ows.)
   1897        (1900 m-2; 1910 m-13, HS w/them;
   BC-1900; ob-ch. OCN-12/26/49, s/o E. V.
   King & neph/o Judge J. M. King; NL M-H)
HILLARY (R.Ows. 23 S b.--) P/--
   [MARY CATHERINE _____ (c16 S b. VA)]
   - July, 1877, Ows.   [NOTE: W-NL on mg.;
   NL 1880; 1900-1910-1920; W/as Catherine &
   Mary C.]
HIRAM (c27 b.Clay) [s/o Moses King & Mary
   - ACB]
   NANCY WRIGHT (c14 b.Est.) P/IN
   c1848        (1860-B, ch-11, 5 & 2, all b.
   Ows.; NL 1850Inx. for this Hiram; B-O ch. &
   B-W ch.; 1870-1880-W)   [HIRAM m2 c1898,
   Hulda (nee _____) Lacy - ACB; 1900-W, Lacy
   s-s]
J[AMES] M[ONROE] (R.Ows. 22 S b.Harl.) P/Harl.
   [s/o Samuel King & Nancy        - 1900 as
   Monroe; later Judge of Boonev.]
   SARAH J. BECKNELL (R.Ows. 21 S b.Ows) P/Ows
   [1889-1961; d/o Wm. Becknell & Nancy Kidd -
   TCS; OCN-5/19/50; 1900; ob-W BE-12/7/61]
   8 May, 1910, Ows. [40th anniv. OCN-5/19/50;
   wid. R.Boonev. 1961]
JEFFERSON WOODARD (c21 S b.Harl) [1868-1958
   Taft; s/o Woodard P. King, Sr. & Elizabeth
   Harris - TCS; ob-H Be-12/11/58]
   SARAH J. THOMPSON (c18 S b.KY) [d/o James
   Riley Thompson & Mary     - TCS]
   1889/90        (1900-1910; TCS; NL M-H/J)
JOHN B. (c31 Judge b.TN)
   SARAH ELIZABETH "SALLIE" EVANS (c23 b.Ows.)
   [c1846-1883; d/o John B. Evans & Rebecca
   - ob-W ME-7/20/83; TCS; 1850-C]
   c1869          (TCS; 1870-J son Dan, 0;
   1880-J; ME-7/20/83 death of Sallie, leaves
   hus. & 5 ch.; NL M-J)   [JOHN B. m2 5/15/84
   Serilda Nicholas - TCS]

(King cont.)

**KING (cont.)**
R. M. (R.Ows. 22 S b.Est.)
    AMANDA SLOAN (R.Ows. 14 S b.Pike)
    21 June, 1855, Ows.
SAMUEL (c33 2nd b.Harl.) [m1 _____ -
    poss m1 2/17/1874 (ML) Rachel Turner - M-H
    2:413; bm. groom & N. H. Hall - MC-NFI]
    NANCY _____ (c21 b.KY)
    1879     (1900-5/80, m-20; NL 1880Sx;
    NL M-H/J)
SAMUEL (R.Ows. 58 3rd b.Harl.) P/Clay [widr/o
    Nancy _____ above]
    MATILDA [nee _____] SMITH (R.Clay 33 2nd
    b.Clay) P/Clay [NOTE: a MATILDA COPE md.
    1/15/95 Clay, E. W. Smith; a TILDA HELTON
    md. 1/16/02 Clay, Richard Smith]
    2 Feb., 1909, Clay [recorded Owsley]
    [R.Owsley 1910-1920]
WOODARD P., JR. (c15-20 b.KY) [s/o Woodard P.
    King, Sr. & Eliz. Harris - TCS; ob-HS BE-
    12/11/58]
    _____ (___ b.___)
    1905-10     [DIVORCED pre-1910] (1910
    Woodard, age 20 Div., w/bro. Jefferson;
    NL M-H/J) [WOODARD m2 c1920 Lizzie -
    TCS; 1920, no ch.; R.Boonev. 1958]


**LACY**
PERRY (c23 b.KY)
    BECKY _____ (c18 b.KY)
    c1845     (1850-4; NL 1870Inx; NL 1880Sx)
**LADY**
ELIJAH B. (c47 2nd b.Est.) [m1 c1865 Sarah
    _____ - 1880-E-14]
    NANCY J. _____ (c21 b.Est.)
    1883/4     (1900; M-O ch.; NL M-Est.)
NEWTON (R.Ows. 22 S b.MO) P/Est. [s/o Elijah
    B. Lady & Nancy J. - 1900]
    LUCY LYNCH (R.Ows. 22 S b.Est.) P/Est.
    17 March, 1908, Ows.
**LAKINS**
WILLIAM (c30 b.TN)
    RUTH _____ (c27 b.TN)
    c1867     (1870-2)

**LAMB**
THOMAS THURMAN (c19 b.TN)
    ANN SMITH (c12 b.KY)
    25 May, 1864, Jackson (M-J 1:343; 1870-3)
**LANE**
JAMES H[ENRY] (R.Ows. 24 S b.Lee,VA) [1836-
    1914 Pow.; s/o John S. Lane & Sarah
    Thompson, who later md. Morgan Francis -
    JA; 1850; M-Scott,VA 1843]
    SARAH J[ANE] NOLAND (R.Ows. 23 S b.Est.)
    [1836-1884; d/o Henry Noland & Nancy
    Snowden - JA; REM]
    15 Dec., 1859, Ows. [R.Ows. 1860; Lee 1870;
    moved to Powell Co. - JA]
    [JAMES m2 Sarah Maxwell Holmes - JA]
JOHN (c26 B'smth b.Sullivan Co., TN) [c1839-
    1877; s/o Thomas Lane & Sarah   - D-O]
    NANCY J. MARSH (c18 b.TN)
    c1865      (1870-4; B-O ch. by H2; NL M-J)
    [NANCY m2 Andrew J. Bowman]
JOHN MELVIN (c20 b.Scott,VA) [raised by
    Morgan Francis & Sarah (nee Thompson) Lane;
    prob. s/o Sarah's dau. Minerva Lane]
    ORPHA SMITH (c15 b.Ows.) [d/o Addison
    Smith & Rebecca Ely - B-O]
    c1868      (1870-L no ch; MS lists son d.
    8/69 @ 1 mo.; B-L ch; 1880-L; TS-Wlf;
    NL M-J)    [JOHN m2 3/20/79 Lee, Delina C.
    Smith - M-L; 1880-L; 3Fks-7/1/87 funeral of
    Mrs. Delina C. Lane W/o John M. Lane will
    be preached]
JOHN S. (c18 S b.KY) [s/o John Lane & Nancy
    Marsh - 1870]
    RHODA C. PETERS (c19 S b.KY) [d/o Wm.
    Peters & Emily Morris - 1880]
    1883/4      (1900 m-16; 1910 m-25; TCS;
    NL M-J)
**LANGDON**
ABNER (c19 b.KY)
    CLARKIE WARREN (c14 b.KY) [1872-1904; d/o
    David S. Warren & Mary Shepherd - TS-TCS]
    1886/7      (1900; TCS; NL M-J)
WILLIAM (c21 b.Perry)
    HANNAH BEGLEY (c16 b.Perry)
    c1866, poss. Perry (1870-P-3; B-O ch-1/76;
    1880-P; M-P do not cover this time period;
    NL M-J)

## LANKFORD

ROBERT [B.] (c21 b.TN) [s/o Benjamin Lankford
   & Temperance Posey - TCS]
   NANCY OSBURN (c17 b.KY) [d/o Enoch Osborne
   & Malinda Farmer - TCS]
   21 June, 1855, Harlan, by T. H. Noe, JP
   (M-H; 1860-4; TCS)

## LATHAM

_____ (___ b.___)
   CYNTHIA E. FLANERY (c23-43 b.VA) [d/o Joel
   P. Flanery & Susan Bailey - 1880]
   1880-1900     (TCS; W-NL w/P 1900;
   NL 1900Sx; NL M-J)
WILES L. (c26 sal.kpr b.Lee, VA) [s/o James
   Latham & Caroline   - TCS]
   AMERICA MOORE (c20 b.Ows.) [prob. d/o
   Jesse Moore & Eliz. Gabbard - TCS]
   Aug., 1869     (1870-1880; B-O ch.; H/as
   Wm. 1x & Wiles 2x; NL M-J)
WILLIAM - see WILES

## LEDFORD

_____ (___ b.KY)
   LULA _____ (c14 S b.KY)
   c1900     (1910 W-remd., son Oscar 9,
   no surname listed; Oscar Ledford - DDN)
   [LULA m2 Brown Deaton - DDN]
JAMES H. (c17 b.KY) [s/o Silas Ledford & Jane
   Wilson - TCS]
   MARTHA McDANIEL (c19 b.KY) [d/o Thomas
   McDaniel & Susan   - TCS]
   1892/3     (1900; TCS; NL M-J)
JOHN C. (c22 b.Harl.) [s/o Wm. Ledford &
   Susan Cawood - TCS]
   NANCY TURNER (c20 b.Ows.) [d/o John Turner
   & Tempy Reynolds - TCS; MMH]
   c1859     (1860-1 mo; REM; 1870; B-J
   ch-1876-78; 1880-J; wid. Nancy 1900-M;
   NL M-J)
JOHN S. (c22 b.Ows.) [s/o John Ledford
   & Malena Skidmore - 1860]
   DELINA CRAWFORD (c23 b.KY) [d/o Wm.
   Harrison Crawford & Isabelle Bowman - TCS]
   c1865, poss. Breathitt (1870-L-4; B-W ch.;
   went to Everett, WA c1875 - MNC; TCS;
   NL M-J)

(Ledford cont.)

**LEDFORD**
SILAS W. (c21 b.KY)  [s/o Wm. Ledford & Susan
   Cawood - TCS]
   E. JANE WILSON (c19 b.KY)  [d/o Robert
   Wilson & Sally Strong - JCH; 1860; TCS]
   c1861        (JCH; TCS; 1870-C; 1880-18;
   NL M-J)  [JANE m2 Jno. "Bangum" Wilson -
   NVP; TCS]
**LEE**
JOHN (c21 b.KY)   [s/o James Lee & Margaret
   - TCS]
   NANCY J. BURRIS (c14 b.IN)  [poss. d/o
   Henry Burris & Eliz. Moore - TCS; DC/sib]
   c1866        (1870-J-3, HM w/them;
   1880-13 wid. Nancy; NL M-J)
WILLIAM (c20 b.Ows.)    [s/o _____ Lee
   & Sarah      - 1880-Lau.]
   RACHEL GREEN (c21 b.Lau.)
   c1870        (1880-Lau-8, HM w/them; B-Lau.
   ch-1876; NL M-J)
**LEGG**
HENRY (c26 S b.VA)
   SOPHIA BELL ROWLAND (c19 S b.KY)  [c1872-
   1938 Ows.; d/o Martin Rowland & Martha
   Evans - 1880; ob-W OCC-12/23/38]
   1890/1       (1910; poss. 1900; ob-W; NL M-J)
**LEWIS**
A. J. (R.Ows. 23 S b.Clay)
   LUCINDIA DANIEL (R.Ows. 14 S b.Est.)  [d/o
   John Marcus Daniel & Wl Louisa Daniels]
   28 Nov., 1855, Ows.
GRANVILLE (c20 b.KY)
   ELIZA _____ (c18 b.KY)
   c1869        (1870-L-5/70; NL 1900Sx; NL M-J)
LARKIN (c16 b.KY) P/KY
   ELIZABETH CARREL (c16 b.KY)  [d/o Benjamin
   Carroll & Levisa      ]
   c1879        (1880 no ch, w/WP; NL 1900Sx;
   NL M-J)
MATHIAS (c26 2nd c.minr b.KY)   [appar. Div/f
   Chaney Fields - M-P 1857]
   ALMIRA _____ (c19 b.KY)
   c1863        (1870-L-6; NL 1900Sx; NL M-J)
**LIONS**
see LYONS

## LOCKARD/LOCKHART
JAMES (c21 b.VA)
    MARY _____ (c12 b.KY)
    c1873      (1880-6 b.MO, next ch. 5 KY;
    NL M-J)
MADISON "MATT" (c23 b.KY) [s/o Thomas Lockard
    & Celia Scalf - TCS]
    SARAH A. JONES (c19 b.KY) [d/o Aswell Jones
    & Mary A. Dickey - TCS]
    c1858      (1860-1; NL M-J)

## LONG
GEORGE (c22 S Hot-kpr. b.KY) [1866-1929 Ows.;
    s/o Henry Long & Sarah Taylor - DC]
    MARTHA ELIZ. "LIZZIE" WOODWARD (c13 S b.KY)
    [d/o Stephen Woodward & Nancy Catherine
    Woods - TCS; 2nd M-L]
    1887/8      (1900-1910-1920; TCS; NL M-J)
    [ELIZABETH (R.Beattyv. 63 wid. b.Ows.) m2
    12/21/37 S(amuel) B. Moore (66 Div. b.Ows.)
    - M-L]
GEORGE (R.Butler Co., OH 39 S b.OH) P/OH
    LAURA BOWMAN (R.Ows 18 S b.Ows) P/Ows-Jack.
    15 Feb., 1910, Ows.
PENDLETON O. "PEN" (c18 S b.TN) [c1868-1939;
    s/o Henry Long & Sarah Taylor - DC/bro.; DC
    lists P/as ---- Long & Sarah Jennings, but
    Jennings is H3/o Sarah]
    MARY EMILY (nee WILSON) ESTEP (c20 b.KY)
    1886/7      (1900 Estep s-d b. 1/85; B-O
    ch.; NL M-J)    [H-remd.]
PENDLETON O. (c43 2nd b.TN) [widr/o Mary Emily
    Wilson above]
    MARY M. (nee _____) JEWELL (c47 2nd b.KY)
    [m1 _____ Jewell]
    1906/7      (1910 m2-2, Jewell s-ch.; 1920;
    H/DC lists W/as Mary Jewell Long)
ROBERT (c19 S b.Ows.) [1889-1979; s/o George
    Long & Martha Eliz. Woodward - 1900; ob-H
    BS-7/5/79]
    MARY J. FIELDS (c21 S b.KY) [d/o John
    Fields & Elizabeth Spence]
    1908      (1910-1 yr., 1 mo., m-1, w/WP;
    R.Boonev. 1959 - ob-WS BE-6/25/59)

## LOVELACE/LOVELESS
COLUMBUS - see JEREMIAH COLUMBUS

(Lovelace cont.)

**LOVELACE (cont.)**
JAMES [M.] (R.No.Fk, Br. 30 S b.Per.) [s/o
    Jeremiah Lovelace & Phoebe Lipps - MT]
    CERILLA [SERILDA] KING (R.Bloody Cr., Br.
    14 S b.Bloody Cr., Br.) [d/o George King
    & Mary Vires - D-W; MT]
    16 Sept, 1855, Breathitt, by S. P. Chandler
    (M-B; 1860 & 1860MS)
J[EREMIAH] C[OLUMBUS] (c24 b.KY) [c1839-1887;
    s/o Jeremiah Lovelace & Phoebe Lipps - REM]
    DEAMY [DIADEMA] McGUIRE (c20 b.KY) [d/o
    Ben McGuire & Diadema Mann]
    11 March, 1863, Ows. (JFB; 1870-B; 1880-L;
    REM P-CW; wid. Demmie 1900-L)
LUM - see JEREMIAH COLUMBUS
**LUCAS/LUCUS**
FLOYD (c23 S b.Lee) [1885-1948 Lee; s/o
    Francis M. Lucas & Margaret Bowman - ob-H
    BE-12/9/48; 1900-L]
    MOLLIE C. PRICE (R.Levi c18 S b.Ows.)
    [d/o Isaac Price & Mildred Kidd - 1900; 2nd
    M-O; BE & OCN as Mollie Eckman]
    15 Dec., 1907        [DIVORCED 1920-31]
    (ob-H; 1910; 1920-B; LNG; NL M-J)
    [FLOYD m2 8/9/29, Pauline Fields - ob-H]
    [MOLLIE (R.Ows. 40 Div. b.Ows) m2 12/24/31,
    Walter Mainous - M-O;  MOLLIE m3 1932-40,
    Gerald H. Eckman - ob-WS&M BE-8/8/40-
    1/20/44; art. BE-2/8/40-10/21/48, OCN-
    11/1/56; Mollie Eckman R.Beattyv. 1940-56;
    ob-WS BE-1/11/62, Mollie listed as SHEEDER
    R.Lex.; ob-WS BE-2/24/66-10/13/66-2/16/67,
    Mollie listed as ECKMAN, R.Lex.]
HARVEY (c23 b.KY)
    AMERICA MANN (c25 b.KY) [prob. d/o John
    Mann & Patsy Tincher - w/James McGuire & wf
    Diadema Mann 1850]
    c1855, Breathitt (1860-B; B-B ch.; 1870-L;
    1880; KY-Exp. 9/94 JJDD interview w/Harvey
    Lucas 1898)
JESSE (c24 b.Lee,VA) [1841-1923 Lee; s/o
    Goolman Lucas & Polly      - JAB]
    MIRIAM JAMISON (c20 b.Est.) [1846-1931 Lee;
    d/o John Jamison & Elizabeth Kelly - JAB]
    1865/6      (1870-L-3; 1880-L; 1900-L m-34;
    1910-L m-42 = 1867/8; ob-ch. OCN-11/10/55)
(Lucas cont.)

**LUCAS (cont.)**
[PLEASANT] PLESANT (22 S b.Lee,VA)  [s/o R.
   Lucas & Mary        - mg.]
   ELLENOR [C. "ELLIE"] MARCUM (18 S b.Lee,VA)
   [d/o Rebecca Marcum - mg.]
   12 June, 1854, <u>Lee Co., VA</u>, by R. W. Wynn
   (M-Lee,VA; 1860-2 1870-1880-1900-L; B-L ch;
   ob-ch. BE-1/23/64)
SAMUEL (c30 b.Lee,VA)  [s/o Wm. Lucas & Cath.
   Markham]
   WINNIE THOMPSON (c20 b.Lee,VA)  [d/o Wm.
   Alfred Thompson - REM]
   1866/7         (1870-1880-1900-L; B-L ch.;
   NL M-J)
S[AMUEL] P. (R.Lee 25 S b.Lee) P/Lee  [1883-
   1934 Garrard; s/o Wm. T. Lucas & Mary Ann
   Plummer - ob-H OCC-3/16/34; 1900-L]
   MINNIE PRICE (R.Ows. 20 S b.Ows.) P/Ows.
   [d/o Isaac Price & Mildred Kidd - 1900; art
   OCN-11/1/56; ob-WS&M BE-8/8/40-1/20/44]
   7 March, 1908, Ows.    [R.Lee 1910 m1-2;
   Mt. Hebron 1934; wid. R.Bourne 1940; Lanc.
   1944; Lex. 1948-1957 - BE-10/21/48 reunion;
   R.Connersville, IN 1962-1966 - ob-WS BE-
   1/11/62-2/24/66-10/13/66]
**LUKER**
JAMES (c20 b.TN)  [s/o Jacob Luker]
   ELIZABETH "BETSY" SEE (c17 b.KY)
   c1844         (1850-5, HF w/them; B-O ch.)
**LUNSFORD/LUNCFORD**
_____  (___ b.___)
   MARTHA (nee BAKER) MOORE (c35 4th b.KY)
   [m1 James Moore - 1900; m2? Shoog Sandlin;
   m3? Wm. Sandlin - TCS]  [d/o James W.
   Baker & Sarah Davidson - 1880]
   1909/10        (1910 w/BiL Logan Duff as
   Martha "Lunc," m4-0 yrs., H-NL, Dan Moore
   neph; TCS; NL M-J)    [MARTHA m5?, Robert
   Horn/Hornsby - TCS]
JOHN (c22 b.KY) P/KY
   RHODA HOLLAND [HOLLINSWORTH] (c24 b.Clay)
   [1840-1917 Jack.; d/o Squire Hollinsworth
   & Sally Potter - DC; P/M-C 1839; 1860-C has
   her b.Pike]
   4 Feb., 1862, <u>Clay</u> (M-C file 12; NL 1870-
   Inx; 1880-13 & Hollinsworth s-Gch.; 1900-J
   m-25; NL M-J)

**LURENSON(?)**
HIRAM (R.Ows. 23 S b.VA) P/TN-VA
  SUSAN HALL (R.Ows. 22 S b.KY) P/VA  [poss.
  d/o Hezekiah Hall & Eliz. Browning - 1860;
  B-O 1855]
  1 April, 1876, Ows., @ A. S. Hall's
  [NL 1870Inx; NL 1880Sx]
**LUTES**
BUFORD N. (c30 b.KY)  [d. C.W.; s/o John Lutes
  & Priscilla Mann - 1850; art. BE-9/1/66,
  by Willie H. Lutes, Kankakee, IL]
  EVALINE TRIMBLE (c30 b.KY)  [appar. d/o
  wid. Mary Trimble, who was w/them 1860]
  c1859        (1860 no ch.; REM)
CHARLES (22 b.KY)  [1827-1871; s/o John Lutes
  & Priscilla Mann]
  LUCINDA PLUMMER (22 b.KY)
  18 May, 1848        (N-L; 1850-2; B-O ch.;
  1860; 1870-L; wid. Lucinda 1880-1900-L;
  ob-ch. OCC-11/10/39)
CHRISTOPHER C. [a/k/a PETER R.] (R.Ows. 21 S
  b.Est.)  [s/o John Lutes & Priscilla Mann]
  LUCINDA ROBERTS (R.Ows. 23 S b.Clay)
  17 March, 1855, Ows.  [R.Owsley 1860; Lee
  1870-1880-1900; wid. Lucinda 1910 Lee;
  ob-ch. BE-4/18/46, OCN-9/29/50-3/22/56;
  H/as Christopher 4x, as Peter 2x]
HARLAN (R.Lee 28 S b.Pul.) P/Pul.
  [MARY] MOLLIE BRANDENBURG (R.Ows. 29 S b.
  Ows) P/Ows.  [d/o Hardin BBurg. & Sarah Ann
  Hall - 1880; ob-W OCC-2/21/41]
  10 March, 1909, Ows.  [R.Lee 1910;
  Primrose, Lee 1911 - BE-4/7/11 Miss Rhoda
  BBurg. visiting sis, Mrs. Harlan Lutes;
  R.Stanton, Powell Co. 1941]
HENRY MANN (c24 b.Est.)  [s/o Charles Lutes
  & Delilah Mann - REM; P/M-E 1821; Est.
  Ct. rec. 11/20/26 James & Arch McGuire
  gdn/o Henry Lutes orph/o Charles Lutes]
  EVALINE TREADWAY (c17 b.Clay]  [d/o Wm.
  Walton Treadway & Margaret Bowman - TCS]
  6 Feb., 1845, Ows.  (JFB; 1850-3; B-O ch.;
  1860)

(Lutes cont.)

**LUTES (cont.)**

JAMES H. (c20 b.KY)   [s/o John Lutes
& Priscilla Mann - TCS; served C.W.
art. BE-9/1/66 by Willie H. Lutes]
CAROLINE CENTER (c14 b.NC)  [c1843-1872/5]
c1857        (1860-2; B-O ch., W/Center;
1870-L; ob-ch. BE-4/4/40 Buford N. b. 4/58;
DC ch. W/Venter)    [JAMES m2 3/6/76 Ellen
Lucas (d/o Goolberry & Mary) M-L; 1880-
1900-L]
PETER R. - see CHRISTOPHER C.
SIMPSON (c29 b.Ows.)  [1858-1941; s/o
Christopher Lutes & Lucinda Roberts -
1880-L; ob-H OCC-8/29/41]
ANNA FRANCES BRANDENBURG (c23 b.Ows) [1864-
1940 Louisville; d/o Hardin BBurg. & Sarah
Hall - 1880; ob-W OCC-8/2/40]
1886/7        (1900-1910-L; B-L ch.;
ob-H&W; ob-ch. BE-1/29/70; NL M-L)
WILLIAM (c19 b.KY)   [c1845-1929; s/o John
Lutes & Priscilla Mann - 1860; art. BE-
9/1/66, Willie Lutes]
SARILDA THOMPSON (c15 b.VA)
1864        (1870-L-5; REM; 1880-L)
[WM. m2 4/5/1883 Frances Jane Hall - M-L]

**LYNCH/LINCH**

B. HARRISON (c19 S b.TN)
LULA MARGARET "LUCY" CREECH a/k/a TACKETT
(c14 S b.KY)  [1878-1900; d/o Enoch CREECH
& Mary TACKETT - B-O; TCS BBG]
1898        (1900 m-1 dau. Cynthia 9 mos.;
H-remd. 1910, Cynthia Lynch 10, w/GP, Enoch
& Mary Creech; TCS; H/as B. H. & Harrison)
B. HARRISON (c20 2nd b.TN)  [m1 Lucy Creech
above - TCS; 1900]
LUCY DUNN (c15 S b.Ows.)  [d/o Wm. Dunn
& Elizabeth Stephens - TCS]
1901/2        (1910 m-8 H-2nd, W-6/6 ch.,
all listed, his dau. Cynthia by W1 NL,
because she is w/WP; B-O ch.; 1920; H/as
B. H. & Harrison)

(Lynch cont.)

## LYNCH (cont.)

CHARLES BENTON "BENT" (c20 S b.Ows.) [1874-
1961; s/o Huldy Lynch - DC; GS/o James
& Minerva Lynch - 1880]
LAURA BELLE NEWMAN (c20 S b.Lee) [1875-
1956; d/o Henry H. Newman & Mary Jane
Partington - REM F's P-CW; ob-W lists
WP/Crittendon & Mary Jane]
1894/5      (1900-1910-1920; B-O ch.;
H-d. Trav. Rest 1961)
DANIEL (c20 b.KY)
SUSAN _____ (c25 b.KY)
1865            (1870-L-4; 1880Sx-E;
1900-E m-34)
EMMERSON - see MAJOR EMMERSON
FRANKLIN - see JAMES FRANKLIN
GRANT - see WILSON GRANT
HARKANIS (R.Ows. 21 S b.Ows.) P/Ows.
AMANDA MULLINS (R.Ows. 24 2nd b.Br.) P/Br.
[m1 _____]
11 June, 1908, Ows.    [NL 1910Sx]
HARRISON - see B. HARRISON
J. SIDNEY (R.Est. 33 2nd b.Est.) P/Est-Mad.
[m1 _____]
JOSEPHINE LYNCH (R.Lee 19 S b.Lee) P/Orange
Co., NC & Ows. [1873-1898; d/o Thomas
Lynch & Nancy BBurg. - 1880-L]
16 March, 1892, Lee @ Thomas H. Lynch's, by
James E. Dunigan; wits. John S. BBurg.,
Ephraim Angel & others  (M-Lee 4:97;
H-remd. 1910, ch. Hattie 16 & Lloyd 14; M-L
1914 son Lloyd; M-L 1927 dau. Hattie)
J. SIDNEY (c42 2nd b.KY) [m1 Josephine Lynch
above]
MARY [CAMPBELL?] (c29 S b.KY) [poss. d/o
John Campbell & Elizabeth Bowman - 1880]
1899/1900          (NL 1900Sx; 1910, ch.
Hattie 16 & Lloyd 14, by W1; 1920-L widr.
Sidney w/son Lloyd)
JACOB (c27 b.KY)
LUCY _____ (c26 b.KY)
1897/8          (1900)

(Lynch cont.)

**LYNCH (cont.)**
JAMES (R.Ows. 22 S b.uk [SC])
   MINERVA [nee BOWMAN] BLEVINS (R.Ows. 24
   wid. b.clay) [wid/o Robert Blevins - D-O
   1855] [d/o Elisha Bowman & Mahulda
   Phillips - REM]
   14 April, 1857, Ows. [wid. Minerva
   R.Owsley 1870-1880-1890-1900-1910]
JAMES FRANKLIN "FRANK" (c19 S b.KY) [s/o
   James Lynch & Minerva Bowman - 1870]
   MARTHA "PATSY" BAKER (c18 S b.KY)
   1879      (1880-10/79; 1900 m-20; 1910
   m-30; ob-ch. BS-1/21/88; H/as Franklin,
   James F. & Frank)
JAMES C. (c21 S b.Trav.Rest) [s/o Wm. R.
   Lynch & Cath. Nancy Salyers]
   LUCY WARD (c20 S b.Maulden, Clay)
   1902/3     (1910 HM w/them; B-O ch.; BC-
   1919; ECP; 1920)
JOHN (c19 b.KY) [1860-1923; s/o James Lynch
   & Minerva Bowman - 1870; TS-TCS]
   MARY ELIZABETH "LIZZIE" MOORE (c19 b.KY)
   [d/o Nicholas Moore & Lucinda McQueen -
   1870; ob-WS OCC-8/18/39-10/18/40]
   1879      (1880-MWY; 1900-7/80 m-18;
   1920; M-L ch-1920; Boonev. 1939-40; ob-ch.
   BS-3/9/95)
JOHN W[ESLEY] (c21 b.Ows.) [s/o Wm. D. Lynch
   & Nancy Cath. Salyers]
   MARY JANE HAMILTON (c13 b.KY) [d/o Randolph
   Hamilton & Susan    - TCS]
   14 Oct, 1879 Jackson Co., by J. B. Rowlett,
   Elder, @ Randall Hamilton's; wits. Julius &
   Russell Spivy, etc.; sur. Randolph Hamilton
   (M-J; TCS; 1880-L; 1900; ECP; H-remd. 1910)
JOHN WESLEY (36 [s/b c46] 2nd b.KY)
   [widr/o Mary Jane Hamilton above]
   NETTIE (nee FOX) McINTOSH (20 2nd b.KY)
   [wid/o Thomas McIntosh - 1900-L; M-L]
   [d/o Isaac Fox, Lucinda BBurg. - 1900-L]
   12 Dec., 1905, Lee @ Ike Fox's, by Wm. P.
   Page, Min.; wits. Lee & Matt Fox (M-L;
   1910 McIntosh s-ch.; ECP; wid. Nettie 1920)


(Lynch cont.)

**LYNCH (cont.)**
LEWIS (c36 b.NC)
_____ (___ b.___) [d. 1855-9]
  c1853              (widr. Lewis 1860-6; H-remd.
  1870-J)
LEWIS (c44 2nd b.NC) [widr/o _____
  above - TCS; 1860 widr.]
    MARY ANN _____ (c26 b.NC)
    1860/1        (TCS; 1870-1880-1900-J)
MAJOR EMMERSON (c21 b.Ows.) [appar. s/o
  Minerva (nee Bowman), wid/o James LYNCH -
  1880; ob-H OCC-2/11/38]
    MARY ANN GOOSEY (c20 b.Ows) [1868-1957 Lee;
    d/o David Goosey & Armina Roach - ob-W OCN-
    12/12/57; DC]
    1888/9          (1900-L; B-L ch.; 1910-L,
    m2-21 both; 1920; ob-ch. BE-10/5/50; wid.
    Mary Ann d. 1957 Lee)
ROBERT (c22 S b.KY)
_____ (___ b.___)
  c1904              (H-remd. 1910-5; NL M-J)
ROBERT (c21 S b.Ows.)
    LOTTIE MEAD (c15 S b.Jack.)
    1905/6        (1910; B-O ch.)
ROBERT (R.Ows. 26 2nd b.Ows.) P/Ows. [m1 _____
    _____ above]
    MARTHA E. COMBS (R.Ows. 26 S b.Ows.) P/Ows.
    [1879-1963; d/o Tinsley Combs & Sarah Ellen
    Goosey - TCS; ob-WS OCC-12/18/36; N-P 4/98
    MGS]
    16 Aug, 1908, Ows.  [R.Owsley 1910-1920]
SIDNEY - see J. SIDNEY
THOMAS (c23 b.Orange Co., NC)  [s/o Joseph
  Lynch & Mary Dishon - TCS]
    NANCY (nee BRANDENBURG) UNDERWOOD (c22 2nd
    b.Est.) [wid/o Wm. Underwood] [d/o Sam
    Dooley BBurg. & Sally BBurg. - TCS]
    1867            (1870-L-8 & 1; 1880-L; B-L
    ch.; 1900-L m-33; 1910-L m-42; WJM; ob-ch.
    BE-6/16/49)
THOMAS (c18 S b.Trav.Rest) [1881-1961 Ows.;
  s/o wid. Nancy Lynch (not wid/o Thomas);
  ob-H BE-1/26/61; P/NL DC]
    SUSAN COUCH (c17 S b.Sturgeon)
    1900/1          (1910-1920; B-O ch.; wid.
    Susan R.Ows. 1961)
(Lynch cont.)

**LYNCH (cont.)**

THOMAS (R.Ows. 20 S b.Ows.) P/-- [s/o James
   Lynch & Martha Baker - 1900]
   ESTHER DUNAWAY (R.Lee 20 S b.Lee) P/-- [d/o
   Wm. Dunaway & Quintilla Ann Estes - 1900-L]
   4 July, 1905, Lee @ Wm. Dunaway's, by Wm.
   Robinson, Judge; wits. Wm. Dunaway & Henry
   Price    (M-L; 1910-L; 1920-14)
THOMAS (24 S b.Est.) P/Est-Jack. [s/o Joseph
   Lynch & Louisa Lakes - mg.]
   LUCY BRANDENBURG (22 S b.Ows.) P/Ows. [d/o
   Jackson Brandenburg & Martha Callihan - mg;
   ob-WS OCN-6/26/58, BE-12/5/63; 1900]
   26 Oct., 1908, Estill Co.; wits. Wm.
   Blevins & Dany Lynch; sur. Elijah Lynch
   (N-EM; R.Chillicothe, OH 1958-63)
WALTER [E.] (R.Lee 22 S b.Lee) [s/o Thos.
   Henry Lynch & Nancy BBurg. - DB; 1900-L]
   KATIE HAMILTON (R.Lee 16 S b.Ows.) [d/o
   John Hamilton & Martha Isaacs - DB; 1900-L]
   10 March, 1904, Lee @ bride's res., by A.
   J. Marcum; wits. Geo. Burk & A. B. Marcum
   (M-L; DB; R.Crestmont 1963 - ob-WS BE-
   11/7/63)
WESLEY - see JOHN WESLEY
WILLIAM D. (22 S b.Orange Co., NC) [s/o
   Joseph Lynch & Mary Dishon - REM]
   CATHERINE NANCY SALYERS (16 S b.Claib,TN)
   [d/o Ben Salyers, Isabella Rose - TCS; REM]
   14 Feb., 1856, Claiborne Co., TN (REM; ECP;
   1860-1870; B-O ch-11/56; wid. Nancy 1880-
   1890; wid. Cath. 1900-1910)
WILLIAM H. (c22 S b.KY) [s/o Lewis Lynch & W1
   - TCS; 1860; 1870-J]
   SARAH ROBINSON (c19 b.KY)
   c1879          (1880-J, no ch; DC-ch. 1976;
   NL M-J; H-remd. 1900-J, 1st ch. 3/85)
WILLIAM (c20 b.KY) [s/o James A. Lynch
   & Minerva Bowman - 1880]
   SALLY LUNSFORD (c16 b.KY)
   1881          (1900-J-7/82 m-18 annot; NL M-J)
WILLIAM (c24 S b.TN)
   ALICE YOUNG (c18 S b.Let.) [d/o Reese Young
   & Eleanor Collins - 1880; P/1870-Let.]
   1889/90          (1900-1910; B-O ch.; DC son)

(Lynch cont.)

## LYNCH (cont.)
WILLIAM H. (c35 2nd b.KY) [m1 to Sarah
   Robinson above]
   SARAH CARMACK (c31 S b.KY)
   20 June, 1892, <u>Jackson Co.</u> (TCS; 1900-J
   "m-10", 1st ch. b. 3/85; 1910 m-18)
WILSON GRANT (c20 S b.Trav.Rest) [1876-1951;
   s/o James A. Lynch & Minerva Bowman - TCS;
   ob-H OCN-12/28/51]
   HOLLY ANN TIREY (c14 S b.Trav.Rest) [1880-
   1965; d/o John Tirey & Lucinda Addison -
   TS-TCS]
   1895/6              (1900-1910; B-O ch.; TCS;
   1920; H/as Wilson & Grant; W/as Holly,
   Polly, Hally & Hallie An)
## LYONS/LIONS
RICHARD "DICK" (c23 b.DeKalb Co., AL) P/Knox
   Co., TN
   LAURA DANIEL (c21 b.KY) [d/o John Marcus
   Daniel & W2 Mary Fraley - 1850; P/M-E;
   art. BE-12/6/51]
   c1868              (1870-L-1; 1880-L; art. BE)
   [RICHARD (R.Proctor 38 2nd carp b.DeKalb
   Co., AL) m2 9/2/83 Letitia York (R.Lee 34 S
   b.Ows.) md. @ Alfred York's - M-L; ob-ch.
   OCN-4/17/58; 1900-1910-L]

# INDEX

A few notes about the index:

Though I have left the spelling in the marriages as it was listed in the record, I have corrected the spelling in the index. So, you will find "Margarite" McGuire as "Margaret" McGuire.

I have standardized the surnames. Thus, you will find Amanda "Sloan" under Amanda "Slone".

If a bride has been married more than once, I have listed her under both her maiden name and married name. For example, Mary Emily (nee Wilson) Estep will be listed in the index under Mary Emily Wilson and under Mary Emily Estep.

If there is discrepancy between records listing a bride's maiden name, I have listed her under both names. For example, Nancy Cornett/Combs was listed in Clay births as Nancy Cornett and on her 1st marriage as Nancy Combs. Thus, she is listed under both Nancy Cornett and Nancy Combs in the index.

If I found records for a bride using both her nickname and Christian name, I have listed her in the index under her Christian name. For example, Martha "Patsy" Baker will be listed under Martha Baker.

If I found records for a bride using only her nickname, she is listed in the index under the nickname, instead of what I might assume the Christian name to be. For example, Lottie Mead was listed in the 1910 census and Owsley

389

births as Lottie (instead Charlotte), so she is listed in the index under Lottie Mead.

A listing of nicknames and the corresponding Christian name is listed in the Preface of this book. A listing of abbreviations used for Christian names is also listed in the Preface.

-A-

A

Aggie - see Agnes
Bam - see Alabama
Becky - see
  Rebecca
Belle - see
  Belvadora
Belle - see
  Isabelle
Betsy - see
  Elizabeth
Betty - see
  Elizabeth
Cassie - see
  Cassandra
Cindy - see
  Lucinda
Demmy/Deamy - see
  Diadema
Edy - see Edith
Eliza - see
  Elizabeth
Ellie - see
  Ellenor
Emily - see also
  Emeline
Fannie - see
  Frances
Frankie - see
  Frances
Haley/Hailey - see
  Mahala
Ibby - see
  Isabelle
Jennie - see
  Virginia
Josie - see
  Josephine
Kate - see
  Catherine

Kitty - see
  Catherine
Lenna - see Orlena
Lillie - see
  Lillian
Linda - see
  Malinda
Lizzie - see Eliza
Lizzie - see
  Elizabeth
Lizzie - see
  Martha Eliz.
Lizzie - see Mary
  Eliz.
Lizzie - see Sarah
  Eliz.
Lottie - see
  Charlotte
Lucy - see Lucinda
Lytha - see
  Talitha
Maggie - see
  Margaret
Manda/Mandy - see
  Amanda
Manervy - see
  Minerva
Mattie - see
  Martha
Mercie - see
  America
Mima - see Jemima
Minie - see Armina
Molly - see Mary
Nan - see Nancy
Patsy - see Martha
Peggy - see
  Margaret
Polly - see Mary
Pop - see Mary
Sally/Sallie - see
  Sarah
Tempy - see

A (continued)
 Temperance
 Tish - see Letitia
 Vina - see Levina
Abner
 Amanda J., 57
 Easter, 9
 Eliza, 29
 Ellen, 193
 Lucinda, 308
 Mariah, 32
 Matilda, 28, 35
 Minerva, 40
 Nancy, 224, 340
 Sophia, 200
 Susan, 11
 Susan K., 42
Abshear
 Emily, 6
 Florence, 15
 Lou, 44
 Sallie Anna, 82
Absher
 see Abshear
Abstane
 see Abston
Acres
 see Akers
Adams
 Sarah Jane, 358
Addison
 Lurinda/Ludy, 295
 Martha, 233
Adkins
 Elizabeth, 96
Ager
 see Eager
Akers
 Emily Jane, 47
 Martha Ann, 372
 Patsy J., 63
Alder?
 Mary Belle, 372
Alexander

Effarilla/Effy,
 168
Allen
 America, 46
 Armina, 120
 Elizabeth, 147
 Lucy, 194
 Margaret, 219, 296
 Martha B., 196
 Nancy, 362
 Rhoda, 231, 360
 Rhoda Jane, 12
 Sarah, 7
 Virginia, 175
Ambrose
 Martha, 291
Amis
 Elizabeth, 25
 Eva, 290
 Nancy, 24
 Sarah, 29
Anderson
 America, 165
 Lucinda, 305
 Mary Jane, 338
 Nancy, 340
Anderson?
 Josephine, 16
Angel
 Amanda, 266
 Catherine, 263
 Eliza Ann, 92
 Elizabeth, 193
 Lucinda, 282
 Lugenia/Logenius,
 300
Arnold
 Amanda, 90
 Minneola/Minnie,
 301
Asbell
 Dema, 92
 Pauline Cath/Kate,
 167

Ashcraft
  Eliza Ann, 8
  Margaret, 209
Ashcraft?
  Emily Ellen, 184
Asher
  Armitta/Mintie,
    234
Austin
  Mary, 213

-B-

Bailey
  Ann, 211
  Emma, 153
  Fannie, 55
  Florence, 194
  Louisa, 22
  Martha, 261
  Mary, 164
  Mary Jane, 243
  Nancy, 182
  Sarah Ann, 214
  Susan, 237
Baily
  see Bailey
Baker
  Christina, 39
  Clara, 270
  Edith, 73
  Eliza Jane, 179
  Elizabeth, 194,
    282
  Ellen, 202
  Elmira, 2
  Emaline, 33
  Esther, 14
  Eveline, 283
  Isabelle, 71, 200
  Joyce, 35
  Levina, 142
  Lulu, 267
  Margaret, 33

Martha, 111, 234,
  381, 385
Mary, 132, 205,
  270
Mary Ann, 72
Matilda, 28
Nancy, 251, 258,
  294
Nancy Ann, 360
Perlina, 265
Rachel, 161
Rebecca Jane, 217
Sarah, 123
Sarah Jane, 1, 73
Sophia, 322
Susan, 38, 71, 121
Susannah, 27
Ball
  Jane, 228
  Martha, 48, 59
Banks
  Cassy Eliz., 252
Barger
  Alabama, 179
  Emily, 225
  Hannah Matilda,
    118
Barker
  Channy/China Jane,
    274
  Clarinda, 61
  Elizabeth, 362
  Martha, 223
  Mary Grace, 358
Barnes
  Matilda, 101
Barnett
  Mary J., 118
Barret
  see Barrett
Barrett
  America, 41
  Annie, 40
  Charlotte, 43

Barrett (continued)
  Dora, 158
  Elizabeth, 72
  Esther, 279
  Fannie, 135(2)
  Florence, 371
  Gilliann, 261
  Jane, 131, 201
  Kezziah, 199
  Louraine, 247
  Lucy, 118
  Martha, 150
  Martha Jane, 78
  Mary, 42
  Mary A/Ollie, 45
  Mary Jane, 312
  Nancy Jane, 280
  Phoebe, 56
  Sally, 269
Bartsfield
  Stella, 106
Baughman
  Eliz. Jane, 364
Beard
  Frances E., 11
  Margaret, 361
Beatty
  Ann F., 323
Beckley
  Rose, 70
Becknell
  Callie, 128
  Elizabeth, 187
  Malvery, 38
  Mary, 132
  Minnie, 131
  Sarah A., 187
  Sarah J., 374
Begley
  Adelia, 223
  Elizabeth, 187
  Ella, 148
  Ellen, 122
  Emma, 149

  Hannah, 376
  Leona/Loney, 68
  Lucy, 150
  Martha, 30
  Mary, 49
  Sarah J., 285
Begley?
  Susan, 30
Begly
  see Begley
Bell
  Martha J., 146
  Rebecca, 192
  Susan Ward, 272
Bennett
  Anna, 369
  Lucinda, 19
Biggs
  Lucy, 13
  Sarah J., 132
Biggs?
  Harriet, 56
Bingham
  Diadama, 252
  Elizabeth, 234
  Ellen, 130
  Minnie/Mintie, 49
Birch
  see Burch
Bird
  see Byrd
Bishop
  Alsey, 112
  Amanda/Amy, 257
  Cassandra, 164
  Charity, 267
  Emily, 30
  Kizzie, 165
  Laura, 43
  Lucinda, 243
  Lucy, 120
  Mary, 152, 255,
    270
  Nancy J., 254

Bishop (continued)
Nancy M., 273
Rachel, 13, 120
Winny, 214
Bishop?
Druscilla, 310
Mariah/China, 2
Blake
Cora, 290
Cora Belle, 70
Hannah, 80
Blevins
Minerva, 385
Blount
Louisa, 221
Boles
see Bowles
Boling
see Bowling
Bond
Margaret, 339
Mary, 78, 81
Minerva, 273
Bonds
see Bond
Booth
Clarinda, 358
Jemima, 361
Botner
Bertha, 65
Dora, 111
Frances, 90
Louisa/Lula, 237
Louvisa/Luvin, 203
Mary, 98
Mary Ann, 175
Mary Frances, 369
Matilda A., 238
Minerva Jane, 77
Nancy Margaret, 61
Nannie, 82
Sarah, 231
Susie, 36
Bowles

Della, 188
Emma, 240
Flora, 188
Jemima Eliz., 68
Lucy Ann, 12
Nancy, 338
Nelly M., 157
Sarah E., 81
Bowlin
see Bowling
Bowling
Adeline/Ada, 86
Charlotte, 29
Elizabeth, 25, 105
Emily J/Jennie,
161
Isabelle, 254
Malinda, 119
Mary, 132
Mary Jane, 262
Sarah Jane, 1
Bowls
see Bowles
Bowman
Addie Hazel, 29
Anna, 154
Callie, 29
Clarinda/Clara
Ann, 155
Dora, 40
Elizabeth, 52, 88,
129, 289, 305
Emily Jane, 129
Fannie, 43
Frankie, 313
Geneva, 246
Hulda, 41
Laura, 51, 379
Lennie Eliz/Betty,
275
Letitia, 274
Lou Emily, 140
Lucinda, 48
Lucy Jane, 36

Bowman (continued)
  Lula, 189, 363
  Margaret, 156, 300
  Martha, 83
  Martha Ann, 77
  Martha J., 277
  Mary, 302
  Mary Bell, 165
  Mary Ellen, 83,
    248
  Minerva, 60, 385
  Minnie F., 189
  Mollie Jane, 231
  Molly, 87
  Nancy, 2, 112
  Nancy Ann, 37
  Nancy J., 145
  Rachel, 251, 317,
    321
  Rachel Ann, 149
  Rhoda, 212
  Sarah, 63
  Susan, 272
  Temperance J., 351
  Temperance Jane,
    249
Brandenburg
  Alpha, 222
  Amanda, 52, 163
  Angelina, 207
  Anna Frances, 383
  Dora, 349
  Edna, 140
  Elizabeth, 206
  Ellen, 307
  Florence M., 264
  Hester, 287
  Jalah, 320
  Josephine, 181
  Kate, 153
  Lucy, 387
  Lucy Jane, 230
  Lurinda/Louisa,
    229

  Margaret, 85, 229
  Martha Ann, 91
  Mary, 49, 382
  Mary Frances, 187
  Matilda, 229
  Mattie, 237
  Nancy, 91, 386
  Nancy Ann, 98, 236
  Nannie, 4, 161
  Nellie S., 66
  Rebecca
    Cath./Katie, 228
  Sarah Ann, 243
  Surilda Jane, 101
Brandenburgh
  see Brandenburg
Branson
  Martha, 228
Brawner
  Emilia, 183
  Lucinda Jane, 317
Bray
  Mary, 290
Breeding
  Fannie, 236
  Nannie May, 47
Brewer
  Letitia, 39
  Lucy A., 313
  Lula, 16
  Martha, 350
  Mary, 117
  Mary Frances, 168
  Mary J., 84
  Nancy Mary, 69
  Sarah Margaret,
    341
Britton
  Emily, 137
Brock
  Martha, 234
  Susan, 46
Brogans
  Martha, 277

Browning
  Luvenia/Luanna, 63
Bruce
  Carrie, 253
Bryant
  Carolina, 124
  Eliz. Jane, 259
  Elvira, 316
  Julia, 176
  Margaret Jane, 18
  Martitia, 207
  Mary, 260
  Sarah, 330
Buckhart
  Nancy, 362
Bullock
  Mary Isabelle, 62
Burch
  America, 67
  Elizabeth, 234
  Malinda Cary, 50
  Martha Ellen, 212
  Mary, 112
  Mary Jane, 336
  Mattie, 49
  Nancy E., 213
  Rhoda, 213
  Sarah, 371
  Susan, 241
Burch?
  unknown, 36
Burke
  Elizabeth, 157
  Mary P., 166
Burns
  Amanda, 216
  Catherine, 289
  Elizabeth, 134
  Isabelle, 41, 132
  Joyce, 1
  Lucinda, 119
  Lydia, 132
  Mallissa/Massie, 120

  Margaret, 369
  Margaret J., 58
  Mariah Matilda, 359
  Martha Ann, 370
  Mary, 298
  Mary Emily, 322
  Nancy, 160
  Nancy A., 283
  Polly, 307
  Rebecca, 232
  Sarah, 59
  Zilpha, 297
Burnside
  Hannah, 142, 356
Burris
  Mary, 254
  Nancy J., 378
Burton
  Agnes, 55
  Elizabeth, 27
  Susan, 55
Bush
  Ann, 321
  Margaret Tandy, 322
  Sarah, 215

          -C-

Cable
  Mary, 325
  Polly, 373
  Sarah Margaret, 143
Cain
  Martha, 359
Caldwell
  Margaret, 179
  Sarah, 179
Callahan
  Malinda, 264
  Marinda, 358
  Martha, 95

Callahan (continued)
Mary, 230
Susan Annie, 227
Callihan
see Callahan
Campbell
Deborah, 25
Dorcas, 133
Elizabeth, 14
Grace, 50
Hannah, 127
Levina, 286
Mary, 224
Sarah, 86, 127
Campbell?
Mary, 384
Cardwell
Maranda Eliz., 151
Carmack
Bertha/Bertie, 59
Eliz. Clementine,
7
Isabelle, 13, 41
Jane, 201
Mary, 159
Mary Eliz., 273
Rhoda, 57
Sarah, 388
Carol
see Carroll
Carrel
see Carroll
Carroll
Elizabeth, 57,
307, 378
Margaret M., 116
Carter
Cynthia, 210
Catron
Hetty A., 140
Caudill
Allie, 295
Lizzie, 301
Louvisa/Louisa, 67

Louvisa/Luvin, 203
Malvery, 212
Nancy J., 256
Cawood
Callie, 184
Druscilla P., 309
Flora Ellen, 311
Mariah, 20
Cecil
Levisa Ann, 89
Margaret Eliz.,
148
Minnie, 137
Center
Caroline, 383
Chambers
Lydia Ann, 309
Rachel Ann, 173
Chandler
Elmina, 289, 295
Hannah, 356
Nancy, 289
Sylvania, 197
Chappell
Barbara A., 226
Charles
Agnes, 55
Childs
Louvina, 320
Martha E., 281
Chouse
see Shouse
Christian
Elizabeth, 329
Circy
see Searsey
Clark
Luvernia, 34
Mariah, 352
Mary, 64, 98
Rachel, 242
Sarah C., 193
Coldiron
Martha, 326

Cole
  Alice, 89
  Amanda, 178
  Elizabeth A., 110
  Kansas Lee, 221
  Laura Eliz., 23
  Leni L., 183
  Louisa, 23
  Lucinda, 126
  Lucy Cath., 58
  Lula, 133
  Margaret, 93
  Martha Ellen, 173
  Martitia, 195
  Nancy J/Sis, 350
  Susan, 107
  Virginia, 33
Coleman
  Susan, 150
Collier
  America, 276
Collins
  Amanda, 212
  Cynthia, 278
  Dora, 357
  Eliz. Alice/Allie, 43
  Eliz. Jane, 357
  Eliza J., 279
  Emaline, 282
  Emily, 190
  Martha, 280
  Sarah, 155
  Sarah M., 44
Collinsworth
  Catherine, 193
Colwell
  see Caldwell
Combs
  Angeline, 135
  Bertie, 272
  Celia, 166
  Eliz. A., 175
  Eliz. Ann, 178

Eliza J., 166
Elizabeth, 23, 354
Emily, 318
Flora Bell, 329
Frances, 215
Isabelle, 255
J. Frances, 195
Jane, 15
Malinda, 148
Margaret, 356
Martha, 103
Martha E., 386
Martha Eliz., 324
Mary, 51, 168, 226
Mary Ann, 15
Nancy, 35, 206
Nancy Ann, 122
Nancy Jane, 323
Nancy M., 16
Nellie, 364
Rachel, 265
Sallie A., 326
Sarah, 267
Sarah Jane, 226
Sarah Kath., 167
Sarah Susan, 348
Susan, 202
Conner
  Martha E., 313
  Permelia L., 342
Conrad
  Elizabeth, 343
Cook
  Lavina, 143
Coomer
  Margaret, 75
  Mary Ann, 89
Coon?
  Susan, 30
Cooper
  Lou Emily, 312
  Martha, 150
  Mary Jane, 257
Cope

Cope (continued)
  Nelley A., 239
Cornelius
  Susan, 9
Cornett
  Elizabeth, 86
  Margaret, 247
  Nancy, 35
  Sarah, 29
  Sarah W., 61
  Susan, 282
  Virginia, 203
Cottongin
  Eliz. Jane, 357
  Margaret J., 154
Cottonhill
  Dorothy/Darcus, 31
Couch
  America, 208
  Ann, 42
  Darrity/Daugherty,
    284
  Lethy, 198
  Levisa, 41
  Marzena, 222
  Nancy, 177, 298
  Nancy Ellen, 100
  Serina/Rena, 39
  Susan, 137, 386
Coulton
  Martha Jane, 108
  Mary M., 237
Crabtree
  Mary W., 181
Crank
  Laura J., 88
  Sarah Ellen, 84
  Telery Julia, 78
Crawford
  Allie, 354
  Ara, 310
  Delina, 377
  Eliza, 349
  Emeline, 347

  Mary E., 84
  Nancy A., 148
Creech
  Dolly, 98
  Dora, 340
  Elizabeth, 371
  Hally, 257
  Lucy Ann, 94
  Lula/Lucy
    Margaret, 383
  Maggie, 186
  Mariah Louisa, 312
  Mary, 328
  Mary Ann, 104
  Mary Ann/Sissie,
    271
  Mary C., 185
  Mary Jane, 260
  Mollie, 136
  Nancy, 236
  unknown, 105
Crook
  Belle, 298
Cumins?
  Josephine, 285
Curby
  see Kirby

-D-

Dalton
  Allie M., 312
  Melissa, 76, 310
  Rebecca, 328
  Sarah, 86
Dameral
  Irene/Rena, 54
  Margaret, 217
  Minnie, 292
Damrell
  see Dameral
Daniel
  see Daniels
Daniels

Daniels (continued)
  Arra/Irie/Ira, 199
  Bettie, 247
  Ellen, 294
  Laura, 389
  Lucinda, 378
Daulton
  Mary, 358
Davidson
  Alabama, 250
  Elizabeth, 335
  Josephine, 276
  Lydia M., 162
  Mary, 53
  Nancy, 319, 329
  Rachel, 154
  Sarah, 28, 120,
    179
  Tabitha, 296
Davis
  Nancy, 204
Day
  Betty, 59
  Lenora/Nora, 54
  Lucy, 144
  Mary Ann, 95
  Rebecca, 57
  Theodoshia, 60
Dayberry
  Mary, 234
Dean
  Alcy Ann, 58
  Cath./Cattie, 119
  Elizabeth, 27
  Mary J., 266
  Rachel, 197
Deaton
  Easter, 135
  Mahala, 28
  Nancy Eliz., 225
  Sarah A., 2
Deeds
  Jane, 134
  Martha, 136

Deeds?
  Eliza, 306
Dezarn
  Catherine, 333
Dickens
  Sarah Jane, 294
Dishman
  Laura, 171
Drake
  Eliza, 332
  Martha, 123
Duff
  Caroline, 289
  Louisa, 325
  Lucy, 90
  Mary Cath., 321
  Sarah, 128
Dunagin
  see Dunigan
Dunaway
  Deamy, 92
  Diadema, 209
  Elizabeth, 251
  Esther, 387
Dunigan
  Elizabeth, 207
  Nancy, 155
Dunn
  Clauda, 50
  Lucy, 383
Dunnigan
  see Dunigan
Durbin
  Emily E., 206
  Nancy Ann, 333
  Zerilda, 210
Durbin?
  Caroline, 246

-E-

Eager
  Mattie G., 142
  Mollie T., 238

Eastep
  see Estep
Eastes
  see Estes
Eden
  Mary Etta, 347
Edwards
  Armina, 369
  Barbara E., 237
  Dicy, 360
  Elizabeth, 252
  Lucy Jane, 71
  Maggie, 174
  Martha, 113
  Sylvania, 115
  Tabitha, 167
  Vashti, 176
Egan
  Martha E., 158
Elkins
  Etta B., 300
Eneline
  Martha, 233
English
  Minerva, 219
Estep
  Elizabeth, 178
  Mary Emily, 379
Estes
  Eliza Jane, 363
  Emily Jane, 216
  Nissinia, 367
  Sarah Ann, 283
Evans
  Carmelia A., 186
  Charlotte, 327
  Druscilla/Zillie,
    22
  Edith, 51
  Elizabeth, 184
  Emily, 147
  Jerusha Alice, 48
  Laura B., 22
  Louisa, 342

Lucinda, 57, 306
Lucretia, 335
Margaret, 90
Mary, 176
Mary Ann, 114
Mary Jane, 49
Nancy J., 160
Nancy Jane, 75
Sarah, 67, 143
Sarah Eliz., 374
Eversole
  Elizabeth, 129,
    261
  Louisa, 23
  Lucy, 253
  Lydia, 133
  Martha, 262
  Mary, 205
  Matilda, 256
  Nancy, 360
  Nancy Ann, 250
  Sarah, 29, 61, 353

-F-

Fairchilds
  Lucy, 20
Falconer
  Tabitha C., 367
Farler
  Dora B., 163
Farley
  Julia, 94
Farmer
  Bertie, 278
  Charlotte, 14
  Clarkie, 91
  Ellen/Ella, 185
  Loudith, 185
  Lucy, 233
  Mary A., 248
  Rebecca, 303
  Rebecca J., 281
Faulkins

Faulkins (continued)
  Sarah F., 105
Feltner
  Rebecca Jane, 128
Fields
  Elsie, 103
  Hannah, 26
  Joana, 57
  Justina/Tina, 34
  Lucinda, 314
  Mary, 264
  Mary J., 379
  Nancy A., 297
  Sarah, 197
Flanery
  Allie Mae, 232
  Cath./Kate M., 21
  Cynthia E., 377
  Linda, 211
  Lizzie, 67
  Lucinda/Lou, 265
  Lucy Ann, 169
  Martha, 132, 288
  Mary Frances, 302
  Mary? Rebecca, 193
  Minerva, 121
  Nancy, 319
  Nancy M., 285
  Rebecca, 328
  Sarah E., 348
  Sarah F., 76
  Sarah Margaret,
    168
  Susan Annie, 126,
    227
  Zinalda Florence,
    190
Flannary
  see Flanery
Flannery
  see Flanery
Flinchum
  Mary, 277
Floyd

  Isabelle J., 77
Ford
  Jemima, 267
  Nancy, 136
Foreman
  Emily, 81
Fowler
  Letha, 184
  Nancy, 317
  Piney, 318
Fox
  Alice, 159
  America, 45
  Cora, 66
  Emma/Emmer, 23
  Ida, 75
  Jalia, 99
  Jane, 96
  Levina, 311
  Nettie, 385
  Talitha, 156, 243,
    325
Fox?
  Lucinda, 282
Fraley
  Emily Cath., 294
  Mary, 194
  Mary J., 209
  Rachel, 217, 330
Francis
  Matilda, 355
Franklin
  Helen, 373
Freeman
  Della, 3
  Eliza, 316
  Maggie, 249
  Mary Jane, 260
  Rosa Belle, 169
  Sarah, 41
  Sarah Jane, 73
  Sarah M., 262
  Scythy, 283
  Susan, 202

Frost
  Eliz. Ann, 262
  Isabelle, 26
  Laura B., 331
  Lucinda/Babe, 205
  Mary Ellen, 318
  Nancy, 346
  Nancy Jane, 162
  Sarah E., 3
  Susan A., 254
Fry
  Rachel, 130
Fulks
  Adaline, 52

-G-

Gabbard
  Agnes Jane, 323
  Annie, 15
  Barbary, 45
  Clara, 10
  Cynthia E., 190
  Delphia, 58
  Dora, 340
  Dora B., 189
  Emaline/Emma, 238
  Hannah F., 321
  Jalie, 206
  Jane, 26, 324
  Jemima, 18
  Larinda, 357
  Laura, 113
  Louetta, 283
  Lucy J., 32
  Lula, 267
  Lydia M., 162, 196
  Mamie, 223
  Margaret, 241,
    316, 336
  Martha E., 185
  Martha Hayes, 269
  Mary, 33, 124, 268
  Mary Belle, 177

  Mary Ella, 171
  Mary Jane, 286
  Nannie L., 358
  Rebecca, 207, 259
  Rebecca A., 350
  Rebecca Jane, 337
  Sarah, 188
  Sophia, 356
  Susan, 25, 114
  Susan A., 67
Gale
  Alice, 61
  Joannah, 130
  Lucy Ann, 61
Garrard
  Catherine F., 332
Garrett
  Amanda Jane, 351
  Catherine, 8
  Ella P., 365
  Mary, 152
  Nancy Josephine,
    36
  Rosa Belle, 351
Gay
  America, 162
  Lottie, 194
  Lula, 200
  Lulie, 195
  Martha, 199
  Mary, 196
  Susan, 275
Gayheart
  Mallie, 256
Gentry
  Martha J., 252
Gibbs
  Lucy, 20
Gibson
  Alabama, 155
  Charlina, 341
  Elizabeth, 278
  Lucy Emily, 108
  Maggie, 147

Gibson (continued)
  Malvina, 53
  Minerva, 280
  Polly J., 325
  Rosa, 201
  Rosy Ann, 287
  Sarilda/Shrilda, 56
  Susan Cath., 62
Gilbert
  Arkie, 258
  Delilah/Lily, 38
  Elizabeth, 177, 244
  Laura, 33
  Lenora, 127
  Lucinda, 117
  Malvery, 258
  Malvina, 202
  Margaret, 173
  Martha, 1, 316
  Mary, 37
  Mattie, 12
  Nancy J., 368
  Patsy, 73
  Rebecca, 242
  Rosa, 266
Gilly
  Phoebe, 303
Gipson
  see Gibson
Glass
  Josephine, 103
Godfrey
  Surrena/Rena, 122
Goodman
  Rosa, 21
Goosey
  Mary Ann, 386
  Sarah Ellen, 166
Gordan
  see Gordon
Gordon
  Elizabeth J., 220

  Mary Jane, 98, 100
Gray
  Armina, 8
  Luvina, 372
  Mary Ann, 123
  Mary Eliz., 69
  Mary Evaline, 347
Green
  Depsey/Debbie, 304
  Rachel, 378
Griffee
  Maggie, 217
  Sarah Ann, 188
Griffey
  see Griffee
Griffith
  Almarinda, 243
Grindstaff
  Catherine, 248
Gross
  Amanda, 4
  Lulie, 10
  Malvina, 17
  Margaret, 357
  Martha Jane, 135
  Mary Jane, 366
  Sarah, 295
Gullet
  see Gullett
Gullett
  Lottie, 163
  Permenia/Vernina/ Perlina, 244
Gum
  Lucinda, 63
  Millie, 51
  Milly A., 352
  Milly Ann, 2
  Sarah, 191
Gumm
  see Gum

-H-

Hacker
  America, 350
  Armilda, 37
  Chaney, 256
  Elmina, 289
  Lenora/Nora, 54
  Nancy, 71, 196
  Rachel, 34
  Rebecca, 196
  Sophia, 129, 346
  Susan, 2
Halcomb
  see Holcomb
Hale
  Martha, 372
  Mary L., 238
Hall
  Araminta, 187
  Elizabeth, 220
  George Ella, 94
  Martha, 320
  Mary Jane, 312
  Melda, 158
  Permelia, 348
  Sarah Ann, 93, 209
  Susan, 382
Hamilton
  Callie, 91
  Cora, 302
  Elizabeth, 57
  Emily/Emma, 97
  Katie, 387
  Margaret, 341
  Margaret Jane, 340
  Mary, 116, 221
  Mary Jane, 385
  Nancy, 49
  Paulina V., 352
  Rebecca Josephine,
    203
  Sarah, 40
  Sarah Elender, 339
Hammond
  see Hammonds

Hammonds
  Margaret Ellen,
    123
  Pattie Ann, 139
Hammons
  see Hammonds
Hampton
  Claudy, 355
Handy
  Mary Cath., 160
  Melissa, 76
Harber
  Sarah, 65
Harbour
  see Harber
Harris
  Millie, 146
Hartsock
  Cynthia, 170
  Julie, 169
Harvey
  Elizabeth, 233
  Lillian, 314
  Margaret/Dollie,
    288
Hatton
  Armina, 198
Hayes
  Elizabeth, 214
  Lucinda, 330
  Serilda, 107
Hays
  see Hayes
Hedrix
  see Hendricks
Heflin
  Mary Van Dyke, 280
Heidenrich
  Cressie, 92
Helton
  Catherine, 19
  Margaret, 9
  Mary Jane, 28
  Sarah Jane, 242

INDEX

Hendrick
Ann, 70
Hensley
Catherine, 273
Elizabeth, 297
Eva, 183
Mary J., 80
Nancy, 42
Rachel, 251
Herd
Cora M., 253
Emily, 300
Flora, 360
Lucy, 287
Margaret, 141
Martha Jane, 204
Mary, 125, 230
Minnie, 174
Sylvania, 229
Herndon
Mary Eliz., 263
Mary P., 166
Sarah J., 305
Hicks
Martha, 42
Martha B., 331
Mary, 254
Minta, 342
Rachel, 317
Rose, 332
Hieronymous
Demerias, 121
Nancy, 197, 204
Sallie J., 345
Hignite
Laura, 152
Mary, 170, 264
Rachel, 264
Sarah, 62
Hill
Dora, 201
Gertrude, 337
Martha, 333
Nancy, 250

Hobbs
Emily E., 139
Mahuldah, 164
Naomi C., 182
Sarah S., 144
Talitha, 156
Hogg
Alice, 225
Belvadora, 308
Ida, 181
Perlina, 104
Sally, 77
Holbrook
Nancy Frances, 327
Holcomb
Clarinda/Clara,
100
Fanny, 150
Mary Ann, 62
Nancy Jane, 334,
368
Paralie Jane, 359
Susannah, 207
Holland
Melissa, 138
Phoebe Jane, 286
Rhoda, 381
Hollingsworth
see Hollinsworth
Hollinsworth
Christina, 172
Rhoda, 381
Hollon
Eliza, 265
Holloway
Lourana, 178
Holmes
Louisa J., 368
Hoover
Lucy, 101
Mary Jane, 300
Horn
Rebecca, 175
Hornsby

Hornsby (continued)
  Catherine, 71
  Druscilla, 261
  Eliza, 142
  Martha Jane, 5
  Sarah J., 5
  Sarah Jane, 358
  Susan, 247
Hoskins
  Amanda J., 113
  Elizabeth, 50
  Emma, 131
  Laura B., 44
  Mattie, 130
Hounshell
  Rebecca, 86
Howard
  Charity, 232
  Elizabeth, 314
  Laura, 152, 322
  Marietta/Mary
    Frances, 287
Howell
  Emeline Barbara,
    368
  Mary S., 228
  Nancy Jane, 368
Howerton
  Serena, 203
Hubbard
  Milly, 60
Hudson
  Mary Ann, 109
  Sarilda/Shrilda,
    115
Huff
  Almilda, 48
  Callie, 323
  Linda, 32
  Lulie B., 72
  Nancy, 136
  Sarah, 29
Hughes
  Alpha, 366

Mary J., 84
Maud M., 108
Hundley
  Amanda, 34, 323(2)
  Mary, 159
  Sarah, 48
  Sophia, 145
  Susan Cath., 161
Hunley
  see Hundley
Hunt
  Mariah, 74
Hunter
  Elizabeth, 337
Hurst
  Nancy E., 192
Hutch
  Rebecca J., 67
Hutchison
  Ella, 9
Hutson
  see Hudson
Hyden
  Dema, 93

-I-

Ingram
  Kizzey, 365
  Susannah Jane, 17
Isaacs
  Abbie, 103
  Dovie, 104
  Lydia?, 263
  Margaret, 351
  Martha, 160, 306,
    308
  Mary Frances, 276
  Mattie, 105
  Mertie, 119
  Sarah, 109, 305

-J-

Jackson
  Fannie, 65
  Harriet, 194
  Martha, 255
  Sarah, 127
Jamerson
  see Jameson
Jameson
  Diana, 198
  Miriam, 380
  Patience, 178
  Phoebe, 64
  Rhoda, 9
Jamison
  see Jameson
Jett
  Deloras, 309
  Jane, 354
  Mattie, 355
  Mattie Lou, 355
  Nancy, 138
  Nannie Lou, 293
  Pender, 310
Jewell
  Caroline, 367
  Mary M., 379
Johnson
  Jaley, 266
  Larinda, 208
  Linda, 215
  Lourany Janet, 316
  Nancy, 39
  Rachel, 349
  Sarah, 244, 299
Johnston
  Rachel Eliz., 268
Jones
  Catherine, 333
  Elizabeth, 79
  Emily, 145
  Ollie, 234
  Rhoda, 10
  Sarah A., 379
Judd

  Amanda, 96
  Bertha, 110
  Cecilia Jane, 174
  Frances, 97
  Hattie B., 363
  Josephine, 373
  Lucinda, 338
  Malvina, 78
  Myra, 217

-K-

Keith
  Margaret, 325
Keller
  Annie, 17
Kelly
  Druscilla, 37
  Frankie, 81
  Mary Ellen, 58
Kendrick
  Josephine, 98
  Nancy Jane, 362
Ketchum
  Armina/Army, 66
  Margaret, 119
Kidd
  Nancy C., 50
  Sarah Eliz., 343
Kilbourn
  see Kilburn
Kilburn
  Nancy, 359
  Rachel, 250
  Tabitha, 176
Kincade
  see Kincaid
Kincaid
  Edith, 130
  Margaret, 358
  Susan/Sudie, 339
King
  Elizabeth, 317
  Hannah, 317

King (continued)
  Mary, 39
  Mary Jane, 146
  Serilda, 380
Kirby
  Delilah, 360
Kirk
  Mildred, 80

-L-

Lair
  Nancy, 51
Lane
  Martha B., 76
  Mary, 111
  Nancy J., 75
Langdon
  Minerva, 21
Lawson
  Mary Ann, 79
Ledford
  Lula, 200
Lee?
  Margaret/Peggy,
    232
Lester
  Malinda, 204
Levell
  Bettie, 355
Lewis
  Emily C., 125
  Malinda, 141
  Mary, 227
  Nancy, 136, 198
  Nancy A., 36, 315
  Vanetta, 269
Linch
  see Lynch
Little
  Emily, 135
  Ida B., 330
  Louisa, 369
  Sarah Jane, 41

Long
  Eliza, 337
Lorton
  Martha Eliz., 170
Lovelace
  Nancy, 143
Loveless
  Linda, 267
Lowe
  Minnie, 89
Loyst
  Mable, 104
Luker
  Sallie, 271
Lunsford
  Sally, 387
Lutes
  Elizabeth, 373
  Nancy, 360
  Siladeth, 222
Lynch
  Emily Jane, 286
  Josephine, 384
  Lucinda, 40
  Lucy, 375
  Margaret, 12
  Melissa Jane, 145
  Minerva, 292
  Rachel Ibby, 263
  Sarah Eliz., 230

-M-

McCarty
  Amanda, 215
McCollum
  Amanda Paralee,
    231
  Ida, 224
  Louisa J., 15
  Maimie, 143
  Martha M., 127
  Rachel, 204
McDaniel

McDaniel (continued)
  Isabelle, 254
  Martha, 377
  Mary, 113
  Mary J., 35
  Nannie, 140
  Rhoda Jane, 122
McDaniels
  see McDaniel
McEwan
  Sallie L., 230
McFarland
  Evaline, 211
McGee
  Lucretia, 162
McGeorge
  Mary, 87
  Sarah A., 281
McGlasson
  Elizabeth A., 311
McGuire
  Anna Frances, 195
  Caroline, 47
  Diadema, 380
  Eliz. Ann, 309
  Elizabeth, 147,
    149
  Emily, 80
  Gilly Ann, 352
  Julia, 221
  Margaret, 372
  Margaret Jane, 186
  Priscilla, 206
  Zarilda Frances,
    361
McIntire
  Mary, 62, 81
  Nancy, 63
McIntosh
  Amanda, 53
  Angeline, 6
  Chaney, 285
  Daisy, 90
  Fanny, 359, 361

  Frances/Fancy, 92
  Isabelle, 244
  Isabelle/Esibell,
    163
  Joana, 57
  Lethan, 2
  Martha, 295
  Mary, 274
  Mary Eliz., 322
  Maud, 25
  Nannie, 113
  Nettie, 385
  Nicy, 38
  Sally Belle, 131
  Sarah, 127, 174
  Tisha, 200
McKiney
  see McKinney
McKinney
  Esther, 276
  Hannah A., 353
  Mary Jane, 302
  Rosannah, 22
McPherson
  Josephine, 364,
    373
  Mary E., 87
  Minerva, 219
  Nannie C., 299
  Virginia Edna, 180
McQueen
  Dora, 234
  Martha, 66
  Mary, 170, 322
  Polly, 306
  Sarah Ellen, 59
  Sophia, 169
McQuinn
  Caroline, 355
McVey
  Elizabeth Jane, 79
  Sarah, 76
McWhorter
  Maggie, 268

Madden
  Mada M., 349
  Nancy, 136
  Rhoda A., 116
Maddox
  Priscilla Bell,
    146
Mahaffa
  see Mahaffey
Mahaffey
  Eliz. Anna, 291
  Elizabeth, 343
  Emma, 235
  Minnie, 116
  Rachel, 109
Mahaffy
  see Mahaffey
Mainous
  Amanda, 235
  Gracie, 306
  Helen, 246, 373
  Jeriah/Honey, 345
  Martha, 303
  Martha Belle, 351
  Nellie, 328
  Virginia, 235
Maison
  see Mason
Malicote
  Rosa Eliz., 335
Maloney
  Cora, 246
  Dora, 245
  Lourana, 178
  Susan, 208
Mangan
  Mary Ann, 265
Mann
  America, 380
Marcum
  Carlista/Callie,
    168
  Elizabeth, 183
  Ellenor C., 381

Flora, 106
Jane, 101
Mary, 170
Sarah Anna, 168
Sarah C., 189
Sarah Cath., 344
Tempa, 6
Margroves
  Barbara, 182
Marian
  see Marion
Marion
  Nancy E., 260
  Rosy Ann, 287
  Serena, 189
Markham
  see Marcum
Marsh
  Nancy J., 75, 376
Marshall
  Ann, 179
  Dora, 125
  Ellen, 173
  Letitia, 3, 126
  Liedora/Dora, 72
  Malinda, 74
  Martha, 275
  Mollie, 3
  Nancy, 250
Martin
  Sadie, 159
Mason
  Catherine, 285
  Julia, 124
  Minerva J., 82
  Rose, 70
Mathews
  Millie Jane, 7
Mathis
  Martha, 80
  Susan, 253
Mattingly?
  Lucy, 340
Mayes

Mayes (continued)
  see Mays
Mays
  Charlina, 341
  Elizabeth, 239
  Isabelle, 24
  Letitia, 117
  Louise/Eliza, 98
  Maggie, 370
  Margaret, 95, 217
  Margaret Jane, 215
  Mary, 18, 120
  Mollie, 218
  Rebecca, 17
  Rhoda, 140
Mayse
  see Mays
Mead
  Lottie, 386
Menefee
  Lena Hazel, 282
Metcalf
  Mary Jane, 260
  Mollie, 55
  Nancy, 144
  Nancy Clark, 96
Metcalfe
  see Metcalf
Miller
  Nancy, 24, 249
  Sarah Lucinda, 249
  Susan, 250
Million
  Hannah, 260
  Lottie, 36
Minter
  Ann Judith, 284
  Cynthia, 240
  Cynthia E., 66
  Fannie J., 153
  Fannie R., 191
  Florence Ellen, 89
  Henrietta, 138
  Jane, 123

  Laura Belle, 327
  Margaret Ellen,
    239
  Maria L., 13
  Matilda E., 138
  Sallie T., 3
Moore
  Ada, 148
  Amanda, 195, 310
  Amanda Frances,
    268
  America, 312, 377
  Caroline, 213
  Elizabeth, 250,
    280(2)
  Emadatha, 112
  Emaline/Emily J.,
    102
  Emily/Emma J., 147
  Emma, 53, 161, 196
  Esther, 125
  Frances, 44, 291,
    303
  Isabelle, 314
  Jane, 128
  Judith, 266
  Kate, 74
  Lucinda, 222, 241
  Lucretia, 159
  Lydia, 218
  Margaret, 93,
    151(2), 226
  Martha, 301, 381
  Mary, 177, 256
  Mary Belle, 371
  Mary E., 96
  Mary Eliz., 385
  Mary Margaret, 288
  Melissa J., 79
  Nancy, 257, 365
  Nancy A., 195
  Rachel, 205, 278
  Rebecca, 276
  Rebecca Jane, 224

Moore (continued)
  Rhoda, 149
  Sarah, 59, 308
  Sarah Cath., 16
  Sarah G., 95
  Stacy, 60
Morgan
  Emily, 224
  Emily Abee, 69
  Mary, 86
  Matilda, 274
  Sarah, 353
Morris
  Easter, 296
  Elizabeth, 297
  Ella, 118
  Emily, 119
  Julia, 78
  Julina, 13
  Linda, 74
  Lucinda, 46, 306
  Lucy J., 58
  Lydia, 347
  Margaret, 197
  Martha, 15
  Nancy, 85, 121
  Rhoda, 85
  Rhoda Eliz., 116
  Rosa, 266
  Sylvania, 16
Mosley
  Angeline, 5
  Armilda, 30
  Malinda, 31
  Martha, 286
Mosly
  see Mosley
Moyers
  Emma Rosa, 255
  Lou Ellen, 83
  Lucy Susan, 272
  Maggie, 48
  Maggie Daisy, 128
  Rebecca Susan, 88

Mullins
  Amanda, 384
  Lula, 180
  Mary, 208, 294
  Rosa, 201
  Rosa Ann, 289
Muncy
  Emily, 67
Murrell
  Docia, 53
  Margaret, 87
  Mollie, 331
  Nancy A., 164
  Orlena, 124
Murrell?
  Laura, 281
Myers
  Jane, 324
Myres
  see Myers

-N-

Nancy
  Anna, 296
Nantz
  Barbara, 189
  Charity, 334
  Emily C., 328
  Martha, 344
  Mary, 86
  Rebecca, 220
Napier
  Elizabeth, 231
  Susan, 328
Neace
  Ida, 199
  Virginia, 1
Neece
  see Neace
Needham
  Lucinda, 330
Neeley
  America, 364

Neeley (continued)
Hannah Louise, 127
Ida, 349
Letitia Margaret, 347
Lucinda, 139
Mary, 110
Mary J., 154
Minerva J., 362
Ruth, 115
Sarah J., 365
Newman
Belinda/Milly, 118
Celia, 215
Chalista, 82
Frances Emma, 363
Laura Belle, 384
Leannah, 334
Marsha/Martha, 216
Martha Ann, 228
Melissa, 74
Millie, 216
Sarah Minerva, 223
Vashtie, 176, 212
Newnam
see Newman
Newton
Dianah, 216
Isabelle, 215
Nancy, 216
Sarah A., 209
Nickels
Lucy, 57
Noble
Ada, 303
Martha, 259
Nancy Jane, 301
Noe
Elizabeth, 317
Sarah, 172
Nolan
see Noland
Noland
Diadema/Demis, 373

Nora C., 101
Rosa, 194
Sarah Jane, 376
Sarah Margaret, 91
Norman
Mary Ann, 133

-O-

Oldham
Emily/Emma, 116
Mary, 49
Olinger
Anne Eliza, 324
Mary Jane, 241
Oliver
Lydia A., 14
Osborne
Druscilla/Drew, 290
Emily, 82
Nancy, 377
Osburn
see Osborne

-P-

Pace
Elizabeth, 231
Emma, 214
Linda, 134
Susan, 311
Talitha, 325
Palmer
Dora, 40
Elizabeth, 149
Hulda, 41
Lou Ann, 71
Maggie, 357
Mary Bell, 73
Nancy Jane, 97
Paris
Sarah, 22
Parker

Parker (continued)
  Daisy, 46
  Sarah, 240
Parmer
  see Palmer
Parnel
  Matilda, 81
Parsons
  Lucinda, 362
  Martha, 140
  Phoebe, 336
Patrick
  Mahala, 111
  Margaret, 64
  Mary, 346
Patton
  Minnie, 330
Payne
  Parrott, 4
Pearson
  Cath. Ann, 342
  Lou Emily, 220
  Minty, 145
Pearson?
  Catherine, 222
Pendergras
  see Pendergrass
Pendergrass
  Bettie, 335
  Elizabeth, 117
  Flora, 292
  Hattie, 88
  Letitia, 117
  Lou, 192
  Louise/Eliza, 98
  Martha Ann, 228
  Sarah, 81
  Vivia, 297
Pendleton
  Catherine, 305
Pennington
  Mahala, 76
  Nancy, 136
Perkins

Lucinda, 330
Surinda, 21
Person
  Delilah, 344
Peters
  Armitta/Mintie, 234
  Catherine, 84
  Dicey Jane, 85
  Eliza Jane, 232
  Elizabeth, 262
  Emily, 371
  Emma B., 105
  Frankie, 202
  Grace, 112
  Ida, 115
  Lucy, 367
  Lula, 28
  Margaret, 28
  Martha B., 106
  Martha E., 190
  Martha J., 108
  Mary, 161
  Mary Ann, 258
  Mary Bell, 245
  Mary M., 99
  Maude Jane, 113
  Prescovy, 371
  Rachel, 269
  Rhoda C., 376
  Sarah Ann, 269
  Sarah Eliz., 106
  Susan, 242
Pettit
  Rachel J., 142
Phillips
  Deborah/Delila, 307
  Elizabeth, 80
  Jemima, 19
  Rhoda A., 152
  Sally, 101
  Susan, 70
  Sylvania, 69

Phipps
  Cynthia/Scyntha, 39
  Josephine, 30
  Julina, 13
Pierson
  see Pearson
Pigg
  Margaret A., 347
Pitman
  see Pittman
Pitt
  Almedia, 190
Pittman
  Nancy, 55
  Sarah Ann, 361
  Susan Jane, 181
Plummer
  America, 184
  Christiana Ann, 122
  Lucinda, 382
  Nancy, 218
  Sarah, 96
Ponder
  Sally, 329
Porter
  Mary, 19
  Rachel, 172
  Rebecca, 86
Portwood?
  Louisa/Eliza?, 186
Powel
  see Powell
Powell
  Nancy, 112
  Sarah Jane, 294
Prather
  Eliza, 90
Price
  Caroline, 32
  Eliza Jane, 272
  Hattie, 218
  Jessie Bell, 144

  Lillie, 203
  Maggie, 147
  Mary, 7, 166, 293
  Minnie, 381
  Mollie C., 380
  Myrtle, 109
Pritchard
  Lucy, 314
  Sarah M., 153
Profitt
  Sylvania, 310

-R-

Raddford
  see Radford
Rader
  Elizabeth, 96
  Mary Jane/Jennie, 266
  Sally, 190
Radford
  Elmina, 289, 295
  Fannie M., 40
  Mary Ellen, 248
Ragan
  Minnie P., 4
Raines
  Levinia, 144
  Nannie R., 308
Raisner
  see Rasner
Rasner
  Margaret J., 154
  Sarah Cath., 160
Reasor
  Naomi C., 182
Rector?
  Frances, 241
Reece
  see Reese
Reed
  Catherine, 315
  Cora, 290

Reed (continued)
  Martha, 358
  Mary, 57
Reese
  Millie, 281
  Sarah, 6
  Susie, 7
Reid
  see Reed
Reins
  see Raines
Reynolds
  Easter, 316
  Elizabeth, 22
  Ella Belle, 4
  Emaline, 30
  Emma, 151, 210
  Jaley, 263
  Jane, 284
  Julia, 205
  Lucinda, 162
  Lucy Ann, 223
  Lula, 356
  Margaret, 73
  Martha, 157
  Mary Bell, 337
  Mary Jane, 21, 243
  Minerva Jane, 163
  Nancy, 157, 206
  Nancy J., 209
  Permelia, 336
  Regina, 354
Rice
  Laura Bell, 270
  Mary Ellen, 199
  Mattie, 311
  Mattie/Dude, 100
  Nannie Bell, 24
Richardson
  Louvina, 270
  Nancy M., 257
  Susannah Jane, 17
Riddle
  Frances, 301

Riley
  Hannah, 244
  Jane, 199
  Loudemia, 284
  Mahala, 11
  Margaret, 25,
    46(2), 361
  Maxaline, 111
  Nancy Malitha/
    Mattie, 146
  Orlena, 154
  Sarah, 19
Roach
  Armina, 288
  Edith, 172
  Mary, 248
  Susan, 288
Roberts
  Anna, 307
  Belle, 244
  Dicey, 304
  Dora, 18
  Elizabeth, 94, 253
  Ellen, 211
  Levisa, 85
  Lucinda, 382
  Mary Ann, 45
  Mary Jane, 312
  Nancy, 196
  Nancy A., 362
  Paulina, 97
  Rebecca, 253
  Ruth, 115
  Susan, 294
Robertson
  Catherine, 361
  Malinda, 13
  Mary Margaret, 333
  Nancy, 35, 85
  Sarah A., 35
Robinson
  Ardenia, 221
  Elizabeth, 224
  Ibba Caroline, 366

# INDEX

Robinson (continued)
    Josephine, 234
    Matilda, 195
    Sarah, 387
Rogers
    Eliza, 182
Rose
    Alice F., 321
    Etta Bell, 72
    Julia, 217
    Lizzie, 310
    Maggie, 124
    Mary Ann, 141
    Nancy Jane, 129
    Rebecca, 126, 141
Ross
    Edna, 150
    Elizabeth, 74
    Liza D., 150
    Lucy Ann, 120
    Lucy E., 192
    Nancy, 279
    Stella C., 151
Rowland
    Catherine, 28, 218
    Charlotte, 299
    Hally, 56
    Martha, 5, 276
    Martha E., 175
    Mary, 54
    Mary A., 27
    Mary Cath., 8
    Sarah Jane, 299
    Sophia Bell, 378
Rowlett
    Josephine, 349
    Sarah, 239
    Sarah F., 76
Russell
    Mahala, 156
    Mary, 292
    Mary Matilda, 222

        -S-

Sageser
    Agnes, 185
Salyers
    Cath. Nancy, 387
Sams
    Elizabeth, 333
Sanders
    Birdie, 192
    Lucinda, 114
    unknown (d/o
        Prof.), 311
Sandlin
    Arminda, 32
    Catherine, 52
    Eliza, 30
    Ella, 318
    Lean, 285
    Margaret, 180
    Mary, 341
    Mary Eliz., 304
    Nancy, 24
    Nancy Jane, 58
    Sarah, 72, 315
    Sophia, 178, 350
Sawyers
    Elizabeth, 251
    Mary Ann, 76
Saylor
    Lula, 117
    Mary Jane, 10
Schoolcraft
    Mary, 333
Schoonover
    Sarah A., 16
Scott
    Alpha, 348
    Phoebe, 348
Seaborn
    Phoebe A., 279
Seal
    see Seale
Seale
    Flora, 268
    Mary, 99

Seale (continued)
  Mary Margaret, 288
  Melissa Frances,
    343
  Mittie, 343
  Ollie, 137
  Theresa, 94
Searcy
  Lucy K., 239
  Mary Eliz., 319
Searsey
  see Searcy
Sebastian
  Julia, 34
  Laura, 299
  Matilda, 121
See
  Amanda, 8
  Elizabeth, 381
  Lydia Ann, 278
Sexton
  Minerva J., 279
Shackelford
  Emadatha, 112
  Mary Ann, 332
  Susan, 255
Shepherd
  Josephine, 31
  Martha, 35, 59
  Mary Ann, 59
  Nancy L., 164
Shoemaker
  Elizabeth, 64, 124
  Sarah J., 325
  Temperance, 324
Shook
  Eliza Jane, 192
  Mary Eliz., 258
Short
  America, 290
  Elizabeth, 155
  Emily, 332
  Fanny, 361
  Martha, 244, 336

Nancy Eliz., 37
Rebecca, 37
Shouse
  Arizona/Zona, 43
  Lula, 39
  Malinda, 366
  Mary Jane, 18
Simms?
  Druscilla, 310
Simpkins
  Jane, 134
Simpson
  Deborah, 19
  Martha, 19
  Mary, 265
  Matilda, 293
Singleton
  Emma/Emily, 116
  Susan/Suda, 213
Sizemore
  Alcy Ann, 293
  America, 10
  Amy, 24
  Catherine, 33
  Cynthia A., 293
  Druscilla/Zillie,
    22
  Florence, 318
  Lucy, 8
  Martha, 200, 213
  Nellie, 31
  Rebecca J., 67,
    344
  Susan, 233
Sloan
  see Slone
Slone
  Amanda, 375
  Elizabeth, 134
  Lucinda, 19
Smith
  Ada Ann, 118
  Anna, 376
  Caroline, 156

Smith (continued)
  Edna, 306
  Ellen F., 22
  Emaline, 343
  Esther, 42
  Esther A., 281
  Fannie, 55
  Laura, 187
  Leah, 102
  Lizzie Bell, 141
  Lucretia, 159
  Lucy Jane, 230
  Lula, 65
  Lydia A., 14
  Margaret, 180
  Martha, 335, 365
  Martha Ann, 97
  Mary, 121, 151,
    298
  Mary Ann, 153, 220
  Mary Ann/Pat, 101
  Mary Cath/Kate,
    221
  Mary Eliz., 288
  Matilda, 287, 375
  Minnie, 273
  Mirtie, 188
  Nancy, 283
  Nannie C., 158
  Orlena, 370
  Orpha, 376
  Polly, 134
  Rebecca, 360
  Rhoda, 9, 70
  Sarah, 7, 353
  Sarah Ann, 148
  Sarah Frances, 223
  Sarah Jane, 243
  Sophia, 94
  Stacy, 60
  Sudie, 65
  Susan, 25, 46
Snider
  see Snyder

Snodgrass
  America, 152
Snowden
  Margaret, 122
  Nancy, 6
Snyder
  Virginia Caroline,
    326
Sparks
  America, 107
  Elizabeth, 183
  Mary, 70
  Mattie, 145
  Mollie Jane, 231
  Nancy, 361
  Perlina, 207
  Phoebe Jane, 56
Spence
  Amanda, 207
  Bertha E., 106
  Elizabeth, 233,
    314, 334
  Minnie, 338
  Mollie, 107
  Permelia, 169
  Rhoda J., 338
Spencer
  Mable, 43
  Malinda, 373
  Mary Jane, 18
  Matilda, 186
  Nancy, 361
  Sarah J., 352
Spicer
  Callie, 70
  Fidelia, 19
Spivey
  Louisa, 139
  Lucy Ann, 125
  Martha, 93, 364
  Nancy, 306
  Sarah Ellen, 109
  Susan, 240, 307
Spivy

Spivy (continued)
see Spivey
St John
Fannie J., 241
Sarah C., 105
Stacy
Betty, 6
Elender, 263
Stamper
Araminta, 19
Elizabeth, 346
Emily, 147
Julia F., 211
Mary B., 246
Nancy, 219
Nancy Jane, 291
Polly, 219
Rebecca, 370
Standiford
Rosa B., 313
Stapleton
Caroline, 213
Nancy, 45
Steel
see Steele
Steele
Amanda, 104
Charlotte, 204
Lusetta/Lucy, 369
Mary Ann, 219
Rebecca, 17
Stephens
Elizabeth, 208
Mary Ann, 84
Stepp
Alice, 86
Elizabeth, 155
Emma Eunice, 332
Fronia Cath., 167
Priscilla, 171
Sternburg
Alice, 91
Stevens
see Stephens

Stewart
Arrilda, 344
Lenilcoti, 166
Stidham
Emily B., 12
Sarah, 241
Sophia, 296
Stivers
Ollie, 234
Strong
Cordelia, 20, 34
Elander, 217
Ellen, 170
Maranda, 176
Mary Jane, 100
Minnie, 143
Rachel, 26
Rebecca J., 220
Rebecca Rachel, 277
Sally, 11
Sarah, 171
Strong?
Mahaley, 204
Stuart
see Stewart

-T-

Tackett
Letitia, 229
Lillie, 99
Lula/Lucy
Margaret, 383
Mary Frances, 186
Taulbee
Martha Ann, 315
Taylor
Belle, 88, 126
Catherine, 17
China, 226
Cornelia/Nealie, 87
Delilah/Lillie,

Taylor (continued)
171
Elma, 174
Harriet, 245
Lucy Helen, 11
Lydia, 275
Margaret Martha,
315
Martha, 22, 92
Sophronia, 332
Terry
Mary, 39
Mary Jane, 356
Thomas
America, 304
Anna, 300
Anna E., 372
Anne, 366
Catherine, 264
Elizabeth, 152,
233
Emily, 302
Jemima, 69
Lucy, 304
Lucy Ann, 12
Margaret, 176, 368
Martha Marcella,
164
Mary, 128
Mary Ann, 95, 106
Mary Cath., 68
Mattie, 23
Nancy Ann, 102
Nissinia, 367
Nona J., 344
Rhoda, 131
Silvania, 77
Susan Jane, 16
Thompson
Sarah J., 374
Sarilda, 383
Winnie, 381
Thuman
Ellen, 298

Tincher
Eliza J., 334
Margaret, 229
Mary, 210
Tirey
Holly Ann, 389
Ibba Caroline, 366
Martha J., 63
Melissa, 158
Treadway
Agatha/Gatha, 44
Cora M., 237
Emily, 9, 89
Eva, 60
Evaline, 382
Laura, 52
Laura Marsh, 211
Louisa, 104
Trimble
Cintha Ann, 373
Evaline, 382
Truett
Sarah, 240
Truitt
see Truett
Turner
Aery, 225
Elizabeth, 83
Emily, 318
Linnie, 17
Mary, 84
Nancy, 377
Tyra
see Tirey

-U-

Underwood
Agnes, 51
Lula, 102
Nancy, 386
unknown
Alafair, 130
Alice, 103

INDEX

unknown (continued)
Almira, 47, 378
Amanda, 34, 37,
  145, 240, 384
America, 290
Angeline, 77, 340
Ann, 354
Annie, 190
Becky, 375
Belle, 198
Catherine, 179,
  357
Christina, 24, 172
Cordia, 99
Delitha, 209
Dolly, 64
Dora, 88
Eady?, 114
Eliza, 54, 56, 90,
  198, 282, 378
Eliza Ann, 251
Elizabeth, 6, 35,
  184(2), 281, 283,
  286, 320, 345,
  346, 355
Emily, 13
Eva, 187
Evaline, 352
Evliney, 313
Feriley, 177
Garnett, 277
Halley, 26
Haney, 133
Hannah, 334
Hannah L., 309
Helen/Ellen, 353
Hetty, 273
Isabelle, 310
Jane, 5, 21, 123,
  250, 284, 297,
  310, 359
Jemima, 133
Joyce, 284
Julia, 121

Larinda, 208, 357
Laura, 319
Leathy, 102
Lener, 357
Levina, 339
Lizzie Bell, 141
Louellen, 185
Louisa, 271, 331
Louisa/Eliza, 292
Lucinda, 10, 205,
  362
Lucy, 13, 112,
  286, 299, 384
Lula, 377
Luvernia, 34
Mahala, 156, 312,
  318
Malinda, 55
Margaret, 47, 162,
  173, 179, 191,
  206, 314
Margaret J., 204
Martha, 43, 48,
  82, 156, 170,
  197, 210, 279,
  308, 326, 333,
  365
Martha A., 326
Martha B., 331
Martha J., 66, 236
Mary, 30, 110,
  124, 140, 161,
  173, 177, 247,
  273, 282, 298,
  327, 341, 345,
  379
Mary A., 27, 31,
  321, 354
Mary A. F., 32
Mary Ann, 252,
  331, 386
Mary B., 54
Mary Cath., 374
Mary E., 34

unknown (continued)
Mary F., 123, 133
Mary J., 31, 32,
    312, 350
Mary Jane, 98
Mary M., 379
Matilda, 38, 142,
    238, 334, 375
Maxaline, 57
Melina/Maxaline,
    30
Melissa, 170
Mima, 311
Minerva, 182
Minia, 292
Minnie, 345
Myrtle, 228
Nancy, 121, 136,
    180, 222, 232,
    247, 296, 316,
    359, 375
Nancy A., 283
Nancy J., 15, 375
Nancy M., 181
Nannie, 251
Orpha, 183
Polly A., 137
Polly J., 325
Rachel, 250, 269
Rachel H., 289
Rebecca, 122, 186,
    295, 370
Rebecca J., 216
Rebecca M., 139
Revella, 271
Rhoda, 278
Ruth, 375
Ryer J., 160
Sallie A., 194
Sally, 153, 298
Sarah, 55, 63, 83,
    87, 107, 148,
    180, 252, 303,
    339, 356

Sarah A., 291
Sarah J., 21
Sarah M., 336
Sceallie, 38
Serena, 189
Serilda, 348
Sudie?, 117
Susan, 107, 165,
    235, 255, 384
Susan A., 32
Susannah, 198
unknown, 14, 15,
    39, 41, 45, 53,
    83, 99, 110, 122,
    131, 164, 191,
    194, 199, 201,
    214, 284, 290,
    300, 302, 319,
    352, 375, 386(2)
Velara, 230
Virginia, 286
Winnie F., 277
Zerilda, 315

-V-

Vanderpool
Eliz. Jane, 172
Vaughn
Nancy, 331
Sarah E., 154
Venable
Dorothy/Dottie,
    138
Ellen, 114
Hattie Lee, 242
Martha, 198
Mary Bell, 227
Nancy, 108
Nannie, 167
Rachel Evaline/
    Dolly, 236
Sarah Minerva, 223
Stella C., 151

Vickers
    Esther, 252
Vires
    Margaret, 45
    Sarah Jane, 371

-W-

Waddle
    Mary, 338
Wadkins
    see Watkins
Wadle
    see Waddle
Wallin
    Nancy M., 10
Ward
    America A. Eliz.,
        123
    Catherine, 289
    Cynthia Lucinda,
        235
    Lucy, 385
    Susannah, 249
    Tempa, 6
Warner
    Nancy, 19
Warren
    Amanda, 202
    Clarkie, 376
    Evaline Margaret,
        62
    Julia, 78
    Lauranda, 65
    Levina, 154
    Margaret, 53
    Mary, 50
    Mary D., 12
    Susan, 313
Watkins
    Emma, 358
Watts
    Mary Jane, 139
Weaver

    Mariah, 184
Webb
    Mary J., 117
Wells
    Jennie, 10
    Martha, 171
    Virginia, 175
West
    Elizabeth, 259
    Nancy, 180
Whicker
    Mary, 342
Whisman
    Mary Ann, 133
Whitaker
    Nancy Jane, 245
    Pearl, 323
White
    Angeline Virginia,
        191
    Elizabeth, 340
    Emma, 107
    Julia, 147
    Leannah, 334
    Margaret, 357
    Margaret A., 114
    Martha, 97
    Mary E., 295
    Perlina, 177
    Sarah Ann, 271
    Sena/Cena, 125
Wilder
    Cora, 249
    Hannah, 249
    Nannie J., 227
    Rebecca, 134
    Sarah Ann, 251
Williams
    Eliza, 275
    Eliza Ann, 258
    Lizzie, 67
    Lucy A., 297
    Lydia, 69
    Margaret Jane, 240

Williams (continued)
  Mary A., 165
  Matilda, 270, 274
  Patsy Ann, 309
  Pattie Ann, 139
  Sarah Bell, 339
  Sophia, 191
Wilson
  Alpha, 14
  America, 125
  Cordelia, 177
  Cushenberry, 93
  E. Jane, 378
  Elizabeth, 329
  Ellen, 364
  Emily, 235
  Emily Amazon, 183
  Isabelle, 145
  Josephine, 208
  Leah Jean, 62
  Lillie, 109
  Lucy, 79
  Lucy Ann, 63, 105
  Lucy Emma, 110
  Maggie, 320
  Mahala, 260
  Margaret, 126,
    137, 176
  Margaret/Mary Ann,
    327
  Martha, 326
  Mary, 23, 227
  Mary Ann, 214
  Mary Eliz., 182
  Mary Emily, 379
  Mary Jane, 264
  Mary P., 329
  Melissa/Lissa/
    Lizzie, 259
  Minnie Belle, 144
  Nancy Ellen, 320
  Nancy Jane, 374
  Nancy Mae, 38
  Rachel, 307

  Sarah Ann, 296
  Sarah J., 110
  Sophia, 338
Winkle
  Almedia, 103
Winkler
  Sarah, 352
Winn
  see Wynn
Withe
  see Wythe
Witt
  Paulina, 75
Wolf
  see Wolfe
Wolfe
  Annie, 107
  Margaret J., 60
Wood
  see Woods
Woodard
  see Woodward
Woods
  Edith, 73
  Elizabeth, 262,
    331
  Isabelle, 71
  Lula, 267, 363
  Mary, 70
  Nancy Eliz., 225
  Nancy Kath., 87
  Rebecca, 27
  Sarah Jane, 165,
    226
  Susan Eliz., 163
Woodward
  Hazel, 81
  Martha Eliz., 379
  Mary J., 77
  Nancy Kath., 87
Wright
  Nancy, 374
  Phoebe, 193
Wyatt

Wyatt (continued)
  Amanda Jane, 123
  Cynthia, 133, 210
Wynn
  Clarinda, 309
  Mamie, 347
Wythe
  Martha Ann, 210

           -Y-

Yates
  Arthina, 47
Yeary
  Etta, 26
  Rhoda, 344
York
  Ada, 96
  Lucy Jane, 118
Young
  Alice, 387
  Amazon, 208
  Lucinda, 319
  Mary, 232
  Mary J., 32
  Susan, 79